1776

A London Chronicle

THE
FEMALE COMBATANTS

OR WHO SHALL

Publish'd According to Act Jan.ᵗ 26·1776. Price 6.ᵈ

1776

A London Chronicle

or

How to Divert Oneself

while Losing an Empire

Edited by

Justin Lovill

The Bunbury Press
2019

First published in 2019
by the Bunbury Press

Selection, material in this form, and
new material © Justin Lovill 2019

ISBN 978-0-9562046-1-5

A CIP catalogue record for this book is available
from the British Library

Printed by T J International Ltd, Padstow, Cornwall

CONTENTS

Afterwards

Some events in the Chronicle

A great frost begins; it continues for the rest of the month — 7 January

The Perreau brothers are executed at Tyburn for forgery — 17 January

Riots break out at Drury Lane Theatre — 1-5 February

Captain Cook agrees to undertake his third great voyage — *c.* 9 February

The first volume of Edward Gibbon's *Decline and Fall of the Roman Empire* is published — 17 February

Mohawk chief Joseph Brant meets the king — 29 February

Adam Smith's *The Wealth of Nations* is published — 9 March

John Wilkes makes a landmark proposal for electoral reform — 21 March

A coach containing dead bodies is stopped on London Bridge — 28 March

A Customs officer is murdered by smugglers at Deptford — 12 April

The trial of the Duchess of Kingston for bigamy begins — 15 April

The Royal Academy exhibition opens and the House of Commons debates the Budget and the American war — 24 April

News arrives of the evacuation of Boston by the king's troops — 2 May

Boswell brings about a meeting between longstanding antagonists Dr Johnson and John Wilkes — 15 May

The first stone of the new Somerset House is laid — 28 May

David Garrick performs on stage for the last time — 10 June

A masquerade is held at Ranelagh Gardens — 14 June

The Countess of Tyrconnel elopes from Hanover Square — 13 July

One of the queen's elephants dies — 24 July

News of the American declaration of independence arrives — 10 August

The Hon. John Damer shoots himself in a Covent Garden tavern — 15 August

A regatta in honour of the Prince of Wales is held at Richmond — 22 August

The last night at Vauxhall Gardens descends into riot — 29 August

The lord mayor is robbed by a highwayman near Turnham Green — 6 September

An attempt is made to abduct actress Ann Brown — 4 October

A hot naval press begins on the river and in the east of the city — 28 October

News arrives of the capture of New York by the king's troops — 2 November

'John the Painter' arrives in London having set fire to the dockyard at Portsmouth — 8 December

Samuel Foote is tried for attempting to bugger his footman — 9 December

A public fast is held to solicit divine assistance in the American war — 13 December

The manuscript of Fanny Burney's *Evelina* is delivered clandestinely to a publisher in Fleet Street — 25 December

Abbreviations and brief Glossary

At the end of most daily sections in the Chronicle short extracts are given from newspapers published on that day, such as might have been read on a visit to a coffee-house. A full list of titles and the abbreviations used can be found in the Bibliography, but the ones appearing most often are as follows:

GA Gazetteer and New Daily Advertiser

LC	London Chronicle	*MC*	Morning Chronicle
MJ	Middlesex Journal	*MP*	Morning Post
PA	Public Advertiser	*SJC*	St James's Chronicle

[>] indicates a cross reference to a Chronicle entry under the date indicated with months given in a short form, for example [> 5 Jan].

| within quotations indicates a paragraph break in the original.

A few old forms of place names have been retained. These include:

Brighthelmstone	Brighton
Caen Wood	Kenwood
Charles Town	Charleston
Marybone	Marylebone
Rumford	Romford
Surry	Surrey

Some other terms which may require clarification:

&c.	et cetera
heavy	(in weather summaries) overcast, cloudy
kennel	channel or surface drain in a street
key	quay
one pair of stairs	first floor (i.e. up one pair of stairs)
ordinary	chaplain
orgeat	a cooling drink made from orange-flower water and barley
passenger	pedestrian, passer by
patriot	Often used derogatively or ironically of those, such as John Wilkes, thought to be seeking personal advancement through populist challenging of the established order. In recording Dr Johnson's remark that 'Patriotism is the last refuge of a scoundrel,' Boswell added: 'He did not mean a real and generous love of our country, but that pretended patriotism which so many, in all ages and countries, have made a cloak for self-interest.'[1]
provincial	American
snow	small sailing vessel resembling a brig
ton, the *ton*	fashion, the fashionable people

Introduction

On 10th August 1776 Lord George Germain, secretary of state for the colonies, received news of the American declaration of independence. On the same day George III was on Wimbledon Common to see an experiment of a method of protecting buildings against fire. The inventor David Hartley had built a house three storeys high incorporating thin iron plates. The lower rooms were filled with faggots, pitch, tar and other combustibles. As the fire took hold and the lower part of the house became engulfed in flames, the king was in a room above, admiring the success of the experiment, quite unaffected by the raging below.

The king in a house on fire provides an emblem of kinds both for his own apparent disconnection from the ferment in America and for the life of his capital city during the American war of independence. 'Our session is over,' wrote Edmund Burke at the end of May, 'and I can hardly believe, by the tranquillity of every thing about me, that we are a people who have just lost an empire. But it is so.' In the city about him masquerades, murders and daily life continued much as usual while across the Atlantic cannon and musket and the fire of liberty all blazed, recasting the political order of the world.[2]

Much has naturally been written about events in America at this time, but what was it like to be living in London? This book seeks to answer that question by way of a daily chronicle in which the stories of 1776 unfold, and its characters emerge, through diaries, letters and newspaper reports.

In many ways it was a golden age, at least for those with command of gold. Britain had emerged from the Seven Years War of 1756 to 1763 as Europe's pre-eminent naval and colonial power, controlling North America and, through the East India Company, holding sway over much of India. The known world was continuing to expand, and with it the opportunities for trade, intercourse and plunder. In 1770 Captain Cook and his crew had landed at Botany Bay, the first recorded Europeans to set foot on the east coast of Australia, and in July 1775 he had returned from a second expedition to the Pacific. As 1776 dawned he was at home in Mile End Road, but a new expedition was in the offing, its aim being further to advance trade by the discovery of a north-west passage between the Atlantic and Pacific oceans.

As trade expanded, wealth and exotic goods poured in. Items imported into London and Bristol between January and May 1776, for example, included elephant teeth from Africa, salt petre and cotton from Bengal, bark and cochineal from Cadiz, whale oil from Canso, cocoa and coffee from Dominica, deer skins and tobacco from Georgia, mahogany from Honduras, rum, sugar and turpentine from Jamaica, anchovies, brimstone and juniper berries from Leghorn, camphire and redwood from Madras, almonds and gum from Mogador, and plums and olive oil from Oporto.[3]

A contemporary guidebook described London as 'the largest and most populous city in Europe, and the greatest mart of trade in the whole world'. Its population was probably still well under a million but the array of talent to be found in it was prodigious. Walking the streets in the early months of 1776 you might encounter, among others, Robert Adam, Beaumarchais, Jeremy Bentham, William Blake, James Boswell, Edmund Burke, Fanny Burney, Thomas Chippendale, James Cook, John Singleton Copley, Charles James Fox, Thomas Gainsborough, David Garrick, Edward Gibbon, Dr Johnson, Angelica Kauffman, Sir Joshua Reynolds, George Romney, Thomas Rowlandson, Richard Brinsley Sheridan, Elizabeth Siddons, Adam Smith, George Stubbs, Horace Walpole, John Wesley, Benjamin West and John Wilkes.[4]

With money at your command you could have your house built or refashioned by the Adam brothers, furnish it with Chippendale furniture and Wedgwood porcelain, and have your portrait painted by Reynolds or Gainsborough. At the theatre you could watch Garrick in his last season and catch up on Sheridan's latest success. London's wealth also attracted foreign performers. 'As a proof to what excess of luxury this country is arrived,' noted the *Morning Post* in November, 'there are now in London the four most capital singers in the world: Signora Gabrielli, Signora Agujari, Signor Manzoletto, and Signor Rauzzini.' As for books, those published during the year included the first volume of perhaps the best known of all histories, Gibbon's *Decline and Fall of the Roman Empire*, and Adam Smith's *The Wealth of Nations*, which has been described as in its ultimate results 'probably the most important book that has ever been written'; not to mention *Common Sense*, published in Philadelphia but written by an Englishman, Thomas Paine.[5]

Wealth was also feeding a building boom. During the year work began on Bedford Square and on the new Somerset House, the old one being pulled down and the Thames nearby embanked. In July Horace Walpole wrote from Strawberry Hill: 'Rows of houses shoot out every way like a polypus; and, so great is the rage of building everywhere, that, if I stay here a fortnight, without going to town, I look about to see if no new house is built since I went last.' The wife of an American refugee, on first encountering the ordinary busy-ness of London's streets, was so taken aback that she asked her husband to stop until the crowd had passed. Foreign visitors were also dazzled by the city's lighting. A few years later one noted that 'even on the most ordinary and common nights, the city has the appearance of a festive illumination; for which they say some German prince, on his first visit to London, actually took it, believing it to have been particularly ordered on account of his own arrival'. When Dr Johnson remarked, in 1775 and 1777 respectively, that 'the full tide of human existence is at Charing-cross,' and that 'when a man is tired of London, he is tired of life,' he was reflecting a sense of the city's size and possibilities, but also of its centrality as the pulsing heart of a busy, connected, expanding world.[6]

As with all golden ages, however, unease and shadows lurked beneath the surface. In 1772 a banking crisis had caused considerable panic. Fears persisted about the unprecedented level of national debt and the increasing reliance on paper money. Perhaps the most widely read new book of 1776 noted that 'nothing can be more delicate or hazardous' than paper currency, which, unlike coin, had no intrinsic value. 'It is an immense fabrick, with its head in the clouds ... and ... like the baseless fabrick of a vision, may in a moment vanish'. This sense of wealth's precariousness was fed by a series of forgeries, the most notorious of which, involving the Perreau brothers and Margaret Rudd, had been uncovered in March 1775 and was still awaiting its denouement.[7]

Meanwhile new fortunes, rapidly made, were unsettling the social order. Nabobs returning from India brought with them 'Asiatic' morals, deep pockets, and a willingness to outbribe their way into parliament. Although the number of nabob MPs was small – only 22 had been returned in the 1774 general election, out of 558 seats – their arrival was felt as a challenge by the landed gentry. At a more modest level, too, new wealth seemed to be encouraging social restlessness. In July the *Morning Post* reported that 'even a dealer in cabbages ... lately took a trip to London, where he purchased an harpsichord, value 20 guineas, in order to instruct his amiable daughter in the charming science of music'.[8]

The solvent of affluence also seemed to be weakening moral and gender boundaries, not least through the flourishing of pleasure gardens such as those at Vauxhall and Ranelagh. 'We cannot help thinking', commented one survey, 'that places of public entertainment have been too numerous in the present age [and] that the prudence and modesty in women, during former times, and the manly assurance in men, was much superior to the practice of the present age, where a promiscuous intercourse takes place amongst the sexes, and all distinctions are jumbled together in one mass of confusion.'[9]

Affluence and its anxieties were only part of the story, however, with poverty all around and prostitution rife. Returning home at night Dr Johnson often saw children asleep in the streets and used 'to put pennies into their hands to buy them a breakfast'. A Prussian visitor marvelled 'that the crowds of poor wretches who continually fill the streets of the metropolis, excited by the luxurious and effeminate life of the great, have not some time or another entered into a general conspiracy to plunder them'.[10]

As London's array of diversions increased some sensed vacancy beneath the gilded merry-go-round. In 1774 the *Critical Review* observed: 'If we cast our eyes upon the upper, or the middle ranks of life, we shall find that the principal business of men and women is the study of dress, and the pursuit of amusements. They lie down to sleep, and rise up to trifle'. In the following year Lichtenberg, visiting from Germany, judged that luxury and extravagance had risen to such a pitch in

London 'as never before in the history of the world'.
Samuel Curwen, a refugee from the troubles in America,
agreed: 'The dissipation, self-forgetfulness, and vicious
indulgences of every kind, which characterize this
metropolis, are not to be wondered at. The temptations
are too great for that degree of philosophy and religion
ordinarily possessed by the bulk of mankind.' London's
money seemed to be going to its head — literally, in the
case of female fashions, with precariously towering
head-dresses proving ripe for ridicule. Lichtenberg
himself sketched the Duchess of Devonshire at the
opera in November 1775 (*right*). 'I assure you that this
is no exaggeration,' he wrote to a friend. 'A single
such feather costs a guinea; they are red, white, and
black.'[11]

Inadequate foundations and resultant instability were also discerned in the
country's political, economic and legal structures, which came under a series of
attacks early in 1776. In January (reprinted in London in late May) Thomas
Paine's *Common Sense* argued that the failings of the British constitution were the
fundamental cause of the supposed oppression of America. In February Richard
Price's *Observations on the Nature of Civil Liberty* argued that true liberty could
not be said to exist when half of the House of Commons was elected by just 5,723
people. In March Adam Smith's *Wealth of Nations* proposed clearing away the
established web of monopolies, tariffs and subsidies and concluded that Britain
could no longer afford the costly, tottering head-dress appendage of its American
empire. Twelve days later John Wilkes proposed a bill in parliament for the more
equal representation of the people, with rotten boroughs to be swept away and
an axe taken to corruption, 'Treasury influence' and 'aristocratical tyranny'. The
prime minister responded by observing jocularly that he could not be serious.[12]

So while Londoners in 1776 might benefit from the world's riches and feel
proud of Britain's pre-eminence, there was also a tempering sense that a reckoning,
or at least an eclipse, might be nigh. A *History of North America*, published during
the year, concluded that 'it would be contrary to the nature of things' for America
to remain under Britain's dominion once it became its equal in riches and population.
Developments on both sides of the Atlantic, including 'the sudden and rapid
decline of our manners and our powers, together with the crimes of princes and
the sufferings of the people', were conspiring towards a 'great disruption ... The
foundations of our tottering empires are sapped; materials are hourly collecting
and preparing for their destruction'. In America, on the other hand, there were
'vigorous, and even virtuous men, who have nothing to lose but their lives ... and
that country rising out of nothing, will be fired with the ambition of appearing
with glory in its turn on the face of the globe, and in the history of the world'.[13]

While history may not repeat itself it sometimes affords strange echoes, and London in 1776 may appear to a modern reader like something glimpsed in a distorting mirror. Many of its surfaces are strange – a world of link boys and sedan chairs, of wigs and candle-light, of highwaymen and public executions – but it reflects something eerily familiar back at us: the stirrings of globalisation, vast new wealth unrooted in land or social obligation, a proliferating array of luxuries and diversions to distract the affluent, conspicuous inequality, and an undertow of political discontent. Governor Hutchinson, the most notable of the American refugees in London, meeting a French diplomat in May 1775, heard from him 'the particulars of a great riot at Paris: and we both observed that a dissatisfaction with government was not confined to America, nor the English dominions, but [was] rather the general temper of the age'.[14]

As far as the international stage was concerned, Britain seemed to be making a historic mistake by insisting on a sovereign right to tax America and so jeopardising a union which brought enviable trading advantages. Domestic opinion was sharply divided on the question, but those aghast at the government's handling of the matter felt themselves powerless to draw the country back from a perceived precipice. For its part America, wishing to free itself from control by a remote colonial power, was intent on liberty and sovereignty, including control of its own trade. There too opinion was divided, however, loyalists wishing to cleave to the reassuring union with the mother country, rebels determined to assert adult independence. Meanwhile France, resenting its own recently reduced place in world affairs, was waiting on the sidelines, ready to exploit any opportunity to undermine British ascendancy.

Fame reassures America

Detail from *Liberty Triumphant; or the Downfall of Oppression,* published *circa* 1774

Arrangement of the book

This introduction is followed by two guides for those unfamiliar with London in 1776: **Briefing Notes for Strangers**, which provides background information on the political situation and on some of the town's notable characters, and then a **Tour**.

There follows the day by day **Chronicle** which is based closely on contemporary records. Details of the editorial approach taken can be found below.

Finally an **Afterwards** section sketches subsequent political developments, the later lives of selected individuals, and the fates of some of 1776's places of diversion.

The Chronicle text

The note of the weather at the beginning of each daily section is drawn from meteorological diaries published in the *Gentleman's Magazine*.[15]

The account of each day's events is given largely in the words of contemporary diaries, letters and newspaper reports, although in places these have been trimmed, condensed and otherwise adjusted. Accounts from different newspapers have often been combined. Details of all sources appear in the notes.

Reports that seem to be implausible or otherwise suspect have been omitted. However, given that the Chronicle is drawn in large part from newspapers, it should be borne in mind that a number of entries will be inaccurate or simply untrue.

Occasional information from modern sources has been inserted where it seems likely that it will be helpful. It is given in a simple modern idiom, no attempt having been made to imitate eighteenth-century prose. Any phrasing that looks 'antique' is so.

At the end of many of the daily sections there are brief extracts from newspapers published on that day, reports from morning papers preceding those from evening ones.

At the end of some months particularly notable events in America are briefly summarised in a 'Meanwhile in America' section.

All material placed within quotation marks, including the newspaper extracts, is given verbatim, although in a few cases minor emendations (such as omission or addition of paragraph breaks, spelling out of contractions, and adjustment of punctuation) have been silently made. Where spelling has been adjusted this is indicated in the notes.

In the rest of the Chronicle text the style of the source material (including original and inconsistent spelling and punctuation) has been largely retained. The reader will therefore encounter, among other things, missing apostrophes, 'less' where we expect 'fewer', 'dutchess' alongside 'duchess', and '£500' as well '500l.', not to mention 'millenium' and other shockers.

A certain amount of standardisation has nonetheless been carried out for the sake of ease of reading. Place and personal names have generally been standardised except within quotations, although some contemporary forms (e.g. Wirtemburg for Württemberg) have been retained. Capitalisation has been greatly reduced, and specific adjustments have been made where it seems likely that the original wording would impede ready comprehension. In art restoration terms the aim has been a fairly light clean with minor retouching.

Books about particular years usually take a different approach, the author identifying themes and subjects and considering them in discrete chapters in accessible modern prose. Such a method tends to remove the background 'noise' of trivial events, to produce a sense of order and context, and to afford scope for wise historical analysis. The Chronicle offers none of these things. Indeed, those faced with it may share the reaction of the fictional countryman 'Squire Randal when, on a jaunt to London in 1776, he ventures to a coffee-house for breakfast and picks up a newspaper: 'What a hodge-podge was there! what a farrago of broken limbs, robberies, lottery-tickets, ladies luxuries, murders, deaths, births and marriages, *higgledy-piggledy* together!'[16]

One particular disadvantage is that coverage of strands and stories is intermittent, so that a reader wanting to follow a particular theme or thread or person must either wade through the entire book or use the index to locate the scattered entries.

The higgledy-piggledy approach does, however, offer some compensations. It enables the reader to see notable events and characters against the wider, day by day canvas of London life. In some respects it may also bring the reader closer to the experience of those alive at the time, for whom history unfolded not neatly by theme but as one thing after or jostling alongside another, and who did not know what would happen next, let alone how things would turn out in the long run. It is also hoped that by relying heavily on contemporary accounts the Chronicle captures at least something of the flavour of that time, its accents and assumptions, in a way that modern paraphrase might struggle to do.

George the III. King of Great Britain.

After a portrait by Zoffany exhibited at the Royal Academy in
April 1771. 'Very like,' noted Horace Walpole in his catalogue.

Briefing Notes for Strangers

31st December 1775*

A: Court, politics, war

i. The Court

The king, **George III**, is 37 years old and has been on the throne since 1760, when he succeeded his grandfather, George II. The first of the Hanoverian kings to be born and educated in England, he is dutiful, personally abstemious, interested in astronomy and clocks, speaks fluent French and German, and dates his letters to the minute. His shyness leads him to fill awkward silences with interjections such as 'What? What?' and 'the oscillations of his body, the precipitation of his questions ... and the hurry of his articulation' lead some to mistake him for a bumbling fool. Closer observers find him to have a solid if not brilliant under-standing. He tends to obstinacy and dislikes opposition.[1]

In 1761 he married **Charlotte** of Mecklenburg-Strelitz, now aged 31, to whom he is devoted. Seeing her recently at the theatre and in Hyde Park, an American refugee noted that she is 'a small siz'd woman, her features very regular, save her nose, which has something of the turn up', and that 'her countenance carries such a sweetness as attracts the esteem of all'.[2]

In 1762 the king bought Buckingham House for her, on the west side of St James's Park. It is now their main home and has come to be known as the Queen's Palace or the Queen's House. From here they make the short journey across the park to St James's Palace for Court functions. The king has a levee at St James's every Wednesday and Friday, and on Monday during the sitting of parliament, while the queen has a drawing-room every Thursday. In summer they also spend time at Kew and at Windsor.[3]

They already have ten children, seven sons and three daughters, and another is on the way. George Augustus Frederick, aged 13, is **Prince of Wales** and already inclined to be troublesome. The next oldest is Prince Frederick, aged 12, who was made **Bishop of Osnaburgh** before his first birthday.

The king's elder sister **Augusta**, aged 38, is abroad, having married the Prince of Brunswick-Wolfenbüttel. He also has two slightly embarrassing brothers with whom he is at odds. William Henry, **Duke of Gloucester**, aged 32, married a widow of illegitimate birth, Maria Waldegrave, in secret ten years ago and they are currently in Italy. Henry Frederick, **Duke of Cumberland**, aged 30, was discovered in bed with Lady Grosvenor in 1769, causing a scandal and a court case. He was found guilty of 'criminal conversation' and had to pay £10,000 damages to the wronged husband. In 1771 he married Anne Horton, née Luttrell,

---

* All quotations are from contemporary sources, details of which may be found in the notes section towards the end of the book.

The Trial of the D. of C. and Lady G-r for Crim. Con.

a widow from a family of political opportunists. The king was so perturbed that he had a Royal Marriages Act passed forcing descendants of George II in most cases to obtain prior consent from the monarch to marry. The Cumberlands are excluded from Court but have set up in style at Cumberland House in the Mall.

There is also **Princess Amelia**, aged 64, the king's aunt. She is little at Court, and instead divides her time between a house in Cavendish Square, her villa at Gunnersbury, and occasional visits to Bath.[4]

The king stands at the head of a vast system of patronage from which he derives much of his power. The most obvious manifestation of this is the royal household. Among the many employed in or by it are a band of musick (master Dr William Boyce); a brusher of the robes; a clerk of the venison warrants; six coal porters; an embellisher of letters to the Eastern princes; a feather-dresser; a gentleman of the wine cellar; a heater of water for the horses; two herald painters; a herb-strewer; keepers of the fire buckets and of ice-houses; makers of harpsichords and sedan chairs; masters of the buck-hounds, of the tennis court, of the revels, and of the horse (the Duke of Ancaster); a master falconer; a mole-taker; a necessary woman; two operators for the teeth; an organ-blower; eight pages of the back stairs; eight postilions; a rat-killer; a sweeper of the courts at St James's; a table decker to the maids of honour and bedchamber women; forty-eight watermen; and a yeoman arras worker at the Great Wardrobe.

In addition the queen's own household includes the Duchess of Ancaster as mistress of the robes, six ladies of the bedchamber, six maids of honour, five bedchamber women, five coachmen, eight footmen, five postilions, four chairmen, her own band of musick, and a bottleman, P. Quin. Her treasurer is the Earl of Guilford, father of the prime minister.[5]

ABOVE Queen Charlotte, with the royal children in the background,
by Benjamin West, 1779.
FACING PAGE A contemporary view of the Grosvenor-Cumberland trial,
with Lady Grosvenor third from the left.

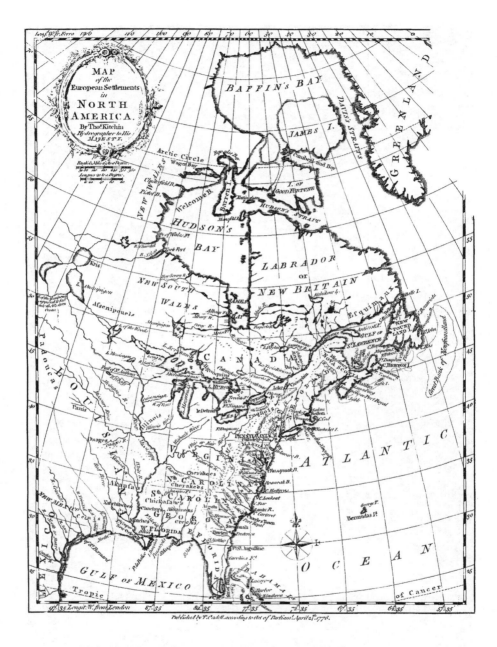

The European Settlements in North America, by Thomas Kitchin
Published by Thomas Cadell in the Strand, 24th April 1776

ii. America

For some time the business of the king's government has been dominated by one issue, the rebellion in America.

The roots of the problem lie largely in success. Increasingly populous, educated, wealthy and confident, colonial America has grown to maturity. Its leading people, many of whom are lawyers, naturally aspire to greater control of its affairs. They consider themselves to enjoy the same rights as Englishmen, and, not being represented in parliament, do not expect to be taxed by it. They are also increasingly resentful of the fact that Britain controls their trade, with the question of sovereignty lying beneath it all. They have been freed to stand their ground in any quarrel by British victory in the Seven Years War, which has removed the threat from France and Spain.

The British government, on the other hand, is still grappling with the cost of that war. The national debt increased from under £75 million at its start to over £130 million at its end, and it seems reasonable to ministers to recover at least some of the cost of protecting America by imposing taxation upon it. Dr Johnson, who receives a government pension, obligingly argued the point in his pamphlet *Taxation No Tyranny*, published in March: 'They, who ... flourish under the protection of our government, should contribute something towards its expence.' More recently Methodist leader John Wesley has argued the same case, first in *A Calm Address to our American Colonies*, then in a letter to an evening newspaper in which he maintained that the Americans 'are not contending for liberty' but for 'the illegal privilege of being exempt from parliamentary taxation'.[6]

The process of taxing America overtly was begun by George Grenville's government with a Sugar Act in 1764, but trouble only really began with the Stamp Act of the following year, which imposed duties on newspapers and legal documents. 'This single stroke has lost Great Britain the affection of all her colonies,' wrote one American. British goods were boycotted and in New York an effigy of the governor was hanged alongside one of the devil.[7]

In March 1766 the government of Lord Rockingham, who had replaced Grenville, responded ambivalently, repealing the Stamp Act but passing a Declaratory Act which asserted the authority of the British parliament over America. In the following year a Revenue Act, promoted by chancellor of the exchequer Lord Townshend, imposed duties on tea, paper and other items imported into America.

Over the next few years resistance rumbled on, mainly in Massachusetts. On 5th March 1770, less than two months after Lord North had taken over as prime minister, British troops stationed in Boston fired on protesters, killing three and fatally wounding two others. The soldiers were tried and acquitted but the incident, soon dubbed 'the Boston Massacre', exacerbated resentment. In April, continuing to appear at once weak and obstinate, the British government repealed the Townshend duties except for that on tea.

In May 1773 a new Tea Act was passed to help the East India Company, which had vast quantities of unsold tea rotting in its London warehouses and was nearing bankruptcy. Export duties were reduced, and for the first time the company was allowed to sell its tea directly in America rather than through middlemen. As a result it could sell its stock at low prices there, undercutting smuggled tea, which was widely consumed.

The Townshend import duty remained, however, so that with cheap tea the Americans were being expected to swallow the principle of colonial taxation. They smelt a rat, and smugglers and merchants, who were directly affected, mobilised popular support. On 16th December, in defiance of Thomas Hutchinson, the loyalist governor of Massachusetts, a group of men dressed as Mohawks boarded three ships in Boston harbour, hoisted 342 chests of tea out of the holds, and emptied them into the sea. Hutchinson judged it 'the boldest stroke which had yet been struck in America'.[8]

Paul Revere's inaccurate but influential depiction of the
Boston 'Massacre', printed and sold in Boston, 1770

News of what later came to be known as the Boston Tea Party reached London in January 1774. It prompted the Coercive Acts, known in America as the Intolerable Acts. The first, the Boston Port Act, provided for the closure of Boston's port until its people had compensated the East India Company for the lost tea. Other Acts went beyond restitution, punitively reducing the role of local government in Massachusetts. In April Hutchinson was replaced by a British general, Thomas Gage, who arrived a month later with four regiments. To many Americans it seemed clear that Britain was intent on destroying their freedoms.

The hard line embodied in the Coercive Acts divided opinion at home while largely uniting it in America. In September and October 1774 the colonies, Georgia excepted, assembled in the First Continental Congress at Philadelphia and resolved to boycott British and Irish goods and East India Company tea. Many Americans saw short term economic hardship as a price worth paying in order to wrest control of their affairs from a remote and unaccountable colonial power. 'Let us eat potatoes and drink water,' wrote John Adams to his wife, 'let us wear canvas, and undressed sheepskins, rather than submit to the unrighteous and ignominious domination that is prepared for us.'[9]

The able Doctor, or America Swallowing the Bitter Draught.

Lord North, with the Boston Port bill in his pocket, pours tea down the throat of a reluctant America. Lord Mansfield holds the victim's arms while the rakish Lord Sandwich secures her ankles and raises her dress to cast an expert eye on the view. In the background, from left to right, France and Spain look on in bemusement, Britannia averts her eyes, and former prime minister Lord Bute holds a sword inscribed 'Military Law'. From the *London Magazine* for April 1774.

The BOSTONIANS Paying the EXCISE-MAN, or TARRING & FEATHERING

Plate I.

London, Printed for Rob.ᵗ Sayer & J. Bennett, Map & Printseller, N.º 53, Fleet Street, as the Act directs 31, Oct.ᵗ 1774.

Bostonians return Lord North's compliment. Print depicting the
treatment meted out to John Malcolm, a Customs officer at Boston,
who was led tarred and feathered to a gallows on 27th January 1774.
Published by Sayer and Bennett, 53 Fleet Street, 31st October 1774.

A SOCIETY of PATRIOTIC LADIES,
AT
EDENTON in NORTH CAROLINA.

London, Printed for R. Sayer, & J. Bennett, N.º 53 in Fleet Street, as the Act directs 25 March 1775.

'We the ladys of Edenton do hereby solemnly engage not to conform
to that pernicious custom of drinking tea …' Satire on a meeting of
25th October 1774 at which fifty-one American women signed a
statement in support of Congress's boycott of imports from Britain.
Published by Sayer and Bennett, 25th March 1775.

Meanwhile in London Lord North brought forward the general election, due in 1775, to the autumn of 1774, putting a new House of Commons in place to handle the anticipated crisis.

The Colossus of the North; or The Striding Boreas.

*See our Colossus strides with Trophies crown'd,
And Monsters in Corruption's Stream abound*

'Methought I was walking up Palace yard, and on a sudden a stream burst forth out of the grand door of Westminster Hall, in which were overwhelmed hundreds of members, all floating down this torrent of corruption, as you have seen dead dogs, cats, and turnip tops in the Thames. Across this stream, strode a colossus ...'

Print from the *London Magazine* for November 1774 satirising North's successful deployment of the usual tools of interest and patronage to retain control of the House of Commons at the recent election. 'Boreas' in the title refers to the Greek god of the north wind, under which name North was often caricatured.

The colossus's feet are fixed upon the shores of *Tyranny* and *Venality*. In one hand he holds papers marked *Places*, *Pensions* and *Lottery Tickets*, and in the other a blazing torch marked *America*. A disconsolate Britannia laments, 'Those that should have been my preservers have been my destroyers,' while the 'patriotic' John Wilkes, an advocate of electoral reform, seeks to counter the torrent with a broom, saying 'I'll stem the stream.'

During the year now reaching its end, 1775, the pace of events has quickened on both sides of the Atlantic.

On 20th January in the House of Lords the ailing Lord Chatham (William Pitt the elder) proposed the removal of the king's forces from Boston but was heavily defeated. He criticised the government for acting out of a combination of ignorance of America's circumstances and anger at its temerity. 'What! shall America presume to be free? Don't hear them, chastise them.'[10]

On 20th February in the House of Commons Lord North made a final attempt to avert war with a conciliatory proposal: if the colonists made satisfactory provision for their own defence and government, parliament would not tax them, although it 'could never give up the right' to do so. For the opposition Edmund Burke described the scheme as 'altogether insidious', calculated not to produce peace but 'to increase the disorders and confusions in America'. It was nonetheless approved by a large majority and dispatched in writing to each of the colonies individually, with a view to dividing them one from another.[11]

On 16th March Lord Camden counselled caution in the Lords and summarised the state of affairs as seen by the opposition. 'To conquer a great continent of 1800 miles, containing three millions of people, all indissolubly united on the great Whig bottom of liberty and justice' was 'an undertaking not to be rashly engaged in'. The one realistic option was a naval blockade, but that would achieve only 'the blocking up their ports, and the suppression of their trade. But will this procure the conquest of America? No, my lords; they are prepared to meet these severities, and to surmount them. They are applying themselves most diligently to agriculture, that great source of strength and independence. ... They have united in the rejection of luxury and superfluous enjoyment. They have suppressed their public diversions ... and every man attaches himself wholly to the great business of his country. Such is the state of America.'

Britain, on the other hand, 'this *civilized, enlightened*, dissipated and debauched country,' was far from prepared:

'How shall the want of American commerce be supplied, of that commerce which contributes the means of your luxury, of your enjoyments, of the imaginary happiness of this country? We may feel the loss of American connection, a loss which nothing can compensate; but America will have little reason to regret her disconnection from England; and, my lords, it is evident that England must one day lose the dominion of America. It is impossible that this petty island can continue in dependence that mighty continent, encreasing daily in numbers and in strength. To protract the time of separation to a distant day is all that can be hoped; and this hope might be obtained by wise and temperate counsels; not by precipitation and violence, uniting America against you. For so it is, my lords. There is not a man in America, who can endure the idea of being taxed ... by a legislature 3000 miles distant, or who can separate the idea of taxation from representation.'

In reply Lord Sandwich, first lord of the Admiralty, foresaw no great difficulty in conquering America. 'Suppose the colonies do abound in men, what does that signify? They are raw, undisciplined, cowardly men. ... Believe me, my lords, the very sound of a cannon would carry them off ... as fast as their feet could carry them.'[12]

Three days later Benjamin Franklin, who had been in England since 1764 and had attempted to mediate with the British government, set out from his house in Craven Street, Strand, to return to America.[13]

On 22nd March Edmund Burke proposed in the Commons that the Coercive Acts be repealed and that, rather than persisting in futile attempts to tax from afar, parliament should accept 'the legal competency of the colony assemblies for the support of their government in peace and ... war'. He argued that 'the use of force alone is but temporary. It may subdue for a moment; but it does not remove the necessity of subduing again: and a nation is not governed, which is perpetually to be conquered. ... | A further objection to force is, that you impair the object by your very endeavours to preserve it. The thing you fought for, is not the thing which you recover; but depreciated, sunk, wasted, and consumed in the contest.' His resolutions were all defeated.[14]

On 10th April the lord mayor, John Wilkes, presented a petition from the City of London to the king at St James's, one of many appeals from those with commercial interests who wish the government to avoid a costly, trade-disrupting war. The country may be divided but the City is vociferously pro-American. There were reportedly 'upwards of fifty thousand persons surrounding the palace and in Pall Mall, who huzza'd the lord mayor and aldermen at their going into the palace, and on their return to their carriages', but a feared riot did not materialise.[15]

On 19th April the war of independence began with skirmishes at Lexington and Concord. Next day the *Cerberus* man of war sailed from Portsmouth with reinforcements for Boston. On board were three major generals, William Howe, Henry Clinton and John Burgoyne.

In early May American forces took the forts of Ticonderoga and Crown Point, vital staging posts for an assault on Canada.[16]

On 15th June George Washington was appointed commander-in-chief of the colonial army. Two days later the British under General Gage won a victory at Bunker Hill, near Boston, but suffered heavy losses. Gage, a veteran of the Seven Years War, reported to London: 'These people shew a spirit and conduct against us, they never shewed against the French ... | They are now spirited up by a rage and enthusiasm, as great as ever people were possessed of, and you must proceed in earnest or give the business up.'[17]

On 7th July members of the Continental Congress signed an 'olive branch' petition to the king. Describing themselves as his 'dutiful subjects' they accused his ministers of abusing his 'royal confidence and authority, for the purpose of

The Political Cartoon for the Year 1775.

Horses named Obstinacy and Pride trample on Magna Carta and the constitution as a somnolent George III is driven towards a cliff-edge by Lord Mansfield, with former prime minister Lord Bute behind them bearing a sword. Lord North (centre) and a crutch-carrying Lord Chatham (right) are among those who appear powerless to prevent the impending disaster. In the foreground voters are distracted by bribes. Above a devil flies away with the national credit, and in the distance America is in flames. Published in the *Westminster Magazine* for April 1775.

An English view of the battle at Bunker Hill, published 1783

effecting our destruction'. They asked him 'to direct some mode' of achieving 'a happy and permanent reconciliation', but offered no concessions.

On 31st July the Congress finally replied to Lord North's conciliatory proposal. The colonies, they said, were 'entitled to the sole and exclusive privilege of giving and granting their own money' and deciding how it should be spent. It was unjust to expect contributions towards the cost of their defence 'while Great Britain possesses a monopoly of their trade. This of itself lays them under heavy contribution. ... If we are to contribute equally with the other parts of the empire, let us equally with them enjoy free commerce with the whole world.'[18]

On 2nd August letters were sent to Boston recalling General Gage and appointing General Howe in his place. It was thought that Gage, whose wife was American, lacked stomach for the fight, the king referring to him as 'the mild general'.[19]

On 23rd August the king issued a proclamation declaring America to be in rebellion.

On 1st September Congress's 'olive branch' petition was presented to Lord Dartmouth, secretary of state for the colonies, by Richard Penn, who had brought it from America, and Arthur Lee, an American-born lawyer and colonial agent. From the government's point of view the petition originated in an illegal assembly and Dartmouth made clear that there would be no reply.

On 5th September Dartmouth wrote to General Howe with instructions to abandon Boston before winter and head south.[20]

On the morning of 23rd October Stephen Sayre, an American banker and former sheriff of the City of London, was arrested at his house in Oxford Street on the order of Lord Rochford, one of the secretaries of state. He was accused of a treasonous conspiracy to seize the king on his way to the state opening of parliament, to take possession of the Tower, and to overturn the government. Evidence was lacking, however, and he was released on bail five days later.[21]

On 25th October John Wilkes dined at the Mansion House with Richard Penn, Arthur Lee, and French playwright and adventurer Caron de Beaumarchais. The last was in England to finesse a difficulty between the French crown and another adventurer, the Chevalier d'Éon, but at about this time he was also developing a cunning scheme whereby France could covertly provide the rebels in America with gunpowder and other military supplies.[22]

On 26th October the king opened a new session of parliament, declaring that 'the rebellious war now levied is ... manifestly carried on for the purpose of establishing an independent empire'. Britain would not 'give up so many colonies which she has ... protected and defended at much expence of blood and treasure'. When 'the unhappy and deluded multitude' became 'sensible of their error' he would be ready to receive them 'with tenderness and mercy'. He intended to appoint commissioners 'to grant general or particular pardons and indemnities ... and to receive the submission of any province or colony which shall be disposed to return to its allegiance'. When copies of the speech arrived in America rebel soldiers besieging Boston burnt them and hoisted their union flag in defiance.[23]

On 10th November Lord George Germain was appointed secretary of state for the colonies, replacing the more conciliatory Dartmouth. Lord Weymouth replaced Lord Rochford as secretary of state for the southern department.[24]

On 11th November the *Adamant* set sail from Quebec for England with Ethan Allen and thirty-three other rebel prisoners of war on board, along with Colonel Guy Johnson, the king's superintendent of Indian affairs, and Mohawk chief Joseph Brant (Thayendanegea).[25]

On 13th November American forces under General Richard Montgomery captured Montreal, forcing the British governor, General Guy Carleton, to retreat to Quebec.

On 14th November General Gage arrived back in London. 'Whatever accounts he brought were sedulously concealed,' according to Horace Walpole. 'All that was learnt was that the troops could not get out of Boston, were to winter there, and were fortifying themselves as strongly as they could, and had few fresh provisions.'[26]

On 29th November the Continental Congress established a committee of secret correspondence to communicate with 'our friends' in Britain and elsewhere. Prominent among these was Arthur Lee.

Early in December Montgomery's troops, joining others under Benedict Arnold, began a siege of Quebec. They will attack it in the early hours of New Year's Day.[27]

On 22nd December an Act to prohibit all trade and intercourse with Massachusetts Bay and other colonies during the rebellion received the royal assent.[28]

On the evening of 23rd December ministers, attended by the attorney general and the solicitor general, met to consider what to do with Ethan Allen and the other prisoners of war who had arrived and were being held in Pendennis Castle, Cornwall. Reprisals affecting British prisoners in America were feared, and within a few days it was decided to send the men back across the Atlantic to Boston, leaving General Howe to deal with the problem.[29]

On Christmas Day Germain's office received a letter dated 20th November from General Carleton noting his retreat from Montreal and the desertion of Canadian peasants and expressing doubt as to his ability to hold Quebec.[30]

On 27th December General Burgoyne arrived in London from Boston. In the evening ministers gathered in the great council chamber at Germain's office in Whitehall to consider dispatches he had brought from General Howe. The news was not good: the order to evacuate Boston had arrived too late and provisions would last only until the beginning of March.[31]

So things stand at the turn of the year, with Boston besieged, Quebec about to be attacked, and the government in London trying to work out how best to wage a distant war.

iii. The ministry

Frederick North, aged 43, has been **prime minister** since 1770 but dislikes the title and tells his children not to use it. He is more often referred to as 'the first minster' or simply 'the minister'. He is a Tory, but again the term is rarely used, faction and interest rather than party being the basis of political loyalties. As the eldest son of the Earl of Guilford he is known by the courtesy title **Lord North** but he sits in the House of Commons. He is also chancellor of the exchequer, in which role he is regarded as an able manager of the nation's finances.[32]

He lives at No. 10 Downing Street with his wife Anne. They have three sons and three daughters, ranging in age from five to eighteen, the eldest being George Augustus, who is at Oxford. North also has a house in Grosvenor Square, which he lets out, but his long-lived father fails to provide him with an adequate allowance and he is constantly in debt.[33]

Although he comes from an old Court and political family, at times he appears a reluctant prime minister. In 1772 he wrote to his father: 'It must always be my wish to be released from a station which is too great for my abilities before I have entirely forfeited the little reputation I may have gained'. According to his daughter Katherine he looks frequently from the Downing Street windows to the nearby Pay Office, where he formerly worked, declaring that he has 'never been happy since he removed from the one to the other'.[34]

He does, however, enjoy a close relationship with the king, who recently described him as 'my sheet anchor'. The king is personally generous to him, fostering his sense of obligation to continue in office. In 1771 Anne North was made ranger of Bushy Park, a sinecure providing a comfortable country house within easy reach of town. In September 1777 the king will offer to pay off North's debts up to £20,000.[35]

He is an effective performer in the House of Commons, his wit and affability making him popular even with opponents, although his humour sometimes exasperates them, Edmund Burke complaining in one debate, 'It is not sufficient, when the first minister shall make you laugh.' Edward Gibbon, on the other hand, dining at Bushy in April, was highly amused: 'If they turned out Lord N. to-morrow, they would still leave him one of the best companions in the kingdom.'[36]

In his government the management of foreign affairs is divided between three secretaries of state, giving rise to some conflict and confusion.

Lord Weymouth (Thomas Thynne, 3rd viscount), aged 41, has been secretary of state for the **southern department** since November and deals with southern Europe including France, Portugal and Spain. He sits in the House of Lords and owns Longleat, the grounds of which he has had improved by Lancelot 'Capability' Brown.

Lord Suffolk (Henry Howard, 12th earl), aged 36, has been secretary of state for the **northern department** since 1771 and deals with countries including Russia,

Lord North, after a portrait by Nathaniel Dance, *circa* 1774

He wears the ribbon and star of the order of the garter, received in 1772. According to memoirist Nathaniel Wraxall, in his person he is 'of the middle size, heavy, large, and much inclined to corpulency'. He has 'a fair complexion, regular features, light hair, with bushy eyebrows, and grey eyes rather prominent in his head. His face might be ... esteemed a caricature of the king'. His eyesight is poor and his tongue is 'rather too large for his mouth', rendering his articulation 'somewhat thick'. In 'speaking, walking, and every motion' he is 'to the last degree awkward'.

Lord Suffolk, also wearing the ribbon and star of the garter, after a portrait by Reynolds, 1778

Sweden, Holland and the German states. On America he takes a robust line. He advocated the arrest of Benjamin Franklin before he left Britain and pressed for the recall of General Gage. His health is poor. He sits in the Lords.

Lord George Germain, aged 59, has been secretary of state for **the colonies** since November. His department deals mainly with Ireland, the Caribbean and America, and is often referred to as the **American department**. He is the minister most responsible for the conduct of the war and takes a hard line which recommends him to the king but sets him at odds with the more peaceable Lord North. He was born a Sackville, youngest son of the 1st Duke of Dorset, but changed his name in 1770 under the terms of the will of Lady Betty Germain, who left him a fortune and the estate of Drayton in Northamptonshire. He also has Stoneland Lodge in Sussex, rented from his nephew, and sits for East Grinstead in the House of Commons. In earlier life he rose to major general in the army, but his reputation was tarnished by accusations of cowardice relating to his command of a cavalry wing at the battle of Minden in Germany in 1759. A court-martial in the following year judged that he had disobeyed orders and was 'unfit to serve his majesty in any military capacity whatever'. Although the evidence tended to support him he is still satirised as 'the Minden hero'. He is married but attended by rumours of homosexuality.[37]

Lord George Germain, with Drayton in the background,
after a portrait by George Romney, 1778

According to his friend Wraxall he was 'near six feet ... muscular, and capable of
enduring much bodily as well as mental fatigue. ... His features were strongly
pronounced and saturnine ... An air of high birth and dignity illuminated by strong
sense pervaded every lineament of his face. ... His voice was powerful and his figure
commanding, though he did not always thoroughly possess himself nor display
the coolness demanded for so trying a situation as that of American secretary.'

Lord Sandwich (John Montagu, 4th earl), aged 57, has been **first lord of the Admiralty** since 1771, his third stint in the post. According to Fanny Burney he is 'a tall, stout man, and looks as furrowed and weather-proof as any sailor in the navy', with 'good nature and joviality marked in every feature'. He is clumsy, his French dancing master apparently asking that he 'would never tell any one of whom you learned to dance'. He is fond of cricket, sailing, fishing and music, holding Christmas musical meetings at his seat, Hinchingbrooke near Huntingdon. His wife was declared insane in 1767, by which time he had already taken as his mistress Martha Ray, who is about twenty-five years his junior and a fine singer. They live more or less openly together and have five surviving children.

He is known as 'Jemmy Twitcher' after a treacherous character in *The Beggar's Opera*, having betrayed his fellow libertine John Wilkes in 1763. In the midst of a political war between the government and Wilkes (see below), Sandwich produced a privately printed copy of Wilkes's *Essay on Woman*, an obscene parody of Pope's *Essay on Man*, in the House of Lords in order to damage him. The hypocrisy and ruthlessness of the act were noticed. His approach to America is robust but his concern to maintain a sufficient force in home waters, to deter any invasion attempt by France or Spain, leads to friction with Germain.[38]

Lord Barrington (William Wildman, 2nd viscount), aged 58, has been **secretary at war** since 1765 having also held the post from 1755 to 1761. His is an Irish title and he sits in the House of Commons. Asked at dinner a year ago about his long tenure while governments changed about him, he replied 'that he could compare the state to a great plum-pudding, which he was so fond of that he would never quarrel with it, but should be for taking a slice as long as there was any left'. Since then his taste for pudding has abated. He has deep reservations about the conduct of the war. During the summer he wrote to the king that the extra troops which the government planned to send in the spring 'cannot possibly be raised', and to Lord North that 'the Americans may be reduced by the fleet, but never can be by the army.' In October he wrote again to the king saying he wished to quit the Commons. Not wanting to lose an able and experienced administrator, the king has so far avoided discussing the matter with him.[39]

Two other figures, not formally part of government, are thought to exert considerable influence.

Lord Mansfield (William Murray, 1st baron), aged 70, lord chief justice of the King's Bench, attends meetings of the privy council and is seen as a hard-line *éminence grise* who encourages the king to defend his prerogative. His country home is at Caen Wood (Kenwood), which he has had expanded and improved by the Adam brothers. His household there includes Dido Elizabeth Belle, aged about 15, the illegitimate daughter of one of his nephews and a black slave. Another of his nephews is Lord Stormont (David Murray, 7th viscount), aged 38, ambassador in Paris.

Lord Sandwich, after a portrait by Zoffany, 1763

Published by Valentine Green, 'engraver in metzotinto to
his majesty', Salisbury Street, Strand, 30th August 1774

Charles Jenkinson, aged 46, another privy councillor, is a protégé of unpopular former prime minister Lord Bute. According to Wraxall, 'Few persons ... have played so important a part behind the curtain of state ... | His intercourse with the king, and even his influence over the royal mind, were assumed to be constant, and sometimes ... subversive of the measures proposed by the first minister.'

Two underlings also play important behind-the-scenes roles.

John Robinson, aged 48, is one of Lord North's secretaries at the Treasury and has responsibility for patronage, managing elections, the East India Company, and other confidential matters. The king approves of him, writing recently that his 'accurateness and expedition in executing whatever he is entrusted with can only be equalled by his zeal and integrity'. Wraxall considered him 'one of the most active and essential functionaries of the executive government. ... His person was coarse, inelegant, and somewhat inclined to corpulency, but he possessed solid judgment and suavity of temper, combined with plain, unaffected, and conciliating manners'.

William Eden, aged 31, an under secretary to Lord Suffolk in the northern department, is a rising man of government business. He has a house in Downing Street, conveniently near Lord North. According to Wraxall, 'His countenance was thin and pale, his features regular and full of intelligence, his manners calm, polite, and conciliating,' but in his manner and deportment there was 'something which did not convey the impression of plain dealing or inspire confidence'.[40]

William Eden

Lord Mansfield
after a portrait by David Martin, 1770

iv. The opposition

Benefiting from extensive powers of patronage the government enjoys overwhelming support in both houses of parliament. The opposition, or minority as it is often known, includes notable talents but lacks unity, numbers and effective leadership. The result is that while the debates on America may appear to favour it the divisions do not.[41]

Lord Chatham (1st earl), aged 67, who as William Pitt dominated politics during the Seven Years War, is away from the fray due to failing health. In his absence **Lord Rockingham** (Charles Watson-Wentworth, 2nd marquess), aged 45, a former prime minister, is the main opposition leader. 'His rank, his integrity, and his vast patrimonial property rather than any intellectual endowments had placed him at the head of his party.' Other prominent opposition peers include the **Duke of Richmond** (Charles Lennox, 3rd duke), aged 40, and **Lord Shelburne** (William Petty, 2nd earl), aged 38.

Edmund Burke, aged 46, an MP for Bristol, is Rockingham's man of business. He stands out among leading politicians both for his intellect and for his modest background as son of a Dublin attorney. His speeches about America tend to be eloquent, vehement and long. He speaks rapidly, 'for his ideas outran his powers of utterance', and his Irish accent is 'as strong as if he had never quitted the banks of the Shannon'.

Charles James Fox, aged 26, is the ageing *enfant terrible* of politics, talented but dissolute. In youth he was indulged by his father Lord Holland, a leading politician, who bought him a seat in parliament and paid off his gambling debts of £120,000. 'His features, in themselves dark, harsh, and saturnine, like those of Charles II, from whom he descended in the maternal line, derived a sort of majesty from the addition of two black and shaggy eyebrows'. His figure is 'broad, heavy, and inclined to corpulency'. Having held junior government posts in the early 1770s he has fallen out with Lord North. When he chooses to spare time from the clubs and gaming tables he has emerged as a leading critic of the government's American policy. In October he described North as 'the blundering pilot who had brought the nation into its present difficulties. ... Lord Chatham, the King of Prussia, nay, Alexander the Great, never gained more in one campaign than the noble lord has lost — he has lost a whole continent.'

Isaac Barré, aged 49, is Lord Shelburne's spokesman in the Commons. A former army colonel, he lost an eye while serving with Wolfe at Quebec and speaks with authority on American matters. 'Severe and sometimes coarse in his censures or accusations, he nevertheless sustained his charges against ministers with considerable force of argument and language.'[42]

Charles James Fox, by James Sayers, 1782

Edmund Burke, by James Sayers, 1782

Also strongly critical of government is classicist, libertine and demagogue **John Wilkes**, aged 50, the most controversial politician of the age.

During the 1760s he engaged in a series of cat-and-mouse struggles with government which saw him imprisoned, prosecuted for seditious libel, expelled from the House of Commons, wounded in a duel, and fleeing to France. Returning in 1768 he was elected for Middlesex but imprisoned in the King's Bench prison, Southwark. Soldiers fired on a mob surrounding the prison, killing several in what became known as the St George's Fields Massacre. After being expelled from the Commons again, re-elected, and excluded again, in the early 1770s he used popular support to gain positions in the City of London instead. He is currently an alderman having recently completed an expensive year as lord mayor. He hopes soon to be elected to the lucrative post of chamberlain in order to repair his finances.

At the 1774 general election he was re-elected to parliament for Middlesex and has since become an outspoken champion of American resistance. To detractors he remains a cynical rabble-rouser, but to admirers he embodies the struggle for liberty, having successfully opposed the use of general warrants and helped to establish the freedom of the press to report parliamentary debates. His struggles have echoed across the Atlantic. Like Americans he has been excluded from parliament and punished for standing up for liberty, while the killings in St George's Fields appear to some to have been a foretaste of the Boston Massacre.

His private life has not been dull. He married a rich older woman in 1747. When they separated ten years later their daughter **Mary**, known as Polly, chose to live with Wilkes. She is now 25, still lives with him, and they remain devoted. He also has what he calls a 'papal nephew', born in 1760 to a former housekeeper.

His mistress for the last two years has been **Marianne de Charpillon**, a dangerous companion for an ageing rake: twelve years ago, aged about 17, she ran tormenting rings around Giacomo Casanova during his stay in London. He claimed to have avenged his humiliation by buying a parrot which he taught to say '*La Charpillon est encore plus catin que sa mère*' ('The Charpillon is an even greater harlot than her mother'), having a servant offer it for sale outside the Royal Exchange, and asking the excessive price of 50 guineas to ensure that its message would continue to be heard day after day.[43]

Wilkes was 'a celebrated beau', according to Henry Angelo, and usually wore 'either a scarlet or green suit, edged with gold'. Wraxall recalled him as 'an incomparable comedian in all he said or did' who 'seemed to consider human life itself as a mere comedy. ... In private society, particularly at table, he was preeminently agreeable, abounding in anecdote, ever gay and convivial ... If any man ever was pleasing who squinted, who had lost his teeth, and lisped, Wilkes might be so esteemed.'[44]

ABOVE. LEFT Wilkes as satirised by Hogarth, 1763. RIGHT With his daughter, by Zoffany, 1779. The dog belonged to Zoffany.

BELOW In his lord mayor's regalia, after a portrait by Robert Edge Pine, 1774.

Corbutt Delin! et fecit.

The HON.^{BLE} S.^R W.^M HOWE.

Knight of the Bath,; Commander in Chief of his Majesty's Forces in America

LONDON: Publifh'd as the Act directs, 10.th Novr 1777, by JOHN MORRIS, Rathbone Place.

Published by John Morris, Rathbone Place, 10th November 1777

v. Army and navy

Major General William Howe, aged 46, son of a viscount, has been a soldier for thirty years and is greatly respected. He has affection for the Americans, having fought alongside them in the Seven Years War, and has been critical of British policy. Early in 1775 he accepted appointment as Gage's second in command in Boston in the hope of succeeding him and promoting reconciliation, but by the time he arrived in late May the war had begun and Boston was surrounded. He is therefore caught in a fight he would not have chosen. His time in Boston is eased by the acquisition of an American mistress, Elizabeth Loring. It is later rumoured that he acquired her from her husband in return for a government contract and that, along with his own inclination for peace-making, her charms distract him from the conflict. Some time after his knighting in October 1776 a ditty will advise:

> Awake, awake, Sir Billy;
> There's forage on the plain,
> Oh leave your little filly
> And open the campaign![45]

His elder brother **Lord Howe** (Richard, 4th viscount), aged 49, is presently in London. He has recently been appointed vice admiral but has fallen out with Lord North over a lucrative sinecure which he claimed North had promised to him but which was given instead to Sir Hugh Palliser, a favourite of Lord Sandwich. Among sailors he is known as 'Black Dick' from his dark complexion. His reputation as a naval officer is high and he will shortly be offered overall command in America. Like his brother he has close connections there and would prefer a peaceful solution to be found.[46]

Major General John Burgoyne, aged 52, is currently in London briefing the king and ministers about the situation in America. Horace Walpole dubbed him 'General Swagger', considering him 'a vain, very ambitious man, with a half understanding that was worse than none'. In 1751 he eloped with and married Lady Charlotte Stanley, a daughter of the Earl of Derby. He is widely distrusted, the political letter writer 'Junius' accusing him of bribery and of 'taking his stand at a gaming-table, and watching with the soberest attention for a fair opportunity of engaging a drunken young nobleman at piquet'. As an MP he has supported the government's American policy. 'I look upon America as our child, which we have already spoilt by too much indulgence,' he said in April 1774, opposing repeal of the duty on tea. Before setting out for Boston in the spring of the current year, 1775, he asked to be allowed to return in the dead part of winter. Now he is here his motives are suspected, not least because in the interim he has been sending ministers a series of letters from America critical of the campaign and leaving little doubt as to his own ambition for a higher command.[47]

Lieut. Gen. John Burgoyne Col. of the 16. Re
of Light Dragoons & Governor of Fort William.

Published some time after his promotion to lieutenant general on 26th March 1776

vi. Public opinion, mercenaries, Mohawks

The country at large appears sharply divided regarding the war, but there is also a sense of detachment from it, as noted by the writer of a letter published in the *Middlesex Journal* in July:

> All England is sitting contentedly a spectator of the American quarrel, as if it had little or no interest in the quarrel. Public divertions are more crowded than ever; new amusements for dissipation are contrived; the drawing-room [is] as splendid and as frequented as ever, and look in the face of every man you meet, there is that happy vacancy in it, which indicates, if not a positive good, at least an exemption from all positive evil; and if a conversation arises, two to one but you hear something thrown out against these *rebellious Americans*. Mr Editor, this national ignorance ... is what has brought us to the verge of ruin.[48]

As the letter indicates, while you will find strong opposition to the war voiced in London and among merchants, it is balanced in the country at large by instinctive patriotism, especially now that fighting has begun. There is reluctance in the fight, however, many seeing it as a civil war against fellow subjects who share British blood and values.[49]

As a result recruits are hard to find and government plans to fill the gap by paying for foreign troops. At first it was hoped they would come from Russia, but on 3rd November the king advised Lord North that he had received a letter from the empress, Catherine the Great, which constituted 'a clear refusal, and not in so genteel a manner as I should have thought might have been expected from her. She has not had the civility to answer in her own hand and has thrown out some expressions that may be civil to a Russian ear but certainly not to more civilized ones.' Attention has now turned to the small German states including Hesse-Cassel, Waldeck, and Brunswick, which promise to be more amenable.[50]

The ministry is also hoping for support from the Indians of the Six Nations. Having crossed the Atlantic in the same boat as the American prisoners of war, **Colonel Guy Johnson**, aged about 35, superintendent of Indian affairs, arrived in town on 27th December. Next day he went to see Lord George Germain and he has already been presented to the king and the queen. He assumed the role of superintendent on the death of his father-in-law, Sir William Johnson, in July 1774, and has come to seek confirmation of the appointment, not least because of conflict with General Carleton regarding both his own role and that of the Indians in Canada. He has been accompanied by Mohawk chief **Joseph Brant**, aged 32, and his warrior companion John Hill, or Oteroughyanento, meaning 'trembling mist between two clouds'. They are eager to secure British support for the recovery of lost Mohawk lands in return for assistance against the rebels.

While exotic to English eyes, Brant is not quite the outsider he seems and his Mohawk name, Thayendanegea, meaning 'two sticks bound together', or 'he who places two bets', is suggestive of his position between two worlds. He attended an English school in Connecticut, fought on the British side in the Seven Years

War, and is a committed Anglican. His elder half-sister Mary, or Molly, was Sir William Johnson's common law wife. Having been favoured both by Sir William and by Guy Johnson, he has recently been appointed an officer in the Indian department and is on its payroll.[51]

vii. France

Louis XVI, aged 21, succeeded to the throne last year and appointed veteran diplomat the **Comte de Vergennes**, aged 56, as foreign minister. Since the outbreak of the American war France has been giving Britain assurances of friendship, but it is no secret that it is still smarting from its defeat in the Seven Years War and is eager to weaken its old enemy. The paradoxical prospect of an *ancien régime* monarchy supporting a democratic revolution is hardly remarked upon, it being assumed that France, like other countries, will act on perceived self-interest rather than on principle.

French assurances have already been undermined by signs of covert and informal support for the rebels. In early August two French officers who had been in America were watched at a hotel in Watling Street. On being 'pumped by a discreet and proper person' they revealed that 'there are at least 200 French amongst the troops of the rebels, who acted as artillerists and engineers'. They had also seen 'seven French ships, masked under English colours' come into different ports with ammunition, and further officers, engineers and gunpowder were expected.[52]

Charles Gravier, Comte de Vergennes

viii. Enter Beaumarchais

More substantial French assistance is being enthusiastically promoted by **Pierre-Augustin Caron de Beaumarchais**, aged 43, whose *Le Barbier de Séville* had its premiere in Paris in February. Acting for Vergennes he has paid several visits to London during the last year, ostensibly to negotiate with the Chevalier d'Éon, who has compromising papers which the French crown wants suppressed, but also to report on the political situation.

At some uncertain date, possibly during November, Beaumarchais wrote to Louis XVI outlining an inventive plan for helping the Americans. His idea is to create a fictional trading company which will take advantage of the scarcity and high price of gunpowder in America on the one hand and of tobacco in France on the other. 'Your majesty will begin by placing one million at the disposal of your agent, who will style himself Roderique Hortalez and Company, this being the business name and signature under which I have agreed to conduct the entire business.' Half of the money would be sent to America and in return Hortalez and Company would receive Virginia tobacco, which the French government's Fermé-Generale would already have agreed to buy at a good price. Hortalez would use the remaining half million 'to procure cannon powder and convey it without delay to the Americans'. Instead of paying the usual market rate of 20 or 30 sols tournois a pound it would buy secretly from the king's registrars at between 4 and 6 sols. The powder would be sold to Congress for 20 sols, and Congress's resulting debt to Hortalez would be discharged by way of more tobacco. By continuing to trade thus advantageously in both directions, Hortalez and Company would be able to multiply the king's initial million repeatedly: 'If the first million produces three, these three millions put back into the business on the same basis, should produce 9, 27, &c.'[53]

At present, however, the young king remains cautious and Beaumarchais is frustrated. He has just returned from Paris, arriving on 29th December.[54]

ix. American spies and refugees

When in London Beaumarchais has been a frequent dining companion of John Wilkes, who has introduced him to **Arthur Lee**, aged 35, from a prominent Virginia family but educated in Britain and now a barrister with lodgings in the Middle Temple. Lee is a fanatical proponent of American independence and in 1774 replaced the more pragmatic Benjamin Franklin as London agent for the Massachusetts assembly. A letter dated 12th December is now on its way to him from Congress's committee of secret correspondence. It appoints him to liaise covertly with a Monsieur Dumas at the Hague and to inform the committee of 'the disposition of foreign powers towards us ... We need not hint that great circumspection and impenetrable secrecy are necessary.' Meanwhile the British government is reading Lee's mail, and he is aware of the fact. Government is also alert to the sympathies of his brother **William Lee**, a City alderman and Wilkes supporter, who was interviewed in the summer regarding an attempt to induce disaffected shipwrights to emigrate to America.[55]

Another expatriate who supports the rebels is **Patience Wright**, aged 50, a celebrated wax modeller with a showroom off Pall Mall. She is quite open about her political sympathies, apparently losing the favour of the king by scolding him for sanctioning the war. She may be sending intelligence to America in wax heads dispatched to her sister in Philadelphia, but one acquaintance describes Patience as 'crazy pated', and it is not clear that the information she sends is of any use.[56]

Also apparently supporting the rebels is **Edward Bancroft**, aged 31, who rents a house in Downing Street. Born in America, he settled in England in 1767 and has become a noted author and chemist, being elected to the Royal Society in 1773. Since the outbreak of the war he has been writing to his friend Benjamin Franklin in terms which seem to leave no doubt as to where his loyalty lies.[57]

London has also become home to a number of loyalist refugees. Theirs is a slightly melancholy existence, spinning out the days in rented lodgings and visits to one another, lacking purpose and status, caught between hope that they will be able to return to America and fear that the world they grew up in has gone for ever.

Most prominent among them is **Thomas Hutchinson**, aged 64, former governor of Massachusetts, who has been in London since June 1774. A year later he received news from one of his sons, who was still in America, that his house at Milton was 'in possession of the rabble: all my letters, books, papers, &c. taken and carried away, and the publication of some of them already begun'. In November he heard that the house had been sold and that Washington 'rides in my coach at Cambridge'. Hutchinson himself has been received cordially by the king and ministers. He urges them to take a hard line with America but is aware that he has little influence.[58]

There is also Cumberland-born **Jonathan Boucher**, aged 37, a former rector of St Anne's, Annapolis, Maryland, where, as a staunch loyalist, he enjoyed the patronage of the governor Robert Eden. He was also a friend of George Washington until politics divided them. When the war began he refused to be intimidated by armed crowds and denounced the rebel cause from his pulpit. His last sermon was delivered with pistols on the pulpit cushion before him. It ended: 'As long as I live, yea, while I have my being, will I proclaim "God save the King!"' He fled in August and reached England in October, bringing with him warm letters of recommendation from Governor Eden to his younger brother William, as well as to Lord Dartmouth and a brace of bishops.[59]

Other refugees include **Jonathan Sewall**, aged 47, former attorney general of Massachusetts, who arrived early this year; **Samuel Quincy**, aged 40, former solicitor general of the same province, who left America in May; **Samuel Curwen**, aged 60, a former merchant at Salem and deputy judge, who arrived in July; and **Edward Oxnard**, aged 28, a former merchant from Maine, who arrived at the end of August having left his pregnant wife behind.[60]

x. India

While most attention is on America, and will remain so during the coming year, there is also trouble in the eastern empire. In India, as in North America, Britain has emerged pre-eminent from mid-century imperial jostling among European powers. It has done so in the guise of the East India Company, which has developed from trading origins into a major military and governmental force. Robert Clive's victories in the 1750s, notably at Plassey, were hailed at home and for a while it seemed eastern riches might ease Britain's financial problems, the company agreeing to pay £400,000 annually to the Treasury. In the last few years, however, the company's finances have deteriorated dramatically, partly because of a severe famine in Bengal. Its stock has fallen, investors have panicked, the Treasury payment has been suspended, and it has had to be bailed out by the Bank of England. Meanwhile individual nabobs are still returning home with envy-inducing fortunes, fostering a sense that Britain, vaunted home of liberty, is sullying itself with eastern corruption and despotism only for rapacious individuals to snaffle the spoils.

Clive himself was subjected to a long and critical inquiry by a House of Commons committee. He was finally exonerated in May 1773, but his already poor health deteriorated and eighteen months later he died in mysterious circumstances at his house in Berkeley Square. Suicide is widely suspected, adding to a sense of something rotten in Britain's eastern adventure.

The government has taken a first step towards controlling Indian affairs with a Regulating Act, passed in June 1773. It appointed a governor general with four councillors to rule Bengal, but the particular nominations made conflict more or less inevitable: on the one side were two old India hands, Warren Hastings as governor general and Richard Barwell, and on the other three councillors sent from England, including an ambitious intriguer, Philip Francis. Since arriving in India a year ago Francis has been undermining Hastings. In March he made use of a letter from a rascally maharaja called Nandakumar which accused Hastings of corruption. Nandakumar was himself then accused of forgery by a third party, arrested, tried before chief justice Elijah Impey (an old school friend of Hastings) and executed on 5th August. While Nandakumar's elimination appeared helpful to Hastings, it has been turned against him. On 15th September the anti-Hastings majority on the council sent a dispatch to the company's headquarters in Leadenhall Street noting that 'the world may perhaps conclude that this man was too formidable a witness to be suffered to appear …'

So slow is passage to and from India, however, that even news of Nandakumar's original accusation against Hastings has only just arrived.[61]

Mrs Abington as Thalia, the Comic Muse
After a portrait by Reynolds, 1764-1768

B: Some notable characters of the town

Frances Abington, née Barton, aged 38, is the leading comic actress of the age. She grew up in poverty near Covent Garden. It is said that aged 12 she earned money by standing on tables in taverns under the piazza reciting Shakespeare, and that later she adopted 'more profligate and degrading means of support'. She first appeared on stage in 1755. Four years later she married James Abington, one of the king's trumpeters, and went with him to Ireland where she had great success on stage, became the mistress of a rich Irish MP, and separated from her husband, who was reportedly paid £500 for her. In 1765 she returned to England with the MP who promptly died, leaving her well provided for. In the same year she was invited by actor-manager David Garrick to join the company at Drury Lane Theatre and she has been a member of it ever since, although her wilfulness makes relations with Garrick fraught.

As recently as 1773 she was listed in *Harris's List of Covent-Garden Ladies*. It noted that she kept a coach and an elegant house in Southampton Street. 'Her salary, though genteel, is not sufficient to maintain her table and manner of living ... The approaches must be made the proper way ... | N.B. She measures gentility by the weight of the purse.' She was still in Southampton Street in late November 1775, but in the coming spring the house there will be advertised for sale and she will address letters from Leicester Fields.

She has many admirers including Sir Joshua Reynolds, who has painted her as the Comic Muse, and Dr Johnson, who likes her jelly. German aphorist G. C. Lichtenberg, in London recently, thought her so remarkable that he could write a small book about her:

> She has, withal, a figure of exquisite beauty, which she displays with the purpose of pleasing. In intellect she is certainly far superior to all the other English actresses. It is evident that the tinsel world of Drury Lane is too narrow for her ... Her face is far from beautiful; she is pale and too proud to paint, her nose is somewhat *retroussé*, and her mouth none the finest. But from beneath their well-shaped brows her eyes shoot such keen glances, often accompanied by a certain indescribable way of smiling at the follies she exposes, that they produce a singularly uncomfortable feeling in those on whom they fall. ... She often, contrary to custom, turns away from the audience. You should see her then, how graceful the undulations of her limbs, every step seemingly intended, in mere wantonness, to whet the hundred eyes that wait upon her ...[62]

Another leading actress, **Ann Catley**, aged 30, also grew up in poverty, in her case near Tower Hill, and is also said to have been a prostitute from a young age. Since her debut at Vauxhall Gardens in 1762 she has been celebrated for a fine singing voice. After early entanglements with a dissolute baronet and others she has been attached since about 1768 to Lieutenant Colonel Francis Lascelles and has several children by him and his predecessors. According to playwright John O'Keeffe, 'She was one of the most beautiful women I ever saw: the expression of her eyes, and the smiles and dimples that played round her lips and cheeks, enchanting. She was eccentric, but had an excellent heart.' Her manner of performing is considered thrillingly bold by some and disgustingly vulgar by others. According to one witness, 'It was the singing of unequalled *animal spirits* ... No other female singer ever gave the slightest notion of her. She was bold, volatile, audacious; mistress of herself, of her talent, and her audience.' She is presently performing in Dublin, where, as everywhere, she commands a high price. Her return will be reported in late April and in September she will appear once more on the London stage.[63]

Teresa Cornelys, née Imer, aged about 52, was born in Venice and began her career as an opera singer. During the 1740s and 1750s she married a dancer and separated from him, performed across northern Europe, took lovers including Casanova and the Margrave of Brandenburg-Bayreuth, had several children, and ran into debt. In 1759 she took refuge in London under the name Cornelys, borrowed from another lover. In the following year she leased Carlisle House in Soho Square and began putting on entertainments aimed at an aristocratic audience. Over the following decade, in Horace Walpole's words, she 'presided over our diversions', outward success hiding considerable debts incurred in enlarging and embellishing the property.

In 1771 she put on a series of operatic performances, illegal without royal licence, and was twice fined £50 at Bow Street magistrates' court. In the following

'Trial of the sovereign Empress of the vast Regions of Taste'
Raised aloft by her lawyer and the Duchess of Northumberland, Teresa Cornelys appears before Sir John Fielding at Bow Street. From the *Oxford Magazine* for March 1771.

'The Whimsical Duet, or Miss C-tl-y teaching her fat dane Bitch to rival Miss Y—g'

Having been unimpressed by the musical efforts of a rival actress (probably Elizabeth Younge),
Ann Catley teaches her dog to sing. The man seated beside her is presumably Lascelles.
From the *Oxford Magazine* for March 1773.

year her ascendancy was challenged by the opening of the Pantheon, built at vast cost in Oxford Street, and her creditors grew restless: in October she was arrested for debt and put in the King's Bench prison, in November she was declared bankrupt, and in December Carlisle House was sold. Over the next few years it was used for various entertainments but without success. From early August this year, 1775, it was advertised repeatedly by Mr Christie the auctioneer as for sale by private contract. However, in late November the *Morning Chronicle* reported 'certain intelligence that Mrs Cornelys is again to shine in her native sphere at Soho', and on 11th December the *Morning Post* added that 'she is once more got into Carlisle House'. A week later she presided over the first masquerade of the present season, and has just announced another, to be held on 8th January.[64]

Georgiana, Duchess of Devonshire, aged 18, eldest daughter of the 1st Earl Spencer, married the 5th Duke of Devonshire in June 1774 on her seventeenth birthday. After attending a ball in January this year Walpole noted that she 'effaces all without being a beauty; but her youth, figure, flowing good-nature, sense, and

Georgiana, Duchess of Devonshire, by Jeremiah Meyer, *circa* 1774

lively modesty, and modest familiarity, make her a phenomenon'. She has already become a leader of fashion. In April the *Morning Post* reported that she is 'the most envied woman this day in the *ton*; not for her personal charms, tho' they are many, nor for her fortune, title, or equipage, tho' they are splendid to a degree; but for a delicious *ostrich feather* lately presented her by Lord Stormont on his arrival from Paris, measuring exactly one yard and three inches'.[65]

Sir John Fielding, aged 54, presides at the public office or magistrates' court in Bow Street, following in the footsteps of his half-brother Henry, who died in 1754. While officially just a magistrate he is also the city's unofficial chief of police, directing a small group of thief-takers and advertising crimes in the newspapers. He has been blind since 1740. His first wife died in 1774 and he remarried soon afterwards. An American refugee, watching him examine prisoners at Bow Street in August, described him as 'a venerable elderly gentleman with hoary locks and blind (as Justice is represented to be) having a black fillet over his eyes, of a mild deportment, ready apprehension and great penetration'.[66]

Fielding as chairman of Westminster quarter sessions
After a portrait by William Peters. Published 12th November 1778.

Samuel Foote, probably aged 55, owns the lease of the Theatre Royal in the Haymarket, known as the Little Theatre, or Mr Foote's theatre. He has a patent allowing him to put on plays there in the summer months, when the main theatres of Covent Garden and Drury Lane are closed.

In 1766 he lost a leg when riding a horse belonging to the Duke of York and he was granted the theatre patent in recompense. According to a contemporary memoir, his 'wooden, or rather cork leg, was so well contrived by springs, that he could move his knee, ancle and toes, and but for a small hitch in his gait, which those who did not know him took for lameness, he might very well have passed as having both his legs'. John O'Keeffe, on the other hand, recalled that 'one could not help pitying him sometimes, as he stood upon his one leg, leaning against the wall, whilst his servant was putting on his stage false leg, with shoe and stocking, and fastening it to the stump: he looked sorrowful, but instantly resuming all his high comic humour and mirth, hobbled forward, entered the scene, and gave the audience what they expected — their plenty of laugh and delight.'

Foote both writes the plays he puts on and takes the leading parts, lampooning contemporary types and characters. 'His productions have the merit of being so many interesting pictures of the manners of the age,' according to a Prussian visitor. 'He usually ... made but little alteration even in the names of those who had the misfortune to fall under his lash. He knew how to imitate with great exactness the gait and conversation of any one, and never forgot to place his hero in the most foolish and ridiculous point of view.' Others sense underlying cruelty in his method and his works have resulted in many feuds over the years. The latest has arisen over a planned satire on the Duchess of Kingston (see below) and is still brewing. Meanwhile, unable to put on plays in London during winter, he is performing in Dublin but will return shortly.

As a young man he married, but his wife has not been in evidence for many years.[67]

Caterina Gabrielli, aged 45, is one of a number of highly paid foreign singers currently in London. Over the last twenty-five years she has conquered and exasperated other European cities. Traveller Patrick Brydone, seeing her in Palermo in 1770, judged her 'the greatest singer in the world', although 'her caprice is, if possible, even greater than her talents ... She is certainly the most dangerous syren of modern times, and has made more conquests, I suppose, than any one woman breathing.' He added that she had been banished from Vienna and most of the Italian cities 'from the broils and squabbles that her intriguing spirit, perhaps still more than her beauty, had excited,' and that 'no art whatever is capable of making her sing, when she does not chuse it.'

In 1771 she was lured to Russia by Catherine the Great. Nathaniel Wraxall, who met her at the Peterhoff palace in July 1774, noted that she had demanded '7000 rubles (or about 1500l. sterling) a year, besides a house and carriage ... They remonstrated with her on the unreasonableness of so enormous a salary,

Samuel Foote
After a portrait by Reynolds, 1767

and … informed her that a field marshal had no more. "If that be the case," said she, "I would advise her majesty to make one of her marshals sing.'"

She has been engaged for the present season as *prima donna* at the opera house, or King's Theatre, in the Haymarket, and has taken a house in Golden Square. She has insisted that her sister Francesca be engaged advantageously as well, although it is said the sister cannot sing.

'Nothing can exceed the impatience of people of all ranks, and all ways of thinking, concerning this so celebrated singer,' wrote Fanny Burney, who was among the crowds filling the theatre on 7th November to hear her intended debut. True to reputation, however, Gabrielli sent word an hour before the doors were to be opened that she was indisposed. The managers begged her to go on, pointing out that a riot might otherwise result. 'She answered very coolly, but with smiles and politeness, that if *le monde* expected her so eagerly, she would dress herself, and let the opera be performed; only, when her songs came to their simphony, instead of singing, she would make a courtesey, and point to her throat.'

On Saturday 11th November she did appear, prompting excitement in the *Morning Chronicle*: 'Gabrielli! the great *Gabrielli!* Signora *Caterina Gabrielli!* has at last made her appearance on an English stage!' Fanny Burney attended again and noted that the peals of applause upon the singer's entrance 'seemed as if they would have shaken the foundations of the theatre. … | She is still very pretty, though not still very young. She has small, intelligent, sparkling features; and though she is rather short, she is charmingly proportioned, and has a very engaging figure. All her notions are graceful, her air is full of dignity, and her walk is majestic. … | She visibly took no pains to exert herself, and appeared so impertinently easy, that I believe she thought it condescension enough for us poor savage islanders to see her stand upon the stage, and let us look at her.'

According to Lady Edgcumbe, 'The ceremony of her quitting the theatre after the opera is over is extremely curious. First goes a man in livery to clear the way; then follows the sister; then the Gabrielli herself; then a little foot-page, to bear her train; and lastly another man, who carries her muff, in which is her lap-dog.'

The *Morning Post* suggested a similar entourage: 'At the opera … she is attended by two females and two gentlemen out of livery, one to bring her coffee or what she calls for, and the other to hold her lap-dog on a small white sattin cushion, while she is on the stage: when she is off, it lies in her lap and there receives the caresses of many a peer.'[68]

David Garrick, aged 58, is manager of Drury Lane Theatre and the most celebrated actor of the age. In 1737, aged 20, he set out for London from his native Lichfield with his former teacher, Samuel Johnson. Four years later he enjoyed a triumphant debut as Richard III and since then has championed the works of Shakespeare and has excelled in both tragic and comic parts. In 1747 he bought a half share in the patent for Drury Lane Theatre and under his management it has achieved pre-eminence. In 1749 he married Eva Maria Veigel,

Signiora G——

ABOVE. LEFT Caterina Gabrielli, from the *Town and Country Magazine* for April 1776. RIGHT Garrick as Macbeth.

BELOW Garrick at the breakfast table, from a drawing by Nathaniel Dance, 16th March 1771. Garrick is said to have considered it 'the best likeness ever made of him'.

a noted dancer. In 1754 he bought a villa beside the Thames at Hampton. He has had it improved by Robert Adam, who has built a temple to Shakespeare in the grounds. In 1772 he bought a town house in the Adelphi, the Adam brothers' new development between the Strand and the river, and now divides his time between there, Hampton, and grand houses such as Chatsworth, where he is a familiar guest. His private life appears without blemish, even Sir John Fielding, with whom he is not on good terms, remarking that 'the chastity of Mr Garrick, as a manager of a public theatre, and his exemplary life as a man, have been of great service to the morals of a dissipated age'.

On stage, according to Lichtenberg, who saw him recently, he 'moves about among the other actors like a living man among puppets'. He is 'rather small than middle-sized', but strong, well proportioned, and nimble.

> As regards his face, even dull physiognomists may read the fine intellectual quality in his well-formed forehead, and his powers of observation and wit in the rapid movements of his brilliant and somewhat roguish eyes. ... When he is serious, the spectators are serious too; they furrow their brow or smile just as he does; and in his private joys and friendly ways, in his asides, when he seems to be taking the audience into his confidence, there is such a sweetness and trustfulness of look that all hearts fly, as it were, to the fascinating man. ...
>
> He went to the same school as Shakespeare ... The school alluded to is London, where a man with such a talent for observation is able to gain more experience in one year than he could in a whole life passed in a little county town ...

Recently he has become concerned about his health and weary of the demands of capricious actresses such as Mrs Abington. He is currently negotiating the sale of his half share in the patent to a syndicate led by a coming young man of the theatre, Richard Sheridan.[69]

Omai or **Omiah** of Otaheite (Tahiti), aged about 22, was brought to England in July 1774 on board the *Adventure*, which had been part of Captain Cook's second expedition to the Pacific. Also on board was James Burney, elder brother of Fanny, who speaks Tahitian and acted as Omai's interpreter during the first part of his stay in England. A writer to the *London Magazine* who met Omai soon after his arrival noted that he is about 5 foot 10 inches tall and 'rather lusty, and strong made ... His hair is jet black, shining and strong, and clubbed behind since he came over ... His hands are tataowed, according to the mode in his native country. ... | A few common expressions he pronounces with fluency, such as, "How do you do?" &c.'

Since then he has stayed with Lord Sandwich at Hinchingbrooke, accompanied him on river trips on the Admiralty barge, been feted by great ladies, and had a suit of armour made for him in the Tower. In November 1774 he visited the Burney family in St Martin's Street, as Fanny Burney recorded:

> As he had been to Court, he was very fine. He had on a suit of Manchester velvet, lined with white satten, a bag, lace ruffles, and a very handsome sword

which the king had given to him. He is tall and very well made, much darker than I expected to see him, but has a pleasing countenance. | He makes remarkable good bows — not for him, but for anybody, however long under a dancing master's care. Indeed he seems to shame Education, for his manners are so extremely graceful, and he is so polite, attentive, and easy, that you would have thought he came from some foreign Court.

A year later, on 14th December 1775, he made a surprise return to the Burney house. 'He now walks everywhere quite alone,' noted Fanny, 'and has lodgings in Warwick Street, where he lives by himself. The king allows him a pension. He has learnt a great deal of English since his last visit, and can with the assistance of signs and action, make himself tolerably well understood.' On being asked if he had seen the king lately he replied, '"Yes; King George bid me, 'Omy, you go home.' Oh, very dood man, King George!" | He then, with our assisting him, made us understand that he was extremely rejoiced at the thoughts of seeing again his native land; but at the same time that he should much regret leaving his friends in England.'

Having gone to America in April on board the *Cerberus*, James Burney has just returned, in good time to join the mooted expedition to the South Seas and convey his friend Omai home.[70]

Omai, 'drawn from nature by W. Hodges'. Published 1st February 1777.

Sir Joshua Reynolds, aged 52, is president of the Royal Academy and the leading artist of the day. His pronunciation is still 'tinctured with the Devonshire accent' of his youth and he relies on an ear trumpet, having been very deaf for over twenty years. He has a house in Leicester Fields (or Square) and another on Richmond Hill. He is unmarried and his sister Frances acts as his housekeeper, although their relations are uneasy and she will shortly be replaced by one of his nieces. He tends to invite too many people to dinner, resulting in scenes of affable chaos. His wide circle of friends includes Garrick, Burke and Dr Johnson. Not included are his two closest rivals, Thomas Gainsborough, aged 48, and George Romney, aged 41, both of whom have recently set up anew in London. He is about 5 foot 6 inches tall and, according to Edmond Malone, 'of a florid complexion, and a lively and pleasing aspect; well made, and extremely active. ... He possessed a constant flow of spirits, which rendered him at all times a most pleasing companion; always cheerful, and ready to be amused with whatever was going forward'.[71]

Richard Brinsley Sheridan, aged 24, has recently abandoned studies at the Middle Temple and emerged as a promising writer for the stage. It is in his blood: his father Thomas is an actor and his mother Frances, now deceased, was a playwright.

His first play, *The Rivals*, fell short when it opened on 17th January 1775 at Covent Garden Theatre, but he quickly revised it and eleven days later it hit the mark. Having previously found some scenes 'insufferably tedious', the *Morning Chronicle* felt that the new version 'encourages us to hope for a very capital play from the same writer at a future season'.

It has been followed by *The Duenna, or, The Double Elopement*, a comic opera, first performed at the same theatre on 21st November, the music being arranged by Thomas Linley senior and junior, his father-in-law and brother-in-law respectively. On its second night it was received with 'the most universal tokens of applause ever known on a similar occasion'. The king and queen share the enthusiasm. 'No dramatic piece ever received greater countenance from royalty than the *Duenna* has,' reported the *Morning Chronicle*. 'Her majesty after the first time of seeing it, ordered a copy of the music with a harpsichord part, to be made out for her by Mr Simpson, and the instance of their commanding it twice successively is unprecedented.' Its run continues, the same paper reporting that the theatre's managers 'have at least cleared 3000l. by the *Duenna*'.

In his own life Sheridan has played the part of romantic hero with success. In 1772 he escorted the 17-year-old **Elizabeth Linley** when she travelled to France to escape the attentions of admirers, including a married dastard called Captain Mathews. In France she and Sheridan were married by a Catholic priest but kept the union secret. Meanwhile Mathews wrote to the *Bath Chronicle* branding Sheridan a liar. Returning to England, Sheridan fought him in two sword duels. He prevailed in the first, at the Castle tavern, Henrietta Street, London, but in the second, upon Kingsdown near Bath, he was seriously wounded.

ABOVE Reynolds, self-portrait, *circa* 1775.

BELOW Sheridan, after a portrait by Gainsborough, *circa* 1785.

The two fathers, Thomas Sheridan and Thomas Linley, were keen to keep the young couple apart, but during Lent 1773, when Elizabeth was appearing in oratorios in London, Sheridan contrived to see her, on one occasion apparently disguising himself as a hackney coachman in order to drive her home from the theatre. Meanwhile her beauty and voice were making her the talk of the town. Horace Walpole noted that the king 'ogles her as much as he dares to do in so holy a place as an oratorio'. According to Fanny Burney, 'The applause and admiration she has met with, can only be compared to what is given Mr Garrick. The whole town seems distracted about her. Every other diversion is forsaken. Miss Linley alone engrosses all eyes, ears, hearts.'

Thomas Linley having relented, the couple were married, or remarried, on 13th April 1773. Thomas Sheridan remained against the match and is still at odds with his son.

As a married woman Mrs Sheridan has ceased to perform in public and now has a young son. Her husband, meanwhile, has ambitions beyond writing. He is currently negotiating on his own and others' behalf to buy Garrick's half share in the patent of Drury Lane Theatre, although he is relying on loans for much of his part of the purchase money.[72]

A scene from *The Duenna*, 1775

Elizabeth Sheridan as St Cecilia, after a painting by Reynolds, 1775

Published by the engraver, William Dickinson, Henrietta Street, 21st May 1776

The music book was provided by Dr Burney. The children were daughters of Bartholomew Coote Purdon, a well connected banker who will go missing in October 1776.

'Most simple and beautiful,' noted Horace Walpole in his catalogue after seeing the picture at the Royal Academy in 1775. It had been painted for Sheridan, who was at first unable to pay. When finally he did so, in January 1790, Reynolds wrote to him: 'It is with great regret I part with the best picture I ever painted'.

C: Current *causes célèbres*: Three intriguing women and an enigma

> We have no Joans of Arc, nor Catharines de' Medici;
> but this age has heroines after its own fashion ...
>
> Horace Walpole, 17th December 1775[73]

i. Elopement: The bewitching Miss Brown

A cast change has recently been necessary in *The Duenna* because the actress who played Clara, the runaway heroine, has herself run away. **Ann Brown**, aged 16, has been performing at Covent Garden Theatre since she was 11 or 12. Early in December she left the house of her father Edward Brown, a coal merchant, and eloped with **Miles Peter Andrews**, aged 33, a man about town, aspiring dramatist, friend of John Wilkes, and owner of gunpowder mills at Dartford in Kent. Having tracked her to the home of a sympathetic aunt, her father brought her and her beau before Sir John Fielding at the public office in Bow Street on 5th December. Asked if he loved Ann, Andrews insisted that he did, 'more than life'. Fielding asked why he did not then marry her. 'Because I am married already,' came the rather unhelpful reply, and Fielding promptly gave custody to Mr Brown.[74]

The runaway was not to be confined so easily, however, as a report in the *Morning Post* on 15th December made clear:

> Yesterday the little Syren of Covent Garden theatre made a second elopement, eluding the vigilance of her father and the managers. A strange hue and cry was made after her but in vain: the father shed fruitless tears for his lost child; the managers too lamented her loss, but finding no bars or padlocks could secure her, they prudently, foreseeing the event, got her part understudied by Miss Dayes, in the new opera, who made her first appearance in the character of Clara last night. Mr Hull came forward, to inform the audience how *very bad* Miss B— was, which was the cause of her non-appearance, but forgot to explain the nature of her disorder; however he graced the solemn occasion with all the mournful honours of his elegiac face. — Several of the female letter-carriers, we find, have been detected, as accessaries to this amour, and are discharged the theatre in consequence thereof.[75]

On 30th December it was reported that 'Miss Brown has been articled as an apprentice, since her elopement from Covent-Garden Theatre, to an Italian, who now claims her, and bids both father and managers defiance.' Her new instructor is Signor Sal Pietro, a well known violinist with lodgings in Dean Street, Soho. A writ of habeas corpus has been or shortly will be issued by the Court of King's Bench demanding that Andrews and 'John Salpietro' bring 'the body of Ann Brown spinster' before Lord Mansfield at his chambers in Serjeants' Inn, Chancery Lane.

Further complicating the situation, both Ann's father and Sal Pietro are thought to want to control her partly for mercenary reasons, her looks, fine voice, and recent success making her a valuable stage commodity.[76]

It is tempting to see her story – of a child approaching adulthood making a bid for freedom from an overly demanding parent – as a metaphor for the struggle between Britain and America, but there is no sign that anybody does.

Ann Brown in the character of Clara
Mezzotint by John Raphael Smith after his own drawing from life.
Published 21st August 1778.

Mr ROBERT PERREAU.

Publish'd as the Act directs, July 2.1775.

Mrs. RUDD.

Mr. D. PERREAU.

Publish'd as the Act directs, August 1st 1775.

From the *London Magazine* for June and July 1775

ii. Fraud: The Perreau brothers and Mrs Rudd

On Saturday 11th March 1775 **Robert Perreau**, aged about 41, a well known apothecary, went to the public office in Bow Street to report a fraud committed by his sister-in-law. All was not quite as it seemed, however. A few days earlier he had been rumbled by bankers Henry and Robert Drummond in trying to pass off a forged bill in the name of an army agent, William Adair. The suspicious Drummonds took Perreau and the bill to Adair's house in Pall Mall. On Adair disowning the bill, Perreau claimed that it had been given to him by the wife of his twin brother **Daniel**. The woman in question, **Margaret Caroline Rudd** (née Youngson), aged about 30, long separated from her husband, was not in fact married to Daniel, but they lived together and had three children. She was sent for, took the fault upon herself, and the Drummonds gallantly relented.

Unhelpfully for the Perreaus and Mrs Rudd, the forged bill was one of many. While Robert Perreau had enjoyed a solid early career, Daniel had become bankrupt as a trader in the West Indies. When he joined his brother in London the two of them began speculating on the stock market and Daniel became attached to the intriguing Mrs Rudd. In 1771 the brothers lost heavily gambling that war would break out between Britain and Spain over the Falkland Islands. Over the next few years a series of forged bonds enabled them not only to stave off ruin but to appear to prosper. Robert lived in Golden Square with Henrietta, his wife of eighteen years, and their three children. Early in 1775 Daniel and Mrs Rudd moved into a house in Harley Street costing £4,000, paid for by a fraudulently secured loan.

According to Mrs Rudd's account, after the sticky encounter at Adair's house the trio feared that word would spread and agreed to flee. Subsequently Robert had second thoughts and decided instead to try to save his own name and that of his brother by casting all the blame onto Mrs Rudd. As a result, on the afternoon of 11th March, when she was sitting in a coach in Southampton Street waiting to head to France, Robert arrived with Sir John Fielding's clerk and she found herself escorted to nearby Bow Street. In the event Robert's plan failed, the sitting magistrate, William Addington, consigning both him and Mrs Rudd to Tothill Fields Bridewell. Next day, Sunday, they appeared before Fielding and soon Daniel Perreau was also taken into custody. Subsequently Mrs Rudd, a much sharper player than either of the brothers, managed to obtain immunity from prosecution by turning king's evidence.

This 'blow-up ... at the west end of the town' attracted huge public attention, partly because of the outward respectability of the prisoners and partly because the affair's opaqueness left ample scope for speculation and the taking of sides. It is still not clear where responsibility lies because since being arrested the suspects have told different stories, the brothers blaming Mrs Rudd and vice versa.[77]

'The late forgeries of the two brothers seem the most remarkable of the kind that ever appeared in this country, or perhaps in the whole world,' reported the *Morning Post* on 21st March. 'All other forgeries were commonly a grand stroke at raising of money and running away with it, but these adventurers appear to have forged one bond to pay off another, and raised it at last to something like a regular branch of trade'. A week later a letter in the *Public Advertiser* complained that 'the *important* affair of the two Perreaus has, at length, driven the American business out of all conversation without doors, and even within.'

When the brothers were tried at the Old Bailey on 1st and 2nd June, 'there was a most amazing crowd, every avenue to the court being filled with well dressed people, who offered very large sums for admittance'. Both men were found guilty, but to Mrs Rudd's dismay the judge 'spoke with much warmth on the impropriety of her having been admitted evidence for the crown by the magistrates of the public office, an act he deemed totally unauthorized, and therefore he refused to admit her, ordering her into the custody of the keeper of Newgate, previous to her trial, as a principal in all the forgeries'.[78]

Over the following months her lawyers appealed against this decision but without success, it being countered that she had failed to provide the crown with

Mrs. Margaret Caroline Rudd
at the Bar of the Old Bailey

Published dec.r 15.th 1775 according to Act of Parliament

a complete account of her involvement. Meanwhile, with a further trial potentially pending, the execution of the brothers was deferred.

On 8th December Mrs Rudd was finally brought to trial. The jury's unusual conclusion was that she was not guilty 'according to the evidence before us'. The *London Chronicle* reported that she was 'neatly dressed in second mourning', 'wrote near 50 notes to her counsel, and displayed a most astonishing composure'. When the verdict was announced 'she appeared confounded with joy at her discharge', and on leaving court 'she stept into a coach, which conveyed her ... to the house of a friend at the west end of the town.'[79]

The verdict leaves the granting of a royal pardon as the only hope for the brothers, who are still in Newgate, and great efforts are being made to save them. Robert Perreau, who has enjoyed a good reputation since becoming an apprentice nearly thirty years ago, enjoys particular support. As for Mrs Rudd, felt by many to be 'the cause of all the mischief', she is rumoured to have become attached to the rakish Lord Lyttelton and is planning to publish an account of her life.[80]

Mess. Robert and Daniel
PERREAU

London Publish'd Jan.ᵗ 20ᵗʰ 1776. According to Act of Parliament.

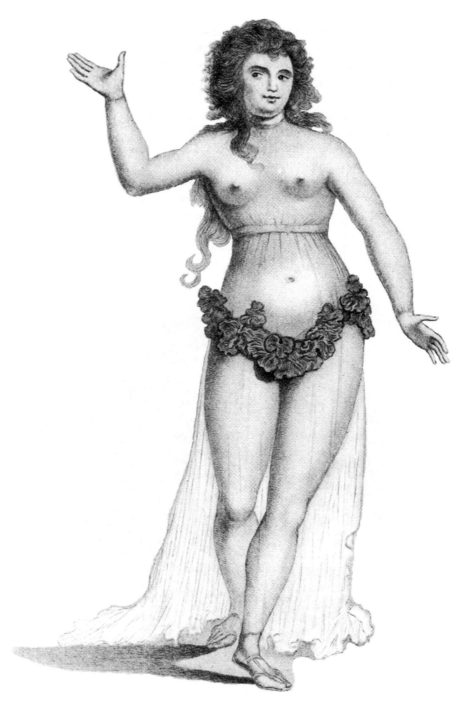

Elizabeth Chudleigh as Iphigenia in 1749, probably at a masquerade on 1st May

iii. Bigamy: The Duchess of Kingston

Mrs Rudd may have emerged from her trial, but the **Duchess of Kingston**, aged 54, is still anxiously awaiting hers.[81]

Born Elizabeth Chudleigh, into a respectable but impoverished west country family, in 1743 she became a maid of honour to Augusta, Princess of Wales. In the following summer she married the Hon. Augustus Hervey, a young naval officer, late at night in a country church before a handful of witnesses. The marriage was kept secret in part to enable her to return to her position at Court, which she did soon afterwards, ostensibly still Miss Chudleigh, Hervey meanwhile sailing for the West Indies. In 1746 he returned from sea and they lived together in London. Next year a child was born, but it died soon afterwards and early in 1749, provoked by Elizabeth's infidelities, Hervey severed all ties.

In the same year she acquired notoriety by appearing scantly dressed as Iphigenia, probably at a subscription masquerade at the King's Theatre in the Haymarket on 1st May, but possibly at a jubilee ball at Ranelagh five days earlier. When an admiring George II asked if he might touch her breasts, she offered to put his hand to a far softer place, and guided it to his own forehead.[82]

Within a few years she had become mistress of Evelyn Pierrepont, 2nd Duke of Kingston, nine years older than her and very rich. By 1758, with his money, she had built herself a fine house on a three acre plot at Knightsbridge, with northerly views over Hyde Park.

Even though she was now comfortably placed, early in 1759 she travelled into Hampshire to make good the lack of church records regarding her marriage to Hervey. His elder brother George had succeeded to the earldom of Bristol and was unmarried. She was therefore only a death away from becoming Countess of Bristol, and seems to have decided that it was worth making sure she could support her claim to the title should the need arise.

The elder brother was in no hurry to die, however, and in 1768 a complication arose when Augustus Hervey began proceedings to obtain a divorce, reportedly with a view to marrying the daughter of a Bath physician. Elizabeth was understandably alarmed: she faced being publicly exposed as an adulteress and as having lived a lie for over twenty years. She could not be sure the Duke of Kingston would stand by her, not least because she was now 47 and he was in need of an heir.

Her lawyers had a solution. Hervey's claim to be her husband could be challenged as false in the ecclesiastical court by a suit of jactitation of marriage (from the Latin *jactitare*, in the sense of to publicly throw out or boast). In response Hervey's proctor sought out the one surviving witness of the secret marriage, a former maid called Ann Craddock, but she refused to testify, saying she was old and could not remember after so many years. It is also possible that Hervey colluded with Elizabeth not to provide effective proof of marriage, it being evident that if her suit succeeded he would be free to marry just as he wished. Governor Hutchinson later heard that the duchess had 'sold a house for £15,000, and it can be proved that money was paid to Hervey'. Collusion or not, on 10th February 1769 the ecclesiastical court judged that Hervey had 'totally failed' to prove marriage, had 'wickedly and maliciously' boasted of matrimony, and was now to have 'perpetual silence' imposed on him and to pay the legal costs of the case, amounting to £100.[83]

Not only did this sentence remove the threat of disgrace from Elizabeth, it prompted the Duke of Kingston finally to make her his wife, the marriage taking place on 8th March 1769, her forty-eighth birthday. On 5th July 1770 the duke made a new will leaving her £4,000 a year, his personal estate without reservation, and a life interest in his real estate. On her death the real estate was to pass to one of the duke's nephews, Charles Meadows, second son of his sister Lady Frances, who had married one Philip Meadows, deputy ranger of Richmond Park. It seems clear that the duke disapproved of the Meadowses in general and in particular of his sister's eldest son Evelyn, born in 1736. According to the duchess, Evelyn was passed over because he had treated his mother badly, had avoided battle while in the army, and was living extravagantly on the assumption that he would inherit.[84]

Elizabeth Chudleigh, after a now lost portrait by Reynolds of uncertain date

In September 1773 the duke died at Bath. Elizabeth's slow, lachrymose progress to London prompted much ridicule, Horace Walpole remarking that 'she moved to town with the pace of an interment, and made as many halts between Bath and London as Queen Eleanor's corpse.' When the duke's will was read in London a month later the Meadowses were not amused. Having borrowed extensively against his expectations, Evelyn found himself cut off with a mere £500 added in a codicil. Determined to have the will overturned, he went on the hunt for proof of Elizabeth's marriage to Hervey. He managed to track down the widow of the clergyman who had performed the ceremony and the former maid Ann Craddock, who had been so reluctant to help Hervey five years earlier but now proved biddable.[85]

Blithely unaware of this, early in 1774 the now dowager duchess set off for Rome where she was warmly received by the pope, Clement XIV. She did not arrive back at Kingston House, as her Knightsbridge home was now known, until early in July. She found that in her absence the duke's will had been challenged in Chancery by a civil bill in the name of Philip and Lady Frances Meadows. It alleged a secret marriage, collusion to deceive the duke, and that she had prevailed upon him to write the will by 'imposition or menaces or undue influence ... or by some other unfair and fraudulent means'. The duchess panicked and fled back to the continent. According to Walpole, 'She decamped in the middle of the night; and six hours after the officers of justice were at her door to seize her.'[86]

By December she was back in Rome. Meanwhile the Meadowses took action in the criminal court as well, a grand jury finding a true bill against her on 8th December for felony in marrying the duke at the time she was actually the wife of Augustus Hervey. In consequence, as the *Morning Chronicle* noted, 'She must appear to take her trial at the Old Bailey as a felon, or an outlawry will issue against her.'

Any temptation there may have been for the duchess to stay abroad was undermined by shortness of cash, Chancery ordering in February 1775 that she should receive nothing more from the duke's personal estate until she had answered the outstanding bill. It was said that, lacking funds for the journey home, and thwarted by a reluctant English banker at Rome, she 'pocketed a brace of pistols, returned to his house, and receiving the usual answer that he was not at home, she sat on the steps of his door, and declared her determined resolution there to remain until he returned'. When he did, 'Money was demanded, not asked. A little prevarication ensued; but the production of a pistol served as the most powerful mode of reasoning: the necessary was obtained, and the duchess instantly quitted Rome.'[87]

On 18th March, while she was heading north, Hervey's elder brother George died of a palsy at Bath. If not a duchess, she was now at least Countess of Bristol, and as a peeress could hope to be tried not at the Old Bailey but before the House of Lords. By April she was in Calais where she was joined by her lawyers. A reply to the Chancery bill was drawn up and she arranged for the Duke of Newcastle and other old friends to stand bail, allaying her fear that she might be put in prison prior to a criminal trial.

She arrived in London on 20th May. Four days later, having moved her indictment by *certiorari** into the House of Lords, she appeared in the Court of King's Bench and gave bail for her appearance when called upon. According to the *Morning Post*, 'Her grace is somewhat thinner than she was before she left England, but looks extremely well, and did not seem the least embarrassed or terrified when she came into court.'[88]

On 27th June the duchess's reply to the Meadowses' civil bill was heard in Chancery. 'Her grace pleaded a sentence of the ecclesiastical court, by which she was declared to be a single woman before the late duke married her, and also the probate of the late duke's will; when after a long and solemn debate of the matter, the lord chancellor was pleased to allow her grace's plea.' This was encouraging: if a civil court accepted the authority of the 1769 decision, why should a criminal one not do the same?[89]

At this point, however, the duchess found herself confronted by a very different problem in the form of actor-manager-playwright Samuel Foote. He was fond of easy targets and this year had lighted upon her. His new play, *A Trip to Calais*, did not echo events in her life but she was evidently the inspiration for one of its characters, Lady Kitty Crocodile: Lady Kitty's surname alludes to the insincere mourning of which the duchess had been accused after the duke's death; she is referred to as being intimate with the pope and as having been decked out 'like another Iphigenia'; and she advises the play's young heroine, Jenny Minnikin, to resort to bigamy to resolve an impasse.[90]

Under the Stage Licensing Act of 1737 plays had to be licensed for public performance by the lord chamberlain, and to Foote's dismay permission was refused. He assumed, probably correctly, that the duchess had brought influence to bear.

There followed an ink war carried out through the newspapers, Foote claiming that the duchess had tried to bribe him to suppress the piece and the duchess claiming that he had tried to blackmail her, offering suppression in return for a substantial sum.

The duchess's campaign was waged largely by the Rev. William Jackson, editor of the *Public Ledger* and a man with a relish for journalistic combat. Importantly for future events, the *Ledger* insinuated that Foote was a homosexual, a series of paragraphs on 16th August alluding to his relations with his theatre treasurer, William Jewell: 'A print of a certain theatrical mimic is now taking. He is represented in a posture of extacy, whilst his purse-bearer, in the form of a Cupid, is pointing an arrow out of the quiver of Love, at an heart vulnerable only by such an archer. ... | A dearer jewel than ever Mr Maddison was now rubs down the Pegasus of wit, and keeps the rampant rogue of genius in wonderful order.'[91]

---

* 'A writ, issuing from a superior court, upon the complaint of a party that he has not received justice in an inferior court, or cannot have an impartial trial, by which the records of the cause are called up for trial in the superior court.' (*OED*)

Foote responded with a letter to the duchess published in the next day's *Morning Chronicle*. Disdaining to answer 'the illiberal attacks of your agents', he repeated his claim that, rather than trying to blackmail her, he had rejected her 'splendid offers' requiring suppression of the play 'with the contempt they deserved'. Towards the letter's end he turned his attention to Jackson and tried his own heavy hand at insinuation: 'Pray, madam, is not J—n the name of your female confidential secretary? and is not she generally clothed in black petticoats made out of your weeds?'[92]

Next day, 18th August, the duchess's chaplain John Forster swore on oath before Sir John Fielding that, when he had visited Foote about the play, the actor had said that unless the duchess 'would give him two thousand pounds, he would publish the *Trip to Calais*, with a preface and dedication to her grace'. The affidavit was published next evening in the *London Chronicle*, and there hostilities ended, for the time being. The actor's friends felt he had triumphed: 'notwithstanding Forster's oath,' wrote Garrick to George Colman, 'Foote has thrown the duchess upon her back, and there has left her, as you or I would do. She is sick and has given up the cause, and has made herself very ridiculous, and hurt herself much in the struggle.' It would be premature, however, for Foote to feel satisfied over the affair, not least because he has acquired a bitter, unrelenting enemy in the viperish Jackson.[93]

In the autumn the duchess's attention returned to the criminal charge of bigamy. On 3rd November the supportive Lord Mansfield presented her petition to the House of Lords asking that the indictment be brought before them as soon as they thought fit, and on the 20th they debated when and where the trial should be held. Pointing out that the prosecution was on behalf of 'private individuals', was 'connected with other disputes about property', and was being pursued 'in defiance of the sentence obtained out of the ecclesiastical court', Mansfield said it could be asked 'whether, in point of justice, there should be any trial at all? A peeress of England was to be tried by her peers. The curiosity of Europe would be excited. Admitting her to be convicted, *cui bono*? ... As to the public at large, would her conviction operate as an example? By no means; for no punishment could be inflicted on her. ... Suppose the lady found guilty. What then? Why then she makes your lordships a curtsey, and you return the compliment with a bow.' The normal punishment for the offence would be burning in the hand, but peers could not be subjected to corporal punishment for anything under a capital crime. 'The lady therefore pleads her peerage, and takes her leave.' He suggested that the trial should be conducted relatively privately, at the bar of the House, on 18th December, and left their lordships to consider whether it should take place at all. Other peers were not so sympathetic and it was agreed that the trial should proceed on the date proposed.[94]

On Sunday 3rd December, during divine service in the Chapel Royal at St James's, the duchess 'was suddenly seized with a faint sickness, which rendered her speechless; her grace was immediately carried out of the chapel between two of the gentlemen belonging thereto to her own coach, which drove home with all speed, when her grace's physicians were immediately sent for'.[95]

On 11th December she was sufficiently recovered to write a petition to the king asking him to intervene. She played on her royal connections, having been a maid of honour for over twenty years and 'esteemed and honoured' by the king's father, but to no avail. On the same day a separate petition was presented on her behalf to the House of Lords asking that the trial be put off for two months in light of her illness.[96]

Next day her physicians were examined by the Lords. Dr Falck told them that her complaint was 'principally ... from a kind of paralytic attack, and a debility of the nervous system, whereby her faculties are impaired and her memory'. Dr Schomberg said that the duchess believed the 'kind of stupor' she had suffered at the Chapel Royal had in fact happened 'at the Asylum'.

Speakers in the debate that followed included not only Lord Mansfield and the lord chancellor but Lord Sandwich and two of the secretaries of state. According to the *Public Advertiser*, the prevailing opinion was that 'Westminster-Hall is the properest place for the trial. It was urged, that the offence was of the deepest dye; that bigamy in some cases might have worse consequences than murder; that therefore the trial ought to be as public and notorious as possible.' It was agreed that proceedings should be deferred until 24th January and that between sessions the duchess should be in the custody of Black Rod, rather than held in the Tower, as had been suggested. The debate resumed two days later when it was decided that the trial should indeed take place in Westminster Hall.[97]

This was bad news for the duchess, who had naturally wanted things kept as close as possible. On 20th December the trial was further deferred, until 28th February, because of practical difficulties in preparing Westminster Hall in time. Two days later the duchess played the last of her many legal cards, her counsel attending the attorney general at his chambers in Lincoln's Inn to ask him to grant a *nolle prosequi* ('unwilling to pursue'), stopping all proceedings against her on the grounds that the ecclesiastical court had already ruled on the matter. They argued in vain and as the year comes to an end the duchess is awaiting trial.[98]

'What this heroic lady will attempt next is very unknown,' wrote Horace Walpole on 17th December. 'If she decamps, outlawry and forfeitures follow. ... If she adheres to frenzy she must retire to a mad-house. If she braves her fate, I shall not wonder if she escapes.' Two days later clubman George Selwyn wrote to Lord Carlisle: 'You will be here for the trial, I take for granted. It will be altogether the most extraordinary one that ever happened in this or I believe any other country. It is a cursed, foul pool, which they are going to stir up, and how many rats, cats, and dogs, with other nuisances, will be seen floating at the top, nobody can tell.'[99]

The married Maid of Honour, or, the
Widow'd Wife and her two Husbands.

D── ─s of K

C── H D── of K

Published as the Act directs 1 Feb.1775. by W. Nicoll, St Pauls Ch. Yard.

*And in each hand
A wanton Lover which by turns caress'd her
With all the freedom of unbounded passion.* Otway

From the *Matrimonial Magazine* for January 1775. 'C' under Hervey stands for Captain.

iv. The strange case of Beaumarchais and the Chevalier d'Éon

Charles Geneviève Louis Auguste André Timothée d'Éon de Beaumont, to give him his full name, aged 47, has been living in England for the past thirteen years. Born into a family of minor French nobility, he enjoyed early success as a soldier and diplomat. In 1762, with the Seven Years War drawing to a close, he came to London as secretary to the Duc de Nivernais, who was charged with negotiating the peace. In 1763, as a reward for his services, he received the order of St Louis and since then has been known as the Chevalier d'Éon. Remaining in London after Nivernais's departure, he was appointed minister plenipotentiary.

For Louis XV the peace was humiliating and, through a clandestine group known as the *secret du roi*, he began to plot revenge. D'Éon was drawn into the work of the *secret* and became privy to sensitive plans for an invasion of Britain, but in October 1763 his rise was checked by the arrival of a new ambassador, the Comte de Guerchy. A bitter feud ensued with d'Éon accusing Guerchy of trying to have him poisoned and kidnapped and of instructing an adventurer, Treyssac de Vergy, to assassinate him. The French government demanded d'Éon's arrest and the seizure of his papers, but were advised that such steps would be contrary to British law. Fearing abduction by his own government, d'Éon moved into lodgings in Brewer Street and barricaded himself in. With him he had correspondence purloined from the embassy and compromising papers relating to the *secret*.[100]

A stalemate ensued, the British government refusing extradition and the French government suspending d'Éon's pension. In response, in March 1764 he published the purloined correspondence comprising letters between Guerchy and himself and senior French ministers. The book, described by Horace Walpole as 'a thousand scandals on M. de Guerchy, in a very thick quarto', sold well and caused a stir. D'Éon was careful not to publish anything relating to the *secret*, and on 23rd March he played this trump card, writing to inform Louis XV that if he was abandoned he would surrender himself and all his papers to the British government. The result, he suggested, would be war.[101]

Guerchy sued for libel over the publication of the correspondence and in July d'Éon was found guilty. He went into hiding and was subsequently declared an outlaw, but in October the tables were turned when the would-be assassin de Vergy apparently sought him out and offered to testify against Guerchy. As a result, on 1st March 1765 a grand jury found a true bill against the ambassador for a conspiracy against d'Éon's life. The matter was never brought to trial but Guerchy returned to France, officially on leave, and died there soon afterwards. His place had meanwhile been taken by François-Michel Durand, a member of the *secret*, who settled the immediate dispute with d'Éon, a pension of 12,000 livres being guaranteed in return for the surrender of one particularly compromising document.[102]

D'Éon remained fearful for his safety nonetheless and in 1769 removed from Brewer Street to new lodgings in Petty France, where he remained for three years before returning to Brewer Street. He also retreated on occasion to Staunton Harold in Leicestershire, seat of his friend the 5th Earl Ferrers.

Meanwhile rumours began to circulate that the chevalier was in fact a woman, and large wagers were laid on the question in the form of insurance policies. The *London Magazine* later recalled that the rumours reached the City 'about the winter of the year 1770, and opened a scene of gaming of the most extraordinary kind'.

From an 'Account of Insurance' among his papers it seems that d'Éon may himself have been involved in a scheme to make money out of the wagers, receiving a quarter share of profits. Outwardly, however, he appeared outraged by the rumours and by the indelicacy of bets being placed on such a question. On 23rd March 1771 he went into the City to challenge those involved, and two weeks later he set about two '*Anglais insolents*' with his cane.[103]

Then, on 7th May, he vanished. Two days later the *London Evening Post* reported that he had left behind 'unquestionable proof of his being of the female sex' and carried a notice of his disappearance placed by his friends. They were apparently 'extremely uneasy on account of his absence' but may also have had a view to stoking interest and encouraging betting.[104]

On 14th May the same paper reported that 'there are upwards of 60,000l. to settle upon the d'Éonic policies'. According to the *Middlesex Journal* two days later, 'very extraordinary discoveries have been made relating to some *policies* which have lately been opened in the City; the *lady* who is the object of them has decamped and left her associates to suffer the punishment of the fraud to which they inticed her'. Another report, on 8th June, also suggested a scam: 'We hear from good authority, that as soon as the sum of 40,000l. (of which the chevalier himself is to have a fourth) is underwritten, the mysterious (or rather the fallacious) matter is to be disclosed.' The quarter share mentioned tallies suggestively with the 'Account' among d'Éon's papers.[105]

If reports are to be believed, d'Éon finally returned to his house in Petty France at about 11 p.m. on 20th June, having taken a trip to Germany. In a private letter he said he had been only to the north of England and to Scotland. In an attempt to counter the suspicions aroused, on 29th June he made a sworn statement before the lord mayor in which he declared that he had 'never had and never will have any part directly or indirectly in the policies of insurance that have been made relating to my person'.[106]

There the question of his/her sex was left, appropriately dangling, along with the outcome of the wagers upon it.

His relations with the French government having eased, in July 1773 he was asked for help in dealing with another troublesome exile, **Charles-Claude Théveneau de Morande**. Morande had arrived in London in 1770 after various scrapes in Paris. In the following year he published *Le Gazetier Cuirassé* [The Armour-Plated Gazetteer], *ou, Anecdotes Scandaleuses de la Cour de France*, which went through several editions and provoked predictable outrage at Versailles. He was soon at work on a biography of Louis XV's mistress, Madame du Barry, titled *Secret Memoirs of a Woman of Pleasure*. After the customary attempted kidnap and other efforts to prevent publication had failed, d'Éon was asked to act as go-between. In the event his efforts also proved fruitless, and in the spring of 1774, with publication apparently imminent, Louis XV and du Barry turned to a more accomplished operator, **Caron de Beaumarchais**.[107]

Born Pierre-Augustin Caron in 1732, the son of a watchmaker, he had first come to notice in 1753 by inventing a novel escapement mechanism. Before long he had been appointed watchmaker to the king, the first of a series of Court roles. In 1756 he married a young widow and soon adopted the grander sounding surname of Beaumarchais. Within a year of the marriage his wife had died of typhoid. In 1766 he married a second widow, who brought him a substantial fortune. Meanwhile he had begun writing for the stage, with moderate success, and been taken up by a rich banker called Duverney, who, in Beaumarchais's words, 'initiated me into the secrets of finance'.

In 1770, however, things began to go wrong. Duverney died in July and his heir accused Beaumarchais of forgery. In November Beaumarchais's second wife died following childbirth, and in 1772 their infant son also died. Early in 1773 Beaumarchais was imprisoned for ten weeks as a result of a feud with the Duc de Chaulnes over a young actress, and while he was in prison a court ruled against him in the forgery case. To make things worse he was accused of trying to bribe the judge and his wife, and in the following February was found guilty and deprived of some of his civic rights.[108]

In the spring of 1774 he was therefore in urgent need of rehabilitation and jumped at the chance to travel incognito to London as the king's agent. For his part Morande was immediately charmed by this new negotiator, whom he found 'adorable'. An agreement was soon reached, and on 27th April 6,000 copies of the *Secret Memoirs* were loaded onto a cart, taken to Marylebone, and burnt in the kiln of a glasshouse. In return for the destruction, and for contracting never again to libel the French Court or monarchy, Morande had large debts paid off and was guaranteed 4,000 livres a year for life. At some point he was also taken on by Beaumarchais as his agent in tracking down and dealing with other libels, which the generous payments he had received naturally encouraged. By June 1775 Beaumarchais was boasting that he had turned Morande from a poacher into a good gamekeeper who would be 'very useful in the interests of the king'.[109]

After the Marylebone conflagration Beaumarchais returned to Paris hoping to be rewarded by the restoration of his rights, only to find that Louis XV was otherwise occupied with dying. Fortunately the new king, Louis XVI, was soon in need of his services, and in June 1774 he was back in London to suppress another libel. He was in Paris for the opening of his new play, *Le Barbier de Séville*, in February 1775, but two months later returned to London to suppress a further libel.[110]

Chevalier D-E-n returnd or the Stock-Brokers outwitted.

ABOVE From the *Oxford Magazine* for August 1771.

BELOW Morande. One of his many enemies later described him as having 'a broad, flat face ... eyes overcast and haggard, expressing fear and perfidy. A flattened nose, with wide and flared nostrils, which seem to breathe the most impudent lechery ... In a word, the face of a tiger, shaved and tanned, but not sated by its carnage.'

Meanwhile the new king had decided to disband the *secret* and conduct a more conventional foreign policy, making it imperative that the compromising papers still held by d'Éon did not come to light. Several attempts were made to agree a final settlement with him, but they foundered, not least because of his insistence that his considerable debts be paid off as part of any deal.

According to d'Éon, in the spring of 1775, hearing that Beaumarchais was in London again, he asked their mutual acquaintance Morande to bring him to Brewer Street, 'and we met, led no doubt by a natural curiosity on the part of extraordinary animals to see one another'. Elsewhere he admitted that 'like a drowning man ... I tried to hang on to the ship *Caron*'. According to Beaumarchais it was d'Éon who called on him and, pleading female weakness, solicited his assistance.

Whatever the precise circumstances, it seems clear that the normally astute Beaumarchais believed from the start that d'Éon was a woman and felt drawn to help 'this astonishing creature'. He also saw a further opportunity to win royal favour, writing to Louis XVI on 27th April to assure him that a deal could easily be done whereby all the papers would be retrieved on reasonable terms. In the same letter, written eight days after the skirmishes at Lexington had ushered in the American war, he offered his services as a source of intelligence at a critical time. 'Having taken steps to destroy ... this nest of vipers,' he wrote, referring to his work against the libel writers, 'I have devoted myself to a more noble undertaking and to more satisfying researches. As my name alone has made me welcome to members of different parties, I have been able to learn from good sources all that relates to the government and the present situation of England.' Characteristically unabashed by the fact that his efforts to gather intelligence would be hampered by his lack of English, he offered to send entertaining and informative reports, succinct or extended, as the king wished, and in return asked only for enduring protection against the enmity of ministers and courtiers.[111]

In June Beaumarchais returned to France and secured agreement to give d'Éon 'all reasonable security ... for the regular payment of his pension of 12,000 livres', although d'Éon's demands for the settling of his debts remained a stumbling block. Back in London, on 14th July he wrote to foreign minister Vergennes: 'I hold to your orders Captain d'Éon ... I will bring to the king the keys of an iron safe secured with my seal, safely deposited, and containing all the papers that it is necessary for the king to have.' The safe or strongbox had been entrusted by d'Éon to his friend Lord Ferrers as security for a £5,000 loan.[112]

Beaumarchais was soon in France and on 25th August a formal commission was issued, signed by the king and Vergennes, for him to treat with d'Éon and 'do all things that he considers necessary' to secure the return of the papers. He was back in London again by early September, dining on the 6th at the Mansion House with d'Éon and others as guests of the lord mayor, John Wilkes.[113]

His shuttling continued with another trip to Paris twelve days later. This time his main purpose was to undermine the ambassador to London, the Comte de

Pub.ᵈ Decᵇ 6 1774

THE BODY SOUL & MIND OF THE GAZETIER CUIRASSE

Satirical view of Morande, published 10th December 1774. His head sprouts vipers and scandal. In one hand he holds the head of a woman, presumably du Barry, and in the other a scale-pan laden with coins, the fruit of his blackmail.

Beaumarchais

Undated portrait by Jean Baptiste François Bosio

Guines, and press for a role in helping France to exploit the American war. On 21st September he wrote to the king that England was in a 'crisis ... within and without', but that, with Guines providing only 'trivial news and very inaccurate notions', French ministers were 'badly informed ... | It is indispensable to have a superior and vigilant man [i.e. *me*] in London at present.' His unrealistic hope of becoming ambassador came to nothing, but Vergennes shared his desire to exploit the American opportunity, and a few days later Beaumarchais returned to London with approval to use French government funds to that end.[114]

An agreement with d'Éon, known as the 'Transaction', was finally signed on 4th November but backdated to 5th October, d'Éon's forty-seventh birthday, apparently as a token of its representing the start of a new life. D'Éon was to give up not only the papers in the strongbox, held by Lord Ferrers at his house in Upper Seymour Street, Portman Square, but also other 'secret correspondence' concealed beneath the floorboards of his bedchamber in Brewer Street. He undertook not only to do this 'without reserving or retaining for myself a single document', but also to remove all doubt regarding his/her sex by making 'a public declaration, clear, precise, and unequivocal' on the subject and resuming female attire before returning to France.

In return d'Éon was to receive a 'safe conduct on parchment', signed by the king and Vergennes, permitting him to return to France and to remain there 'under the special and direct protection of his majesty'. The annual pension of 12,000 livres was to be converted into an annuity and 'other larger sums' would also be remitted by Beaumarchais, 'for the settlement of her debts in England'.

D'Éon added a request for 'a sum of money for the purchase of my female outfit, this unexpected expense, extraordinary and compulsory, not being my idea', and Beaumarchais agreed at his own discretion to provide 2,000 crowns for the purpose.[115]

While d'Éon's interest in dressing and being treated as a woman is not in question, it seems clear that the conditions in the Transaction requiring a decisive and public resolution of his/her sex were included on the initiative of Beaumarchais and the Court. The advantages for the Court were evident: a line would be drawn under an embarrassing saga and d'Éon as a woman would be easier both to control and to protect once back in France. The son of his old adversary the Comte de Guerchy, for one, had announced an intention to challenge him, and ministers believed the young count's sense of honour would prevent him from proceeding if d'Éon was believed to be a woman. The advantage for Beaumarchais was covert: it would enable him and his agent Morande, through their inside knowledge, to make a great deal of money in the market for insurance policies on d'Éon's sex.[116]

Within days of the Transaction Beaumarchais set off for Paris with the prize of the secret papers, but according to d'Éon his approach to them was recklessly cavalier. First, he sent Morande to Upper Seymour Street on his own to retrieve the strongbox, thus placing considerable temptation in the way of a notorious scandal writer and blackmailer. Then, embarking at Dover on the night of 9th November, and suffering from what d'Éon called 'a cruel venereal malady' (which may just have been a bad cold), he was so overcome that he left 'my other particular *cassette*,' formerly kept under the floorboards, 'containing my secret correspondence with the late king ... on a vessel next to his'. Fortunately 'the English sailors, who were more attentive, threw it from one boat to the other and it escaped falling into the sea.'[117]

D'Éon would soon find further cause for complaint. With Beaumarchais barely out of the country, on 10th November the *Morning Post* reported: 'The Chevalier d'Eon is absolutely recalled home, by the express order of the king his master, who means to load him, or rather *her*, with honours; for it is now proved to a demonstration, that this prodigy is of the feminine gender.' Next day came another report in the same paper: 'A new policy is preparing in the City *to do* the *she* Chevalier d'Eon; betts now run 7 to 4 a woman against a man; and a nobleman well known on the turf, has pledged himself to bring the matter to a clear decision before the expiration of fourteen days.' It seems likely that both reports originated with Morande, acting independently or on Beaumarchais's instructions, the aim being to shift the betting odds and so increase the value of policies held by the pair.[118]

Realising what was going on, d'Éon responded with a letter from Brewer Street which appeared in the same newspaper in French on the 13th and in translation the next day:

> The Chevalier d'Eon desires with most earnest intreaty the people of England ... not to renew any policies on his sex ... He is convinced that there are among the Great in France, some that abuse the perfect knowledge they have of his sex, so as to engage certain bankers in Paris, to correspond with certain bankers in London ... Whatever are the grounds of fresh reports, the Chevalier d'Eon publickly declares ... that he has recently refused great sums of money, which have been offered to him to be concerned in such policies; offers that he could never hear of, but with the most sovereign contempt. He declares that he will never manifest his sex, till such time as all policies shall be at an end. If that is impossible, the Chevalier d'Eon will be forced to quit secretly a country which he deems second to his own, as it has proved a bulwark against the persecution of his malicious enemies ...[119]

This of course ran directly counter to the Transaction and jeopardised whatever lucrative schemes Beaumarchais and Morande had in play. As a result, according to d'Éon, 'Morande, greatly agitated and in great consternation, hurried to the house of my lawyer Vignoles, then came with him to my house in order to tell me that Beaumarchais would be furious with me because of this announcement, that it would ruin all the *good plans* he had for me, that I was nobody's friend, and that I was my own worst enemy, etc.'[120]

Furious or not, Beaumarchais remained in France for over a month, urging the king to intervene in support of America and seeking instructions as to how to handle outstanding details relating to d'Éon. He finally arrived back in London two days ago, on 29th December, and spent the day with his confidant Morande. Invited to dine with them next day, d'Éon found them laughing and joking. Beaumarchais sang a song which he said he had composed for d'Éon while in Paris, where it was rumoured that the two were to marry. He then turned the conversation to d'Éon's letter to the *Morning Post*. D'Éon said he had written it only because people *whom Beaumarchais knew well* had placed earlier paragraphs designed to 'relight the fire of the policies on my sex'. At this Beaumarchais stood up in anger, put his hat on, and told d'Éon that not only was the letter badly written, humourless, and impertinent, but that he had broken his word of honour — a reference to the undertakings of the Transaction. D'Éon rose in turn, also put his hat on, angrily told Beaumarchais that the negotiation and the negotiators could go to the devil, and walked out. Next day, New Year's Eve, Beaumarchais wrote a rather patronising letter in hope of reconciliation, unaware that the agitated d'Éon had left town, taking a post-chaise for Staunton Harold. He will arrive there on 2nd January and find comfort in 'the good reception, the good food, and the good claret of my lord'.[121]

It should in fairness be noted that there is no certain proof that Beaumarchais and Morande are involved in betting on d'Éon's sex. However, given their opportunistic characters, it would be odd if they are not seeking to exploit their inside knowledge to make money in this way, and the anger they showed when d'Éon refused to play his part tends to support the assumption that they are. One account suggests they have committed as much as £100,000, for themselves and Paris bankers, in which case they are seriously exposed.[122]

During the year about to begin the arising feud will have dramatic consequences for d'Éon and Morande. As for Beaumarchais, his main energies are now otherwise engaged, in the small business of shaping the history of the world.

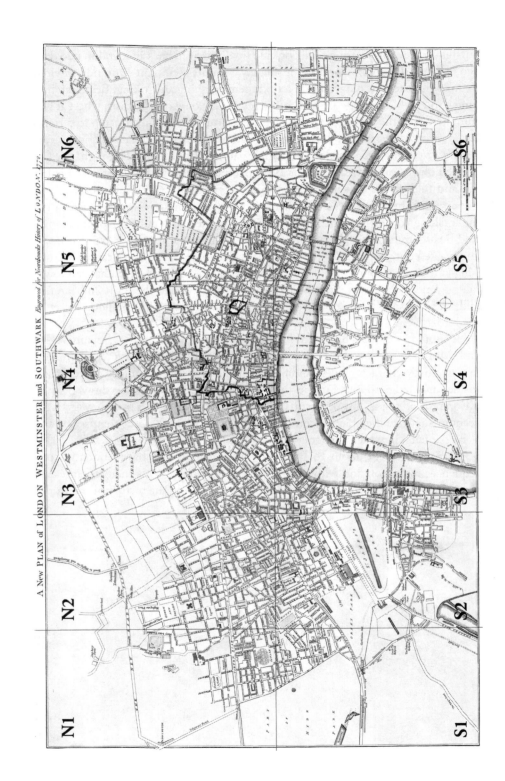

A New PLAN of LONDON WESTMINSTER and SOUTHWARK *Engraved for Nordonode's History of LONDON 1772.*

A Tour of London
1776

The tour is in two parts, a north route and a south route, both travelling west to east across the city. Each route is divided into six sections corresponding to sections of the map opposite: 'A New Plan of London, Westminster and Southwark', dated 1772 and engraved for John Noorthouck's *History of London*, which was published in the following year.

The routes are marked on the map sections by a thin grey line. Some street names have been added, and a few details have been inserted from a slightly later map which appeared in Walter Harrison's *New and Universal History, Description and Survey of the Cities of London and Westminster*, published in 1776-1777. The Harrison map is generally less detailed but includes 'the additional buildings to the year 1777'.

The 1772 map is also supplemented by extracts from two much more detailed plans: the first by John Rocque, surveyed from 1739 and published in 1747, and the second by Richard Horwood, surveyed from 1791 and published between 1792 and 1799.[1]

Quotations are drawn from guidebooks and other contemporary sources, details of which may be found in the notes. Unless otherwise indicated all trader information is drawn from the alphabetical listing in *The London Directory for the year 1776*. Names of individuals who may be of general interest and/or who feature notably in the Chronicle are in **bold**. Ages given are as at the start of the year and have been included for some notable figures not covered in the Briefing Notes. House numbers where given are those in use in 1776 and may not tally with modern numbering.

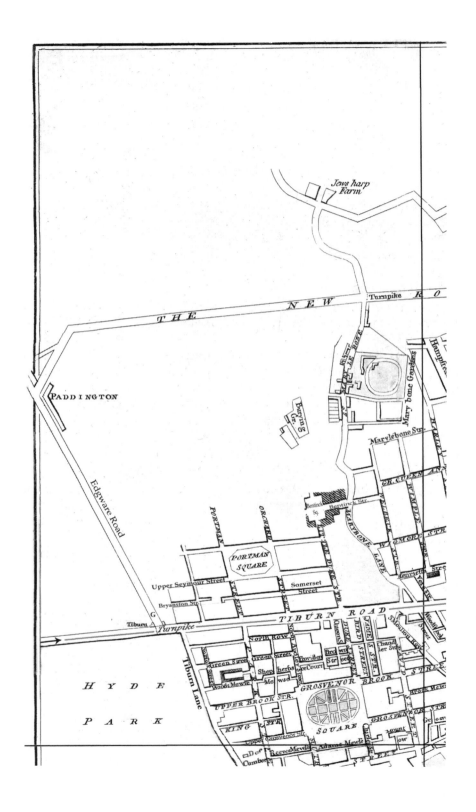

N1

As we approach from the west, on our right **Hyde Park** is 'encompassed with a wall' and 'well stocked with deer'. Ahead of us - depicted by Rowlandson above - is one of many **turnpikes** placed around the edge of the city. The toll house beside it also serves a second turnpike across the south end of **Edgware Road**, where a coach can be glimpsed heading north.

The toll house is roughly where **Tyburn gallows** stood until 1759, when a 'new moving gallows' was introduced which could be carried off in a cart once the bodies had been cut down. The new gallows may therefore only be in evidence on execution days and its location may vary. Its usual site has been the subject of debate, but it seems it was a short way north of the old site, with the gallows being set up more or less in the middle of Edgware Road, roughly where G is on the map opposite.[2]

A fictional countryman's account of a visit to London in 1776 describes a typical execution day scene, pickpockets included:

> All the doors and windows leading to Tyburn were hung with faces, eyes, and noses, to enjoy the glorious sight of a fellow-creature going to be swung by the neck. Many people who had a notion of staying to see the end of it, had provided themselves with pockets full of neat-tongues, slices of ham, oranges, and what they here call *polonies* ... and just as the cart was drawn away, and the man began to dangle like a joint of meat on a string, the folks began to eat and shout like furies, and a general cry ran through the croud of 'Take care, gentlemen and ladies, of your pockets; the hangman-day villains are at work ...'[3]

From here onward the first part of our route will follow in reverse the last journey of those condemned to die.

As we reach the corner of the park, running south is **Tyburn Lane**, also known by its modern name **Park Lane**. Ahead is **Tyburn Road**, also known as **Oxford Road** or **Oxford Street**.

To the south, **Grosvenor Square** is 'reckoned the finest square in and about London'. It has 'an equestrian statue of King George I finely gilt' at its centre, along with 'many trees and fine rows of hedge nicely cut which serve as a shelter for the birds who take up their residence in this spot and amuse the inhabitants with their agreeable melody'. Among those with town houses here are **Lord North**, who lets his out; opposition leader **Lord Rockingham**; **Lord Grosvenor**, estranged from his wife **Henrietta (Harriet)** since the discovery of her affair with the Duke of Cumberland; and **Lord Stanley** and his lively wife **Lady Betty** (née Hamilton), aged 23 and 22, in a house recently refurbished by Robert Adam. 'Their suppers are magnificent, but their hours are abominably late'. Lady Betty has recently taken to the game of commerce, and 'makes all the world ... play at it till five o'clock in the morning'.[4]

North of Tyburn Road, **Lord Townshend**, master general of the Ordnance, has a house in **Portman Square**. In March he and officers experiment with a hand grenade in the square and baggage waggons destined for America are painted there. The square is still a work in progress: indeed, all the streets west of **Marybone** or **Marylebone Lane** have been built since the time of Rocque's survey. The 5th Earl Ferrers, vice admiral and friend of the Chevalier d'Éon, has a house in **Upper Seymour Street**, not far from Tyburn, where in 1760 his elder brother was hanged for murdering his steward. In **Orchard Street** live **Richard Sheridan**, his wife **Elizabeth** (née Linley), and their one-year-old son. Painter **George Stubbs**, aged 51, has a house in adjoining **Somerset Street** (No. 24), on a site now covered by Selfridges. **Little** or **New Duke Street** is home to scandal writer **Charles Théveneau de Morande** (No. 40), aged 34, who is employed as an agent by Beaumarchais.

In September 1775 an American refugee found the area 'rather disagreeable as they are building large rows of houses and that which is intended for a square is fill'd up with rubbish'. He was probably referring to **Manchester** or **Bentinck Square** (as it is named on Harrison's map), which is being developed at this time. In adjoining **Bentinck Street**, **Edward Gibbon**, aged 38, MP for Liskeard in Cornwall, is putting the finishing touches to the first volume of his great history, to be published in February. He keeps his own carriage and has half a dozen servants.[5]

A detour up Marybone Lane would lead us to **Marybone** (or **Marylebone**) **Gardens**. Dating back to 1650, it offers 'evening amusements during the summer season', with music, fireworks, and 'vaulting on the slack rope'. It is less fashionable than its rivals Ranelagh and Vauxhall and this will be its final year of opening.[6]

ABOVE Tyburn with the old fixed gallows, as drawn by Hogarth. This view was subsequently engraved as plate 11 of his *Industry and Idleness* series, published in 1747, but reversed so that the gallery for spectators appears on the right. In the plate the gentle slopes in the distance become two hills, probably those of Hampstead and Highgate, suggesting that the viewpoint is looking broadly northwards up Edgware Road.

BELOW Marylebone Gardens by John Donowell, 1755,
with the Great Room on the left and the Orchestra on the right.

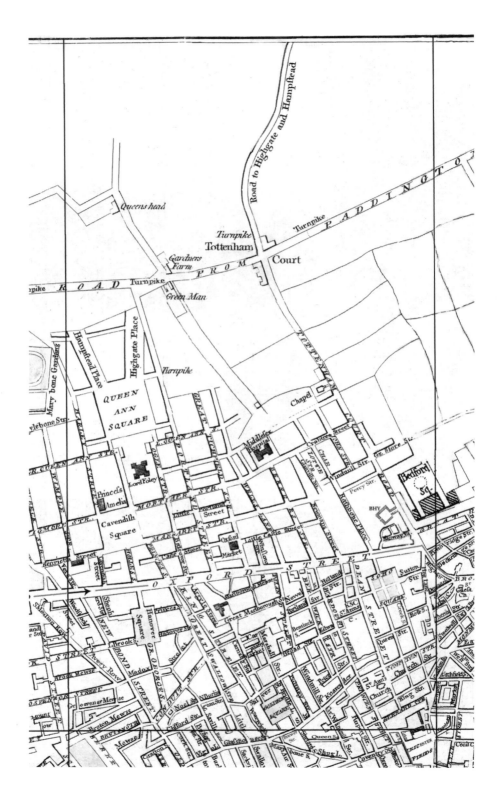

N2

Continuing eastward, **Oxford Street** is 'the longest and handsomest street in the city of London. It is regularly paved, and when the lamps, which are regularly placed on the houses ... are lit up in the evening, there is a most beautiful prospect'. At No. 160 is the troubled bank of Sayre, Purdon and Co. One partner, American **Stephen Sayre**, has recently been imprisoned for an alleged plot to kidnap the king, while the other, **Benjamin Coote Purdon**, disappears in October, apparently drowned in the Thames. Also in the street are Gillow and Co.'s cabinet and upholstery warehouse (No. 176) and James Showell, whip-maker to their majesties (No. 322).[7]

About half way along on the north side, **Oxford Market** is a small covered market for meat, fish and vegetables. Slightly further east, on the south side, on a site now occupied by Marks and Spencer, is the **Pantheon**, marked P on the map opposite, its facade shown above. It is 'a superb building, of which the principal part is a grand rotunda, crowned with a fine dome. This edifice is ... dedicated to the nocturnal revels of the British nobility'. Its entertainments 'are chiefly in the winter season, and consist of musical pieces, both Italian and English; masquerades, balls, concerts, &c.' According to Gibbon, 'The Pantheon, in point of ennui and magnificence, is the wonder of the eighteenth century and of the British empire.'[8]

At Oxford Street's east end, near the corner with Tottenham Court Road, is one of many **pillories** to be found around the city. To the south runs **Hog Lane**, now Charing Cross Road. To the east, **Bainbridge Street** is home to one of the city's several **cockpits**: 'a main of cocks, for two guineas a battle and ten the odd, between Surry and Middlesex', begins here at 5.30 p.m. on 2nd January.[9]

ABOVE Interior of the Pantheon, after Charles Brandoin. Published 1772.

BELOW Two details. LEFT The organ, orchestra, and dancing. RIGHT One of several suggestive hats, pointing to the underlying purpose of such assemblies.

George Romney
self-portrait
circa 1784

Areas adjacent

i. North of Oxford Street, west to east

On the north side of **Cavendish Square** lives the king's aunt **Princess Amelia**, although she removes to Gunnersbury House in Ealing for the summer. On the east side lives judge and orientalist **William** (later Sir William) **Jones**. Painter **George Romney** has recently moved into a large house on the south side, four doors east of Holles Street, and his name is on the door. The house formerly belonged to another portrait painter, Francis Cotes, and has a large painting room and a gallery where visitors and prospective sitters can view completed works. Romney will charge you 18 guineas for a 'three-quarter' portrait (30 inches by 25) rising to 70 guineas for a whole length, substantially undercutting Sir Joshua Reynolds, who charges 35 and 150 guineas respectively. On the square's west side, toward the south end, lives **Lord Barrington**, secretary at war.[10]

To the north, on the west side of **Harley Street**, 'just above the mews', is the house of **Allan Ramsay**, aged 62, principal painter in ordinary to the king, whose studio consists of 'a set of coachmen's rooms and haylofts gutted, all thrown into one long gallery'. Unfortunately his health has entered a decline and he is currently in Italy seeking a cure. On the same side of the street, No. 48 is 'an elegant new-built house ... exceedingly well finished, and fitted up and ornamented at a great expence'. Unfortunately its owner is fraudster **Daniel Perreau**, presently in Newgate awaiting execution. The house is offered for sale in March.[11]

To the east, sculptor **Joseph Nollekens** lives at No. 9 **Mortimer Street**. **Great Titchfield Street** (No. 30) is home to **Madame de Charpillon** and her daughter **Marianne**, current mistress of John Wilkes. Writer **Giuseppe Baretti**, aged 56, also has lodgings in the street. In the first half of the year he spends much of his time at the Southwark and Streatham homes of Henry and Hester Thrale, being tutor to their elder daughter, but in July he flounces out and it seems likely that thereafter he is here more often.[12]

Further east, American **Benjamin West**, aged 37, historical painter to the king, lives and works in a house on the east side of **Newman Street** (No. 14), opposite Castle Street. In **Goodge Street** (shown with its earlier name of Crabtree Street) lives **Miles Peter Andrews**, who has recently caused a stir by eloping with actress **Ann Brown**. Running south, parallel to Charlotte Street, **Glanville Street** is involved in another notable elopement during the year, the **Countess of Tyrconnel** lodging here incognito in July.[13]

To the south-east, off the west side of **Tottenham Court Road**, is **Black Horse Yard** (BHY on the map), where human body parts are discovered in sacks at the end of March. Construction of **Bedford Square**, east of Tottenham Court Road, is reported in June. In July two of the labourers argue, one of them striking the other 'so violent a blow' that he falls from the scaffold and expires immediately.[14]

Near the north end of Tottenham Court Road, a short distance beyond the junction, is another **turnpike** (Rowlandson's view of which is on p445). North-west of the junction lie the **Adam and Eve** tavern and **Joshua Brookes's Menagerie**. In April Brookes advertises 'a fine assortment of new and curious South American birds, wild turkies, pheasants, poultry, and variety of water fowls,' along with Alderney cows and a range of 'curious fancy deer'. His is probably the 'collection of birds and beasts' at Tottenham Court Road visited in December by Edward Oxnard and other American refugees. Oxnard considers most of the collection 'hardly worth seeing' but is impressed by 'a bird from East Indies of the Turkey kind, tho' as big as 5 of them', and by a lioness and a camel.

In July 'the original Sampson, lately from Vienna' announces that he 'has just opened his Riding-School, the back of the Adam and Eve'. Every evening except Sunday, weather permitting, he undertakes 'divers feats of activity upon a camel, never before performed in England'. Whether the camel is borrowed from Brookes's is not clear.[15]

ii. South of Oxford Street, west to east

In **Hanover Square** 'carriages have a narrow ill-paved street to pass round in, and the middle has the air of a cow-yard, where blackguards assemble in the winter, to play at hussle-cap, up to the ancles in dirt.' Visiting in March, Edward Oxnard encounters 'a number of dogs, traind to dance to music'. **Great Swallow Street** and **Little Swallow Street** broadly occupy the site of modern Regent Street. Running west, **New Burlington Street** is home to the lord mayor **John Sawbridge** (north side) and naturalist **Joseph Banks** (south side). Banks is well placed to keep an eye on **Omai** the Otaheitean who has been installed in lodgings in **Warwick Street** a short way south-east.[16]

To the north, **Argyle Street** is home by the end of the year to the precariously fashionable parson **William Dodd**, aged 46 (east side). In February 1777 he will be arrested here for forgery. In adjoining **Great Marlborough Street** live actor Thomas Sheridan (No. 38), father of the playwright, and widower Sir James Porter,

Dr Dodd, in
an engraving
commissioned
by himself

a former ambassador to Constantinople, with his children including eldest daughter **Anna Porter**, aged 17.* In February **Colonel Guy Johnson**, superintendent of Indian affairs, takes lodgings in the street during his stay in London.[17]

Paul Wentworth, an American merchant secretly employed by the British government, has a house in adjoining **Poland Street**. In nearby **Bentinck Street** lives engraver **Francesco Bartolozzi**. Early in the year a notice seen in the window of 'a reputable house' in **Broad Street, Soho**, to the south, is printed in newspapers: '*Logins and Bord for Singel Laddys that dus not car to be cumbred with men,*' it announces in one version; '*To prevent scandal, bord and logins for singel ladys that dus not care to be mad whores and means to pay,*' in another.[18]

* Anna Porter's journal shows her to have enjoyed a fairly typical round of diversions during the year. She attended the drawing-room at St James's five times and was at the ball held there on the queen's official birthday. She saw Garrick perform in his last season, went to *The Duenna* twice, and heard Gabrielli at the opera house. She went to Almack's several times, to the Royal Academy's annual exhibition, to Mr Lever's museum of curiosities in Leicester Fields, and to Mrs Wright's wax-work gallery off Pall Mall. In early summer she went several times to Ranelagh before heading to Bath for much of July and August with her ailing father. She also kept notes of the sermons she heard, particularly enjoying one in February by a Mr Harvey 'on the depravity of the times, the love of wealth leading to sin'. In April she attended the Duchess of Kingston's trial and left a notable account of it. She also met Omai the Otaheitean, 'who seemed to me silly', and Mohawk chief Joseph Brant, by whom she was more impressed.

Residents of nearby **Golden Square** include **Robert Perreau** (west side, third house from north-west corner), except that he is presently in Newgate with his brother Daniel; Bavarian envoy Count de Haslang (west side); MP and inventor of fireproofing systems **David Hartley** (south end of west side); **Angelica Kauffman**, aged 34, who lives with her father Joseph, also an artist (centre of south side); and opera singer **Caterina Gabrielli**, who has 'put a plate upon her door, on which she has had engraven, "Mrs Gabrielli"'.[19]

To the east, **Princes Street Coffee-house** has recently been under government surveillance, subversive letters having been left

Angelica Kauffman
after a portrait by Reynolds, *circa* 1777

there for collection. In March the bird-shop in the same street advertises 'an exceeding good talking parrot, parroquets, Virginia Nightingales, canary birds, bullfinches and goldfinches', along with a small monkey and a range of dogs. In adjoining **Gerrard Street** are Gibson and Gisborne, playing-card makers, and Mrs Mary Welcker's Old Musick Shop (No. 17) which boasts 'New Musick, and the greatest assortment of any shop in London'. Mr Baldwin's, at No. 26, is used by **Boswell** as his base during his visit to London in the spring. In **Church Street** to the north is Dodo Tollner, organ builder.[20]

Further north, at the upper end of **Dean Street** (No. 3) is the shop of Mary Smith, 'mother to Robert Smith, deceased, late rat-catcher to her royal highness the Princess Amelia', who continues the business. Those troubled with rats 'may be supplied with Mr Robert Smith's Books of compleat Rat and Vermin Catching, at 10s. 6d. or a small book at 5s. 6d. each, and every thing necessary; and gentlemen, servants, and others instructed to catch those vermin the same as in Mr Smith's life-time'. In **King's Square Court** (KSC on the map) lives sculptor **Agostino Carlini** (No. 36).

To the east, **Soho Square** is home to **Carlisle House** (south-east corner, north end), where **Teresa Cornelys** presides over elaborate masquerades. Other residents of the square include Venetian ambassador Signore Moroni (north-east corner, west end), and playwright and theatre manager **George Colman** (south side). In adjoining Greek Street are Nicholas Sanders, chocolate maker, and Josiah Wedgwood and Thomas Bentley's Staffordshire warehouse.[21]

ABOVE Golden Square from the south. Published 1754.

BELOW The scene at Carlisle House on 6th February 1771, from the *Oxford Magazine* for that month. The bear was a Mr Hodges.

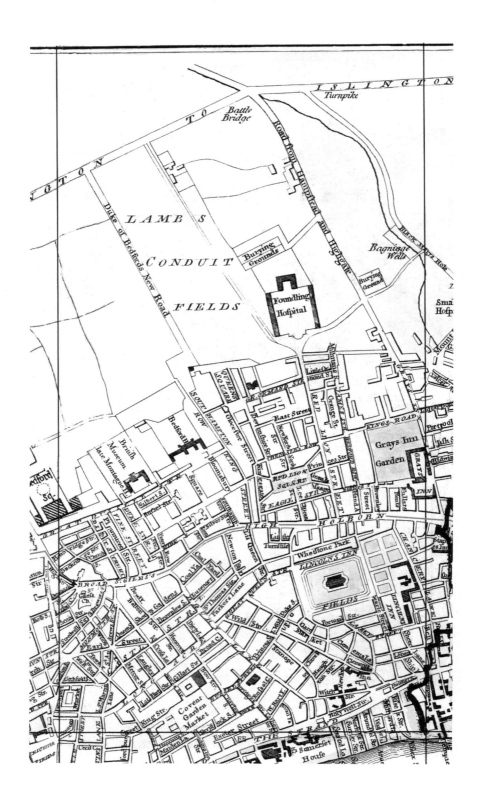

N3

We head south-east into **Broad Street St Giles**, passing **St Giles's Church** on our right. Among traders in Broad Street are William and Henry Shakespear, cheesemongers. Further east, at No. 326 **Holborn**, almost opposite Gray's Inn gate, is Mr Wildman's Bee and Honey Warehouse, where 'the finest virgin honey-comb' may be had for 1s. 6d. per pound. Also available are his Compleat Guide for the Management of Bees as well as 'new-invented mahogany, cedar, glass, and straw hives, both for chamber and garden, and any quantity of bees, which may be seen working in the different hives'. In September a nearby pastry cook is reported as bringing 'an action for special damages' against Wildman for not keeping his bees at home, they having made 'strange depredations on the tarts and cheese-cakes of the complainant'.

In past years Daniel Wildman has also been a noted showman: in 1772, at the Jubilee Gardens, Islington, he performed standing on horseback 'with a curious mask of bees on his head and face'; in 1773 he exhibited his bees at a grand levee at Cumberland House in Pall Mall; and in 1774 he performed at the Colysée in Paris.[22]

Areas adjacent

i. North of route, west to east

The **British Museum** is 'one of the greatest collections of natural history, an-tiquities, books, &c. in the world' and 'has a garden of near eight acres behind it'.

The British Museum, with a beggar cap in hand

'The curious, by applying to the porter at the museum gate, will be informed of the method by which admission is to be obtained.' The process is slow, however, and those who apply for tickets in April are still waiting for them in August. Once inside, on the staircase you will pass a variety of fish skeletons, a young whale, and a large crocodile. **Great Russell Street** is also home to the lord chancellor, **Lord Bathurst**, and to eminent 'mad doctor' William Battie. In **Bloomsbury Square** (east side, north end) lives **Lord Mansfield**. Nearby **Bedford House** is London home to the widowed Duchess of Bedford. 'Behind it has a beautiful garden, and a prospect of the fields.'[23]

To the east, **Red Lion Square** is home to **John Harrison** (south-west section, east end), inventor of a timekeeper for determining longitude at sea, who dies here in March. The square has a gloomy air, a writer in 1771 claiming never to have entered it without thinking of his own 'latter end' because of 'the four watch-houses, like so many family vaults, at the corners, and the naked obelisk that springs from amidst the rank grass'.[24]

Due north, the **Foundling Hospital** consists of 'two large wings directly opposite to each other, one of which is for the boys, and the other for the girls. ... In the front is a large piece of ground, on each side whereof is a colonade of great length ... These colonades are now enclosed, and contain ranges of workshops, where the children are taught to spin, weave, and exercise other handicrafts.' In the chapel is an altarpiece showing the Wise Men making their offerings to the infant Jesus, held in his mother's arms. Until recently there was also 'a fine organ, presented by the great Handel, who had sacred oratorios frequently performed here to brilliant and crowded audiences', producing 'a considerable revenue to the hospital'. This organ having become defective, a new one has lately been installed. It is played 'by one of the children, who, having had the misfortune to lose his sight, has been educated to music'.[25]

To the south-east, 'the principal ornament' of **Gray's Inn** 'is a well laid-out and spacious garden, to which all persons of a decent appearance have free access every day at certain hours. It is composed of gravel walks between vistas of very lofty trees, as well as of grass plots, agreeable slopes, and a long terras, having at each end a portico.' During the year lamps are placed along the road from the end of **Gray's Inn Lane** to Highgate and lit for the first time, with watch-boxes to follow, so that the road may 'be travelled at all hours in safety'.[26]

On the way to Highgate you might visit **Bagnigge Wells** (see Plate 15). 'Hither the invalids of London, &c. repair every morning from April till November, to drink away their disorders; and in the evening the company resorting to the tea-rooms and gardens are more numerous than at any other public place of the kind. In the center of the gardens is a fountain in the midst of a bason of water, which contains hundreds of gold and silver fish.' On 23rd March a newspaper notice announces: 'The Royal Bagnigge Wells are opened for the season. Tea, coffee, and hot loaves, as usual.'[27]

ABOVE The Foundling Hospital from the south.
After Louis Philippe Boitard. Published 1753.

BELOW The Hospital chapel. Engraving by John Sanders. Published 1774.

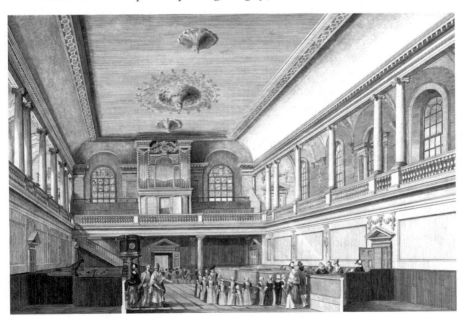

ii. South-west: Covent Garden &c.

Due south from St Giles's Church, **Litchfield Street** is home to one of several **rotation offices**, 'where two or more magistrates sit daily, in the morning, from ten to three, to hear complaints'.[28]

To the east, **Long Acre** is rich in coach-makers, with at least nine, as well as Thomas Jones, livery lace-man (No. 39), Hadley and Nuttall, engine makers to his majesty (No. 63), and Robert Evans, gold-beater (No. 74). At No. 5 **James Street**, leading south into Covent Garden, is Ferdinand Gillard, feather merchant.[29]

Covent Garden itself is home to 'the greatest market in England for herbs, fruit and flowers. It is surrounded by a wooden rail, and in the center is a column, on the top of which are four sun-dials.' After dark other trade prevails. 'There are some parts of this great town which should never be visited towards evening,' warns one guidebook, and it has Covent Garden in mind. It is 'the great square of Venus, and its purlieus are crowded with the votaries of this goddess. One would imagine that all the prostitutes in the kingdom had pitched upon this blessed neighbourhood for a place of general rendezvous.'[30]

On the square's west side, **St Paul's Church** 'was designed by Inigo Jones, and though plain, is accounted elegant, having a noble portico on the east side, where the poll is taken for members for the city and liberty of Westminster'.

The westernmost house on the square's north side, 'next King Street', is **Low's Hotel**, opened in 1774 by former peruke-maker David Low. Here may be found 'spacious and airy rooms, good beds, elegant furniture, constant attendance, and a strict attention to preserve the good character of the house ... | Also good stables and coach-houses for the use of the gentlemen who frequent the hotel.'

In **King Street** itself, Mr Martyn advertises in February for any curious foreign birds that have died in the winter season as he is making a collection of stuffed ones: 'from half a crown to half a guinea will be given for each, according to the rarity and preservation'.[31]

In **Henrietta Street**, to the south of the church, Clay's paper manufactory is visited by the queen in June. Also here, near Southampton Street, and perhaps on the corner with it, is **Mrs Sledge's print shop**. In addition to selling prints she will herself execute your portrait in shadow, 'in the highest taste and perfection',

FACING PAGE Covent
Garden from the south,
by Thomas Bowles.
Published 1751.

RIGHT 'What Frolicks
are here ...' May Day in
Covent Garden, with
Low's in the background.
Published 1778.

What Frolicks are here   HUMOURS of   E'en Banter and Baud
So Droll and so queer   MAY DAY. Pl 2.   Unite, to applaud
How joyful appeareth the Day   And celebrate first of the May.
London, Printed for R. Sayer & J. Bennett Map & Printsellers N.º 53 Fleet Street, as the Act directs 1 Aug.º 1776

and has done as much for 'most of the foreign ministers and first people of fashion in England'. One sitting of five minutes is sufficient and prices range from 1s. 6d. up to 4s. 6d. for a portrait 'neatly framed and glazed'. Here too ladies may be taught grotto and shell work and how to paint flowers, portraits and landskips. The versatile Susanna Sledge also sells remedies for common ailments and a range of cosmetic aids including 'fine fresh bears grease', 'a curious liquid for changing red or grey hair', and a tooth powder 'which infallibly cures the scurvy in the gums, and renders the teeth as white as ivory'.[32]

At No. 46 **Maiden Lane** is Mr Burgess's Academy for Drawing and Painting, with an evening school for drawing three days a week and 'a separate room entirely for ladies'. Actress **Frances Abington** was living on the west side of adjoining **Southampton Street** in November 1775 but has removed by March.[33]

In the north-east corner of Covent Garden, under the colonnade, is the entrance to the **Theatre Royal, Covent Garden**. Managed by Thomas Harris, it is one of two winter theatres with royal patents to put on plays, the other being Drury Lane. The doors of both are usually opened at five or half past with performances beginning an hour later. Bills consist of a main piece and a lighter after piece.

Sheridan's *The Rivals* had its premiere here in January 1775, followed in November by *The Duenna*, which is the hit of the moment and will run for seventy-five performances in this its first season. According to Edward Oxnard, 'The commonality ... take upon them to determine the merits of a performance. If it does not suit their taste they express it by hissing. Should that prove ineffectual they pelt the actors with apples till they make some apology', failing which they 'drive them from the stage'.[34]

South of the theatre's entrance is the Shakespeare or **Shakespeare's Head** tavern, and south of that is the **Bedford Coffee-house**, where you might encounter Garrick or Sheridan. It is sometimes confused with the **Bedford Arms**, on the square's south side (second house east from Southampton Street), where the Hon. John Damer shoots himself in August. The houses on this south side, from Southampton Street eastwards, form **Tavistock Row**, home to portrait painter **Nathaniel Dance**, who has Captain Cook sit to him here in May.[35]

Heading north-east along **Russell Street**, on our left we pass **Bow Street**, where the magistrates' court or **public office** is on the west side, the fourth house from the south excluding the corner house. Blind magistrate **Sir John Fielding** presides and he lives here when not at his house at Brompton. Proceedings can be rowdy, one frequent visitor noting that on public days 'the custom ... is constantly adopted of laughing, and turning into ridicule the defences and manner of delivery of the unfortunate culprits who are brought to the bar'.[36]

Looking south-east across the north-east corner of the piazza, after Thomas Sandby, *circa* 1768. Ahead, on the left of the picture, is the entrance to the Shakespeare's Head tavern. To its left, out of view, is the entrance to Covent Garden Theatre. To the tavern's right, obscured by columns, is the Bedford Coffee-house.

Dodd delin.   Taylor sculp

View of the **PUBLIC OFFICE** *Bow Street, with Sir John Fielding presiding, & a Prisoner under examination*

From *The Malefactor's Register*, 1779

In **Bridges Street** to our right is the new facade of the **Theatre Royal, Drury Lane**. It is part of internal and external renovations by Robert Adam recently completed in advance of the last season of the theatre's actor-manager **David Garrick**. The *Middlesex Journal*, which has its office opposite (No. 5), thought the alterations did 'infinite honour to the fine taste of Mr Adam ... and the spirit of the manager, who has now converted an old barn into the most splendid and complete theatre in Europe'. Not everyone was so impressed, a poem in the *Public Advertiser* asking, 'Why, Garrick, why this waste of gold? | These tinsel'd mirrors glaring? | You surely won our hearts of old, | Plain Nature's dress by wearing.'

If you want to see Garrick perform, be prepared to do battle. 'At 4 we set out, tho' an hour before the play began,' noted Oxnard. 'We found full 500 people waiting for the doors to be open'd. When they were, the croud was so great that I was in great danger of being squeasd to death.'[37]

Continuing east, the narrower part of Russell Street is sometimes known as **Little Russell Street**. Drury Lane's prompter **William Hopkins** lives here, opposite the theatre's stage door, with his wife Elizabeth, an actress. Probably still living with them are their daughters Elizabeth and Priscilla, also actresses.[38]

iii. South-east: Lincoln's Inn Fields &c.

Crossing **Drury Lane** we continue north-east towards Lincoln's Inn Fields. To the north, **Great Queen Street** is home to the oil-shop of Partridge and Mose (No. 4), where may be bought 'new-invented flambeaux (equal to wax) with the

Robert Adam's designs for Drury Lane Theatre, 1775
ABOVE The Bridges Street facade. FACING PAGE The auditorium.

peculiar advantage of not dropping while using on carriages'. Also in the street are coach-makers Tooke and Toovey (No. 33), paper-hanging manufacturer John Brooks (No. 74), and, in a house on the north side, engraver James Basire, with whom the 18-year-old **William Blake** is currently serving his apprenticeship. On the south side, near the middle, **Freemasons' Hall** is under construction: the foundation stone was laid on 1st May 1775 and the Hall opens on 23rd May 1776. The street is also home to the **Office for Hackney Coaches and Chairs**. Its commissioners 'are impowered to licence 1000 hackney-coachmen ... every proprietor to pay the weekly sum of 5s. to the receiver at the office every month'.[39]

In **Stanhope Street** to the south you can visit 'The justly celebrated Mrs Corbyn, from Germany, at her original Turkey Wash and Perfumery Warehouse, the Golden Ball, No. 5 ... | She undertakes still to answer all legal astrological questions, in a most surprizing manner, and far superior to the vague practice of Quacks and Pretenders to Scientific Astrology. She continues to give amazing accounts of all persons by sea and land.'[40]

In **Lincoln's Inn Fields** 'the houses are very fine, especially on the west side, and the area has a large bason of water in the centre, and is surrounded with an iron palisade on a dwarf-wall.' The square is home to Sardinian ambassador the Marquis de Cordon (west side, by Duke Street) and to several notable lawyers: **Alexander Wedderburn** (south side, towards west) and **Edward Thurlow** (south side, central), solicitor general and attorney general respectively, and **Sir William Blackstone** (west side). On the square's east side, **Lincoln's Inn** itself is home to **Jeremy Bentham**, aged 27.[41]

At No. 10 in nearby **Carey Street** is Joseph Earle, bricklayer, who promises to cure 'smoaky chimnies ... as can be attested by the first persons in this kingdom'. To the south, between Witch or **Wych Street** and **Holywell Street**, is **Lyon's Inn**. 'It consists of one small court, with a neat hall; and is an inn of Chancery belonging to the Inner Temple.' Here the **Rev. William Jackson**, editor of the *Public Ledger* and baiter-in-chief of Samuel Foote, has chambers 'elegantly furnished' at the expense of one of the paper's owners.[42]

To the south-west, in the middle of the road, is **St Mary le Strand**, completed in 1717 but still known as the New Church in the Strand. **St Clement Danes**, also in the middle of the road, is further east.

At No. 297 **Strand**, 'nearly opposite Norfolk-street', is Thomas Tiffin, 'real and only surviving son-in-law to Mr George Bridges, bugg destroyer to his majesty, first inventor of that art', who continues the eradication of 'those nauseous vermin out of rooms, bedsteads and furniture &c. without damaging the same, as many thousands can and will testify'. In **Norfolk Street** itself live the musical Linley family headed by **Thomas Linley** senior, father-in-law of Sheridan. On the corner of the Strand and **Arundel Street** is the **Crown and Anchor** tavern, an occasional haunt of Boswell and Johnson, who sup here in April with Sir Joshua Reynolds. In Devereux Court, east of the northern part of **Essex Street**, is Mary Twining's tea warehouse.[43]

ABOVE Lyon's Inn, by Samuel Ireland, 1800.
BELOW St Mary le Strand from the west, by Thomas Bowles, published 1753.
In the foreground on the left is a watch-house with two sedan chairs beside it
waiting for custom. In the distance is the steeple of St Clement Danes.

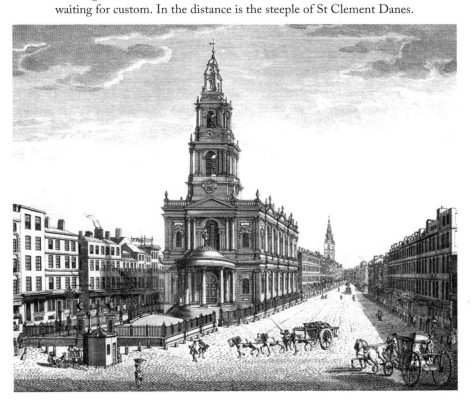

N4

The heavy black lines on the map section opposite show the boundaries of the City of London and of the liberty of St Martin's Le Grand, added by an old hand on the copy of the map used.

Continuing eastward, at the King's Arms on **Holborn Hill** may be found Andrew Cooke, 'bugg-destroyer' to the Foundling Hospital and the Asylum, both of which he has 'entirely cleared'. In January at the nearby Crown and Horseshoe Joseph Stone offers a range of birds, 'wholesale and retail'. They include 'a choice collection of goldfinches', and, 'just come to town from Norwich, a fresh cage of stout well-bred canary birds ... fine in feather, and full in song; they sing the nightingale and titlark's note exceeding fine, and many other delightful strokes.'[44]

Snow Hill is home to Moore and Co., gingerbread-bakers (No. 5), Buskin and Dunn's looking-glass warehouse (No. 63), and Abraham Atterbury's coffin-plate manufactory (No. 71). As the road turns south we pass the west end of **Cock Lane**, where in 1762 the daughter of the clerk of St Sepulchre's Church heard the knockings and scratchings of a celebrated ghost.[45]

Wending round and then continuing broadly eastwards, on our left we pass **St Sepulchre's** (*above*). At midnight before execution days the bellman tolls the church's great bell and calls aloud to nearby Newgate prison: 'You prisoners that are within, who for wickedness and sin, after many mercies shewn you, are now appointed to die to-morrow ... I beseech you for Jesus Christ's sake, to keep this night in watching and prayer, to the salvation of your own souls, while there is yet time and place for mercy; as knowing to-morrow you must appear before the judgement seat of your Creator'.

The bell is tolled again from 7 a.m. to 10 a.m. as the passing bell. The carts carrying the condemned to Tyburn stop by the churchyard and the bellman delivers an exhortation and a prayer: 'All good people, pray heartily unto God for these poor sinners, who now are going to their death, for whom this great bell doth toll. You that are condemned to die, repent with lamentable tears; ask mercy of the Lord, for the salvation of your own souls, through the merits, death, and Passion of Jesus Christ ... *Lord have mercy upon you, Christ have mercy upon you, Lord have mercy upon you, Christ have mercy upon you.*' According to Noorthouck, 'These exhortations however are not extended to murderers.'[46]

A detail from Rocque (*right*) shows the position of the old **Newgate prison**, spanning the west end of the street that bears its name. As shown below, it boasted 'a well-contrived ventilator on the top of it to expel the foul air ... to prevent an engendering of that pestilential malady called the Gaol-Distemper'. However, a replacement prison is being built which faces west onto the northern part of **Old Bailey**. On 25th March the workmen begin 'to pull down that part of the ancient prison called Newgate,

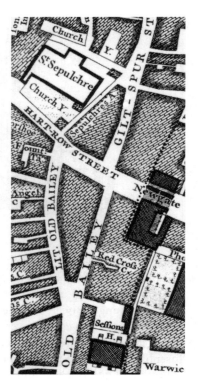

nearest adjoining to the new-erected fabric'. On 16th July, 'as a piece of timber was letting down from the top of old Newgate, it ... fell upon the head of one of the labourers, and killed him on the spot'. On 3rd September the lord mayor makes a detour en route to Smithfield, 'on account of the old gate being pulling down in Newgate-street'.[47]

Newgate's unfinished state is noted by William Smith, MD, in a report on the state of London's prisons published in November. He describes it as 'filled with nasty ragged inhabitants swarming with vermin, though **Mr Akerman**, the keeper, is extremely humane, and assiduous in keeping the place as wholesome as possible'. The humanity of Richard Akerman (*right*) is also attested by Boswell and Dr Johnson, among others. His house is in the middle of the prison's new 300 foot frontage on Old Bailey.[48]

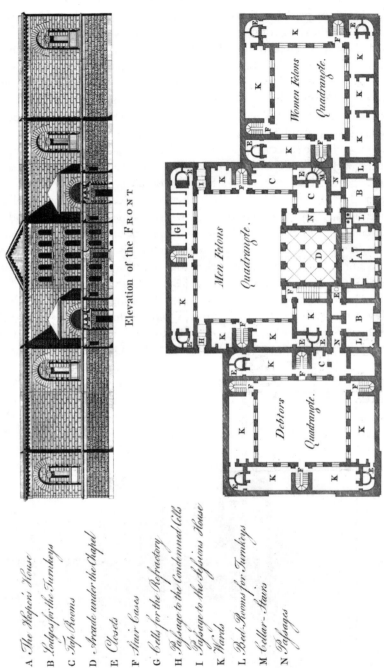

NEWGATE.

Elevation of the FRONT

GROUND PLAN.

Men Felons Quadrangle.

Women Felons Quadrangle.

Debtors Quadrangle.

A The Keeper's House
B Lodges for the Turnkeys
C Tap Rooms
D Arcade under the Chapel
E Closets
F Stair-Cases
G Cells for the Refractory
H Passage to the Condemned Cells
I Passage to the Sessions House
K Wards
L Bed-Rooms for Turnkeys
M Cellar-Stairs
N Passages

Facade and plan of the new prison

From John Howard's *State of the Prisons in England and Wales*, 1777

Adjoining the prison to the south is the **Old Bailey Sessions House** (*below*), where trials are held eight times a year. 'It has lately been rebuilt entirely of stone, and is brought so much forwarder than the old one as to be parallel with the street. On each of the sides is a flight of steps that leads to the court-room, which has a gallery on each side for the accommodation of spectators. The prisoners are brought to this court from Newgate by a passage that closely connects between the two buildings'. American refugee Peter Oliver attends in July, 'but, to the disgrace of Justice, I was obliged to give two shillings for a seat in the gallery. There were 8 criminals tried for their lives in the space of two hours, and I never as yet have seen fairer trials.'

At the back of the Sessions House there is 'a convenient passage covered over for the judges and counsellors that attend the court; close adjoining to which stands **Surgeons' Hall** [*facing page, below*]. ... There is an ascent to the principal floor by a double flight of steps, between which below is a door level with the ground, for the convenience of bringing in dead bodies after execution, in order to be dissected. ... The theatre for dissections and anatomical lectures is an octagon, in each side of which is a niche intended to receive skeletons of the most distinguished criminals that are sent to the Hall ... several of which are already occupied.'[49]

Returning to **Newgate Street**, at No. 1 lives the ordinary or chaplain of Newgate, the **Rev. John Villette**. Refugee **Edward Oxnard** took lodgings at No. 51 in September 1775 but in January he removes to the Strand (and thence to Bread Street in June and to Brompton in September). The **Queen's Arms** is the regular meeting place of the Society for Free Debate. On 6th December, for example, they debate 'What influence have lotteries on the morals of the people?' and 'Is it possible, consistent with the nature of the British government, that it can be conducted without bribery and corruption?' At the street's east end is **St Martin's Le Grand**, in former times a distinct liberty and place of sanctuary.[50]

Continuing south-east into **Cheapside** we find Longman, Lukey and Broderip, musical instrument makers (No. 26) and John Boydell, print seller (No. 90). At No. 73 Joshua Long will sell you 'dry candied ginger, that excellent stomachic for gentlemen to have in their pockets when hunting or shooting', 'the finest Barbadoes sweetmeats', 'fine Italian apricots in large boxes', 'pine apples both candied and preserved', 'Portugueze quince marmalade', 'new cocoa nuts full of milk', 'large green and yellow mangoes', 'real Gorgona anchovies', 'fine Westphalia hams', and 'Brunswick puddings', 'with many other things cheaper and in greater variety than any shop in town'. On the south side the building shown west of **Bow Lane** is **St Mary le Bow** (*right*), which 'obtained its name from being the first church in London built with stone arches, then vulgarly called bows'. The church's steeple, 'spiring to the height of two hundred and twenty-five feet, is the highest of any parish church in the city' and is crowned by a polished brass weather-dragon. 'Though the dragon ... is ten feet long, and proportionably bulky, yet it is turned by the least wind.'[51]

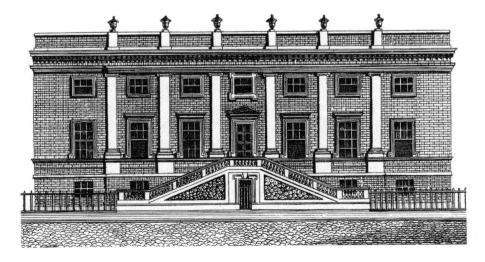

Areas adjacent

i. South-west: Fleet Street &c.

A section from Rocque (*opposite*) adds some detail here.

At the west end of **Fleet Street** is **Temple Bar**, on the top of which the heads of traitors were formerly displayed, but none now remain. It has a postern on each side for pedestrians, but these 'serve only to harbour bad women and pickpockets, who prey on the unwary passenger late in the evening'.

At the nearby **King's Head**, late the Ship and Dolphin, items for sale at an auction in June include 1,500 walking canes, 1,700 mangoes, and '30 pounds of long human hair'.[52]

A short way east of Temple Bar are two notable wax-works. At No. 197 Fleet Street, between Temple Bar and Chancery Lane, is **Rackstrow's Museum**. Here for two shillings you may see an array of 'celebrated figures resembling Life', including the Norfolk dwarf, a rhinoceros, 'the stupendous skeleton of a whale', and 'a new anatomical figure of a woman with child, shewing the circulation of the blood by liquors flowing through glass tubes'. An advertisement in July boasts that 'persons of all ranks and denominations (even the most tender and delicate of the fair sex) daily croud to see them', the sight being 'solemn, yet delightful and instructive'.[53]

To the east, at No. 189 Fleet Street, between Chancery Lane and St Dunstan's Church, is **Mrs Salmon's Royal Wax-work**, often referred to as simply **the Wax-work**, not least because Mrs Salmon died more than thirty years ago. Among the figures here are Peter the Wild Boy, Henry VIII and Anne Boleyn, and King Arthur at the Round Table. In 1767 'strong and striking likenesses' of murderess Elizabeth Brownrigg and her husband were added, and before long they will be joined by John the Painter, 'who fired the dock-yard at Portsmouth'.[54]

Also in Fleet Street are bankers Robert Child and Co. (No. 1) and Hoare brothers (No. 37). Sayer and Bennett's print and map shop is at the sign of the Golden Buck (No. 53), and the street also boasts at least twelve booksellers including John Murray (No. 32, opposite St Dunstan's churchyard) and Thomas Lowndes (No. 77), who in December receives an anonymous manuscript, the first volume of Fanny Burney's *Evelina*. Abraham Stevens, hatter and sword-cutler, is at No. 17, one of at least six in the street who combine the two trades.[55]

At the sign of the Rose (No. 131), Sharp, hair-dresser and perfumer, informs the public in November 'that he is returned from Paris, and will dress ladies hair in the most fashionable and elegant manner during the winter season'. It being impossible for him to attend every lady himself he has engaged 'several of the best hair-dressers in Europe to assist him'. At No. 155 is Mrs Green, pen-cutter to his majesty, who keeps 'a large assortment of good and well cut pens, with a variety of quills, both Dutch'd and in the rough' and offers 'most money ... for all kinds of quills, whether swan, goose, raven, or crow'. In March, recently widowed, she advertises for 'three good cutters. Encouragement adequate to merit will be given.'[56]

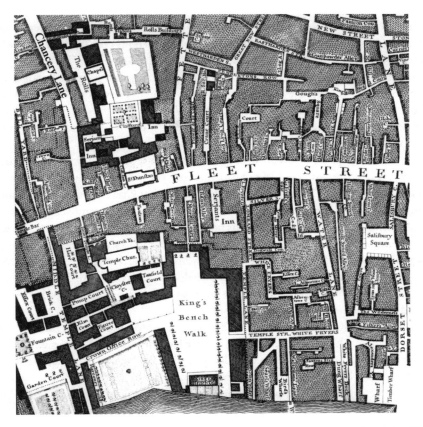

TOP Rocque detail. LOWER LEFT Temple Bar. RIGHT Mrs Salmon's Wax-work.

To the south, off the west side of **Middle Temple Lane**, No. 2 **Garden Court** is home to American lawyer **Arthur Lee**, aged 35, who is conspiring with Beaumarchais to secure French assistance for the American rebels. To the east, in chambers off **King's Bench Walk**, lives **Daines Barrington**, judge, antiquary and naturalist, who during the year receives some of the letters from Gilbert White which will later be published as *The Natural History and Antiquities of Selborne.* Further east, 'No. 62, **Dorset-street**, Salisbury-Court,' is home to the *Morning Chronicle*, edited by William Woodfall.[57]

Off the north side of Fleet Street, No. 7 **Crane Court** is home to the **Royal Society**. They dine at the **Mitre** tavern, across the road and a short step west, which is also favoured by Boswell and Johnson. East of Crane Court are **Johnson's Court** and **Bolt Court**. Early in 1776 **Dr Johnson**, aged 66, removes from No. 7 in the former to No. 8 in the latter. His household includes his black servant Francis Barber and Anna Williams, a blind and elderly poet who suffers 'very much from a pain in the head'. Behind the Bolt Court house is a garden which Johnson 'took delight in watering; a room on the ground-floor was assigned to Mrs Williams, and the whole of the two pair of stairs floor was made a repository for his books, one of the rooms thereon being his study'.[58]

At No. 4 Bolt Court lives James Ferguson, inventor and natural philosopher. On 3rd January he gives a lecture here 'on Electricity; in which, besides all the common experiments, he will set models of mills, clocks, and orreries, in motion by Streams of Electrick Fire ... Several entertaining experiments will be added, with instructions how to apply electricity towards curing many bodily disorders. Admittance 1s. each person. No gold changed, nor bad silver taken.' He dies here on 16th November.

To the north, in **New Street** is **William Strahan**, MP and printer. During the year, in conjunction with Thomas Cadell in the Strand, he publishes both Adam Smith's *Wealth of Nations* and the first volume of Gibbon's *Decline and Fall*.[59]

Returning to the 1772 map, running north-south is **Fleet Market**, which was built over the upper part of Fleet Ditch in the 1730s and where meat and vegetables are sold. It comprises two lines of shops, one storey high, with a covered walk between them lit by skylights. In February Mr Payne, a constable well known for his efforts against vice, pays a visit 'to **George-alley**, in Fleet-market, that common receptacle for whores and thieves', where he apprehends a young woman for inveigling a young man into 'a notorious house'.[60]

On the east side of Fleet Market, towards its south end, named simply 'Fleet' on the map, is the **Fleet prison**, 'allotted for the confinement of debtors from any part of the kingdom, and for such as are guilty of a contempt of the Court of Chancery and King's-Bench. There is an area inclosed by high walls, in which the prisoners divert themselves, together with a kitchen, and a coffee-house.' According to William Smith, 'There are 100 rooms, and sometimes 350 prisoners. No bath or bathing-tubs ... | The turnkeys are pretty careful to prevent spirituous

Dr Johnson's
house in
Bolt Court.
Watercolour by
J. T. Smith.

liquors from being brought in, but the prisoners may drink as much beer as they please, quarrel when they have a mind, and afterwards settle their disputes as they can. ... There are few hours of the night without riots and drunkenness.'[61]

Prison reformer John Howard visits in April and notes 241 debtors 'in the house' and 78 in the surrounding 'rules', where prisoners are allowed to live under certain conditions. He finds the prison crowded with the prisoners' wives, 'women of an appellation not so honourable', and children, and notes the wide array of diversions available. In a large room over the chapel is 'a dirty billiard-table, kept by the prisoner who sleeps in that room ... | They also play in the yard at skittles, missisippi, fives, tennis, &c. And not only the prisoners: I saw among them several butchers and others from the market, who are admitted here as at another public house. ... | On Monday night there is a wine-club, on Thursday night a beer-club, each lasting usually till one or two in the morning. I need not say how much riot these occasion, and how the sober prisoners are annoyed by them.'[62]

To the south, **Bridge Street** runs down to Blackfriars Bridge. On the street's west side, formed of two courts, **Bridewell** is both a hospital and 'a house of correction for night-walkers, pickpockets, vagrants, and disobedient apprentices and other servants'. The prisoners are set to work 'by a hemp-dresser, who has the profit of their labour, an apartment in the prison, and a salary of £14. ... The hours of work are in winter from eight to four, in summer from six to six, deducting meal-times.' The hospital is home to twenty decayed tradesmen, with apprentices who 'wear blue doublets, with trowsers of the same coarse cloth, and white hats, excepting those who have entered the last year of their servitude, whose hats are black'.[63]

THE HUMOURS OF THE FLEET

Prison life

ABOVE In the Fleet. BELOW Looking west over Bridewell.

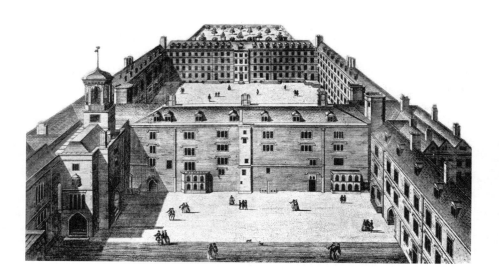

ii. South-east: Ludgate Hill and eastwards

On the north side of **Ludgate Hill** is the celebrated **Belle Sauvage** inn. At No. 29, near Old Bailey, is the lottery office of Bailey, Jaques and Co., which is attacked in December when it is rumoured they have refused to pay money due on a winning ticket. To the east, Thomas Longman is one of several booksellers in **Paternoster Row** (No. 39). There are further booksellers in **St Paul's churchyard**, which is also home to Peter Dollond and Son, opticians (No. 59), who have a second shop in the Haymarket (No. 35). You may also find fruit for sale: in August Edward Oxnard sees 'some good apricots and peaches' and haggles over the price. **St Paul's Cathedral** may be seen gratis at prayer time, but you will need to pay twopence for access to each of the curiosities including the Whispering Gallery. **St Paul's School**, where 155 boys are educated free, borders the east end of the churchyard. In nearby **Watling Street** are Long and Son's burial crape and bunting warehouse (No. 68) and James Miller, whalebone merchant (No. 77).[64]

A typical city club meeting at the Belle Sauvage. The assembled members include an attorney, an auctioneer, a bricklayer, a broker, a distiller, a print seller, a sausage-maker, and a silver-smith. The young man front left, who proffers a copy of the *Morning Chronicle*, is probably William Law Hamilton, clerk to the paper's printer, who during 1776 helps build a libel case on behalf of Samuel Foote. The newspaper being read on the other side of the room is the *Morning Post*. The figure on the right with arm aloft is Robert Dighton the younger, who painted the picture from which the print is derived. Published 1st November 1778.

South of the cathedral, the buildings shown to the south of **Knightrider Street** are **Doctors' Commons**, home to 'the spiritual courts of the Archbishop of Canterbury, and the Bishop of London, for civil and ecclesiastical causes'. Matters treated here include 'ordination, celebration of divine service, tythes, oblations, blasphemy, adultery, simony, incest, matrimony, divorces, bastardy and the like'. Here also are offices in which wills are deposited and searched. On **St Bennet's Hill** to the east is Robert Morris, herald painter to his majesty, who paints 'atchievments, escutcheons, trophies for funerals, companies banners, streamers, &c. and carries on every branch of the herald painting business; likewise arms painted on vellum, in the most accurate manner'. He is well placed for the College of Arms or **Heralds' Office**, which is on the east side of the Hill.[65]

iii. North-west

Largely beyond the map's north edge is **Islington**, 'formerly a pleasant village, situated at some distance to the north of London; but it has been so considerably enlarged within these few years by the addition of new buildings, that it now almost joins the metropolis'. Refugee **Samuel Curwen** lodges here, 'at Mrs Wilson's opposite Hornsey Row'.[66]

To the south, the 'diversions' of **Sadler's Wells** begin in April and include singing, dancing, tumbling, 'many surprising balances on the wire', and the occasional pantomime. 'Great numbers of people resort' here, 'and as the price is but small, it is no uncommon thing to see the girl who draws beer in a public house seated as a young lady by the side of a tradesman's daughter; and the girl who drives a wheelbarrow jostling the elbow of a kept mistress.' At the end of April the *Morning Chronicle* cites the presence of the Duchess of Chandos 'and other persons of distinction' as a sign that the entertainments, while affording 'the highest satisfaction to the middling and lower order of the people', are 'not unworthy the attention of ... those of superior rank'. In June an American visitor notes 'some very good comick dancing, with other exhibitions, all which were well worth seeing, once'. In August 'the celebrated Signor Rossignol ... so much followed for his excellent imitations of various birds' is engaged to perform twelve nights.[67]

The nearby Tunbridge Wells, or New Tunbridge Wells, is also known as **Islington Spa**. A genteel tea-garden, it is the subject of a farce by George Colman performed at Drury Lane Theatre in March. From the neighbouring **New River Head Water-works** water is carried through wooden pipes to the city.[68]

The Spa Fields **Pantheon** to the south opened in 1770. According to Noorthouck, writing three years later, 'Here apprentices, journeymen, and clerks, dressed to ridiculous extreams, entertain their ladies on Sundays, and ... affect the dissipated manners of their superiors.' The owner has since gone bankrupt and in September the fixtures are auctioned. They include '74 mahogany drinking-tables', 'a very capital Buzaglo stove', and 'a stout kitchen range, with wind-up cheeks'. In 1777 the building will reopen as a chapel. In nearby Coldbath Fields is the **Smallpox Hospital**, founded in 1746.[69]

TOP St Paul's School. Engraving by Benjamin Cole, 1756. MIDDLE Sadler's Wells from the south-west, after a drawing of 1792. BOTTOM The Smallpox Hospital.

A short way east is **Clerkenwell Bridewell** or **New Prison**. According to William Smith, 'The number of prisoners seldom exceeds 180. The wards are dark, dismal, and want air. There are no ventilators nor bathing-tubs. ... The gaol is repairing, and to be enlarged.'[70]

To the south-west, **Cross Street**, off Hatton Garden, is home to John Wall-du-Val's Hatton House Academy: 'Grown persons taught to dance the minuet, cotillons, and English country dances, as privately as they please, at any hour ... Persons of a common capacity are perfected in this necessary accomplishment, to appear with a graceful, easy deportment at the genteelest assemblies, in a few lessons, (no enquiry of persons, names, or places of abode)'. He also teaches fencing and, 'for the convenience of ladies and gentlemen at the west end of the town', has another academy 'a little above Air-street, Piccadilly'.[71]

iv. North-east

The Charterhouse, formerly a Carthusian monastery and refounded in 1611 as a school and hospital, is 'one of our noblest charities'. It has forty-four gownboys or scholars (including Fanny Burney's younger brother Charles) and maintains 'eighty decayed gentlemen, soldiers, and merchants, who live in a collegiate manner, dining together in a great hall, in a most plentiful way. They have a physician, apothecary, steward, cooks, butler, &c.' A short way south-west, the building in the middle of **St John's Street** is the Middlesex sessions house known as **Hicks's Hall**, after Sir Baptist Hicks, at whose cost it was built in 1612.[72]

At the south end of the street, **Smithfield** is 'the greatest market in Europe for black cattle, sheep, and horses' and 'a very considerable market for hay and straw'. (It is formally known as West Smithfield to distinguish it from East Smithfield, which lies to the east of the Tower.) In September a newspaper reports that a post and bell have been erected 'for the better regulating the market', but that it has been 'stuck with tenter-hooks' and 'the savages of Smithfield ... seize every cat they can find, and throw it upon these hooks, where the poor unoffending animal expires in all the excess of torture. Several were hanging there last week, some by their jaws, some by their feet, and others by their ribs.'[73]

Smithfield is also home to **Bartholomew Fair**, which begins on 3rd September (formerly 24th August) each year. Visiting in 1780, Samuel Curwen will consider it 'a meer rabble rout ... conducted by men, women and children in painted masks, and merry andrew awkward dirty tawdry dresses, amusements consisting in jumping, dancing, riding in round about horses without leggs, speech making &c. &c.'[74]

At nearby **St Bartholomew's Hospital** 'the sick and lame poor have every necessary provided for their relief, and able physicians and surgeons appointed ... besides a number of matrons and nurses'. Between the hospital and Newgate Street, **Christ's Hospital** is a charity so extensive 'that there have sometimes been above a thousand children, boys and girls, supported by it at the same period. ... Their dress is a blue coat, with a petticoat of the same colour, yellow stockings, and bonnets instead of hats. There are ten pounds given with each, on being put out an apprentice.' Other children here are taught mathematics and navigation towards their serving at sea.[75]

To the east, Jonathan Delver, whalebone boiler, is at No. 11 **Fell Street**, which runs west off **Wood Street** near its north end. Towards Wood Street's south end, on the east side, is **Wood Street Compter** (WSC on the map), where debtors are confined. According to William Smith it is 'full of filth and vermin' and 'in a very ruinous state'. He gives the number of prisoners as 'from 260 to 300' but John Howard gives much lower figures: 107 when he visits in March and 72 in May.[76]

A short way north, on the north side of **Lad Lane**, is the **Swan with Two Necks** inn ('necks' being a corruption of 'nicks', a reference to the swan mark of the Vintners' Company). Mohawk chief **Joseph Brant** is lodged here temporarily on arrival in late December 1775 or early January and chooses to stay until his departure in May. It is busy with coaches: for example the 'Dover and Canterbury Machines, in one day, set out ... every morning at four o'clock, Sunday excepted', and in summer coaches 'for those delightful places, Ramsgate and Margate ... may be had at any hour, by applying at the coach-office'.[77]

A dancing academy. The notice on the far wall reads: 'Grown gentlemen taught to dance, & qualify'd to appear in the most brilliant assemblies: at the easy expence of 1l. 1s. 6d.' After a painting by John Collet. Published 1768.

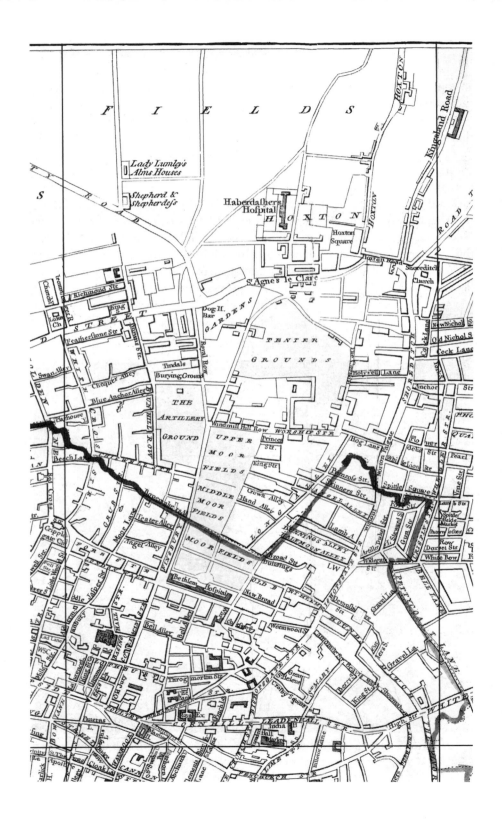

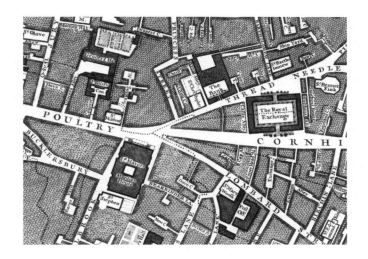

N5

Continuing east we pass from Cheapside into **Poultry**. The hospitable booksellers Charles and Edward Dilly are at the sign of the Rose and Crown (No. 22), where **Boswell** stays at the start of his visit to London in the spring and a celebrated encounter between Dr Johnson and John Wilkes takes place in May. Off the street's north side is the **Poultry Compter**, shown in the detail from Rocque above. Visiting in March John Howard notes seventy-two debtors and six felons. According to William Smith, 'The prison is very dirty, old, confined, and extremely unhealthy. ... Men and women, felons and disorderly people, are crammed together in one ward in the day, and at night lie on dirty boards in filthy holes almost unfit for swine.'[78]

On the other side of the road and a short way east is the **Mansion House** (*below*), scene of City feasting.

Nearby **Threadneedle Street** is home to the **Bank of England**. 'There are large vaults under it, made secure by strong walls and iron gates, for preserving the treasure therein contained.' The back entrance, shown by Rocque, is from **Bartholomew Lane**, 'through a superb gate-way that opens into a spacious court-yard, which proves very commodious for waggons, coaches, &c. coming frequently thither with loads of silver and gold bullion'. Money-laden waggons leave here during the year, under escort for Portsmouth with funds for the American war. The lane is also home to the **New England Coffee-house**, much favoured by American refugees.[79]

On the other side of Threadneedle Street, the **Royal Exchange** is the City's great meeting place for merchants. Its distinct **walks**, shown opposite, give a sense of the range of business, with 'arcades all round, paved with black and white marble, to which the merchants may retire from the sun and rain'. If you have cargo to transport to Venice or Naples, for example, the Italian Walk is the place to find the commander of a ship soon setting out (the *Betsey*, lying off the Tower, 'will absolutely sail' for Venice by the end of January). The Exchange is open from noon until 3 p.m., outside which hours merchants tend to do business in the nearby coffee-houses (**New Lloyd's Coffee-house** is over the north-west part of the Exchange). Beneath the Exchange 'are vaults occupied by the East India Company as pepper magazines', and in its turret towards Cornhill 'is a good clock, with four dials, which is well regulated every day, so as to become a standard of time to all the mercantile part of the town; and it goes with chimes at three, six, nine, and twelve o'clock, playing upon twelve bells'.[80]

Cornhill is home to John Bowles, print seller (No. 13), to Gerard Crawley's umbrello warehouse (No. 45), and to the **Portugal**, **Rainbow** and **Union** coffee-houses. Opposite the Royal Exchange's south front is **Exchange Alley**, home to **Garraway's Coffee-house** (No. 4), which has an auction room on the first floor. In February 'a capital sugar plantation in Dominica ... with negroes, cattle, and stock of all kinds' is sold here, and in August 'the property of Richmond Theatre, with the scenery, cloaths, &c.' fetches £3,700.[81]

The **General Post Office** is on the south side of **Lombard Street**, west of Abchurch Lane. Its staff include six messengers, twenty-five sorters, sixty-seven letter carriers, a watchman (John Whale), a door-keeper to the postmaster general, a deliverer of the letters to the House of Commons, two inspectors of the mis-sent and dead letters, and a window-man and alphabet-keeper on the general days. Here letters to and from suspected American sympathisers are intercepted and copies made which are sent to the American department in Whitehall. Anthony Todd, secretary to the postmaster general, has recently pointed out that this involves a great deal of work bearing little fruit.[82]

Lombard Street is also home to Pigou, Andrews and Grueberd, gunpowder merchants (No. 4), Whitworth and Yates's Birmingham manufactory of coffin furniture (No. 5), **Lloyd's Coffee-house** (No. 16), and Barclay, Bevan and Bening,

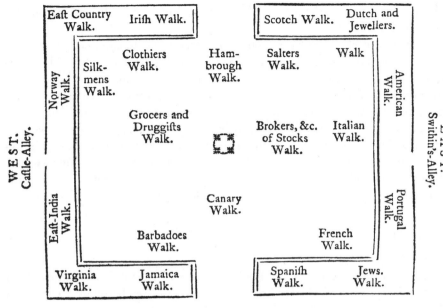

NORTH.
Threadneedle-Street.

| East Country Walk. | Irish Walk. | | Scotch Walk. | Dutch and Jewellers. |

Silk-mens Walk. Clothiers Walk. Ham-brough Walk. Salters Walk. Walk.

Norway Walk.

American Walk.

WEST.
Castle-Alley.

EAST.
Swithin's-Alley.

Grocers and Druggists Walk. Brokers, &c. of Stocks Walk. Italian Walk.

East-India Walk.

Canary Walk.

Portugal Walk.

Barbadoes Walk. French Walk.

Virginia Walk. Jamaica Walk. Spanish Walk. Jews. Walk.

Cornhill.
SOUTH.

UPPER The walks of the Royal Exchange. LOWER Its arcades, after a drawing of 1777.

bankers (No. 56). To the east, in **Birchin Lane** are George Rutt, hatter and stock-broker (No. 11), and the **Carolina Coffee-house** (No. 25), where in July may be bought 'some very fine green turtle, just arrived from New Providence after a short passage'.[83]

From Cornhill our eastward route continues along **Leadenhall Street**. Off its south side, **Leadenhall Market** 'is not only the largest in the City of London, but perhaps throughout the world, and consists of five considerable squares, or rather courts ... The avenues leading to the above markets from Gracechurch-Street, and Lime-Street, are crowded with dealers in provisions of every sort. This market is a real object of curiosity for any stranger to form an idea of the extensiveness, as well as cleanliness of English butchery, and the almost immense consumption of meat by the natives of this realm'. East of the market is **East India House**, where the East India Company's business is carried on under twenty-four directors. John Peppercorn is accomptant and Gabriel Snodgrass is surveyor of shipping.[84]

Areas adjacent

i. North-west

In **Aldermanbury** (north-west of Poultry) Richard Ryder at the Axe inn will sell you 'the best green native Colchester' oysters for 3s. 3d. per barrel, and 'exceeding fine Pyfleet' ones for a little more, 'fresh from the beds three times a week'. His surname is branded on the top of each barrel and you can have them delivered to any part of the town, within two miles, porterage free. 'No bawling at my warehouse door, or puffing the goodness of my oysters, they will recommend themselves. I have been concerned in the barrelled oyster business upwards of thirty-three years.'[85]

The large building east of Aldermanbury is **Guildhall**, home to various courts, including the lord mayor's. It is also used 'for feasting our kings, queens, and other potentates, foreign ministers, &c.' and 'for chusing the City officers, and members of parliament, it being capacious enough to contain 7000 persons. And here the **lotteries** are drawn.'

State-run lotteries are a familiar part of London life, having been used to help finance a range of projects, including Westminster Bridge and the British Museum, and to mitigate the national debt. The 1775 lottery began drawing in November and is about to end. The 1776 lottery begins in November. Tickets cost £10 each, beyond the reach of most purses, and the usual practice is to buy a share of a ticket from a lottery office. Take care, however, because unscrupulous office keepers sell duplicate shares or shares of tickets they do not possess and then, a day or two before the end of the drawing, shut up shop and decamp.

There are 60,000 tickets and the largest prize is £20,000. The lottery wheels are brought under guard from the Lottery Office in Whitehall to Guildhall, where the tickets are drawn by boys from nearby Christ's Hospital. 'There are two large wheels,' noted an American visitor recently. 'A Blue Coat boy stands at each, draws a ticket out, lifts his hand over his head and delivers it to another who cuts it. He delivers it to one of the commissioners, who declares the number ... Vast numbers daily attend in hopes of being the fortunate possessor of the £20000. Anxiety is strongly express'd on their countenances whenever the word *prize* is declard.'

A fraud has recently been detected, one of the boys confessing that 'he was prevailed on to take out a number the night before, and after the man had wrote it down, the boy the next morning pretended to put it in the wheel and drew it out; by which the man has been paid upwards of 400l. and would have received 3000l. had all the offices paid him, but some of them suspected a fraud.' It was reported that the boy in question was clemently not discharged from the school, 'but confined there with an heavy log on one of his legs'.

On 12th December 1775, 'for preventing the like wicked practices in future', it was ordered 'that every boy before he is suffered to put his hand into either wheel, be brought by the proclaimer to the managers on duty, for them to see that the bosoms and sleeves of his coat be closely buttoned, his pockets sewed up, and his hands examined; and that during the time of his being on duty, he shall keep his left hand in his girdle behind him, and his right hand open, with his fingers extended'. On 16th January further precautions are added, including delaying nomination of a group of boys to go to Guildhall until the morning of the drawing, having 'the two who are to go on duty at the wheels ... taken promiscuously from amongst the whole number', and employing additional managers to watch them at the wheels.[86]

A lottery wheel, 1776

Drawing a lottery, 1780

In **Coleman Street** to the east are William May, ink maker, Claude Bosanquet, Turkey merchant (No. 28), and William Gwillam (or Gwillim), funeral feather man (No. 61). North-east, at the bottom of **Moorfields**, is **Bethlehem** or **Bedlam Hospital**. 'There are about two hundred cells, or rooms for patients, which are furnished with beds, when they are found capable of using them; or with clean straw every day, when they are mischievous. ... | This hospital was formerly open for the admission of the public, to the great prejudice of many of the unhappy patients; but by a wise regulation lately made, no person is admitted without a ticket signed by one of the governors.' In April an annual report records that 187 lunatics have been admitted, 190 cured, 17 buried, and 244 remain under cure.[87]

Bethlehem Hospital from the north

In **Chiswell Street**, west of Moorfields, are Samuel Whitbread, brewer, William Caslon and Son, letter-founders (No. 61), and Samuel Parkes, chemist and druggist (No. 68), of whom can be bought 'genuine fox's lungs ... for the cure of coughs, catarrhs, and defluxions on the lungs ... sold in pots (with directions)'. Round the corner in **Bunhill Row** are Mr Linch, harpsichord maker, who dies in February, and John Walford, buckram stiffener and dyer.[88]

To the east, on the north side of **Windmill Hill Row**, is the **Foundry**, a former cannon foundry leased by **John Wesley**, aged 72, which has been the centre of his operations since 1740. The lease expiring, in 1778 he will move to a new chapel in the City Road.[89]

ii. North-east

On the west side of **Bishopsgate Street**, 'within two or three doors from Cornhill', stands 'that grand spacious house of public entertainment', the **London Tavern**.

Further north-east the street becomes **Bishopsgate Without**, home to Strange and Parker, cheesemongers (No. 2), and Letitia Clark's hat warehouse (No. 29). On the west side is the **London Workhouse** (LW on the map), 'a large commodious building, established for the relief and employment of the poor, and the punishment of vagrants and disorderly persons'. Children 'found begging in the streets, pilfering on the keys, or lying about in glass-houses, and uninhabited places' are taken in, 'dressed in russet cloth, with a round badge upon their breasts, representing a poor boy and a sheep, with this motto, *God's providence is our inheritance*. And when arrived at a proper age, the boys are bound out apprentices, to trades or sea service, and the girls placed in honest families.' In the keeper's side 'are confined beggars and vagrants ... and lewd women taken up in the streets, who are kept to hard labour, in beating of hemp and washing of linen'.[90]

In **Spitalfields** to the east the manufactures of silk 'are rich beyond conception; but the numbers of workmen employed are frequently discontented with their wages, and troublesome'. Among traders in this area are William Cazaly, who has a stocking manufactory at the corner of Spital Square, Joshua Green and Son, shag weavers (No. 41 Crispin Street), Susanna Lamy, handkerchief weaver (No. 40 Gun Street), John Randall, tabby-waterer (No. 7 Elder Street), Guy Bryan and Co., scarlet dyers (Vine Court), and Abraham Thorpe, ferret and galloon weaver (No. 8 Widegate Street).[91]

To the north, behind the Hare at **Hoxton**, Wilson's Pleasure-Bath offers bathing, swimming, and angling. 'There is a large temperate bath, where gentlemen may learn to swim without danger; and a small bath for young gentlemen, about three feet and a half deep, with a paved bottom, quite transparent; a cold bath, supplied by a cold spring, and allowed the best in the kingdom: also a large fish-pond, well stocked with carp, tench, and a great variety of other fish.'[92]

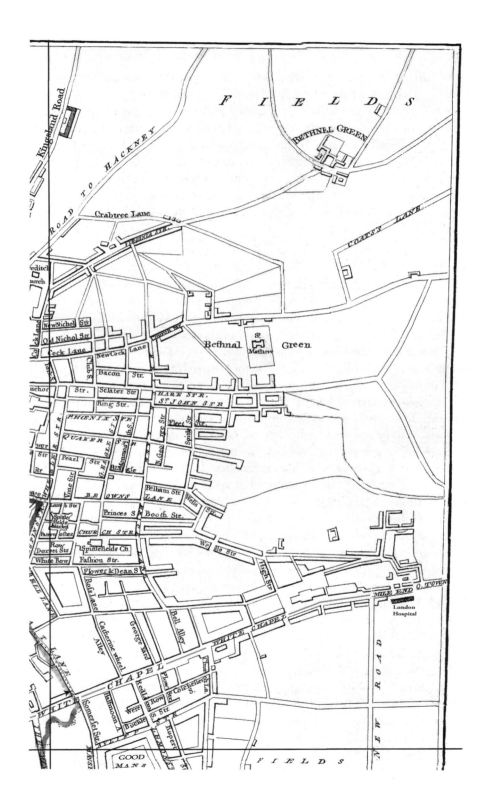

N6

Approaching the city's eastern fringe, **Whitechapel** 'is a fine wide street, and is the principal eastern entrance into London from the great Essex road'. Its south side 'is used for a hay market three times a week; and is no less a market for meat, being crouded with the shops of carcase butchers'. The street is also home to tobacco pipe maker William Scourfield, bell-founders Pack and Chapman, an aqua fortis and colour maker, a white-lead works, and an indigo blue manufacturer.[93]

On the south side of **Mile End Road**, the **London Hospital** 'hath about an hundred and sixty beds for the reception of the sick'. Mile End is also home to Charington and Moss, brewers, and, when he is not at sea, to **James Cook**, aged 47, and his wife Elizabeth. Cook's house, No. 7 Assembly Row, is on the south side of the main road, a short way beyond the edge of the map. Boswell visits in April and is given tea in the garden.[94]

Over the fields to the north, beyond **Bethnal Green** and the edge of the map, is **Hackney**, 'a very large and populous village ... so remarkable for the country seats of rich citizens, that it is said there are not less than an hundred carriages kept in it. ... | It is from this village that the coaches let to the people in London first received the name of Hackney coaches; for in the last century such numbers of people were frequently going in visits to see their friends here, that it occasioned them often to hire horses or carriages for that purpose'.

Among prosperous inhabitants hereabouts is magistrate **James Penleaze**, whose house opposite the Nag's Head in **Hackney Road** is the scene of a violent burglary in April and of subsequent intrusion attempts.[95]

The London Hospital, 1753

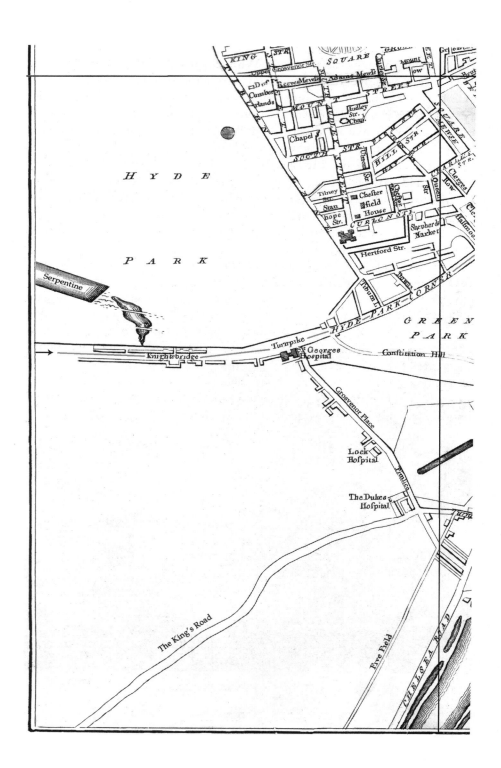

S1

Behind us, beyond the edge of the map to the west, the **Duchess of Kingston** lives in **Kingston House** (west of modern Ennismore Gardens, on the south side of Kensington Road). The photograph above shows it with Regency additions in 1937, before its demolition. 'Her house can justly be called a gem,' noted a visitor in 1762. 'It contains a quantity of handsome and costly furniture and other curiosities and objects of value, chosen and arranged with the greatest taste, so that you cannot fail to admire it greatly. There is hardly a place in the whole house left bare or without decoration, like a doll's house. Everything is in perfect harmony. The view, in front over Hyde Park, and at the back over Chelsea, is considered with truth one of the finest that could be pictured.'[1]

South of us the **King's Road** is his majesty's favoured route to Kew. It is the king's private road, and will remain so until 1830, although you may use it on production of a copper pass.[2]

Beyond the edge of the map to the south is the 'pleasant and populous' riverside village of **Chelsea**, 'where is a wooden bridge, lately erected across the river to Battersea', for crossing which a toll is charged. In nearby Cheyne Walk is **Don Saltero's Coffee-house**, famous for its rarities which include a pair of nun's stockings, the King of Morocco's tobacco pipe, and 'a starv'd cat, found between the walls of Westminster Abby when repairing'.[3]

Looking north-east to the wooden bridge at Chelsea

A short way east are the **Physic Garden**, 'the most capital of its kind in England', and **Chelsea Hospital**, for old and disabled soldiers, where many casualties from the war in America arrive during the year. 'The pensioners, which are very numerous, wear red coats lined with blue, perform duty as in a garrison, and are provided with cloaths, diet, cleanly lodging, washing, fire, and one day's pay in every week for their expences. Every person admitted must prove that he has been disabled in the service of the crown, or has served twenty years in the king's army.' Among the staff are a master cook, a second cook, three under cooks, a master butler, a master baker, a master barber, a master lamplighter, a scullery man, two sweepers, a matron (Miss Joanna Pitt), a clock keeper (Mr Fitter), a sexton (Henry Medley), and a canal keeper and turncock (W. Brett).[4]

Adjoining its grounds on the east is **Ranelagh Gardens**, shown below by Rocque, who gives the Hospital its old name of Chelsea College. Ranelagh is 'a place of amusement and dissipation' with 'a fine **rotunda**, resembling the pantheon at Rome'. In the middle of the rotunda 'is a chimney having four faces, which makes the room warm and comfortable in bad weather; and the upper part of it helps to support the roof'. Dr Johnson was impressed: 'When I first entered Ranelagh, it gave an expansion and gay sensation to my mind, such as I never experienced any where else.' According to Gibbon, after 'the brilliancy of the first moment ... it very soon grows insipid', although he acknowledged it 'the most convenient place for courtships of every kind. It is certainly the best market we have in England.' The rotunda and gardens may be seen on every day except Sunday for a shilling. They are also open in the evenings from April to July, when the charge is half a crown and entertainment is provided by 'a well-chosen band of music,

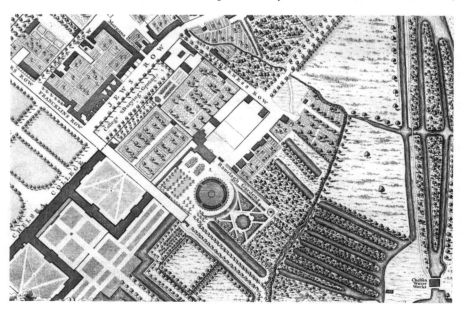

with an organ, accompanied by the best voices that can be got'. Tea and coffee are served, but no liquor. The road from London 'is all the way lighted with lamps', and an advertisement in June mentions a 'horse patrole', but highway robberies upon visitors are common.[5]

East of Ranelagh lies the **Chelsea Water-works** which, by way of reservoirs in Hyde Park and Green Park, supplies the west end of the town.

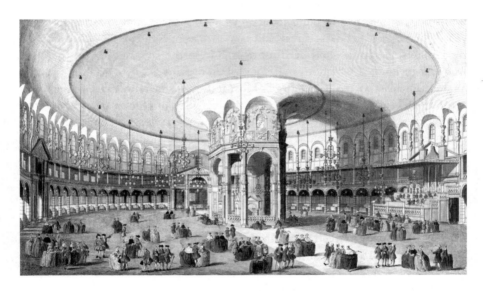

ABOVE 'An inside view of the Rotundo', after a painting by Canaletto, *circa* 1751.

BELOW Chelsea Hospital from the river, by Thomas Bowles, with the rotunda on the right.

Returning to the 1772 map, on our north side is **Hyde Park**, where 'gentlemen and ladies ... resort ... in coaches, on horse-back, and on foot, to take the benefit of the air'. During a great freeze in January the **Serpentine river** is the scene of skating matches. In June peace officers appointed by the park ranger apprehend several persons for 'the very indecent practice of bathing ... for they stripped themselves stark naked on the banks in the middle of the day, when numbers of passengers of both sexes were going by'. Hand-bills are stuck up to try to put a stop to this and other nuisances, but later in the month other transgressors are apprehended for fishing in the river, 'the punishment of which offence is transportation for seven years'. The park also boasts 'a reservoir near Grosvenor-gate, a grove towards the top, some fine springs, and herds of deer: and in the summer season there are frequent reviews, at which his majesty is often present'.[6]

Heading east we pass **St George's Hospital**. In **Grosvenor Place** to the south is the **Lock Hospital**, 'solely adapted for the reception of such as are afflicted with the venereal disease'. In 1774 **Beaumarchais** was planning to take a house in Grosvenor Place, and if he did so it may still be his London base.[7]

On the east side of the junction we pass through a **turnpike** before reaching **Hyde Park Corner**. To the north, **General John Burgoyne**, just returned from America, has a house in **Hertford Street**. His wife Lady Charlotte, a daughter of the Earl of Derby, has apartments in Kensington Palace, where she dies in June. **Evelyn Meadows**, arch antagonist of the Duchess of Kingston, is also a sometime resident of Hertford Street, appearing in rate books for 1774, 1775 and 1779 but not for 1776. Further north, residents of **Tilney Street** include the **Hon. John Damer**, whose house and clothes are in the most expensive taste and who shoots himself in a Covent Garden tavern in August.[8]

Chesterfield Street, east of Chesterfield House, is home to **George Augustus Selwyn**, clubman and enthusiastic attender of executions: he need only take a short chair ride north to reach Tyburn. He has been an MP since 1747 but has not yet spoken in a debate. To the north, residents of **Hill Street** include libertine **Lord Lyttelton** (Thomas, 2nd baron); Corsican exile **General Paoli**, whose friend **Boswell** stays here; and bluestocking **Elizabeth Montagu**, 'in the highest style of magnificence,' according to Hannah More, 'her apartments and table ... in the most splendid taste'.[9]

Further north, in **Mount Street** apothecary James Berry will sell you 'Mr Hill's Medicine for the Bite of Mad Dogs ... at 5s. 3d. each dose'. Dentist Martin van Butchell is in the 'upper part' of the street, his name in white marble on the door. He has a sideline in selling 'elastick garters' and 'springs ... which, by their pleasing elasticity, will cause wigs to be more comfortably used'. Should he consider you a friend he may show you the corpse of his wife who died a year or so ago. She has been expertly embalmed 'after an entire new method' by Dr Hunter and has 'a most striking appearance of life'. She is kept in the parlour, 'decently laid in a very handsome box', in the lid of which 'are glasses over her face and legs'.[10]

Some Mayfair residents

Elizabeth Montagu
after a portrait by Reynolds, 1775.
Engraved and published by John
Raphael Smith, 10 Bateman's
Buildings, on the south side of
Soho Square, 10th April 1776.

Lord Lyttelton
after a portrait by Richard Cosway, 1780.
Above his right hand is the figure of a woman
said to have appeared to warn of his death.
He died three days later, in 1779, at the
age of 35, providing scope for much moral
reflection on his rakish life.

George Selwyn
by Hugh Douglas Hamilton, 1770

General Paoli
after a portrait by Susanne Caron, 1769

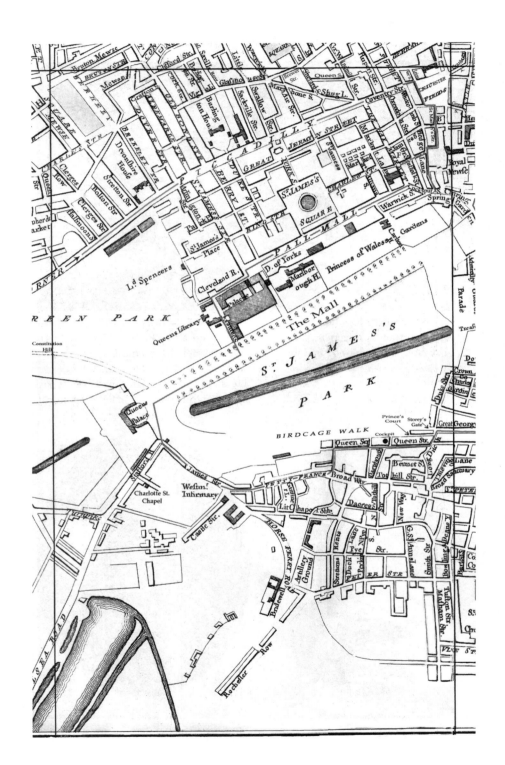

S2

i. Green Park, Piccadilly and northwards

Heading north-east from Hyde Park Corner, on our right is **Green Park**, which has 'a fine and pleasing ascent up to that health-restoring eminence called Constitution Hill, where the deer rove about with a kind of familiarity'. The idyll does not survive nightfall, however, thefts becoming common after dark in spite of the sentries posted about the park.[11]

After passing the **reservoir** in the park's north-east corner, on the other side of **Piccadilly** we come to **Devonshire House**, home to the Duke of Devonshire and his wife **Georgiana**. To the north, **Berkeley Square** is home to Augustus Keppel, vice admiral and an awkwardly vocal critic of the government (east side, towards south end). Confectioner Dominicus Negri trades at the sign of the Pot and Pine Apple in the south-east corner. On the south side is **Shelburne House**, the palatial town house of **Lord Shelburne**, a leading opposition figure and patron of **Joseph Priestley**, who is often here in winter, pursuing his philosophical and chemical researches. On the west side are: **Lord Rochford**, until recently a secretary of state, who favours conciliation with America and is visited by Beaumarchais one evening in April (fifth door north from Charles Street); **Lady Clive**, widow of Robert Clive, who died here in mysterious circumstances a little over a year ago (fourth door south of Hill Street, which is marked 'H'); and the Duke of Ancaster, master of the horse (third door north of Hill Street). 'The east and west sides of this square are well paved,' notes a 1783 guide, 'and the buildings, though without much order, are of a reputable class. But the north side is infamously the reverse. Small irregular edifices, among which are an open fishmonger's-stall, and a lottery-office, contribute their mutual deformities to disgrace this finely elevated spot.'

Looking south over the Green Park reservoir, *circa* 1760. In the distance, the towers of Westminster Abbey are slightly to the left and the Queen's Palace is on the right.

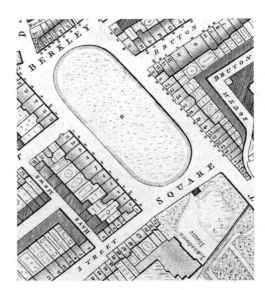

Detail from Horwood showing the spacious setting of Shelburne (later Lansdowne) House, with its own lodge facing Berkeley Square

East of the square, **Grafton Street** is home to **Lord Howe**, another vice admiral. In the spring he mulls here whether to accept appointment as commander-in-chief in the American war.[12]

Continuing east along Piccadilly, **Burlington House**, home to the Duke of Portland, 'is fenced from the street by a brick wall about 220 feet in length, in the course of which are three gates for the admittance of carriages. ... Behind the house is a spacious garden.' The forbidding frontage has led one contemporary writer to wonder, 'How many are there, who have lived half a century in London, without knowing that so princely a fabrick exists. It has generally been taken for a jail. None, I am confident, ever passed under its gloomy wall, late at night, without thinking of ghosts, robbery, and murder.'[13]

Opposite Burlington House, on the south side of Piccadilly, is the shop of **John Almon**, bookseller, a centre of American and opposition information. In May he publishes the first English edition of Thomas Paine's *Common Sense*, omitting the passages considered most incendiary. Also opposite Burlington House is William Mackay, oil-man. In March he advertises 'Just imported, and the last this season, some fine Peregord pyes, with truffles, &c.'* as well as 'potted chad from Westmoreland'. The *Court and City Register* lists **Charles James Fox** as living in Piccadilly in 1776, and he is said to have lodged at some point at Mackay's, perhaps drawn by the pies. Also in Piccadilly are John Quick, lottery office keeper (No. 5), John Chew, paper hanging manufacturer, and Charles Fortnum, grocer.[14]

---

* A 1788 recipe for a Périgord Pie features three brace of partridge, a pound of fat bacon, half a dozen fresh truffles, half a pint of fresh mushrooms, six shallots, and 'some good gravy that will jelly'.

To the north, philosopher **David Hume** lodges briefly in **Brewer Street** in May ('at Mrs Perkins ... and next door to Mr Forbes the surgeon') before returning to Scotland to die. Also living in the street, in the house of wine merchant Joseph Lautem (No. 38), is the sexually ambiguous **Chevalier d'Éon**, who has his windows broken. **John Sangster**, who in May accuses Samuel Foote of attempted sodomy, is lodging at the Fox in nearby **Sherard Street** in July when he is bound over to prosecute.[15]

ii. North-east corner: Haymarket, Leicester Fields, &c.
Reaching the east end of Piccadilly, on our left is **Great Windmill Street**, where **William Hunter**, physician extraordinary to the queen, has a house complete with an operating theatre in which he delivers anatomical lectures.[16]

To our right is the **Haymarket**, 'so called from its being a great market for hay and straw, every Tuesday, Thursday, and Saturday'. In Barto Valle's Old Italian Warehouse (No. 21) you will find, among other things, freshly imported orange and lemon trees, 'Roman brocolo and Malta colliflower seeds', 'apricots and prunelloes', 'macaroni and vermicilli', and Italian cordials. Also in the street are Henrietta Pike, brandy merchant, and, at the bottom, James Oliphant, hat maker. George Baker's 'Electrical Eel, or Numbing Fish of South America', is a popular attraction at the Great Room (No. 28) from August, admission five shillings. An advertisement in late October boasts that the eels 'are now in the greatest perfection' and have 'met with the applause of the highest personages, who received the shock with pleasure and astonishment'. A later notice refers explicitly to their having received 'the approbation of their majesties'. By late November the eels have been removed to 'Mr Baker's new apartments in Piccadilly, nearly opposite St James's-street'.[17]

On the west side, the large building near the south end is the **opera house** or **King's Theatre in the Haymarket**. 'The stage is more spacious than that of any other theatre in England, and therefore processions and other gaudy pageants are seen here with peculiar advantage. ... | Italian operas are exhibited in the winter, the most celebrated instrumental and vocal performers, and the most capital dancers in Europe being engaged at very extravagant salaries. The house is frequented by the first personages in the kingdom; and there is no place of public entertainment so often honoured with the presence of the royal family.'[18]

Across the road, on the east side and slightly to the north, is the **Theatre Royal** in the Haymarket (F on the map), also known as the **Little Theatre**, 'in which **Mr Foote**, for several years past, has entertained the town during the summer season' (his patent limits him to the period between 15th May and 15th September). One of the advantages of working in London, according to Gibbon, is that 'when I am tired of the Roman Empire, I can laugh away the evening at Foote's theatre'. It is connected to Foote's town house which is on the west side of **Great Suffolk Street**. Foote also has a villa at North End, Fulham, at the corner of modern North End Road and Lillie Road.[19]

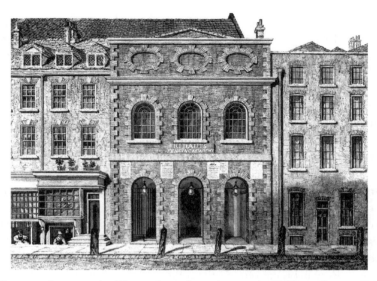

The opera house in the Haymarket, after a drawing by William Capon, 1783

Continuing eastwards along **Coventry Street**, on our right we pass **Oxendon Street**, home to one of the opera house's celebrated singers, **Giovanna Sestini**. On 1st May she is safely delivered of a daughter here. At No. 1 **Whitcomb Street** are Vaughan, Holmes and Griffin, sedan chair makers.[20]

On the north side of **Leicester Fields** (already sometimes known as **Leicester Square**) is **Leicester House**, a former royal residence. It is now occupied by **Mr Lever's Museum of Natural Curiosities**, which is open every day from 10 a.m. to 4 p.m., admission 5s. 3d. An advertisement during cold weather in January reassures the public that 'there are good fires kept in all the house'. Among exhibits noted by Fanny Burney's sister Susan on a visit in 1778 are scorpions, bats, birds of paradise, pelicans, flamingos, peacocks, a penguin, an elephant, 'a tyger from the Tower', a Greenland bear and its cub, two or three leopards, a young crocodile, and 'a room full of monkeys', one of which 'is put in the attitude of Venus de Medicis, and is scarce fit to be look'd at'.[21]

On the east side of the square, American artist **John Singleton Copley**, aged 37, moves into the fourth house from the south end early in the year with his wife, father-in-law and young children, and during the year he works on his 'Copley Family' here (see Plate 6). **Jane Hogarth**, widow, lives two doors to the south in a house she shared with her husband William for over thirty years until his death in 1764.

Across the square, near the middle of the west side, lives **Sir Joshua Reynolds**, whose prices range from 35 guineas for a head to 150 guineas for a whole length. His younger sister **Frances**, who also paints, lives with him as housekeeper. He also has two pupils, James Northcote and William Doughty, and a trusted senior

Looking north across Leicester Square. By Thomas Bowles. Published 1753.

servant, Ralph Kirkley, who has been with him for over a decade. There is a separate painting room behind the house, with its own fireplace, and in the dining parlour is kept a large macaw which appears in several portraits. Reynolds's retreat from town is Wick House, a villa on Richmond Hill.[22]

Actress **Frances Abington** may also be living in the square during the year as she addresses letters from here in March and April. In March it is reported that explorer **James Bruce** has arrived 'at his house in Leicester-square, from his seat in Scotland'.[23]

Heading south we go down **St Martin's Street**, home to musician and author **Dr Charles Burney**, aged 49, and his family including daughter **Fanny**, aged 23. Their house, shown to the right and marked B on the map, was formerly occupied by Sir Isaac Newton and still has his observatory on the roof. It is Fanny Burney's 'favorite sitting place, where I can retire to read or write any of my private fancies or vagaries'. During the year she works on *Evelina* here.[24]

The king's stables in the Mews

Heading down towards Charing Cross we skirt the Royal or **King's Mews**, where the National Gallery and the north part of Trafalgar Square now stand. In **Hedge Lane**, 'next to the Meuse Gate', lives decorative painter **Giovanni Cipriani**.

The present Meuse is a large and sumptuous edifice of brick and stone, before which is a very large gravelled court-yard, reaching down to Charing-cross, for exercising the horses, and a convenient pond in the middle for watering them.

The building consists of a double range of stables, with many of the finest horses in Europe on each side of each range. The names of the principal horses are affixed over their respective stalls. Here are kept the horses which draw his majesty's state coach. Most of the horses in these stables are very fine animals, many of them brought from his majesty's German dominions, and others are presents from foreign powers. ...

The Meuse is well worthy the visits of the curious; but the servants, who shew the noble beasts, expect a present for indulging their curiosity.[25]

We turn sharply west into **Cockspur Street**, where at the Exhibition Room in February can be seen the new Italian company of Breslaw, a famous juggler, along with other entertainments: 'Each night will be different surprising performances, the particulars of which are inexpressible. The room is fitted up in an elegant manner, and will be illuminated with wax lights.' Edward Oxnard attends and thinks Breslaw's 'tricks are exceeding great and appear to have the aid of the Devil'.

The street is also home to **Thomas Pinchbeck**, inventor, and his son William, toy-man, with whom he does not get on: his will of 1779 leaves a guinea a week 'to my undutifull and afflicting son Will Pinchbeck (whom I am unhappy to say has never done one single thing to oblige me since his infancy)'. The elder Pinchbeck is esteemed by the king and in March is granted a patent 'for his new-invented, simple addition to those very useful domestic machines called *snuffers*, by which the disagreeable circumstance of their dropping the wick after snuffing the candle ... is totally prevented'. Trading next door is Pinchbeck's son-in-law William Hebb, snuff-man. Actress **Ann Catley** is at No. 12 in the autumn while in London to perform at Covent Garden Theatre. Also in the street is the **British Coffee-house**, frequented by Scotsmen including **Adam Smith**, who uses it as his London base.[26]

iii. Pall Mall and St James's

Proceeding west along **Pall Mall**, on the south side, opposite **Market Lane** (now the Royal Opera Arcade), is the **Royal Academy exhibition room**, shown above in 1771. From the Academy's foundation in 1768 it occupied a house here but three years later its schools and library removed to Somerset House and the lease of the Pall Mall building passed to auctioneer James Christie, with a covenant stipulating that in April and May each year space should be available for the Academy's annual exhibition. The exhibition will continue to be held here until 1779, removing in 1780 to the new Somerset House.[27]

On the same side of Pall Mall, just to the west, **Chidlies** (or Chidley or Chudleigh) **Court** is home to American wax modeller **Patience Wright**, who moved to England in 1772. In May a newspaper puff describes her as 'one of the most extraordinary women of the age' and notes that her present exhibition includes busts of the king and queen, the Duke of Cumberland, Lord North, and John Wilkes. Young Anna Porter is among the visitors to her showroom during the year. She is 'delighted with her astonishing figures', but considers Wright herself 'a greater curiosity than any of her works'.[28]

To the south, **Carlton House** was occupied by the king's mother, Augusta, dowager Princess of Wales, until her death in 1772, and enjoys extensive gardens. In September it is reported that the king and queen have visited 'to view the alterations which are making for the reception' of their two eldest sons, but the house will not formally pass to the Prince of Wales until 1783.[29]

Off the north side of Pall Mall, attorney **Joseph Hickey** has his home and offices in **St Alban's Street**. In July his wayward son **William** visits his sisters here when he knows his father is away. To the west, **St James's Square** 'is pretty large, has fine houses on all sides, inhabited mostly by the nobility, and is well paved, with a noble bason in the center, surrounded with a pallisade'. It is home to **Lord Dartmouth** (William Legge, 2nd earl), recently replaced as American secretary and now lord privy seal; **Lord Bristol** (Augustus Hervey, 3rd earl), first husband of the Duchess of Kingston; Sir Sampson Gideon, son of an eminent financier; Count Walderen, the Dutch envoy; Richard Terrick, Bishop of London (London House, east side); and the Duke of Norfolk (Norfolk House, south end of east side).[30]

In **Jermyn Street** to the north lives **John Hunter**, surgeon and anatomist and brother of William. American refugee **Peter Oliver**, former chief justice of Massachusetts, lodges at a sadler's in the street on arriving in June. At the corner of **Eagle Street**, which runs north to Piccadilly (between the 'y' and 'n' of Jermyn on the map), William Pilton, wire-worker, has 'some very fine piping bullfinches' for sale in March.[31]

Continuing west along Pall Mall, and using an extract from Horwood for detail, on the **north side** are:

1 **Sir Hugh Palliser**, rear admiral and a lord commissioner of the Admiralty.[32]

2 **The Cocoa Tree**.[33]

3 **Almack's**, in a house leased by William Almack. William Brooks became the manager *circa* 1774 but the original name is still in use and will linger until the completion of a new club house on the west side of St James's Street in 1778. Edward Gibbon is elected a member on 20th May, paying a subscription of £7 7s. Women are admitted: during the year Anna Porter attends several times and the Duchess of Devonshire is reported as dancing here.[34]

4 **Boodle's**. Run by Benjamin Harding. Founder Edward Boodle died in 1772, but the old name remains. The club will remove to the east side of St James's Street in 1782 or 1783.[35]

5 **King's Place**. According to a Prussian visitor, 'there are many noted houses ... in the neighbourhood of St James's, where a great number [of women] are kept for people of fashion. A little street called King's Place is inhabited by nuns of this order alone, who live under the direction of several rich abbesses. You may see them superbly clothed at public places; and even those of the most expensive kind. Each of these convents has a carriage and servants in livery; for the ladies never deign to walk any where, but in the park.'[36]

6 **Smyrna Coffee-house**.[37]

North side residents also include Caesar Hawkins, sergeant surgeon to the king, and Sir John Pringle, physician in ordinary to the king and president of the Royal Society. James Dodsley, bookseller and publisher of the *Annual Register*, trades here towards the western end.[38]

ABOVE Patience Wright, from the *London Magazine* for November 1775.

BELOW Detail from Richard Horwood's map published in the 1790s.

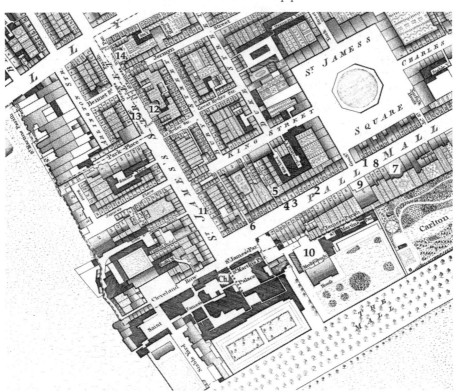

On the south side of Pall Mall are:

7 **Cumberland House**, home to one of the king's younger brothers, Henry Frederick, **Duke of Cumberland**, and his wife Anne.[39]

8 **Mr Christie's Great Room**. During the year **James Christie**, aged 45, founder of the auction house, advertises frequent sales 'at his Great Room next Cumberland House'. He owns two houses here and at the rear has had built a lofty auction room which is approached through a passage between them. He also holds other sales 'at his Great Room, the Royal Academy, in Pall-mall' (see above).[40]

Caricature of James Christie, published 1782

9 **Schomberg House**, which is divided into three. The western portion has been home to **Thomas Gainsborough** and his family since they moved from Bath in 1774. He paints in a large extension over the garden to the south, using brushes with six-foot handles. His nephew, Gainsborough Dupont, is his studio assistant. He also keeps several servants including a footman and has, or shortly will have, his own coach. In a letter to his sister dated 26th December 1775 he wrote that his expenses were running 'at a full thousand pounds a year', and, while he would 'work hard and do my best', only time would tell 'what will become of me'. His

Gainsborough by Zoffany, *circa* 1772, and Schomberg House, from a drawing of 1793. Gainsborough occupied the right-hand portion.

daughters Mary (or Molly) and Margaret, aged 25 and 24, are still at home and causing concern by their shared enthusiasm for his handsome friend Johann Christian Fischer, a noted musician in his early forties. (In the same letter Gainsborough confided: 'I have detected a sly trick in Molly by a sight I got of one of her letters, forsooth, to Mr Fischer ... I have never suffered that worthy gentleman ever to be in their company since I came to London; and behold while I had my eye upon Peggy, the other Slyboots, I suppose, has all along been the object. Oh, d—n him, he must take care how he trips me off the foot of all happiness.')[41]

10 **Marlborough House**, the town house of George Spencer, 4th Duke of Marlborough.[42]

Also on on the south side is the town house of the American secretary, **Lord George Germain**. During the year he takes an additional house in Kew Lane, Richmond, presumably in part to be near the king at Kew.[43]

Among Pall Mall's traders is Scarbrough, perfumer to the Duke of Cumberland, whose offerings include 'a very fine bloom tooth-powder, with roots of dragon's blood, and all sorts of brushes for the teeth'. In February Mr Dalmain's Tambour Warehouse, near Carlton House, has 'elegant masquerade dresses, consisting of a Sultan and Sultana dress, and two for attendants, to be sold reasonable'.[44]

Off the south-west corner of Pall Mall is **St James's Palace**, 'an irregular brick building, without one single beauty on the outside to recommend it'. According to one guidebook:

> In the front [i.e. from St James's Street] it appears like an old gate-house, which is an entrance into a square court, with a piazza on the west side of it, leading to the grand stair-case: this stair-case leads to the gallery where persons resort every Sunday about noon, to see their majesties and the nobility go to the royal chapel. If you are desirous of seeing the king and queen, &c. this is the best place ... Make no hesitation, but walk immediately up stairs; though sometimes you are obliged to give the centinels a few pence first.
>
> Under this piazza is a door, leading to the chapel; where, by knocking and slipping a shilling each person into the hand of the verger ... you may have admittance, and stand, during divine service, in the presence of their majesties; and for one shilling each person more, you may sit ... not in pews, but on turn-up seats on the outside of them ...
>
> Beyond the first court are two others, which have not much the air of a royal palace. The windows, however, look into a pleasant garden, and command a view of the park.

Service in the **Chapel Royal** (marked 'Ch.' on the detail from Horwood) 'is like that in cathedrals; and for that end there belongs to it a dean, a lord-almoner, a sub-dean, forty-eight chaplains, who preach in their turns before the royal family, twelve gentlemen of the chapel, two organists, ten children, a serjeant, a yeoman, a groom of the vestry, and a bell-ringer'. Refugee Samuel Curwen paid a shilling for admission on Christmas Day 1775 and found it 'about the bigness of our assembly room at Salem, the king and queen in a gallery opposite the altar hung round with red velvet with two rows of gold lace and a deep fringe'.[45]

In **St James's Street** to the north are:

11 **Lock's the hatters**, here since 1765, in the building still occupied by the firm.[46]

12 **The Savoir Vivre**'s new club house which opens on 4th March. The club was formed in 1772 at the Star and Garter in Pall Mall, removing to the west side of St James's Street a short time later. The new building will be taken over in 1782 or 1783 by Boodle's, which has occupied it ever since.[47]

13 **Thomas Hutchinson**, most eminent of the American refugees, is lodging in a house hereabouts at the start of the year. In August it becomes 'scarcely habitable' as building work begins on what will become **Brooks's Club** on the corner with Park Place, and he removes to No. 147 New Bond Street.[48]

14 **White's**, here since 1755.[49]

To the west, **Arlington Street** is home to **Horace Walpole**, aged 58, east side, when he is not at Strawberry Hill, Twickenham. **Lord Weymouth**, secretary of state for the southern department, also has a town house here. His office, along with that of **Lord Suffolk**, secretary of state for the northern department, is a short way south in **Cleveland Row**.[50]

In **Park Place** lives **General Thomas Gage**, recently returned from America. His house suffers a 'most daring and impudent burglary' between 4 and 5 p.m. on 10th December: 'the villain got in at the parlour window, whilst the servant was gone below stairs to order the dinner to be served up, during which time he … handed off five silver waiters, a silver mustard pot, a large silver fork, and two elegant candlesticks … and got off '. To the south, **St James's Place** is home to **Mrs Delany**, letter writer and creator of cut-paper illustrations of flowers and plants.[51]

Looking east to Pall Mall, with St James's Palace on the right. Published 1753.

iv. St James's Park and the Queen's Palace

Returning to the 1772 map, and wending our way through St James's Palace, we emerge to **the Mall** and **St James's Park**. 'The park is the usual place of exercise in a morning for fine gentlemen and ladies, who resort thither to see and to be seen; and the Mall is one of the finest gravel walks in Europe.' A German visitor in 1782 will be astonished by the number of people in the park 'towards evening, in fine weather ... for the most part well dressed and handsome', although he considers the canal 'a marshy pond'.

An earlier visitor (1765) noted the park's rustic air, with cows and deer grazing. 'Most of these cows are driven about noon and evening to the gate, which leads from the park to the quarter of Whitehall. Tied in a file to posts at the extremity of the grass-plat, they swill passengers with their milk, which, being drawn from their udders upon the spot, is served, with all the cleanliness peculiar to the English, in little mugs, at the rate of a penny a mug.' The cows are still here, an American noting in June that 'at one corner of the park is a place for the milking the cows, and seats for persons of all sexes and ages who go there to drink the milk warm'.

The park is particularly popular with such refugees. One day in May Governor Hutchinson notes meeting twelve fellow New Englanders by chance here and seeing two or three more at a distance. In January 1777 Samuel Quincy will write home to his mother that, because of the number of familiar faces, 'St James's Park wears an appearance not unlike the Exchange in Boston.'[52]

Only people with permission are allowed to ride in their carriages through the park gates. A select few, including senior ministers and the Archbishop of

Looking east, with the south front of St James's Palace on the left,
the Mall on the right, and the dome of St Paul's Cathedral in the distance

Canterbury, have ivory tickets engraved 'Horse Guards', with their names in red characters, which allow them through Horse Guards and all the various gates. The French and Spanish ambassadors have the same freedom without tickets at any time, but other ambassadors only while the king is away at Kew in the summer. A third group, including royal physicians, ladies of the bedchamber, 'musicians to the king', and 'operators for the teeth to the royal family', are 'allowed to pass in their carriages only through the gates in the stable yard into and out of St James's Park'.[53]

Do not be surprised if you see the king taking his morning ride in one of the parks. A visitor in the spring of 1777 will note seeing him wearing 'a plain suit of red with yellow buttons, a very large hat in which was a cockade, but no other ornament. His horse, a very bony, showy black one, a bob-tail, no way decorated; a couple of footmen, and one gentleman by way of companion, were all his retinue.'[54]

You may also see the king and queen being carried between St James's Palace and the **Queen's Palace**, also known as the **Queen's House**, formerly Buckingham House, at the west end of the park. In August 1775 Samuel Curwen saw them returning from a drawing-room at St James's, the king in a sedan chair 'adorned with a crown atop. He was reading a paper, that he held so near his face as to prevent a distinct sight of it; in lieu of which I saw the whitest hand my eyes ever beheld ... The queen soon appeared in a chair carried by two porters, more richly decorated than the king's and with a crown set on the center of the top.' While the king 'appeared neglectful of the crouds that formed two lines through which he passed, the queen observed, smiled, and bowed'. Their chair journeys are not

Looking west to the Queen's Palace from St James's Park
From the *London Magazine*, 1762

Robert Adam's 1771 design for a sedan chair for the queen,
with a crown on top as mentioned by Samuel Curwen

always so decorous: in June 1777 a well dressed madwoman, with 'something of great importance to communicate to the king', will cause a panic by beating her hands through the side-glass of his chair in Pall Mall.[55]

The king bought Buckingham House in 1762 for £28,000, 'and it began to be called the Queen's Palace, from the particular pleasure' she took in it. In 1775 it was formally settled on her by Act of parliament. Visiting in June, Curwen notes that 'the rooms are large, lofty, and extreamly well filled with pictures, many of which are said to be capital ... The king is so excessively fond of clocks that not a room but has one and some 2 or 3 in a variety of shapes and forms and movements.' In the garden at the back is a canal, and a terrace affording 'a fine prospect of the adjacent countries ... On the south side of the garden, almost adjoining to the road, hath been built a spacious and elegant **Riding-House**' (the building shown above Stafford Road on the map). The **queen's elephants** are housed nearby until the elder one dies in July, after which the surviving elephant is removed to the stable-yard at Kensington Palace.

According to Governor Hutchinson, who visited the elephants in May 1775, they are 'in a stable at some distance behind Buckingham House' and 'are fed with hay in winter, and in summer chiefly with grass and herbs out of the queen's gardens, just by the stables'. Samuel Curwen visited two months later and sat on the back of one elephant, 'he having been made to lye down for that purpose. They are very docile and tractible, of the height of 7 feet, and of the most clumsey and uncouth figure. They manage their trunks with great dexterity as men do their hands ... taking up so small a thing as a sixpence as quickly and readily as any one could.' In December 1775 a third refugee, Edward Oxnard, noted that the keeper had taught them to do 'almost any thing he bid them'.

Some payment is expected from visitors, Lord North reportedly remarking that 'there was as much raised by seeing the elephants, as ever had been or ever would be paid by all America'.

Other 'curious beasts' are also kept here, a beautiful young leopardess arriving from Africa in February.[56]

The road more or less opposite is **Charlotte Street**, named after the queen. The fashionable **Chapel** here was built for **Dr Dodd** and opened in 1767, but it has not brought him the hoped for income or royal favour, and on 24th February he sells most of his interest and relinquishes his role as its morning preacher.[57]

v. Westminster, west part

From the palace we head south-east along **James Street** (now Buckingham Gate) and **Petty France**. To the south is **Tothill Fields Bridewell**, 'a house of correction for loose and disorderly persons'. According to William Smith, 'There are sometimes 150 prisoners confined ... a miserable set of objects; some of the very lowest order of abandoned women, covered with filth and vermin, eat up with the bad distemper, and broke down by every species of intemperance. Debtors, felons, fines, and disorderly people, are all huddled together.' He adds that the keeper is 'a sober, careful, and pious man' who 'reads prayers and exhorts the prisoners every day' but 'complains that it is out of his power to keep them from rioting and drunkenness'.[58]

Bearing left then right we go through **Queen's Square** (now Queen Anne's Gate) into **Queen Street**. In April Boswell visits the notorious **Margaret Caroline Rudd** in her lodgings at No. 10 and she is still here in June when she places a newspaper advertisement disowning a spurious memoir.[59]

The small round building on the edge of St James's Park is the **Royal Cockpit**. At the park's south-east corner is **Prince's Court**, where **John Wilkes** lives with his daughter **Mary**. His house, for which he pays 50 guineas rent a year, is No. 7, at the west end of the north side, 'the last house next to the Birdcage walk ... small, but exceedingly pleasant'. According to Henry Angelo, 'He had a good library there, and the parlour looking into the Bird-cage walk was hung with Hogarth's prints.' On the east edge of the park, **Duke Street** is home to **Lord Suffolk**.[60]

We pass into **Great George Street**, built in the 1750s, which includes the house of the **Spanish ambassador**, Prince Masserano. In late January he is attended by four physicians, who pronounce him 'in the most imminent danger', and an express is sent off to Madrid, but in June he is well enough to give a dinner for the king's birthday and to have 'very grand fireworks ... played off' before the house. In October he is 'confined to his room' by the gout. Chevalier d'Escarano is secretary to the embassy.[61]

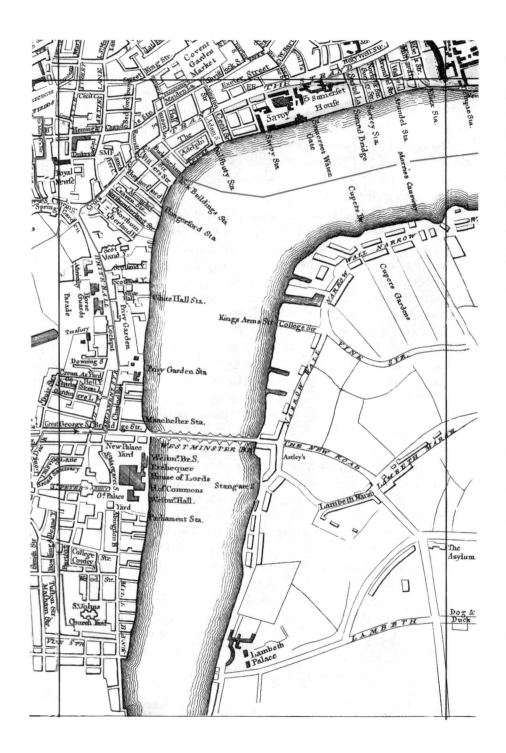

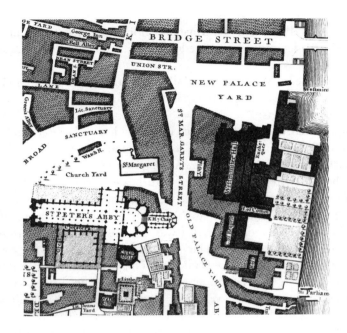

S3

i. Westminster, east part

Heading east towards the river we cross **King Street** where Reid, surgeon, can be found at the Apothecary's Shop every Tuesday, Thursday and Saturday. He 'undertakes to cure, or prevent the further growth of crookedness in children under 12 years of age' and offers 'instruments for all deformities'. At the south end of the street is **Broad Sanctuary**, home to **Edmund Burke**.[62]

Another section from Rocque (*above*) shows the area towards the river in greater detail.

St Peter's or **Westminster Abbey** is closed to casual visitors for part of the year while a 'superb and elegant choir' is erected. On 3rd October it is reported that having 'been shut up so many months' the Abbey 'is to be opened on Sunday, but is to be no more a thoroughfare'. If you do find it open expect to pay to see 'the wax-work ... as also the tombs of the kings ... The man who shews them will ask for a few halfpence for himself, but this is optional.' The wax-work's effigies of kings and queens 'formerly were ornamented with coronation robes, and the ensigns of royalty; but these tawdry figures are now almost stripped of their coverings'.

If you are in the Abbey and see a young man standing on a monument to view it from above it is probably **William Blake**, who devotes the warmer months during his apprentice years 'to zealous sketching, from every point of view, of the tombs'. According to a Victorian biographer, 'Shut up alone with these solemn memorials of far off centuries – for, during service and in the intervals of visits from strangers, the vergers turned the key on him – the spirit of the past became his familiar companion.'[63]

South of the Abbey is **Westminster School**, 'where great numbers of the young nobility and gentry have their education. ... At present there are above four hundred scholars.'[64]

To the north-east, **Westminster Hall** 'is reckoned the largest room in Europe unsupported by pillars, being 270 feet in length, and 74 in breadth', and houses the following law courts:

• **King's Bench**. In theory concerned with cases in which the crown has a direct interest, it has evolved into the leading court of common law. Its lord chief justice, **Lord Mansfield**, is paid £4,000 a year. Among its officials are a clerk of the errors, a clerk of the outlawries, a bag-bearer, a train-bearer, a chief cryer, and three tip-staffs. In December Samuel Foote is tried here in his absence for attempted sodomy.

Visiting recently, Edward Oxnard 'was not a little surpriz'd to see with what decision the causes were determin'd. I was not there above thirty minutes and three causes were deliv[ere]d to the jury and determin'd ... Lord M— appears very authoritative, will not beare a contradiction. The jury he does not suffer to leave their stands, but stay and determine as he advises — tho' I must say the three verdicts I heard appeard to be very just. His lordship is of a middling stature, [with] something sterne in his countenance that strikes with awe.'

• **Chancery**. The court of the lord high chancellor, **Lord Bathurst**. A court of equity, its intended purpose is to mitigate the rigours and injustices of the common law.

Two other courts adjoin the Hall:

• **Common Pleas**, another common law court, handling civil cases between subjects. It is reached through a door on the Hall's west side, having removed from the Hall itself in 1740-1741. Its chief justice is paid £2,500 a year. **Sir William Blackstone** is one of its judges. John Walker is hereditary chief proclamator and Rowland Lickbarrow is clerk of the judgements and reversals.

• **Exchequer**, a third common law court, concerned with revenue cases. It is above stairs to the north-east of the Hall. Its name derives 'from a chequered cloth, which antiently covered the table where the judges or chief officers sat' and which was used for setting out how much money was owed to the crown. Horace Walpole is clerk of the estreats (a sinecure), George Rose is surveyor of the green wax, and the busy John Walker is hereditary chief usher.[65]

The Hall is a bustling and often noisy place. The two views on the facing page both look southward. The upper view shows the Hall as it was earlier in the century: booksellers' stalls line the sides, the courts of King's Bench and Chancery are at the far end, left and right respectively, and the Court of Common Pleas is in the foreground on the right. However, in 1739 the first two courts were divided from the rest of the Hall by the erection of a screen designed by William Kent, and, as noted, Common Pleas removed a short time later. The screen was subsequently raised in height and is shown in the lower view, by Pugin and Rowlandson, published in 1809.

In April the Hall is turned into a single grand court for the trial by the House of Lords of the Duchess of Kingston for bigamy. Before and after proceedings the duchess makes use of the **New Palace Yard** house of her friend the **Duke of Newcastle**, which adjoins the Hall.[66]

South-east of the Hall, oriented west to east, is the **House of Commons**, 'to which there is a communication and an ascent from Westminster Hall, by a dark entry and double flight of stone stairs'. It was formerly St Stephen's Chapel, 'having been originally a chapel founded by King Stephen, and dedicated to that saint ... | The benches for the members gradually ascend one above another, and are covered with green cloth: the floor is matted, and round the House are galleries supported by slender iron pillars'. Visiting in March Edward Oxnard considers it 'a small and mean room' and judges the Speaker's chair 'greatly inferior' to the one in the house of representatives in Massachusetts. According to a German visitor in 1782:

The House of Commons
from the river

> The members ... keep their hats on, but the spectators in the gallery are uncovered. | The members ... have nothing particular in their dress; they even come into the House in their great coats, and with boots and spurs. It is not at all uncommon to see a member lying stretched out on one of the benches while others are debating. Some crack nuts, others eat oranges, or whatever else is in season. There is no end to their going in and out; and as often as any one wishes to go out, he places himself before the Speaker, and makes him his bow, as if, like a schoolboy, he asked his tutor's permission.[67]

Do not expect to be able to watch debates concerning America as visitors are often kept out on these occasions. On 1st December 1775 Samuel Curwen tried to enter the gallery 'to hear the third and last reading of the bill prohibiting all commerce with America', but was informed that 'it is to remain shut to all strangers. The pretended reason is that the House being too small, the gallery is necessary for the use of the members'. In November 1776 Edward Oxnard also tries to get in but finds the doors shut.[68]

A short way south is the **House of Lords**, 'a spacious lofty room ... hung with fine old tapestry, which ... represents the defeat of the Spanish Armada'. Sir Francis Molyneux is gentleman usher of the black rod, Robert Quarme is yeoman usher, Miss Blackerbys is housekeeper, and there are seven door-keepers.[69]

FACING PAGE. UPPER The Commons in the session of 1741-1742, looking east.

LOWER Westminster from the river. The Abbey looms in the background; the long roof of Westminster Hall dominates the middle ground; the House of Commons is in the foreground on the left.

ii. Whitehall

Returning to the 1772 map and heading north, **Parliament Street** is home to Lord North's two secretaries at the Treasury, **Grey Cooper**, who claims a baronetcy and styles himself 'Sir', and **John Robinson**, whose house is burgled in June when he is out of town. To the east, Manchester Buildings in **Cannon Row** (Channel Row on the map) is home to **Isaac Barré**, a notable opposition orator in the Commons. To the west, in **Charles Street**, author, letter writer and former slave **Ignatius Sancho** runs a grocery shop with his wife, having been helped to set up in business by the Duke of Montagu.[70]

Lord North himself lives at No. 10 **Downing Street** with his wife and children. He is paid £4,000 a year as first lord of the Treasury plus £1,800 as chancellor of the exchequer. Also in the street are rising political figure **William Eden** and **Edward Bancroft** (No. 4), American, chemist, and spy. In December 'John the Painter' comes knocking on Bancroft's door after setting Portsmouth dockyard ablaze.[71]

A plan dated 1793 (*opposite*) provides a closer view of the area directly to the north. It includes the offices of the secretary of state for the **American department** (although by 1793 this was an anachronistic reference). In 1776 the department's staff includes two under secretaries (John Pownall and William Knox), a gazette-writer (William Fraser, £300 a year), an embellisher, a secretary of Latin language, and a decypherer of letters (Edward Willes, £1,000 a year). It has a great room and views onto Whitehall: in November 1774 Governor Hutchinson looked on from here as the king processed to parliament in the state coach.[72]

To the west is the **Tennis Court**, a remnant of Whitehall Palace which still serves its original purpose. In July 1777 it will be reported that Charles Fox 'is become as conspicuous in the Tennis Court as in the Senate, or at any of the fashionable clubs in the neighbourhood of St James's. When he leaves off play, being generally in a violent perspiration, he wraps himself up in a loose fur coat, and in this garb is conveyed to his lodgings.' A year later he will apparently lose 3,000 guineas in a bet when a celebrated player manages to hit a pillar supporting the court's 'penthouse' or gallery. Nearby is the **Tennis Court Coffee-house**.[73]

To the north, a narrow passage leads from Whitehall to the **Treasury**, built on or near the site of Henry VIII's cockpit at Whitehall Palace. The name **Cockpit** is still used to refer to the Treasury and in particular to the adjoining privy council chamber. In February Lord North has a levee 'at the Cockpit' and Lord George Germain has one 'at the great council chamber at the Cockpit'. Elizabeth Shaw is housekeeper to the levee rooms, and William Watson is bag-bearer and ranger of books.[74]

FACING PAGE. UPPER Plan dated 1793. LOWER The Treasury from the north.

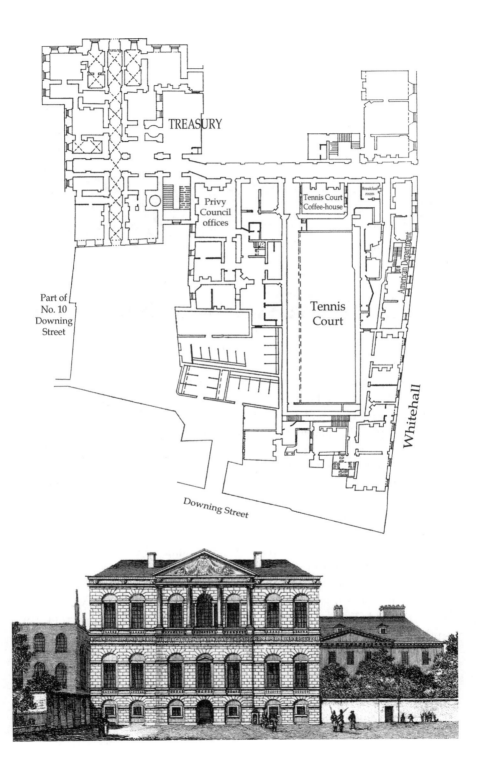

TREASURY

Privy
Council
offices

Tennis Court
Coffee-house

Breakfast
room

Tennis
Court

American Department

Part of
No. 10
Downing
Street

Whitehall

Downing Street

ABOVE Looking north-east towards Horse Guards, by Samuel Hieronymus Grimm. FACING PAGE. UPPER Rocque detail. LOWER The Admiralty, with the Adam screen.

A final detail from Rocque provides a more general view of Whitehall. F indicates a house 'adjoining to the Horse Guards' occupied by the **French ambassador** (now known as Dover House and occupied by the Scotland Office). In January there are 'remarkably splendid' illuminations in front of it in honour of the queen's official birthday. In February the ambassador the **Comte de Guines** leaves here 'with a very grand retinue' having been recalled. His successor, the **Marquis de Noailles**, does not arrive until October. **Charles Jean Garnier** acts as chargé d'affaires in the interim, but his letters are addressed from Duke Street St James's. The American rebels consider Garnier 'extremely intelligent and friendly to our cause'.[75]

North of **Horse Guards** is the office of **Richard Rigby**, paymaster general of his majesty's forces. Continuing north, 'the clumsiness of the architecture' of the **Admiralty** as seen from Whitehall 'is now happily concealed by an elegant screen ... contrived by Mr Adam, the architect'. **Lord Sandwich** is first lord of the Admiralty, enjoying a salary of £3,000 a year and a house with views onto St James's Park. He lives here with his mistress **Martha Ray**, whose portrait hangs in pride of place above a chimney-piece. In February a dinner is held here at which is sealed the appointment of **James Cook** to undertake what will prove his final voyage. Among the Admiralty staff are Philip Stephens, secretary, and George Jackson, deputy secretary, both of whom have detailed dealings with Cook as he prepares for the voyage. Further north, also on the west side of the road, between the Admiralty and Charing Cross, is the **Salopian Coffee-house**, where Edward Bancroft meets 'John the Painter' in December.[76]

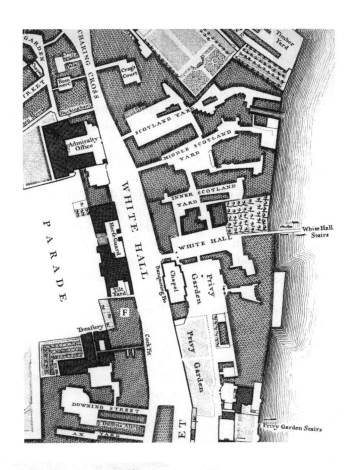

On the east side of Whitehall, the **Banqueting House** 'has been for some time converted into a chapel for divine service'. Visiting in January, Edward Oxnard notes that the ceiling 'painted by Rubens ... is much defac'd, but there remains sufficient to convince you of his abilities'. Later in the year **Giovanni Cipriani** is at work on it. In April he informs the Board of Works that he is 'at leisure to proceed with the painting of the ceeling at Whitehall Chapel and could wish to begin the same directly'; in October it is reported that 'the celebrated historical pictures in the cieling ... (painted by Rubens) having suffered much from time, and the dampness of the situation, have for some time past been cleaning and repairing by that eminent artist Signor Cipriani'; and on 1st December the chapel opens 'for the first time since it has been repaired and new beautified'.[77]

The building attached to the Banqueting House's south end is the **Lottery Office**. Here are housed 'two wheels about six feet in diameter, and twelve or eighteen inches thick, so that the sides, being thin, reserve a sufficient cavity for containing the tickets; they have also convenient openings in the sides for putting in the hand to draw them, and are suspended on their centers in a manner very convenient for shaking or mixing them'. The drawing takes place at Guildhall, the wheels being conveyed there and back under military escort.

The adjacent **Privy Garden** belonged 'to Whitehall Palace before it was burnt down; but now it is quite open, and on some parts of it houses have been built by several noblemen, who have obtained grants of it for that purpose from the crown'.[78]

North of the Banqueting House, 'opposite the Horse-Guards', is Thomas Thrale, pastry and kitchen cook, who in July advertises 'a large quantity of fine chicken turtle'. In October refugee **Samuel Quincy** takes lodgings at Thrale's having previously lodged in the Strand.[79]

Further north, **Scotland Yard** is home both to the **War Office**, presided over by **Lord Barrington**, and to the **Board of Works**, where architect **Sir William Chambers** is comptroller and clubman George Selwyn is paymaster of the works, a sinecure paying £500 a year. Other staff include a clerk of the king's private roads, an engine-maker to the palaces (Ephraim Brookes), engine keepers at Whitehall and St James's, a tin-man (Gideon Dare), a wire-worker (Sarah Bacon), three blacksmiths (including Mary Hartley), a master carver, a mat-layer and turner, a pump-maker, and a master plumber and keeper of waters at Hampton Court. The master gardener at Hampton Court is L. ('Capability') Brown.[80]

iii. Charing Cross &c.

Returning to the 1772 map we continue north to the bustle of **Charing Cross**: 'Fleet-street has a very animated appearance,' remarked Dr Johnson in April 1775, 'but I think the full tide of human existence is at Charing-cross.' We turn right past **Northumberland House**, town home of the **Duke** and **Duchess of North-umberland**. It is 'one of the largest and most magnificent buildings in or about London, although in the Gothic taste ... The house contains many elegant, large,

ABOVE Looking north-east up Whitehall to the Banqueting House, with the Lottery Office on its south side. By Thomas Sandby, *circa* 1760.

BELOW Looking east to Northumberland House, from what is now the southern side of Trafalgar Square. After a view by Canaletto, *circa* 1752.

and very commodious apartments, enriched with the most valuable furniture, paintings, &c. [which] are worth getting a view of. Between the south aspect of the house and the Thames is a pleasure garden'. In Charing Cross, opposite the house, is an Office for Hiring Servants where 'gentlemen, ladies, and others, may be suited with men and women servants, from the highest station to the lowest, for town and country, on the shortest notice, with undeniable characters'.[81]

A short way north is the 'very elegant edifice' **St Martin in the Fields** (marked SMF on the map), which has 'a good ring of bells' in its steeple. Beyond the church, cabinet-maker **Thomas Chippendale**, aged 57, has his house and workshop on the east side of **St Martin's Lane**, opposite **Old Slaughter's Coffee-house**. In the summer of 1776 he retires to a modest house in Lob's Fields, now Derry Street, Kensington, leaving the business in the hands of his son and namesake.[82]

Continuing north-east from Charing Cross we pass the end of **Craven Street**, where Benjamin Franklin lived before returning to America. Current inhabitants include Dr John Leake, who gives lectures at his house here on the theory and practice of midwifery. A little further along on the same side, on a site now occupied by Charing Cross railway station, is **Hungerford Market**. It has 'a good market-house, which was formerly well furnished with meat, as were also the other parts of the market with vegetables, &c. but it now turns to very little account'. **Joseph Bull**, tried at the Old Bailey in January for murder, works in a slaughter-house here.

Having turned right into **Buckingham Street** we arrive at **York Buildings Stairs**, at the top of which is 'a very handsome terrace walk planted with trees'. At the south-west end of the terrace is 'a high wooden tower called **York Buildings Water-works**, erected for raising water for the supply of that neighbourhood'.[83]

iv. Looking south from York Buildings Stairs

The river before us is busy. A 1782 visitor will note 'countless swarms of little boats passing and repassing, many with one mast and one sail, and many with none, in which persons of all ranks are carried over. Thus there is hardly less stir and bustle on this river, than there is in some of London's crouded streets.' South-east across the water, near King's Arms Stairs, Lambeth, is **Coade's Artificial Stone Manufactory**, where 'are executed all sorts of ornaments, as statues, chimney-pieces, tombs, vases, capitals, frontispieces, frizes, enriched facia, pallera's, ballusters, &c.'[84]

Further south, **Westminster Bridge** consists of thirteen main arches plus a very small one at each end. It was opened in 1750, much of the cost having been raised by lotteries, and is a source of considerable pride. It boasts thirty-two lamps and twelve watchmen who 'do duty every night, to prevent robberies and irregularities'.[85]

On the Lambeth side, a short way south-east of the bridge, is **Astley's Riding School**. Here ladies and gentlemen are 'instructed in the polite art of riding on horseback at 2s. 6d. per lesson' and horses are 'carefully reduced to obedience'. In early evening may be seen 'Mr Astley's surprising dexterity on one, two, three, and four horses', with other 'feats of horsemanship and activity' and a variety of

ABOVE St Martin in the Fields, completed in 1726 on the site of a former church.

BELOW Looking broadly south across the terrace of York Buildings. In the distance on the left is Westminster Bridge. Along the terrace is the Water Gate, with the tower of the Water-works beyond. The steps on the right lead up to Villiers Street.

spectacles. Mrs Astley also performs, being 'well known for her surprising command' over bees. In April 'the company of Spaniards ... perform their various new, manly entertainments, really beyond conception'. In September 'Madam Rossi, from the South of France' appears 'with several large serpents in a surprizing manner', and on her last night, 'besides the usual entertainments', there is 'a comic race in sacks, by four capital performers, to run, jump, or tumble'.[86]

To the south, **Lambeth Palace** is home to the **Archbishop of Canterbury**, Frederick Cornwallis.

If you venture due south of the palace, beyond the edge of the map, you will find **Vauxhall Gardens**, a rowdier and more colourful alternative to Ranelagh, admission one shilling. It opened *circa* 1660 and was named the New Spring Gardens to distinguish it from the Spring Gardens near Charing Cross. It is now more often referred to as Vauxhall Gardens or simply Vauxhall. According to one guide:

> In very fine weather the best passage from the city is by water, but hundreds go either on foot or in carriages. They open in May, and are shut up in August, and on the last night of admission there are commonly from three to four thousand spectators, and a kind of riot generally ensues ... so that we would recommend sober country visitors to avoid the last night ...
>
> There is an elegant Orchestra, filled with a fine band, and many of the best singers, who entertain the company with catches and glees. On the sides of several parts of the garden are boxes, ornamented with paintings, where tables are spread, and the company regaled with hams, chickens, pies, tarts, &c. with wines of the best kind.

In this respect 'Vauxhall differs widely from the prudish and abstemious Ranelagh, where one is confined to tea and coffee'. Prices in 1774 were burgundy 6s. a bottle, champagne 8s., a chicken 2s. 6d., and a custard or a cheesecake 4d. 'When it grows dark the garden near the Orchestra is illuminated, almost in an instant, with about 1500 glass lamps, which glitter among the trees, and render it exceeding light and brilliant.'[87]

Also on the Lambeth side of the river are three notable charitable institutions. A short way east of Westminster Bridge, on the north side of the road, is the **Westminster New Lying-in Hospital**, founded in 1765 by Dr Leake. To the south-east is the **Asylum**, or **House of Refuge for Orphan Girls**, where those aged eight to twelve are 'employed in reading, knitting, sewing, and in the business of the kitchen', the aim being to rescue 'the forlorn of the fair sex from the ensnaring and seductive paths of vice'. For those already ensnared, to the north-east there is the Magdalen Hospital — see section S4 below.[88]

FACING PAGE. TOP Exterior of Astley's, facing Westminster Bridge Road, after a drawing by William Capon, July 1777.
MIDDLE Lambeth Palace.
BOTTOM Detail from Horwood showing the layout of Vauxhall in the 1790s. The circular shape above the 'ar' of 'Gardens' is the Orchestra.

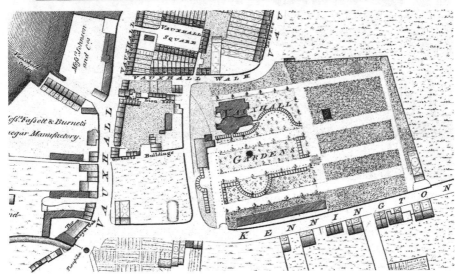

ABOVE. UPPER Vauxhall Gardens looking east, with the Grand Walk ahead on the left and the Orchestra on the right. From the *Gentleman's Magazine*, 1765.

LOWER 'The Citizen at Vauxhall', published 1784.

FACING PAGE The Adelphi, with the Terrace above and wharfs and warehouses below, 'being so contrived as to keep the access to the houses level with the Strand'. Published 1770.

v. Savoy and Somerset House

Taking boat and heading east along the river, on our left we pass the **Adelphi**, recently built by the Adam brothers, *Adelphoi* being Greek for brethren. Architecturally bold but financially reckless, the scheme had to be bailed out by a state lottery. A 1775 guide noted that 'this surprizing work was begun in June 1768, and is not yet entirely compleated ... Before the lower part of [the] front is a spacious and commodious wharf, on which a number of lofty arches are raised, (which form a kind of piazza) supporting a terras, (called the *Royal Terras*) which joins with the main streets, leading to the Strand. ... The space between the roof of the piazza, and the terras, is filled up with convenient offices and counting-houses, for different tradesmen, who land coals, wood, &c. at this wharf, and at the back of the piazza are warehouses and store-houses for goods and merchandize.' Occupants of the Royal or **Adelphi Terrace** include Topham Beauclerk, literary idler and friend of Boswell (No. 3), **Robert Adam** (No. 4), and **David Garrick** and his wife (No. 5).[89]

A little further east is the **Savoy**. Once a palace, 'here are now a great many private houses, a prison for deserters and other offenders, barracks for the guards and recruits, and chapels for the French and German protestants.' During the year there are repeated escape attempts by the prisoners, and in March a serious fire forces the removal of the barracks to the stables of Somerset House next door. Visiting the prison in March John Howard finds '119 prisoners, of whom 49 were transports. I saw many sick and dying. The gaol was so infected by them, that the distemper has been caught there by many since: and if it be not thoroughly purified, it will destroy many more.' He returns in May to find only thirty-seven prisoners, 'many of them sick of the gaol-distemper, in the rooms where I saw the sick and dying in March'.[90]

Next along the riverbank is **Somerset House**, 'a large antique palace, extremely dark'. It has been 'so far neglected as to be suffered to fall to ruin in some of the back parts ... | The garden was adorned with statues, shady walks, and a bowling green: but as none of the royal family have resided here since Queen Catharine, dowager of Charles II, several of the officers of the Court, and its dependants, are permitted to lodge in it; and great part of it has been lately used as barracks for soldiers. The garden, after being spoiled by the exercising recruits in it, has been shut up and totally neglected'.

The **Royal Academy** presently occupies what are known as the royal apartments. Among its students is **Thomas Rowlandson**, aged 18, who on one occasion is nearly expelled for startling a female life model by effective use of a pea-shooter. According to another student, writing home in March 1777, 'There is one large room for the Plaster academy; one for the Life, where two men sit two hours each night, by turns, every week; a large room, in which lectures are given every Monday night, by Dr Hunter on anatomy, [Samuel] Wale on perspective, Sir Joshua Reynolds on painting, and Thomas Sandby on architecture; and, among many other apartments, there is a choice library.' In February landscape painter **Richard Wilson**, aged 62 or 63, is appointed librarian. For his surveillance of the books he will be dubbed 'Old Cerberus' by one student and have his mulberry nose, hobbling gait and gruff voice mimicked by another: '"What are you about, what are you doing?" "I am sketching, sir." "Sketching! take your hand off the book, boy. And what are *you* about?" (addressing another). "Drawing from this print." "Drawing! Don't paw the leaves, sirrah! You'll spoil the book. What! have you got eyes in your fingers, boy?"'[91]

The buildings are about to be replaced by new ones which will house government offices along with the Academy and other public bodies. On 9th March it is reported that workmen 'have begun to pull down Somerset-house, and the buildings adjoining', and on 28th May the first stone of the new building is laid.[92]

FACING PAGE The Savoy Prison, 1793.

BELOW. UPPER North or Strand front of old Somerset House. Published 31st March 1777.

LOWER Strand front of the new building, from the *Gentleman's Magazine* for January 1779.

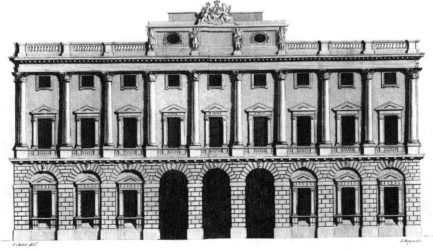

Front View of the ROYAL ACADEMY, ROYAL & ANTIQUARIAN SOCIETIES &c. in the Strand.

vi. The Strand

Beyond these old riverside palaces to the north is the **Strand**. Like nearby Covent Garden it is frequented by prostitutes at night. One guidebook notes: 'To observe these, who but a little while ago were some of the fairest works of the creation ... rotting alive with the most loathsome of all diseases, yet importunately inviting to the act of lust ... is altogether shocking to humanity!'

Among the street's more respectable traders are Mary and Mathias Darly, printmakers (No. 39), who in January publish 'Darly's Comic Prints, Characters, Caricatures, &c. Price 4l. 4s. ... consisting of three hundred prints: being the most entertaining book ever published'. Their shop is shown in the print below, published by them in 1772. Also in the street are Isaac Barnes, ivory and hardwood turner (No. 41); Henry Jaffray, undertaker and glover (No. 65); and Thomas Cadell, bookseller and co-publisher of Gibbon's *Decline and Fall* and Adam Smith's *Wealth of Nations* (No. 141). On the south side, opposite Southampton Street, is Samuel Lund's umbrella warehouse, where may be bought 'umbrellas upon an entire new construction to put on a walking stick, and take off at pleasure'. Also available are 'oiled silk socks, which keep the damp from the feet', and 'oiled silk bootikins', to protect against the gout, rheumatism and dropsy.[93]

Opposite the Savoy is **Exeter Exchange** (EE on the map), 'erected for the purposes of trade ... The lower floor is laid out in small shops ... and the upper one is used for auctions, and other temporary purposes.' Between here and **Catherine Street** to the east is a **pillory**. On the west side of Catherine Street, about halfway between the Strand and Exeter Street, is the entrance to **Blake Court**, home to the *Morning Post*.

Opposite Somerset House trades Abraham Buzaglo, famous for stoves, who 'for ready money only' also sells 'sedan and carriage patent warming machines, particularly calculated to warm ladies and gentlemen, whilst sitting in the opera-house, or in pews, or in libraries, and in their carriages and sedans'.[94]

THE MACARONI PRINT SHOP.

Pub......... by M Darly Strand July 14.ᵗʰ 1772

ABOVE Old Somerset House from the river, by Canaletto, *circa* 1750.

BELOW The new river frontage, by Samuel Ireland, 1791.

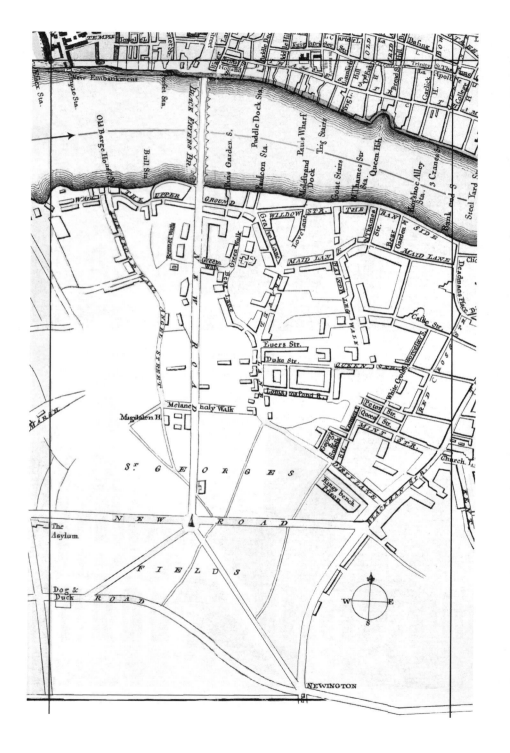

S4

Continuing east along the river we are rowed under **Blackfriars Bridge**. Completed in 1769, it 'is lighted with elegant lamps, and attended by four watchmen and a labourer' as well as by toll collectors. In January it is reported that, in the takings 'as adjusted at Christmas, there appeared about 40l. in bad shillings, and upwards of three tons of bad half-pence'. In the same month a Marshalsea court officer is taken before the lord mayor at Guildhall for assaulting the toll collectors 'and refusing to pay the toll the preceding evening', but is let off, promising 'not to do the like in future'. In June 1780 the toll gates will be burnt down and plundered during the Gordon Riots.[95]

South of the river, west of **St George's Road** (New Road on the map), is the **Magdalen Hospital** or **House**, 'for the reception of penitent prostitutes', who are employed 'making their own cloaths, both linen and woollen; knitting and spinning; making lace, artificial flowers, and childrens toys ... &c.' In December 1775 there were 100 in the house. According to a 1782 guide, 'The windows are so contrived as effectually to exclude the penitents from the view of passengers.' Divine service in the chapel on Sundays is a fashionable attraction, 'when collections are made for the benefit of the charity. The Magdalens are heard to join the responses, &c. and they also sing psalms and hymns,' but the two galleries in which they sit are

'View near Black Friers Bridge. From a picture in the possession of David Garrick Esqr.' After William Marlow. Published by John Boydell, Cheapside, 20th February 1777.

'concealed from the rest of the congregation by pieces of green canvas, stretched upon frames, and placed at the front of each gallery'. The screening may not be as effective as this suggests, one visitor noting that 'the unfortunate young women were in a latticed gallery, where you could only see those who chose to be seen'.[96]

A short way south, the meeting of five roads at the centre of **St George's Fields** is marked by a stone obelisk. To the south-west, the **Dog and Duck** public house is noted both for 'a mineral water, which is said to give relief in the scurvy and many other cases', and as a place 'for women of the town to assemble at, to pick up culls'.[97]

East of the obelisk is the **King's Bench prison**, 'for the confinement of debtors, and those sentenced by the Court of King's Bench to suffer imprisonment for libels and other misdemeanors ... | The building is very extensive, and is surrounded by a lofty brick wall, which excludes any prospect from within, even from the uppermost windows.' For a fee, however, prisoners can buy freedom of the 'rules', a surrounding area of three square miles. One foreign visitor describes the prison as a republic 'existing in the bosom of the metropolis, and entirely independent of it', with 'apartments which would not disgrace a palace' as well as its own shops, public houses and a coffee-house. 'They have even been known to give balls and concerts.'

According to William Smith, 'There have been no less than 30 gin-shops at one time in the King's Bench, and I have been credibly informed ... that upwards of two hogsheads or 120 gallons of gin, which they call by various names, as *vinegar, gossip, crank, mexico, sky-blue*, &c. [are] sold weekly, besides other spirits in proportion.' John Howard notes smallpox among the prisoners and that during the summer 'it was so crowded ... that a prisoner paid five shillings a week for half a bed, and many lay in the chapel. In May 1776 the number of prisoners within the walls was 395; and by an accurate list which I procured, their wives (including a few only called so) were 279, children 725, total 1004: about two thirds of these were in the prison.'[98]

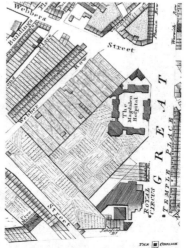

ABOVE. UPPER The Magdalen Hospital from the east.

LOWER A Magdalen, from an account of the hospital published in 1776.

FACING PAGE. LEFT Stone sign of the Dog and Duck. RIGHT Detail from Horwood showing location of the Magdalen Hospital, where Webber Street meets modern Blackfriars Road. The octagonal structure at the hospital's south-west corner is the chapel.

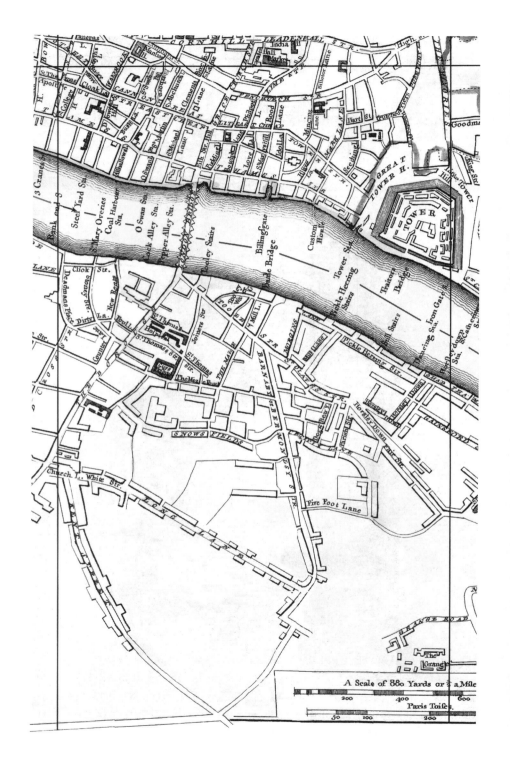

A Scale of 880 Yards or ½ a Mile

200   400   600

Paris Toises

50   100   200

S5

i. South of the river

A short way from the river, west of **Deadman's Place**, is **Henry Thrale's brewery**, with a nearby dwelling house in which Thrale and his wife Hester entertain Dr Johnson, among others. Johnson has 'an apartment ... appropriated to him' both here and at the Thrales' villa at Streatham.[99]

Running south-west from London Bridge is 'the High-street which is frequently called **the Borough**, and which on the west side is chiefly occupied by butchers'. To the east of it are **St Thomas's Hospital** and **Guy's Hospital**. Among the staff of the latter are an apothecary, a butler, a beadle, a keeper of the lunatic men, and a keeper of the lunatic women.[100]

The E-shaped building to the south-west is the **Marshalsea**, in which are confined 'persons committed for crimes at sea, as pirates, &c. and for debt by land'. According to William Smith, over a thousand prisoners enter each year, usually for small sums and short periods, and there are sometimes as many as 340 inmates. 'Several prisoners occupy rooms, who might have taken the benefit of the last insolvent Act [an amnesty for debtors]; and one prisoner has been eighteen years in gaol, which is very inconvenient when the prison is crouded, and many obliged to lay in one room. The place is in bad repair, and the stairs so dark and ruinous, that it is dangerous to go up and down without a candle. The deputy keeper is pretty attentive to prevent riots and confusion as far as he is able'.

John Howard visits in March and May and notes as follows:

> The yard is well supplied with water. In it the prisoners play at rackets, misisippi &c. and in a little back court, the *Park*, at skittles. | The tap is let to a prisoner in the rules of the King's Bench prison: this prison being just within those rules. I was credibly informed, that one Sunday in the summer 1775, about 600 pots of beer were brought in from a public house in the neighbourhood (Ashmore's), the prisoners not then liking the tapster's beer.[101]

A short way south-west, on the same side of the high street, is the **New Gaol, Southwark**. According to Smith, it is 'pretty clean and airy', with 'between 90 and 100 felons and 30 or more debtors sometimes confined. ... A clergyman faithfully attends, and takes great pains to give the felons a sense of their crimes.'[102]

ii. London Bridge and north of the river

Before us on the river, **London Bridge** is 'now rescued from the pendulous deformity of old ruinous houses, that rendered it so long a disgrace to the city'. The bridge's central arch has been greatly enlarged 'by making two arches into one, and this judicious widening renders the navigation up and down the river considerably safer than before'. Like the other bridges it is 'handsomely illuminated with lamps, from the setting to the rising of the sun, and guarded by a number of watchmen in the night'.[103]

Not all of the bridge's nineteen arches are passable, 'two on the south side, and four on the north, being taken up with the **London-bridge Water Works**. Those on the south side, erected within a few years, to supply the Borough with water, are worked in the same manner as those on the north, but are much smaller.' The machine on the north side 'raises 2,052 gallons of water in a minute, that is 46,896 hogsheads in a day, to the height of 120 feet, where it is received in a bason, on the top of a tower, and conveyed to almost every part of the city'.[104]

Having passed under the bridge, on our left we come to **Billingsgate**, 'the only port for fish in London. It is a large water-gate, dock, or port for small vessels, laden with fish of all sorts, oranges, lemons, Spanish onions, and other commodities. It is likewise the port for Gravesend boats and wherries to take in their fares; from whence they are to depart at the ringing of a bell'. A 1786 guide will advise that, for those who 'live convenient', Billingsgate 'is the place to buy sea-fish at, whether you want little or much'. Market days are Mondays, Wednesdays and Fridays, but these are 'the dearest days. You may often buy them fresh, and forty per cent. cheaper, on the intermediate days.'[105]

Further east is the **Custom House** (*opposite*). 'To a stranger, it appears one continual scene of noise and confusion, yet everything is transacted with the greatest order and regularity; without doors the quays (which are rather too confined) are likewise in a continual bustle, nearly choaked up with the goods and merchandize which either have been imported, or are going to be exported, and are a testimony of the vast trade carried on in this city.'[106]

To the north, in **Fenchurch Street** are Thomas Bateman, grocer, tea-man and chocolate maker (No. 2), Akerman, Scrivenor and Shaw, china-men (No. 3), James Season, trunk maker and fire bucket warehouse (No. 26), and John Baker, slop seller (No. 30). In adjoining **Rood Lane** (No. 10) is Newbrough Swingland, cork cutter.

To the east, in **Crutched Friars** is the **Navy Office**, 'a plain building the appearance of which gives the spectator no idea of its importance'. Among its staff are over eighty clerks, four watchmen (earning £12 a year each), a bargemaster, a rat-catcher (Edmund Jenkins, £4 a year), Thomas Sabe, who takes care of fourteen lamps (50s. per lamp), and Tresby Collins, who attends the back gate (1s. per day).[107]

To the south, and back by the river, **the Tower** contains 'the offices of ordnance, the mint, the keepers of the records, the jewel office, the Spanish armory, the horse armory, the new or small armory, barracks for the soldiers, and handsome houses for the chief officers who reside there'. At the **Mint** George Selwyn holds another sinecure as surveyor of the meltings and clerk of the irons, receiving £132 10s. for himself and a clerk. John Chambers is surveyor of the money presses.

The Tower also houses the **Menagerie**, which 'those who are inclined to see the rarities ... generally take a view of', entrance sixpence. This 'noble collection of wild creatures' includes Pedore, 'a beautiful lioness brought from Senegal'; her brother Caesar, who 'is three years and a half old, and supposed to be the finest lion ever seen in England. ... His mouth opens wide, and discovers a frightful set of teeth; and when he roars, he may be heard at a great distance'; Miss Groggery, 'a beautiful leopardess, about twenty years of age'; Sukey, a North American bear; Phillis, 'a large wolf, brought from Boulogne in France'; and a large brown Eagle, brought from Norway. 'The keeper generally relates some melancholy truth which has arisen from the indiscretion of people going too near the dens of the lions. We should, therefore, advise those who [visit] to stand at a proper distance from the dens'. In December it is reported that the collection is presently 'the largest and most curious ... that has ever been seen' in the Menagerie and includes 'two royal tygers from Bengal, the only males that were ever brought into England'.[108]

You may wish to watch where you walk in the surrounding area. According to a German visitor in 1782, 'Nothing in London makes so disgusting an appearance to a foreigner, as the butchers' shops, especially in the environs of the Tower. Guts and all the nastiness are thrown into the middle of the street, and cause an insupportable stench.'[109]

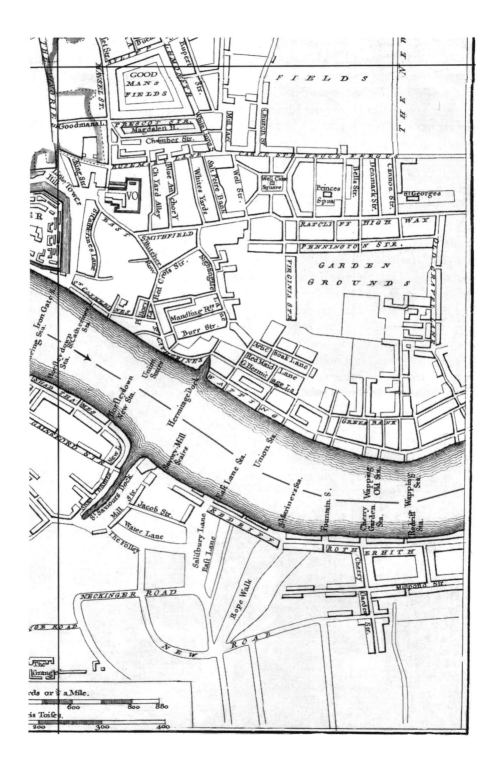

S6

Just east of the Tower is the **Victualling Office** (marked VO on the map), 'a very large building, situated on the upper part of Tower-hill ... It contains houses for ... certain officers, separate apartments for offices, store-rooms, slaughter-houses for oxen and hogs, a brew-house, and a house for salting and barrelling provisions.' W. Harwood is master butcher earning £40 a year.[110]

In **Rosemary Lane** to the north is **Rag Fair**, depicted above by Rowlandson, 'where old cloaths are sold every day by multitudes of people standing in the streets'. Many of the nearby shops 'deal for great sums in cast off apparel'.[111]

As our boat carries us on and London's bulk slips away behind us, the traders on both sides of the river are increasingly those concerned with shipping and the sea. In **Wapping**, for example, are Robert Wilson, anchorsmith, Joseph Clark, mast and oar maker, and Henry Cock, biscuit baker. Passing through Wapping in November 1775, refugee Edward Oxnard considered it 'a place well calculated for the persons who inhabit it — whores, rogues and sailors'.

As the detail below from a wider map shows, if we followed the slow snake of the river further east it would take us through the naval centres of **Greenwich** and **Woolwich** to **Gallions Reach** and round to **Long Reach**. Here, in late March, guns and stores will be loaded onto the *Eagle* prior to its carrying Admiral Howe to America, and two months later Captain Cook will moor here with the *Resolution* and the *Discovery* ahead of his final voyage.[112]

BOREAS.

I Promise to reduce the Americans.

Lord North caricatured as Boreas, Greek god of the north wind, the eye-glass alluding to his lack of physical and political vision. From the *Oxford Magazine* for September 1774.

CHRONICLE

New Year's Eve, falling on a Sunday, was celebrated without the usual rout and revelry. News brought from America four days earlier by General Burgoyne had added to the press of government business, clerks spent the whole day preparing papers, and the cabinet met to discuss the true state of the army. In the evening a messenger was dispatched to request the immediate attendance in town of Lord Sandwich, first lord of the Admiralty, who had been celebrating Christmas in Huntingdonshire in his usual style, with a music festival and his mistress.

January

1st January, Monday Cloudy day, wet evening
At the Queen's Palace, George III was awake well after midnight, writing a brief note to his prime minister, who was suffering from inflammation in one of his eyes. 'Lord North. It is very unpleasing to me to have you troubled with the smallest complaint. I therefore very strongly recommend your keeping as quiet as possible for a couple of days and I trust to see you well on Wednesday'.[1]

In the morning the king and queen, with the 13-year-old Prince of Wales and three of his younger brothers, made the short journey to St James's Palace for the customary New Year celebrations. The king was dressed in a claret-coloured suit, his wife in a robe of silver tissue and coloured flowers, with a necklace of valuable brilliants. The drawing-room was attended by the lord chancellor, the Archbishop of Canterbury, the Prince of Hesse, exiled Corsican leader General Paoli, foreign ambassadors, generals Gage and Burgoyne, Colonel Guy Johnson, and many nobility, including Lady North but not her husband. Forty Christ's Hospital boys, educated in navigation, were presented to the king.

At noon the king and queen entered the great council chamber and an ode by William Whitehead, poet laureate, set to music by Dr Boyce, master of the king's band of musicians, was performed. Their majesties arrived earlier than usual, with the result that several of those attending came too late to hear the ode's tear-eyed Britannia addressing the American rebels:

> 'Sheathe, sheathe the sword which thirsts for blood,
> (She cried) deceived, mistaken men!
> Nor let your parent, o'er the flood,
> Send forth her voice in vain!
> Alas, no tyrant she,
> She courts you to be free:
> Submissive hear her soft command,
> Nor force unwilling vengeance from a parent's hand.'

Whether any of the listeners wondered how the Americans were supposed to be at once submissive and free is uncertain. An alternative ode, reflecting a widespread sense that the fault lay at home, had appeared in a morning newspaper: 'What have the generous Trans-Atlantics done, | That blood and murder should defile their shores? | Why should the parent arm against the son? | Madness directs the vengeance that he pours.'

The gathering at St James's continued till past four o'clock, after which the royal party returned to the Queen's Palace to dinner.[2]

Some of the age's notable figures marked the day in characteristic ways. 'About eighteen hundred of us met together in London,' noted John Wesley, Methodist leader, 'in order to renew our covenant with God: and it was, as usual, a very solemn opportunity.' Samuel Johnson composed a New Year prayer, as was his custom: 'Almighty God, merciful father, who hast permitted me to see the beginning of another year, grant that the time which thou shalt yet afford me may be spent to thy glory and the salvation of my own soul.' Meanwhile John Wilkes dined with his mistress Marianne de Charpillon and others at the house of her mother in Great Titchfield Street.[3]

At the public office in Bow Street the 'blind beak' Sir John Fielding was at work as usual. He received information that one Robert Williams, wanted since October for the murder of a coachman, had been spotted officiating as a constable at a puppet-show in Panton Street. It was thought that if any of the people usually employed by the magistrates were sent, it would cause such an alarm as might enable him to escape. To avoid this, Justice Addington went with a person not known and seized Williams, who was so much confounded, that it was some minutes before he recovered his speech. He was escorted to Bow Street, examined by Fielding, and committed for further questioning next day.[4]

At home in Great Marlborough Street, Anna Porter, 17-year-old daughter of a former ambassador to Constantinople, wrote in her journal: 'Now I enter on a new year let me a little consider how I will spend it. ... I will do every thing with the intention of doing right. I will endeavour to please all. Converse with the men unaffectedly without flirting — with the women with good humour and complaisance, attention and kindness. Prudence guide me! Duty animate me!' She went on to warn herself against 'frivolous squandering' of time and spending money 'giddily'.[5]

At his lodgings in Newgate Street, American refugee Edward Oxnard wrote in his diary: 'Heaven grant this new year may restore peace to my unhappy country.'[6]

In the evening *Macbeth* was performed at Drury Lane Theatre, with Mrs Yates as Lady Macbeth. The lady mayoress, the third Mrs Sawbridge, was in the king's box, very richly dressed, where she attracted the eyes of the audience; her diamonds were supposed to be worth five thousand pounds sterling.[7]

At Covent Garden, Thomas Sheridan, father of the playwright, took the title role in *Richard III*. Over thirty years earlier, as a young man, he had received

Mrs Yates as Lady Macbeth

glowing reviews in the same part for his debut at Smock Alley Theatre, Dublin, but his stock had long since fallen. The house was not above a fourth part full and the reviews were not kind: 'Perhaps there never was a man that wanted more of the requisites to constitute a great actor ... The town are now acquainted with Mr Sheridan's peculiarities, and it cannot be expected that, at his time of life, he can divest himself of them'.[8]

With day's end the city fell quiet and its criminals emerged, as they did every night, like mice in an old house, scuttling purposefully in the dark.

About ten o'clock, two footpads knocked down a poor old man in Thames Street, near the Custom House, and ran off with his whole stock in trade, consisting of a basket stored with gingerbread, cakes, &c.[9]

A coach to Manchester was robbed just going out of London, and stopped again before it had got forty miles; but the passengers telling the last highwaymen they were come too late, as they had already been robbed, they rode off without saying anything further.[10]

The newspapers carried various reports touching America, one linking the crisis to a domestic *cause célèbre*.

GA 'It is said that General Burgoyne ... has opened the eyes of the ministry, both with respect to the personal courage of the Americans, and the number of well-disciplined troops which our armies will have to beat if this war is continued; but it is supposed that able officer will remove the present infatuation of the ministry, and convince them that peace and not war with our colonies, is the true way to make them good subjects of Great Britain.'[11]

GA 'Some very valuable presents are preparing to be sent to Quebec, which are to be distributed amongst the Indian chiefs, with a view of bringing those savages over to the side of government.'[12]

GA 'It is confidently asserted at the west end of the town, that the scaffolding which is now preparing to be erected in Westminster-hall, for the trial of the Duchess of Kingston,* will be left standing till after an enquiry is made in parliament concerning the persons who have been the cause of the disputes with America'.[13]

2nd January, Tuesday A very cloudy moist day

In the morning a great quantity of gunpowder and other naval stores were shipped off from the Tower for America.[1]

The quarter sessions for Westminster were held at Guildhall, King Street, with Sir John Fielding as chairman. It was ordered that all the vagrants lately apprehended be examined, and those able to serve the king be sent to houses of rendezvous for that purpose. A housekeeper and his wife in Russell Court, Covent Garden, were indicted for keeping a disorderly house by admitting women of the town to lodge with them. It was proved that the girls used to stand at the window and invite company out of the street. The court ordered both the man and his wife to be imprisoned for three months and to stand in the pillory near where they lived within a fortnight.[2]

A bricklayer's labourer went home unexpected to his lodging near Moorfields and caught his wife in an indecent situation with his landlord. The poor fellow cut his own throat and expired soon after. The woman has been out of her mind ever since.[3]

At Covent Garden Theatre Sheridan's comic opera *The Duenna* resumed its long run. At Drury Lane, the young Sarah Siddons made her second London appearance as Portia in *The Merchant of Venice*. Her debut four days earlier had received mixed notices. The *Middlesex Journal* said it gave no room 'to expect any thing beyond mediocrity', and detected 'a vulgarity in her tones'. According to the more prescient *London Chronicle*, 'Her figure is a fine one, her features are beautifully expressive, her action graceful and easy, and her whole deportment that of a gentlewoman ... She cannot fail to rise to great eminence in her profession.'[4]

MC 'By a letter from Cork, dated Dec. 23, we are informed, that the *Marquis of Rockingham* transport, that sailed from Portsmouth, with the thirty-second regiment on board, was wrecked between Cork and Kinsale, the 22nd, when Lieutenant Marsh, Ensign Sandiman, the captain of the ship, all the crew except four, with women and children, and upwards of an hundred soldiers, were drowned.'[5]

MC '*Extract of a letter from Boston, Dec. 1, by the* Queen of Naples, *arrived at Dover.* "The works of this place have been repaired and fortified as far as art can go. There is no part of them but what is mined, even the Castle itself; should therefore the provincials, when the frost sets in, think proper to make a desperate attack, they will meet with a reception which their rashness merits. ... The reports of a play-house here is true; the officers have acted several pieces, and very laudably given the receipts of the houses to the soldiers who had families, and were in want of assistance."'[6]

---

* For the background see pp58-65.

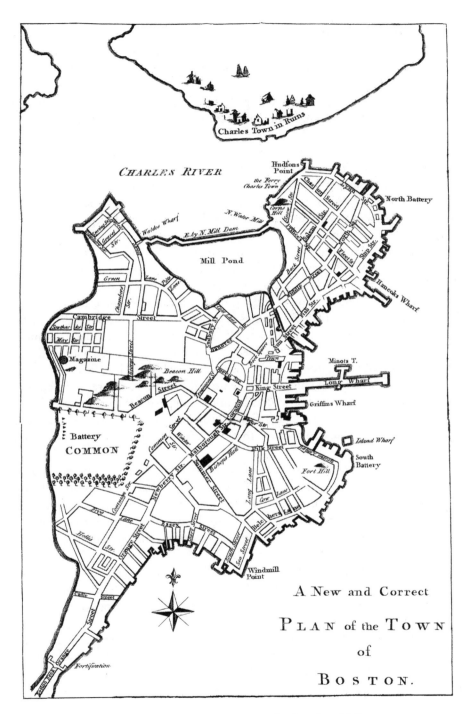

From the *Gentleman's Magazine* for October 1775

3rd January, Wednesday Cloudy morning, bright afternoon

At St James's, after a very thin levee and a council, Lord North held a long conference with the king, having been prevented from attending any public business for several days past.[1]

At the public office in Bow Street, Robert Williams was put to the bar on suspicion of murdering Henry Stubbings, coachman to John Pratt, Esq., on Sunday morning the 15th of last October, in his master's stable-yard in Percy Street, Bloomsbury. Mr Vincent and his wife, who reside close to the yard, testified to hearing cries of *Murder* and seeing from their window a struggle between Stubbings and a man without hat and wig who threw him upon his back and ran away. Stubbings pursued the man for about ten yards, then fell, calling out that he was murdered. He was afterwards removed to St Bartholomew's Hospital, where he died in a very short time.

Mr Vincent produced the murder instrument, which appeared to be the iron head of one of the pikes carried by the sheriff's officers who attend executions at Tyburn. Its blade was bent almost double, apparently turned by the fall of the deceased. The hat and wig, found in the yard after the murder, were also produced. They were sworn to by Daniel Hopkins (a prisoner, on a charge of burglary) who deposed that he knew them to belong to Williams, and that the murder instrument was lent to Williams from his house. He said he was well acquainted with Williams and had heard of the murder from Williams's girl, who told him 'Bob had killed the coachman,' and begged him not to mention it to any one. Laurence Robinson, a barber, knew the wig, and proved its identity by deposing (before he saw it) that previous to the murder he had sewed a red ribbon into it. The ribbon appeared as he had described. He also declared that he shaved the prisoner's head just about the time of the murder.

Desired to look at the prisoner stedfastly, Mrs Vincent said she did not believe him to be the murderer, on account of the quantity of hair on his head. It being discovered he had false curls, he was ordered to take them off, and after their removal his hair appeared to be just equal to the probable growth since the fact was committed. Williams, after receiving a most solemn admonition from Sir John Fielding, was committed to Newgate.[2]

The lottery finished drawing at Guildhall, when no. 43979 (as last drawn) was entitled to £1,000. 'Tis computed that upwards of 400 clerks, employed at Guildhall to take down the numbers, and also in the several offices, will now be out of employ.

At about two o'clock a party of horse grenadier guards escorted the lottery wheels to the Lottery Office at Whitehall, where they were examined in the presence of the commissioners. It appeared that no other ticket had been secreted but that confessed to in December by one of the Bluecoat boys who draw the lottery.*[3]

---

* For the December fraud see p123.

The Eloped Clara

The Combustible Lover

Actress Ann Brown and gunpowder mill owner Miles Peter Andrews,
from the *Town and Country Magazine* for January 1776.
For the background see pp52-53.

The father of Miss Brown, the runaway syren of Covent Garden Theatre, apprehended the wanton truant at her aunt's in the city, and forcing her into a coach, drove off with her into the country. However, she had not been carried above five miles before her cries raised the inhabitants of a village, whom she soon worked to her purpose, by declaring that the man (her father) was carrying her away by force, in order to ship her for America. In consequence of this artful tale, the peasants released her, on which she ran to town across the country, and has not since been retaken.[4]

Writing from his house in Bentinck Street to his stepmother in Bath, Edward Gibbon mentioned the forthcoming publication of his *Decline and Fall of the Roman Empire*:

It will probably make its appearance about the middle or end of February ... The public, I know not why, except from the happy choice of the subject, have already conceived expectations, which it will not be easy to satisfy: the more especially as lively ignorance is apt to expect much more than the nature and extent of historical materials can enable an author to produce. However, if the first volume is decently received in the world, I shall be encouraged to proceed; and shall find before me a stock of labour and of amusement sufficient to engage my attention for many years. The prosecution of some scheme is in my opinion the circumstance the most conducive to the happiness of life, and, of all schemes, the best is surely that, the success of which chiefly depends on ourselves. ...

I say nothing of public affairs. Never did they wear a more melancholy aspect. We much fear that Quebec will not hold out the winter. The provincials have everywhere displayed courage and abilities worthy of a better cause; and those of my ministerial friends who are the best acquainted with the state of America, are the least sanguine in their hopes of success for next year.[5]

In the evening their majesties went to view Mr Droz's *Spectacle Mechanique* in King Street, Covent Garden, where they staid two hours, during which time the king seem'd struck with the mechanical movements of three surprizing figures, and tried various methods to discover upon what principles they acted, but in vain. When they came to a little drawing boy, Mr Droz shewed him two or three little designs that it drew, and asked which he would be pleased to have it execute. The king answered the head of Louis XV. Mr Droz replied that the urchin sometimes was *mechànt*, and would not do as commanded. However, in a few minutes it finished the heads of *our* king and queen, finely shaded. After expressing the utmost amazement, they condescended to accept them, and went away highly charmed with their entertainment.[6]

About six or seven o'clock in the evening Sheridan called on Garrick at his house in Adelphi Terrace to discuss purchase of the actor's share in the patent for Drury Lane Theatre. They agreed to meet again two days later.[7]

Died Mr John Perrineau, in Golden Lane. He had lived a misanthrope for many years, and never kept company with any person whatever. When dead, upwards of £40 were found sewn up in the seat of his breeches, and nearly as much more quilted up in the back of his waistcoat, both which he wore constantly for seven years past.[8]

4th January, Thursday Frost in the night, an exceeding wet day
Sheridan wrote to his father-in-law Thomas Linley, one of three joining him in the planned purchase from Garrick, to say that agreement had been reached in principle. In a postscript he alluded to dark rumours circulating about actor Samuel Foote, who was currently in Ireland: 'You have heard, I suppose, that Foote is likely never to show his face again.'[1]

MC 'Last week a bricklayer's labourer that was at work at one of the houses building in Great Russell-street, Bloomsbury-square, fell from the top of the house to the bottom, and broke a joist in every story through which he fell; there were five in number. He got up without being any ways hurt by the fall, and went to the Blue Boar publick house just by, and drank a pint of beer.'[2]

5th January, Friday Very moist mild day. Full moon
Lord George Germain, the American secretary, wrote from his office in Whitehall to General Howe in Boston. Recruiting was, he regretted, going on slowly and negotiations with Russia for troops had failed, but treaties were now in train with other states for upwards of 17,000 men. He hoped that by the middle of March they would be able to send at least 10,000 to General Carleton in Canada.[1]

At St James's, after a levee, lords North, Suffolk, Germain, the lord chancellor, the Bishop of London, &c. attended a council which sat upwards of three hours upon the report by the recorder on the convicts under sentence of death at Newgate. Eight were ordered for execution on Wednesday the 17th instant including Robert and Daniel Perreau, for fraud;* Richard Baker and John Radcliffe, for counterfeiting silver coin; John Davis, for breaking into a dye-house in Spitalfields and stealing a quantity of silk; and George Lee, for a robbery on the highway near Gunnersbury Lane. Six others were respited.

The council did not break up till past four o'clock and were reportedly much divided respecting the fate of the Perreaus, several being inclined to mercy, but an eminent lawyer turned the scale by insisting they should suffer the sentence of the law. The king himself was much moved, and walked about the room in great agitation.

Mr Recorder was greatly distressed from the extraordinary time he was obliged to stand, as he is greatly imbecilitated from the gout; and as it is contrary to etiquette to permit him to sit or withdraw before the king's resolution is declared, a noble lord, from a sympathetic feeling of that disorder, went and brought him his crutches, which were thankfully accepted.[2]

A man who has begged for years, with a long beard and patched coat of many colours, was apprehended in St Giles's as a vagrant, and it was proposed to shave him. He begged not to lose his beard, for he should not long survive it. He was, however, shaved, and died next day, Saturday.[3]

MC 'A gentleman just arrived from Boston informs us, that the provincial army consists of resolute, stout, hearty young men, well clothed and disciplined, plenty of cannon and small arms, but no mortars. He thinks there is not the least probability of conquering them.'[4]

6th January, Saturday, Epiphany Very heavy foggy day, wet evening
Early in the morning the body of Mr Simkins, stationer, in Hill Street, Southwark, was taken out of the river, drowned amongst the shipping.[1]

This being Twelfth Day, after divine service in the Chapel Royal, in the absence of his majesty, the lord chamberlain made the usual offering at the altar of frankincense, myrrh, &c. and also of a purse of gold, to be distributed among the poor.[2]

Having paid a brief visit to Bristol, John Wesley returned to London 'just in time', as he noted, 'for on Sunday, 7th, the severe frost set in, accompanied with so deep a snow, as made even the high road impassable'.[3]

PA 'A number of flat-bottomed boats are now constructing at Deptford Yard, but for what purpose is kept an absolute secret.'[4]

PA 'A correspondent observes, that the inflammation in Lord North's eyes, which prevented him from attending public business these few days past, is no new disorder, it being very well known his lordship could not see things clearly for a long time.'[5]

* For the background regarding the Perreaus and Mrs Rudd see pp54-57.

MP 'On Sunday morning last was run the famous match between Mr Hetherington's and Mr Higgs's ponies (twenty miles on the Uxbridge road) for fifty guineas, each riding his own poney, and his own weight; which, as it was a crossing and jostling match, afforded great sport to the spectators; it was won by half a head by Mr Higgs, who jockied Mr Hetherington twice into the ditch. Also the same day Mr Shadrach's famous horse Shuffler, and Mr Mishach's famous horse Monkey, trotted two miles on the Rumford road, for fifty guineas, which was won with great ease by the former'.[6]

7th January, Sunday Rain all night, and snow all day
Henrietta Perreau, wife of Robert, accompanied by her children and a gentleman and a female friend, all dressed in deep mourning, waited to deliver petitions to their majesties as they passed to the Chapel Royal. The youngest child, a girl about three years of age, dressed in a neat white frock and black ribbands, kept looking her mother in the face, and though the unhappy woman endeavoured to conceal her grief, yet the girl watched her so narrowly that she always partook of her sorrow whenever the mother was unable to stifle it. As soon as Mrs Perreau had delivered the petitions she was very much agitated. Her friend immediately assisted her with a smelling bottle of salts, and thereby in all probability saved her from going into fits. Her majesty seemed very much concerned at the appearance of this disconsolate woman and her children.[1]

The Chevalier d'Éon wrote a thirty-eight page letter from Staunton Harold in Leicestershire to Beaumarchais in London. They had fallen out at the end of December over a contract they had made, known as the Transaction, in which Beaumarchais had acted on behalf of the French government. Under its terms d'Éon was to surrender secret documents, declare himself a woman, and adopt female attire, and in return was to receive an annual pension and settlement of his debts to an unspecified amount. D'Éon had become incensed that Beaumarchais and his agent, Charles-Claude de Morande, were trying to make use of their inside knowledge of the deal to profit in a market that had developed for bets, in the form of insurance policies, on his sex. It seems they had committed large sums, some on behalf of Paris bankers, in the erroneous belief that he was a woman.* Concerned for his honour, d'Éon now wrote that he did not wish, 'on any account or for any sum in the world, that the public should believe that I am myself interested in the infamous policies ... | It may be that the wits and financiers of Paris make fun of my delicacy ... and regard my situation as an opportunity to pillage the pockets of the English. That is something to which I will never consent'.[2]

There began, attended with a high easterly wind, what the *Gentleman's Magazine* described as 'the greatest fall of snow that has been known in England in the memory of man'.[3]

* For the background see pp66-75.

8th January, Monday Hard frost, and strong snowy night, heavy day
Two men were whipped at the cart's tail round Covent Garden for stealing pewter
pots from public-houses in that neighbourhood.[1]

'The snow lay all day to-day in the squares and parts of the streets, tho' not very
cold,' noted Governor Hutchinson, the most eminent of the American refugees,
in his diary.[2]

Another loyalist, the Rev. Jonathan Boucher, wrote to a friend in his native
Cumberland in a letter which indicates some of the difficulties faced by the refugees.
Recommendations furnished to Boucher before his departure from Maryland by
Governor Eden had brought him 'sufficiently flattering' notice from Lord Dart-
mouth, William Eden, and the bishops of Bangor and London, but to date he
had received 'only promises'.

> The excuse of government people is, that they have so many circumstanced
> as I am on their hands, that, not being able to provide for all, they are unwilling
> to give umbrage by singling out one; and, besides, as there are still thousands
> behind, suffering for their loyalty, I am far from sure that their fears are ground-
> less, that were those, already driven away, provided for, many more would not
> soon contrive to follow. I think I have myself seen, now in London, 15 or 16
> refugee American clergymen; and it is calculated that there are two or three
> thousand in the kingdom of other characters.
>
> To put me still more forward, Mr Eden ... introduced me to Lord George
> Germaine, the new American secretary, who talked pretty fully to me concerning
> that country. At his desire also I gave him, in writing, a pretty copious detail
> of all my sentiments and advice on the subject. All this, at the distance you
> live from great men, you would think promising, yet nothing has come
> of it, nor in my present judgment will come of it, save that I was thanked for
> it by his lordship, and, as I have lately heard, some of it was thought well of
> by Lord North.
>
> The Bishop of London seems not to be of a very liberal or exalted way of
> thinking, any more than his grace of Canterbury, to whom also I have been
> introduced. They are cold and formal, and seem to think they do wonders
> when they give you a dinner.

He added the common lament that while he had enjoyed 'some character and
note' in America, 'here every body I see eclipses me'. He had, however, just accepted
a curacy at Paddington, to begin in February. He understood it might be worth
about £70 a year, and, importantly, would not require him to leave London: 'It
is thought best that I should not get far out of sight of these people, on whom I
am alas! to rely for bread, lest, peradventure, they might wholly forget me — an
infirmity to which such men, it seems, are pretty frequently subject.'[3]

In the evening Mrs Gaul, an elderly woman, endeavouring to reach something
off the chimney-piece at her house in Wormwood Court, Oxford Street, set her
cloaths on fire, which burnt her so dreadfully that she expired on Tuesday morning

in great torture. By this misfortune an estate of £100 per annum devolves to her daughter, a widow with five children, whom she had not spoke to for nine years.[4]

Mrs Cornelys held her second masqued ball for the season at Carlisle House in Soho Square. The house was opened at ten, and the rooms, with the side boards, at midnight.

Among several entertaining characters disposed through the apartments were Hecate and five witches, Sallino, Marino, Jenino, Peggino, and Tabino. They had 'just whisk'd over in a whirlwind from Scandinavia' to dance 'the famous Lapland quadrille, as performed before all the sovereigns of the universe, and to the astonishment of all beholders', according to a hand-bill distributed by Hecate. There was also an American Rifleman in one of the provincial hunting shirts; a Canadian warrior, who gave the war-hoop on entering the rooms; a Grand Turk, who got violently drunk; a Chimney-sweeper, who beat a fine solo on shovel and brush; and two Waggoners, one alive and merry, the other so fatigued with the business of his character that he fell fast asleep on a sopha as soon as the rooms opened, and remained there perfectly composed till six in the morning.[5]

Meanwhile the *Solebay* set sail from Cornwall with Ethan Allen and other American prisoners of war on board. It proceeded from Cork on 12th February and reached Cape Fear, North Carolina, on 3rd May.[6]

9th January, Tuesday Hard frost day and night, great show for snow. *The frost will continue for the rest of the month.*

As a waiter at the St James's Hotel, Jermyn Street, was sweeping the snow from the top of the house he fell off. His fall was broke by lighting upon the roof of a coach which was standing at the door, but he was very much bruised.[1]

On arriving in town Lord Sandwich was met by the melancholy news of the death of his second son at Lisbon, where he had gone for the recovery of his health. That, at least, was the official story, but according to a letter from a well connected army officer, Sandwich heard the news earlier: 'Shocking as it is, yet it is most true that he concealed the account of his son's death two or three days that it might not stop the amusements and entertainments which he was then making at Hinchinbroke.'[2]

Not having received the Chevalier d'Éon's letter of the 7th, Beaumarchais wrote from London to warn him not to to break any of the conditions in their contract. Should he do so, 'from that moment your happiness and your honour would be destroyed'. He appended a list of secret documents d'Éon had agreed to surrender but which were missing and demanded that he send them as soon as possible.[3]

In the evening a remarkable figure appeared in the stage box at Covent Garden Theatre. It was thought by most of the audience to be a Turkish ambassador, but turned out to be no other than Captain Roper in the dress which he wore at the masquerade the preceding night.[4]

Captn. Toper

Noted masquerader Captain Roper, satirised as Toper,
from the *Town and Country Magazine* for July 1777

GA 'Richard Baker, one of the coiners under sentence of death in Newgate,
is gone out of his mind. This unhappy man has a wife and three children.'[5]

MC 'A few days since a porter was employed to carry a hamper to a gentleman's
house in Marybone. At his arrival there, he found the family were all in the country,
except a maid servant, to whom he delivered his trust, with a charge, as it contained
goods of consequence, that it was to be deposited in the best parlour till her master's
return. The servant mistrusting nothing, asked him what the porterage came to?
He said the gentleman had satisfied him; and then went his way. This hamper
contained a man, who secreted himself there till night, and then uncorded himself,
and (with two or three others that he let in) stripped the house of all the plate,
jewels, and other valuables, to a considerable amount, and got off undiscovered.'[6]

GA 'We are assured, that since the American disputes, several ladies of distinction in this metropolis have come to a resolution not to drink any tea till such
times as the disputes are amicably adjusted; and at the same time have offered
their servants double wages to leave off that pernicious custom, which has been
the cause of all the disputes with the colonies.'[7]

10th January, Wednesday

A very heavy day

Lord Sandwich wrote from the Admiralty
to inform the king that, following the
death of his son, he would not be able
to attend him till Sunday next. The
letter was accompanied by a rebel flag
which he thought the king might wish
to see. It had been captured from an
American ship and featured a green
pine tree on a white background, with
the motto, 'Appeal to Heaven'.[1]

Struggle for an American pine tree banner,
from a map published at Paris in 1776

On the first day of the Old Bailey
sessions twenty-five prisoners were tried,
three of whom were capitally convicted,
including Thomas Williams, for robbing
a woman in Queen Street of half a guinea
and a piece of poplin. When he was
brought in guilty the court was alarmed
with the shrieks of a woman in the gallery,
who proved to be his wife. She was carried
away in strong fits. Seven other prisoners were convicted of transportable offences;
but as the Americans will not receive any of our *exports*, they were ordered to be
burnt in the hand and kept to hard labour. Three were ordered to be whipped,
and twelve were acquitted.[2]

Captain Cook wrote from his house at Mile End to the Rev. John Douglas,
a canon of Windsor, who was assisting him in writing up the journals from his
recent voyage for publication:

> With respect to the amours of my people at Otaheite and other places, I think
> it will not be necessary to mention them at all, unless it be by way of throwing
> a light on the characters or customs of the people we are then among, and
> even then I would have it done in such a manner as might be unexceptionable
> to the nicest readers. In short, my desire is that nothing indecent may appear
> in the whole book, and you cannot oblige me more than by pointing out
> whatever may appear to you as such.[3]

About seven o'clock, the Norwich stage coach to London was attacked about
two miles on the other side of Newmarket, by a single highwayman, who ordered
the coachman to stop. As he advanced to the window, the inside passengers, who
were armed, bid him come on, for they were prepared for him; but this menace
he disregarded, and on his coming nearer, a gentleman discharged a pistol and
shot him thro' the body, and the coachman instantly drove on. When the coach
arrived at Newmarket, messengers were dispatched in search and the highwayman

was found near the spot where he had stopped the coach, crawling on his hands and knees, mortally wounded, and on the verge of death. Being asked if he had any accomplices or fire arms, he declared he had none. He was placed on a horse, but died before he reached Newmarket.

He proves to be one John Walker, whose mother a few years ago kept an inn at Newmarket. He was placed an apprentice to a bookseller at Norwich, but coming into possession of a considerable sum of money, quitted his profession, repaired to London, took up a dissolute course of life, and soon consumed it. He was about 23 years of age and has left a wife and children now in London.

It appears that he came to Cambridge on Tuesday, put up his horse at one inn, lay at another, and did not rise till late the next morning. He was cautious of being seen and quite poverty struck, having only a few halfpence in his pocket. He seemed much dejected, and said before he departed, it would not be so the next time he came, as he would soon be among people who had money, and went away about three o'clock that afternoon. He had a countryman's shirt over his cloaths when he attempted this robbery, and part of an iron candlestick for a weapon.[4]

MC 'Last week died at Rotherhithe, Mrs Giles, a maiden lady, who about five years ago was laid out for dead, but on going to remove her into the coffin, the maid perceived some signs of life, on which she was put into a warm bed, and a surgeon sent for, who bled her; after which she recovered and made her will. She left her whole fortune to the above servant, provided she was kept a fortnight after her decease, and not buried till her head was cut off.'[5]

11th January, Thursday A great deal of snow
At 10.33 a.m. the king wrote from the Queen's Palace to condole with Lord Sandwich on the loss of his son and to encourage greater urgency in naval preparations: 'We must shew that the English Lion when rouzed has not only his wonted resolution but has added the swiftness of the Race Horse.' He reminded him of an idea of buying coal vessels and fitting them out as ships of war. He said that every means should be adopted 'to cover the sea with vessels' and so prevent the Americans from importing that 'essential article' for the next campaign, gunpowder.[1]

John Wilkes and his daughter dined at home in Prince's Court, Westminster, with Miles Peter Andrews, lover of the now notorious Miss Brown, and other guests including two MPs outspokenly critical of the ministry. Beaumarchais had been invited but wrote to excuse himself, afflicted as he was with a sore throat 'in your country of colds'.[2]

MP 'They write from Ireland that the desertions from the ninth, the thirty-fourth, and fifty-third (three of the regiments under embarkation orders for America) are so numerous that, tho' each corps was complete before the receipt of these orders, the officers do not now expect to land half their compliment of effective men on the American continent.'[3]

GA 'So very great is the distress of the general part of the prisoners now confined in the King's Bench prison, that one of them was obliged to dress a cat a few days since to prevent himself and family from starving.'[4]

LC 'There have been killed, since September last, for the use of the navy, at London, Portsmouth, Plymouth, and Dover, for sea stores and harbour meat, 8000 oxen, and 18,000 hogs, besides a large quantity of sheep.'[5]

12th January, Friday
Snow all night and day

About two o'clock in the morning (probably, and not before) died at his lodgings at Newington Butts, Mr Thomas Weston, comedian, of the Theatre Royal, Drury Lane. His disorder was a galloping consumption, arising from an ulcer which had formed upon his lungs, and baffled the skill of the most eminent physicians. The *Morning Post* next day noted his 'propensity to scenes of dissipation' but judged that 'as a comic actor he stood in the foremost rank'. Lichtenberg, writing in October 1775, considered him 'one of the most comical fellows I have ever set my eyes on. His figure, his voice, his whole bearing excite laughter, although he never seems to intend it, and never laughs himself.'[1]

Thomas Weston as Billy Button in Foote's *The Maid of Bath*, from the *London Magazine* for February 1776

In the morning the Condemned Sermon (as it is called) was preached at Newgate chapel before the Perreau brothers and other convicts awaiting execution. After which they received, with great seeming devotion, the sacrament of the Lord's Supper.[2]

Mrs Perreau and her three children, dressed in deep mourning, attended at the Queen's Palace, and procured another petition to be presented to her majesty.[3]

At half past twelve the king went from the Queen's Palace to St James's for a levee in his private coach, attended by two footmen only, on account of the severity of the weather. The chairmen could by no means have carried his majesty across the park without falling.[4]

Several City of Westminster magistrates met at Sir John Fielding's, and taking consideration of the weather and the distresses of many of the industrious poor, entered into a subscription to furnish proper food for them.[5]

Upwards of 400 large bullocks were brought up for the use of the transports and men of war fitting out for America. Next day, the 13th, they began killing and salting them at the Victualling Office on Tower Hill.[6]

At the Old Bailey twenty-five prisoners were tried, of whom three were capitally convicted, including Robert Williams, for the murder of Henry Stubbings, coachman. The evidence against him was much as had been heard at Bow Street nine days earlier. He was sentenced to be executed on Monday next, and his body to be anatomised.[7]

At night the sewer in Grub Street broke in, by which accident two men fell to the bottom. A woman also fell, but, hanging by her cloathes, was taken up unhurt. The men are supposed to be lost, as the sewer is remarkably deep in that place.[8]

GA 'To so great a pitch of luxury is this age arrived, that a hair-dresser near St James's has set up an elegant carriage, in which he constantly attends his customers.'[9]

13th January, Saturday Some scattering snow

A well-dressed man was found dead in the snow at Pimlico, with a gun by his side, and boots on. It is supposed he had been shooting, got intoxicated, and fell. Two other men were found dead in the snow in the marshes at East Ham. One stood upright in a ditch with his gun on his shoulder, and the water up to his breast. It is imagined the smoothness of the surface deceived him. The other lay half covered with snow at some distance off.[1]

The remains of Miss Mary Ann Bunce, who died the 6th instant in Abingdon Street, Westminster, only daughter and heiress of Sir James Bunce, bart., were going to be deposited in the family vault in the church of Kemsing, Kent. The hearse, however, with the attendants, could proceed no further than Farnborough and was obliged to return to town, the snow being near ten feet deep at the bottom of Farnborough Hill, where the mail, a chaise, and a waggon lay buried.[2]

In Newgate, Robert Perreau was visited by his wife and wrote a letter to his former employer Mrs Tribe, of Oxendon Street, insisting on his innocence: 'I neither know of, or had the least intention of defrauding Messrs. Drummonds, but was the unhappy deluded tool of others, and acted upon by the most premeditated, artful wickedness that can be devised.'[3]

Refugee Samuel Curwen rode to London from his lodgings at Islington and then took a hackney coach to the house of the other condemned brother, Daniel Perreau, in Harley Street, to view his effects prior to auction. He found 'a very large company of genteel, well dressed people most of whom were of the feminine gender, on the same errand as ourselves, to view the house and furniture, the former of which is in the highest and most expensive taste'.[4]

At the Old Bailey three prisoners were capitally convicted including Joseph Bull, who worked in the slaughter-house at Hungerford Market, for the murder of Catherine Guy, a woman with whom he had cohabited some years.

The first witness, William Doran, deposed that being in his apartment in Crown Court near Hungerford Market on the evening of 24th December last, he heard Bull, who lodged in the next room, enter and demand money from the deceased, which he said he had given her to pay the rent. She answered that she had not spent it, upon which Bull swore he would destroy her: 'You bloody bitch, I will knock your bloody liver out, and your bloody melt.'* The partition between the rooms being only lath and plaister, Doran heard Bull strike and kick at the deceased. She cried out for mercy and said, 'Joe, my dear Joe, do not treat me so, I have not spent the money.' Doran then heard her fall down on the floor with such force that it shook the plates in his room.

Anne Doran confirmed her husband's evidence and said she had called to Bull and begged for God's sake he would stop. 'He bid us be d—d and keep our own apartment. I heard nothing more pass that night, but I went down at about a quarter after seven in the morning. I told my landlord and landlady, that I did suppose Bull had killed his wife, for she lay in a deplorable condition; for I had opened my own door and saw her weltering in her blood, with her hair all about her ears ... She lay and moaned in such a manner it terrified me; that was Christmas Day in the morning.'

Bull later returned and, without any concern or remorse, stepped over the deceased, looked for a shirt, and bargained with a person who came along with him for an old deal box, before going out a second time. He was later apprehended by a constable at the Cannon public-house in Hungerford Market.

The deceased lived until the Tuesday morning. Susannah Young, who sat with her, deposed that 'she called for Joe and God a quarter of an hour before she died. They were the last words she ever spoke.'

Mr Harding, apothecary, and Mr Jarvis, surgeon, attended the deceased on Christmas Day and gave evidence that the blows and subsequent neglect were undoubtedly the cause of her death. Another witness produced the prisoner's shirt with some blood on it.

Bull's defence was a flat contradiction of all that had been sworn by the witnesses. He claimed that while he lay in bed the deceased came home drunk, threw herself upon him, and insisted upon coming to bed. He drew his foot out of bed and pushed her on the floor, threw the water in the chamber-pot over her, dressed himself and went out. 'I went home again about eleven o'clock. There she laid upon the floor with her head bent down upon her knees, and about a large spoonful of blood at her nose and frothing at her mouth. I lifted her upon the bed. I did not think but she was in her fits as usual when she has been in liquor. She has often laid three or four days together in that way, when she had been a-drinking. I expected to have found her in Bridewell, as I frequently have done.' He added,

---

* Probably meaning *tongue*. Joseph Wright's *English Dialect Dictionary* (1905) offers this definition with the example, 'I'll knock the melt out of you.'

'My shirt being bloody does not signify any thing. Sometimes it is full of blood. I am in the slaughter-house carrying beef every day.'

Mr Justice Nares summed up the evidence, during which the prisoner, with the utmost composure, put his hand in his pocket, pulled out his tobacco pouch, and put a quantity of tobacco into his mouth.

The jury went out a short time and on their return found him guilty. He was sentenced to be executed at Tyburn in two days' time, the 15th instant, his body to be afterwards dissected and anatomized.[5]

GA 'A correspondent hopes that Mrs Rudd will immediately make and publish a solemn oath to the truth of the transactions between herself and the Mess. Perreau, regarding the forgeries; and as the full discovery of the truth, though it may tend to criminate herself, can do her no personal injury,* this duty is the more incumbent on her. It is now the prevailing opinion that Robert Perreau is totally innocent, and great doubts remain whether Daniel be guilty. Mrs Rudd is, probably, the only person in the world who knows the whole truth of the matter, and it is her duty, at whatever expence to herself, and however it may wound the delicacy of her feelings, to declare it.'[6]

LEP 'The distress of the troops and people at Boston exceed the possibility of description. There are advices in town of December 14; not a coal ship was then arrived. The inhabitants and troops literally starving with cold. They had taken the pews out of all the places of worship for fuel; had pulled down empty houses, &c. and were then digging up the timber at the wharfs for firing. No provisions nor cloathing. Expecting every day the provincial generals to storm the town; and that it would be burnt. In short, no words can describe the horror and miserable condition of the place. They have been eating horse flesh for some time. *But the — goes to the play, and laughs as usual. Jemmy Twitcher sings catches with his whores at Huntingdon. Lord George Minden says it is all wrong; if he were minister, he could do wonders. Sly old Jefferies drops hints for spilling more blood; more blood, more blood, the old fox whispers.*'†[7]

LC 'We learn from Cork, that the officers saved on board the *Rockingham* transport were, Capt. Clover, lieuts. Booth and Carter, and the doctor's mate. It is impossible to paint the distress of the officers and soldiers who were saved, the greatest part of whom, being cast on the rocks, had their flesh tore in a shocking manner, and instead of receiving the least assistance from the inhabitants, were attacked by some thousands of the common people, who carried away every article that could be saved from the wreck.'[8]

---

* Because she had already been tried and acquitted.

† The references are to the playgoing king; Lord Sandwich, known as Jemmy Twitcher; Lord George Germain, disgraced at the battle of Minden; and Lord Mansfield, whose predecessors as lord chief justice of the King's Bench included Judge Jeffreys.

14th January, Sunday Snow all night and day

At Newgate the two sons of Robert Perreau, aged fifteen and eight, were admitted to take leave of their father. When the ordinary, Rev. John Villette, returned for evening prayer, Perreau told him, with tears in his eyes, that he had hardly been able to disengage himself from them, 'owing to their tender affection and feeling for their poor father's miserable situation and impending catastrophe'.[1]

In the evening the black man who walked upon his stumps, and has supported himself many years by begging, was found dead in Oxford Street, supposed to have perished by the inclemency of the weather.[2]

15th January, Monday A little scattering snow

In the morning an express returned to the General Post Office, that was sent away on Sunday for Dover. The post-boy could get no farther than Northfleet, where the snow was above twelve feet deep, and he and his horse were obliged to be dug out.[1]

A melancholy procession left Newgate at a quarter past nine o'clock, carrying the two prisoners to be executed at Tyburn, Robert Williams, for the murder of Mr Pratt's coachman, and Joseph Bull, for the murder of Catherine Guy. Afterwards the bodies were brought to Surgeons' Hall in the Old Bailey for dissection. Lectures will be read upon them — one on the viscera, and the other on the muscles.[2]

A petition in favour of Robert Perreau, signed by seventy-eight capital bankers and merchants, was delivered to Lord Weymouth, one of the secretaries of state. It argued that Robert's crime was less serious than that of his brother and asked that his sentence be reduced to transportation. Meanwhile Mrs Rudd was also writing to Lord Weymouth, to try to undermine such pleas for clemency. Robert Perreau's conduct to her had, she said, 'obliterated every sentiment' of tenderness in her breast. She provided evidence that he 'actually benefited by the forgeries', bonds having been converted into cash at Drummonds Bank to pay off a debt of his to a lace-man in the Strand.[3]

Robert Perreau's wife Henrietta waited on the Countess of Egremont and Lady Weymouth, ladies of her majesty's bedchamber, with a petition for each, praying their intercession in behalf of her husband, and they both immediately went to the queen.[4]

Henrietta Perreau could not refrain from returning to Newgate to take a last farewell of her husband. Villette noted seeing Robert Perreau afterwards, 'towards the evening', when 'he appeared as well composed as could be expected, after the shock he must have undergone'. Villette then informed the brothers that two Jews who were also to be executed 'were to be separated from them and the other convicts, and that a mourning coach was to be provided by the sheriffs, without any expence to their family'. At this 'they jointly shewed unusual satisfaction, and told me, that I could not sufficiently express for them their gratitude to

Mr Reynolds, the under sheriff, the kind proposer of this act of benevolence. Accordingly an additional gallows was erected, in order to prevent any disturbance their minds might have been subjected to, from their opposite principles of religion, in their dying moments.'[5]

The sale began of Daniel Perreau's furniture at his house in Harley Street, which was uncommonly crowded. Eight cabriole chairs sold for 17 guineas and a commode dressing table of a curious construction for 11 guineas.[6]

A poor woman with an infant by her side perished with cold in an empty house in Spitalfields. The woman had some signs of life when discovered, but expired before assistance could be got.[7]

The committee of Westminster magistrates sat by adjournment at the Piazza Coffee-house to consider the best methods of carrying into speedy execution the plan to furnish food for the industrious poor. The committee will sit every day at noon for the reception of subscriptions and the delivery of tickets during the severity of the weather. Each ticket will entitle the bearer to half a bushel of coals. On Wednesday food ready dressed will be delivered out between two and five o'clock at the workhouses in Portugal Street, Exeter Street, Castle Street, and Poland Street, and some is to be brought every day to be tasted by the committee.

The long lists of subscribers' names published by newspapers during the rest of the month included the Duke of Newcastle (£21); the lord chancellor (one guinea per day during the hard weather); the Duchess of Kingston, David Garrick and Horace Walpole (five guineas each); and Dr Johnson and John Wilkes (one guinea each).[8]

About twelve o'clock one Bateman and his wife, lately convicted [> 2nd] of letting apartments in their dwelling-house in Covent Garden to common prostitutes, were put in the pillory in Bridges Street, opposite York Street. The man hid his head in the pillory and the woman, being with child, was allowed to stand without putting hers in. After continuing there a full hour they were taken to undergo the remainder of their imprisonment. A great number of constables attended to prevent them from being ill-used, and their case being looked upon as pitiable, having a family of seven children, a collection was begun for them. It would have turned out to greater advantage had it not been interrupted by the mobility, who, being told that the informer was Mackenzie, who keeps the cook-shop hard by, they went to his house, preceded by a person carrying a calf's head suspended on a pole. They broke his windows and destroyed his furniture, after which several of the culprits were secured by the peace officers. It seems the prosecution was commenced at the instigation of Mackenzie's wife, who was jealous of her husband for going to the house where the girls of the town lodged.[9]

A man and his wife, of Angel Court, were excommunicated at the New Church in the Strand (St Mary le Strand) for calling a woman a whore.[10]

At Cassel a treaty was signed with the Landgrave of Hesse-Cassel for 12,104 troops.[11]

MC 'The naval force destined to act against America will, we hear, consist of 56 ships of war, from fifty to sixteen guns each, besides sloops, bombs, &c. and will be manned by 16,000 seamen, and 3000 marines: the expence of which will be 1,800,000l. The army will consist of 34,000 effective men, which will cost 1,500,000l., so that the whole of the armaments for America, by sea and land, for the year 1776, will be 53,000 men, and the expence 3,300,000l.'[12]

16th January, Tuesday Snow most part of the day
In the morning the master of a coach yard in Wardour Street, Soho, who had been missing since Sunday the 7th, was found buried in the snow in Marybone fields, with his head bruised in a shocking manner. It is supposed he was robbed and murdered near that place. Two persons who were the last seen in his company are in custody on a suspicion of being the perpetrators.[1]

An old woman, who sold gingerbread cakes, and lived in Paddington, was found dead near Tyburn turnpike, supposed to have died through the inclemency of the weather, being very aged. A poor old woman, who sold ribbons and laces, &c. about the country for a livelihood, was found frozen to death near Lambeth.[2]

The Thames was almost frozen over near London Bridge, and all the arches except the middle one stopped up. It was entirely frozen over at Mortlake, where several persons walked over the ice, and one man ran in imminent danger of losing his life, by wheeling a barrow of dung from Mortlake to the opposite shore, for the trifling wager of five shillings.[3]

As they were crowding in the avenues of Surgeons' Hall, to see the bodies of the murderers executed on Monday, several persons lost their watches and money.[4]

The sale of Daniel Perreau's goods continued. Two large plate glasses sold for £185 each, and the total paid for the furniture of the dining room came to £617.[5]

All the constables belonging to Westminster received summonses to attend the execution to-morrow at Tyburn, a circumstance never before known.[6]

In the afternoon several persons of distinction met at a tavern in St James's Street and one of the company went to the Queen's Palace, returning in about two hours. It was supposed that his business had been to intercede in favour of the Perreaus.[7]

Harris's List of Covent-Garden Ladies, or, Man of Pleasure's Kalendar, for the Year 1776, 'containing an exact description of the most celebrated Ladies of Pleasure who frequent Covent Garden, and other parts of this metropolis', was published by H. Ranger, No. 23 Fleet Street, opposite St Dunstan's Church, price 2s. 6d. sewed.[8]

MC 'Within these few days a very commodious snow house has been erected in the vicinity of Oxford Market, which the builders and proprietors immediately opened with the sale of porter, purl, and other liquors, and to which much company, out of curiosity, daily resort.'[9]

GA 'The custom of gambling on matters of life and death, was never more shockingly conspicuous than in the case of the Perreaus, immense sums having been *done* (as it is phrased) and large bets having been made at several coffee-houses on the fate of the unhappy brothers. | Bets of 100 guineas to five were offered and refused at a coffee-house near St James's, that Robert Perreau would receive his majesty's clemency before twelve o'clock this day.'[10]

17th January, Wednesday A little scattering snow

The Rev. Mr Villette arrived early at Newgate and the Perreau brothers, having spent the night in the same cell, sent their servant with a request to speak with him. 'When I entered ... they shewed me their declarations, which they intended to deliver to me at the fatal tree, and which Daniel particularly protested were strictly true.' They asked for 'refreshment, as they had not gone to rest the whole night', and were indulged with 'a little toast and warm wine'.

About eight o'clock, genteelly dressed in deep mourning, with their hair dressed and powdered, the brothers joined the rest of the convicted men in the chapel, where they received the holy sacrament. Afterwards they went to the room for the reception of malefactors, to have their irons knocked off, previous to going forth to execution.

The number of people that made application to be let into the room was incredible, but Mr Akerman, the keeper, attended at the gate himself, and refused even his most intimate friends. Six gentlemen only, friends of the convicts, were admitted. Daniel came in first, bow'd to the company, and went to the fire, where he warmed himself with great composure. Robert followed, and looking at his brother for a moment, wiped off a falling tear, which he seemed anxious to hide. He turned to a little table, where lay the ropes with which they were to be bound. His emotions were then so strongly painted in his countenance, that the surrounding spectators gave vent to their sympathy in loud lamentations. Daniel assisted in putting the ropes properly round himself, but when he saw the officer do the same for his brother, it quite unmann'd him and he sigh'd and wept. They then took a last farewell of their friends, came out of Newgate without any person holding their halters (as the custom is), and seated themselves in the coach, after Robert had given the turnkey three guineas.

Whilst the bellman was repeating the usual verses at St Sepulchre's churchyard, the mob were extremely pressing to gain a sight of the brothers in the coach, which then stood still. The glasses being up, it was necessary to get close to do so, but as everybody could not be gratified at the same time, the consequence was confusion and disturbance. Robert Perreau, observing their anxiety, with the utmost composure put down the glasses of the coach, so that in an instant the mob ceased their clamour, their attention being engaged with a view of the unfortunate sufferers.

A little after nine o'clock the melancholy procession began. An infinitely larger number of spectators than ever was known waited at the press-yard gate of Newgate, lined the streets and windows from thence to Tyburn, and filled the galleries and sheds erected for the curious.

In a cart, preceded by the city marshals, sat Lyon Abrahams and Saunders Alexander, convicts for burglary, with George Lee, convicted of highway robbery. Next followed the hurdle, on which were drawn Baker and Radcliffe, coiners, who went in that form as prescribed by the law for those guilty of petty treason. There followed a number of sheriff's officers, after whom came slowly on a mourning coach, in which were Robert and Daniel Perreau, with Mr Villette and a sheriff's officer. According to Villette:

> Almost immediately after the coach moved, they applied themselves to prayer, and at proper intervals, conversed with me, and sometimes took notice of the spectators, among whom they recognized several of their acquaintance. Robert said, he hoped that wicked woman Mrs Rudd, was not a spectator, and when we drew near the place of execution, he added, he should not wonder if she was. But Daniel appeared confident she would not [be]. ...
>
> The people in general as they passed along, demonstrated their pity by their tears and prayers for them, and the only reflection thrown out against them, was from a miscreant, who exclaimed, 'Damn 'em, hang them both together,' which being overheard by Robert, he meekly returned the opprobrious execration with a blessing; indeed the whole of their temper and deportment, in their last moments, strongly indicated lively hopes of a speedy deliverance from this Vale of Misery, and an entrance into a blessed immortality.

The Jews and coiners behaved with becoming decency, but on leaving Newgate Lee put on an air of vulgar heroism. He appeared to be about 18 years of age, a handsome slim lad, genteelly dressed in a ruffled shirt, pompadour coat, white waistcoat, buff breeches, silk stockings, and a round hat with a small gold lace round it. He had previously been fitted out by his friends to go to a voyage in a West India ship in the capacity of steward, but getting acquainted with a young prostitute, he spent all his money, and, being unwilling to ask his friends for more, went on the highway and committed the robbery for which he suffered. It is said it was his first offence. In imitation to a criminal that suffered some time ago, he stiled himself *Sixteen String George*, and the neatness of his person and dress removed all suspicion. During his confinement before trial, his attention was more taken with ornamenting his irons with ribbons than providing for his defence, and at the bar he affected an indifference, so that when the fatal word 'guilty' was announced he carelessly twirl'd his hat to his head, and turned his back on the court with the most determined contempt.

As the procession passed through Holborn, Lee pulled off his hat to a young woman in a hackney coach, genteelly dressed in white, who immediately burst into tears.

Another young woman, who was big with child, standing in Holborn to see the malefactors go by, just as they passed gave a loud shriek, was taken in labour, and delivered immediately in the street of a fine boy. The mother and the infant were put in a hackney coach and driven to her habitation near the Mint, Southwark.

In a cart that stood in High Holborn two women were so much intoxicated with gin, that they fell to fighting even while the unhappy convicts were passing by them.

The procession arrived at Tyburn about half past ten. The crowd was immense. Thousands had assembled an hour before the convicts came, and at that time so many additional thousands poured in, that it was with the utmost difficulty that the constables kept a clear space about the gallows, though there were scarce less than 300 of them. Several noblemen were present in their carriages to see the execution of the brothers.

The gallows was divided into two parts by a middle post. The Jews, Abrahams and Alexander, were tied up by themselves under the left-hand one, a circumstance not remembered before, and had a Hebrew priest to pray with them.

Lee got out of their cart and ascended the other: in getting up the steps placed at the tail of the second, he hit his leg a violent blow, which seemed to pain him very much.

The Perreaus waited in the coach till everything was settled for their reception in the cart under the gallows. Jack Ketch opened the coach door and the two brothers got out with books in their hands. They ascended the same cart as Lee and the coiners, where they joined them and the ordinary in some select ejaculations, which seemed to be offered with great piety and energy. 'Towards the conclusion,' according to Villette, 'Robert did not forget to offer up an ejaculation for his wife and children; and Daniel again prayed for her who had deceived and betrayed them.' Each then delivered a paper to Villette, and held a serious conference with him for full ten minutes, during which Daniel placed his right hand upon his heart, and lifted his eyes towards heaven. Little was said that could be heard, owing to the great concourse of people present, thousands coming away without being able to get near.

About half after eleven, having given Ketch and his deputy some money, Robert Perreau turned and kissed his brother and they embraced with great affection. Their caps being now put over their eyes, they joined hands, which being a signal of their resignation, both carts were immediately drawn away, and they were launched into eternity. Their hands remained clinched together about half a minute after the cart was drove away, when, by the motion of their bodies, they separated. Thus two brothers in the same moment quitted that world which they had entered together. They behaved with a firmness and resolution rarely met with at the hour of death.

The Perreaus were both handsome men and about 5 feet 9 inches high. Their bodies were put into different shells, which were conveyed by a hearse and four to the house of Robert Perreau in Golden Square.

Notwithstanding the awful solemnity of the occasion, the crowd behaved with the most inhuman indecency, shouting, laughing and throwing snow balls at each other, particularly at those few who had proper compassion for the misfortunes of their fellow creatures.

It was computed that there were near 40,000 people present. There were many reports of accidents: part of two galleries gave way, by which one woman and two children were killed on the spot; a young woman, said to have been a prostitute, was thrown down and trampled to death; a man was trampled to death by a horse; another man was squeezed to death, his entrails being almost forced out at his mouth; another man was almost bruised to death, by being jammed between two coaches; a soldier had his leg broke, by standing upon the wheel of a coach; a lad of 16, nephew to Mr Batty, gardener, near Whitechapel Church, fell off a coach and was crushed to death by the crowd; and many others had their limbs broke, or were terribly bruised. Some reports were probably exaggerated, although according to next day's *Gazetteer*, 'it is supposed about a dozen people lost their lives'.[1]

Among others attending was James Northcote, apprentice to Sir Joshua Reynolds. Eight days later he wrote to his brother in Plymouth describing the furore:

> I went with all the world to see the Pereaus hung ... Miss Reynolds* thinks of nothing else and thinks them quite innocent and that they have been hardly used. Of late it has been the subject of every bodys talk. Miss Reynolds went to see Daniel Pereaus house in Harly Street before the sale and was surprized at the vast elegance of the furniture. As they went in a mourning coach I was not able to distinguish their faces and the crowd was so very great that I was afraid to go too near, for there was one young man killed in the mob and others hurt. Sir Joshua went to see them at Tyburn.[2]

Among the American refugees, Edward Oxnard watched the Perreaus pass on their way to execution and Governor Hutchinson met the returning crowds afterwards. 'Everybody agrees that Mrs Rudd ought to have been hanged,' he noted in his diary, 'as being the most guilty, but the jury had not evidence before them to convict her.'[3]

Meanwhile:

Between one and two o'clock in the morning some housebreakers attempted to rob a gentleman's house in Newman Street, but fortunately there was an alarm-clock and, the first door they opened, it was set in motion, and waked the family. The thieves made a precipitate retreat, leaving behind them a dark-lanthorn,† some picklock keys, and a horse-pistol.‡[4]

In consequence of printed notices to the inhabitants of London and Westminster, concerning the cleaning and sweeping the foot pavements, men, women, and

---

* Frances, Sir Joshua's sister.
† A lantern with a slide or other means by which the light can be concealed. (*OED*)
‡ A large pistol carried at the pommel of a saddle when on horseback. (*OED*)

children employed themselves in cutting, digging up and removing the condensed snow and icey matter from before their shops and houses. Nothing was to be heard for some hours but a confused clink and rattling of iron crows, paving shovels, tongs, pokers, and fire shovels.[5]

About one o'clock, betwixt two and three hundred poor people were waiting at the Duke of Northumberland's at Charing Cross in hope of relief from their graces' munificence.[6]

Several poor fishermen, out of employ through the severity of the frost, drew a boat about the streets at the west end of the town, begging for relief. Likewise a number of gardeners with carts dressed with black flags went about the environs of the city, begging charity for their wives and families, as they cannot work during the inclement weather.[7]

In the afternoon eight coaches filled with felons, who had been put on board a vessel in the river, in order for transportation, were brought back under a guard of soldiers and lodged in the Savoy; 'tis said that they are to be incorporated with the regulars employed against the Americans. 'A hopeful acquisition indeed!' commented the *Morning Chronicle*.[8]

MP 'So dreadful and impassable are the northern roads, that Lord George Germaine's carriage was preceded all the way from Northampton by a large party of pioneers, who cut occasional passages for it thro' the snow, or otherwise his lordship could not have arrived in town to have assisted at the privy council, which was held on Monday last.'[9]

MC 'Great Britain, it is now supposed, has not 10,000 regular troops from Portsmouth to Fort George, nor eight ships of the line ready to proceed to sea at five days notice. There are at this instant 22,000 troops, the flower of the French army, within three days march of Dunkirk, and fourteen ships of the line, and eighteen frigates lying in Brest Water, fitted, victualled, and ready to put to sea. ... Hear this, ye Britons, and tremble!'[10]

18th January, Thursday Very heavy, but no snow

This being observed as her majesty's birth-day,* there was a numerous and splendid drawing-room at St James's, notwithstanding the severity of the weather, which confined many families in the country. The lord chancellor appeared in his state coach, which had been newly gilt and painted. The most superb carriage was Lord Stanley's vis-à-vis, which cost 1,100l. Among others present were the dukes of Chandos and Argyle, the duchesses of Bedford and Gordon, lords Germain and Mansfield, generals Gage and Burgoyne, the lord mayor, Governor Hutchinson, and Mr and Mrs Garrick.

* She was born on 19th May 1744 and the king on 4th June 1738 (new style). Her birthday was marked in January to avoid the celebrations falling too close together.

Most of the ladies wore rich silks of English manufacture. Their heads were not dressed with their usual feathered plumage but with artificial flowers and fruits. The amazing quantities of these made the drawing-room appear like the decorations of a *fête champêtre*. 'The dresses of the ladies were exceeding rich and their heads were studded with diamonds to a very great amount,' noted refugee Edward Oxnard, who went to survey the scene. 'Some single lady's I dare say had 5000' (i.e. diamonds worth £5,000).[1]

During the drawing-room the Earl of Mexborough had an Order of the Bath, containing diamonds of immense value, cut from his ribbon in the presence chamber, the second that has been stolen this year in the palace. It is supposed to have been done by one of a gang of sharpers who dressed themselves for the occasion.[2]

In honour of the birth-day lords North, Weymouth and Germain gave grand entertainments to the nobility at their respective houses, and the Bishop of London gave a dinner to upwards of fourteen bishops at his house in St James's Square. The lord mayor had the portico of the Mansion House illuminated with 300 glass lamps. The illuminations in the front of the French ambassador's house, adjoining to the Horse Guards, were also remarkably splendid.[3]

Edward Gibbon wrote from Bentinck Street to his friend J. B. Holroyd, later Earl of Sheffield, who was at Sheffield Place, later Park, in the wilds of Sussex:

> How do you do? Are you alive? Are you buried under mountains of snow? I write merely to triumph in the superiority of my own situation, and to rejoice in my own prudence, in not going down to S. P., as I seriously but foolishly intended to do last week. ...
>
> We proceed triumphantly with the Roman Empire, and shall certainly make our appearance before the end of next month. I have nothing public. ... The higher people are placed, the more gloomy are their countenances, the more melancholy their language. You may call this cowardice, but I fear it arises from their knowledge (a late knowledge) of the difficulty and magnitude of the business. Quebec is not yet taken. I hear that Carleton is determined never to capitulate [to the] rebels. A glorious resolution if it were supported with 50,000 men.[4]

Having received the Chevalier d'Éon's long letter of the 7th, Beaumarchais responded with an ultimatum: 'I give you eight days to cool yourself down, to reconsider, and to repent. But if that term expires ... I will be compelled to leave and to break off all relations with you. My only regret will be to carry back to France the unwelcome conviction that your enemies know you better than your friends.'[5]

In the evening the Duke of Devonshire arrived in town from the seat of his father-in-law, the Earl Spencer, at Althorpe. Having rode three miles from Northampton, and finding the roads impassable for carriages, his grace and three other noblemen got out and walked all the way to Devonshire House.[6]

At Drury Lane Theatre Mr Garrick performed the part of Abel Drugger in *The Alchemist* by Ben Jonson to a brilliant and overflowing house. It is said to be his last time in this character and astonishing bursts of applause attended his performance. When Face asked Drugger whether he had any interest with the players, he answered, 'I had once, but I don't know whether I have now or not.' This was deemed behind the scenes a confirmation of his having sold his share of the patent.[7]

Hannah More, bluestocking and aspiring dramatist, who had been taken under the actor's wing, wrote:

> Let the Muses shed tears, for Garrick has this day sold the patent of Drury Lane Theatre, and will never act after this winter. *Sic transit gloria mundi!* He retires with all his blushing honours thick about him, his laurels as green as in their early spring. Who shall supply his loss to the stage? Who shall now hold the master-key of the human heart? Who direct the passions with more than magic power? Who purify the stage? and who, in short, direct and nurse my dramatic muse?[8]

Hannah More, after a portrait by Frances Reynolds, *circa* 1780

A gentleman passing outside the theatre before the performance, not knowing of the charitable tickets which Sir John Fielding had issued, was importuned repeatedly by the poor and ragged for a *ticket*. At which he exclaimed, 'Good heavens, what universal popularity hath this great actor, when the very beggars solicit tickets to see him!'[9]

A ball for the birth-day was held at St James's, beginning soon after nine o'clock and ending before twelve. After the king and queen entered it was opened with a minuet danced by the Prince of Hesse and Lady Betty Stanley, who was the best dressed woman in the room in a mouse-coloured sattin, embroidered with variegated flowers. Lady Gideon sported an extraordinary head, which forced a smile from her majesty; the lower part of her hair was like a man's wig, and the upper part terminated in a lofty peak, like a grenadier's cap, with a bouquet on the top of all. Two female Quakers (one Mr Barclay's daughter, of Cheapside) were noticed for the elegance and simplicity of their dress.[10]

RIGHT 'Mr Garrick in the character of Abel Drugger', after a painting by Zoffany, 1770

19th January, Friday

Strong frost, heavy snow early

Two young watermen of Rotherhithe, belonging to the Customs, appeared on their skaits on the Serpentine river in Hyde Park, in the habits of a Dutch man and woman, and supported their characters to the satisfaction of some thousands of assembled spectators.[1]

At night some villains broke into Limehouse Church and stole the sacramental plate, the communion table cloth, and the clerk's gown. They attempted to steal a clock from inside the church, but could not unscrew it.[2]

PA 'The Dutch have refused the request made to them by our Court, for a body of their troops to be sent to America. All Europe is laughing at the folly, and despising the applications of the British ministry for troops.'[3]

MC 'David Garrick, Esq., has signed and sealed for the sale of his share in the patent and property of Drury-lane theatre. The purchasers are Dr Ford, Mr Ewart, Mr Linley, and Mr Richard Sheridan. The purchase money is 35,000l. The publick may now, therefore, depend upon it, that this will be the last season of Mr Garrick's performing.'[4]

20th January, Saturday Strong frost, bright mid-day
Jonathan Sewall, former attorney general of Massachusetts, wrote from No. 1 Brompton Row to his friend Edward Winslow in America:

> I verily believe your sufferings are drawing near a period. You will undoubtedly have, early in the spring, an army of 40,000 and a fleet of upwards of 70 ships, and then the mettle of the rebels will be try'd. ...
>
> I wish you were here Ned, with money enough in your pocket. You can have no idea what a noble country this is for a gentleman. Every thing is upon an immense scale. Whatever I have seen in my own country, is all miniature, yankee-puppet-show. I was at Court the day before yesterday, being the queen's birth day, (I am now at the 20th) and I believe in my conscience, the prime cost of the dresses I saw there, was sufficient to have purchased our whole Continent. The wealth of this country is truly astonishing, but unless a gentleman can get his share of it, he has no business here. £600 per annum is but as a drop in the ocean — the man is lost — he is nothing — less than nothing, and vanity, and his contemplation of his own comparative littleness, is vexation of spirit — but, humiliating as it is, I wish to stay here for the sake of giving my boys a chance for the grand prizes which every profession presents to view ... As to Massachusetts Bay, I wish it well, but I wish never to see it again till I return at the millenium. No, believe me, Ned, the mad conduct of my countrymen has given me a dose I shall never get over. God mend them, and bless them — but let me never, never be cursed with a residence among them again.[1]

At Drury Lane Theatre *The Discovery*, a comedy by the late Mrs Sheridan, mother of Richard, was revived to enable the queen to see Mr Garrick in the part of Sir Anthony Brainville. Mrs Abington played Lady Flutter. Garrick's intention of retiring from the stage being generally known, the house was filled in a few minutes after the doors were open. After the play he stepped forward and delivered a poetical address to the ladies, in character, which was received with great applause.[2]

MC 'The guards at St James's, the Queen's Palace, Whitehall, Savoy, Somerset, and all the public offices, are accommodated with fur gloves at the king's own expence, and for the course of the week have been relieved every two hours by his order.'[3]

MC 'A correspondent desires us to recommend to every person who has occasion to walk the streets, to have a piece of felt or old hat nailed to the bottom of the heels and soals of their shoes ... He has tried several other methods to prevent his falling, but finds nothing answers the purpose so well as this. Taking short steps, and reclining rather forward, was recommended in the last great frost, and is most certainly very proper to prevent accidents.'[4]

21st January, Sunday Strong frost

In the evening a great crowd gathered about the door of the late Robert Perreau in Golden Square. About half past nine the bodies of the two brothers were put in separate hearses. The coffins were covered with black cloth, and black nails, with a black plate on each, on which were inscribed their names, day of death, and age, which on both was 42, being born within ten minutes of each other. Then followed two mourning coaches. In the first were the two sons of Robert and two brothers-in-law, and in the second were four friends.

The procession made its way to St Martin in the Fields without lights or parade, but attended with a great throng of people. To avoid too large a gathering it was ordered that the great bell should not toll till the ceremony was over, but when the procession arrived at the church the crowd was so large and rude that it was with difficulty the bodies and mourners could get entrance.

When the coffins were taken out of the hearses they were covered with plain velvet palls, and followed by the eight mourners, and several servants in livery. There was great curiosity to see the unfortunate youths, who followed their father to his untimely grave with becoming dignity.

The party were stopped a considerable time waiting for the minister and parish officers. It is remarkable that both the churchwardens who officiated were on the jury on Robert Perreau's trial, and one of them was foreman.

Service having been performed in the church, the bodies were carried down to the vaults, where very few were admitted, the rest being with great difficulty kept out. The coffins were placed near others of the family in vault no. 4, those of Robert's deceased children being laid over his. After this the mourners waited some time in the vaults, till the churchwardens had driven away the crowd. They were then conducted to the vestry and refreshed with wine, waiting till the crowd was nearly dispersed. They were conducted to the coaches, and returned to Robert's house, where a crowd was again assembled.

According to the church's burial posting book, Robert Perreau had '6 men, great bell, prayers and candles' at a cost of £6 14s. 6d. Daniel also had six men, the great bell, and prayers, but no candles, the cost being £6 7s.[1]

On the same night the remains of actor Thomas Weston were carried in a hearse from his lodgings at Newington and interred in the burying ground of his family at St James's Church. His corpse was attended to the grave by several performers of the Theatre Royal, Drury Lane.[2]

22nd January, Monday Strong frost

Mr Alderman Peckham sat at Guildhall. There was not one prisoner brought before him, owing, it was imagined, to the lower set of people keeping within doors this severe season.[1]

In Edinburgh, Boswell read an account of the execution of the Perreaus and lay awake with gloomy thoughts of the deaths of himself and those he loved.[2]

23rd January, Tuesday Strong frost, heavy day, some scattering snow

A contract was made with a merchant in the city for five million cabbages, to be delivered at different times within two months, to make sour crout for the forces in America.[1]

MP 'It is observed by a correspondent (to the honour of the human heart) that there was a greater crowd of servants yesterday at the committee of the Westminster Charity, to obtain tickets for their masters and mistresses subscriptions to relieve the industrious poor, than ever was known in memory of man, to procure tickets for a ridotto, masquerade, or any other public entertainment that ever was exhibited. A striking proof this, that Charity, not Dissipation, is the characteristic of the English in the year 1776.'[2]

24th January, Wednesday Strong frost

About one o'clock in the morning, while a number of Irish people were watching a dead body in a house in Spitalfields, the floor fell in, by which means the corpse and near thirty persons fell into the cellar, which, being a kind of warehouse, had a great quantity of earthen pans and crockery in it. Several people were very much bruised and one man had an arm broke.[1]

The Thames below London Bridge was so frozen that the sailors walked to and from their ships on the ice. In the morning a boat was discovered between Deptford and Greenwich, froze in, with the waterman dead, and sitting upright stiff at the helm.[2]

In the evening a chairman (by appearance) carried a basket to Lord Stanley's, in Grosvenor Square, which he said contained a hare; but the porter being absent, the servant who answered the door refused it. The basket was then carried to the next door, Lord Abercombe's, and his lordship being at home it was received. When opened, it proved to contain a male child about two months old, which his lordship went with in person to the parish workhouse, and ordered it to have a proper nurse, and the greatest care taken of it.[3]

At half after nine the doors opened for a masqued ball at the Pantheon, tickets two guineas each. According to the *Morning Post*, 'The company, as usual, was of the mixed kind, composed rather too much of the lower orders, on account of the severity of the weather,' which had confined 'many families of distinction at their country seats'. At twelve o'clock there were about 1,200 persons collected, about two-thirds in dominos. Mr Vernon, Mr Reinhold, and several other musical gentlemen entertained the company with catches, glees, and airs, and a Harlequin danced an excellent hornpipe.

Among the characters, two Quakers, one said to be a beautiful countess who lives not a thousand miles from Cavendish Square, held forth with great humour to a congregation of Friars, Goddesses, Weird Sisters, and Indians. They were soon *drove* from their station, however, by the *jee hoa*s of a Waggoner from Margate. The Indians were inimitable. They gave the war-hoop with its terrors, and were a large party. One in particular, a New Zealander, was so much in character that it was some time before Omiah the Otaheite (who was in a fancy dress of light green and gold) could be convinced that he had not met a countryman. Capt. J—nes supported the part of a wild American with true natural ferocity. He could scarcely be kept from using his tomahawk upon the most trivial occasions, and towards morning became both dangerous and troublesome.[4]

LADY BETTY BUSTLE and her MAID LUCY preparing for the MASQUERADE at the PANTHEON.

Printed for Carington Bowles Map & Printseller N.º 69 in S.ᵗ Pauls Church Yard, London . Published as the Act directs. 13.ᵗʰ May 1772.

25th January, Thursday Strong frost, a heavy day

At half past one their majesties went to St James's, where there was a brilliant drawing-room, during which Dr Burney presented the first volume of his *General History of Music* to her majesty, to whom it is dedicated.

Sheets of the work would be ready for collection at the author's house in St Martin's Street six days later. Among the 857 subscribers gathered by the sedulous Burney were the Prince of Wales, the Elector of Bavaria, ten dukes and duchesses including Georgiana, Duchess of Devonshire, five bishops, Lord Sandwich and William Beckford (5 copies each), Warren Hastings (3 copies), David Garrick, Horace Walpole, Dr Johnson, Sir Joshua Reynolds, and Jean Jacques Rousseau.[1]

UPPER Charles Burney. Engraving by Bartolozzi, after a portrait by Reynolds, 1781.
LOWER Orpheus and Eurydice. Engraving by Bartolozzi, after Cipriani,
from Burney's *History of Music.*

In the afternoon officers of the Board of Works were examined by a committee of the House of Lords relative to preparations for the trial in Westminster Hall of Elizabeth, calling herself dowager Duchess of Kingston. Mr Shakespeare, master carpenter, said that a fit and proper place for the trial could not be built in less than thirty days, especially at this season of the year. It was agreed that the trial be put off until 15th April.[2]

MC 'In a field near Galley Wall, Rotherhithe, which has been overflowed, and frozen over for some time, several matches of cricket have been played by persons in skaits, on Monday, Tuesday, and yesterday, the many droll circumstances arising from the precarious footing of the several parties producing much laughable entertainment to the numerous spectators, who sometimes have been reputed at between two and three thousand.'[3]

MP 'The deluded Miss Brown has compleated the Double Elopement, the first from her father, and the second from her new music master; she went off last Wednesday, and poor Sal Pietro has not been able hitherto to find out where, or with whom she is gone. He is terribly shagreened at the evaporation of his golden dreams: he had already treated for a ready furnished house for her accommodation, and had devised other projects of grandeur, all which was to have been paid [for] by the vast sums of money he was sure to get by her singing every where. However, she was so kind as to send him last Saturday the following laconic *billet doux*, to comfort him: "Sir, I have been obliged to take this sudden step, to quell in part the public clamour against me; when this is completed, and I have settled my affairs, PERHAPS I may learn music from you. — Yours, &c."'[4]

The *London Chronicle* published a letter from Boswell, dated 'Edinburgh, Jan. 19' and signed 'Borax', in which he took his countrymen to task:

> As an instance how very highly the grand American controversy is considered in the northern metropolis, I send you the following original hand-bill, which was given about in Edinburgh:
> 'To be sold by Peter Williamson, at his penny-post-office, entry to the Royal Exchange; or at the coffee-room in the Parliament House,
> A pair of fine young grey Squirrels, lately brought from North America; and are become very diverting, in ringing of music bells, by turning a wheel. They are extremely tame and tractable, and against next spring will make an excellent breed, as they are of the best kind.
> N.B. As all commerce with North America is now shut up, it is hard to say when an opportunity may offer to get two such well matched handsome Squirrels. It is therefore hoped the curious will not disappoint themselves.'
> I could wish to know if Juvenal himself could have pointed any thing more characteristically of coldness and thoughtlessness about the public interest. What! have the people of Scotland nothing else to regret while all commerce with America is shut up, but that they cannot get handsome squirrels who can ring bells and turn a wheel ...[5]

From *The Macaroni and Theatrical Magazine* for March 1773

26th January, Friday Strong frost, some snow early, bright day
In the morning a girl of the town was found dead in the Back Lane, Whitechapel, supposed to have perished through want. A sailor was found dead on the Deptford road, with his throat cut from ear to ear. It appeared he had been robbed and murdered.[1]

In the afternoon a duel was fought behind the Foundling Hospital by two officers in consequence of a quarrel at the late masquerade. One of them received a shot in the arm which divided the artery. He was carried home to his apartments in Piccadilly in a very dangerous condition.[2]

Colonel Guy Johnson wrote from his lodgings in Brewer Street to Lord George Germain concerning Indian affairs. After initial visits to Germain and the Court at the turn of the year Johnson had been 'seized with the influenza', as a result of which he was 'repeatedly blooded, blister'd, &c. and confined the greatest part of the month'. His health now improved, he set out at length his view of what needed to be done to ensure Indian support against the rebels, with particular emphasis on his own role: 'Without a proper authority the super-intendant can be expected to do very little ...' He added: 'The Indian chief who accompanied me, with his companion, are persons of character and influence in their country; they can more at large speak on any matters that may be required of them.'[3]

French ambassador the Comte de Guines wrote to his foreign minister, the Comte de Vergennes, in Paris:

Lord George Germain pushes actively all the preparations for the next campaign. I was assured that he was gaining more and more the king's confidence and that Lord North's credit was decreasing. Indeed, I received him and his family at my home on the same day I received Lord North and his family and they both avoided each other in marked manner. The re-assembly of parliament will tell us more about it within a few days. I do not expect anything interesting during the course of the next week. The weather is so bad and the cold so severe that no one is in a hurry to leave his country home and get on the road to return to London.[4]

27th January, Saturday Strong frost, snow most part of the day
Thirty thousand pairs of shoes came by the Wellingborough waggon to the Windmill Inn, St John's Street, intended for the use of the troops in North America.[1]

MP 'The die is cast at last, and an embarkation of the guards is finally resolved upon; a draft is therefore ordered immediately to be made out of the three regiments of guards, to complete a battalion of 1000 men. ... The consternation this has occasioned amongst the military *petit maitre* is almost incredible: Lady *Squab*, Countess *Fizzle*, and Lady *Trimmer*, are driving about from minister to minister, to procure leave of absence for their *pretty* sons and nephews, alledging that the *delicacy* of their frame and constitution will not be able to bear up against the severity of the climate and service; hitherto however to the honour of the premier, no excuse whatever has been admitted.'[2]

28th January, Sunday Intense frost, a great deal of snow. Stormy
In the morning a boy about nine years of age was found up to the neck in a pond near Bethnal Green, froze to death.[1]

A corn vessel ran foul of the starlings of London Bridge. The corn was hoisted by tackle and loaded into waggons on the bridge. Soon afterwards three other vessels ran foul of the bridge, and there appeared no other way of saving the people in them from perishing in the cold but by rope ladders, which being let down all the men came up with ease, but one, who was so benumbed that it was with the utmost difficulty he held to the ropes, crying all the way as he ascended, 'O Lord! O Lord! I am lost, I shall perish.' However, he reached the top in safety, and was dragged over the balustrades.[2]

Prison reformer John Howard (*opposite, left*) visited the King's Bench in Southwark. It was the first recorded of many visits he made to London's prisons during the year, particularly in March and May, providing material for his *State of the Prisons in England and Wales*, published in May 1777.[3]

Horace Walpole (*opposite, right*) also spent a characteristic day, in his case in the rather different setting of Strawberry Hill, Twickenham. He received a gift from the Countess of Albemarle, 'the red hat of Cardinal Wolsey, found in the Great Wardrobe by Bishop Burnet when clerk of the closet', and wrote to his old friend Sir Horace Mann, British resident at Florence, who was thinking of paying a visit to England after long absence.

North front of Strawberry Hill, by William Marlow, *circa* 1784

I am almost afraid to frighten you with an account of our winter; but then it is such a winter as I never saw. I was with you at Florence in 1741, and those ever since have been springs, and sometimes summers. This was made for the north pole, has lasted three weeks, and grows every day worse and worse. It caught me at Lord Ossory's, in Bedfordshire, and locked me up there above a fortnight. At last it gave me the gout in both hands, on which I set out directly for London through mountains of snow and quarries of ice. ...

The government is straining every nerve to muster a great army in America, though it must combat for its very landing. Fifteen thousand Hessians and Brunswickers are retained. This force, if half of it can get thither and land, must be maintained from hence. ... Guess at the millions this will cost; and come and see your country before all its splendour is at an end! Boston is famishing: what is the fate of Quebec, we do not yet know. The parliament is met, but two-thirds of the members are frozen in the country. Omiah, the native of Otaheite, breakfasted with Mr Conway to-day, and learns to skate. He had no notion of ice, and calls it stone-water; a very good expression.[4]

29th January, Monday Intense frost, an exceeding bright day
About 4 a.m., as the watchman was going his round in Holborn, he observed a
coach upon the stand without any driver. Examining the coach he found the man
dead in the boot.[1]

'A Watchman with his lanthorn by moonlight'. Etching by John Bogle
after his own painting which was exhibited at the Royal Academy, 1776.

A woman stood for an hour in the pillory at the corner of Russell Street, Drury Lane, for having kept a house of ill fame in Nag's Head Court in that lane. The extreme coldness of the weather prevented any great crowd from gathering, but a small collection amounting to about five shillings was made for her. She underwent the sentence with strong marks of anger, kept up by a good portion of gin, taken as she mounted the rostrum. Her arms were observed to be turned almost black through the cold before she was taken out. Afterwards she was taken to Bridewell to undergo the remainder of her sentence, imprisonment for eleven months.[2]

Gibbon wrote again to J. B. Holroyd: 'Hares &c. arrived safe; were received with thanks, and devoured with appetite: send more, *id est*, of hares. ... What think you of the season? Siberia, is it not? ... Roman Empire (first part) will be finished in a week or fortnight. ... Embrace my lady. The weather too cold to turn over the page. Adieu.'[3]

In the afternoon the river was frozen at Kew, and people walked over the ice instead of paying the toll to go over the bridge.[4]

In the evening a boat, in which were two boys, was jammed between the ice just above London Bridge. The boys' cries were soon heard by the persons on the bridge, but no method was contrived for their release, till a gentleman passing in his carriage, and enquiring into the affair, offered five shillings to any one who would attempt it. On this a sailor offered his assistance and some ropes and three or four hurdles were procured. Persons on the bridge held a rope, and the tar descended, placed the hurdles on the ice, and getting as near the boys as possible, threw a rope to each of them, which they made fast around their bodies, and coming forward on the hurdles, all the parties were drawn up safely at ten o'clock. The boys had not left the boat five minutes before it was drawn under the ice by the force of the tide.[5]

Lord George Germain gave a grand supper and ball to upwards of 300 nobility and gentry at his house in Pall Mall. Some gentlemen expressed their surprise, declaring they should have thought him the last person for such kind of entertainment. 'How so,' cried Mr Charles Fox, 'I never heard the Minden Hero disliked any ball but a cannon ball.'[6]

30th January, Tuesday Intense frost

At 11 a.m. a House of Commons committee met to try the merits of a petition concerning the 1774 general election contest at Worcester, one of several challenged on grounds of corruption. The plaintiff was Sir Watkin Lewes, who had been outbribed by two wealthy nabobs, John Walsh and Thomas Bates Rous.

The petition was read by the clerk and set forth complaints against the city's magistrates and sheriff, who was returning officer, for abusing their authority, and against the sitting members, Mr Rous and Mr Walsh, for bribing and attempting to bribe voters. One of the witnesses, formerly waiter at Hooper's Coffee-house in Worcester, swore to having seen Walsh give two farmers two guineas each on the promise of their votes. He also said he heard Walsh declare that he would have his election, though it cost him 20 guineas a man, and at other times that he would spend a tub full of money.

A female witness swore that Walsh went to a butcher's house with his agent Brown, who in Walsh's presence gave money to the butcher's wife on her promising her husband's vote. Mr Mansfield, counsel for Walsh, was rather ill-natured in cross-examining this last witness, yet the laugh went heartily against him. On being asked what money Brown gave the butcher's wife, she said she could swear to some silver. He asked how she knew there was no gold among it. Because, says she, gold is *yellow* and silver is *white*. And pray, says he, what brought you up to London, thinking she was paid by Sir Watkin, to which she replied, *the Leominster waggon*. The committee adjourned at half past three.[1]

The Chevalier d'Éon replied from Staunton Harold to Beaumarchais, referring to him as 'the cleverest and most agreeable monkey that I have ever met'. He defended his failure to hand over all the secret papers on the ground that his debts had not been settled, and he challenged Beaumarchais again over his betting schemes.[2]

SJC 'It is said that the Duchess of Kingston is very liberal to the poor during this severe season, and her benefactions in food and coals have saved some hundreds from perishing by cold or hunger; an example well worthy the imitation of her sex among the nobility — and Charity hides a Multitude of Sins.'[3]

31st January, Wednesday Intense frost, foggy morning, bright later
In the morning, the Thames being totally frozen over above Putney Bridge, they began to erect booths on the river.

A boat was found in Blackwall Reach with two men frozen to death in it.

Two boys fell under the ice at Symonds's Wharf, and were both got out, but one of them was so terribly cut by the ice, that it became necessary to amputate the leg above the knee.

Mr Wilson, a smuggler hunter, who had been missing a week, was discovered, put under some ice in a creek near Dartford; by marks on the neck it appears he had been strangled.

Coal porters began to unload the lighters, and bring the coals in sacks over the ice.

Many persons of the first rank appeared among the skaiters on the Serpentine river in Hyde Park, and the banks were lined with carriages filled with ladies viewing the performances. A gentleman dressed in furs *à la mode de Russe* was very capital, and a sailor from Rotherhithe was distinguished by cutting out any figure or letter of the alphabet on the ice. Omiah the Otaheitean tried to skait, but was very awkward. Booths were erected, and large quantities of provisions were sold, the venders of gin and gingerbread meeting with the greatest success.

In the afternoon a man in liquor attempted to walk over the Thames at Rotherhithe, slipped down when near the middle, and the ice breaking, he fell in and

Some effects of the freeze

Kew Bridge, where the toll was avoided by people by walking over the ice

Skaters on the Serpentine, as depicted by Rowlandson, probably in the 1780s

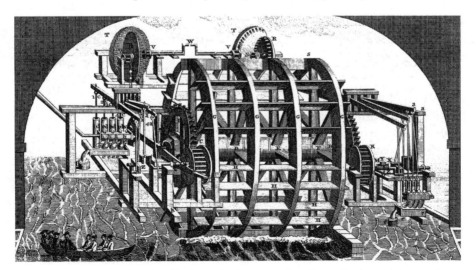

The water-works at London Bridge, which were reduced to a single working section

was drowned. It is said he was a journeyman carpenter, and has left a wife and five children.[1]

In the evening Vanbrugh's *The Provoked Wife* was performed at Drury Lane Theatre. Mr Garrick, in the part of Sir John Brute, exhibited an extraordinary lady's cap, ornamented with such a plume of feathers, ribbons, oranges and lemons, flowers, &c. and so formidable a toupee, that the audience gave repeated bursts of applause and such peals of laughter that the roof of the theatre seemed to be in danger. 'The female head-dress has now reached the highest degree of ridicule,' noted the *Gazetteer* a few days later. 'It was time for the stage to lay hold of such extreme folly, and to expose it to the derision of the public. ... The ladies in the boxes drew back their heads, as if ashamed of the picture; and it is to be hoped that for the future they will take a reef in, as the sailors say, and lower their topsails.'[2]

MC 'Sunday one of the birds, called a bald coote, fell into the yard at Mr Brookes's, watchmaker in St John's-lane, and was taken; on Saturday four brace of partridges were shot in St George's Fields; on Sunday a team of wild ducks were seen under the centre arch of Black Friars Bridge; near a thousand sea gulls were seen from London Bridge on Sunday; and many wild ducks were shot from the lighters at Queenhithe. These are strong proofs of the extreme rigour of the season.'[3]

GA 'The arches of London-bridge are so choaked up with ice, that only one division of the water-works can perform their operations; it is therefore now more than ever incumbent on the master and servants in all families to be careful to prevent fires, which in a scarcity of water can hardly fail to be attended with dreadful consequences.'[4]

LP 'His majesty, since Monday, rides every morning in the riding-house at the Queen's Palace, the roads being so very bad as to render it very dangerous to venture farther on horseback. | Notwithstanding the severity of the weather, the queen, and all the princes and princesses, walk near an hour every day in the garden at Buckingham-house.'[5]

Meanwhile in America

1st January. Norfolk, the best sea-port and most flourishing town in Virginia, was burnt to ashes after the king's forces had been driven out by the rebels.[1]

10th January. Thomas Paine's *Common Sense*, 'written by an Englishman', was published anonymously in Philadelphia. It described George III as 'the royal brute' and argued that reconciliation was now 'a fallacious dream'.[2]

COMMON SENSE:
ADDRESSED TO THE
INHABITANTS
OF
A M E R I C A,
On the following interesting
S U B J E C T S.

I. Of the Origin and Design of Government in general;
with concise Remarks on the English Constitution.
II. Of Monarchy and Hereditary Succession.
III. Thoughts on the present State of American Affairs.
IV. Of the present Ability of America, with some miscellaneous
Reflections.

Written by an ENGLISHMAN.

Man knows no Master save creating HEAVEN,
Or those whom choice and common good ordain.
THOMSON.

PHILADELPHIA, Printed.
And Sold by R. BELL, in Third-Street, 1776.

Garrick as Sir John Brute
Published for Bell's British Theatre, 1st June 1776

February

1st February, Thursday Intense frost. Appearance of a thaw in the afternoon Below bridge the river was froze over and some thousands of people walked across. A sailor boy venturing too near the bridge, the ice gave way and he fell in, but he was got out safe by the throwing ropes to his assistance.

A number of people skated on the river, especially from Westminster Bridge to the horse-ferry at Millbank.

At Fulham the river was so much frozen over that booths were erected on the ice, and a kind of fair was held, to which great numbers resorted.[1]

There was a very numerous drawing-room at St James's, by the arrival of many of the nobility in town from their country seats, who had been detained on account of the badness of the roads.[2]

Lord George Germain wrote from Whitehall to General Howe in Boston to assure him that every effort was being made to bring forward preparations for the next campaign, 'though the severity of the weather, almost beyond what has ever been known in this country, very much obstructs the service in the naval department'.[3]

The *Morning Chronicle* carried an advertisement for the first volume of Edward Gibbon's *Decline and Fall*, to be published on the 17th of the month. Meanwhile in Bentinck Street the author wrote the brief preface: 'It is not my intention to detain the reader by expatiating on the variety, or the importance of the subject, which I have undertaken to treat ...'[4]

In the evening a new comic opera, *The Blackamoor Washed White*, was performed at Drury Lane Theatre. The plot concerned Sir Oliver Oddfish's attempts to prevent Frederick, a young man of fortune, from gaining access to his daughter Julia. He widens his canal and plans to replace all his male servants with black ones. Disguising himself as one of these, Frederick enters the house and, after several scrapes, gains Sir Oliver's consent to marry Julia, who was played by Mrs Siddons.

The audience expressed strong marks of disapprobation during the performance. Captain Roper of the guards, coming a little elevated into the front boxes, roared out to the performers, 'God d—n you, am I to pay five shillings for seeing a man walk about with a clout* upon his head? I'll bring an action against your manager for my five shillings. I'll *white-wash* him I warrant you.' Hopkins the prompter noted in his diary that there was 'much hissing and crying out "No more, no more!" ... As soon as the *Blackamoor* was given out for the next night, they kept a great noise and call'd for another farce to be given out. At length they ... went away vowing vengeance on it the next night.' The reviews were also critical, the *London Magazine* judging it 'as a literary composition ... the most execrable that was ever attempted to be represented on an English stage'.[5]

* A piece of cloth , especially a small or worthless piece, or of clothing. (*OED*)

The problem, however, probably lay less with the play than with the author, the Rev. Henry Bate. He was notorious as editor of the *Morning Post*, widely regarded as a scandal-sheet, and for his part in the so-called Vauxhall Affray of 1773, in which his spirited defence of an actress at the pleasure gardens had led to conflict with a group of macaronis, led by George Robert Fitzgerald. On that occasion Bate had roundly defeated Fitzgerald's footman in a boxing match, and his enemies now evidently sensed an opportunity to discomfit him.

Henry Bate
After a portrait by Gainsborough exhibited at the Royal Academy in 1780

2nd February, Friday Heavy, a gentle thaw
The wind, which had been easterly during the severe weather, changed to the south, and a gentle thaw came on. Governor Hutchinson noted the change: 'More moderate to-day than for 3 weeks past, and some rain, but the Thames is froze over at Richmond, and the streets of London are covered with a body of ice 6 or 8 inches thick in some places, and as hard as the pavement.'[1]

At 10 a.m. the committee on the Worcester election met again. John Evans, a freeman of Worcester, gave evidence that the mayor, Mr Mathers, had offered him two guineas if he would *serve* Messrs. Walsh and Rous. He was near three hours under examination, for being deaf, one of the door-keepers of the House of Commons stood behind him, and bawled every question that was put to him very loud at his ear. One of the committee members desired him to be asked if he was always so deaf, to which he replied, 'No, only in very cold weather.'[2]

The committee's exhaustive hearings continued over the following weeks until it gave its determination on 4th April [>].

In the morning Lord North wrote to warn the king that Vice Admiral Lord Howe was planning to demand an audience that day 'to signify his intention of quitting the service'. Howe was a popular and experienced figure and, North added, the idea that he was about to be appointed to a command in North America had 'begun to get wind' with 'a very good effect in the public'. He asked the king to do what he could to prevent Howe from 'taking a hasty step'. At 5.46 p.m., before going to dinner, the king wrote back to reassure his anxious minister: 'Things are very far from desperate [so] that if no one will interfere I do not dispair of bringing things to rights ... Therefore rest satisfied till you hear more from me.'[3]

In the evening the author of *The Blackamoor Washed White* convened a large number of what the *Morning Chronicle* called 'well ordered, though not very well-dressed friends' to support his opera. With their assistance, and some alterations and curtailments, it was heard to the end, and left in possession of the stage.[4]

GA 'The guards are every day practising the use of the rifle gun in Hyde Park; the barrels of these new-fangled instruments of death are on so particular a construction, that a pistol carries 300 yards; and some of the men are already so dexterous, that they can hit the center of a small target at that distance. Whether they will be such good marksmen when there is a rifle gun opposed against them, is another question.'[5]

3rd February, Saturday Bright day, thaw continues
Some lads, out of a bravado, went upon the ice just below London Bridge. The ice gave way, they all fell in, and three of them were drowned.[1]

At 3.01 p.m. the king wrote from the Queen's Palace to Lord North: 'I have seen Lord Sandwich and I think settled the command of the N. American fleet agreably to Lord Howe's proposal to me yesterday ... Lord Sandwich deserves commendation for being so very complying.' Howe was to replace Admiral Shuldham, who had commanded the fleet since September 1775 and was favoured by Sandwich.[2]

Corbült delin.^t et feci^t.

The RIGHT HON^{BLE} RICHARD LORD HOWE.

Commander in Chief of his Majestys Fleets in America.

LONDON: Publish'd as the Act directs, 16th Novr 1777, by JOHN MORRIS, Rathbone Place.

The Theatrical Dispute, or the Parson BAITED.

A view of this night's fracas

The Blackamoor Washed White was performed for the third time at Drury Lane Theatre. Several exceptionable passages were omitted and it went off very well till the second act, when Captain Roper and another gentleman came into the boxes. Being a little mellow, they showed their disapprobation in a vociferous manner, which was so resented by the rest of the house that an universal uproar ensued, and those who attacked the piece were salted with volleys of oranges, apples, and even halfpence. Capt. Roper struck at somebody in the pit, and his companion jumped upon the stage. Numbers of the audience followed him there, blows ensued, several persons were knocked down, and many turned out of the house. A man was thrown from the gallery, but saved himself by hanging on the chandelier, and a lady of high rank was struck in the face with an orange. 'In short,' according to *Lloyd's Evening Post*, 'the whole scene was more alarming than any that has occurred on such an occasion.' 'I thought they would have pulled the house down,' noted prompter Hopkins in his diary.

The affray lasted about half an hour, after which the principal part of the audience (the ladies excepted, who had retired in great agitation) returned to their seats, and the entertainment was concluded as well as could be expected. Mr Garrick did not hear of the dispute time enough to arrive before it was over.[3]

'There are now about eight thousand cart loads of snow and ice,' reported the *Morning Post*, 'that have been carried out of the streets of this city, deposited in

Moorfields; every cart has a ticket given it at entrance, like a turnpike ticket, containing the name of the owner of the cart, and the ward from whence they came. These tickets are to be produced at Guildhall, where there will be some allowance per load made to each scavenger. Eight thousand loads, at 5s. each, is 2000l.' In the event the bill was not so high. On 23rd July the commissioners of sewers presented an account of the demands of rakers and others employed during the frost. It came to 1,129l. 17s. 11¼d. and it appeared that between 17th January and 6th February 8,728 cart loads had been cleared away.[4]

LC 'Lord Howe is to have the command of the fleet against the Americans, and his brother being commander by land, the most spirited conduct is expected next campaign.'[5]

4th February, Sunday Heavy, thaw increases, exceeding moist air. Full moon
In the morning Captain Roper and Mr B— waited upon the Rev. Mr Bate with an apology for causing a riot the previous evening, assuring him that it was merely inebriation which led them into so wanton a frolic, and not any prejudice against the author or his piece.[1]

In the afternoon a clergyman during his sermon pulled out of his pocket a newspaper, and read out of it the following paragraph, viz. 'On Sunday the 18th of January, two ponies ran on the Uxbridge road, 20 miles for 20 guineas, and that one gained it by about half a head; both ponies were ridden by their owners.' He also read another paragraph of the like kind, of a race on the Rumford road on a Sunday.* He made apology for reading part of a newspaper in the pulpit, said he believed it was the first instance of the kind, and he sincerely wished that there never might be occasion for the like again. He then pointed out the heinous sin of Sabbath-breaking, and what a scandal it was that such actions should be practised in a Christian country by men of property, who ought to set a good example to the lower class of people, and that it should pass unnoticed by those who had authority to punish such offenders. He added that such wickedness would have been severely punished by Mahometans; how much more ought it to be by Christian magistrates.[2]

In the evening Captain Roper and some other gentlemen waited upon Mr Garrick to apologise to him. After expressing concern for the phrenzy of the preceding evening, Capt. Roper said he hoped no damage was done to the theatre? Mr Garrick, with great politeness and good humour, answered, 'very trifling, he believed; only a sconce or two beat down, and a glass pannel broke'; to which the captain replied, 'If that's all, Mr Garrick, a very particular friend of mine in the Royal Irish has had his jaw broke; so if you please we'll set the broken glass against the broken jaw-bone, and balance the account.'[3]

* The original reports have not been found but this is perhaps a garbling of the *Morning Post* paragraph quoted under 6th January above. If the races did occur later, 18th January was a Thursday but 28th January was a Sunday.

5th February, Monday Several smart showers, a very bright day. Stormy
At the levee at St James's, Lord Howe kissed the king's hand upon being appointed commander-in-chief of his majesty's forces in North America.[1]

John Wilkes and his daughter dined at home with Beaumarchais and Arthur Lee, who had much to discuss.[2]

Early in the evening an officer arrived with dispatches from General Howe at Boston. At 6.20 p.m. Lord George Germain wrote to the king enclosing the dispatches and reporting that when the officer had left Boston on 29th December the army was 'well and in good spirits. The rebels had erected a battery and fired upon the town, but it was soon dismounted.'[3]

Drury Lane Theatre was exceedingly full in every part shortly after the doors were open. As soon as the overture began, there was a most discordant noise of clapping, hissing, shouting, and knocking of sticks, which continued in full chorus while it was played. When Mr Vernon and Mr Davies appeared to open *The Blackamoor*, the noise increased so much that they could not be heard. At length Mr Garrick came forward and, after waiting some minutes for silence, addressed the house to the following purport: 'Ladies and gentlemen, my situation as a manager is at present exceedingly critical. I wish to please the publick and I wish to preserve the author's property. The opinion of this audience shall be complied with as soon as I can gather it; but suffer me to say, my theatrical life will be but short, and I beg I may end it in peace.' A man in the pit cryed out, 'If you have a mind to die in peace, don't let *The Blackamoor* be played again.'

A violent clapping met Mr Garrick's words, and 'The piece, the piece,' being re-echoed through the theatre, Mr Vernon and Mr Davies again attempted to begin, but in vain as before. Mr King then came on the stage with a paper in his hand, and after standing the brunt of the house, as his manager had done before him, he informed the audience that the author of the opera 'begged to withdraw it, for the sake of restoring peace to the theatre, and for the sake of convincing the public that he not only lamented the disturbance which happened in the house on Saturday evening, but that he was not by any means concerned in promoting it, as had in the most unmanly manner been alledged in some of the morning prints'. Mr King was saluted with a lighted candle from the boxes, and an orange from some other part of the theatre, on which he very prudently retired, after a repetition of claps, hisses, &c.

Mr Vernon and Mr Davies returned to their duty, but without the wish'd for effect. The audience for some time employed themselves in fighting with their sticks, shoving against each other, and dealing out abuse. Mr King again appeared, and said he came immediately from Mr Bate, who intreated his friends in particular, and the audience in general, to suffer him to withdraw the piece. A noise, if possible more violent than before, ensued upon this; and a person in a one pair of stairs side box being observed to take a candle from a sconce and throw it on the stage, those who filled the front of the two shilling gallery attacked him with oranges, apples, &c. He for some time stood their fire, but at length was obliged to retire. Soon afterwards a battle began between three young officers in the corner one pair of stairs box and some of the gallery, in which the latter were victorious, and the box champions were obliged to remove their quarters. Some of them went into the stage box, and jumped upon the stage, where there was a public fight; but the managers immediately fastened the stage doors, sunk the lights and dropped the curtain.

The audience passed their time in perpetual noise and skirmish till near eleven o'clock, when Mr Garrick once more came on the stage, and was likely to return without being heard, till a gentleman hallowed out, 'Pay some respect to Mr Garrick,' which immediately lulled the audience into silence. Mr Garrick then declared that 'the author, in order to restore peace to the theatre, had taken the copy of his opera from the prompter, and gone away with it; that he would not suffer them to act it; all that lay in his power, therefore, was to prepare any other entertainment the audience pleased, and to assure them that he would wait there patiently till five or six in the morning to receive their commands.' This speech had the desired effect,

Thomas King, in his later role as Puff in Sheridan's *The Critic*. After a painting by Zoffany, *circa* 1780.

and those who had been so loud and riotous for either the new or an old farce, so long a time, quietly withdrew, without there being any performed.

While Mr Garrick was on stage, some rude person threw an orange at him.

The noisiest part of the audience was a collection of officers, bucks, bloods, &c. (many of them much intoxicated) who came to the theatre without any impulse of friendship or enmity to the new piece, but merely, as they called it, 'to make sport, and kick up a dust'.[4]

A detachment of these bloods later sallied forth, and after breaking about five and twenty lamps, lay siege to a house in the Strand, mistaking it for Mr Bate's. They endeavoured to force the doors and shutters, uttering the severest denunciations against the author, but the watch were roused and soon put them to flight.[5]

Henry Angelo was a young man about town at this time and in his memoirs described a *Blackamoor* riot. He was, however, writing many years later and mistakenly said the play was performed only once. It seems likely that his description relates to the final performance on this night, although it could relate to the one on Saturday the 3rd:

> Mr Bate had mustered several friends, who were distributed at different parts of the house, among whom I was of the number. My station was in one of the corner boxes, on a line with the gallery. The clamour commenced with the party against the author, cat-calls, hisses, and yells; which were met by the other with clapping of hands, and exclamations of 'turn them out'. But what enraged the opposers, and begot them the alliance of the galleries, was a most indiscreet act on the part of Mr Bate. His friends, whom he had got behind the scene, assisted by some well known pugilists, in the midst of the disturbance crossed before the curtain from one stage door to the other, doubling their fists, and using other menacing gestures at the audience. This was the signal for a general charge upon Bate's party. The box in which we were crowded was attacked with showers of apples, oranges, and other such missiles; and some of the gallery heroes, leaning over, contrived to reach our box with bludgeons, which soon cleared it, with the exception of the late celebrated dentist Monsieur Dumergue, who hid himself in the back of the box, the wax lights having been knocked out, until being discovered by the opposite side, he too was pelted from his retreat. ... It was asserted, and pretty generally believed, that this riotous opposition had been planned and put into force by Fitzgerald, and the others concerned in the Vauxhall Affray.[6]

6th February, Tuesday A bright day, some little rain. Stormy

In the morning the body of a woman, about 30 years of age, was taken up in the river near Execution Dock. There was a fracture on her skull, a plain gold ring on her finger, and a few shillings in her pocket. It is imagined she had been thrown overboard from some vessel in the river.[1]

At a full court of aldermen at Guildhall Sir Stephen Janssen, bart., resigned as chamberlain, opening the way for a contest to replace him.[2]

GA 'Advice is received from Berlin, that several experienced Prussian engineers embarked a few weeks since for America, they being engaged on very advantageous terms by the American Congress.'[3]

MC 'Wednesday, many gentlemen of the navy, &c. at Portsmouth and Gosport, had a very genteel masquerade on the ice in skaits, with proper dresses. The whole afforded a pleasing sight to a great number of spectators.'[4]

7th February, Wednesday A fine day, chiefly bright

Died suddenly, after eating a hearty breakfast, Mr Tomkyns, wholesale tobacconist in Thames Street. About two hours after his decease his wife was delivered of twins.[1]

8th February, Thursday An exceeding wet day

At the King's Theatre in the Haymarket there were not above 400 persons for a *Fiera in Mascherata*. The stage and audience part of the house formed one grand room which was handsomely illuminated. The lower boxes and adjoining range on each side were converted into little shops and parades for different shewmen. Mat. Darly's prints, articles of plate, *bijouterie*, millinery, &c. were exhibited to sale, and to please the eye and tickle the ear there were Lawrence's Company of Fire-eaters, Salt-box Players, &c. with their noisy trumpeter. Among those present were the dukes of Devonshire and Ancaster, Lord and Lady Betty Stanley, Lord Lyttelton, and Lady Grosvenor.[1]

GA 'His majesty's ships of war now fitting out for America, from frigates of thirty-six guns down to the smallest vessels, are all to be provided with boarding-nets, hand-grenadoes, stink-pots, &c. | Every transport which is going to America is to carry over a number of live sheep for the use of his majesty's army.'[2]

9th February, Friday Fair morning, wet afternoon. Stormy

On or about this day occurred a dinner at which was confirmed Captain Cook's undertaking his third and final great voyage, relinquishing as a result his position as a pensioner of Greenwich Hospital. His first biographer, Andrew Kippis, described the circumstances some years later from information provided by Lord Sandwich.

> For the conduct of an enterprize, the operations of which were intended to be so new, so extensive, and so various, it was evident that great ability, skill, and experience were indispensably necessary. That Captain Cook was of all men the best qualified for carrying it into execution, was a matter that could not be called in question. But, however ardently it might be wished that he would take upon him the command of the service, no one (not even his friend and patron, Lord Sandwich himself) presumed to solicit him upon the subject. The benefits he had already conferred on science and navigation, and the labours and dangers he had gone through, were so many and great, that it was not deemed reasonable to ask him to engage in fresh perils. At the same time, nothing could be more natural than to consult him upon every thing relative to the business; and his advice was particularly requested with regard to the properest person for conducting the voyage.
>
> To determine this point, the captain, Sir Hugh Palliser, and Mr Stephens* were invited to Lord Sandwich's to dinner. Here, besides taking into consideration what officer should be recommended to his majesty for accomplishing the purposes in view, many things were said concerning the nature of the design. Its grandeur and dignity, the consequences of it to navigation and science, and the completion it would give to the whole system of discoveries, were enlarged upon in the course of the conversation. Captain Cook was so fired with the contemplation and representation of the object, that he started up, and declared,

---

* Philip Stephens, secretary to the Admiralty.

that he himself would undertake the direction of the enterprize. It is easy to suppose, with what pleasure the noble lord, and the other gentlemen, received a proposal which was so agreeable to their secret wishes, and which they thought of the highest importance towards attaining the ends of the voyage. No time was lost by the Earl of Sandwich, in laying the matter before the king; and Captain Cook was appointed to the command of the expedition, on the tenth of February, 1776. At the same time, it was agreed, that, on his return to England, he should be restored to his situation at Greenwich ...[1]

10th February, Saturday Some excessive heavy showers. Stormy

Captain Cook went on board the *Resolution* and, as he noted, 'hoisted the pendant, and began to enter men. At the same time, the *Discovery*, of three hundred tons burthen, was purchased into the service, and the command of her given to Captain Clerke, who had been my second lieutenant on board the *Resolution*, in my second voyage round the world, from which we had lately returned. | These two ships were, at this time, in the dock at Deptford, under the hands of the shipwrights; being ordered to be equipped to make farther discoveries in the Pacific Ocean, under my direction.'

Meanwhile a flurry of orders issued from the Admiralty: both ships to be victualled for twelve months, except beer, for which one month only was to be supplied, with brandy in lieu for the rest of the year; both ships to be fitted with a camp forge and copper oven and with 'Lieut. Orsbridge's machine for rendering stinking water sweet'; twelve long musquetoons to be supplied to *Resolution* and eight to *Discovery*; guns to be put on board when the ships arrived at Gallions Reach; and frames of two decked vessels to be packed in cases for exploring, surveying or emergency.[1]

Observations on the Nature of Civil Liberty, The Principles of Government, and the Justice and Policy of the War with America by Richard Price, a dissenting minister and political radical, was published. Expecting it might 'sink in the first edition', he suggested to the printer, Thomas Cadell in the Strand, that 500 copies would be sufficient, but on learning that Price was prepared to put his name to the book, Cadell said he would venture to print 1,000. They sold out within three days. On 16th February Cadell was told that if he reprinted he would be prosecuted by the directors of the Bank of England, and was apparently intimidated, but Price was advised 'without fear, to print as many copies as the public demanded'. The fifth edition appeared on 18th March and cheaper editions followed with smaller type and fewer pages, selling at sixpence rather than two shillings to make it affordable to a wider audience. By the end of the year an estimated 60,000 copies had been sold, not allowing for editions in Dublin, Edinburgh and America. As a result it was probably the most widely read new book of the year in England. Among those impressed by it was James Aitken, later known as John the Painter, who was in London at this time engaged in petty crime.[2]

ABOVE The *Resolution*.

BELOW Richard Price, from the *London Magazine* for May 1776.

In the book's opening section Price challenged the domestic political system. The 'very idea of Liberty' was lost in a country in which votes were often paid for, half the House of Commons was elected by just 5,723 people, MPs were subject to no control by constituents, and there was a 'higher will', that of the monarch, 'on which even these mock representatives themselves depend, and that directs their voices'. In such circumstances it was 'an abuse of language to say that the state possesses Liberty'.

He also argued for a form of European government. Each state should continue independent 'with respect to all its internal concerns', but 'a general confederacy' should be formed with 'a senate consisting of representatives from all the different states'. This senate should have 'the power of managing all the common concerns of the united states, and of judging and deciding between them, as a common arbiter or umpire, in all disputes'.[3]

His main concern, however, was the struggle being played out on the other side of the Atlantic:

> This is a contest from which no advantages can possibly be derived. Not a revenue: for the provinces of America, when desolated, will afford no revenue; or if they should, the expence of subduing them and keeping them in subjection will much exceed that revenue. Not any of the advantages of trade: for it is a folly, next to insanity, to think trade can be promoted by impoverishing our customers, and fixing in their minds an everlasting abhorrence of us. It remains, therefore, that this war can have no other object than the extension of power. Miserable reflection! To sheath our swords in the bowels of our brethren, and spread misery and ruin among a happy people, for no other end than to oblige them to acknowledge our supremacy. ...
>
> The truth is, we expected to find them a cowardly rabble who would lie quietly at our feet; and they have disappointed us. They have risen in their own defence, and repelled force by force. They deny the plenitude of our power over them, and insist upon being treated as free communities. It is this that has provoked us; and kindled our governors into rage.[4]

He went on to outline his concern that the financial system was highly vulnerable to shocks arising from the war given the size of the national debt (which he estimated at £137 million), the scarcity of coin, and the reliance on paper money. It was this aspect of the book that most alarmed government and gave rise to the warning to Cadell.

> Our circulating specie ... appears to be greatly decreased. But our wealth, or the quantity of money in the kingdom, is greatly increased. This is paper to a vast amount, issued in almost every corner of the kingdom; and, particularly, by the Bank of England. ...
>
> Coin is an universal sign of wealth, and will procure it every where. It will bear any alarm, and stand any shock. On the contrary, paper, owing its currency to opinion, has only a local and imaginary value. It can stand no

shock. It is destroyed by the approach of danger, or even the suspicion of danger. ...

Nothing can be more delicate or hazardous. It is an immense fabrick, with its head in the clouds, that is continually trembling with every adverse blast and every fluctuation of trade; and which, like the baseless fabrick of a vision, may in a moment vanish, and leave no wreck behind. The destruction of a few books at the Bank; an improvement in the art of forgery; the landing of a body of French troops on our coasts; insurrections threatening a revolution in government; or any events that should produce a general panic, however groundless, would at once annihilate it, and leave us without any other medium of traffic, than a quantity of specie scarcely equal in amount to the money now drawn from the public by the taxes. It would, therefore, become impossible to pay the taxes. The revenue would fail. Near a hundred and forty millions of property would be destroyed. The whole frame of government would fall to pieces, and a state of nature would take place.[5]

Later in the book he returned to the American war and considered the chances of success.

Our own people, being unwilling to enlist, and the attempts to procure armies of Russians, Indians, and Canadians having miscarried, the utmost force we can employ, including foreigners, does not exceed, if I am rightly informed, 30,000 effective men. Let it, however, be called 40,000. This is the force that is to conquer half a million at least of determined men fighting on their own ground, within sight of their houses and families, and for that sacred blessing of Liberty, without which man is a beast, and government a curse. All history proves, that in such a situation, a handful is a match for millions. ...

Were we, therefore, capable of employing a land force against America equal to its own, there would be little probability of success. But to think of conquering that whole continent with 30,000 or 40,000 men to be transported across the Atlantic, and fed from hence, and incapable of being recruited after any defeat — this is indeed a folly so great, that language does not afford a name for it. ...

In this hour of tremendous danger, it would become us to turn our thoughts to Heaven. This is what our brethren in the colonies are doing. From one end of North-America to the other, they are fasting and praying. But what are we doing? Shocking thought! we are ridiculing them as Fanatics, and scoffing at religion. We are running wild after pleasure, and forgetting every thing serious and decent at Masquerades. We are gambling in gaming houses; trafficking for boroughs; perjuring ourselves at elections; and selling ourselves for places. Which side then is Providence likely to favour?

In America we see a number of rising states in the vigour of youth, inspired by the noblest of all passions, the passion for being free, and animated by piety. Here we see an old state, great indeed, but inflated and irreligious, enervated by luxury, encumbered with debts, and hanging by a thread. Can any one look without pain to the issue?[6]

The book 'made a great sensation', according to Horace Walpole, and 'all the hireling writers were employed to answer'. Joseph Priestley, given a copy just before publication, sat up reading till after one in the morning and sent a copy to Benjamin Franklin in America. The *Gentleman's Magazine* also approved: 'He has considered coolly and candidly the grand question in contest between the American colonies and the parent state, and endeavoured to shew the pernicious consequences of pursuing violent measures to establish what he thinks an inequitable claim.' The *Town and Country Magazine* was not so impressed: 'The author's language is good, his arguments trite, and his conclusions most frequently chimerical.' John Wesley was also uneasy. In early April, on a preaching tour in the north, he began to write 'an answer to that dangerous tract, Dr Price's "Observations upon Liberty"; which, if practised, would overturn all government, and bring in universal anarchy'.[7]

Two men who presumably approved of the book, Beaumarchais and Arthur Lee, dined at Wilkes's again, this time joined by the Comte de Lauraguais, who was an old friend of Beaumarchais and was acting as an observer in London for the Comte de Vergennes.[8]

In the evening the king and queen went to the King's Theatre in the Haymarket for a new serious opera called *La Vestale*, the principal characters played by Signor Rauzzini and Signora Gabrielli. Anna Porter attended and was 'charmed with Rauzzini' but found Gabrielli 'more fine than pleasing'.[9]

MC 'The candidates for chamberlain are already reduced to two, namely, Mr Alderman Wilkes and Mr Alderman Hopkins; 'tis thought therefore that it will be a very sharp contest.'[10]

11th February, Sunday Heavy black clouds, and some little rain
In open defiance of the Sabbath day two men, partly naked, walked for a wager along the Mall in St James's Park, in the face of the numerous congregation from Charlotte Chapel who were coming into the park at the Queen's Gate. The congregation were not a little obstructed in their way home by the disorderly behaviour of the rabble who attended the prize walkers.[1]

In consequence of the late heavy rains, the melting of the snow, and the spring tide, Bushy Park was so much overflowed as to oblige the park keeper to have his food conveyed to him in a boat, and handed in at the one pair of stairs window.[2]

12th February, Monday Smart frost in the night, very fine bright day
Wishing to communicate knowledge of the Scriptures and the English language to Omai the Otaheitean, Granville Sharp, a Christian reformer who advocated American rights and the abolition of slavery, went to the Admiralty to request permission. Lord Sandwich gave his consent and Sharp set off to call on Joseph Banks, who had taken Omai under his wing. Next day, Tuesday, Sharp had the first of a series of meetings with Omai.[1]

13th February, Tuesday Fine bright morning, wet afternoon

At 9 a.m. a sale of animal skins began at the New York Coffee-house in Sweeting's Alley, Cornhill. Included were 10,600 bear skins, 10,100 cat, 15,000 Indian half-drest deer, 7,250 fox, 49,600 martin, 7,740 mink, 16,130 otter, 160,400 raccoon, and 5,430 wolf.[1]

Joseph Priestley sent Benjamin Franklin a parcel to be conveyed by a Major Carleton, brother to the governor of Quebec:

> By the same hand you will receive a most excellent pamphlet by Dr Price, which, if any thing can, will, I hope, make some impression upon this infatuated nation. An edition of a thousand copies has been nearly sold in two days; but, when Lord George Germain is at the head of affairs, it cannot be expected that any thing like *reason* or *moderation* should be attended to. Every thing breathes rancour and desperation, and nothing but absolute impotence will stop their proceedings. We therefore look upon a final separation from you as a certain and speedy event.[2]

Two less straightforward letters to America were written by Arthur Lee, perhaps at his residence, 2 Garden Court in the Middle Temple, and sent by private messenger to Boston. The outer, covering letter was unsigned and in evidently feigned handwriting:

> The inclosed will easily explain itself. The intelligence you should observe, and take measures accordingly. A fund for necessary expenses should be fixed here, in such hands as can be confided in. You know who is to be trusted. From experience I can say ... the New England men are fittest to be trusted in any dangerous or important enterprise. Show this only to R. H. L.,* of Virginia, and he will guess from whence it comes.
>
> The intelligence, if it gets to hand in time, should be communicated as soon as possible to every part of America, that she may be prepared.

The inner letter was addressed to a royalist, Lieutenant Governor Colden of New York, presumably as a cover in case it should fall into the wrong hands:

> You will be curious to know what are the ministerial intentions, and their force for the next campaign. The following is their army upon paper: Hessians, 12,000; Brunswickers, Woolfenbutlers, and Waldeckers, 5,000; six regiments under Lord Cornwallis, 3,000; eight more to sail in the spring, 4,000; Highlanders, 2,000; now in America, 8,000. ...
>
> The English and Irish troops go with infinite reluctance, and strong guards are obliged to be kept upon the transports to keep them from deserting by wholesale. The Germans, too, I am well informed, are almost mutinous; but the Landgrave of Hesse is an absolute tyrant, and must be obeyed. It is therefore conceived that, if the Congress have proposals prepared in English and German, to distribute among them when they land, which no precautions can prevent, multitudes will desert.

---

* His brother, Richard Henry Lee.

Upon the whole, the ministry, if every thing favours them, may have about thirty thousand men in America by the latter end of June. ...

I am well assured that the French Government will wink at the exportation of arms and ammunition. ...

Let me have your opinion of all these things. The opposition gains ground, and the nation begins to feel; but America must trust to her own arm and Heaven for protection. ... Cover mine and address it to 'John Horsfall, Treasurer, Middle Temple'.[3]

14th February, Wednesday Fine bright morning, wet afternoon

John Wilkes marked St Valentine's day by dining with his mistress Mademoiselle de Charpillon alone.[1]

Captain Cook wrote from his house at Mile End to John Walker, one of two Quaker merchant brothers of Whitby who owned the ship on which he had served his apprenticeship:

I should have answered your last favour sooner, but waited to know whether I should go to Greenwich Hospital or the South Sea. The latter is now fixed upon. I expect to be ready to sail about the latter end of April ... I know not what your opinion may be on this step I have taken. It is certain I have quitted an easy retirement for an active and perhaps dangerous voyage. My present disposition is more favourable to the latter than the former, and I imbark on as fair a prospect as I can wish. If I am fortunate enough to get safe home there's no doubt but it will be greatly to my advantage.[2]

In the House of Commons the report of a committee on the late Shaftesbury election was considered. Sir George Yonge, chairman, said that the most notorious bribery, corruption, and perjury had been carried out, not secretly and as if ashamed, but openly, with pomp and parade, by sound of trumpet, ringing of bells, and public processions. It appeared to have been the practice for many years back for the voters at Shaftesbury to expect money from the candidates at elections, and that nothing was to be done without it. It was resolved that subornation of perjury had been practised and the most wilful corrupt perjury committed. It was moved that six men, including Francis Sykes and Thomas Rumbold, the late sitting members, both nabobs, were guilty of these crimes. This produced much debate but resolutions against all six were at last agreed, and it was resolved that the attorney general be directed to prosecute them.[3]

Horace Walpole wrote from Strawberry Hill to Edward Gibbon, who had sent him an advance copy of his *Decline and Fall*. After gushing praise he concluded: 'You have, unexpectedly, given the world a classic history. The fame it must acquire will tend every day to acquit this panegyric of flattery.'[4]

A letter in the *Morning Post* accused the owners of the Pantheon of seeking unfairly to undermine their competitor, Teresa Cornelys, by announcing a masqued ball for the 19th of the month, when she was due to hold one at Carlisle House.

'If you persist in having your ball on the same day with hers, it must indisputably be with the most unmanly design of overwhelming a female with ruin — overwhelming too, not a little ungratefully, the very person to whom, as proprietors of the Pantheon, you owe even your present being. Had her yet unequalled talents in elegant entertainment never appeared in this kingdom, ye, in your proprietary capacity, had never been known.'[5]

15th February, Thursday Fine bright morning, wet afternoon

The Runaway, a new comedy and the first play by Hannah Cowley, was performed at Drury Lane Theatre. According to the *Morning Post,* 'Never was a piece received with more universal applause,' but the *London Magazine* was not impressed by Mrs Siddons in the part of the heroine, Emily Morley: 'If a certain appearance of stupidity and want of animation be a sure token of love in a female Quixote, Mrs Siddons acquitted herself very well'. An epilogue by Mr Garrick, which aimed its satire principally at the modern fashion of dressing the ladies heads, was well spoken by Miss Younge.[1]

The greatest number of the nobility seen together for many years attended a benefit for decayed musicians at the King's Theatre in the Haymarket. It was so crowded that benches were set on the stage for near 300 that could not find room in any other part of the house. Messrs. Baumgarten, Cervetto, Florio, Fischer, Lide and La Motte played solos and concertos. Signors Trebbi and Rauzzini, and Signoras Galli and Gabrielli, sung in turns.[2]

16th February, Friday Fine bright day, some trifling rain

Governor Hutchinson wrote in his letter book, into which he transcribed correspondence:

> It is certain that a prodigeous armament is preparing, and will be very soon sailing in one large body after another, until the whole is gone for America ... and under Providence, I think we may found a reasonable hope for a more favourable summer than the last. We Americans are plenty here, and very cheap. Some of us at first coming, are apt to think ourselves of importance, but other people do not think so, and few, if any of us are much consulted, or enquired after.[1]

The *Gazetteer* carried a notice by Teresa Cornelys in which she lamented that the owners of the Pantheon had 'cruelly, not to say illiberally' chosen to hold a masqued ball on the same day as her. While she was 'unequal to the task of combating with so powerful a body', she intended to throw herself 'into the arms of a people, whose characteristic is a detestation of oppression, and an exalted benevolence to the oppressed. I shall boldly persevere in my designs; and I pledge myself, that on Monday next the entertainment shall be such as to merit and deserve the approbation and protection of the nobility, gentry, and public.'[2]

Caricature by C. W. Bampfylde, published 15th February 1776

The scene depicted appears in Christopher Anstey's poem *An Election Ball*, published during the year, in which a father writes to his wife of looking on as their fashionable daughter prepared for a ball:

> What a wonderful sight did I see in her chamber!
> As sure as I live there was Madge in her smock,
> Laying hard at the tail of our old dunghill cock!
> She pluck'd it — and pull'd it — and tore from the stump
> All the feathers that cloath'd his unfortunate rump,
> And away to her toilet her image to view,
> On the wings of Impatience and Rapture she flew ...

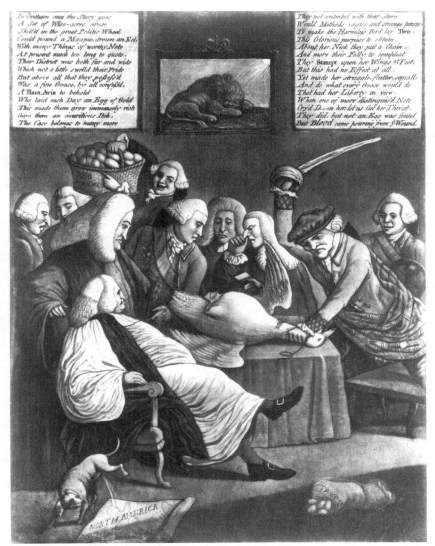

THE WISE MEN *of* GOTHAM *and their* GOOSE-

Another fowl in peril. The verses on the wall relate that the wise-acres of Gotham (government ministers) had a rare goose (the colonies) 'who laid each day an egg of gold' (trade). As a result they grew 'immensely rich' and developed 'an avaritious itch' to have her lay two eggs instead of one (taxes as well). At this the goose struggled for liberty, prompting one of the men to suggest they cut her throat. 'They did, but not an egg was found | But blood came pouring from ye wound.' Former prime minister Lord Bute, still used by satirists to embody government absolutism, wields the sword but the models for the other figures are less certain. Between the verses on the wall the British lion slumbers, while in the foreground a dog urinates on a discarded map of America.

Published by William Humphrey, Gerrard Street, Soho, 16th February 1776.

17th February, Saturday Wind continually shifting. An exceeding wet day
A very full council was held at the Cockpit on American affairs, upwards of eighty
privy councillors being present. The result was immediately laid before his majesty
by Lord North, and in the evening a messenger was dispatched with orders to
the masters general of the ordnance of Ireland, for expediting the provision of all
warlike stores for the troops going to America.[1]

Lord George Germain wrote from Whitehall to Governor Carleton, assuring
him that priority had been given to 'sending as early as possible a relief to the
town of Quebeck, in case you should have been able, with the small garrison you
had collected together, to maintain possession of it during the winter; such relief
to be followed by a body of troops sufficient to retake the town in case it should
have fallen into the hands of the rebels'. He hoped that a larger additional force
would have embarked by 20th March, to consist of eight regiments, 'together with
four companies of artillery, and a large battering train; the whole to be under the
command of Major General Burgoyne, who, together with Major General Lord
Cornwallis, is appointed by the king to serve under you on the side of Canada'.[2]

The first volume of Edward Gibbon's *History of the Decline and Fall of the
Roman Empire* was published, 'elegantly printed in quarto, price one guinea, in
boards'. The author recalled its appearance in his autobiography:

> The volume of my history ... was now ready for the press. After the perilous
> adventure had been declined by my timid friend Mr Elmsley, I agreed, on very
> easy terms, with Mr Thomas Cadell, a respectable bookseller, and Mr William
> Strahan, an eminent printer; and they undertook the care and risk of the
> publication, which derived more credit from the name of the shop than from
> that of the author. ... So moderate were our hopes, that the original impression
> had been stinted to five hundred, till the number was doubled by the prophetic
> taste of Mr Strahan. During this awful interval I was neither elated by the
> ambition of fame, nor depressed by the apprehension of contempt. My diligence
> and accuracy were attested by my own conscience. History is the most popular
> species of writing, since it can adapt itself to the highest or the lowest capacity.
> I had chosen an illustrious subject; Rome is familiar to the schoolboy and the
> statesman, and my narrative was deduced from the last period of Classical
> reading. I had likewise flattered myself that an age of light and liberty would
> receive, without scandal, an enquiry into the human causes of the progress
> and establishment of Christianity.
>
> I am at a loss how to describe the success of the work without betraying
> the vanity of the writer. The first impression was exhausted in a few days; a
> second and third edition were scarcely adequate to the demand, and the book-
> seller's property was twice invaded by the pyrates of Dublin. My book was on
> every table, and almost on every toilette; the historian was crowned by the
> taste or fashion of the day; nor was the general voice disturbed by the barking
> of any profane critic.[3]

The reviews were indeed full of praise, with some noting the subject's relevance to contemporary affairs, but Gibbon's treatment of the rise of Christianity caused misgivings.

> His plan is very extensive, and his views of the Roman history more comprehensive and accurate than any historian who has preceded him. His style also is manly, perspicuous, and in a degree elegant. His observations are judicious, and seem strongly pointed to the decline and fall of the British, as well as Roman, Empire. The same causes which brought on the ruin of the last, are too visible in the other, corruption, luxury, ambition, and standing armies. (*London Magazine*)[4]

Gibbon
after a portrait by Reynolds, *circa* 1779

> As far indeed as the narrative extends, we can impartially bestow a panegyric. Sorry we are to add, that the two last chapters cast a shade over the work ... In these the author professes to make 'a candid, but rational enquiry into the progress and establishment of Christianity' ... And here, notwithstanding the art with which it is infused, the venom of our author's tenets is too apparent ... Detesting its principles as much as we admire its style, we shall waive entering into farther particulars, or extracting the poison here diluted, satisfied with having warned our readers of the main design, and too fashionable principles of this too fashionable work, whose danger is enhanced by its ingenuity ... (*Gentleman's Magazine*)[5]

18th February, Sunday A black, wet, churlish day
Died during the service in Lambeth Church, Mr Robert Chinery, wharfinger and importer of juniper berries.[1]

19th February, Monday A heavy wet morning, bright afternoon
In the morning a young lady, about 15 years of age, daughter to a gentleman of fortune near Limehouse, jumped out of her room window, two stories high, into a paved yard, and was killed on the spot. She had been disordered in her senses, owing to a contusion she received in her head by a fall from her horse a few days since.[1]

The tide was so high that the water was near two feet deep in Westminster Hall, and all the persons attending the Court of King's Bench were obliged to go in and out by the House of Commons.[2]

Lord Weymouth, secretary of state, received a letter dated 14th February and marked 'Most secret' from Lord Stormont, ambassador in Paris:

Tho' I am persuaded, my lord, that France does, and must see our difficulties with that secret pleasure, with which it is natural to behold a rival's distress, and tho' I believe it highly probable, that she does, and will contrive to give the Americans such secret assistance, as may tend to feed the rebellion, and waste our strength by a long and difficult war; yet I must say, my lord, that I do not think it likely, that the present French ministry will take a bold, and open part against us. I rest this opinion chiefly upon M. de Maurepas' want of enterprize, and love of ease ...*[3]

In the evening the world of masqueraders united to shew that they thought Mrs Cornelys merited their protection, for there were perhaps upward of 1,200 persons at Carlisle House, many more than at the rival entertainment at the Pantheon. The Carlisle House masquerade was universally allowed the best that has been given there, which some ascribed to a spirit of opposition calling forth all the powers of Mrs Cornelys.

A band of music was placed in each apartment, and tea, lemonade, iced creams, and orgeat were plentifully distributed. Among those present were the Duke and Duchess of Devonshire, Lord and Lady Spencer, and Lord and Lady Grosvenor, in different parties as may be supposed. Many gentlemen assumed characters in female habits and so got in by pairs for a single ticket, it having been advertised that a ticket admitted one gentleman or two ladies.

The *Gazetteer* said it had been 'confidently assured that the celebrated Mrs Rudd' would be present but it was 'not at liberty' to mention the character she would appear in. Among those who certainly did appear were Lady Betty Stanley as Reuben's Wife; the Hon. Mrs Fitzroy, half an officer and half a parson; Captain Roper, a female preaching Quaker; two Laplanders, accoutred with their snow shoes and fuzees; a Harlequin, who broke his shins in endeavouring to shew his agility; a Chinese, who sacrificed liberally to Bacchus; an American Rifle-man; a pretty Oyster-wench; and two tattered Beggar Girls, who being asked in what character they appeared, ingenuously answered, 'they had no character'. The fun arose chiefly from these low characters who quarrelled, scolded, wept, fought, and rioted in the true spirit of Billingsgate. A black livery servant and his fond wife, in the character of a strapping Cook, afforded much diversion with a mock minuet which did credit to their dancing. Also to be seen were Running Footmen, Pilgrims, Witches, Turks, Persians, and Nosegay Girls in plenty. The beautiful Madam Lambert appeared in an elegant slave dress, which added greatly to her natural charms.

About one o'clock trumpets and kettle-drums announced the opening of the supper rooms, to which the company were preceded by Bayes's new-raised regiment of cavalry, who came prancing and galloping through the passages and round the rooms, affording no small surprize and laughter. There was mirth and good humour at supper, particularly at the table where the beautiful Mrs Dawson, pretty Mrs

* Jean Frédéric, Comte de Maurepas, was the French first minister.

Kennedy, and Mr Mahon sung catches and glees. Claret, burgundy and champaign flowed in abundance till six in the morning, at which time the pyramids of ice, which had been expected to dissolve from the heat of the room and the company, were seen still to stand erect.

Numberless *filles de joie* from every part of the town attended in the course of business, and doubtless found their return. The rival nunneries of King's Place gave up their *treasures*, which caused no small contention between the parties.

The masks had not all left the house at nine o'clock in the morning, and even then it was evident they retired with regret.[4]

MC 'So anxious are the ministry to disappoint Mr Wilkes in the chamberlainship of London, and so sedulous to make Mr Hopkins head of the City treasury, that they have strained every nerve in favour of the latter and not only employed all their usual agents, but have even insisted upon their pickled cabbage and sour crout merchants using their utmost endeavours to serve the favourite candidate, under the penalty of not being honoured with future contracts during the American war; nay, they have even engaged his majesty's chimney-sweeper to use his interest with his black-faced gentry of the brush and shovel in the City to poll in his favour.'[5]

20th February, Shrove Tuesday A heavy wet morning, bright afternoon
There was perhaps the most numerous appearance of liverymen in Guildhall ever known, estimated at full 4,000, for the election of a chamberlain. About one o'clock the lord mayor, attended by the two candidates, Mr Wilkes and Mr Hopkins, the two sheriffs, &c. ascended the hustings. After the common cryer had opened the business the candidates were put up. The shew of hands appearing to be in favour of Mr Wilkes, the sheriffs declared him elected. A poll was immediately demanded, and voting continued until the 27th of the month [>].[1]

The lobby and all the avenues leading to the House of Commons were extremely crowded, in expectation of admission into the gallery during the debate on a motion by Mr Fox relative to America; but before the House proceeded to public business, the Speaker gave orders to have the gallery door locked, and the key laid on the table. The only exceptions made were in favour of members of the other House, a few Irish members* and about thirty ladies, most of whom sat out the whole evening, and a good part of the succeeding morning.

At half after three Mr Fox rose. He spoke with much warmth and great abilities for upwards of an hour, giving a full and pointed recapitulation of the errors of administration. He concluded by moving, 'That it be referred to a committee to enquire into the causes of the ill success of his majesty's arms in North America; as also into the causes of the defection of the people in the province of Quebec.'

* Ireland had its own Commons and Lords which sat in Dublin.

Lord North, Lord Howe, General Burgoyne, and Mr Burke spoke in the debate which lasted till half after two in the morning. At 3 a.m. Lord North wrote from Downing Street to inform the king that Fox's motion had been rejected by a considerable majority, ayes 104, noes 240.[2]

MP 'The anti-nabob party in the House of Commons have given great offence to the lawyers in voting Mess. Sykes and Rumbold guilty of subornation of perjury — a crime equal in magnitude and punishment to perjury itself. ... | The country gentlemen in the House of Commons have so great enmity towards the nabobs, that they want to have a thorough *roast* of them. Indeed, there is no great wonder that this spirit should have arisen. These Indian overgrown fortunes have purchased out many old families, with circumstances of great ostentation, and then overpowered and trampled upon all the natural interest around them; exhibiting at the same time, in their own persons, so much illiterate ignorance and illiberal manners, that the meanness of their origin can never be doubted. There are exceptions to this rule, but not many.'[3]

21st February, Ash Wednesday Fair morning, very wet afternoon
The Comte de Guines, French ambassador, took leave of his majesty. M. Garnier has been appointed chargé d'affaires till another ambassador arrives.

Ostensibly recalled for incompetence, de Guines had fallen victim to a factional struggle at Versailles. He was favoured by Marie Antoinette, and his fall was engineered by her political adversaries, including the Comte de Vergennes. His position had not been helped by rivalry from Beaumarchais, who, in a memoir to Louis XVI, had criticised him for indolence and for providing only trivial intelligence about the American crisis.[1]

22nd February, Thursday Coarse day, some heavy rains. Stormy
A letter from General Howe, dated 23rd January at Boston, arrived with welcome news:

> By intelligence received this morning from the enemy's quarters, I learn that about the 1st of this month the rebels, headed by Mr Montgomery, made an assault upon Quebeck, and that they entered the town, but were repulsed with considerable loss by their own acknowledgment. Mr Montgomery, with many other officers, and seventy men, were killed; Colonel Arnold and three hundred wounded and taken prisoners.

The letter was addressed to Lord Dartmouth, replaced as American secretary by Germain on 10th November, indicating the slowness with which that news had reached Boston.[1]

In the morning Edward Oxnard went to Guildhall to witness the polling for chamberlain. 'When a party appeard in favor of Mr Wilkes the mob were very noisy with shewing their approbation, but a party in favor of Mr Hopkins would disconcert them much and produce groaning, hissing, and every mark of disrespect

The NEW FASHIONED PHAETON.
Sic Itur ad Astra.
London *Printed for* R. Sayer & J. Bennett. *N.º 53 Fleet Street, as the Act directs, 22.ᵈ Feb.ʸ 1776.*

Published by Sayer and Bennett, 53 Fleet Street, 22nd February 1776. On the same day Mrs Delany wrote from St James's Place to her daughter in Derbyshire: 'The ladies head-dresses *grow daily*, and seem like the Tower of Babel to mean to reach the skies!' She added: 'I hope Miss Madge in the *Election Ball* has made you laugh.'

they could shew.' Later he dined at the Crown and Anchor in the Strand with twenty fellow refugees belonging to the New England Club and heard the news from Quebec.[2]

23rd February, Friday Fair morning, wet afternoon
In Westminster Hall workmen began to erect the scaffolding for the trial of the Duchess of Kingston.[1]

At St Paul's Church, Covent Garden, Sarah Goff, 'a negro aged about 14 years', was baptised.[2]

At 6.30 p.m. the Lent oratorios under the direction of Mr Stanley and Mr Linley senior commenced at Drury Lane Theatre with *Acis and Galatea*, by command of their majesties, the music by Handel. The principal vocal performers included the two younger Linley daughters, Mary and Maria, and Miss Draper (Mr Stanley's pupil from the Foundling Hospital, who sung last season). The king was dressed in purple and the queen in a black sack with white ribbons. Edward Oxnard was among the audience. Next day's *Morning Post* praised the Linley sisters, aged 18 and 12: 'Miss Linley must please that part of the musical world, who prefer the natural exertions of a melodious voice, to the affected and laborious transitions, which too often captivate the *cognoscenti*. ... The youngest sister, a child in a frock, has a very fine pipe; the little creature seemed much alarmed in her first song, yet she ran through some very difficult and capital divisions, which were universally admired.' Their brother Thomas, aged 19, led the instrumental band 'very steadily and masterly; he has got however an extraordinary wriggle in his head, since his last exhibition in town, which the public could readily dispense with.'[3]

24th February, Saturday A very wet day
In the morning the Comte de Guines set out from his house at Whitehall with a very grand retinue on his return to France.[1]

A young leopardess, of a very singular and beautiful colour, lately brought from Africa, was carried through the city on a sledge to the Queen's Palace, and put in the house where the curious beasts are lodged.[2]

MP 'A few days since the daughter of a gentleman of very considerable fortune eloped from her father's house with a black servant that lived in the family; her unhappy parent is inconsolable, as his unfortunate child is within a few weeks of being at age, at which time she is intitled to an independent fortune. Every enquiry has been made to discover the place of their retreat, but without effect; it is thought that as soon as the daughter is of age, she will marry her Ethiopian lover.'[3]

MJ 'The inhabitants of the apartments in Somerset House have received notice to quit at Lady Day next, immediately after which that antient fabric is to be pulled down, and the following offices to be built on the scite of it, viz. Stamp, Victualling, Navy, Pay, Salt, Coach, and Hawkers and Pedlars. ... Sir William Chambers is the architect.'[4]

The three younger Linleys who performed at Drury Lane on the 23rd.

RIGHT Thomas, after a portrait by Gainsborough, *circa* 1772.

BELOW Mary, from Gainsborough's portrait of her and her elder sister Elizabeth, *circa* 1772.

RIGHT Maria, after a portrait by Richard Westall.

All three died relatively young: Thomas in a boating accident in 1778, aged 22; Mary from tuberculosis in 1787, aged 29; and Maria of a fever in 1784, at the age of 20 or 21.

25th February, Sunday Bright morning, cloudy afternoon, with some rain
In the morning a young lady near Queen Square was found hanging in her garter
at the foot of her bed; by some letters found in her pocket, it is supposed it was
for the love of a young man lately set out a volunteer for America.[1]

On or about this day Beaumarchais wrote a long and impassioned letter to
Louis XVI. He then probably took it to Paris himself. On 29th February it was
submitted under a loose seal to Vergennes, who shortly presented it to the king.

> Sire, The famous quarrel between America and England, which will soon
> divide the world and change the system of Europe, imposes upon each power
> the necessity of considering carefully how the outcome of this separation will
> affect it, for good or ill. But the most interested of all is certainly France, whose
> sugar islands have been, since the last peace, a constant object of regret and
> hope to the English ...
>
> Today, when a violent crisis is advancing upon us with great strides, I am
> obliged to warn your majesty that the conservation of our American possessions,
> and the peace which France seems to desire so much, depend solely upon this
> single proposition: It is necessary to aid the Americans. It is this that I am
> going to demonstrate.
>
> The King of England, the ministers, the parliament, the opposition, the
> nation, the English people, the parties which tear this state to pieces, all agree
> that they can no longer flatter themselves that the Americans can be brought
> back into the fold, even if the great efforts being made today for their subjection
> should succeed. ...
>
> Besides, Mr L.* (M. de Vergennes will tell your majesty his name), secret
> agent of the colonies in London, absolutely discouraged by the uselessness of
> the efforts he has made through me to obtain from the French ministry the
> aid of powder and munitions, said to me today: 'For the last time, is France
> absolutely decided to refuse us all assistance and to become the victim of England
> and the laughing stock of Europe by this incredible inaction?' Obliged myself
> to give a definite reply, I await your final response in order to give mine. 'We
> offer to France, for the price of secret assistance, a secret treaty of commerce
> which will bring to her, for a certain number of years after the peace, all the
> benefits with which we have for the last century enriched England, plus a
> guarantee of her possessions dependent on our strength. Do you not want
> that? ...
>
> 'Go, monsieur, go to France, set before them this picture of affairs. I am
> going to shut myself up in the country until your return so as not to be forced
> to give a reply without having received yours. Tell your ministers that I am
> ready to follow you there, if necessary, to confirm these declarations. Tell them
> that I hear the Congress has sent two agents to the Court of Madrid for the
> same purpose, and I can assure you they will have received a very satisfactory
> response. Will the council of France today exercise the glorious prerogative
> of alone being blind to the glory of the king and the interests of his kingdom?'

* Arthur Lee.

Beaumarchais added that it was important if possible 'to send Lord Stormont back to London, as, through his connections in France, he is in a position to inform, and does daily inform, England of all that is said and proposed in your majesty's council'.[2]

Beaumarchais seems also to have been involved at this time in a late, half-hearted attempt to resolve the impasse with the Chevalier d'Éon. According to d'Éon, on 20th February Beaumarchais had a mutual friend, a rich banker called Duval, write to ask him to come to London for a final meeting in the neutral setting of Duval's house. Once d'Éon arrived, however, Beaumarchais put the meeting off, and a few days later d'Éon was told that he had gone to Paris at short notice 'on a matter of the greatest importance' — perhaps to carry the letter quoted above.[3]

Lord Stormont
by James Sayers, 1784

In the evening the body of Mr Charteris, who kept the livery stables in Wardour Street, Soho, and had been missing a considerable time, was taken out of the Serpentine river in Hyde Park, supposed to have been robbed and murdered, his head being terribly beat and mangled. He was found by a gentleman who saw his hat in the water, and sent his Newfoundland dog to fetch it. The dog fetched the hat, and then went in again and dived to the bottom, from whence he brought up a wig. It is supposed that he moved the body in fastening upon the wig, as it immediately floated to the surface. Some money was found in the dead man's pockets, and silver buckles in his shoes. The body was carried to the George in Upper Grosvenor Street for the coroner's inquest to sit on it. This it did on Wednesday evening, 28th February, the verdict accidental death.[4]

26th February, Monday Bright and cloudy at intervals, some heavy showers Governor Hutchinson walked from his lodgings in St James's Street to Guildhall, which he entered at the same time as 'Wilkes's mob, who ... were as great blackguards as can well be conceived, and seemed ripe for a riot. ... Never was so near Wilkes, to have so full a view since I have been in England.' Fellow refugee Samuel Curwen was also present. 'Being thoroughly tired with the noise, huzzas and bustle, I made off,' he noted in his diary, 'with my pocket full of libellous and dirty reflections on the candidates ... Returned home drenched in rain at 3 o'clock'.[1]

MP 'So great is the curiosity to hear the trial of the Duchess of Kingston, that tickets are already *done* at five guineas each, and yet they admit but for one day, fresh tickets being ordered to be delivered out every day of the trial.'[2]

27th February, Tuesday Tempestuous night, coarse day, some heavy showers At 10 a.m., when the picquet guard was off duty, twenty-four prisoners escaped from the Savoy by breaking through a back window next the water side and getting over the wall, the tide being down. As they were passing over the craft on the river a soldier bid them stop, but on their refusal he was ordered to fire and did so. The ball passed through the left side of the back of the last deserter, penetrated through the heart, and came out of his body. The wounded man turned round, looked at the man that shot him, and fell down instantly dead. By jumping into the Thames one man was carried down the river by the current and drowned. Fifteen others were apprehended in the course of the day, one of whom had got as far as Kentish Town.[1]

Samuel Curwen returned to Guildhall for the close of the poll for chamberlain. Alderman Hopkins was elected by 2,887 votes to 2,710, 'to the no small mortification of the Wilkites,' Curwen noted, 'who by far in numbers, amongst the lower class, exceeded the friends of the successful candidate'. After the poll a man in King Street was rolled in the kennel by the populace, and beaten so unmercifully that he died as he was carrying to an hospital. After the sheriffs and great part of the livery had left Guildhall, a mob rushed in and, under pretence of attacking those who wore Mr Hopkins's cockades, picked many pockets and committed other violences.[2]

*GA 'Extract of a genuine letter from an officer in the king's army at Boston, to a near relation in London, dated Boston, Jan. 20. ... "*On the 8th inst. between eight and nine o'clock at night, we were alarmed by some of the enemy, who came over a small neck of land by a mill upon Charles-town side, and came into some houses that were not destroyed on the 17th of June,* where they surprised and took one serjeant and three private men prisoners, who belonged to a wooding party, after which they set fire to the houses, and retreated under a heavy fire of cannon and musquetry from one of our redoubts. ... But what is most extraordinary, a new farce was that night to have been acted in Boston, called *The Blockade of Boston*; the play was just ended, and the curtain going to be drawn up for the farce, when the actors heard from without that an attack was made on the heights of Charles-town, upon which one of them came in, dressed in the character of a Yankee Serjeant (which character he was to play), desired silence, and then informed the audience that the alarm guns were fired; that the rebels had attacked the town; and that they were at it tooth and nail over at Charles-town. The audience thinking this was the opening of the new piece, clapped prodigiously; but soon finding their mistake, a general scene of confusion ensued. They immediately hurried out of the house to their alarm posts, some skipping over the orchestra, trampling on the fiddles; and in short, every one making his most speedy retreat, the actors (who were all officers) calling out for water to get the paint and smut from off their faces; women fainting, &c. ... We expect a reinforcement in spring, when I hope we shall give the scoundrels a hearty thrashing, and put an end to the business. Provisions here are amazingly

---

* At the battle of Bunker Hill.

dear; one small cabbage was sold the other day for three shillings, and every thing also in proportion; however, we are all in good spirits, and hope for better times."[3]

28th February, Wednesday Stormy night, strong showers, hail and rainy day
A singular cause was concluded at Doctors' Commons. It was brought by Mrs Kingsman, formerly Dorothea Maunsell, against her husband Mr Tenducci, a celebrated Italian singer, whom she alleged to be a eunuch. The couple had eloped and married in secret in Ireland ten years earlier, when Dorothea was 15 or 16, but had subsequently parted. In 1773 she had married another man, William Kingsman, and in May 1775 had begun the long legal process of establishing the nullity of her first marriage. The facts being proved, the judge pronounced the first marriage 'absolutely null and void' by reason of impotency and condemned Mr Tenducci in costs.[1]

At 9 p.m. the lady mayoress's ball was opened at the Mansion House by the Duke of Manchester and the Duchess of Richmond. The entertainment and decorations were splendid, elegant and costly. Among about 600 persons attending were Lord Shelburne and almost all the minority lords, and many ladies of the first distinction. The dancing continued till one o'clock.[2]

29th February, Thursday Clouds and sunshine at intervals, some showers
There was a full drawing-room at St James's, at which the Indian chief and his companion lately come over were introduced to their majesties by Colonel Johnson and graciously received. They were dressed in the habits of their country and made a splendid and most warlike appearance. They were accompanied to and from their lodgings by Johnson and Captain Tice, who came over from America with them. 'I have had the honour to be introduced to the King of England,' Joseph Brant recalled years later, 'a finer man than whom I think it would be a truly difficult task to find.'[1]

Governor Hutchinson attended a levee given by Lord North, who 'intimated the probability of the troops leaving Boston. I said what I could in behalf of the inhabitants, &c., and of the council's leaving the province, which was like giving up the government. He said it was much the same thing to have no power, or room to exercise the powers of government.'[2]

The House of Commons met at half after two o'clock, and before any other business, Lord North moved that the treaties with the Landgrave of Hesse, the Duke of Brunswick, and the hereditary Prince of Hesse be taken into consideration. He went into the detail of the treaties, and the services to which the foreign troops were destined, and his speech, with the reading of the treaties, took upwards of three hours. Lord George Germain, Colonel Barré, and Mr Burke also spoke. The debate was very languid till after nine o'clock, when Mr Fox put new life into it by a most pointed attack on Lord North, whom he held out in a thousand ridiculous lights. At a quarter after two in the morning Lord North's motion was put, and agreed to by a majority of 242 to 88. The gallery doors were locked all day, and the key was left on the Speaker's table.[3]

Solutions to the sedan chair problem provided in 1772 (above) and
1777 (below) by printmaker Matthew Darly of No. 39 in the Strand

March

1st March, Friday Smart frost in the night, fine bright day

About noon Alderman Hopkins with some sixty supporters came into Guildhall, preceded by a band of music. About one o'clock the sheriffs, with Wilkes, Hopkins, &c. ascended the hustings, and the result of the election for chamberlain was declared. Hopkins was then conducted to his house in Broad Street in a grand procession including constables and the City marshal; aldermen and the grand committee, with blue cockades in their hats; the committee's standard, with the words 'Honesty Rewarded' and 'Hopkins for ever'; the standard of England and the City's arms; and music, consisting of kettle drums, trumpets, French horns, clarinet, and bassoon.[1]

Mrs Harris, wife of James Harris, MP, wrote from Piccadilly to her son, also James, envoy extraordinary at Berlin, saying that many doubted whether the Duchess of Kingston would stay for her trial, 'but true it is that the scaffolding is begun in Westminster Hall, and that she has attended and looked to it more than once; some say she goes daily'.[2]

GA 'By a letter from Edinburgh we are informed, that several sedan chairs have been obliged to be made of a large size, on purpose to accommodate the ladies of fashion in that metropolis, whose heads are arrived at such a magnitude, that the usual chairs could not contain them.'[3]

2nd March, Saturday Heavy black day, but no rain

The Duke of Wirtemburg* arrived in town from Germany with a very grand retinue. It is said he is come over to make a tour of Great Britain. While in London he will stay at the hotel in Suffolk Street.[1]

At 9 p.m. a fire broke out in the warehouse of Messrs. Cox and Bigg, printers, in the Savoy. The journeymen had just left the office and were at a neighbouring public-house, from whence they observed the flames. The fire raged so violently that in a short time the large building, which formed the printing office and the dwelling-houses of the two partners, was consumed, together with a warehouse filled with books belonging to Mr Cadell of the Strand, and several adjoining erections. It was with the utmost difficulty that the two new German chapels were saved. Happily through the vigilance of two captains, and the activity of the Savoy guard, the gunpowder was moved in time to prevent the fire catching it. Several engines played with water, but in particular two that were floating upon the river, which had more effect than all the rest. No lives are said to be lost, though the fire continued till near 4 a.m. Somerset House was in great danger, and several of the remaining inhabitants, especially those in the stable-yard, let the firemen enter and take their furniture from the premises.[2]

* Karl Eugen, Duke of Württemberg, born 1728. His interests included agriculture, travel and mistresses. He fathered around a dozen illegitimate children.

3rd March, Sunday Frosty night, foggy, bright, and cloudy, snowy evening
As soon as they could see in the morning, men were at work painting upwards
of twenty baggage waggons in Portman Square, that they might be got dry to be
shipped on board the transports the ensuing week.[1]

General Burgoyne wrote from Kensington Palace to Lord George Germain
to request that his embarkation for Canada be delayed. The spirits of his ailing
wife, Lady Charlotte, had been weakened by the recent death of her father, the
11th Earl of Derby, and by that of her mother two days later. In addition, that
morning, 'by the mistake of a servant in the delivery of a note', she had received
'suddenly and totally unprepared' the news that a favourite sister, Lady Margaret
Stanley, had also died, and that another sister, Lady Mary, 'would not survive a
week'. Burgoyne judged that if he left for Canada immediately 'these combined
sorrows' would convey his wife 'to the family grave before it is closed'.[2]

4th March, Monday Turbulent night, sunshine and showers at intervals
Early in the morning some thieves attempted to break into Mr Wyat's, silk-dyer,
in Elder Street, Spitalfields, but were overheard by the journeyman, who discharged
a blunderbuss and shot the first man's brains out. The rest made their escape. On
searching the dead man a chisel, tinder-box, and a bunch of picklock keys were
found.[1]

The Indian chief and his companion, with Colonel Johnson, breakfasted with
Lord Townshend at his house in Portman Square, and afterwards visited several
of the nobility.[2]

During February Mrs Abington and the managers of Drury Lane Theatre had
wrangled about which night during the season should be allotted for her benefit,
and, to her vexation, 16th March had been settled upon. She now wrote to Garrick
from Leicester Fields: 'Sir, As it has been for some time my fixed determination
to quit the stage at the conclusion of the present season and not return to it again,
I thankfully accept your very obliging intention to play for my benefit in May;
you will therefore please to dispose of Saturday the 16th inst. in any manner
most agreeable to yourself.' Transcribing the letter, Garrick added: 'The above
is a true copy of the letter, examined word by word, of that worst of bad women
Mrs Abington, to ask my playing for her benefit'.[3]

Above a hundred of the first people of fashion attended the opening of the
Scavoir (old spelling) or Savoir Vivre, a new house lately built on the east side of
St James's Street. According to Hannah More, on this night, 'the very first time the
rooms were ever used, the enormous sum of sixty thousand pounds was lost'. Horace
Walpole wrote disapprovingly of the club and its founder, General Richard Smith:

> This man had from a cheesemonger's son risen to an insolence of wealth by
> plunder in the Indies. His wife was covered with chains of pearls and diamonds,
> and he himself, who had been drawn by Foote, in *The Nabob*, under the character
> of Matthew Mite, was the deepest of all deep gamesters in London. Being

excluded from the fashionable club of young men of quality at Almack's, and wishing to plunder them like the Indies, he and a set of sharpers had formed a plan for a new club, which, by the excess of play, should draw all the young extravagants thither. They built a magnificent house in St James's Street, furnished it gorgeously, and enrolled both the clubs at White's and that of Almack's. The titular master of the house the first night acquainted the richest and most wasteful of the members that they might be furnished in the house with loans of ready money, even as far as forty thousand pounds. This pernicious seminary, erected, in defiance of so many laws, at the very gate of the king's palace, and menacing ruin to their heirs to the most opulent of the legislature, was tolerated by a Court that delighted in seeing the great lords and commoners reduced to a state of beggary and dependence ...[4]

The Savoir Vivre, built in the fashionable Adam style on the site of three 'old and very low houses' at a cost of some £10,000. The architect and builder was John Crunden. Since *circa* 1782 the building has been occupied by Boodle's.

5th March, Tuesday Bright morning and evening, very wet mid-day. Stormy. Full moon

In the morning three boats full of market women and goods, attempting to go through the great arch under London Bridge at the same time, ran foul of each other. In the scuffle two of the boats were overset, and a waterman and two women were drowned.[1]

Edward Oxnard strolled in St James's Park and 'drank some milk from the cow — many poor people keep them here for this purpose'. He then saw the guards relieved 'after performing a few evolutions before the Prince of Wertemburg, who is a man of middling stature, well featured, but remarkably red in the face'.[2]

Dr Johnson wrote to Boswell, who was feeling melancholic in Edinburgh: 'My counsel you may have when you are pleased to require it; but of my company you cannot in the next month have much, for Mr Thrale will take me to Italy, he says, on the first of April. ...

The Duke of Württemberg,
on a coin of 1776

Fix your thoughts upon your business, fill your intervals with company, and sunshine will again break in upon your mind. If you will come to me, you must come very quickly'.[3]

In the House of Lords the Duke of Richmond moved that a humble address be presented to the king, praying that he would countermand the march of the troops of Hesse, Hanau, and Brunswick, and give directions for an immediate suspension of hostilities in America, in order to lay a foundation for a permanent reconciliation between the contending parts of this distracted empire. He said he hoped the brave Lord Howe was not sent to America for the dishonourable and barbarous purpose of burning their towns, in reply to which Lord Talbot, with a *sang froid* that disgusted all that heard him, said their docks and towns *ought* to be burnt. After a long debate the motion was defeated by 100 to 32.[4]

In the evening a young watch movement maker, who lived in a court near Moorfields, and lately had 100l. left him by a relation, lost the whole at cards at a public-house in Westminster. Next morning, Wednesday, he went home to his lodgings and hanged himself.[5]

MJ 'It is calculated that the ensuing campaign against the American colonies will cost Great Britain at least four millions sterling. | A further tax upon windows is talked of, and also a tax upon dogs, horses, and carriages.'[6]

6th March, Wednesday Exceeding wet, black, cold, churlish day

A complaint was exhibited at the public office, Bow Street, against John Cooper, driver of hackney coach No. 96. Hannah Willis, of Shenfield, Berks, arrived in town on the evening of 28th February, to go to a service in Great Marybone Street. She called a coach at the White Horse Cellar, Piccadilly, but after the coachman had driven her to a considerable distance, he got down, said he could not find the house, got into the coach, and behaved rudely to her. She cried out, and some person coming up, she insisted on being driven back to the White Horse Cellar, where she paid the coachman 2s. 6d. in the presence of Mr Hatchet the landlord. Mr Hatchet swore to the number of the coach, but could not recollect the driver's person, neither could the girl. For the defence, George Mearson, servant to Mrs Raper, of Norfolk Street, swore that the prisoner took up his lady at No. 10 in the Poultry and drove her home about the hour of the supposed violence. John Batton, who attends the coach stand at the end of King Street, Cheapside, swore to Cooper's being there that evening. On the whole it seemed that some person, in wanton wickedness, had put another number 96 on a coach, and been guilty of a fault for which Cooper was likely to have suffered. He was discharged.[1]

As the soprano Signora Gabrielli was drinking coffee with several persons of quality, at her house in Golden Square, she received two notes. One was from the porter's wife at the opera house, informing her that her husband was suddenly taken ill, and could not attend at the door this evening. The other was from Signor Celestino, first fiddler at the opera house, in which he let her know that he would not lead the band for her benefit, because she had affronted him by saying there was no more comparison between Celestino and Giardini than between a frog and an elephant.* The company laughed heartily, but Signora Gabrielli with the greatest composure drew out her purse, and sent five guineas to the porter, then gave the other note to her lap-dog, which tore it to pieces.[2]

Captain Cook sent the Admiralty a list of articles required for gifts to natives, either to gain their friendship or 'to exchange for refreshments'. It included 3 dozen scissars, 5 dozen old shirts (not patched), 6 dozen long knives, 7 dozen small tooth combs and 32 dozen large ones, 9 dozen glass and metal buttons, 20 dozen looking-glasses with frames, 20 dozen yards of ribband to string medals, 32 dozen fish hooks, 40 kettles or potts, 340 yards of red baize, and 500 hatchets. Beneath the table of these goods Cook added: 'A pair of Fearnought trowsers and a jacket for each man, and four or five good watch-coats to each ship.'[3]

MP 'To shew to what an expence polite education is arrived, the following parts of that of a young lady not an hundred miles from Grosvenor-square is laid before the public: Dancing five guineas entrance, and half a guinea a lesson. Music six guineas entrance, and half a guinea a lesson. Drawing five guineas entrance,

---

* Eligio Celestino (1739-1812) and Felice Giardini (1716-1796) were both celebrated violinists. The latter was leader and musical director at the opera house.

and half a guinea a lesson. Italian three guineas entrance, and a quarter of a guinea a lesson. The same lady is allowed 500 guineas a year for dress; she is only 15, and means to be sure to marry a duke.'[4]

7th March, Thursday Heavy black day, with much rain
Garrick, rightly doubtful as to whether Mrs Abington intended to leave the stage, sent a reply 'by Ralph' to her letter of 4th March:

> Madam, At my return from the country, I found your letter upon my table. I read it with great surprise, and can yet scarce believe that you are in earnest. It would perhaps be as vain as impertinent in me to caution you against being too rash in determining upon so serious a matter. My reasons for quitting the stage are many, and too strong to be withstood; you can have none but will be easily conquered by your inclination. It will therefore be worth your while to consider seriously; and if you have the least reason to repent of your late determination, the best night for a benefit, which is the last night of acting before the holidays, and which the proprietors have purchased, is at your service. If you are still absolutely resolved to quit the stage for ever, I will certainly, in May, do for Mrs Abington what I have done for others who have made the same resolution.[1]

About one o'clock their majesties went from the Queen's Palace to St James's, where there was a very grand drawing-room, some hundred of the nobility being present on account of her majesty's not appearing any more before her lying-in. The Prince of Wales and the Bishop of Osnaburgh went in separate chairs, the prince dressed in a suit of scarlet, the bishop in light blue. The Duke of Wirtemburg, with the lords of his bedchamber and aides de camp, was introduced to her majesty. Two German ladies who came over with the duke were introduced by Lady North and graciously received.[2]

Nearby in St James's Street Governor Hutchinson had visitors: 'Mr Clarke and Auchmuty called on me, and were anxious to do something to shew the sense of the Americans in London, of the removal of the troops from Boston, and particularly the difficulties to which the inhabitants would be exposed.' Hutchinson himself had a brother and a son there. 'I went to Lord Suffolk, and let him know how uneasy we were. He gave me more encouragement than I have had before, that they would not be removed. His lordship told me at the same time, that he had said to the king that I proposed desiring an audience, to represent to him my losses in New England, and the distresses of my family, but was unwilling to give him the trouble. The king answered, "I hope the time of retribution is not far off."'[3]

Also on this day Suffolk wrote from Duke Street, Westminster, to Lord George Germain, who was threatening to resign in a dispute over the instructions to be given to the Howe brothers as the king's commissioners in America. Germain wanted the instructions to require a declaration of submission from the rebels, but Lord North had proposed alterations to soften the demands. Suffolk advised Germain not to make 'any hasty resolution' and balanced support with a call for pragmatism:

If Lord North can ever insist upon anything derogatory to the authority of parliament, I shall be against him. If he can mean to make a *paix plâtrée*,* I shall be against him. If to get out of the war at any rate can be his object, he will find a very different intention mine; but if the substance of what we are contending for is obtained, if submission is shown by the laying down of arms, the dissolution of congresses, and the restoration of legal government, and Lord North should deem this a virtual acknowledgment of their disobedience and our pretensions, may it not deserve your lordship's full and fair consideration whether it is worth opiniatring† the declaration he objects to?

In the evening another colleague, solicitor general Alexander Wedderburn, also wrote in support to Germain: 'To end the war without finishing the dispute is much worse than to have given up the point without a struggle.'[4]

Captain Cook was admitted a member of the Royal Society, having been elected unanimously on 29th February, and in the evening a paper he had written at Mile End on 5th March was read. Addressed to the society's president, Sir John Pringle, it discussed the method taken for preserving the health of the crew of the *Resolution* during her late voyage round the world.[5]

8th March, Friday A bright day, with some smart showers

Omai visited Granville Sharp for three hours. This was the longest of their meetings, according to Sharp's notes, and was perhaps the occasion of a conversation which Sharp recalled in a speech many years later:

> When sitting with him at table one day after dinner, I thought it a good opportunity to explain to him the Ten Commandments. I proceeded with tolerable success in reciting the first six commandments. He had nothing to object against any of them, though many explications were required before he understood all the terms; and he freely nodded his assent. But when I recited the seventh commandment, 'Thou shalt not commit adultery,' he said, 'Adultery! what that? what that?'
>
> 'Not to commit adultery,' I said, 'is that, if a man has got one wife, he must not take another wife, or any other woman.' 'Ohh!' says he, 'two wives very good, three wives very, very good.' 'No, Mr Omai,' I said, 'not so; that would be contrary to the first principle of the law of nature.' 'First principle of the law of nature,' said he, 'what that? what that?' 'The first principle of the law of nature,' I said, 'is, that no man must do to another person any thing that he would not like to be done to himself. And, for example, Mr Omai,' said I, 'suppose you have got a wife that you love very much; you would not like that another man should come to love your wife.' This raised his indignation: he put on a furious countenance, and a threatening posture, signifying that he would kill any man that should meddle with his wife. 'Well, Mr Omai,' said I, 'suppose, then, that your wife loves you very much; she would not like that you should love another

---

* 'Plastered peace', unlikely to endure.
† *Opiniatre*, to maintain or insist on obstinately.

woman; for the women have the same passions, and feelings, and love toward the men, that we have toward the women; and we ought, therefore, to regulate our behaviour toward them by our own feelings of what we should like and expect of faithful love and duty from them toward ourselves.'

This new state of the case produced a deep consideration and silence, for some time, on the part of Mr Omai. But he soon afterwards gave me ample proof that he thoroughly comprehended ... the proper conduct and behaviour which we owe to other persons. There was an ink-stand on the table, with several pens in it. He took one pen, and laid it on the table, saying, 'There lies Lord S——' (a nobleman with whom he was well acquainted, and in whose family he had spent some time); and then he took another pen, and laid it close by the side of the former pen, saying, 'and there lies Miss W——'* (who was an accomplished young woman in many respects, but, unhappily for herself, she lived in a state of adultery with that nobleman); and he then took a third pen, and placing it on the table at a considerable distance from the other two pens, as far as his right arm could extend, and at the same time leaning his head upon his left hand, supported by his elbow on the table, in a pensive posture, he said, 'and there lie Lady S——, and cry!'[1]

Leaving the Adelphi for his country villa, Garrick scrawled a hurried note to Edward Gibbon:

Whenever I am truly pleased I must communicate my joy. Lord Camden called upon me this morning and ... declared that he never read a more admirable performance than Mr Gibbon's History. He was in transport, and so was I. The author is the only man to write History of the Age — such depth — such perspicuity — such language, force, variety, and what not! I am so delighted with him, continues he, that I must write to thank him — I should be happy to know him. My lord, I have that honour, and will contrive, if possible, to bring you together. Said I too much? My coach is at the door — my wife bawling for me, and every thing impatient — so hey for Hampton till Monday ...[2]

During a debate in the House of Commons on the extraordinary expenses of the army, Colonel Barré proposed that copies of the requisitions by the commander-in-chief in North America, on which sums had been advanced, be laid before the House. Lord North said that whatever could be provided would be, but that as yet no account could be given for the principal part. He added that in some cases it might be improper to lay the reasons for the demands before the House, as they might concern the future conduct of the campaign. Col. Barré said that perhaps a great sum might be for *secret service*, adding in irony that 100,000l. might be distributed among the Congress. 'If you have such secrets,' said he, 'don't tell them. We must give you credit, that as the known conduct of the war has nothing but absurdity in it, the wisdom of it is in the *secret* management.' The ministry amended his motion for papers by adding the words *such as can be made up*, and then it passed.[3]

---

* The references are of course to Lord Sandwich and Martha Ray, or Wray.

AN

INQUIRY

INTO THE

Nature and Caufes

OF THE

WEALTH OF NATIONS.

By ADAM SMITH, LL. D. and F. R. S.
Formerly Profeffor of Moral Philofophy in the Univerfity of GLASGOW.

IN TWO VOLUMES.
VOL. I.

LONDON:

PRINTED FOR W. STRAHAN; AND T. CADELL, IN THE STRAND.
MDCCLXXVI.

LEFT Isaac Barré, after a portrait by Hugh Douglas Hamilton.
RIGHT Title page of *The Wealth of Nations*.

9th March, Saturday Bright at times, but a great deal of rain

An Inquiry into the Nature and Causes of the Wealth of Nations by Adam Smith was published, 'elegantly printed in two volumes, quarto, price 1l. 16s., in boards'. Smith had spent most of the preceding three years in London, where it is thought much of the final version was written, his base being the British Coffee-house in Cockspur Street. There were few reviews but the book sold better than publisher William Strahan had expected and the print run, unknown but thought to have been 500, was exhausted in six months.

According to Smith, a nation's wealth consisted 'not in the unconsumable riches of money' but in 'the annual produce of the land and labour of the whole country'. This produce would be greatest where trade was unfettered and individuals were left to act in their own self-interest. 'Every individual necessarily labours to render the annual revenue of the society as great as he can. He generally, indeed, neither intends to promote the publick interest, nor knows how much he is promoting it. ... He intends only his own gain, and he is in this, as in many other cases, led by an invisible hand to promote an end which was no part of his intention.'[1]

Attempts to protect or direct trade by means of monopolies, tariffs, and subsidies made economies less efficient. 'Every derangement of the natural distribution of stock [i.e. capital] is necessarily hurtful to the society in which it takes place; whether it be by repelling from a particular trade the stock which would otherwise go to it, or by attracting towards a particular trade that which would not otherwise come to it.' It was in the public interest that trades should be open to free competition.

'People of the same trade seldom meet together, even for merriment and diversion, but the conversation ends in a conspiracy against the publick, or in some contrivance to raise prices.' Nations, meanwhile, were mistaken if they believed 'that their interest consisted in beggaring all their neighbours' by seeking to disadvantage their trade. On the contrary, 'A nation that would enrich itself by foreign trade is certainly most likely to do so when its neighbours are all rich, industrious, and commercial nations.'[2]

He traced much of the recent increase in Europe's wealth to two factors. The first was increased efficiency and trade arising from the division of labour. An unwelcome consequence was that simple, repetitive tasks would tend to make those engaged in them 'as stupid and ignorant as it is possible for a human creature to become' unless education provided mental variety and stimulation. Another consequence was that adult humans, unlike other animals, became more or less incapable of existing independently. Barter and exchange of goods and services became essential, rooted in every case in self-interest. 'It is not from the benevolence of the butcher, the brewer, or the baker, that we expect our dinner, but from their regard to their own interest. We address ourselves not to their humanity but to their self-love'.[3]

The second, related factor contributing to modern wealth was the emergence of a global market. 'The discovery of America, and that of a passage to the East Indies by the Cape of Good Hope, are the two greatest and most important events recorded in the history of mankind. ... By uniting, in some measure, the most distant parts of the world, by enabling them to relieve one another's wants, to increase one another's enjoyments, and to encourage one another's industry, their general tendency would seem to be beneficial.' Unfortunately the full potential benefits were not being enjoyed because of monopolies such as that granted to the East India Company.[4]

He also considered at length the pressing matter of Britain's relations with America. While Britain had been more liberal in its approach to its colonies than other European nations, and as a result had seen them flourish in comparison, it nonetheless reserved to itself 'the more advanced or more refined manufactures' and the 'exclusive privilege of supplying the colonies with all the goods which they wanted from Europe'. The maintenance of this monopoly had hitherto been 'the sole end and purpose' of Britain's dominion over her colonies and 'the principal badge of their dependency'. The vast cost of the wars Britain had fought against Spain and France in the last forty years to protect the colonies had been 'in reality, a bounty which has been given in order to support a monopoly. The pretended purpose of it was to encourage the manufactures, and to encrease the commerce of Great Britain. But its real effect has been to raise the rate of mercantile profit, and to enable our merchants to turn into a branch of trade, of which the returns are more slow and distant than those of the greater part of other trades, a greater proportion of their capital than they otherwise would have done'.

Not only was this way of running an empire economically inefficient, it led to a damaging level of national debt. Moreover, to prohibit the Americans 'from making all that they can of every part of their own produce, or from employing their stock and industry in the way that they judge the most advantageous to themselves, is a manifest violation of the most sacred rights of mankind'. As yet the restrictions had not proved very damaging, but 'in a more advanced state they might be really oppressive and insupportable'.[5]

It would therefore be sensible for Britain to 'give up all authority over her colonies'. She would be immediately freed of the expense of protecting them, and 'might settle with them such a treaty of commerce as would effectually secure to her a free trade, more advantageous to the great body of the people, though less so to the merchants, than the monopoly which she at present enjoys. By thus parting good friends, the natural affection of the colonies to the mother country ... would

The Author of the Wealth of Nations

quickly revive.' However, such a measure 'never was, and never will be adopted, by any nation in the world', because while it was in Britain's interest it would be 'mortifying to the pride'.[6]

If on the other hand Britain should act upon her claimed right to tax the colonies without the consent of their assemblies, there would be no enduring peace. 'The leading men of America, like those of all other countries, desire to preserve their own importance. They feel, or imagine that if their assemblies, which they are fond of calling parliaments, and of considering as equal in authority to the parliament of Great Britain, should be so far degraded as to become the humble ministers and executive officers of that parliament, the greater part of their own importance would be at an end. They have rejected, therefore, the proposal of being taxed by parliamentary requisition, and like other ambitious and high spirited men, have rather chosen to draw the sword in defence of their own importance.'[7]

To address this problem Smith suggested that 'each colony, which should detach itself from the general confederacy' should be granted a number of representatives in the British parliament in proportion to their contribution 'to the public revenue of the empire'. In this way 'a new method of acquiring importance, a new and more dazzling object of ambition would be presented to the leading men of each colony. Instead of piddling for the little prizes which are to be found in what may be called the paltry raffle of colony faction, they might then hope, from the presumption which men naturally have in their own ability and good fortune, to draw some of the great prizes which sometimes come from the wheel of the great state lottery of British politics.'[8]

He concluded that America was 'a sort of splendid and showy equipage' that Britain could no longer afford:

> The rulers of Great Britain have for more than a century past amused the people with the imagination that they possessed a great empire on the west side of the Atlantic. This empire, however, has hitherto existed in imagination only. It has hitherto been, not an empire, but the project of an empire; not a gold mine, but the project of a gold mine; a project which has cost, which continues to cost, and which if pursued in the same way as it has been hitherto, is likely to cost immense expence, without being likely to bring any profit ... It is surely now time that our rulers should either realize this golden dream ... or ... awake from it themselves, and endeavour to awaken the people. If the project cannot be compleated, it ought to be given up. If any of the provinces of the British empire cannot be made to contribute towards the support of the whole empire, it is surely time that Great Britain should free herself from the expence of defending those provinces ... and endeavour to accommodate her future views and designs to the real mediocrity of her circumstances.[9]

In the morning several thousand beds and blankets were shipped from the Tower for the use of the Hessian troops going to America. Meanwhile the soldiers of one of the regiments of guards assembled in the Birdcage Walk in St James's Park, and drew lots who should be drafted for the American service.[10]

10th March, Sunday Fair day, and in general bright

In the morning the prisoners in the Savoy again attempted to break out and four of them made their escape.[1]

A boat crossing the river from Execution Dock to Princes Stairs overset, being overloaded with passengers, by which accident nine men were drowned.[2]

The anniversary sermon for the Society for the Recovery of Persons Apparently Drowned was preached by the Rev. Dr Dodd at St Andrew's, Holborn, before a large and respectable congregation. He took his text from the first book of Kings, chapter 17, verses 21 and 22: 'And he stretched himself upon the child three times, and cried unto the Lord, and said, *O Lord, my God, I pray thee let this child's soul come into him again.* And the Lord heard the voice of Elijah, and the soul of the child came into him again, and he revived.' He very pathetically related the case of a poor wretch who, borne down by the weight of misfortunes, had lately attempted to drown himself, but had been restored to his wife and children by the means held out by the society. There was scarcely a dry eye in the church and the contribution was a very liberal one, amounting to 45l. 15s. 3d. Twelve of the persons who had been recovered through the means of the society attended, among whom were an elderly man, who had been fifty-five minutes under water, and a fine little boy.[3]

The body of a child, supposed to have been born before its time, was found by some boys in the canal in St James's Park. It was tied up in a handkerchief, together with some iron bed-screws, in order to sink it.[4]

11th March, Monday Slight frost in the night, fine bright day

In the morning 2,000 horses, purchased for the army, passed over Westminster Bridge on their way to Woolwich, where they are to be embarked on transports bound for America.[1]

A number of baggage waggons upon a new construction were drawn from Portman Square to Tower Wharf, also to be shipped for America. They are made to take to pieces, so that each waggon will fill up but little room on board, and are with great ease put together again.[2]

A married soldier of the guards, on whom the lot fell to be draughted for America, expressed his emotions at the thought of leaving a wife and infant family, on which a single man of his corps generously stood forth and offered to go in his room. This was gladly accepted of by the married soldier, who gave the other all the money he had about him.[3]

The House of Commons debated the extraordinary expenses of the land forces in America. Mr Burke drew several comparisons between the records of Mr Pitt and Lord North, and contended that the campaign which gave the great continent of North America to this country, though the force consisted of 40,000 men, fell considerably short of the expence of maintaining 8,000 wretched men, starved, disgraced, and cooped up in the single town of Boston. He paid very high compliments to General Montgomery, who in one campaign had conquered two-thirds of Canada for the Americans. Mr Fox vied with Mr Burke in his eulogium of the general. Lord North censured what he called this unqualified liberality of praises bestowed by the opposition upon a rebel. He admitted that he was brave, he was able, he was humane, he was generous, but he was still a rebel. Mr Fox rose a second time and said the term rebel was no certain mark of disgrace, for that all the great assertors of liberty, the saviours of their country, the benefactors of mankind, in all ages, had been called *rebels*; that they even owed the constitution, which enabled them to sit in that House, to a *rebellion*.[4]

From his house in Arlington Street Horace Walpole sent some gossip to a friend: 'The Duke of Wirtemburg is arrived with a mistress, whom he got made Countess of the Empire. The Queen of France would not receive her: she has been received at Court here; the man who keeps the *hotel garni* in Covent Garden would not lodge her for the reputation of his house.' The woman in question was Franziska von Hohenheim, the duke's official mistress since 1772, who had been made Imperial Countess (of the Holy Roman Empire) in 1774. The reluctant hotel owner was probably David Low of Low's Hotel.[5]

In the evening Governor Hutchinson went with his daughter Peggy 'to the Pantheon, being the first time I had seen it; and though it is thought as magnificent a show as any in Europe, or rather, as grand and elegant a room, yet I have no inclination to go a second time'.[6]

MC 'The landing-place at Somerset Gardens, and that noble piece of architecture, the gateway, done by the celebrated Inigo Jones, was last week entirely demolished. The chief parts thereof now lay under the garden wall to help make good the intended embankment into the Thames'.[7]

MP 'A correspondent assures us that the excess to which pleasure and dissipation are now carried amongst the *ton*, exceeds all bounds, particularly among our women of quality. The Duchess of D—e has almost ruined her constitution by the hurrying life which she has led for some time; her mother Lady S—r has mentioned it with concern to the duke, who only answers "let her alone — she is but a girl." Lady D—y is in the same situation, and full as determined to *keep it up!*'*[8]

12th March, Tuesday Heavy misling day, bright evening

Mrs Stokes, charged with marrying seven husbands, was examined before the lord mayor at Guildhall. Henry Dean, a black man, her first husband, was present and said he had been married to her seventeen years, that he followed the sea for a livelihood, and when he came home was always arrested for debts she had contracted during his absence. A Mrs Stace, who came from Rumford as an evidence, said she was a witness at the defendant's wedding in 1771 to one Coxhall,

* The dashed names are Devonshire, Spencer, and Derby. Lady Derby was the former Lady Betty Stanley, whose husband had succeeded to the earldom in late February.

River front of old Somerset House, showing the gateway and stairs

who died about five months since in a prison, where he was confined for debt. Several others gave evidence that in 1775, six months before the death of another husband in the Westminster Infirmary, the defendant was married at Rumford to one Stokes. She was remanded to Wood Street Compter till she could get bail.

According to a later report, she was subsequently acquitted and released, but was apprehended again on 31st August and returned to Wood Street Compter on a new charge of having married two further men since her enlargement.[1]

Edward Oxnard went to Westminster Hall with a friend 'to see the scaffolding erecting for the tryal of the Dutchess of Kingston'. After dining they went to

Drury Lane Theatre to see *Woman's a Riddle* with Mrs Abington as Miranda. It was performed as a benefit for Thomas King, who played Sir Amorous Vainwit.[2]

The Society for the Recovery of Persons Apparently Drowned held their anniversary dinner at the London Tavern. Among those present were the lord mayor, John Wilkes, Dr Dodd, and about 250 respectable gentlemen. Mr Evans entertained the company on the harp and Mr Griffith played a few tunes on the harpsichord. Many gentlemen joined in catches, glees, and songs, and every person present appeared to participate of the general happiness.[3]

Lady North gave a ball. Among those attending was Mrs Harris, who wrote from Piccadilly to her son in Berlin a few days later: 'One card-table pleased me, which was Lord Suffolk and Lord North playing whist against Sir Grey Cooper and Mr Eden.* Their lordships, as you may guess, were triumphant, just as the archbishop used to be when he played against his chaplains.'[4]

At night four silver pheasants and six gold ones were stolen from Osterley Park near Brentford. Next day the owner Mr Childs offered £20 reward for information that would bring the offender or offenders to justice.[5]

At Salisbury, General Richard Smith (founder of the Savoir Vivre) and Thomas Brand Hollis, who had been elected as MPs for Hindon in Wiltshire at the 1774 general election, were found guilty of notorious bribery. The corruption of the contest had been flagrant even by the standards of the time, expectant electors referring to Smith as 'General Gold'. He and Hollis will appear in Westminster Hall for sentencing on 17th May.[6]

MP 'Nothing has disturbed administration more than Colonel Barré's un-expected motion last Friday on the Boston extraordinaries, when there were some strangers in the gallery. The junto cannot bear to have the world know the real situation of affairs, and therefore lock the gallery whenever they know American affairs to be coming on'.[7]

LC 'The officers who are ordered for America are to wear the same uniform as the common soldiers, and their hair [is] to be dressed in the like manner, so that they may not be distinguished from them by the riflemen, who aim particularly at the officers.'[8]

13th March, Wednesday Heavy day, with some trifling rain

The *Morning Post* carried an advertisement for 'an elegant new-built house, situated on the west side of Harley-street, Cavendish-square, (No. 48) late in the occupation of DANIEL PERREAU, with suitable and convenient offices, double coach-house, and stabling for seven horses behind the same. The premises are exceedingly well finished, and fitted up and ornamented at a great expence ...'[1]

---

* Cooper was a secretary to North at the Treasury and Eden was under secretary to Suffolk in the northern department.

14th March, Thursday A very fine bright day
Mohawk chief Joseph Brant and his companion Oteroughyanento, a warrior, were received by Lord George Germain, to whom Brant delivered a speech: 'Brother Gorah. We have cross'd the great lake and come to this kingdom with our superintendant Col. Johnson from our confederacy the Six Nations and their allies, that we might see our father the Great King'. He went on to complain that in the past, in return for loyal support, the Mohawks had been cheated out of land. 'We hope these things will be considered and that the king or his great men will give such an answer as will make our hearts light and glad before we go, and strengthen our hands'. According to Brant, Germain replied 'in few words', saying he would have 'all those matters settled to our satisfaction whenever the troubles in America were ended', and that he 'hoped the Six Nations would continue to behave with that attachment to the king they had always manifested; in which case they might be sure of his majesty's favour and protection'.[1]

A very full House of Lords being assembled by three o'clock, the Duke of Grafton rose to propose that an address be presented to his majesty, beseeching him to issue a proclamation declaring that if the colonies, within a reasonable time, presented a petition setting forth what they consider their rights and grievances, he would consent to a suspension of arms, and such petition would be considered and answered.

The duke said affairs had come to such a crisis that the fate of the empire depended on the conduct of government. With great uneasiness he found that administration grew more and more adverse to America. Lord Dartmouth had formerly declared in that House that it was not the meaning of ministers to reduce America by conquest, but the person who now filled the American department (Lord George Germain) had as positively declared, in another House, that nothing should be accepted but unconditional submission, so that it was plain the present idea was of conquest alone. The appointment of commissioners was a farce, if nothing was to be

The Duke of Grafton
by James Sayers, 1782

accepted but unconditional submission. Treaty would do every thing that arms could achieve, and in a better manner. The way to have those offers come from America, which every body wished to receive, could only be by pointing out to the leading people there some way of making propositions, and to hold out to them certainty that their petitions should not be rejected. But he observed that after they had been so often deceived, it was not to be expected that they would be contented with the word or assurances of a minister — the authority must be that of parliament.

In reply Lord Dartmouth, now lord privy seal, said more vigorous measures had been embraced not out of choice but necessity, it being plainly proved that America must either be reduced by force or left an independent empire, which had so long been the great object of its leaders. Upon division, after long debate, the motion was defeated by 91 to 31.[2]

At night between five and six hundred people of fashion, and most of the foreigners of note, attended a rout at Northumberland House.[3]

15th March, Friday Heavy day, bright evening

A little after 4 a.m. the York fly was attacked two miles from London by three footpads, who cut the reins of the horses' bridles. One of them held a blunderbuss to the coachman, another held a pistol in each hand, whilst the third, a little man, got into the coach and robbed the passengers of about 25l. and two watches.[1]

The draughts from the three regiments of foot guards marched from Birdcage Walk to Tooting and the neighbouring villages, where they are to be quartered prior to proceeding to Portsmouth, in order to embark for America.[2]

In the evening James Boswell arrived in London from Edinburgh, his journey an anxious one after recent highway attacks. 'The coachman bid us keep a look-out. Some fellows wanted him to stop under pretence of wanting to be up on the outside; but he drove quickly on, and some of us looked out on each side.' He parted with his fellow travellers in St John's Street, Smithfield, and took a hackney coach to Dilly's, a bookselling partnership run by brothers Charles and Edward Dilly at No. 22 Poultry. After being shaved, and having put on a clean shirt, he went to see Sir John Pringle, returning after midnight to sleep at Dilly's. He held off calling on Dr Johnson, fatigued as he was by the journey and knowing he might not get away till late.[3]

Their majesties went to see *Alexander's Feast* at Drury Lane Theatre. Among the performers were the Linley sisters and Mercy Draper, a blind foundling who had become an accomplished singer under the instruction of composer John Stanley, who was also blind. The morning's *Gazetteer* had carried a letter expressing concern for her:

> A Frequenter of Oratorios wishes to know what may be the particular destination of the Female Foundling, who, in the last and present seasons has figured away at Drury-lane theatre. Whether is she intended to be perfected in

the art of *mop-squeezing* or of *music*? In other words, is she for houshold service or the stage? On Wednesdays and Fridays Miss Draper (as we now call her) is exhibited in the oratorios at the Theatre Royal in the habit of a woman of fashion. On Sundays, behold her reduced to psalm-singing at the Foundling Hospital, in the habit of a pauper. Having the appearance of being a modest, amiable young person, who can help pitying her alternately travelling in two such opposite walks of life, as never yet led to happiness in the same individual?

Three days later another correspondent noted that Miss Draper 'yesterday sung in the Foundling Chapel *not* in the habit of the Hospital; which, with great propriety, she seems now permitted to lay aside'.[4]

From the *London Magazine* for August 1776, part of the Court Beauties series. It seems likely that the Miss Draper depicted is the Foundling singer. Verses accompanying the portrait provide no real clue but do refer to her as 'chaste', perhaps limiting the field.

At night the housemaid of a gentleman in the city suddenly went raving mad, and broke a looking-glass, and several of the windows, by which she cut her hands and arms in a terrible manner. She was at length, with difficulty, secured. No cause can be assigned for her being attacked by this shocking disorder; but three or four days before it shewed itself, she told her fellow servants she was afraid she was going mad, and desired them to be aware of her.[5]

MP 'So great is the business at the Admiralty, that the clerks are ordered to attend every night; a circumstance unusual even in time of war.'[6]

16th March, Saturday   An exceeding fine bright day
About 9 a.m. Boswell set out to wait on Dr Johnson, 'but found he was removed from Johnson's Court, No. 7, to Bolt Court, No. 8, still keeping to his favourite Fleet-street'. Learning from Johnson's black servant, Francis Barber, that his master was with the Thrales, Boswell took a boat at Blackfriars Bridge and headed for their house in Southwark, where he found Mrs Thrale and Johnson at breakfast.

> I was kindly welcomed. In a moment he was in a full glow of conversation, and I felt myself elevated as if brought into another state of being. ...
>
> He seemed very happy in the near prospect of going to Italy with Mr and Mrs Thrale. 'But, (said he,) before leaving England I am to take a jaunt to Oxford, Birmingham, my native city Lichfield ... I shall go in a few days, and you, Boswell, shall go with me.' I was ready to accompany him, being willing even to leave London to have the pleasure of his conversation. ...
>
> I mentioned Dr Adam Smith's book on *The Wealth of Nations* which was just published, and that Sir John Pringle had observed to me, that Dr Smith, who had never been in trade, could not be expected to write well on that subject any more than a lawyer upon physick. JOHNSON. 'He is mistaken, sir: a man who has never been engaged in trade himself may undoubtedly write well upon trade, and there is nothing which requires more to be illustrated by philosophy than trade does. ... A merchant seldom thinks but of his own particular trade. To write a good book upon it, a man must have extensive views. It is not necessary to have practised, to write well upon a subject.' ...
>
> We got into a boat to cross over to Black-friars; and as we moved along the Thames, I talked to him of a little volume, which, altogether unknown to him, was advertised to be published in a few days, under the title of *Johnsoniana, or Bon-Mots of Dr Johnson*. JOHNSON. 'Sir, it is a mighty impudent thing.' BOSWELL. 'Pray, sir, could you have no redress if you were to prosecute a publisher for bringing out, under your name, what you never said, and ascribing to you dull stupid nonsense, or making you swear profanely, as many ignorant relaters of your bon-mots do?' JOHNSON. 'No, sir; there will always be some truth mixed with the falsehood, and how can it be ascertained how much is true and how much is false? Besides, sir, what damages would a jury give me for having been represented as swearing?' BOSWELL. 'I think, sir, you should at least disavow such a publication, because the world and posterity might with much plausible foundation say, "Here is a volume which was publickly

advertised and came out in Dr Johnson's own time, and, by his silence, was admitted by him to be genuine.'" JOHNSON. 'I shall give myself no trouble about the matter.' ...

I observed, that Foote entertained us with stories which were not true; but that, indeed, it was properly not as narratives that Foote's stories pleased us, but as collections of ludicrous images. JOHNSON. 'Foote is quite impartial, for he tells lies of every body.'

They landed at Temple Stairs and parted. Boswell went to arrange lodgings in Gerrard Street, where he had stayed the previous year. Walking in the streets he met Charles Fox, whose lack of warmth led him to reflect that he could not expect all men to like him. Having dined with exiled Corsican leader General Paoli, he met a girl in the Strand, took her for a glass of wine at the Fountain tavern, and then went to Dr Johnson's again, where he was treated with raw oysters and porter. He was back at Dilly's shortly after midnight.[1]

17th March, Sunday Some flying clouds, fine bright day, frosty night
Lord North gave a grand dinner at his house in Downing Street to the Duke of Wirtemburg, the two foreign ladies, and a great number of the nobility of both sexes.[1]

William Bligh, aged 21, later to command HMS *Bounty*, was appointed master of the *Resolution* for Captain Cook's impending voyage.[2]

18th March, Monday Frosty night, bright morning, heavy churlish afternoon
In the morning a party of Custom House officers detected a gang of smugglers bringing a large quantity of tea, and other prohibited goods, to a house near the end of Poland Street, on which a desperate battle ensued. Mr Tankerd, one of the officers, had his horse shot from under him, and another officer was wounded. The smugglers escaped without their booty, which was carried in a cart to the Custom House.[1]

Boswell, after George Langton, *circa* 1790

Workmen began to drive piles for the embankment of the river Thames, about fifty foot nearer to low water mark than the garden wall of Somerset House.[2]

Lord Sandwich went in the Admiralty barge to Woolwich, accompanied by the Duke of Wirtemburg, to see experiments made on several pieces of cannon of a new construction, after which they dined at the Royal Academy.[3]

An usher to a boarding school at Hammersmith hung himself, having been accused by his master of assisting the elopement of his wife, and being ordered on that account to quit his service.[4]

At 5 p.m. a great main of cocks began at the Royal Cockpit, Westminster, 'to continue all the week, between the gentlemen of Middlesex and Essex, for five guineas a battle and one hundred the odd battle'. Champ and Lister were the feeders.[5]

Boswell visited Dr Johnson again. Johnson 'took occasion to enlarge, as he often did, upon the wretchedness of a sea-life. "A ship is worse than a gaol. There is, in a gaol, better air, better company, better conveniency of every kind; and a ship has the additional disadvantage of being in danger. ... Men go to sea, before they

The Royal Cockpit as depicted by Hogarth, 1759
The shadow across the centre of the table is of a defaulter suspended
in a basket. He is dangling his watch in hope that it will settle the debt.

know the unhappiness of that way of life; and when they have come to know it, they cannot escape from it, because it is then too late to choose another profession; as indeed is generally the case with men, when they have once engaged in any particular way of life.'"[6]

Later Boswell visited Sir Joshua Reynolds in Leicester Fields, and between ten and eleven at night called on Garrick at his house in the Adelphi. He found him sitting with Mrs Garrick and Hannah More and stayed till near twelve, 'drinking port and water and eating bread and a Hampton nonpareil' (a variety of late ripening apple, from the garden of Garrick's villa by the Thames). He found Garrick 'quite easy and gay as usual. ... He was clear that he should never play any more, but be quite the gentleman, and not partly the player; and that he should not any longer subject himself to be hissed or to be insolently treated by the performers whom he used to rule with a high hand, and who would gladly retaliate.'[7]

MP 'For the *Morning Post*. | To Mrs Abington. | Madam, Excuse the liberty I take in thus publickly addressing you; but the current report of the *important* Mrs Abington's leaving the stage is a concern and consequence of too national, great, and melancholly a moment, to be passed over in privacy and silence. As an individual, therefore, feeling with my agonizing country from this sudden and heavy stroke, inform me, I intreat you, if the report is true; or only one of the many *Abingtonian manoeuvres* practised by you with so much success, from your earliest *padding* it, to your present easy sedan, with *Monsieur Canton** preceding it on particular occasion ... | I am, Immortal and Important Madam, | Yours till death, | SHELL | March 17, 1776. | P.S. My spirits are greatly relieved and elevated by a piece of intelligence a friend has this instant brought in with him, who tells me, (and he is in the secret of matters) that you are actually to have a meeting this day, *at one*, with the new managers elect — to treat for a three years campaign. The highest bidder, he says, will be the buyer; but I fear my friend is a wag.'[8]

19th March, Tuesday Chiefly cloudy, some little sun
Between eight and nine in the morning Boswell met Dr Johnson at the Somerset Coffee-house in the Strand to take the Oxford coach. They were accompanied by two other passengers including John Gwynn, architect of Magdalen Bridge, which was being rebuilt at this time. Once aboard, as Boswell noted, 'We soon got into conversation; for it was very remarkable of Johnson, that the presence of a stranger had no restraint upon his talk. I observed that Garrick, who was about to quit the stage, would soon have an easier life. JOHNSON. "I doubt that, sir." BOSWELL. "Why, sir, he will be Atlas with the burthen off his back." JOHNSON. "But I know not, sir, if he will be so steady without his load."'[1]

---

* Perhaps an allusion to a Swiss servant, being the name of a character in George Colman and David Garrick's *The Clandestine Marriage* (1766).

In the morning the king, escorted by a party of light horse, went in his chaise and four to Wimbledon Common to review Colonel Matthews's brigade of the guards, consisting of 1,000 men. Among those on the roads going to Wimbledon were the Indian chief and his companion, accompanied by several ladies and gentlemen of distinction, the whole consisting of nine carriages and upwards of twenty attendants on horseback. One of the Indians was habited in the dress of his country, over an English suit of clothes. He wore an ensign's breast-plate, his face was painted as with streaks of blood, and he carried a war-hatchet in his hand.

Also present were the Prince of Wales, dressed in regimentals and on horseback, the Bishop of Osnaburgh, the Duke and Duchess of Northumberland, the Duke of Wirtemburg, foreign ambassadors, ministers of state, and a vast concourse of people of inferior rank. Several parties of horse, grenadier and foot guards lined the field to prevent improper persons from breaking in.

The soldiers under review made a fine appearance, the officers in the same uniforms as their men. After marching by the king to the Grenadiers' March they went through their evolutions with great dexterity, first forming themselves into squares, after which they made a general running fire, in imitation of a pursuit, and took possession of several posts on the declivity of a woody hill, from which they kept up an incessant firing, advancing by platoons, the light infantry scouring the wood upon the right and left, and the main body marching on in a column.

According to the *London Chronicle*, 'An American Indian, a very shrewd one, who has been only three months from New-York, seemed much affected with the scene, and exclaimed in a pathetic manner, "This may do here, but it won't do in America."' The Indian in question was probably Joseph Brant.

His majesty nonetheless expressed great approbation of the display, and seemed particularly pleased at the chearfulness in the countenances of the soldiers to embark for their intended expedition. After he had complimented Colonel Matthews, the Duke of Wirtemburg rode up to that officer and paid him likewise a very elegant compliment in French, which the colonel however could not return, as he was totally ignorant of the language. He stood for a considerable time exceedingly embarrassed, which his majesty perceiving, he turned to the duke with a smile, and apologised for the unfortunate situation of his colonel.[2]

In Whitechapel and the streets adjacent a person who had the appearance of insanity sold an inflammatory paper respecting America, and with great vociferation repeated the contents to the multitude who followed him.[3]

20th March, Wednesday In general cloudy, but a fair day
MP 'The new gambling society that have erected the superb building in St James's-street, carry play to a height to which it never yet arrived in this kingdom. Such sums as from 9000 to 16,000l. have been lost there in one evening by one person. Rouleaus are made up only for thousands, and machines contrived for moving them about the rooms.'[1]

THE PREPOSTEROUS HEAD DRESS,
or the FEATHERD LADY.

Pub. by M Darly. 39 Strand March 20 1776.

Published by M. Darly in the Strand, 20th March 1776

21st March, Thursday A fine, bright, warm day

In the House of Commons, at a little after three o'clock, Mr Wilkes rose and introduced a motion for leave to bring in a bill for a more fair and equal representation of the people. Confining his calculations to England, he argued that, allowing for absences arising from sickness, service in foreign parts, travelling, et cetera, 254 members were usually required to achieve a practical majority in that House. It had been demonstrated that such a number 'are actually elected by no more than 5723 persons ... Is our sovereign then to learn the sense of his whole people from these few persons? Are these the men to give laws to this vast empire, and to tax this wealthy nation?'

It would be objected, he said, that all efforts at this time should be employed in extinguishing the intestine discord in North America. On the contrary, the American war was one of the strongest arguments for the regulation of our representation:

> 'In our late disputes with the Americans, we have always taken it for granted, that the people of England justified all the iniquitous, cruel, arbitrary, and mad proceedings of administration, because they had the approbation of the majority of this House. The absurdity of such an argument is apparent, for the majority of this House we know speak only the sense of 5723 persons, even supposing ... the constituent had been consulted on this great national point, as he ought to have been. ... The people in the southern part of this island amount to upwards of five millions. The sense, therefore, of five millions cannot be ascertained by the opinion of not six thousand, even supposing it had been collected. The Americans with great reason insist, that the present war is carried on contrary to the sense of the nation, by a ministerial junto, and an arbitrary faction, equally hostile to the rights of Englishmen, and the claims of Americans.'

He argued that places such as Old Sarum and Gatton, populous towns when the right of representation was given them, but now desolate, should be disenfranchised, and rich and populous manufacturing towns, such as Birmingham, Manchester, and Leeds, should be equitably represented. The disfranchising of the mean, venal, and dependent boroughs would be laying the axe to the root of corruption, Treasury influence, and aristocratical tyranny.

> 'I wish, sir, an English parliament to speak the free, unbiased sense of the body of the English people, and of every man among us ... The meanest mechanic, the poorest peasant and day-labourer, has important rights respecting his personal liberty, that of his wife and children, his property, however inconsiderable, his wages ... We ought always to remember this important truth, acknowledged by every free state, that all government is instituted for the good of the mass of the people to be governed; that they are the original fountain of power, and even of revenue, and in all events the last resource.'

In opposing the motion Lord North was very jocular. He supposed the honourable gentleman was not serious. If he should prevail it would cause great discontent; and he would find it no easy task to prevail on those who had an interest in the boroughs, on which he bestowed so many hard names, to sacrifice to ideal schemes of reformation, so beneficial a species of property. He thought the proposition could do no good, and might do much harm.

The question being put, it passed in the negative, without a division.[1]

In the evening several inhabitants in the King's Mews and Charing Cross went to the rotation office in Litchfield Street and laid a complaint before the magistrates of the great nuisance of some lewd women who are every night in that neighbourhood. In consequence several peace officers went and apprehended twelve women, with two notorious pickpockets. They were all committed to the house of correction for one month, except one young woman, who being sensible of her wicked life, begged the magistrates to recommend her as a proper object for admission to the Magdalen Hospital in St George's Fields, to which they complied.[2]

About eleven o'clock at night a fire broke out on board the brigantine *Hibernia*, lying off the Tower, loaded with porter and hemp bound to Dublin. She drove under London Bridge in flames and was on fire near six hours. The engine belonging to the Royal Exchange Assurance at length extinguished the flames, but not before the brig was nearly burnt down to the water's edge.[3]

22nd March, Friday Very bright morning, cloudy afternoon

A proclamation was issued at St James's for encouraging seamen to enter themselves on board his majesty's ships of war on or before 30th April: able seamen between 18 and 50 years to receive a bounty of £3, ordinary seamen £2.[1]

At one o'clock the lord mayor, Mr Sawbridge, with the sheriffs, chamberlain, and other officers went in procession from Guildhall to St James's to present a petition to his majesty on behalf of the City of London. It said that they looked with horror at 'that dismemberment of the empire; that increase of the national debt, and of burthensome taxes; that loss of our most valuable resources; those distresses of our merchants and manufacturers; those deficiencies of the revenue; that effusion of the blood of our countrymen and brethren; that failure of public credit, and those dreadful calamities and convulsions which must follow a civil war'. They asked that a clear offer of 'just and honourable terms' be made to the colonies before 'the dreadful operations of your armament. Every colour and suspicion of injustice and oppression will then be removed from the proceedings of the mother country'.

The lord mayor had the night before been seized with the gout, and it was with great pain and difficulty he got up to the drawing-room.[2]

In the House of Commons Mr Jolliffe moved for leave to bring in a bill to lay a tax on dogs. They were, he said, one of the most proper objects of taxation, for their numbers were really a nuisance, they devoured great quantities of provisions, which would enable numbers of industrious poor to subsist, and, from the luxury and absurdity of the age, such a tax would yield a considerable revenue. Mr Rigby treated the notion with a degree of humour and contempt, saying that if the bill were brought in he would move for the words *tabby cats* to be inserted. The motion was nonetheless passed, ayes 24, noes 19.[3]

A fishwoman at Billingsgate undertook to drink nine quarterns (two and a quarter pints) of gin, but expired before she drank seven.[4]

Horace Walpole wrote to Sir Horace Mann in Florence:

> We know nothing new from America ... However, had the ministers any good news, they would be eager enough to divulge it. The season is far advanced, yet their expeditions are much behindhand, and the troops that do go will arrive during the dangerous heats. Indeed, I do not think the general language is so prophetic of certain success as it was three months ago, and people seem to grow much more clear of the unpromising state of affairs than they were.
>
> What else can I tell you? That dissipation and gaming continue to stride before the war? Yes, verily. A new club is opened in St James's Street, that piques itself on surpassing all its predecessors. ... But it is the nation that is really gaming deep — we have set twelve provinces on the cast of a die.[5]

23rd March, Saturday A very fine, bright, warm day

Whilst Master Thrale, son of Henry Thrale, Esq., brewer in the Borough, was running his hoop upon a green platt before his father's door, he dropped down dead, to the great surprize and distress of all the family. He was nine years old. The cause of death was a ruptured appendix.

Giuseppe Baretti, tutor to another of the Thrale children, later recalled the news arriving at his lodgings in Great Titchfield Street, brought by a servant of Count Manucci, 'a young nobleman from Florence' who was on his travels and happened to be at the Thrales' house at the time. Baretti ran at once to the house, where he found 'Mr Thrale, both his hands in his waistcoat pocket,' sitting 'on an arm-chair in a corner of the room with his body so stiffly erect, and with such a ghastly smile in his face, as was quite horrid to behold'. Mrs Thrale, meanwhile, had suffered a succession of fainting fits and was with difficulty kept 'from going frantic'. For three days Baretti and Manucci stayed with the bereft parents, 'quite immersed in sorrow, as the boy had been a favourite with us all, and had well deserved to be so'.[1]

MJ 'The Duke of Wurtemburg is at present in England, negotiating a treaty with our Court, for a body of his troops to be kept ready to march for the succour of Hesse, if required; or under certain circumstances, to be sent to America, during the course of the summer. The family of Wurtemburg has been long in the French interest, but the system of œconomy lately established in the finances of France, having cut off all foreign subsidies, he set himself to create new connections of the profitable kind.'[2]

LC 'Lord Howe is making preparations for his departure for America; and the *Eagle*, of 60 guns, on board of which ship he is to hoist his flag, is fallen down to Long Reach to take in her guns and stores, after which she will sail for the Downs to proceed on her voyage.'[3]

LEFT Henry Thrale in happier times, depicted as 'The Southwark Macaroni', 1772.
RIGHT Mrs Thrale, after a painting by Reynolds, *circa* 1777.

24th March, Sunday A very bright warm morning, cloudy afternoon
Died, aged 83, at his house in Red Lion Square, Mr John Harrison, inventor and
constructor of the famous time-keepers for ascertaining the longitude at sea.[1]

25th March, Monday, Lady Day Fine bright day, cutting wind
In the morning a duel was fought in Hyde Park between two officers. Their quarrel
had arisen from a dispute whether Gabrielli or Sestini was the better singer and
the handsomest woman. One of the parties was wounded in the sword arm, which
put an end to the affair.[1]

The greatest number of fishing boats ever known at one time was on the river
between London and Chelsea bridges, owing to the wind and tide being so
favourable for smelting.[2]

At the levee at St James's, Lord George Gordon, youngest brother of the
Duke of Gordon, and future riot inciter, was introduced to his majesty.[3]

In the evening there was an elegant masquerade at the Hon. Mrs Hobart's at
Richmond, at which were present some remarkable good characters, particularly
a Mr Baker in the character of a Lady with a modern head-dress; it was four feet
in height, and adorned with large Portugal onions, roots of celery, radishes,
carrots, with an endive in the center of the cap, finely blanched, and several other
kinds of garden stuff. The wearer supported the character with great humour,

though several ladies were vexed to find themselves the ridicule of young men, as well as of dowagers and old maids that have no hair on their heads. At twelve o'clock Mr Hobart, in the character of a Cook, with a tureen in his hand, introduced the company into a room where a genteel supper, with all kinds of wines, adorned the tables. A revival of spirits soon took place, and an adjournment was made to the drawing-room, where dancing and good spirits flourished till five o'clock in the morning.[4]

26th March, Tuesday Frosty night, exceeding bright day, cutting wind
On about this day the pulling down of the ancient fabric of Somerset House began.[1]

In the morning a clerk belonging to a public office was found dead in his bed at his lodgings near Moorfields, with his throat cut in a shocking manner. His having been connected with a gang of swindlers, who had involved him in many difficulties, is said to have been the cause of this rash action.[2]

In Portman Square Lord Townshend and several other general officers made an experiment of a piece of ordnance called the Hand Grenade. It is round like a common ball, of about the weight of twelve pounds, and filled with shell powder and all sorts of combustibles, and when thrown at any distance is supposed to kill a great number of persons. Many thousands of them are made to send to America, and in particular to Quebec.[3]

Gibbon wrote to his stepmother: 'I have the satisfaction of telling you that my book has been very well received by men of letters, men of the world, and even by fine feathered ladies, in short by every set of people except perhaps by the clergy, who seem (I know not why) to shew their teeth on the occasion. A thousand copies are sold, and we are preparing a second edition, which in so short a time is, for a book of that price, a very uncommon event.'[4]

Mrs Harris wrote from Piccadilly to her son in Berlin: 'Your schoolfellow Jolliffe tried to bring a bill into the House for a tax upon dogs ... [He] was most violently attacked last night by nine young ladies at once, for his inhuman intention; these ladies so *worried* him that he had not a word to say, and they fairly barked him off.'[5]

Lord Howe wrote from his house in Grafton Street to Lord George Germain, returning his draft commission and instructions and expressing grave reservations about them. He was concerned in particular that he was not to engage in any discussion with the Americans until they had complied with the government's demands. He was, he said, 'disqualified from engaging as a commissioner in the execution of instructions framed on that plan'. Germain appears not to have been greatly concerned. At 8.10 p.m. he wrote to the king from his house in Pall Mall: 'Lord Howe has many difficultys about the instructions; however at all events he will not decline the command of the fleet; upon hearing that circumstance your majesty may not be very anxious whether he accepts of being one of the commissioners.'[6]

ABOVE Looking south across the outer courtyard of old Somerset House.

BELOW Looking west across the same courtyard, with demolition work in progress and lead sheets laid ready to support new paving.

27th March, Wednesday Smart frosty night, bright day, misling evening
At the Royal Exchange and Holborn Bars the common cryer read the king's proclamation for a further encouragement to sailors to enter on board the ships of
war. It was afterwards stuck up in divers parts of the city.[1]

Also at the Royal Exchange, and in several other places, an extraordinary
macaroni character of the doubtful gender appeared, exciting the attention of the
public. It seemed to be about 30 years of age, wore a small round hat with a silver
spangled band, its own black hair unpowdered, blowing about its face and falling
loose upon its shoulders, a black ribband with a large rose knot about its neck, a
light blue silk coat, a tissue waistcoat, rose coloured sattin breeches, white cotton
stockings, and thin dress shoes with red heels. Finding the spectators were
growing troublesome it went through the King's Arms tavern, down Abchurch
Lane, and into Cannon Street, where the offended multitude obliged it to take
shelter in a public-house, from whence it was, with difficulty, conveyed to its
lodgings in a hackney coach.[2]

An ordinary macaroni in the fashion of 1776

'A Hint to the Ladies to take Care of their Heads'

The setting is the interior of the rotunda at the Pantheon in Oxford Street.
Published by Sayer and Bennett, 53 Fleet Street, 28th March 1776.

28th March, Thursday A black, heavy, churlish day

Between three and four o'clock in the morning two Custom House officers, on horseback, saw a hackney coach driving furiously on London Bridge, which gave them a suspicion that run goods were concealed therein. On their calling to the coachman to stop, he drove the faster, on which one of them presenting a pistol, and threatening to fire, two men jumped out and ran away, and the coach stopped. The officers proceeded to examine it for their supposed prize, but to their great astonishment they found the bodies of an elderly man and woman in separate sacks, quite naked, each with a rope tied round their neck. There were three bruises about the body of the man, and neither of them had been dead a long time.

The coachman was conducted to the Poultry Compter and later brought before the lord mayor at Guildhall. In his defence he said he drove the coach for another person, that on taking up two men in Cornhill he was ordered to drive to Shoreditch, where two other men came from behind some carts, and as he thought put two large parcels in at the coach windows, after which they immediately disappeared, and the persons in the coach ordered him to drive to St Thomas's Hospital. He added that he did not know the parties, having never seen them before, and that he had lost his fare by their running away. He was discharged, and ordered to drive the bodies, which were still in his coach in Guildhall yard, back to Shoreditch in order that they might be relaid in their graves. There they were found to be those of two paupers who had lately died in the workhouse, and which were supposed to have been stolen out of the poor's burial-ground in Hackney Road, for the use of the surgeons.[1]

Died, aged 30 years, at the sign of the White Raven, a public-house in Mile End Road, the famous white raven that was hatched in the year 1745.[2]

At night, in consequence of an information being given to the parish officers of St Pancras, of a cart often going loaded into the Black Horse Yard, Tottenham Court Road, at a very unseasonable time of night, a watch was set to examine the same.* About eleven o'clock the cart came, which they stopped. On searching it they found three sacks and a large hamper, containing the bodies and limbs of several dead persons. On searching two stables in the yard there were discovered several human bodies, cut and mangled in a terrible manner, and hung on hooks, each joint having a label on it. A large copper was found fixed in one part, as supposed for the purpose of boiling the bones. The driver was secured.[3]

29th March, Friday Heavy morning, clear afternoon

At 9 a.m. Joseph Brant sat (or rather stood) for George Romney at his house in Cavendish Square; another sitting followed on 4th April. The resulting portrait shows him life size, in hunting dress, with a head-dress of red feathers and a tomahawk in his right hand.[1]

---

* It seems likely that the information arose from the London Bridge incident earlier in the day, but the connection is not made in the original report.

Joseph Brant
Mezzotint by John Raphael Smith, 1779, after the portrait by Romney

At some point his warrior companion John Hill also sat for a portrait, in his case to Alice Richardson, crayon painter, of No. 4 College Street, Westminster. The resulting work was exhibited at the Royal Academy's annual exhibition as 'Portrait of Oteronganente, one of the American chiefs now in London', but its subsequent history is unknown.[*2]

In the morning a quantity of beds and bedding was burnt on Tower Hill, on a suspicion of being infected. They were taken from a ship wherein some persons had died under suspicious symptoms of the pestilence.[3]

Also in the morning, Mr Sherrard, harpsichord maker, of Petty France, Westminster, dropped down dead as he was walking along Parliament Street.[4]

The driver of the coach stopped the night before near Tottenham Court Road was examined at the rotation office in Litchfield Street. He said he took up his load at a cellar in Carnaby Street and was ordered to drive to Black Horse Yard by two men, and had not the least knowledge of what his cart contained. Several inhabitants of Tottenham Court Road attended, and gave an account of the proceedings in the above yard, and of the disagreeable smells which had for some time past come from the stables. They were advised to indite the occupier of the stables for a nuisance if a stop was not immediately put to those proceedings. As nothing appeared to affect the driver, he was discharged. A mob assembled at the yard, broke open the stables, and attempted to pull down the building, but by the interference of Mr Clay, the high constable, and a number of petty officers, they were prevented from committing any further outrage.[5]

A subsequent report said alarm in the area subsided when 'it was discovered that the place had been taken by some persons employed to remove the subjects after their dissection at a celebrated anatomical lecturer's', a reference perhaps to William Hunter of Great Windmill Street.[6]

The French chargé d'affaires, M. Garnier, wrote to the Comte de Vergennes with various news: 1,000 men from the guards were embarking at Portsmouth for Boston, General Burgoyne was readying to sail with English and Brunswick troops for Canada, and Hessian troops were expected. 'Everywhere transport ships

---

* There may also have been a third portrait painted during the Mohawks' stay. A well known work in the National Gallery of Art, Washington, attributed to Benjamin West and dated to 1776, has been given the title 'Colonel Guy Johnson and Karonghyontye (Captain David Hill)' (see Plate 8). David Hill was John's brother. The ascribed date arises from the attribution to West and the fact that Johnson is only known to have been in London with Indians during his visit of 1775-1776. Unfortunately there is no evidence that David Hill was ever in London, and contemporary references seem to make clear that his brother John and Joseph Brant were the only Indians who accompanied Johnson. If the picture was painted during the visit perhaps it was John Hill, rather than his brother, who stood for the figure of the Indian warrior. The question is discussed in an extended note, 'How many Mohawks came to London?' (pp645-647).

THE ANATOMIST OVERTAKEN by the WATCH   CARRYING OFF MISS W— in a HAMPER

William Hunter's appetite for dead bodies had been noted in this print of 1773. A watchman, rattle in hand, interrupts a bodysnatcher who points incriminatingly towards a scarpering surgeon who has dropped a paper titled 'Hunter's Lectures'.

are hurriedly chartered and ships and frigates are fitted out. Everything bustles with activity ...'[7]

Dr Johnson and Boswell arrived back in London, Johnson having received a letter while in Lichfield informing him of the death of the Thrales' son. They stopped at Dilly's in the Poultry where they parted, Johnson taking a hackney coach to visit the Thrales in Southwark. In the evening Boswell called at Johnson's house, having promised to let his elderly companion Mrs Williams know of his safe return. 'To my surprize, I found him sitting with her at tea, and, as I thought, not in a very good humour: for, it seems, when he had got to Mr Thrale's, he found the coach was at the door waiting to carry Mrs and Miss Thrale, and Signor Baretti, their Italian master, to Bath. ... They had, I found, without ceremony, proceeded on their intended journey.'[8]

Baretti gave a rather different account of the incident, according to which, on Mrs Thrale announcing her plan to go to Bath, he selflessly offered himself as a male companion. When Johnson arrived Baretti expected that 'he would spare me the jaunt, and go himself to Bath ... but he made no motion to that effect; therefore, after the sad exchange of a few mournful periods, as is customary on such occasions, we got into the coach and were soon out of sight'.[9]

In the afternoon Albany Charles Wallis, a 13-year-old pupil at Westminster School, drowned in the Thames. He was said to have been of a sprightly, intelligent disposition, and advancing rapidly in his studies. He was the only son of Albany Wallis, Esq., of Norfolk Street, an eminent attorney whose clients included David Garrick. The boy's mother Elizabeth had died three years earlier.

According to one account, fearing for his son's safety Wallis had constantly exhorted him not to go on the water in parties, as Westminster boys were in the habit of doing. A clergyman of Wallis's acquaintance passing by on the day before the accident, Thursday, saw the boy in a boat, and knowing his father's fears, called to him, and reproved him very much for his conduct, and obtained a promise from him never to do the like again. This morning, Friday, the clergyman waited on the headmaster, Dr Smith, and made him lecture the boy on the matter, but no sooner did the boy leave school than he and some other Westminster boys procured a boat at Westminster Bridge and diverted themselves on the water till Wallis, in attempting to leap to a larger vessel, fell into the river and was drowned.

A second, slightly different account said that the young Wallis had already left the school for the Easter holidays, and that in the morning he and a school-fellow had hired a boat and rowed as far as the Pleasure-house near Lambeth. 'In attempting to quit the boat Master Wallis fell overboard, but recovering from his surprise, he was swimming towards the shore, when a boat, passing with great velocity, struck him on the head, and he sunk for a second time, then recovered, when the bye-standers on shore threw him a rope, of which he caught hold, but the rope breaking, he sunk with a part of it in his hand, and was seen no more.' A later report said that the man in the boat that struck him on the head had been trying to save him.

To the great grief of his father his body has not yet been found.

On 2nd April Garrick wrote, 'I have been wholly engaged for these three days in comforting an almost distracted friend.'[10]

About 5 p.m. a young clerk who had been charged with an unnatural crime, of which he was innocent, dreading the loss of reputation, jumped from the balustrade of the center arch of Blackfriars Bridge with an intent to drown himself. Instead, however, he fell into an empty coal lighter that was passing, and was bruised in a terrible manner. With his limbs broken, and blood streaming from different parts of his body, he was taken to St Bartholomew's Hospital, where he died next day.[11]

Following his visit to Bolt Court Boswell made up for his absence from London. After dinner he went to the park 'in a kind of brutal fever' and 'was relieved by dalliance'. At supper he drank a bottle of claret by himself which made him 'brutally feverish' again so he returned to the park. Afterwards he was picked up by a 'strumpet' called Jenny Taylor at the top of St James's Street and 'lay with her' in a passage off Hay Hill. He got home to General Paoli's in Hill Street, a short walk across Berkeley Square, at around three in the morning.[12]

Albany Charles Wallis, by Reynolds, *circa* 1774

30th March, Saturday A fine day, in general bright, frost in the night
Dr Johnson crossed the river again to visit Mr Thrale, but 'was made to understand
that when I was wanted I should be sent for'. He wrote a letter of condolence to
Mrs Thrale: 'Only by degrees, and those perhaps sufficiently slow, can the pain
of an affliction like yours be abated. ... Do not indulge your sorrow; try to drive it
away by either pleasure or pain; for, opposed to what you are feeling, many pains
will become pleasures. Remember the great precept, *Be not solitary; be not idle*.'[1]

Boswell woke 'very ill with sickness and headache', got up at ten, and break-fasted with Paoli and Anthony Poggi, an Italian portrait painter. Before noon, afraid that he had caught 'the venereal disorder', he went in search of Jenny Taylor in St Peter Street, Westminster, where she had told him she lived, but finding no trace he concluded she had probably lied about her name and residence. About three o'clock, making his way back through the park, he met a girl who said her name was Nanny Smith and that she lived as a servant-maid in New Bond Street. He took her to the One Tun at Chelsea, 'a house of lewd entertainment in a garden ... and there I enjoyed her'.[2]

At twenty minutes past noon Lord George Germain wrote to the king regarding a lucrative sinecure, the office of receiver general of Jamaica, which had become vacant. 'Lord George would be infinitely obliged to your majesty if you would be graciously pleas'd to grant that office to his youngest son George Germain. It is said to be worth six hundred pounds a year.' At 4 p.m. Lord North joined battle with his own note to the king: 'It is a revenue place, and, therefore, I believe, by law is given by a warrant countersign'd by the Treasury. By some mistake, however, some of the warrants have been issued by the American secretary, and it is probable that his majesty will have an application for the disposal of it; Lord North hopes that his majesty will not countersign any warrant till the point is clear'd up.'[3]

About 3 p.m., having taken leave of the king the day before, General Burgoyne set out in a post-chaise from Kensington Palace for Portsmouth, in order to embark for America.[4]

31st March, Palm Sunday Slight frost in the night, fine day, in general bright
At 8.10 a.m. the king wrote from the Queen's Palace to Lord North saying that he was ready to assist regarding the receiver generalship of Jamaica, 'provided the appointment be made out in favour of one of your sons. As you seemed to expect Lord George Germain wrote to me in favour of his second son; but I instantly answered that I was apprized of the vacancy, but could not think of any appoint-ment until it was clearly proved that it had been usually prepared in his office ... You will never find any occasion of providing for your children that I shall not be more happy if possible than yourself to provide for them. It has not been my fate in general to be well served, by you I have and therefore cannot forget it.'

In the event, however, the place was given to Germain's son and heir Charles, who was eight years old. He was to hold it until 1815.[1]

Fanny Burney went for a walk which she recalled in a letter written a day or so later to Samuel Crisp, a family friend who lived at Chessington.

> Mr Burney, Hetty and I took a walk in the park on Sunday morning, where among others, we saw the young and handsome Duchess of Devonshire, walking in such an undressed and slaternly manner, as, in former times, Mrs Rishton might have done in Chessington Garden. Two of her curls came quite unpinned, and fell lank on one of her shoulders; one shoe was down at heel, the trimming

of her jacket and coat was in some places unsown; her cap was awry; and her cloak which was rusty and powdered, was flung half on and half off. Had she not had a servant in a superb livery behind her, she would certainly have been affronted. Every creature turned back to stare at her. Indeed I think her very handsome, and she has a look of innocence and artlessness that made me quite sorry she should be so foolishly negligent of her person. She had hold of the duke's arm, who is the very reverse of herself, for he is ugly, tidy, and grave. He looks like a very mean shopkeeper's journeyman.

Omai, who was in the park, called here this morning, and says that he went to her grace, and asked her why she let her hair go in that manner? Ha, Ha, Ha! Don't you laugh at her having a lesson of attention from an Otaheitan?[2]

After dinner and a visit, 'the whoring rage' came upon Boswell again and he went to Charing Cross Bagnio with 'a wholesome-looking, bouncing wench' called Nanny Cooms. Having satiated his desires 'by repeated indulgence' he became restless and left, but not before 'she had honestly delivered to me my watch and ring and handkerchief, which I should not have missed I was so drunk'. He took a hackney coach to Berkeley Square, 'and went home cold and disturbed and dreary and vexed, with remorse rising like a black cloud without any distinct form'.[3]

Meanwhile in America

16th March. Silas Deane sailed from Delaware Bay having been appointed by Congress's committee of secret correspondence to open negotiations with the Court of France.[1]

17th March. British troops under General Howe evacuated Boston.[2]

Silas Deane, *circa* 1780

April

1st April, Monday Slight frost in night, cloudy day, bright intervals

In the morning a large body of the guards marched from St James's Park with colours flying, music playing, and drums beating, to the foot of Blackfriars Bridge, where lighters lay ready to take them down to the transports at the Nore, where they will embark for America. The taking leave of their wives, children, and friends, exhibited an affecting scene of distress.[1]

Lord Howe wrote again from Grafton Street to Lord George Germain regarding the draft instructions. He thanked him for adjustments that had been made but reiterated his concern about the very limited role allowed to the commissioners.[2]

Worried again, Boswell went to Duck Lane, Westminster, found Nanny Cooms, and persuaded himself that she was not infected. 'But whom did I see in that blackguard lane but my pretended servant-maid, Nanny Smith, in a drummer's coat by way of a morning jacket! I was abashed and mortified at my simplicity.' Nanny Cooms and another girl told him that Smith had lived with them for three months, 'and they could not answer for her, for the young man who lived with her, a corporal, was now in the hospital. This made me almost sick with fear.' He recovered sufficiently, however, to send for and enjoy 'a pretty fair girl who was on call', which he thought would be 'the last act of this fit of debauchery'.[3]

Samuel Curwen walked to town to pay his respects to Governor Hutchinson, 'whom I found alone reading a new pamphlet entitled "An Enquiry whether Great Britain or America is most in fault".* He invited me to dine on a pudding and a bit of roast mutton, which I accepted.' Later, returning through Leicester Square, 'I called in at Mr Copley's to see Mr Clarke and the family,† who kindly pressed my staying to tea, and in the meantime was amused by seeing his performances in painting. He was then at work on a family piece containing himself, Mr Clarke, his wife and 4 children, of all of whom I observed a very striking likeness' (see Plate 6). At tea they were joined by Benjamin West. 'He is the kings history painter, was kind enough to put me into a way of obtaining a sight of the Queen's palace ... Returned with Mr Clarke ... as far as Temple barr, where by good fortune I got into a full coach, taking a very agreeable young lady in my lap, who was obliging enough to accept it rather than turn me out of the coach, she having taken a place first. ... Arrived at home at 8 o'clock after the pleasantest passage up I ever experienced.'[4]

2nd April, Tuesday An exceeding bright day, hot sun, cool air

At 9 a.m. Edmund Burke sat for Romney. It is thought to have been his last sitting for a now lost portrait from which the engraving opposite may derive.[1]

* Probably *An Enquiry, whether the guilt of the present civil war in America, ought to be imputed to Great Britain or America* by John Roebuck.
† Richard Clarke was Copley's father-in-law.

Edmund Burke

Mezzotint by John Jones, 1790, after a portrait by Romney

In the morning the last division of foot guards for the American expedition marched from their quarters in the neighbourhood of Fulham, Putney, Wandsworth, and Mortlake, to the no little joy of all the publicans, who were troubled with them longer than they expected.[2]

Germain replied to Lord Howe that he was 'very ready to explain verbally his ideas upon the construction of any of the articles, but he cannot take upon himself to make any material alterations in them without the previous concurrence of the ministers, as this last draft was settled with and approved by them, in hopes that it would have been satisfactory'. Politely ruling out further negotiation, he added that he would be happy to hear that Howe was willing to be one of the commissioners.[3]

Two men, Patrick Hastings and John Clark, were brought from Newgate and at one o'clock put in the pillory at the end of Margaret Street, Cavendish Square, where they stood for an hour, for extorting money from a gentleman under the pretence of his wanting to commit an unnatural crime with one of them. A great number of people assembled and the two men were pelted in a severe manner with apples, potatoes, rotten eggs, dirt, &c. till they were almost dead. They were afterwards taken down, put in a coach, and carried back to prison to undergo the remainder of their sentence, two years' imprisonment.[4]

Boswell dined at Sir John Pringle's in Pall Mall, where James Cook and his wife were also among the guests:

> It was curious to see Cook, a grave steady man, and his wife, a decent plump Englishwoman, and think that he was preparing to sail round the world. ...
>
> Cook told us that Omai, whom he was to carry home, begged to have two things for himself: port wine, which he loved the best of any liquor, and gunpowder; but the captain said he would not let him have the power of fire-arms, which he supposed he wished to have from some ambitious design. He said that for some time after Omai's return home he would be a man of great consequence, as having so many wonders to tell. That he would not foresee that when he had told all he had to tell, he would sink into his former state, and then, the captain supposed, he would wish to go to England again ('Britannia', the Otaheite people say, as they cannot pronounce 'England'), but that the captain would take care to leave the coast before Omai had time to be dissatisfied at home.[5]

DROWNED,
On Friday afternoon last, near Lambeth,

A youth, thirteen years of age, from Westminster school. Whoever brings him to his father, Mr WALLIS, in Norfolk-street, Strand, shall have THIRTY GUINEAS reward.

It is anxiously requested of all watermen, fishermen, and others on the river, to be assiduous to find him.

N.B. The person who first brings intelligence of his being found shall have FIVE GUINEAS.

Morning Chronicle[6]

3rd April, Wednesday Frost in the night, fine bright day

In the morning the daughter of a tradesman near Piccadilly was found dead in her bed. It appeared her father had discharged his young clerk, thinking there was too great an intimacy between his daughter and the clerk, and she out of revenge destroyed herself by taking a dose of laudanum.[1]

Boswell called on Dr Johnson:

I found him very busy putting his books in order, and as they were generally very old ones, clouds of dust were flying around him. He had on a pair of large gloves such as hedgers use. His present appearance put me in mind of my uncle Dr Boswell's description of him, 'A robust genius, born to grapple with whole libraries.'

I gave him an account of a conversation which had passed between me and Captain Cook ... at Sir John Pringle's ... I told him that while I was with the captain, I catched the enthusiasm of curiosity and adventure, and felt a strong inclination to go with him on his next voyage. JOHNSON. 'Why, sir, a man does feel so, till he considers how very little he can learn from such voyages.' BOSWELL. 'But one is carried away with the general grand and indistinct notion of A Voyage Round the World.' JOHNSON. 'Yes, sir, but a man is to guard himself against taking a thing in general.'[2]

Edward Gibbon received £65 'by two lottery tickets'. That it was a useful sum can be seen from some of the entries he made in his pocket-book during the next few months.[3]

Week of	Item	£	s.	d.
1 April	To Caplin [valet] ... for a year's wages	35	0	0
22 April	Easter offerings	0	10	6
	Window tax	1	10	6
	Box-keepers at Drury Lane	1	10	0
	For a year's wages &c. of a house maid	7	12	0
6 May	For a Stilton cheese	0	16	0
13 May	For 3 dozen of Champagne	10	10	0
20 May	For Poor's rates paving and lighting	5	17	0
	Door keepers of the House of C.	1	1	0
	Dinner &c. at Boodles	1	10	0
	Won at Whist	4	4	0
27 May	Subscription to Almacks	7	7	0
3 June	Lamplighter's bill	1	10	0
1 July	To Sherwood the Hatter	18	9	0
8 July	To Coachman for wages	4	4	0
	To Mr H. Walpole for a gold snuff-box from Paris	37	5	6
22 July	Lost at the [Lewes] races	2	2	0
29 July	Lost at Commerce	10	0	0
12 August	For the Coachman's breeches	1	4	0

4th April, Maundy Thursday Frost in the night, bright and cloudy intervals, sharp air. Full moon

At 9 a.m. Joseph Brant sat for Romney again. He was followed in the afternoon by Brownlow North, Bishop of Worcester and half-brother of the prime minister.[1]

Being Maundy Thursday, his majesty's bounty was distributed in Whitehall Chapel to thirty poor men and women in the usual manner, to each three ells of holland, a piece of woollen cloth, a pair of shoes and stockings, thirty shillings in a purse, thirty twopences and threepences, a loaf of bread, and a platter of fish.[2]

At 5 p.m., after sitting forty-five days, the House of Commons committee on the Worcester election finally determined that the sitting members, Thomas Bates Rous and John Walsh, were duly elected. It was computed that the election had cost the parties upwards of £20,000. According to the *Morning Chronicle*, news of the decision 'after so many glaring proofs of — threw every hearer into astonishment'. It went on to lament that 'the power of nabob gold in the present age' appeared so strong 'that of late we have not been able to behold, old or young, rich or poor, possessed of virtue sufficient to withstand its influence. ... | *O Tempora! O Mores!*'[3]

5th April, Good Friday Frost in the night, bright and cloudy intervals

About five o'clock, as a poor woman was going through St Giles's, crying hot cross buns, she was accosted by two ruffians. One took away all her buns, and the other took sevenpence halfpenny from her pocket, and then made clear off.[1]

'Being good Friday,' noted Samuel Curwen in his journal, 'had at breakfast *Cross buns*, or buns with a cross marked on the top, it being a custom, the reason of which I cant explore'.[2]

A sailor fell from the shrouds of a ship near the Tower into the river, and was drowned.[3]

GA 'The crew of one of the transports which sailed some time since for America, are said to have turned pirates, and run away with the vessel for the coast of Africa.'[4]

6th April, Saturday Black heavy day

In the morning a servant maid about 15 years of age, who worked for a publican and had been missing near a fortnight, was taken out of the New River, near Islington, at the back of Pullen's farm. A contusion appeared on her head, and her hands were clasped in each other. She was brought to Clerkenwell Church to be owned.[1]

Under this day Granville Sharp noted: 'Omai was so taken up with engagements that I could have no more opportunity of giving him lessons, which were but fifteen in all. However, in that time I taught him the use of English letters'.[2]

In Paris the comptroller general of finances, Anne Robert Jacques Turgot, wrote a memoir arguing against the interventionist policy of Beaumarchais and

The Maundy service in Whitehall Chapel (the Banqueting House), 1773. The sub-almoner distributes to the poor while the king and queen look on from the royal box.

Vergennes. He warned Louis XVI that war with Britain would be 'the greatest of all evils, because it will make impossible for a very long time, and perhaps for ever, a reform that is absolutely necessary for the prosperity of the state and for the relief of the people'. His pregnant advice was ignored.[3]

7th April, Easter Day Black heavy day

At Strawberry Hill Horace Walpole, who issued tickets as a way of managing the flow of visitors to the house, had trouble with his Swiss footman, David.

> As I came to breakfast, he told me coolly the Duke of Wirtemburg had called at eight o'clock and wanted a ticket for Strawberry Hill. 'Bless me!' said I, 'and what did you say?' 'I told his grace you was not awake, and bad him come again at ten.' 'Good God!' said I, 'tell him to call again! Don't you know he is a sovereign prince?' 'No, I did think he was only a common duke!' I could not help laughing, though I was so shocked. In short, he had called again, and had again been sent away, nor can David yet conceive that I was to be waked. I was forced to write a thousand lies and excuses, and swear I was bedrid with the gout, and could not pay my duty to his serene highness ...[1]

The day was observed at Court as a high festival. At noon his majesty, preceded by the heralds and pursuivants at arms, went to the Chapel Royal. After receiving holy communion, according to annual custom he made a present of the Byzant, or wedge of gold, for the benefit of the poor. Her majesty was not present, but heard divine service at her own palace.[2]

After breakfast at the Chapter Coffee-house in Paternoster Row Boswell attended St Paul's Cathedral. He sat next to Henry Thrale and 'received the holy sacrament, being a sincere Christian in faith, and hoping to be better in practice'. Afterwards he dined with Dr Johnson, according to his Easter custom.

> After coffee, we went to afternoon service in St Clement's Church. Observing some beggars in the street as we walked along, I said to him I supposed there was no civilised country in the world, where the misery of want in the lowest classes of the people was prevented. JOHNSON. 'I believe, sir, there is not; but it is better that some should be unhappy, than that none should be happy, which would be the case in a general state of equality.'[3]

When alone, Johnson composed an Easter prayer, reflected on his own failings, and recorded his resolutions. 'My reigning sin, to which perhaps many others are appendant, is waste of time, and general sluggishness, to which I was always inclined ... | I go now with hope, | To rise in the morning at eight. | To use my remaining time with diligence. | To study more accurately the Christian religion.'[4]

8th April, Easter Monday A coarse day, hail, rain, and snow, and some sunshine
Being Easter Monday, the river was as usual crowded with boats carrying the holiday-makers to Greenwich, and the road from Kent Street to Greenwich was lined with apprentices and their girls, pickpockets and demi-reps, going to enjoy the diversion of rolling, at the hazard of their necks, down the hill in the park. A boat with nine people in it was overset near Execution Dock, and three were drowned. At Greenwich a young woman, running down the hill, fell down and broke her arm. Several others had their ancles sprained, knee-pans put out, &c.[1]

Governor Hutchinson was aghast to find extracts from *Common Sense* reprinted in the *Public Advertiser*. They did not include any of the more colourful passages, and, as he noted, seemed to have been selected simply 'to shew open declaration against all plans of reconciliation', but he felt that 'a loyal subject would not reprint' any part of a book that contained 'the most shocking abuses of the king — *Royal Brute*, &c.'[2]

At noon the lord mayor, preceded by the City officers, the governors of Bridewell, Bethlem, and Christ's hospitals, and a band of musick, went in procession from the Mansion House to St Bride's Church in Fleet Street, according to annual custom, and heard the Spital sermon preached by the Bishop of Rochester. By the report for the last year, laid before the lord mayor as usual at the church, it appeared that

> • All the patients cured, relieved, buried, and remaining under cure in St Bartholomew's Hospital amounted to 10,155, those in St Thomas's to 7,957.
> • In Christ's Hospital 142 boys had been put out and provided for, seven had died, and 1,132 remained.

• In Bridewell 1,084 vagrants had been provided for, and 33 apprentices had been maintained at trades, &c.

• In Bethlem 187 lunatics had been admitted, 190 cured, 17 buried, and 244 remained under cure.

Mr Payne the constable apprehended several pickpockets in the church, and immediately took them to be lodged in the Poultry Compter.[3]

In the evening the season at Sadler's Wells began with the usual diversions of singing, dancing, and tumbling. There was a new performance called *La Danse des Oeufs*, or the Egg Hornpipe, the whimsical plan of which is to dispose twelve eggs at equal distances on the stage, among which the dancer, being first publickly blindfolded, goes through the various steps of the hornpipe, without breaking one. Afterwards a new musical piece called *Easter Monday* was sung before a pictur-esque scene, representing the end of the field, and the fruit-stall in the way from town to the Wells. The characters were a Jolly Tar with his Doxey; a City Sneak and his termagant Spouse; and a sportive Gardener. According to the *Morning Chronicle*, 'If we may judge from the hearty laughs which the partakers ... repeatedly burst into, the diversions of this place will continue to be frequented by all who are fond of swallowing pills to cure melancholy, or wish to dissipate care with a chearful glass.'[4]

The same evening some young men and women assembled at a public-house at Bethnal Green to perform the play of *The Drummer, or The Haunted House*, but when the piece was about half finished, the room being crouded with spectators, the floor gave way, by which fifty or sixty people fell through into a room under-neath. One man had an arm and leg broke, and two women were so terribly bruised that they died as they were carrying to an hospital.[5]

9th April, Tuesday A coarse day, a great deal of hail, rain, and snow

The landlady of a public-house in Park Lane was tried at the Westminster quarter sessions for assaulting a Jew and greasing his beard with pork. It appeared in the course of the trial that the Jew went into the prisoner's house and offered to sell her some lemons. She was at dinner with two men and they asked him to have some pork, which he refused; but being resolved to give him some, the two men held him, while the prisoner rubbed it over his mouth, which made it so sore, that he could not eat any thing but spoon victuals for a month after. The jury, after withdrawing near two hours, returned their verdict for the Jew, with 10l. damages and costs of suit.[1]

Captain Cook wrote to the Admiralty to ask that *Resolution* and *Discovery* each be supplied with 'an apparatus for recovering drowned persons' and *Resolution* with 'two puncheons of double-distilled spirit, in order to preserve from putrefaction such curious birds, fish, and other animals we may happen to meet with in the course of the voyage'.[2]

At Battersea a number of women ran a race for a Holland smock, there was a race of asses for a silver laced hat, and seven men grinned for three pounds of tobacco, each of the grinners having a horse-collar round his neck. According to the *Middlesex Journal*, 'The successful wry-face-monger has a countenance not to be matched, at least in the county of Surry.' Just before the women started for

The Grinning MATCH a humourous SCENE at a Country FAIR

Publish'd Sep.r 5. 1775 by W.m Humphreys S.t Martins Lane

the smock, a temporary stage fell down, by which Mr Stanhope of Greek Street, Soho, had his leg broke, and several others were bruised in a terrible manner.[3]

Lord Stormont, ambassador to France, arrived in town from Paris on private business, having left his secretary Horace St Paul as chargé d'affaires in his absence.[4]

At night, one of the prostitutes who stroll about St James's Park was assaulted in the Birdcage Walk by two ruffians, who cut her in a dangerous manner in several parts of her head and face. She was conveyed to an apothecary's in Westminster, where her wounds were dressed. Upon being cleansed of her blood she appeared to be not above 14 years of age, and extreamly beautiful.[5]

MC 'We hear that last Friday several of Mess. Rous and Walsh's constables, and others, surrounded the house of Sir Watkin Lewes, with cockades in their hats, and other marks of triumph, crying out, "Corruption and Perjury for ever!" — "Confusion to all honest men!"'[6]

MJ 'The Duke of Wirtemberg has expressed some surprize at not being more magnificently received at the Court of London; there are two circumstances which he seems to forget, first, the avowed prejudice he always shewed for France, in whose pay his troops were during all [the] last war, and secondly, the impropriety of putting off a female favourite as a mere woman of rank.'[7]

10th April, Wednesday Smart frost in the night, fine bright day
In the morning the Duke of Wirtemburg set out for Newmarket in a coach and six, with three postilions, attended by two coaches and four, and a great number of servants on horseback.

Meanwhile the *Morning Post* observed that 'the longer he stays, the more disgust he will give, from taking too much state upon him. At Ranelagh he appeared with three gentleman attendants, one always walking exactly before him, and one on each side, to prevent the company from presuming to touch the hem of his garment; and thus in true German stiffness, he makes his rounds.'[1]

11th April, Thursday Heavy black morning, fine bright day
In the morning Boswell called on Garrick, who was to perform Abel Drugger in *The Alchemist* for the last time that evening. 'Garrick talked of Abel Drugger as *a small part*, and ... added, with an appearance of grave recollection, "If I were to begin life again, I think I should not play those low characters." Upon which I observed, "Sir, you would be in the wrong; for your great excellence is your variety of playing, your representing so well, characters so very different."'

Afterwards Boswell dined with Dr Johnson at General Paoli's and mentioned the exchange.

> JOHNSON. 'Garrick, sir, was not in earnest in what he said; for, to be sure, his peculiar excellence is his variety: and, perhaps, there is not any one char-acter which has not been as well acted by somebody else, as he could do it.'
> BOSWELL. 'Why then, sir, did he talk so?' JOHNSON. 'Why, sir, to make

you answer as you did.' BOSWELL. 'I don't know, sir; he seemed to dip deep into his mind for the reflection.' JOHNSON. 'He had not far to dip, sir: he said the same thing, probably, twenty times before.'

Following the death of their son, the Thrales had decided not to proceed with their planned journey to Italy and Boswell found that the matter was still in Johnson's thoughts. 'A man who has not been in Italy,' he said, 'is always conscious of an inferiority, from his not having seen what it is expected a man should see. The grand object of travelling is to see the shores of the Mediterranean. On those shores were the four great empires of the world: the Assyrian, the Persian, the Grecian, and the Roman. All our religion, almost all our law, almost all our arts, almost all that sets us above savages, has come to us from the shores of the Mediterranean.'[1]

All the constables belonging to the City of Westminster received orders to be on duty at Westminster Hall by eight o'clock on Monday morning next, to keep the peace during the trial of the Duchess of Kingston.[2]

Charles-Claude de Morande dined with the Chevalier d'Éon in Brewer Street in company with three other Frenchmen. According to a later statement signed by d'Éon and the three others, the conversation turned to the revival in late 1775 of the policies on d'Éon's sex. D'Éon declared that Beaumarchais and Morande had wanted him 'to act in concert with them in the traffic of these policies, representing it to him as an infallible way of making large sums of money'. Morande apparently admitted that in October 1775 he had indeed proposed to make such common cause and that, d'Éon refusing, he had consulted several 'well known English lawyers to establish whether, in the event of winning on those policies, the law would allow one to compel the losers to pay what they owed'. Their 'unanimous reply in the negative' had led him, he claimed, 'to renounce the project'. According to the four witnesses, 'he showed a good deal of ill-humour at the persistent refusal of the Chevalier d'Éon to lend himself to the shameful transactions'.[3]

The *Morning Chronicle* reprinted a report from a *Bristol Journal Extraordinary* of 8th April: 'This morning came up to the key, the snow *Dickenson*, William Meston, master, from Philadelphia, bound to Nantes in Old France, where she was to discharge her loading, and take in a cargo of warlike stores and ammunition for the use of the Continental [i.e. American] army.' On discovering this, 'the mate and people on board ... took the vessel, and instead of proceeding to France, determined to make the first British port. They accordingly brought her into Bristol ... and the mate is immediately going off for London, and will take all the letters and papers which were on board the said vessel, for the inspection of government.' The letters to French merchants mentioned '1500 stands of arms, with bayonets, and steel ramrods' and '15 tons of good gunpowder'.

In the evening John Sands, mate of the *Dickenson*, arrived at the Admiralty, where he stayed for several hours. He also gave information at Lord Weymouth's office in Cleveland Row.[4]

Garrick as Abel Drugger.
Published for Bell's
British Theatre,
29th December 1777.

At Drury Lane Theatre Governor Hutchinson and his daughter Peggy were among the audience to see Garrick as Abel Drugger. Also there was Hannah More, who found herself 'not only in the best place, but with the best company in the house, for I sat next the Orchestra, in which were a number of my acquaintance (and those no vulgar names), Edmund and Richard Burke, Dr Warton, and Sheridan'.*

Next day's *Morning Post* described the scene:

We were not surprized to find the house full as soon as the doors were open, and the most astonishing overflow we ever remember.

His performance of this character was always an exquisite treat to all palates, but last night he seemed determined to give it a gout that should not soon be forgotten. The bottle, and boxing scenes, he carried so high that the plaudits of the audience repeatedly shook the house. When Face asked him whether he has any interest with the players? he replied, 'Yes, I play the fool now and then' — But your worship! — 'They say I'm old enough to be wiser; so I intend to leave off now, and grow melancholy and gentlemanlike.' This stroke was universally taken and had a fine effect. However when he had finished his part, a murmur of sorrow run thro' the house as general as the applause had done during the performance.

Garrick himself, writing to his brother George next day, said he thought 'ye audience were mad, and they almost turn'd my brain'.[5]

* Richard Burke, aged 42, was a political writer and a younger brother of Edmund. Joseph Warton, aged 53, was headmaster of Winchester and a poet and critic.

12th April, Friday Chiefly cloudy, but little sun

Late on Thursday night, having intelligence of some run goods, four Custom House officers made their way to Deptford. Between two and three o'clock this morning they were surrounded and chased by a group of smugglers armed with sticks and bludgeons. Having become detached from the other officers, William Anchor and Joseph Pearson headed towards the watch-house for safety, but before they could reach it they lost sight of each other and Pearson was attacked. Anchor heard him cry out 'O dear,' at the first blow, but heard nothing more.

According to the later trial evidence of Samuel Whiting, one of the smugglers, when they came to the bottom of Hughes's Field their leader, Gypsy George, seized Pearson by the collar, and said if he did not tell his name, he would cut his throat. He knocked Pearson down with his stick, 'then we all hit him with our sticks', one blow each, except Gypsy George, who kept hitting Pearson for about quarter of an hour as he lay on the ground, saying 'D—n his eyes, if you kill a dozen of them, there is no sin in it.' Pearson begged for his life, saying he had a wife and four small children. They left him on the ground and headed off, but Gypsy George went back and hit him again, the other attackers begging him to stop. Gypsy George summoned two other smugglers, saying, 'Come up, my men, and hit him a blow a-piece for me,' which they did.

John Dicey, a waterman who lived nearby, heard noises at about a quarter before three o'clock. 'I first heard them hallooing out, making a terrible noise, then I heard a man cry terribly, "Oh! oh! oh!" ... I ran naked into the street. I came up to the people as they were beating the man. I cried out, "You villains, are you going to murder the man?" They ran away immediately and left him.' Another man who came to help asked Pearson how he could be beat in such a barbarous manner without discharging his pistol. Pearson answered that he was loth to take life, though they took his. A surgeon was fetched and Pearson was put on a boat and taken to the London Hospital, dangerously ill.[1]

Also in the morning, James Langar and Samuel Whitlow were executed at Tyburn, the former for a robbery in Hyde Park, the latter for a burglary. They were both very well-looking young men and extremely intent in their devotions.[2]

At half past noon the king came to St James's for a levee, after which Lord Sandwich laid the papers brought from the *Dickenson* before his majesty in council.[3]

The *Dickenson* revelations were also concerning M. Garnier, the French chargé d'affaires. He sent an account to the Comte de Vergennes in Paris, noting that 'ill-intentioned persons are trying to show that it is a proof of our friendly relations with the Americans'.[4]

Printer William Strahan wrote to philosopher David Hume in Edinburgh. Hume had written four days earlier praising two of Strahan's recent publications, *Wealth of Nations* and *Decline and Fall of the Roman Empire*, but adding that he had told Adam Smith that his work required 'too much thought' to be as popular as Gibbon's. 'What you say of Mr Gibbon's and Dr Smith's books is exactly just,'

Strahan replied. 'The former is the most popular work; but the sale of the latter, though not near so rapid, has been more than I could have expected from a work that requires much thought and reflection (qualities that do not abound among modern readers) to peruse to any purpose.'[5]

The *Morning Post* reported that 'The Dutchess of D— lies dangerously ill, and we hear the physicians have ascribed her indisposition to the reigning fashionable irregularities of the age.' However, four days later it assured the public that 'the Duchess of Devonshire has not been the least indisposed; the report ... was occasioned by the straw that was laid in Piccadilly, upon account of Lady Lincoln's being brought to bed.' The duchess did suffer a miscarriage at around this time, but was well enough to attend the first day of the Kingston trial on the 15th.[6]

MC 'We are authorised to assure the public, that the Duchess of Kingston hath not been at Westminster Hall to see the scaffolding. This, like many other reports to her grace's disadvantage, was maliciously propagated by her enemies.'[7]

13th April, Saturday A cloudy coarse day

Two days before the trial of the Duchess of Kingston, there was an astonishing concourse of people in and about Westminster Hall to survey the scene.[1]

Boswell and Johnson supped at the Crown and Anchor tavern in the Strand with Sir Joshua Reynolds and others and discussed the effect of drinking upon conversation. Reynolds said 'that a moderate glass enlivened the mind, by giving a proper circulation to the blood', and made people talk better. Johnson disagreed: 'Before dinner men meet with great inequality of understanding; and those who are conscious of their inferiority, have the modesty not to talk. When they have drunk wine, every man feels himself happy, and loses that modesty, and grows impudent and vociferous: but he is not improved; he is only not sensible of his defects.'[2]

14th April, Sunday In general cloudy, very little sun

On the eve of her trial the Duchess of Kingston attended divine service at the Chapel Royal and received the sacrament. Afterwards there was a grand drawing-room which Boswell attended, having made the short journey to St James's in a chair. He wore a suit of black clothes belonging to a Florentine castrato, not yet having had a full suit made for himself.[1]

The Earl of Rochford sent tickets for the trial to Beaumarchais with a request that he call on him at his house in Berkeley Square. Rochford was a political and diplomatic veteran who favoured friendly relations with France and a conciliatory approach to the Americans. Having found himself increasingly isolated in cabinet, he had resigned as secretary of state for the southern department in November 1775. His friendship with Beaumarchais dated back over a decade to a time when he had been ambassador at Madrid and Beaumarchais had been there on a mission to salvage the honour of one of his sisters.

Beaumarchais reported on the resulting visit to Berkeley Square in a letter to Vergennes two days later. Rochford had raised the news from Bristol concerning the apparent trade of American merchandise for French munitions. 'This,' Rochford went on, 'joined to the fact that two French gentlemen have been in secret communication with the Congress on behalf of your ministers and have, it is said, secret liaisons with persons in London, has greatly alarmed our council. Some ill-informed people have even sought to make suspicion fall on you. But the king is so little convinced, that it is on his behalf I am discussing it with you. What do you think of all that?'

Beaumarchais replied with characteristic spirit, asking what right England had to restrict French commerce. 'I see, monsieur,' responded Rochford, 'that you are crimson with anger.'

'Milord, you who are English and patriotic, should not find it bad that a good Frenchman should have pride for his country.'

'No offence is taken, but at least you will agree that your minister must deal severely with those Frenchmen who are negotiating with the Congress in the name of your government.'

'I do not believe any of this news, my lord. ... If you can discover the names of these supposed agents and the least proof that they have called themselves agents of our government, I can assure you they will be disavowed and even punished, if they can be arrested.'

Feeling that his defence had worked, but fearing that he was himself under suspicion, Beaumarchais prepared the way for bringing into play a cover story concocted to explain his presence in London. 'The d'Éon affair does not occupy me any more,' he said. 'Whether he goes back to France or not, no one on our side is interested. His decision is his own business and no longer mine. You are going to ask me what brings me here?'

'No, monsieur, because I know in advance what you will reply.'

'I see, my lord, that my letters are opened.'

'My friend, we are too old hands at politics, you and me, not to be aware that one writes what one wishes.'

'I have nothing to hide from you, my lord,' Beaumarchais replied, proffering a letter from a French minister concerning the supply of Portuguese coins for France's American colonies. 'Here is what the king has asked me to do.'

Rochford read the letter several times, apparently with great attention, and after further conversation the two men parted on good terms. Beaumarchais congratulated himself that, to add flesh to his cover story, he had previously called on several London bankers to discuss the buying up of Portuguese coin.[2]

The same evening four young gentlemen, very much in liquor, coming from Greenwich in a boat, ran foul of a rope in the tier opposite the Tower. One of the men fell into the river, but fortunately they had a water spaniel in the boat, which being put in the river, dived and brought the man up, by which means he was saved.[3]

15th April, Monday Cloudy day, fine bright evening

Anna Porter, recently turned 18, rose at 5 a.m. Two hours later, after 'attending my hairdresser', she began a letter to a friend: 'I can absolutely settle to nothing. No chaos ever equalled my head at present, and I will venture to pronounce the heads of half ye people in this great town. This day the Duchess of Kingston is tried for bigamy — the whole town has talked of nothing else for this week past.'[1]

About eight o'clock the judges, and some of the nobility and gentry, began to assemble at the Great Russell Street house of Lord Bathurst, lord high steward for the duration of the trial, where an elegant breakfast of cold tongue, &c. with choice of rich wines was provided. Shortly after nine o'clock the procession to Westminster began, at which time the bells of St Giles's Church struck up a merry peal at odds with the solemnity of the scene. Constables went before, followed by five of Bathurst's coaches, four painted green and the fifth white, all the coachmen and footmen having new liveries. Next came the state coach, drawn by six black horses decorated with blue ribbands, in which travelled Bathurst, in a gold gown, accompanied by garter king of arms, &c., four footmen walking on each side. The coaches of the judges and masters in Chancery followed.[2]

So great was the curiosity to see the lord high steward and the rest of the nobility pass that windows in the lower part of Westminster had been let at one guinea each. Refugee Samuel Curwen and a friend went to Parliament Street to see the procession, but to their disappointment found it had already passed.[3]

In Old Palace Yard, within thirty yards of Westminster Hall, the axle-tree of the state coach broke, but luckily his lordship received no hurt, only being much frightened.

The Duchess of Kingston had left Kingston House at eight o'clock in her chair. According to one report she was met on the road to Westminster by the Duke of Newcastle's coach, which took her the rest of the way. She arrived at the duke's house in New Palace Yard at half past eight, and waited there for the lord high steward and peers to convene in the Hall.

Anna Porter had been invited to sit in the lord high steward's box, and, after setting her letter aside, she left home to meet Lady Bathurst 'at a coffee house adjoining ye House of Lords, where she has taken a room whilst the tryal lasts. Here her company ... assembled, a breakfast was prepared, &c. but I amused my self in seeing the peers and peeresses coming into ye Hall from their carriages, which were mostly elegant ones, and ye horses full harnessed and ornamented.'

Detachments of horse and foot guards had been posted round Old and New Palace yards to keep order, but the crowds of spectators and multiplicity of coaches resulted in several accidents. A man, who appeared rather aged, was thrown down at the end of Parliament Street, a cart going towards Scotland Yard ran over his head, and he was killed on the spot. Meanwhile a poor woman with child was flung down and trampled on, by which she was so much bruised that she died as she was taking to the hospital.

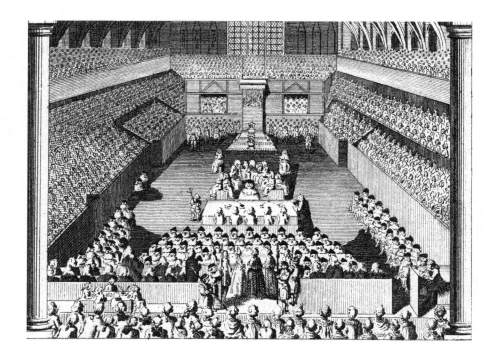

Inside Westminster Hall the crowd was more orderly. By nine o'clock the peeresses, foreign ambassadors, &c. had all taken their seats. The ladies seemed to outvie each other in the richness of their dresses and the brilliancy of their ornaments. None was more distinguished than the Duchess of Cumberland, who came in with the duke, and finding no place set apart for her, sat among the peeresses on the ducal side. The Duchess of Devonshire, showing no sign of being indisposed, attended in company with the Duchess of Argyle and Lady Derby. The Duke of Wirtemburg sat in the foreign ministers' box, as did the ladies who came over with him, about whom there has been so extraordinary a Court buzz. There were several other foreigners of distinction present, including a Countess Castiglione from Milan. It was computed that no less than 4,000 persons were present, that out of that number 2,500 were ladies, and that the jewels they wore were worth upwards of four millions of money.[4]

Among the throng were Governor Hutchinson's daughter Peggy, who attended 'from between 7 and 8 in the morning till 6 or 7 in the evening', and James Boswell, who had been given a ticket by Lady Eglinton. He relished the whole scene, particularly 'the beautiful exhibition of ladies. I did not think there had been so many fine women in the universe; and I thought the mode of dressing, with a deal of hair and feathers and flowers of various colours, more beautiful than what I had ever seen before.' Unfortunately he could hear very little and left at about two o'clock. Also present was Beaumarchais, presumably using the tickets provided by Lord Rochford.[5]

A REPRESENTATION *of the Building in* Weſtminſter-Hall,
for the TRIAL *of the* DUCHESS *of* KINGSTON.

Court of KING'S BENCH. High Court of CHANCERY.

Seats for Peers Tickets.	Seats for Peers Tickets.
Seats for Peers Tickets.	Seats for Peers Tickets.
Seats for Peers Tickets.	Seats for Peers Tickets.
Seats for Peers Tickets.	Seats for Peers Tickets.
Seats for Peers Tickets.	Seats for Peers Tickets.

Gallery — Seats for the Honourable House of Commons — Foreign Miniſters — Duke of Newcaſtle's

The Royal Box, with ſeats covered with crimſon, and a rich velvet chair for his Majeſty, if he comes, and the Lords, &c. in waiting.

His Grace the Lord High STEWARD, ſeated under a rich canopy of State.

A Box with ſeats lined and covered with crimſon for his Royal Highneſs the Prince of Wales, Lords in waiting, &c.

Heralds. — Heralds. — Heralds. — Heralds.

Viſcounts — Great Officers of State. Dukes, Marquiſes, Viſcounts — Seats for Peereſſes. Seats for Lords Tickets. Seats for Lords Tickets. Seats for Lords Tickets.

Judges — Judges ſeated on Woolpacks. — Judges

Maſters in Chancery.

Bishops. — Bishops. — Bishops.

Earls Earls Earls — Earls Earls Earls — Earls Earls Earls

Barons — The Repeater. — Barons

King's Council. — Council.

Solicitor General. — Uſher of the Black Rod. PRISONER. — The Priſoner's

Attorney General. — Evidence. — The Manner

they ſtand at the Bar.

Seats in the — Tickets, and Board of Works. — Windows — for the Vice- — Chamberlain.

Princeſs Amelia. — Gallery — Duke of Newcaſtle's — Speaker of the Houſe of Commons. — Seats for the Honourable Houſe of Commons.

| Hon. Houſe of Commons. | | Tickets. |
| Seats for the Members of the | Ladies. for the Box Duke of Ancaſter's the His Grace | Seats for Peers |

His Grace the Duke of Ancaſter's Seat.

Weſtminſter-Hall Gate.

ABOVE Layout of the Hall, from the *London Chronicle*, 18th April 1776.
FACING PAGE 'Representation of the Trial of the Dutchess of Kingston', undated.

The start of proceedings was delayed while the Lords debated a legal nicety in their own House. Meanwhile, according to the *Morning Chronicle*, two ladies in one of the galleries, waiting eagerly for the Lords to appear, 'on hearing a noise towards the entrance, went to the extremity of the gallery to learn the cause of it'. Unfortunately a board was missing from the flooring in that corner, 'and the ladies sunk precipitately through the vacuity. One of them by her fall totally destroyed ... a female's head-dress, who sat in the seats beneath, dissipating the mock grass, flowers, fruits [and] uncasing the wool ... This was not all; the lady's heel grazed the cheek of the unfortunate fair one, whose proud tower of capillary ornament had been levelled, and her bare bum squatted on a gentleman's head. The other lady only did herself mischief; she hung suspended ... and it is feared has broke one of her ribs.'

The king was not present but the queen, attended by the Duchess of Ancaster and Lady Charlotte Finch, with the Prince of Wales, the Bishop of Osnaburgh, the princess royal, &c. went privately in coaches to the Duke of Newcastle's house. At half after ten they took their places in the elegant centre box of the duke's gallery, to which there was an entrance from his house.

About eleven o'clock the Lords in elaborate procession finally came into the Hall. The serjeant at arms called out, 'Oyez, oyez, oyez! Usher of the black rod, bring forth Elizabeth Duchess Dowager of Kingston, your prisoner, to the bar, pursuant to the order of the House of Lords,' and her grace was brought to the bar, at which point Lady Harrington, known for her own amorous history, ejaculated, 'The Devil confound her! How brazen the wretch looks!' When the duchess approached the bar she made three reverences, and then fell upon her knees before being told she might rise. She was dressed in a very becoming manner in a mourning Polonese, trimmed with black flowers, her head-dress a black hood, her hair without powder. 'She really looked handsome,' noted Anna Porter. She was attended by Mrs Egerton and Mrs Barrington, who were both dressed in white sattin, and by her chaplain, physician, and apothecary.[6]

ELIZABETH *Dutchess Dowager of* KINGSTON.

Taken at the Bar of the House of Lords, on the 15 of April, 1776.

Publish'd as the Act directs, May 20, 1776.

ABOVE The duchess at her trial.

FACING PAGE 'Iphigenia's late Procession from Kingston to Bristol —
by Chudleigh Meadows.' A satirical view of the duchess's entourage.

The charge against the duchess, for feloniously marrying Evelyn Pierrepont, late Duke of Kingston, she being then married to Augustus John Hervey, now Earl of Bristol, was read. She pleaded not guilty, after which Mr Dunning, lead counsel, and Mr Thurlow, attorney general, opened for the prosecution. They were followed by Mr Wallace and Dr Calvert on behalf of the duchess, who argued that a decision of the ecclesiastical court in February 1769, that their client was not married to Hervey, was final.[7]

After initial dismay the duchess seemed chearful and composed, displaying a fortitude and dignity that commanded general admiration. Her attendant Mrs Barrington, however, was so fatigued with standing that she was seized with violent hysterics, which continued for a considerable time.

Boswell was not alone in retiring early. According to one report the queen also left at around two o'clock. Mrs Harris and her daughter Gertrude headed off 'extremely fatigued' when yet another lawyer got up to speak, having not being able to hear a word for four hours. 'By the assistance of an officer of the guards, who walked before us with his sword drawn, we got safely through the crowd.'[8]

At about half past six the trial was adjourned till next day. The prisoner was conducted back to the Duke of Newcastle's, where she took refreshment, and then returned to Kingston House, accompanied by Sir Francis Molyneux, black rod, to whose custody she was committed. At night he slept in the next room to her in case she should try to abscond.[9]

During the day Mrs Delany wrote from St James's Place to her daughter Mary in Derbyshire:

> At present I am in as quiet a solitude (excepting London cries) as if on the top of Bunster or pinacle of Thorp Cloud, for all the world, great and *small*, are gone to Westminster *Hall* ... The solicitude for tickets, the distress of rising early to be time enough for a place, the anxiety about hairdressers, (poor souls hurried out of their lives), mortifications that feathers and flying lappets should be laid aside for that day, as they would obstruct the view from those who sit behind — all these important matters were discuss'd in my little circle last night. Bernard* dined here, Mrs Boscawen† came by appointment in the evening to settle their going together this morning to the tryal; here they met at seven, and went together in Mrs Boscawen's coach. ... I bravely refused a ticket for the queen's box ... for I feared the bustle my spirits would be in now unused to such splendid appearances, and doubted whether my eyesight and hearing would have been at all gratified, as both those senses are a little clouded by old Father Time. So I content myself with my own chimney corner, and have resigned my place to one more worthy of it. My young men return hither to a mutton chop as soon as the busyness of the day is over.

* Probably her nephew, Bernard d'Ewes (1743-1780).
† Frances Boscawen (1719-1805), letter writer and literary hostess.

Next day she added:

At seven they came starved, having been twelve hours fasting, and eat their little dinner voraciously (mutton chops and lamb pye, lobster and apple puffs), drank their coffee between eight and nine, and then came to my little drawing-room ... The shew of the tryal was *awfull*, and *splendid* beyond imagination, but very little more done than a preparation for what's to come, and nobody can guess yet what time it will take.[10]

MP 'The tickets issued by the nobility upon the ... solemn occasion, are meaner than those generally delivered for a puppet-shew. On the top is the Duke of Ancaster's crest ... | Beneath are the duke's arms: the whole is wretchedly engraved, and printed upon a narrow slip of paper; in short it has more the appearance of a wrapper of *Hebb's* best Virginia, than an admission ticket to the supreme tribunal of this great empire.'[11]

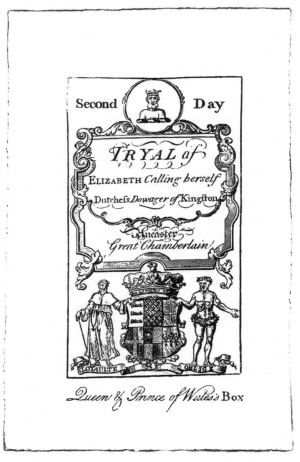

Ticket for the trial's second day. William Hebb, alluded to in the *Morning Post*'s description, was a snuff and tobacco man in Cockspur Street.

16th April, Tuesday A fair day, very wet evening

The trial resumed at eleven o'clock. None of the royal family were present, their majesties taking an airing to Kew and returning to the Queen's Palace to dinner.

Those who did attend included Anna Porter, 'in the gallery belonging to the Board of Works', for which her family had two tickets for the duration of the trial; Boswell, this time with a ticket which admitted him close to the bar; Governor Hutchinson, who left at 4 p.m.; and Hannah More, who described events in detail in two letters written next day from Garrick's house in the Adelphi.

The actor, who was to perform at Drury Lane Theatre in the evening, had given More his ticket and she and Mrs Garrick 'were in full dress by seven. At eight we went to the Duke of Newcastle's, whose house adjoins Westminster Hall, in which he has a large gallery ... You will imagine the bustle of five thousand people getting into one hall, yet, in all this hurry, we walked in tranquilly.' Another advantage was that 'we had only to open a door to get at a very fine cold collation of all sorts of meats and wines, with tea, &c., a privilege confined to those who belonged to the Duke of Newcastle. I fancy the peeresses would have been glad of our places ... for I saw Lady Derby and the Duchess of Devonshire with their workbags full of good things. Their rank and dignity did not exempt them from the "villainous appetites" of eating and drinking.'

More thought it 'impossible to describe the magnificence of the spectacle'. The Hall 'was lined with matting and red cloth and portioned out into galleries and boxes. In the two front rows sat all the peeresses and their daughters, and in the other seats people of fashion of both sexes. The present mode of dressing never perhaps appear'd to so much advantage ... as there was so great a space filled in such regular order with curls, ribbons, flowers, feathers, fruits and jewels. Hoops were prohibited as occupying too much room.'

She and Mrs Garrick were in the Hall early, but as on the first day the procession of peers did not begin until about eleven, with Lord Bathurst and the Duke of Cumberland the last to pass, both having their trains borne. The duchess was then led in by black rod and James Laroche, one of those who had stood bail for her. She was dressed 'in deep mourning, a black silk sacque trimmed with crape, black crape handkerchief, a hood of the same put on becomingly, like a veil, ruffle cuffs, treble black gauze ruffles, black silk gloves and black fan. There was nothing white about her, and had it not been for the remains of a handsome face you wou'd have taken her for a bale of bombazine.' On her curtseying three times to the judges, Bathurst called out that she might rise, and 'the peers made her a slight bow. They sat in their hats the whole time, only when any lord had any thing to propose he rose, took it off, and when he had done speaking put it on again and sat down.'

The attorney general (Thurlow), the solicitor general (Wedderburn), and Mr Dunning spoke tellingly and at length for the prosecution. Anna Porter was impressed by the first two but not by Dunning: 'To an exceeding bad person is joined the false conviction of being perfectly handsome. Imagine ye ridiculous composition this forms!' Boswell, on the other hand, as a lawyer, appreciated the 'shrewdness and vivacity' of Dunning's contribution. Hannah More agreed with both views:

> Dunning's manner is insufferably bad, coughing and spitting between every three words, yet he said more to the purpose than all of them. His sense was strong and pointed to the last degree ... He made her grace shed tears, and I really believe unfeigned ones, tho she is such an actress it is impossible to determine positively on that. In imitation of her great predecessor Mrs Rudd, of pious memory, she affected to write a great deal, tho I plainly saw she only wrote as they do love letters on the stage, without marking the paper with a letter, but I suppose she thought it would give her an air of business, and understanding.

Some time after four o'clock, as Mr Wallace was about replying on behalf of the duchess, Lord Talbot proposed that they adjourn, the sitting having been so long: 'I think we have already heard more than we can retain; at least I honestly confess for my own part I have.' Some disagreement followed, with cries of *Proceed! Proceed!* Lord Camden then drew the attention of the House to the indisposition of the duchess, saying her physicians had been sent for and a surgeon to bleed her. Hannah More was not convinced:

> She was taken ill (politically) when she thought things seemed to look unfavourably, and got her council to whisper it [to] Lord Camden, who desired aloud that they might adjourn, the noble lady at the bar being taken very ill. It was good natured in my lord, who really believed it, but tho a good actress she did not perform so well, but she was detected, as she was gay and smiling the minute before. As soon as they had given her leave to retire, and seemed disposed to go on after she shou'd be withdrawn, she recover'd all at once ...

Their lordships then retired to the parliament chamber, where, after deliberating for three quarters of an hour, they agreed to adjourn till Friday. Information of their decision was not received in Westminster Hall till half after six, at which point the counsel withdrew and the duchess retired in the custody of black rod.

'There was a great deal of magnificence, a great deal of ceremony, and a great deal of nonsense,' concluded More. 'They adjourned upon the foolishest pretences imaginable, and did *nothing* with such an air of business as was really ridiculous. However, I am very glad to have seen it, as probably it will be the only thing of the kind that will ever be seen ... | When it will end nobody can even guess'.[1]

In the evening, perhaps appropriately, *Much Ado About Nothing* was performed at Drury Lane Theatre, with Garrick as Benedict and Mrs Abington as Beatrice. Boswell looked on from the shilling gallery, the only place he could find, 'so that I saw imperfectly, though I heard pretty well'. Hannah More and Mrs Garrick 'drove directly' to the theatre from Westminster Hall. They arrived in time to see the second act, in which, according to More, Garrick 'as usual was delightful, and I think I never saw any thing so admirable as his dancing was ... Never did five and twenty exhibit more grace, vivacity and elegance.'[2]

17th April, Wednesday Wet morning, fair day, bright evening

Horace Walpole wrote from Arlington Street to Sir Horace Mann in Florence:

> You may think of America, if you please; but we think and talk but of one subject, the solemn comedy that is acting in Westminster Hall. Deep wagers had been laid that the duchess-countess would decamp before her trial. This, with a million of other stories, have been so spread, that I am determined to believe no one fact but what I shall read in the printed trial; for at it I have not been, though curious enough about so august a mummery, and so original a culprit ...[1]

Lord Fife visited the Duchess of Kingston. Next day he wrote home to Scotland that he had 'found her pretty easy and in tollerable spirits. She has ever been very civil and obliging to me for these twenty past years, and I own I wish her to beat them, for I consider her cause more as a Persecution than a Prosecution. They were offering 30 and 25 guineas for a ticket the first and second day.'[2]

A severe trial of manhood was held in Whitechapel between two butchers' porters. After they had mauled each other to a dreadful degree, or in the butchers' phrase, were properly *cut up*, they were taken from the field of battle in a couple of wheelbarrows, totally helpless and senseless. One of them is said to be since dead.[3]

The *Gazetteer* featured a further advertisement for the recovery of the body of the drowned son of Albany Wallis, offering an additional incentive: 'Mr Wallis has left TEN GUINEAS with Mr Tremmell, in Northumberland-street, Charing-cross, to be distributed amongst those who shall in future be most assiduous in their endeavours to find the body.'[4]

GA 'The trial of a peer is certainly one of the most splendid spectacles which can be formed by the human imagination; but it is one of the dullest also. Neither the pleadings, nor any other parts of the process, are heard by nine tenths of the company; so that when the eye has been satiated by the magnificence of the scene, the spirits immediately flag, curiosity gives way to languor, and in a little time people discover that the fatigue is by much too high a price for the gratification.'[5]

18th April, Thursday A fair day, bright evening

The house in Harley Street lately belonging to Daniel Perreau was sold by auction for 4,000l.[1]

At the Old Bailey Christopher Saunders, a ship's cook, was tried for carnally knowing a cow. Abraham Denning, of Limehouse Marsh, deposed that at about six in the morning on Sunday 10th March he was in the hayloft of a cow-house when, hearing movement in an adjoining barn, he looked through a chink in the boards and saw Saunders stroking and patting a cow. 'He went to the other end of the barn and fetched a tub to put behind the cow; it stood up edgeways; then he got up on the top of the side of the tub. I saw him unbutton his breeches and his trowsers ... I saw him put his hands upon the cow's back, and wriggle himself about. He was about ten minutes in that posture. I believe it might be more.' The prisoner, who appeared upwards of 60 years of age, denied the charge, but in spite of witnesses to his character as a sober honest man, he was found guilty and sentenced to death.[2]

The Duchess of Kingston, attended by Mr Quarme, deputy black rod, was seen in several parts of the town, particularly in Holywell Street (very near Lyon's Inn, home to the Rev. William Jackson) and at the chambers of Mr Wallace, one of her advocates, in Lincoln's Inn. Her appearance drew together a vast number of people, who attended her return to her coach at Lincoln's Inn, many expressing their hearty wishes for her deliverance.[3]

In the afternoon the body of Master Wallis was found floating off Tower Wharf by a boatman, who took it into his boat. While he attended to the body his brother went and gave the information, so that they would have the rewards between them. The body was then carried in a hackney coach to Mr Cecil's in Norfolk Street, from whence it was soon after moved to the house of the afflicted father. The boy's watch and money were in his pocket, and his buckles in his shoes. His face was but little swelled, and there was no other appearance of a wound about him but at the back of his head, where it is supposed the keel of a boat struck him a violent blow.

During the time the body was being taken out of the Thames, a young man belonging to one of the Dublin traders fell from a boat's edge into the water, and was drowned.[4]

A Fragment on Government was published anonymously. Written by Jeremy Bentham, aged 28, it criticised what he saw as the confused and complacent view of the British constitution set out in the introduction to Sir William Blackstone's *Commentaries on the Laws of England* (1764-1769). Stating that 'a system that is never to be censured, will never be improved', he argued against the 'abject and indiscriminating homage' paid to existing laws. In his view 'the principle of utility' was 'the sole and all-sufficient reason for every point of practice', and 'the only clew to guide a man through these streights'.[5]

Boswell and General Paoli dined at the Mitre tavern with Sir John Pringle and other members of the Royal Society. Boswell sat next to Captain Cook and had a long conversation with him during which Cook described a New Zealander eating human flesh in his presence. At the meeting of the society that followed, a letter from Cook to Pringle, concerning the tides in the South Seas, was read.

Afterwards Boswell went with Paoli to a subscription ball at Haberdashers' Hall. There, among 'a goodly company of city ladies and gentlemen', he met Mohawk chief Joseph Brant, with whom he talked briefly. He also got into conversation with Captain Tice, who with Colonel Johnson had conducted Brant to England, and who happened to have served with a cousin of Boswell's in America. Perhaps already having in mind an article that he would write for the *London Magazine*, Boswell asked if he could pay a visit. Tice said he would be glad to see him 'any morning to drink tea with the chief and him at the Swan with Two Necks in Lad Lane'.[6]

MC 'The baggage of the general officers alone of the Hessian troops, 'tis said, would freight two transports of 300 tons each. The above gentlemen have not only their coaches on board, but have laid in such quantities of every kind of camp and other furniture, with Rhenish wines, old hock, Westphalia hams, and other stores, that they rather seem to be going to settle in America than to serve as soldiers.'[7]

MJ 'To so extravagant a pitch has the present age arrived, that no less a sum than fifty guineas have been offered for admittance into Westminster Hall to-morrow.'[8]

19th April, Friday Bright and cloudy at intervals, cold wind

As he headed back along Piccadilly after a walk in Hyde Park, Boswell was overtaken by Samuel Foote, who invited him into his 'chariot'. Boswell accepted and they talked of Dr Johnson and the Kingston trial. Foote was incensed that the lord chief justice, Lord Mansfield, seemed to be showing partiality towards the duchess.[1]

Boswell does not seem to have attended the trial this day, but crowds of others did, including Anna Porter and John Wilkes. The carriages were so numerous in Palace Yard that many ladies had to alight a great distance from Westminster Hall and walk through the croud, conducted by the guards. Greater care was taken than on previous days to prevent admission of improper persons. It being suspected that tickets had been forged, they were strictly examined, counterfeits detected, and two or three persons who had sold them were taken into custody.[2]

It was half past eleven before their lordships had taken their places in the Hall. After the usual proclamations Mr Wallace spoke on behalf the duchess for upwards of two hours and a half, followed by Dr Calvert. The peers then adjourned to their own House, whither the chief justice of the Common Pleas was carried in a chair, on account of his lameness, and the prisoner withdrew to the room provided for her during the trial.

The Lords debated whether the previous ruling of the ecclesiastical court, that the duchess had not married Augustus Hervey, was conclusive in law if it was proved that it had been obtained by fraud or collusion. Having decided it was not, they returned to Westminster Hall and Edward Thurlow, attorney general, opened the indictment fully.

He said bigamy was a crime of 'malignant complexion and pernicious example'. For the duchess, 'dry lucre was the whole inducement, cold fraud the only means to perpetrate that crime'. It was 'a matter of perfect indifference to the prisoner which husband she adhered to' as long as 'the profit to be drawn from this marriage, or from that, was tolerably equal'.

He described the wedding on 4th August 1744, in a small parish church in the grounds of Lainston House, near Winchester, of Elizabeth Chudleigh, as the duchess then was, to the Hon. Augustus Hervey. It was conducted at night, one of the witnesses 'holding the taper in his hat', and kept secret largely to enable her to retain her position at Court as a maid of honour. Not long afterwards Hervey set sail with the navy for the West Indies, but on his return in October 1746 the couple lived together in Conduit Street, London. In 1747 a child was born but knowledge of its existence was suppressed. It did not survive long, and nor did the marriage, Hervey breaking off all relations a short time later.

In 1751 Hervey's elder brother succeeded to the earldom of Bristol. In 1759 the infirm state of his health 'seemed to open the prospect of a rich succession, and an earldom. It was thought worth while, as nothing better had then offered, to be Countess of Bristol; and for that purpose to adjust the proofs of her marriage.' The prisoner therefore travelled to Winchester, where Mr Amis, the rector who had conducted the wedding, was living in declining health. She sought a certificate of the marriage, but an attorney advising this was not the best way to prove the matter, a 'book was bought, and the marriage was registered. The book was entitled, Marriages, Births, and Burials in the parish of Lainston. ... The prisoner was in great spirits. She thanked Mr Amis, and told him, it might be a hundred thousand pounds in her way. She told Mrs Amis all her secrets; of the child she had by Mr Hervey; a fine boy, but it was dead; and how she borrowed 100l. of her aunt ... to make baby clothes. It served the purpose of the hour to disclose these things.'

Soon after, however, Lord Bristol recovered his health, and the register was forgotten until 1768, when Hervey wished for a divorce in order to marry another woman. Elizabeth, now mistress of the Duke of Kingston, had in view a richer match. Thurlow said that the couple therefore colluded. Elizabeth instituted a suit of jactitation (or false declaration) of marriage, to which Hervey responded with a cross libel, claiming the rights of marriage, but supporting his claim so weakly that in February 1769 judgement was given in her favour. 'A grosser artifice, I believe,' said Thurlow, 'was never fabricated. ... | Thus was the way paved to an adulterous marriage; thus was the Duke of Kingston drawn in to believe, that Mr Hervey's claim to the prisoner was a false and injurious pretension; and he gave his unsuspecting hand to a woman who was then, and had for twenty-five years been, the wife of another.'

Next the solicitor general examined the first witness for the prosecution, Ann Craddock, formerly a servant to Mrs Hanmer, the duchess's aunt. She said she had witnessed the marriage at Lainston, had been employed to take care that the other servants should be out of the way, had seen the couple in bed together, and had later been told of the existence of a child both by the duchess and by Mrs Hanmer.

For the duchess, Mr Wallace sought to undermine this damaging testimony by suggesting that Craddock expected reward from the prosecutors, the Meadows family, for giving it. Mrs Craddock seeming evasive, this suspicion was pursued by several peers who also questioned her. The last of them, Lord Hillsborough, extracted the admission that she had received a letter from a Mr Fozard telling her that a gentleman of his acquaintance 'would get me a sinecure'. John Fozard was a former servant of the Duke of Kingston who had quitted the duke's service on the duke's marriage to Elizabeth Chudleigh. He now owned a livery stable at Hyde Park Corner at which Evelyn Meadows kept his horses.

It having grown so dark that it was impossible for the short-hand writers to take down the evidence, the court was adjourned until next day.[3]

There being no levee nor any publick business at St James's, on account of all the nobility being at the duchess's trial, their majesties took an airing as far as Kew, where they stayed and dined, and did not return to the Queen's Palace till seven o'clock.[4]

20th April, Saturday Many heavy clouds, but a fine day

The trial of the duchess resumed in Westminster Hall at about eleven o'clock. Governor Hutchinson attended, noting in his diary that the trial 'engages the attention of the town, and little is said of America'. Also present was Sir John Fielding, who was called out briefly to examine someone arrested for selling a ticket wrongly thought to have been forged. One absentee was Anna Porter, who stayed away, 'imagining ye evidences would be rather unfit for a female ear'.

Proceedings began with the conclusion of Ann Craddock's testimony, after which eminent surgeon Caesar Hawkins was called. Initially reluctant to disclose information gained in a professional capacity, he admitted that he believed Hervey and Elizabeth to have been married, had attended their son at least once, and had understood that both the marriage and the birth were to be kept secret.

The Hon. Sophia Fettiplace, a sister of Lord Howe and a former lady of the bedchamber to Augusta, Princess of Wales, also admitted that she had understood the marriage to have taken place – 'In Hampshire, in a summer house, in a garden' – but made clear that she knew, or was willing to reveal, nothing else of the matter.

The next witness, war secretary Lord Barrington, was even more reluctant: 'I feel that any private conversation entrusted to me is not to be reported again.' Reminded that he had taken an oath to 'declare the whole truth', he was evidently torn, not wishing to commit perjury, and prompting an intervention from the duchess: 'I do release my Lord Barrington from every obligation of honour.' His sense of honour was not so easily to be laid aside, however, and only after much further pressing did he admit that he had understood 'there had been a matrimonial engagement entered into,' but he added at once that 'whether it amounted to a legal marriage or not, I am not lawyer or civilian enough to judge.'

Judith Phillips, widow of the Rev. Mr Amis but now remarried to a dismissed steward of the Duke of Kingston, exhibited no such qualms. She told in detail of the duchess's visit to Winchester in 1759 and of the making of the register to provide proof of her marriage to Hervey. She was challenged as to whether Evelyn Meadows was paying for her and her husband to live at the Turf Coffee-house in St Mary Axe, and admitted that she had been in company with Meadows at Mr Fozard's.

Other, minor witnesses were examined and at seven o'clock the trial was adjourned. One elderly lady sitting behind the peeresses and their daughters had by this time fallen asleep, and it was with some difficulty she was awaked.[1]

Meanwhile, about noon, the remains of Master Wallis were removed in funeral state from his father's house in Norfolk Street, to be interred in the east cloister of Westminster Abbey. The hearse was followed by his father in the first coach, accompanied by David Garrick and two other gentlemen.

Among accidental spectators of the solemn progress was Samuel Curwen, making his way to the Strand from Westminster Hall, where he had been allowed a glimpse of the splendour of the Kingston trial's setting. He noted that the procession was led by six men on foot 'with black rods, like halberts'; then came 'a man with a tablet on his head covered with black cloth and charged with tufts of white ostrich feathers'; next came the hearse, with '6 or 8 tufts of the same feathers' on the top and 'carried by six horses covered with black cloth and white ostrich feathers on their heads'; and finally '10 or 12 coaches'.

The body was met in the cloisters and was preceded by the headmaster, Dr Smith, and followed by the young gentlemen of the school. The pall was supported by six king's scholars in white scarfs. When they arrived at the grave, the doctor performed the funeral service before a great concourse of people. The scene was truly affecting, most of the boys shedding tears for the loss of their schoolfellow, particularly the youth who was with him in the boat and witnessed the accident. Mr Wallis expressed a desire to see him after the ceremony to soothe his mind, but Dr Smith, it is imagined, thought it not prudent for either party at that time.

The *Morning Post* reported that 'an inscription is intended to be engraved on the tomb, as an awful memento, to his surviving companions.' In 1777 a marble tablet, commissioned by Garrick, was duly installed. Its Latin inscription referred to Albany Charles as his most loving father's 'only hope', noted that he had been captivated by the forbidden waters of the Thames, and closed with an injunction: 'Stay, young man! Contemplate his end!'[2]

Boswell visited the Swan with Two Necks to see Joseph Brant. Returning to Dilly's he had his feet washed, wrote to John Wilkes asking to see him for chocolate, thought of having a portrait print of Brant done, and went to speak again with Brant who agreed to sit for one.[3]

The article arising from Boswell's encounter with Brant appeared with accompanying portrait in the July issue of the *London Magazine*, published on 1st August:

> This chief had not the ferocious dignity of a savage leader; nor does he discover any extraordinary force either of mind or body. ... Upon his tomahawk is carved the first letter of his Christian name, *Joseph*, and his Mohock appellation thus, *Thayendaneken* (pronounced *Theandenaigen*) the *g* being sounded hard as in

get. His manners are gentle and quiet; and to those who study human nature, he affords a very convincing proof of the tameness which education can produce upon the wildest race. He speaks English very well; and is so much master of the language, that he is engaged in a translation of the New Testament into the Mohock tongue. Upon his arrival in London, he was conducted to the inn, called the Swan with two Necks, in Lad-Lane. Proper lodgings were to be provided for him; but he said the good people of the inn were so civil, that he would not leave them; and accordingly he continued there all the time he was in London. He was struck with the appearance of England in general; but he said he chiefly admired the ladies and the horses.[4]

From an Original Drawing in the Possession of James Boswell Esq.

JOSEPH THAYENDANEKEN

The Mohawk Chief

Housebreakers, after Thomas Rowlandson, 1788

21st April, Sunday Fine bright day, hot sun, cold wind

Between two and three o'clock in the morning four villains with black crape over their faces, armed with pistols and cutlasses, broke into the dwelling-house of James Penleaze, Esq., magistrate, opposite the Nag's Head in Hackney Road, through a back parlour window next the fields. Among items taken were a silver tea-kettle and coffee-pot, silver snuff boxes, candlesticks and butter boats, four diamond rings set in gold, a brilliant diamond breast buckle in shape of a heart, a gold repeating watch, and eight enamelled watches. At trials arising from the burglary Mr Penleaze put his losses at 'between 4 and 500l.' and his wife Elizabeth gave a detailed account of what had happened.

> I heard an attempt at the door where I lay. As I did not suppose any body belonging to me would attempt to open my door without speaking, I waked Mr Penleaze, and said, 'For God's sake, for God's sake, here are rogues.' Mr Penleaze jumped up in his bed and asked fiercely, 'Who is there?' But before an answer could be made, the door, with a part of the wainscot, came down, and four men rushed in with a kind of a yell. One had a dark lanthorn in his hand, and one had a bit of gauze under his nose over his mouth, tied behind his head. They were upon the bed almost immediately. Two mounted up upon the bed at the feet, and came almost close up to me. The other two went to the head of the bed, one on each side. One held a pistol to my head, and the other stood with a cutlass before me. We never lie with our curtains drawn, as Mr Penleaze is asthmatical.

They said, 'Your money, your money, tell us where your money is.' I screamed very much, being terrified with the pistols and cutlasses which shone much. I kept up in the bed, begging for God's sake they would not hurt us, and they should have what money we had. Mr Penleaze too said so, and begged they would use us well. They said they would, but as I did not lie down immediately, one of them struck at me with a cutlass, which missed my head and cut in at the head of the bed. I said, 'I will lie down, I will lie down immediately,' and drew the cloaths over my own head ...

They asked Mr Penleaze again where the money was, and he directed them into the room where it lay. I was astonished to hear Mr Penleaze direct them to the room where almost every thing was kept that we had that was valuable. I immediately directed them to another room. I put the cloaths off my head that they might hear me speak the clearer, and that I might have a little breath. I said, 'There is a little more money in the house, there is some gold, I believe, if you will please to go into the next room, gentlemen, and open the drawers in the chest of drawers, and look about the middle drawer, perhaps you may find it there.' This I did to gain time, for then the clock had struck three, for I was in hopes, it being cowslip time, that people going out early in the morning might see them, and they might be prevented from doing any kind of mischief.

Two of the men went to look, but after a brief search they returned, and Mrs Penleaze could only listen as her husband revealed that their son had received a little money the day before and his room was up another pair of stairs. 'I was frightened for my son's life. He is fond of shooting. He always lies with a couple of guns in his room. I begged of them for God's sake not to hurt my son. They said they would not.' Meanwhile her son, woken by the noise, 'came down stairs to see what was the matter'. Two of the men seized him, and Mrs Penleaze 'screamed out to a violent degree', thinking they were going to hurt him, 'but ... they only led him into my room'.

The men ransacked the house and left about a quarter past three, with dreadful menaces of death to any of the family who should attempt to watch them. In their hurry they dropt some silver-handled knives and forks in the garden.

One of the villains, Benjamin Bates, was taken up that evening. Next day another, John Green, was taken and brought before Mrs Penleaze. 'I knew him immediately, and he trembled like an aspin leaf as soon as he saw me'.[1]

In the morning the Duke of Wirtemburg went to the Queen's Palace and took leave of her majesty, and afterwards went to the Princess Amelia, and took leave of her, and then went to St James's, and took leave of his majesty. Next day he set out on his return home.[2]

At night at Kingston House, after Sir Francis Molyneux, black rod, had been some hours in bed, he got up in a violent fright, ran out of his room with nothing on but his shirt, and caught a housemaid in his arms, crying out '*The Duchess is gone off!*' The maid said he might see the duchess, for that she was not undressed, as her counsellors had just left her, but recommended his putting on some other garment. So, in his hurry, he threw his powdering dress over his shoulders and went into the duchess's room, after which he went down and saw that all his officers were on duty, and then he went to bed again.[3]

Sir Francis Molyneux, gentleman usher of the black rod, and his deputy, Robert Quarme, yeoman usher. By James Sayers, 1782.

22nd April, Monday A very fine, bright, warm day

The trial in Westminster Hall resumed a little after eleven o'clock. The prisoner rose, and having curtesied respectfully, read her defence, which took forty-six minutes, and which she delivered in a very pathetic and distinct tone of voice, although frequently so agitated and distressed that she could hardly see for her tears. In seeking to undermine the critical evidence of Ann Craddock she asked, rather revealingly as to her own *modus operandi*, 'Can your lordships believe, that if I [had] a conviction in my own mind of a real lawful marriage between Mr Hervey and myself, that I would not, at any expence, have taken care to have put that woman out of the way?'

Anna Porter had resumed attendance, but she was not impressed by the sincerity of the duchess's claim that she prized 'neither riches nor titles' other than as testimony of her late husband's esteem:

> Oh Woman! Woman! How could you utter such untruths! Much greater rhapsodies than these did she spout. She told us that it was the dukes will enraged her ennemies, but she said so far was she from having had any hand in it, he had unknown to her made 3 wills at different periods, every one more favorable to her — 'encreasing years encreased his good opinion of her'. So little did she instigate his dissensions with Evelyn Meadows whom he disinherited, that she endeavoured to reconcile them — that their first quarrel was on Evelyn's leaving the army ignobly, and the second his not fulfilling his engagements with Miss Bishop — she brought up that old tale which harrow'd up my soul. Oh I rejoiced at all she said against the vile man, for of all those on whom ye name of Man is prostituted he is doubtless ye vilest and so far is his mind from being after ye image of our Creator's, I am sure ye Devil has marked him for his own. ... She ended all, by saying 'twas not for life, for riches, for worldly goods she pleaded; 'twas to beseech them to defend her <u>honour</u>, her <u>innocence</u>. She laid great stress on the words that they might be convinced she had not made a mistake when she took ye sacred names in vain.

From this it emerges incidentally that Anna Porter had close knowledge of Evelyn Meadows, perhaps being a friend of the abandoned Miss Bishop.

A few further witnesses were called for the defence, including Ann Pritchard, who contradicted the evidence of Mrs Craddock: 'She told me, she did not hear the marriage ceremony read.' While she was speaking the Duke of Richmond desired, as he had frequently done earlier in the trial, that the witness might be removed further from the prisoner. He observed that the witness hesitating what answer to give, he saw her look towards the prisoner, and the prisoner's lips move, as if instructing her what to say. Mr Wallace, the duchess's counsel, assured their lordships that no such thing had happened, and this was confirmed by Mr Quarme, who stood behind the prisoner and the witness.

Anna Porter thought Pritchard 'as arrant a femme d'intrigue as ever lived', but did not notice anything amiss. Her brother, however, who also attended, 'saw the whole' and said the duchess 'did not speak, but *fixed* the witness, looking at her most stedfastly and making her signs'.

During the evidence of the final witness, James Laroche, the duchess fainted. According to Anna Porter, this 'most horrid fit ... made a sad hub bub in ye Hall; I never saw any thing more shocking. She was carry'd out, and ye proceeding stopped for half an hour. ... Sensibility is not an inhabitant of her breast, but disappointed ambition and humiliating guilt are dreadful harpies. It shocked me to see that most of the women spectators called her an actress, and were entertained with her situation. 'Tis strange that we are generally ye hardest on ye errors of our own sex.'

After the conclusion of Laroche's evidence, and a reply by the solicitor general, the peers adjourned to their House. On returning they were each asked in turn whether the prisoner was guilty or not guilty. Several peers absented themselves, but all those remaining answered 'Guilty, upon my honour,' except the kindly Duke of Newcastle, who said 'Guilty erroneously, but not intentionally, upon my honour.'

The lord high steward asked if the prisoner had anything to allege against judgement being pronounced, on which she delivered a paper in which she prayed the benefit of the peerage according to statute. The attorney general made a long speech arguing that the privilege did not extend to women, and after much debate the peers adjourned again to consider this matter. On their return the lord high steward informed the prisoner that the lords had decided she should be allowed the benefit. He added, rather optimistically, that 'although very little punishment, or none, can now be inflicted, the feelings of your own conscience will supply that defect.' He added further, in case she should be thinking of committing bigamy again, that 'you can never have the like benefit a second time, but another offence of the same kind will be capital. Madam, you are discharged, paying your fees.'

The serjeant at arms called 'Oyez, oyez, oyez!' and commanded all present to return home in the peace of God. Black rod delivered the white staff to the lord high steward, who stood up, uncovered, and holding the staff in both his hands, broke it into two, and declared the commission dissolved.

Newspapers reported that 'the lady, whom we must now call Countess of Bristol, made a curtesy to the lords and to all the spectators, and then with great composure retired, and was conducted to the Duke of Newcastle's in New Palace Yard.' However, according to writer Joseph Cradock, who assisted the duchess, she did not go so gracefully:

> After the trial, and she was told she might withdraw, with great warmth she said to her attendant friends, 'No: not till I have spoken daggers to one lord, who has been throughout my most inveterate enemy, yet is conscious that he received from me every assistance and benefit in early life.' As a nobleman passed she reached forwards, and seemed to speak in great rage to him: we did not distinctly hear what was said, but he did seem to writhe under the wounds.

The court rose a few minutes after seven o'clock. Outside the crowd in the adjoining streets was excessive, and the disappointment of those gentlemen and ladies who had obtained tickets for the next day was very great.[1]

At quarter past seven Lord Suffolk wrote from nearby Duke Street to inform the king that the trial was over. 'The prisoner made a long and most curious speech,' he noted, 'which terminated in an hysteric fit, or was very soon after follow'd by one (I forget exactly which). The speech is transcribing for your majesty — and for the public advantage the prisoner soon happily recoverd out of the fit.'[2]

Other letter writers also spread the news. 'I have the great satisfaction of telling you,' wrote Hannah More from the Adelphi, 'that Elizabeth, calling herself Duchess-dowager of Kingston, was this very afternoon *undignified* and *unduchessed*, and very narrowly escaped being burned in the hand. If you had been half as much interested against this unprincipled, artful, licentious woman as I have, you will be rejoiced at it as I am.' Edmund Burke, who attended the trial, wrote to a friend in Bristol lamenting lack of progress on a House of Commons motion regarding damage to imported currants: 'The lady is cast this day; indeed, from the beginning there was little doubt of the event. ... | This troublesome business of the trial has so completely engaged every body, that I could do nothing about the fruit: secretaries, clerks, every body engaged; and all affairs totally suspended with all sorts of people. We forgot, for a while, war and taxes, and every thing else ...'[3]

Meanwhile:

Boswell went early to see Captain Cook at his house at Mile End. He arrived too late for breakfast but was given tea in the garden, where a blackbird sang pleasantly. Returning to town he saw Arthur Lee, and then Joseph Brant, before going to Westminster Hall, where it seems he tried to obtain a trial ticket for one of the Dilly brothers. Then, fascinated by the celebrated Mrs Rudd, and having heard that she had taken lodgings in Westminster, he went and knocked on the door of No. 10 Queen Street. Learning from a maid that her mistress was not at home but would be in the evening, he declined to leave his name, asking only that she be told that 'a friend of Mr Macqueen's from Scotland had called and would call again'. The mutual acquaintance in question may have been Robert Macqueen, a Scottish lawyer.[4]

It was reported on 'Change that the French had landed 14,000 men on Jamaica, near which they have a large fleet. This news, whether true or false, had a great effect on the price of stocks.[5]

An elderly woman, who lived in George Yard, was brought before the lord mayor for holding a girl, only 12 years of age, upon a bed in her house whilst a man committed a rape upon her body. The prisoner had taken in the girl under a pretence of friendship, and the poor creature was so much injured that she was obliged to be sent to St Bartholomew's Hospital. Another complaint was laid by the parents of another girl, only 11 years of age, that the prisoner had decoyed her away from them, and introduced men to her; that having a fine set of teeth, two of them were drawn out, and sold for two guineas,* which the prisoner told her should buy her fine cloaths, that she might make a genteel appearance when any gentleman came to her. His lordship recommended one of the girls to the Magdalen Hospital, and the old woman was committed to Wood Street Compter to await her trial.†[6]

Between five and six o'clock their majesties had a private review of the exhibition by the Royal Academicians in Pall Mall.[7]

In the evening a man who lodges near Dowgate Dock, having some words with his wife, threw himself out of a two pair of stairs window into the dock, to avoid her provoking insolence. Fortunately for him, the tide being up, he received no other injury than a good ducking.[8]

At quarter after nine Boswell called again at Mrs Rudd's lodgings, only to learn that she had gone out but would be back in half an hour. Declining to wait, he sauntered to Westminster Bridge and returned at ten. She was still not home, but this time he agreed to go upstairs and wait. He was shown into a modest dining room lit by tallow candles. 'My fancy began to form fearful suppositions in this solitary situation. I thought the ghosts of the Perreaus might appear. I thought that there might be murderers or bullies in the house. But then the street was too public for that.' He looked at her books, which included *Johnsoniana*, two copies of her own *Genuine Letter to Lord Weymouth*, and Pope's *Essay on Man* and *Essay on Criticism* bound together. Having sat reading for about half an hour he heard her coming up the stairs. 'There entered rather a little woman, delicately made, not at all a beauty, but with a very pleasing appearance and much younger than I imagined.' She was dressed in black with a white cloak and hat. He apologised for intruding, said he was a friend of Mr Macqueen's, and asked how she was. 'As well as could be expected,' she replied, and, without prompting, related her unhappy history, insisting on her own innocence.

> I said it was shocking that the Perreaus had died denying as they did. 'Yes,' said she, 'it must shock everybody who has any tenderness of conscience. They should have died in silence.' ...

---

* The poor sometimes sold healthy teeth to be transplanted as false teeth into the mouths of the rich.
† The accused may have been Elizabeth White or Whites, tried at the Old Bailey on 25th May, whose case as reported differs in some respects but is sufficiently similar to suggest it may be the same. Whites was accused of assisting a rape on 14th April upon Elizabeth Cobb, aged 13. She did not deny the charge, but suggested Cobb was already upon the town at the time of the incident. According to the *Morning Post*, 'The jury took the whole of the girl's conduct together, particularly her not making an immediate discovery, and her going the next day to dispose of her teeth, to an eminent dentist in Soho-square, and acquitted the prisoner.'

I said she was reckoned quite a sorceress, possessed of enchantment. She smiled and did not contradict me as to the past, but said she could enchant nobody. I begged her pardon and, with exquisite flattery, said, 'My dear Mrs Rudd, don't talk so. Everything you have said to me till now has been truth and candour'; and I told her I was convinced she could enchant, but I begged she would not enchant me too much, not change me into any other creature, but allow me to continue to be a man with some degree of reason. I was as cautious as if I had been opposite to that snake which fascinates with its eyes. ... She said she had formerly deluded herself with hopes of enjoying happiness. She now was satisfied with insensibility, not however in the extreme, but comparatively speaking. 'You must not be insensible,' said I, and rose and seized her silken hand, and afterwards ... kissed it. This was all experiment, and she showed neither prudery nor effrontery, but the complaisance, or compliance if you please, of a woman of fashion.

Later she said that many stories were made up about her, for example that she lived with Lord Lyttelton, but she claimed she did not know him even by sight. Boswell told her he thought 'love would be the best remedy for her. She said very gently she did not think so.' On his asking for leave to call again, she said she was 'always at home'. He wished her good night 'with a kiss which she received without affectation of any kind'. He concluded that she was probably upon the town and wondered what she thought of him. 'I imagined I was very agreeable, and it pleased me much that she never asked my name or anything at all about me, which showed perfect good breeding. I would not for a good deal have missed this scene.'[9]

23rd April, Tuesday A very fine, bright, warm day

In the morning many ladies and gentlemen went down full-dressed to Westminster Hall, having read in the *Daily Advertiser* that the trial was not ended and the duchess was this day to receive sentence. Meanwhile the part of the temporary court in the Hall which stopped up the entrance of the courts of Chancery, King's Bench, and Common Pleas, was taken down. The rest of the scaffolding would remain in place until the end of July as it was thought the noise of its dismantling would disturb the barristers in the various courts.[1]

Horace Walpole provided a final report on the Kingston affair to his friend William Mason:

The wisdom of the land has been exerted five days in turning a duchess into a countess, and does not think it a punishable crime for a countess to convert herself into a duchess. ... So ends that solemn farce! which may be indifferently bound up with the State Trials and *The History of Moll Flanders*. If you write to her you must direct to the Countess of Bristol. The earl, they say, does not intend to leave her that title, nor the house of Meadows a shilling, but there will be quaeres to both designs. The ecclesiastic court, full as guilty as the culprit, I dare to say, will escape as well. Adieu! ... I am glad to have done with her.[2]

'Mrs Rudd. Drawn from the Life.'
From the *Town and Country Magazine* for September 1775

As for the duchess-countess, it was probably on this day that she set out for Dover, reportedly having received private notice that the Meadows family were seeking a writ of *Ne exeat regno* to stop her leaving the country (although their intention was hardly a secret, having been noted in the *Morning Chronicle* in early February). According to different accounts she travelled in a hired post-chaise or in James Laroche's carriage. Meanwhile, to cover her design, she had invited a party of friends to dine at Kingston House and caused her cousin, Miss Bell

Chudleigh, and another lady, to be driven about the most public streets of the metropolis in her carriage or vis-à-vis. According to one account, 'The duchess's carriage being so well known, and Miss Bell so much like her grace, many considerable betts were lost by people who believed her to be the duchess.' At Dover the fugitive was met by Mr Harding, the captain of her yacht.[3]

The Worshipful Company of Apothecaries set out on their first botanical excursion in search of such medicinal plants and herbs as may have escaped the notice of the curious. After visiting Dulwich, Norwood, Penge Common, &c. they dined at the Grove House at Camberwell, many seeming better satisfied with their dinner than with the botanical pursuit.[4]

Henry Quirforth, an agent in the kidnapping business, and a man and wife of the name of Dennison, who kept what is called a flesh house in Finch Lane, were tried before the recorder at the Old Bailey. They were charged with conspiring to detain 17-year-old Elizabeth Brickleband against her will in the above house, and forcing her on board the *Nancy* brig and transporting her to America. It appeared that for several weeks after the girl was first missing, in June last year, her wretched mother was deprived of her reason, running up and down the streets and enquiring of every one the fate of her unhappy child. At length, learning where she had been confined, she went to Dennison's house, where she was insulted, a young man saying, 'What do you do here again about your whore of a daughter? I debauched her at school; and I took her on board the ship, and there I debauched her again, and gave her a flogging.'

The mother went to the lord mayor, got a warrant to take the culprits up, and they were put in gaol. They sought to defer their trial in hopes of procuring the girl's return. Being asked in court why he did not in some degree atone by sending for the girl, Quirforth said he had been informed by a Mr Roberts, a merchant, that in consequence of severe treatment during the voyage, she died in ten days after her arrival in Maryland. Upon this information, which was the first the mother had heard of her daughter's death, she fell into loud lamentations, and sank down as if herself dead, which filled the court with pity and resentment. The counsel for the defence strove hard to exculpate Quirforth from the charge of conspiracy, but the jury, incensed against the whole party, found them all guilty. Those present waited with impatience to hear a sentence adequate to the crime, but the court only ordered the defendants to be imprisoned for one month (Quirforth) and three months (the Dennisons), and to find security for their good behaviour for one and two years respectively.[5]

Boswell wrote up his account of the previous night's visit to Mrs Rudd and later went to the annual dinner of the Royal Academy, held among the pictures in its exhibition room in Pall Mall. Other guests included the dukes of Devonshire and Dorset, Joseph Banks, Edmund Burke, Samuel Foote, David Garrick, and Horace Walpole. Sir Joshua Reynolds presided, the king's health was toasted, and 'God save the King' was sung.[6]

24th April, Wednesday A very fine, bright, warm day

The annual exhibition of the Royal Academy was opened in Pall Mall. The *Morning Post* judged it 'as capital a collection of modern paintings as ever was exhibited in this country,' adding comments on individual works. Among twelve entries by the Academy's president, Sir Joshua Reynolds, were portraits of the Duke of Devonshire (marked by 'a beggarly kind of madness ... whether owing to his grace, or the artist we cannot say'); the Duchess of Devonshire, descending a flight of steps (see Plate 3); David Garrick, with thumbs together, painted for Mrs Thrale ('certainly a likeness, but there is a primness about the mouth, which prevents its being a striking one'); and Omai in the habit of his country ('a strong likeness, and finely painted'). Benjamin West's altarpiece, 'Devout men taking the body of St Stephen', was 'the best historical painting we ever beheld from the pencil of an English artist ... The dead flesh is uncommonly fine.' There were four paintings each by Angelica Kauffman and George Stubbs. 'We do not think that Mr Stubbs has any equal in this line. The "Tygers at Play" is a fine picture, well drawn and coloured.' Less impressive was James Barry's 'Death of General Wolfe': 'We do not recollect to have seen so wretched a collection of legs, faces, and eyes, as this piece so glaringly represents us.'[1]

In the House of Commons, soon as prayers were over, an amazing crowd of people got into the gallery. At a little after 3 p.m. Lord North rose, and in an elaborate speech entered upon the particulars of what is called the Budget. He proposed the following taxes, which he said he had contrived to fall upon articles of luxury such that they would hardly be felt.

• A duty of 5l. on stage coaches, which had been exempted before.

• An additional duty of 20s. on four-wheel carriages, which men who enjoyed them would hardly lay aside for this trifling addition.

• An additional stamp duty of 1s. on all deeds.

• An additional halfpenny on newspapers. With this article he made very merry, as a great luxury, and expressed his astonishment that under a despotic minister 12,230,000 newspapers should be stamped yearly at the Office. He was confident that, rather than lose the pleasure of seeing ministers daily abused, the curious and the politicians would with pleasure give the other halfpenny.

• An additional stamp duty of 6d. per pack on cards and 2s. 6d. on every pair of dice, which, in this gay, gaming age, he hoped it would not be thought improper to demand.

His lordship calculated the whole computed produce of these taxes at 73,000l. He added that contingencies might arise, and unforeseen incidents, which might require a larger supply, and therefore he gave notice to the House that he should desire a vote of credit for £1 million.

During his speech he mentioned Dr Price's pamphlet on Civil Liberty and refuted several of that writer's calculations. Speaking of the American war, he said he did

Three prints after works exhibited at the Royal Academy exhibition

ABOVE Omai by Reynolds. Mezzotint by John Jacobi (or Jacobé), published by him at Mrs Sledge's, Henrietta Street, 15th August 1777. 'Very good,' noted Horace Walpole in his catalogue after seeing the original work, which was sold at Sotheby's, London, in 2001 for £10.3 million.

FACING PAGE. UPPER Garrick by Reynolds. Mezzotint by Thomas Watson, published 18th March 1779. LOWER 'Tygers at Play' (detail). Etching by Stubbs after his own painting, published by him 25th February 1780. The 'tygers' are in fact leopard cubs. The original work was sold at Sotheby's in July 2015 for £7.7 million.

not wish it to go abroad as his opinion, or that of others in office, that America should not be treated with temper and moderation, and even with affection. He denied reports that the spirit of the nation was sunk, and that a general backwardness to the war was apparent, saying they were grounded on the inflammatory language of opposition, who vilified their countrymen by assertions of their languor and want of courage. It was true that several persons, from what they thought principle, had declined to serve against America, but others had eagerly pressed forward to fill their places and he saw no appearance of a general disinclination.

In reply Governor Johnstone observed that the noble lord's speech seemed rather addressed to the strangers in the gallery than to members of the House. He begged to know why the public, who had a right to hear what passed, were only admitted on one day in the season.

Mr Charles Fox followed the governor, and, with his usual warmth, said he would not vote for the grant of any money for the carrying on what he termed the present unjust and oppressive war. He asked if the strangers were admitted only for one day because the minister could, with tolerable preparation and prudence, so contrive as to appear consistent for one day, and not, according to his usual custom, say one thing positively, and afterwards deny that he had even urged it. He entered into the great American Question at large, and arraigned administration in the most severe terms, after which he spoke to the taxes proposed. He objected to that on newspapers, although he confessed their abominable licentiousness, and the intolerable disturbance to the peace of private families which they occasioned; all which he ascribed to the bad example of administration, who made the press the vehicle of every scurrility in abuse of opposition.

Mr Rigby, paymaster general, was extremely violent against America, and contended that Great Britain ought never to make any specific promise, or agree to any conditions, till the people of America threw down their arms; and if they should obstinately persist, Britain ought to persevere till America was subdued.* It was plain, from the pamphlet called *Common Sense*, written by a member of the Congress,† that America aimed at independence.

Colonel Barré desired to know if Lord Howe was to go to America, and if so whether it would be with powers sufficient to treat on terms of conciliation with the colonies, because he understood from his lordship that he would not go unless he had such powers. No answer was given to this question, and it being half after eight o'clock, the House adjourned.[2]

It was probably on this day that the now Countess of Bristol reached Calais at noon. The cannon of her yacht were fired on reaching the harbour. She was

---

* His belligerence coincided fortunately with self-interest. A week earlier the *Morning Post* had reported that 'Mr Rigby's profit by this year's war, has been calculated at twenty-four thousand pounds.'
† A widespread assumption at this time as to the authorship of Paine's work.

Lord North (left) and Richard Rigby (right), by James Sayers, 1782

at once waited on by the principal persons in the town, who attended her on shore, and shewed her every mark of respect. Meanwhile *Lloyd's Evening Post* reported talk that the Meadowses had filed a bill in Chancery to set aside the Duke of Kingston's will 'as being obtained under false suggestions'.[3]

In the evening there were upwards of 2,000 persons at Ranelagh, many of whom, after they had partook of tea and the round-about walk, left in order to dress for a masquerade at Carlisle House.[4]

Governor Hutchinson went with his daughter Peggy to see *The Conscious Lovers* at Covent Garden Theatre. He noted in his diary that the boxes were 'not a quarter filled. Masquerades, Ranelagh, concerts and many other diversions take up the town. Never was a time when so great a part of the people spend so great a portion of their time and estates in amusements and dissipation.'[5]

About eleven o'clock the queen was taken ill and the great officers of state, &c. were sent for to her palace; but her majesty being much better by twelve, they all went home, except Dr Hunter and the queen's midwife.[6]

Meanwhile the masquerade at Carlisle House had begun. The Bridge-room was converted into an elegant garden, the sides full of shrubs and flowers. In the centre, hung with festoons of silk, stood an elegant pavilion to which the company ascended by a temporary stair-case, and where was spread a table for a dozen persons, in the middle of which was a fountain and a reservoir, with gold and silver fish swimming about. In the Ball-room lofty pines stood at equal distances along the sides, and branched to each other at the top. The middle of the room exhibited an elegant erection of Gothick arches and lamps of variegated colours, under which were circular tables and side boards covered with hot fowls and asparagus, cold ham, pies of different sorts, crawfish, prawns, strawberries, sweetmeats, &c.

There were about 800 persons present, among them several of the first fashion. The characters included Lady Grosvenor as a Hay-maker, Captain Horneck as a Hussar officer, several feather-headed females, a long-tailed Devil, and two double masks, one an Old Woman behind and a Girl before, the other an emblem of the Modern Macaroni, half Ganymede, half Hebe.[7]

25th April, Thursday Many flying clouds, but a fine day, cold wind
About 6 a.m. her majesty was taken with labour pains. Notice was immediately sent to the Archbishop of Canterbury, the secretaries of state, and several of the nobility, and at seven her majesty was safely delivered of a princess. The archbishop, several lords of the privy council, and the ladies of her majesty's bedchamber were present. This great event was soon after announced to the public by firing of the Tower guns, &c. and expresses were sent off to all the Courts in Europe.[1]

A warrant having being granted against a man for keeping a house of ill fame in Miles's Lane, Cannon Street, Mr Payne, the constable, entered the house to apprehend him. Finding himself closely pursued through every room, the man at length sought refuge up a chimney, but even there he was followed, and brought down, the blackness of his figure producing a highly laughable scene. He was taken before the lord mayor, and promised to quit his house within a week.[2]

In the House of Commons Sir James Lowther proposed, 'That it is the opinion of this House, that the introducing of foreign troops into any part of the dominions of the crown of Great Britain, without the previous consent or approbation of ... parliament ... is contrary to the principles of the constitution, and not warranted by law.' Thomas Townshend criticised the recruiting of foreigners in the Hans towns, known to be the asylum of all the rogues and vagabonds of Germany. He said it was folly in the extreme to suppose that when such men arrived in America they would fight cordially for this country and its right. They would enlist with the best paymaster, or join whichever party held out the best prospects of improving their present situation or future fortunes. The motion that the question be now put was nonetheless defeated by 149 to 88.[3]

26th April, Friday A very fine bright day, cold wind
It was so confidently reported that Jamaica had been taken by the French or Spaniards, or both, that bets ran fifty pounds to five in the neighbourhood of the Royal Exchange.[1]

At St James's upwards of 500 of the nobility paid their compliments to his majesty upon the safe delivery of the princess, and all had caudle and cake.[2]

Beaumarchais wrote to the Comte de Vergennes in Paris:

I am taking advantage of a secure opportunity to address you with freedom on the sole truly important affair of today: America, and all that pertains to it.

I reasoned for a long time, the evening before yesterday, with the man you believe should be prevented from travelling to France.*... | He asks incessantly if we are going to do absolutely nothing for them? And ... he tells me simply, 'We need arms, powder, but above all we need engineers. There is no one but you who can save us, and it is greatly in your interest to do so. And what we need most is some engineers.' I reply to him, that the last article is excessively difficult because one cannot send men without giving them a commission: men talk, and we would be compromised ... 'Then give us money,' he replies, 'we will hire some German engineers, some Swedish, some Italian, etc, and you will not be compromised.' That, Monsieur le Comte, is where we are. What do you want me to reply? ...

Will you not have the goodness to show once more to the king how he can win, without firing a shot, in this one campaign? And will you not try to convince his majesty that the miserable assistance that they seek, and over which we have debated for a year, should bring to us all the fruits of a great victory, without the dangers of a combat? That this help can restore to us, while we sleep, all that we lost by the shameful peace of 1762,† and that the success of the Americans, reducing our rival to nothing more than a second rate power, will restore us to the premier rank, and give us for a long time pre-eminence in the whole of Europe? ...

In spite of the danger I run in writing these bold things to you from London, I feel myself twice as French here as in Paris. The patriotism of the people here reawakens my own. It even seems that the precarious and dangerous state that I find myself in, by the suspicions and the close watch that is kept on all that I do, makes my zeal more ardent.

However, do not neglect, Monsieur le Comte, to press M. de Sartine‡ on the question of my safety. It is the least that is due to me. The king and he had the goodness to provide for it; but the same merchants, bankers, courtiers, gold dealers, etc, who, when questioned secretly by the ministry, have testified that I was negotiating a currency exchange with them, will not fail soon to respond that this is a decoy, a bird trap, if they do not see me bring the plan to fruition and pass from order to purchase. Two suspected Irishmen have been arrested here. I wish to be in a position to defend myself on my own and without involving the king or you, should the same thing happen to me ...[3]

In the evening the Duchess of Devonshire gave an elegant rout to the nobility and gentry, which was exceedingly crowded.[4]

---

* Arthur Lee. Vergennes presumably feared his presence would attract British attention.
† The Treaty of Paris, signed in February 1763, which marked the end of the Seven Years War and in which France ceded substantial American territory to Britain.
‡ Antoine de Sartine, the French navy minister and a former lieutenant general of the Paris police.

27th April, Saturday As yesterday

In the evening Garrick played Hamlet at Drury Lane Theatre. Before the performance, when Lord Mansfield entered the stage box, he was received by the audience with a general clap of applause. Lord and Lady North also attended. Two days later a Treasury secretary wrote to Garrick to say they had commanded him 'to thank you in the most particular manner for that high entertainment', adding that 'their appetite is so much increased by it' that they wished for a box to see him perform again next day, the 30th.[1]

GA 'Strict orders have within these few days been sent to the commissioners of the different dock-yards, not to admit any foreigners, nor any persons whatever into those yards, excepting such as have immediate business there.'[2]

28th April, Sunday As yesterday

About 1 a.m. two luminous bodies, apparently balls of fire, were observed to pass over Smithfield, Clerkenwell, &c. travelling south to north at about the rate of a mile a minute.[1]

29th April, Monday Many flying clouds, but fair; sharp, cutting wind

A party of soldiers, who had taken a deserter and were conducting him to the Savoy, stopped to drink and play at skittles at a public-house in St George's Fields. A young man in company with them, conjecturing the situation of the delinquent, plied his guards so plentifully with gin royal and brown stout that the deserter decamped, and left them in the lurch.[1]

In the evening a masquerade at the Casino, Great Marlborough Street, was attended by about 200 persons, among them the Duke of Cumberland. Although the number present was but small, the character masks excelled those of any late masquerade. Among the best was a figure representing Folly, who ran from place to place to shew that Folly was to be found every where.[2]

30th April, Tuesday Frost in night, many clouds in day, cutting wind

In the morning Lord Howe was sent for to the Queen's Palace, where he had a long private conference with the king. At some point during the day Lord George Germain wrote from his Whitehall office to inform the Treasury that Lord Howe and General Howe had been appointed commissioners for restoring peace in North America.[1]

In the evening Vanbrugh's *The Provoked Wife* was performed at Drury Lane Theatre. Mrs Abington was Lady Fanciful, and Mr Garrick took the part of Sir John Brute for the last time. Among the audience were Lord and Lady North and Sir Joshua Reynolds. James Northcote, about to leave his position as apprentice to Reynolds, also got in, but 'so great was the crowd ... it was with considerable difficulty'.[2]

In the play's Covent Garden scene Garrick wore a head-dress which kept pace with the present reigning taste, the addition of yellow streamers to the rampant plumes having a whimsical effect which provoked loud bursts of laughter from every part of the house. According to next day's *Morning Post*:

> This celebrated dramatic constellation seems resolved to set in the fullest splendor of his dramatic glory; for it is universally allowed that he gave his last Abel Drugger and Sir John Brute the highest comic colourings he ever bestowed on those admired characters. When Colonel Bully's song was encored last night in the drunken scene, Sir John cried out, 'Colonel, I insist upon your singing it again, for two reasons: the first is, you are bound to oblige your best friends: and secondly, I don't believe that I shall ever be in this good company again.' It is astonishing what applause attended the observation; even the ladies in the stage and front boxes joined their fair hands in the final plaudits due to the departure of their favourite, the inimitable *Sir John Brute*.[3]

Garrick as Sir John Brute, after a painting by Zoffany, 1763-1764

May

1st May, Wednesday Frost in night, many clouds in day, cutting wind

Lord Howe attended the levee at St James's, and afterwards the council, and took leave of his majesty. Colonel Guy Johnson, superintendent of Indian affairs, also took leave of his majesty previous to his departure for North America.[1]

A cook to a family at Hackney, who had for some time past complained of a dropsy, delivered herself of a bastard child. A fellow servant who suspected the fact acquainted their mistress, and diligent search was made. The infant was found with its head severed from the body and sewed up in some rags in the mother's trunk. The mother will be committed to prison as soon as it is proper to move her.*[2]

Philosopher David Hume, 65 years old and mortally ill, arrived in Brewer Street after a ten day journey from Scotland. At Morpeth he had been met by chance by Adam Smith and dramatist John Home, who were heading home to Scotland from London. Home generously offered to change his plans and accompany Hume south.[3]

MC 'They write from Lewes, in Sussex, that on Wednesday morning last the Hessian transports, with the troops on board destined to America, passed by Winchelsea and Hastings, with drums beating and music playing, the sound of which drew a number of people to the sea side to see their fleet pass, most of whom, though pleased with the effect, lamented the unhappy cause.'[4]

2nd May, Thursday Many clouds, but a fair day

Government concluded contracts for 200,000 gallons of rum for the use of his majesty's troops in North America.[1]

Revenue officers being informed that smuggled tea was lodged in a public-house in Oxford Street, they went there and seized twelve bags, which they put in a hackney coach to convey to the Custom House. The alarm was given to a notorious gang of smugglers who reside in the neighbourhood of St Giles's. They went out armed with pistols, cutlasses, &c. and stopped the coach in St Giles's, took off the tea, broke the coach to pieces, and wounded the officers in a terrible manner, one having an ear cut off, and another his face cut with a hanger. One of the gang was taken and carried before the magistrates in Litchfield Street, who committed him to Newgate, and diligent search is making after the rest.[2]

At about 4 p.m., returning to his lodgings in St James's Street, Governor Hutchinson was surprised to find 'Col. Browne arrived from Boston, having left it the 26 March in the *Lord Hyde* packet, and arrived at Falmouth the 31st April'. He was even more surprised to learn that his own eldest son Thomas and his family,

---

* Under the 1624 Act to prevent the destroying and murthering of bastard children, a woman concealing the death of her illegitimate child was presumed to have murdered it and treated accordingly.

'May-Day in London'
Engraved by William Blake, after Samuel Collings. Published 1784.

and his eldest daughter Sarah, had been on the packet, 'and that the troops had quitted Boston, and were embarked, and many of them sailed with the packet to Halifax, and the rest to sail the next day'.[3]

The news from Boston reached Lord George Germain at about 5.30 p.m. in the form of dispatches from General Howe brought by a 'Mr Brown', perhaps Hutchinson's friend Colonel Browne. They included a letter dated 21st March from on board the *Chatham* in Nantasket Road. It was addressed to Lord Dartmouth, replaced as American secretary in the previous November.

> It is with great regret I am obliged to inform your lordship, that ... the enemy, by taking possession of and fortifying the commanding heights on Dorchester-Neck, in order to force the ships by their cannon to quit the harbour, has reduced me to the necessity either of exposing the army to the greatest distresses by remaining in Boston, or of withdrawing from it under such straitened circumstances. The importance of preserving this force when it could no longer act to advantage, did not leave any room to doubt of the propriety of its removal ... which was executed on the 17th following in the forenoon, without the least molestation from the rebels ...
>
> Halifax, though stripped of provisions during the winter, and affording few conveniences to so numerous a body, is the only place where the army can remain until supplies arrive from Europe. ...

> I shall ... detach three regiments to Quebeck as soon as the navigation of the river St Lawrence becomes practicable, if I do not, in the mean time, hear anything to the contrary from Europe. The remainder of the army, which, after these detachments are made, may consist of about five thousand men, including sick, will be held in readiness to proceed to New-York, when enabled by a supply of provisions, and an addition of transports sufficient for that undertaking ...
>
> I beg leave to remark, that the last commands I had the honour to receive from your lordship are dated the 22d of October, which will serve to show the difficulties ships bound to this port have met with ...

At 6.05 p.m. Germain forwarded the papers from his house in Pall Mall to the king, informing him that he had 'summoned the cabinet to meet at nine o'clock this evening'. They were to discuss in particular 'whether any alteration should be made in the destination of the Hessians', Germain believing that 'the possessing of Rhode Island by the guards and the Hessians' would assist Howe's plan to attack New York.

The meeting was held at Germain's office in Whitehall and did not break up till past midnight. Governor Hutchinson was summoned with Colonel Browne and they waited outside, 'but we were not called nor any inquiries made'.[4]

Meanwhile about 600 masks assembled at Carlisle House, drawn by a reduced price of one guinea and a half per ticket. Among the characters were a May Day Chimney-sweeper, a Gypsy with her sooty-faced infant, two Bag-pipers playing a variety of comic tunes, actress Sophia Baddeley as Lady Jane Grey, and, as a Hay-maker again, Lady Grosvenor, who had her rake broken.

There was little wit before supper, but a good deal of fun afterwards. About five o'clock a gentleman of the City, exhilarated by the hour, the place, the music, the wine, &c. spoke a little freely, tho' not indecently, to Lady Grosvenor. The affront was cruelly resented by some of her attendants who held the gentleman's hands whilst he was assaulted by an unmasked domino, who proclaimed himself a member of parliament, as if the privilege of making laws implied also that of breaking them. They pursued the man into the street, where one of the assailants, who had laid aside every disguise, came from behind and struck him to the ground with so much violence that he received a contusion, if not a fracture, in the scull, which may prove of serious consequence.

Excepting the above *fracas* the evening was a pleasant and convivial one. It concluded with a grand chorus of 'God save the King', and the company were all gone about eight o'clock in the morning.[5]

Another masquerade was held at the Casino, but only twenty-eight people attended, and, being tired of the insipidity, they fell off by degrees to leave the place a melancholy deserted scene. The *Middlesex Journal* hoped that 'this second instance of the public disapprobation, may shew the managers ... the folly of attempting to injure the favourite priestess of taste and elegance in Soho Square, by endeavouring to make a little white-washed room vie with the most superb, and enchanting apartments ever exhibited in this kingdom'.[6]

Lady Grosvenor (née Henrietta Vernon), after a portrait by Francis Cotes

Published by Carington Bowles, 69 St Paul's Churchyard, 8th February 1774

'Such is the vigorous damsel's zeal,
She tries each species of the eel ...'
The Torpedo, a Poem to the Electrical Eel, 1777

3rd May, Friday Chiefly cloudy, but fair churlish cold evening. Full moon
Lord George Germain wrote from Whitehall to General Howe, passing on the
king's approval of the withdrawal from Boston and informing him of progress
regarding reinforcements: the Highland corps of 8,200 men and a detachment of
guards would probably sail from Spithead within a day or two, and transports for
Burgoyne's regiment of light cavalry, and for about 800 draft horses, were fitting
in the river. He added that the plan to attack New York 'is becoming that spirit
and vigour with which you always act', but that it would be better to wait until
reinforcements had arrived, 'that your force may be so increased as to render your
success more certain'.[1]

Beaumarchais wrote to the Comte de Vergennes:

> There is nothing very important here but the news of the evacuation of Boston ...
> The government meets this with an air of approbation, of mystery, and even
> of intelligence. It would very much like it to be regarded as a ruse ordained by
> ministers; but that does not take. It is too certain that the impossibility of
> holding Boston any longer, from lack of provisions, has driven the English
> away. It reminds me that last winter, in France, when my information was that
> the English lacked for everything, milord Stormont broadcast, with sublime
> imposture, that the king's troops were easy and at peace, drinking punch, their
> feet by the fire, while the insurgents endured cold and hunger, he said, in the
> midst of the snow. In the end everything reveals itself; and then one is so
> ashamed!

He said that the evacuation, along with other favourable news, confirmed what
he had noted in his last dispatch, 'that the Americans are well placed in all respects,
engineers and powder excepted. Ah, Monsieur le Comte, powder and engineers
please! I do not believe I have ever wanted anything so much.'

He added that he had nothing to report concerning the Chevalier d'Éon, whom
he seems still to have believed a woman, 'because she continues to talk twaddle,
which would absolutely annoy me if I was to listen to it. However, her brother-
in-law has arrived. He is an agreeable man, and if my heroine does not prove a
hateful and ungrateful creature, it is through him that I hope to bring her to reason.'
The brother-in-law in question was Thomas O'Gorman, Chevalier O'Gorman
in the French nobility, aged 43, who was married to d'Éon's sister. A former army
officer with interests in wine, antiquarianism, and genealogy, he was over 6 foot
5 inches tall, prompting Beaumarchais to dub him 'Ogreman'.[2]

David Hume wrote to Adam Smith at Kirkcaldy:

> I find myself very much recovered on the road, and I hope Bath waters and
> farther journeys may effect my cure.
>   By the little company I have seen, I find the town very full of your book,
> which meets with general approbation. Many people think particular points
> disputable; but this you certainly expected. I am glad that I am one of the
> number; as these points will be the subject of future conversation between us.

I set out for Bath, I believe, on Monday, by Sir John Pringle's directions, who says that he sees nothing to be apprehended in my case.[3]

At Covent Garden Theatre, after the play, a new dance was introduced called *The Humours of Newmarket Races*. The race ground, with its posts, &c. was represented, and the horses were of the human variety. According to the *Morning Chronicle*, it 'was sufficiently ridiculous, but at the same time so laughable, that there was scarcely a fixed muscle in the theatre'.[4]

4th May, Saturday Cloudy day, smart shower in the evening

LG 'Whitehall, May 3. General Howe, commander in chief of his majesty's forces in North America, having taken a resolution on the 7th of March to remove from Boston to Halifax with the troops under his command ... the embarkation was effected on the 17th of that month, with the greatest order and regularity, and without the least interruption from the rebels.'[1]

MP 'The obelisk that is erecting in the center of the great room at the Pantheon, against the masquerade on Monday next ... will have sixteen transparent paintings in it, be 70 feet high, and there will be two setts of horns and clarinets, also catch and glee singers in the gallery of it; the whole is to be illuminated with a prodigious number of lamps, and no doubt will have a very fine effect.'[2]

Coffee-house customers are dismayed by bad news from America in the *London Gazette*
By Henry Bunbury, 1780

5th May, Sunday Several smart showers, hail and rain, very cold evening

In the morning Viscount Stormont, ambassador to the Court of Versailles, aged 48, was married by a special licence to Miss Louisa Cathcart, aged 17, at Lord Cathcart's house in Grosvenor Place. Their majesties and the rest of the royal family wore favours on the occasion. The couple afterwards set out for the seat of the groom's uncle, Lord Mansfield, at Caen Wood. Stormont's first wife had died ten years earlier.[1]

Boswell spent the early part of the day with Edmund Burke, watching him shave and breakfasting with him. He found Burke 'elated' by the news from Boston. Later, probably while at Dr Johnson's house, Boswell secretly transcribed onto a quarto sheet several entries from a large diary kept by Johnson. He later drew on them in his Life, the original diary having been burnt by its author shortly before his death.[2]

In the evening Lord Howe finally set off for Portsmouth. According to the *Morning Post*, 'His going affects his lady so much that his lordship was obliged to go without taking leave of her.'[3]

6th May, Monday Clouds and sunshine at intervals, little rain, cold wind

In the morning John Sangster, recently dismissed from his place as footman to Samuel Foote, went to the public office in Bow Street to accuse his former master of attempting to commit acts of indecency upon him. Mr Bond, one of the clerks, took him to an inner apartment where he conversed with Sir John Fielding, who then dictated the words of an information which Bond wrote down and Sangster signed. Foote was sent for, but the performers for the ensuing season at his theatre in the Haymarket had been summoned to meet at one o'clock this day, and it was not until about 5 p.m. that he attended. He was accompanied by William Jewell, his trusted treasurer, and perhaps by his attorney, Joseph Hickey, father of memoirist William Hickey. Foote was ordered to appear at the next quarter sessions for Westminster, provided bail of two sureties in a bond of £200 each, and was allowed to leave.[1]

At Guildhall the lord mayor committed a girl to Bridewell for fourteen days to hard labour, on the oath of Mr Payne the constable, for singing ballads in St Paul's churchyard, thereby obstructing the way and collecting a great crowd for the convenience of pickpockets.[2]

Letters patent passed under the great seal appointing Lord Howe and General Howe 'Commissioners for restoring peace to his majesty's colonies and plantations in North America, and for granting pardon to such of his majesty's subjects there, now in rebellion, as shall deserve the royal mercy'. They were sent off to Lord Howe at Portsmouth by messenger.[3]

Lord Weymouth, secretary of state, received a letter dated 1st May from Horace St Paul, who was deputising for Lord Stormont at the British embassy in Paris:

Lady Stormont

Mezzotint by John Raphael Smith, 1780, after George Romney, 1776

The portrait was painted for her father shortly after she had left home:
she sat to Romney on 16th, 19th and 21st May and again on 19th June.

I have good grounds to believe that for some months past, there have been French agents in England, endeavouring to procure sums of money for the rebels in America, from their friends in England, in order to convey them in French ships to the French Islands, and from thence to the Congress. M. de Beaumarchais is I understand concerned in this business, but he is not alone. Within these 18 months he has made 8 voyages to London and in the space of 3 weeks he went twice. I have employed some persons here, to follow up this object and to let me know all the particulars they can learn about it.[4]

Meanwhile the *Morning Chronicle* published a letter signed 'L'Amateur Francois' and written by Beaumarchais. It related how, on 29th April at the Pantheon, 'during the dancing, I found under my feet a woman's black taffeta mantle', which he wished to return to its owner. He had not seen her but provided a description deduced in Holmesian fashion from the mantle and the circumstances: 'She is tall and well made; her hair is a silvery blonde; her skin is dazzlingly white; she has a neck fine and free, a slender form, and the prettiest feet in the world. I also noted that she is very young, quiet lively and distracted, that she walks lightly, and that she has, above all, a decided taste for dancing.' He added some verses addressed to this woman he had never seen. A following note informed readers that 'a letter directed to C. B. at the York Coffee-house ... shall be duly answered', indicating that he frequented the St James's Street establishment.[5]

Edward Gibbon gave 'a great dinner at home' for Suzanne Necker, to whom he had been romantically attached as a young man, and her husband Jacques, future finance minister to Louis XVI. From his pocket-book it appears he may have borrowed his friend Topham Beauclerk's cook for the purpose, at the cost of a guinea.[6]

At about 5 p.m. in the House of Commons the order of the day was read for going into a committee of supply to consider a request from his majesty for a vote of credit. Colonel Barré got up, holding a paper in his hand cut from the *London Gazette* of 4th May, which he said contained the only account of the troops quitting Boston. He moved that an humble address be presented to his majesty requesting that all the dispatches received from 1st March last from General Howe and Vice Admiral Shuldham be laid before the House, so that it had full and authentic information of the present state of the war in North America, before proceeding to grant any further supplies for carrying it on.

He had been informed that there was a capitulation agreed between General Howe and General Washington, by which Howe was to leave his stores and not to burn the town, but the *Gazette* did not mention this circumstance, nor did it give any reason for his quitting Boston. He said the only paper published by authority was become a disgrace to the nation. The most shameful efforts had been made to mislead the people without doors; that House had been grossly misled in every communication which had come from ministers; and whenever any information had been desired it was refused. 'Here,' says he, 'we have already voted upwards of nine millions. We are going to give a vote of credit for another million. I dare say, inaccurate as the minister is in his general assertions, he will hardly venture to rise and pledge himself to the House, that five millions more will defray the expences of the present campaign. What then, in the name of decency, are we about? Shall we vote fifteen millions of the public money, without knowing whether there is the least prospect of success?'

Lord North said the contents of the *Gazette* were true. The army was not compelled to abandon Boston; the stores, ammunition, &c. were not abandoned; the army suffered no loss either immediately before or in its embarkation; the troops embarked with all possible coolness and regularity, and even perfectly at their ease; but that nevertheless it would not be proper, in his opinion, to lay all the dispatches before the House, because it might be the means of defeating, or at least of impeding, the operations of the present campaign.

Mr Hartley said the Americans were averse to independency unless driven to it by necessity. They were determined never to submit to be taxed by the British parliament, and desired no more than recognition of those rights they enjoyed to the year 1763. He insisted that General Howe was driven from Boston, and that nothing but a dread of having his whole army cut to pieces, or made prisoners, induced him to make so precipitate a retreat. He said, we have closed the first book of the American war; shall we proceed to the second with our eyes open?

Mr Burke took a short view of the conduct of the war from its commencement, and jocularly observed, that if he had not the highest opinion of the integrity and probity of the noble lord and his colleagues in office, he should be inclined to suspect that they were secret friends to America, and had been bribed to betray the honour and military reputation of this country; for from the first embarkation of troops to this instant, every measure which had been adopted or pursued was directed to the impoverishing this country, and emancipating America.

Lord George Germain said as long as the House thought it proper to support the war, he thought it would be right to pursue it, and no longer. When he came into office, the nation was already engaged in it; he did not begin it.

During the long and animated debate the doors were strictly locked and nobody admitted. It ended after eight o'clock, the motion being defeated by 171 to 54. Charles Fox was absent at Newmarket, and other members of the minority in other places. Afterwards the House went into committee and voted one million credit.[7]

Above 1,000 persons were present at a masqued ball at the Pantheon, including the dukes of Cumberland, Devonshire, Ancaster, and Manchester, Mr Garrick, and Omai in a pink domino. There were a great many fine women, fine jewels, and fine dresses, and the temporary obelisk in the centre of the great room was universally admired. The best of the character masks were a Grand Sultan, with a female Slave, as elegant and beautiful as can be conceived; a tatterdemalion Ballad Singer, a perfect master of the St Giles's slang; a young Butcher, doatingly fond of a smart Orange Girl; two Indian Warriors, with tomahawks; a Newsman with a horn, crying the *Morning Post* and distributing a printed paper stuffed with jests upon government; two Sybils (Mr and Mrs Sheridan); three Watchmen, one particularly noisy with his rattle; and a lady with her head dressed agreeable to Darly's caricature of a head, so enormous as actually to contain both a plan and model of Boston, and the provincial army on Bunker's Hill, &c.

Between five and six in the morning a *dust* was *kicked up* as usual, originating from the grape, but no ill consequences ensued.[8]

7th May, Tuesday Cloudy day, wet evening, very cold wind
Joseph Brant had a further audience with Lord George Germain, delivering a formal reply to the assurance of help Germain had given on 14th March. 'Brother. We return you thanks for this promise, which we hope will be performed, and that we shall not be disappointed, as has often been the case'.[1]

Mrs Abington having written to Mr Garrick that she intended to quit the stage at the end of the season, never to return to it again, he played for her benefit at Drury Lane Theatre. He took the part of Archer in Farquhar's *The Beaux Stratagem*, for the last time, and she was Mrs Sullen. Doors were opened at half after five and the play began at half after six. Samuel Curwen tried to get in, 'but the croud was so greet that suffering thumps, squeezes, pushes, elbowings, and almost suffocation, for near two hours, to save bones, perhaps life, [I] was obliged to return without effect'. Leaving after the performance was also a problem: according to the *Morning Post*, 'the concourse of people of fashion was so great ... that many of them were not able to get to their carriages by one o'clock the next morning.'[2]

8th May, Wednesday Several smart showers, hail and rain, bright intervals
Beaumarchais wrote again to the Comte de Vergennes, having the letter carried to Calais by a man he trusted. Despite the British government's attempts to pretend that the evacuation of Boston had been planned, it was clear, he wrote, that the rebels would soon be masters of their own house. 'If the Americans have the upper hand, as everything invites us to believe, will we not infinitely regret, Monsieur le Comte, not having acceded to their prayers?' He urged once more that France should provide 'engineers, engineers and powder, or the money to buy them!'[1]

9th May, Thursday Chiefly cloudy, but fair. Cold wind
A sailor fell from the top of the main-mast of a ship in the river and was killed on the spot. He was in liquor, and went aloft for a trifling wager.[1]

The House of Commons debated a convicts' bill, as Mrs Harris noted next day in a letter to her son in Berlin: 'Our prisons at present are very full of convicts, for since this American war they know not where to send them. Mr Eden moved they might be put on board transports on the Thames, to work in irons for the purpose of clearing the river of all rubbish, and all that impedes the navigation, and to be fed with common food, none for less than three years, or more than ten.

BUNKERS HILL
or America's Head Dress

Published by Matthew Darly in the Strand on 1st March (or possibly 19th April) 1776. A companion design, 'Noddle-Island, or How are we decieved' [*sic*], published on 12th May and satirising the evacuation of Boston, appears on the cover of this book.

This you may easily guess set the patriots talking: "the liberty of the country would be at an end, men working in irons was slavery, &c."'

In spite of such opposition the bill was passed by the Commons on 14th May and became law nine days later. Its preamble understatedly noted that 'the transportation of convicts to his majesty's colonies and plantations in America ... is found to be attended with various inconveniencies'.[2]

At Drury Lane Theatre Garrick played Benedick in *Much Ado About Nothing* for the last time, Mrs Abington playing Beatrice. It was followed by a farce, *The Rival Candidates*, during which, as prompter Hopkins noted, 'the whole set of clouds fell down upon the stage but did no damage'.[3]

10th May, Friday As yesterday

The *Public Ledger* published ten paragraphs drawing attention to the recent accusations against Samuel Foote, referring to him by name in five of them. He was described as 'one of the most flagitious characters that ever exhibited a deformed picture of human nature'. Homosexuals were 'a swarm of unnatural vermin' and 'it would not be cruelty' to wish they 'had but ONE neck, and that neck was encircled by an halter'. Further paragraphs directed at Foote followed on 11th, 13th and 14th May.[1]

Boswell breakfasted with other guests at Garrick's in the Adelphi. He and Garrick competed in imitating Dr Johnson, everyone judging in favour of Garrick except his wife, presumably out of politeness. Later Boswell called on the real Johnson and found him with literary editor George Steevens. On Boswell relating the rumours about Foote, Steevens said he would rather have the character of a sodomite than of an infidel. Boswell disagreed, and Johnson said he too would prefer to be known as an infidel, if he were to choose.[2]

At Gravesend the baggage belonging to Omai was put on board the *Resolution*.[3]

In the evening a gentleman, who had a mind to ridicule the present mode of the ladies wearing yellow ribbons, ornamented the head and tail of a large mastiff dog with them, and went with him into the large room at the Dog and Duck in St George's Fields, which was full of company. The dog's appearance afforded much mirth to the gentlemen, but was very ill relished by the ladies, many of whom were put to the blush, and appeared greatly mortified.[4]

The first part of *Henry the Fourth* was acted at Covent Garden Theatre for the benefit of Edward Shuter, who played Falstaff. He had been a feted comic actor for over thirty years but latterly his indolence and liking for hot gin had contributed to illness and decline. He played the part with great spirit, and the other performers appeared desirous of supporting him as much as possible. He afterwards repeated the Cries of London and performed an epilogue while sitting on an ass, with his usual spirit and humour. His benefit amounted to 276l., of which 194l. was ready money.[5]

Publish'd for Bells Edition of Shakespeare Febr. 28th 1770.

'Mr Shuter in the character of Falstaff'

Elsewhere, David Hume wrote to William Strahan from Bath, whither he had travelled a few days earlier with John Home.

> When we pass'd by Spine hill near Newbury we found in the inn Lord Denbigh, who was an acquaintance of my fellow traveller. His lordship inform'd him, that he, Lord Sandwich, Lord Mulgrave, Mr Banks, and two or three ladies of pleasure had pass'd five or six days there, and intended to pass all this week and the next in the same place; that their chief object was to enjoy the trouting season; that they had been very successful; that Lord Sandwich in particular had caught trouts near twenty inches long, which gave him incredible satisfaction ...
>
> I do not remember in all my little or great knowledge of history ... such another instance; and I am sure such a one does not exist: That the first lord of the Admiralty, who is absolute and uncontrouled master in his department, shou'd, at a time when the fate of the British empire is in dependance, and in dependance on him, find so much Leizure, Tranquillity, Presence of Mind and Magnanimity, as to have amusement in trouting during three weeks near sixty miles from the scene of business, and during the most critical season of the year. There needs but this single fact to decide the fate of the nation. What an ornament would it be in a future history to open the glorious events of the ensuing year with the narrative of so singular an incident.

Hume's criticism was echoed by the *Morning Post* a week later. However, it is rather undermined by the facts as the only gaps in Sandwich's recorded public activity in this period, of sufficient length to allow for worthwhile jaunts, are from Sunday 28th April to Wednesday 1st May and from Sunday 19th May to Wednesday 22nd May.*[6]

11th May, Saturday Fine, bright, warm morning, cloudy afternoon
Joseph Pearson, revenue officer, died in the London Infirmary of the wounds he received by a party of smugglers on 12th April.[1]

In the afternoon Dr Johnson went to visit the younger Thrale daughters, Susanna and Sophia, who were at Kensington while their parents were away at Bath. It was feared the children had contracted chickenpox, and later he wrote to inform Mrs Thrale that he had 'found them indeed a little spotted with their disorder, but as brisk and gay as health and youth can make them. I took a paper

---

* He attended each day of the Kingston trial (15th, 16th, 19th, 20th, 22nd April) and was also in the House of Lords on 25th April and on the 10th, 13th, 16th, 17th and 23rd May; his name is appended to Admiralty instructions dated 18th, 26th and 30th April and 3rd, 4th and 14th May; he wrote from the Admiralty to the king on 25th April, 2nd May (at 8.30 p.m.), 5th May and 23rd May; he visited the *Discovery* on 27th April and passed the *Resolution* in the Admiralty barge on 11th May and again on 18th May; he spoke with the French chargé d'affaires on 6th May; he attended a full board of Admiralty on 7th May, waiting on the king afterwards; and he attended a general court of East India proprietors on 15th May.

Can you forbear Laughing.

London Printed for R.Sayer & J.Bennett N° 53 Fleet Street, as the Act directs 14 June 1776.

1. One of many satires on head-dresses published during the year.

2. ABOVE Queen Charlotte, by Benjamin West, 1777.

3. FACING PAGE Georgiana, Duchess of Devonshire, by Sir Joshua Reynolds.
Painted *circa* 1775-1776 for the sitter's father, Lord Spencer, and exhibited at
the Royal Academy's exhibition in Pall Mall in April 1776.

4. ABOVE Elizabeth, Countess of Derby, by George Romney, 1776-1778. It was painted for the sitter, whose first appointment at Romney's house in Cavendish Square was on 27th November.

5. FACING PAGE. UPPER The Derbys with their son Edward, by Angelica Kauffman, *circa* 1776. A second child, a daughter, was born in October and christened at their house in Grosvenor Square.

6. LOWER 'The Copley Family' by John Singleton Copley, 1776-1777. The artist is shown with his wife Susanna, their four children, and his father-in-law Richard Clarke. Visiting Copley at his house in Leicester Square on 1st April 1776, fellow American Samuel Curwen found him at work on the picture and observed in it 'a very striking likeness' of all the sitters.

7. ABOVE Mrs Abington as rural *ingénue* Miss Prue in Congreve's *Love for Love*, painted by Sir Joshua Reynolds early in 1771. Horace Walpole, who saw the picture exhibited at the Royal Academy in the same year, thought it 'easy and very like'. The actress took the part again in November 1776, the *Morning Post* noting that she was 'the true natural *hoy ti! toy ti* in Miss Prue'.

8. FACING PAGE A double portrait by Benjamin West, said to have been painted in 1776 and to depict Colonel Guy Johnson and Karonghyontye (Captain David Hill). As superintendent of the department of Indian affairs Johnson was responsible for securing native support in the war against the American rebels. He was in London early in the year accompanied by two Mohawks, Joseph Brant and Oteroughyanento (John Hill), but almost certainly not by John's brother David. The difficulty is discussed in an extended note, 'How many Mohawks came to London?' (pp645-647)

9. ABOVE 'A Sunday Concert' by Charles Loraine Smith, showing a musical gathering at the house of the Burney family in St Martin's Street. In July 1776 Smith eloped with the Countess of Tyrconnel and several of those depicted also played a part in the year's events. The violinist at the centre is Signor Sal Pietro, who tutored runaway actress Ann Brown. On his left is oboist J. C. Fischer, who was dallying with Gainsborough's daughters. In the foreground is Dr Burney, father of Fanny, his hands apparently intent on Mary Wilkes, daughter of John. Published 4th June 1782.

10. FACING PAGE. UPPER Italian artists who had made London their home, tools of their crafts in hand. From left to right: sculptor Agostino Carlini; engraver Francesco Bartolozzi; decorative painter Giovanni Cipriani. During the year Carlini created the celebrated 'Smugglerius' cast for the Royal Academy. Cipriani restored the ceiling of the Banqueting House and designed an enticing masquerade ticket which was engraved by Bartolozzi. Carlini and Cipriani also worked on the new Somerset House, begun during the year under architect Sir William Chambers. Mezzotint by John Raphael Smith, after a painting by J. F. Rigaud. Published 5th March 1778.

11. LOWER 'The Portraits of the Academicians of the Royal Academy', shown as if they are attending a Life school, after a painting by Johan Zoffany, 1771-1772. Zoffany himself is front left, palette in hand. Behind him Cipriani, hat in hand, is talking to Benjamin West, who turns awkwardly to hear. Towards the middle is Reynolds holding his ear trumpet, with Sir William Chambers standing on his right. On the other side of Reynolds is anatomist William Hunter, hand on chin, then Bartolozzi holding Carlini by the arm. The larger portrait on the wall right is of Angelica Kauffman, who, as a woman, was not permitted to attend a nude Life class in the presence of men. Mezzotint by Richard Earlom, published 1st August 1773.

12. ABOVE 'A General Prospect of Vaux Hall Gardens', 1751, looking east, with the Orchestra central.

13. BELOW Vauxhall by Thomas Rowlandson, *circa* 1784, showing the larger, more elaborate Orchestra erected 1757-1758, with Frederika Weichsel, a Vauxhall favourite, singing from the balcony. Several of those depicted played a part in events in 1776, including: in the supper box on the left, intent on his food, Dr Johnson; in a pale dress, slightly left of centre, facing the viewer, the Duchess of Devonshire; also in a pale dress, right of centre, with a hand to a trinket about her neck, actress Mary Robinson, attended on her left by the Prince of Wales.

14. ABOVE Ranelagh, looking broadly south-east 'at the time of the Jubilee Ball', perhaps the one held there on 26th April 1749. Visitors entered through Ranelagh House, on the left, with a covered way leading into the rotunda. In the distance on the right is the canal. Ranelagh was the setting for another notable masquerade on 14th June 1776.

15. BELOW 'The Bread and Butter Manufactory, or the Humors of Bagnigge Wells', showing the interior of the Long Room, 1772.

16. Night life part 1. In the gallery at the Pantheon, which opened in Oxford Street in 1772. Published 20th January in the same year. The opening lines below read:

The Romans as all bards agree on | Bedeckt with gods their grand Pantheon
And our Pantheon brings to light | A store of goddesses as bright …

An EVENINGS INVITATION; with a WINK from the BAGNIO.

Printed for Carington Bowles, Map & Printseller, N° 69 in St Pauls Church Yard, London. Published as the Act directs

17. Night life part 2. A scene characteristic of, and perhaps set in, Covent Garden after dark. Two prostitutes engage a fashionably dressed man while in the background a woman beckons from a bagnio. Published *circa* 1773.

18. ABOVE Looking west across St George's Fields towards Westminster. The obelisk centre left marks the meeting of five roads. On the horizon, right of centre, are the towers of Westminster Abbey. The walled building in the middle distance on the right is the Magdalen Hospital for penitent prostitutes. Watercolour by Samuel Hieronymus Grimm, 1776.

19. BELOW Looking west along the riverbank at Chelsea during the annual 1st August rowing race for Doggett's coat and badge. Chelsea's wooden bridge can be seen in the distance, with the church tower to its right. Undated watercolour by Edward Francis Burney, a cousin of Fanny Burney.

Two views by William Marlow
20. ABOVE Blackfriars Bridge with St Paul's Cathedral beyond, *circa* 1771.

21. BELOW Looking north up Whitehall, *circa* 1775. The Banqueting House looms on the right, with the Lottery Office on its south side. Repairs such as those being made in the foreground seem to have been often required: according to the *Public Advertiser*, 22nd May 1776, 'The pavement [i.e. roadway] between Charing-cross and Parliament-street is supposed to be the worst in England.'

22. Print showing John Molesworth, who claimed that his 'calculations' predicted which lottery tickets had a greater than average chance of winning prizes. In October the Robin Hood Society debated whether his calculations were 'of advantage to adventurers, or an imposition upon the credulity of the public', and decided in his favour.

of sweetmeats, and spread them on the table. They took great delight to shew their governess the various animals that were made of sugar; and when they had eaten as much as was fit, the rest were laid up for to-morrow.'[2]

MP '*Extract of a letter from Portsmouth, dated May 9.* "This morning Lord Howe went on board the *Eagle* man of war at Spithead, which saluted him by firing three rounds as soon as he got on board; several other ships that lay off this place likewise fired their guns, and in the afternoon they weighed anchor, were under sail about six o'clock this evening, and are now out of sight. It is imagined they will join the fleet about Scilly."'[3]

MC 'On Wednesday next a court is summoned at the India-house, when 'tis said that matters of the greatest moment will be brought on the carpet; no less, than the recalling of two governors from Bengal.'[4]

12th May, Sunday A good deal of gentle rain, but a fine warm day
At the age of 29 painter James Northcote left Sir Joshua Reynolds's house in Leicester Fields, 'to take my chance in the world'. He had been Reynolds's pupil since shortly after arriving in London five years earlier, but had grown frustrated by his poverty and restricted role. In a letter home some two months earlier he had complained that Reynolds 'never gave more than a hundred guineas and thin board to any one, and it will be a sad story for me if I cannot get more than that besides being employd so much more to my likeing, by painting heads instead of sattin gowns and silk curtains, which I hate because any body could do that'. The parting was nonetheless marked by 'great cordiality', and Northcote found it 'impossible to quit such a residence as Sir Joshua's without reluctance, a house in which I had spent so many happy hours' and which was 'the constant resort' of the eminent.[1]

Edward Gibbon 'dined and lay' at Strawberry Hill. 'Mr W. read his unpublished chapter on modern gardening — agreable.'[2]

13th May, Monday A very fine, bright, warm day
While breakfasting with Dr Johnson, Boswell's habitual enquiries prompted an outburst. 'You have but two topicks,' said Johnson, 'yourself and me, and I'm sick of both.' Later Boswell called on Strahan the publisher, met John Wilkes, called at Mrs Rudd's but found she was out, and had wine, tea and supper with Edmund Burke.[1]

William Law Hamilton, clerk to William Woodfall, printer of the *Morning Chronicle*, went to the office of the *Public Ledger* in Globe Court, Shoe Lane, 'ten doors from Fleet-Street', as its masthead noted, and bought a copy of the day's paper from Thomas Brewman, who worked for the *Ledger*. The paper contained twelve paragraphs against Samuel Foote. Hamilton's services had presumably been provided by Woodfall as a favour to Foote towards the gathering of evidence for a libel suit: the *Chronicle* had supported Foote in his tussle with the Duchess of Kingston in August 1775, and in July Woodfall will stand personal surety for him.[2]

At the sign of the London Infirmary, a public-house facing the hospital of that name on the Whitechapel road, a coroner's jury sat on the body of Joseph Pearson and gave a verdict of wilful murder. A warrant was issued and several officers of the police set off to apprehend one Joseph Bland of Lewisham, thought to be the principal in the murder.[3]

A man undertook to jump in a sack three miles on the Islington road within an hour, for a wager of five guineas, and performed it within six minutes of the time allowed.[4]

At Drury Lane Theatre Garrick played King Lear. 'The people flock'd about the doors by two o'clock,' noted prompter Hopkins. 'There never was a greater overflow. Mr G. was never happier in Lear. The applause was beyond description, 3 or 4 loud claps succeeding one another at all his exits and many cry'd out *Garrick for ever* &c. &c.' Edward Gibbon was among the audience.[5]

At night, accompanied by their protector Captain Tice, the two Indians set out from the Swan with Two Necks for Falmouth, where they are to embark for their native country. 'Their behaviour here has been remarkably polite and generous,' noted the *Gazetteer*.

Anna Porter, who saw Joseph Brant frequently during his stay in London, agreed. Noting that he 'wore his coloured blanket, Indian cap, belt, tomahawk &c.,' she added: 'He spoke English very well, had erudition, having been employ'd in some translations. He was a sensible, well behaved man, grave and gentle. Spoke short sentences, and in a very low tone. Being asked why he spoke so low, he answered, "Our brothers always speak low to friends — we are loud in war alone."' She was not so impressed by his companion: 'Another Indian with him was rough and ignorant.'

According to one account, during his stay Brant had by order of government been shown 'all the remarkable places and curiosities about London and vicinity, with which he was very much pleased, in particular the Tower'. He also attended at least one masquerade in Mohawk dress. 'An English nobleman came up to him and asked him if ever he intended to lift the tomahawk which he held in his hand against the Americans. Joseph guessing at his sentiments answerd No, on which the nobleman replied, he was glad to hear it, he hoped all the Indians were of the same way of thinking, for the Americans were an injured people, and with a seeming degree of satisfaction kissed his tomahawk.'

Lord Townshend made Brant and his companion each a present of two rifle-barrel guns of a curious construction, which so far took their fancy, that before they went off they were expert in the use of them. Brant also took with him a watch and a silken banner, gifts from the king.[6]

14th May, Tuesday Chiefly cloudy, with bright intervals
William Law Hamilton returned to the offices of the *Public Ledger* and again bought a copy of the day's paper. Foote's lawyer Joseph Hickey also visited and

showed a copy of the paper dated 10th May to Thomas Brewman. Next day, the 15th, Thomas Hawkins, who seems to have worked for Hickey, visited to try to buy copies of the papers dated 10th and 11th May. Brewman told him there were none left and that he could have sold many more than were printed.[1]

According to annual custom the society of Cockneys met at the Ship tavern in Ratcliff Highway, from whence they went in procession, preceded by a band of music, and colours flying, to Stepney Church, where a sermon was preached. Afterwards they went in the same order to the assembly room at Mile End, where an elegant entertainment was provided.[2]

In the evening an oyster-woman detected two well-dressed men committing a crime of a detestable nature in a court in Goodman's Fields. She raised a mob about them, which conveyed them to a nearby horse-pond, where they were so severely ducked that one of their lives is despaired of.[3]

Between eight and nine o'clock Boswell visited Mrs Rudd again. Later he met John Wilkes, who took him into Parliament Street 'to see a curious procession pass: the funeral of a lamplighter attended by some hundreds of his fraternity with torches'.[4]

15th May, Wednesday Coarse day, some few showers

Having conceived 'an irresistible wish' to bring Dr Johnson and John Wilkes together, Boswell achieved his goal. As he noted, 'two men more different could perhaps not be selected out of all mankind', and they had 'attacked one another with some asperity in their writings', so how to manage it was 'a nice and difficult matter'. The dinner that resulted formed perhaps the most celebrated episode in his Life of Johnson.

> My worthy booksellers and friends, Messieurs Dilly in the Poultry, at whose hospitable and well-covered table I have seen a greater number of literary men, than at any other, except that of Sir Joshua Reynolds, had invited me to meet Mr Wilkes and some more gentlemen on Wednesday, May 15. 'Pray (said I,) let us have Dr Johnson.' — 'What with Mr Wilkes? not for the world, (said Mr Edward Dilly,) Dr Johnson would never forgive me.' — 'Come, (said I,) if you'll let me negociate for you, I will be answerable that all shall go well.' DILLY. 'Nay, if you will take it upon you, I am sure I shall be very happy to see them both here.'
>
> Notwithstanding the high veneration which I entertained for Dr Johnson, I was sensible that he was sometimes a little actuated by the spirit of contra-diction, and by means of that I hoped I should gain my point. I was persuaded that if I had come upon him with a direct proposal, 'Sir, will you dine in company with Jack Wilkes?' he would have flown into a passion, and would probably have answered, 'Dine with Jack Wilkes, sir! I'd as soon dine with Jack Ketch.' I therefore, while we were sitting quietly by ourselves at his house in an evening, took occasion to open my plan thus: 'Mr Dilly, sir, sends his respectful compliments to you, and would be happy if you would do him the

honour to dine with him on Wednesday next along with me, as I must soon go to Scotland.' JOHNSON. 'Sir, I am obliged to Mr Dilly. I will wait upon him.' BOSWELL. 'Provided, sir, I suppose, that the company which he is to have, is agreeable to you.' JOHNSON. 'What do you mean, sir? What do you take me for? Do you think I am so ignorant of the world, as to imagine that I am to prescribe to a gentleman what company he is to have at his table?' BOSWELL. 'I beg your pardon, sir, for wishing to prevent you from meeting people whom you might not like. Perhaps he may have some of what he calls his *patriotick* friends with him.' JOHNSON. 'Well, sir, and what then? What care *I* for his *patriotick* friends? Poh!' BOSWELL. 'I should not be surprized to find Jack Wilkes there.' JOHNSON. 'And if Jack Wilkes *should* be there, what is that to *me*, sir? My dear friend, let us have no more of this. I am sorry to be angry with you; but really it is treating me strangely to talk to me as if I could not meet any company whatever, occasionally.' BOSWELL. 'Pray forgive me, sir: I meant well. But you shall meet whoever comes, for me.' Thus I secured him, and told Dilly that he would find him very well pleased to be one of his guests on the day appointed.

Upon the much-expected Wednesday, I called on him about half an hour before dinner, as I often did when we were to dine out together, to see that he was ready in time, and to accompany him. I found him buffeting his books, as upon a former occasion, covered with dust, and making no preparation for going abroad. 'How is this, sir? (said I.) Don't you recollect that you are to dine at Mr Dilly's?' JOHNSON. 'Sir, I did not think of going to Dilly's: it went out of my head. I have ordered dinner at home with Mrs Williams.' BOSWELL. 'But, my dear sir, you know you were engaged to Mr Dilly, and I told him so. He will expect you, and will be much disappointed if you don't come.' JOHNSON. 'You must talk to Mrs Williams about this.'

Here was a sad dilemma. I feared that what I was so confident I had secured would yet be frustrated. He had accustomed himself to shew Mrs Williams such a degree of humane attention, as frequently imposed some restraint upon him; and I knew that if she should be obstinate, he would not stir. I hastened down stairs to the blind lady's room, and told her I was in great uneasiness, for Dr Johnson had engaged to me to dine this day at Mr Dilly's, but that he had told me he had forgotten his engagement, and had ordered dinner at home. 'Yes, sir, (said she, pretty peevishly,) Dr Johnson is to dine at home.' — 'Madam, (said I,) his respect for you is such, that I know he will not leave you unless you absolutely desire it. But as you have so much of his company, I hope you will be good enough to forego it for a day; as Mr Dilly is a very worthy man, has frequently had agreeable parties at his house for Dr Johnson, and will be vexed if the doctor neglects him to-day. And then, madam, be pleased to consider my situation; I carried the message, and I assured Mr Dilly that Dr Johnson was to come, and no doubt he has made a dinner, and invited a company, and boasted of the honour he expected to have. I shall be quite disgraced if the doctor is not there.' She gradually softened to my solicitations, which were certainly as earnest as most entreaties to ladies upon any occasion, and was graciously pleased to empower me to tell Dr Johnson, 'That all things considered, she thought he should certainly go.' I flew back to him, still in dust, and careless of what should be the event, indifferent in his choice to go or stay; but as soon as I had announced to him Mrs Williams's consent, he roared, 'Frank,* a clean shirt,' and was very soon drest. When I had him fairly seated in a hackney-coach with me, I exulted as much as a fortune-hunter who has got an heiress into a post-chaise with him to set out for Gretna-Green.

When we entered Mr Dilly's drawing room, he found himself in the midst of a company he did not know. I kept myself snug and silent, watching how he would conduct himself. I observed him whispering to Mr Dilly, 'Who is that gentleman, sir?' — 'Mr Arthur Lee.' — JOHNSON. 'Too, too, too,' (under his breath,) which was one of his habitual mutterings. Mr Arthur Lee could not but be very obnoxious to Johnson, for he was not only a *patriot* but an *American*.† He was afterwards minister from the United States at the Court of Madrid. 'And who is the gentleman in lace?' — 'Mr Wilkes, sir.' This information confounded him still more; he had some difficulty to restrain himself, and taking up a book, sat down upon a window-seat and read, or at least kept his eye upon it intently for some time, till he composed himself. His feelings, I dare say, were aukward enough. But he no doubt recollected his having rated me for supposing that he could be at all disconcerted by any company, and he, therefore, resolutely set himself to behave quite as an easy man of the world, who could adapt himself at once to the disposition and manners of those whom he might chance to meet.

The cheering sound of 'Dinner is upon the table,' dissolved his reverie, and we all sat down without any symptom of ill humour. There were present, beside Mr Wilkes, and Mr Arthur Lee, who was an old companion of mine when he studied physick at Edinburgh, Mr (now Sir John) Miller, Dr Lettsom, and Mr Slater the druggist. Mr Wilkes placed himself next to Dr Johnson, and behaved to him with so much attention and politeness, that he gained upon him insensibly. No man eat more heartily than Johnson, or loved better what was nice and delicate. Mr Wilkes was very assiduous in helping him to some fine veal. 'Pray give me leave, sir: — It is better here — A little of the brown — Some fat, sir — A little of the stuffing — Some gravy — Let me have the pleasure of giving you some butter — Allow me to recommend a squeeze of this orange — or the lemon, perhaps, may have more zest.' — 'Sir, sir, I am obliged to you, sir,' cried Johnson, bowing, and turning his head to him with a look for some time of 'surly virtue' but, in a short while, of complacency.

Foote being mentioned, Johnson said, 'He is not a good mimick.' One of the company added, 'A merry Andrew, a buffoon.' JOHNSON. 'But he has wit too, and is not deficient in ideas, or in fertility and variety of imagery, and not empty of reading; he has knowledge enough to fill up his part. One species

* Francis Barber, Johnson's black servant.
† As Boswell recorded elsewhere, Johnson's attitude towards the colonists was robust: 'Sir, they are a race of convicts, and ought to be thankful for any thing we allow them short of hanging'; 'I am willing to love all mankind, except an American.'

of wit he has in an eminent degree, that of escape. You drive him into a corner with both hands; but he's gone, sir, when you think you have got him — like an animal that jumps over your head. Then he has a great range for wit; he never lets truth stand between him and a jest, and he is sometimes mighty coarse. Garrick is under many restraints from which Foote is free.' ...

Mr Arthur Lee mentioned some Scotch who had taken possession of a barren part of America, and wondered why they should choose it. JOHNSON. 'Why, sir, all barrenness is comparative. The *Scotch* would not know it to be barren.' BOSWELL. 'Come, come, he is flattering the English. You have now been in Scotland, sir, and say if you did not see meat and drink enough there.' JOHNSON. 'Why yes, sir; meat and drink enough to give the inhabitants sufficient strength to run away from home.' All these quick and lively sallies were said sportively, quite in jest, and with a smile, which showed that he meant only wit. Upon this topick he and Mr Wilkes could perfectly assimilate; here was a bond of union between them, and I was conscious that as both of them had visited Caledonia, both were fully satisfied of the strange narrow ignorance of those who imagine that it is a land of famine. But they amused themselves with persevering in the old jokes.

Boswell claimed a superiority for Scotland over England on the grounds that 'no man can be arrested there for a debt merely because another swears it against him ... and that a seizure of the person, before judgement is obtained, can take place only if his creditor should swear that he is about to fly from the country, or, as it is technically expressed, is *in meditatione fugae.'*

WILKES. 'That, I should think, may be safely sworn of all the Scotch nation.' JOHNSON (to Mr Wilkes), 'You must know, sir, I lately took my friend Boswell and shewed him genuine civilised life in an English provincial town. I turned him loose at Lichfield, my native city, that he might see for once real civility: for you know he lives among savages in Scotland, and among rakes in London.' WILKES. 'Except when he is with grave, sober, decent people like you and me.' JOHNSON (smiling), 'And we ashamed of him.' ...

After dinner we had an accession of Mrs Knowles, the Quaker lady, well known for her various talents, and of Mr Alderman Lee.* Amidst some patriotick groans, somebody (I think the alderman) said, 'Poor old England is lost.' JOHNSON. 'Sir, it is not so much to be lamented that old England is lost, as that the Scotch have found it.' ...

Mr Wilkes held a candle to shew a fine print of a beautiful female figure which hung in the room, and pointed out the elegant contour of the bosom with the finger of an arch connoisseur. He afterwards, in a conversation with me, waggishly insisted, that all the time Johnson shewed visible signs of a fervent admiration of the corresponding charms of the fair Quaker.

This record, though by no means so perfect as I could wish, will serve to give a notion of a very curious interview, which was not only pleasing at the

---

* William, brother of Arthur.

Dr Johnson, after a portrait by Reynolds thought to have been painted in the mid 1770s
Mezzotint by William Doughty, published 24th June 1779

time, but had the agreeable and benignant effect of reconciling any animosity, and sweetening any acidity, which in the various bustle of political contest, had been produced in the minds of two men, who though widely different, had so many things in common – classical learning, modern literature, wit, and humour, and ready repartee – that it would have been much to be regretted if they had been for ever at a distance from each other.

Mr Burke gave me much credit for this successful *negociation*; and pleasantly said, that 'there was nothing to equal it in the whole history of the *Corps Diplomatique.*'

I attended Dr Johnson home, and had the satisfaction to hear him tell Mrs Williams how much he had been pleased with Mr Wilkes's company, and what an agreeable day he had passed.

I talked a good deal to him of the celebrated Margaret Caroline Rudd, whom I had visited, induced by the fame of her talents, address, and irresistible power of fascination. To a lady who disapproved of my visiting her, he said on a former occasion, 'Nay, madam, Boswell is in the right; I should have visited her myself, were it not that they have now a trick of putting every thing into the news-papers.' This evening he exclaimed, 'I envy him his acquaintance with Mrs Rudd.'[1]

Meanwhile there was a very numerous general court of the East India Company at their house in Leadenhall Street. The clerk read a resolution agreed by eleven against ten on the 8th instant, that Warren Hastings, governor of Bengal, and Francis Barwell, one of the council, be recalled. In defence of Hastings it was said that the country was overrun with venality and peculation before he went there and that he had in great measure restored it to good order. From papers read it appeared that no direct charge of criminality against him had been made good, and accusations of corruption made by Nandakumar, a maharaja, had come to nothing, the accuser having himself been found guilty of forgery and hanged for it the previous year. The council in Bengal was, however, irretrievably divided, and the directors were determined to recall that party which was most obnoxious, which they agreed was Governor Hastings and Mr Barwell.

According to the *Morning Chronicle*, 'This was one of the most important debates perhaps ever agitated in that court,' and it did not break up until two in the morning. A motion was called for, but it being thought improper to bring on a question of such importance at such an hour, it was referred to a ballot, to commence that morning (Thursday) at eleven o'clock and close at six the same day. The directors were powerfully sustained by Lord Sandwich, Mr Robinson, Grey Cooper, and many others friends of government who were present.

Their recommendation that Hastings and Barwell be recalled was nonetheless rejected, the ballot proving in favour of those gentlemen by a majority of 106.[2]

16th May, Thursday Coarse day, several showers, hail and rain, cold wind
Being Ascension Day, the churchwardens and other officers of St Bride's, Fleet Street, perambulated the boundaries of the parish, and afterwards held their triennial dinner at the Globe tavern, Fleet Street, with near 100 of the inhabitants.[1]

On his last day before returning to Scotland, Boswell called on Dr Johnson but found him in company and left without a word exchanged. He went to see Mrs Rudd, who showed him a miniature of herself, taken when she was in prison, 'in case of any accident'. He asked if she meant being hanged. She assured him that would never have happened: she had 'taken care of that' and was not afraid of death. She pressed him to stay. Delirium rising, he said, 'You could make me commit murder,' asked if a 'pretty ankle' was one of her perfections, and adverted to her eyes. 'Poets and painters have told me enough of them,' she rejoined. He took a kiss, snatched several more with passion, said 'Adieu' twice, and at last 'God bless you.' Later he visited Samuel Foote.

In the evening, returning to take leave of Johnson, he complained that nothing had been said between them that day, to which Johnson replied that there seldom was. 'Why then meet?' asked Boswell. 'To eat and drink and promote kindness,' replied Johnson, adding, 'Take care of yourself. Don't drink. ... You may do what you deserve to be hanged for next day. ... Don't talk of yourself or of me. ... Don't make yourself and me a proverb.' Boswell thanked him warmly for all his kindness. 'Sir, (said he,) you are very welcome. Nobody repays it with more.'[2]

Warren Hastings, after a portrait by Reynolds, 1766-1767
Mezzotint by Thomas Watson, published 20th March 1777

The entertainments at the Spring Gardens, Vauxhall, opened for the summer season. There were more people than was expected considering the coldness of the weather, and they were so complaisant as to make the singers repeat every song and catch twice over. A solo on the violin was played by Mr Barthelemon, and a concerto on the hautboy by Mr Parke.[3]

GA 'Extract of a genuine letter from Philadelphia, received by a gentleman of undoubted veracity, dated March 12. ... "The ministry have often unjustly accused us of looking after Independency; but what they pretend to dread, their measures will in a short time bring forth. *Common Sense*, which I herewith send you, is read to all ranks; and as many as read, so many become converted; tho' perhaps the hour before were most violent against the least idea of Independence. This summer's campaign will, I make no doubt, set us

The Vauxhall Syren

From the *Town and Country Magazine* for August 1776. The syren's identity is not known. Count de B—, a foreign envoy, was said to be captivated by her and to attend Vauxhall 'every night whilst she sings'.

free from the shackles of education; and the King of Britain, instead of being the idol of Americans, will be of little more importance here than to frighten little children. | You will see by the papers, that our people have opened their batteries on Boston, which is destined to the flames. I wish I could convey to you a small idea of the ardour which inflames our young men, who turn out with more alacrity on the least alarm, than they would to a ball.'"[4]

17th May, Friday Coarse day, but no rain

Before 9 a.m. all the avenues leading to the Court of King's Bench were uncommonly crowded. About noon General Smith and Thomas Brand Hollis appeared to receive sentence for bribery and corruption at the late election for Hindon. The attorney general entered fully into the nature and heinousnesss of the offence, and prayed that the sentence should be proportionate. Counsel for the defendants, particularly for the general, alledged the notorious infamy of the borough, and that however improperly the general might have conducted himself, he had been deceived by the aptitude, venality and artifice of the burghers. Lord Mansfield said it was the first prosecution of such a nature, that he would take until the first day of the next term to consider, and committed the defendants until that

View of the Orchestra in Vauxhall Garden.

Pub.d by J.Bew 1 May 1778.

time [> 8 Jun]. They were taken into the custody of the tipstaff, and conveyed to the King's Bench prison.

Meanwhile, unabashed, Smith had the day before been re-elected in a new contest at Hindon.[1]

At the chambers of Judge Edward Willes in Serjeants' Inn, Samuel Foote, William Law Hamilton, and Thomas Hawkins swore and signed an oath to which copies of the *Public Ledger* dated 10th, 11th, 13th and 14th May were attached. Hamilton and Hawkins detailed their visits to the *Ledger*'s office and swore that they believed the Rev. William Jackson, of Lyon's Inn, was an editor of the paper and that William Faden, of Peterborough Court, Fleet Street, was its printer and publisher. Hamilton and Foote swore to their belief that forty or so paragraphs marked up in the newspapers related to Foote, and were designed to make people believe he was guilty of the crimes he had been accused of, and to prevent him from opening his theatre for the summer season.

On the same day Foote, by his counsel Mr Wallace, moved the Court of King's Bench for a rule obliging the printer of the *Public Ledger* to shew cause why an information should not be filed against him for publishing false, scandalous, and malicious paragraphs, tending to defame Mr Foote's character and injure him in the public opinion. The court, on hearing only two of the paragraphs read, ordered the rule to be granted.[2]

Hannah More wrote from the Adelphi to a friend about Garrick's recent performances:

> On Monday night he played King Lear, and ... it was the universal opinion that it was one of the greatest scenes ever exhibited. I called to-day in Leicester Fields, and Sir Joshua declared it was full three days before he got the better of it. The eagerness of people to see him is beyond any thing you can have an idea of. You will see half a dozen duchesses and countesses of a night, in the upper boxes: for the fear of not seeing him at all has humbled those who used to go, not for the purpose of seeing, but of being seen, and they now courtesy to the ground for the worst places in the house.[3]

18th May, Saturday Coarse day, some trifling showers

In the evening a new opera called *Antigono* was performed at the King's Theatre in the Haymarket, but its effect was considerably impaired by Signora Gabrielli being so hoarse as to be incapable of singing. This celebrated female, notwithstanding her constitutional haughtiness, seemed to feel the disapprobation shewn her. The storm growing louder, she came forward, and went through a song in a kind of *mezza voce*. The numerous and brilliant audience appeared so exceedingly irritated that Mrs Yates came on in a dishabille, and apologized for the accident, which was not known to the managers in time to apprise the public, said she was exceedingly sorry, and could only offer to return the money to such ladies and gentlemen as might chuse to take it. This address was received with approbation, and the opera went on uninterrupted, except a few hisses which attended Signora Gabrielli when she appeared.[1]

19th May, Sunday Cloudy day, with a good deal of small rain

In the morning the noted Miss West attempted to pick a gentleman's pocket at the popish chapel in Duke Street, Lincoln's Inn Fields. After running about several of the neighbouring streets with a rabble at her heels, many of whom were apparently no better than herself, she got clear off.

A notice written *circa* 1778 described the woman in question as as 'one of the most notorious and artful pickpockets that modern times have produced', and added a helpful description:

> She is of the middle size, genteelly grown, her countenance is of the oval form, and rather ruddy; her hair of a moderate brown, her eyes hazle coloured, and her nose inclined to the aquiline; but she is best to be distinguished by a remarkably broad west-country accent, which she cannot disguise. She dresses gay, and is about thirty-five years of age; but looks rather younger.
>
> Persons who may see such a woman crouding into the playhouse, or may happen to sit next her in the gallery, will do well to be cautious, or the pocket will be picked before any suspicion can arise. She will look a man hard in the face, ask him some unmeaning question, and ease him of his cash in an instant.[1]

About noon the king went to St James's for divine service and a drawing-room. It being her majesty's thirty-second birth-day he received the compliments of the nobility, &c. on the occasion.[2]

Dr Johnson dined with Sir Joshua Reynolds and the Bishop of St Asaph at Wick House, Reynolds's retreat on Richmond Hill.[3]

Reynolds's house on Richmond Hill
Aquatint by J. C. Stadler, 1793, after a drawing by Joseph Farington

Princess Mary with five of her siblings, after a painting by Benjamin West, 1776
Mezzotint by Valentine Green, published 29th September 1778

Between six and seven in the evening their majesties came to St James's with all their children. The bed of state was erected in the great council chamber, and a little after seven o'clock the recently born princess, Mary, was christened by the Archbishop of Canterbury.[4]

At night one of the Bow stages was robbed near the Artichoke, Mile End Road, by a single highwayman, who thrusting his pistol through the coach window, demanded the passengers money. They could only muster about five shillings amongst them, with which he rode off much dissatisfied, crying, 'D—n such Sunday gentry.'[5]

20th May, Monday Wet night, cloudy mild day, with trifling rains
In the forenoon in the Court of King's Bench the rule was made absolute against the publisher of the *Public Ledger* for having published false, scandalous, and malicious paragraphs, tending to defame and injure Samuel Foote. Lord Mansfield observed that the licentiousness of the press was in no instance more intolerable than in attempting to corrupt justice, by pre-judging a cause and poisoning the minds of the publick with inflammatory articles against a person who was to stand trial.[1]

In the evening Mr Foote opened the season at his theatre in the Haymarket. Many persons assembled before five, and long before six the streets were crowded with hundreds wishing for admission. As soon as the doors were opened, the crowd pressed eagerly in, affording a considerable harvest for pickpockets. The pit was filled in six minutes, and there was not a single woman in it. Many of the boxes had been taken for ladies of distinction, but on their entering, the galleries made a violent noise, in consequence of which they prudently retired, and were followed by most of the other females in the house. In less than half an hour, there were not twenty ladies of any kind present, and not a place to be had in pit, boxes or galleries.

All was peaceable enough till the end of the second music, and the drawing of the curtain, when Mr Foote came forward, dressed in the character of Sir Robert Riscounter, which he was to play in *The Bankrupt*. He attempted to address the audience, but was prevented for several minutes by an intermixture of hissing, clapping, groaning, and huzzas. He appeared in great agitation of mind, but the signals of approbation were predominant and at length he delivered himself in the following words:

'Gentlemen, It was not my intention, after the charge that had been made against me, to appear before the public till I had an opportunity of proving my innocence; but as the charge was made at the critical point of time when I usually opened my theatre, and having engaged as good a set of performers for your entertainment as I could procure, it was the unanimous advice of my friends that I should open my house, in confidence that the public were too noble and generous to discard an old servant for a mere accusation.

'I am ready to answer every charge that can be brought against me, and have pursued such legal steps to clear my reputation from the virulent attacks of a public paper, as will speedily bring that matter to an issue, the Court of King's Bench having this day made the rule absolute against the publisher.

'I beg leave to return my thanks for the marks you have now given me of your candour, humanity, and justice, in thus giving me a fair and patient hearing. Permit me therefore to assure you, that I will never disgrace your protection. I — I — I can say no more.'

He retired weeping from the stage, amidst such plaudits as are seldom heard.

The comedy now commenced, and Mr Foote's motive for opening with *The Bankrupt* cannot escape the observation of those who know that its satire is chiefly levelled against printers, and conductors of newspapers. It went through with a regularity beyond what could be expected, and both players and manager received uncommon outbursts of applause. According to the *Morning Chronicle*, the audience 'was one of the most respectable that ever was convened in a play-house. Most of the men of rank, of letters, and of distinguished abilities now in town, were present, and they all joined in shewing their detestation of calumny and injustice, by supporting Mr Foote'. The *St James's Chronicle* added that at 11 p.m. an express went off from the theatre for Calais, where the Countess of Bristol was residing, 'with an account that the house is still standing, and the manager has been able to keep his legs by the favour of his friends and the justice of the public'.[2]

21st May, Tuesday Bright chearful day, but very cold

In the morning, if things went as he had planned, Beaumarchais left London for Paris, 'secretly with all my papers'. Before doing so he had a worried visitor, as he later explained in a letter to Vergennes: 'The demoiselle d'Éon rushed to my house in a very alarmed state, and confided in me that one Mr Swinton,* a London wine merchant, had several years before advanced her 200 louis'. The money had been given as the first part of a scheme under which Swinton and others 'were to give her 10,000 louis for revealing her sex to them in the country, to the end that they would buy all the policies in London and win immense sums of money'. After five days, however, the man supposed to bring the 10,000 louis had not arrived and they had all returned to town, d'Éon retaining the 200 louis.

D'Éon now told Beaumarchais that earlier in the day Swinton had come to reclaim the money: Swinton apparently believed d'Éon was about to return to France and had threatened to have him arrested and to make the intrigue public. According to Beaumarchais, 'She went down on her knees, and begged me to extract her, before my departure, from this new embarrassment.' He lent the 200 louis and later passed d'Éon's receipt to Vergennes to support claiming it back on expenses.[1]

SJC 'Omiah, it is said, is become quite the fine gentleman. Query, says a correspondent, would it not have been better to have taught him Mechanics than Gentility, and would it not be of more use to him when he returns, to know how to make a wheel-barrow than a bow?'[2]

22nd May, Wednesday As yesterday

The sessions began at the Old Bailey. Nineteen prisoners were tried, of whom six were capitally convicted, including Benjamin Bates and John Green for a burglary in the dwelling-house of Mr Penleaze on 21st April.[1]

In the Commons General Conway proposed that copies of the instructions given to Lord Howe and General Howe, for making peace with America, be laid before the House. He said that any offer to America should be agreed to by parliament because the Americans had good reason not to trust government. He read out a circular to all the governors in America from Lord Hillsborough, then a secretary of state, dated 13th May 1769, assuring them that his majesty's administration had 'at no time entertained a design to propose to parliament to lay any

---

* Samuel Swinton. A former navy lieutenant, in 1776 he founded *Courier de l'Europe*, a newspaper with which Beaumarchais would become closely involved. It was printed in London and distributed in England and on the Continent. From 1778, if not before, Swinton was also a British secret agent.

further taxes upon America'. The Americans had been deceived and would not be duped again. 'Are not these rebels of a different kind?' he added. 'Who is there among you, that would not combat any power upon earth, invading in the same manner your privileges and rights?'

A long debate ensued in which Lord North, Mr Burke, Mr Fox, Lord George Germain, and Colonel Barré spoke. Closing the debate, Governor Johnstone insisted that Germain had in express terms required unconditional submission, while Lord North was for treaty and conciliation almost on any terms so long as Great Britain could derive advantage from it, and that these opinions were irreconcilable. What might be made out of the hodge-podge of both jumbled together, he left to the House to consider, and to events to prove. On the question being put, 85 were for the motion, 171 against it.[2]

23rd May, Thursday Cloudy morning, bright afternoon, very cold
Early in the morning a man walked blindfold from Charing Cross to Temple Bar for a wager of two guineas. He was allowed an hour, and performed it in three minutes less.[1]

Sangster the footman was approached by a wealthy stranger, Samuel Clay Harvey, who told him that if his allegations against Foote were true he would 'stand my friend and support the prosecution'. Harvey was closely involved with the *Public Ledger*, and at this time or slightly later was among its owners. Following Foote's libel writ the paper had a natural interest in seeing Sangster prevail, and Harvey would prove true to his word, supporting the former footman over the months that followed.[2]

The new hall belonging to the Society of Free Masons, in Great Queen Street, was dedicated in solemn form by Lord Petre the grand master and other officers of the grand lodge, in the presence of upwards of 160 ladies and 400 brethren. An oration on the antiquity, extent, and utility of masonry was delivered by Dr Dodd. The hall consists of one lofty and spacious room with an organ at the upper end. The pillars and openings are embellished with the emblems of masonry. There are five glass chandeliers and at the center of the ceiling are the twelve signs of the Zodiac.[3]

In the afternoon his majesty went to the House of Lords, gave the royal assent to seventeen bills, and made a speech to both Lords and Commons. 'We are engaged in a great national cause, the prosecution of which must inevitably be attended with many difficulties, and much expence: but when we consider that the essential rights and interests of the whole empire are deeply concerned in the issue of it ... I am convinced that you will not think any price too high'. Afterwards parliament was prorogued to 1st August.[4]

Arthur Lee wrote to Beaumarchais in Paris, using the cover identity for him of Roderique Hortalez & Co. 'I pray you to consider, in your arrangements at the Cape, that the want of tobacco ought not to hinder your sending out your supplies to the Americans, for ... the essential object is to maintain the war.' The letter's handwriting appeared to be that of a woman and it was signed 'Mary Johnston'. Beaumarchais replied from Paris on 6th June: 'I am about to send to Cape François, on the island of San Domingo, a ship loaded with merchandise to the value of twenty-five thousand pounds sterling, besides cannon powder and stores. ... On your part, do not fail to send a ship loaded with good Virginia tobacco, and let your friend [code for Congress] send in the ship an intelligent, discreet, and faithful person, with powers to receive the money or merchandise and powder and to make the remittances in tobacco'.[5]

In the evening Colonel Guy Johnson, superintendent of Indian affairs, left London for Falmouth, where Joseph Brant and his companion were waiting for his arrival in order to embark for America. Johnson made a leisurely progress, taking in the curiosities at Wilton House, and only arrived on the 29th. His party sailed in the *Hyde* packet on 2nd June but did not reach Staten Island until 29th July. Johnson explained in a letter to Germain that for the last three weeks of the voyage they had suffered 'much molestation from the rebel vessels ... one of which attacked us near Bermudas ... My surgeon is shot thro' the leg, and 5 others slightly wounded ... My officers and the Indians behaved very well and were very usefull at small arms.' According to another account, 'Joseph and his companion, John of the lower Mohawk town who attended him, having brass rifle guns, made them a present from my Lord Townsend, were so dexterous and good marksmen as to pick off those on board the rebel ship whom by their dress they took to be officers, and after an engagement of two glasses the privateer thought proper to sheer off.'[6]

24th May, Friday As yesterday

Orders were given for 10,000 dozen of tallow candles to be immediately delivered into the Victualling Office on Tower Hill, for the use of the king's ships going to America.[1]

A remarkably fine sturgeon, measuring 7 feet and 4 inches in length, was presented by the water bailiff to the lord mayor, who sent it immediately to his majesty at St James's.[2]

A mad dog ran over Blackfriars Bridge and bit several people in his way. He got as far as the Borough before he was killed.[3]

Benjamin Harley, Thomas Henman, and Joseph Bland were tried at the Old Bailey for the murder of Joseph Pearson, Custom House officer, at Deptford on 12th April last. The indictment also charged J. George, alias Gypsy George, F. George, alias Butcher George, and others not yet taken. After hearing the evidence the jury in less than one minute declared Harley and Henman guilty and acquitted Bland. The judge pronounced sentence of death with awful solemnity. His lordship seemed extremely affected, and forgot that part of the sentence respecting the dissecting and anatomizing the bodies, upon which the miserable convicts were brought a second time to the bar to hear that horrible remainder.[4]

25th May, Saturday Bright frosty night, clouds and sunshine in the day
About 11 or 12 o'clock, at the request of Joseph Banks, Captain Cook called
upon Nathaniel Dance in Tavistock Row to sit for the portrait engraved below,
in which he points to the east coast of Australia on the map before him.[1]

By J. K. Sherwin, 1784, after Nathaniel Dance

According to David Samwell, surgeon on the *Discovery*, 'the plate engraved by Sherwin,
after a painting by Dance, is a most excellent likeness of Captain Cook; and more to
be valued, as it is the only one I have seen that bears any resemblance to him'.

William Knox, under secretary at the American department, forwarded to Lord Weymouth's office and the Admiralty an extract from a letter sent two days earlier from Brighthelmstone. It was written by Lord North's half-brother, the Bishop of Worcester, to his father Lord Guilford. 'The Dieppe pacquet arrived to day, and in it a fugitive American sailor, who says he ran away from a ship freighted by the Congress, and now loading with arms and ammunition at Havre de Grace. He says they have many ships loaded there with arms, which come in concealed packages from the interior parts of France, and that by way of blind, they do not clear out for Philadelphia, but for Lisbon, and thus escape suspicion.'[2]

26th May, Sunday Clouds and sunshine at intervals, a fine pleasant day
In the morning the body of Mr Cain, deputy serjeant of the vestry to the Chapel Royal, St James's, was found hanging in a place called the Pump-room, which supplies the palace with water. He got up the same morning at five o'clock, appeared perfectly in his senses, and laid out the communion cloth and plate in the chapel as usual. From his not having been seen afterwards till dead, it is supposed he went immediately from the altar, and committed this rash action.[1]

Being Whit Sunday, at one o'clock his majesty went to the Chapel Royal, preceded by the heralds, pursuivants at arms, &c. and according to custom made a present of a purse of gold for the benefit of the poor. Her majesty was not present, but heard divine service and received the sacrament at her own palace.[2]

27th May, Monday Chiefly cloudy, but fair
In the morning Benjamin Harley and Thomas Henman were executed at Tyburn for the murder of Joseph Pearson. It being a holiday for working men and apprentices, great multitudes attended, and not content with that sight, many returned to see them dissected at Surgeons' Hall.[1]

It seems likely that one of these two corpses was destined for artistic immortality.* John Deare, a 16-year-old apprentice to a carver in Piccadilly, and in later life a sculptor, wrote to his father at about this time: 'I have seen two men hanged, and one with his breast cut open at Surgeons' Hall. The other being a fine subject, they took him to the Royal Academy, and covered him with plaster of Paris, after they had put him in the position of the Dying Gladiator.' The result was probably the celebrated *écorché* figure described by Baretti a few years later in a guide to the Royal Academy:

> *Smugglerius.* A jocular name given to this cast, which was moulded on the body of a smuggler for the use of the Academy. As Dr Hunter, professor of anatomy to the Academy, was going to dissect that body in one of his lectures to the young students, it was observed, that many parts of it were very fine

* The conflicting evidence is set out in an extended note, 'Who was "Smugglerius"?' (pp647-648).

and worth preserving. Signor Carlini was therefore directed to mould it, and he chose to give it the posture of the Dying Gladiator.

The original cast has been lost but nineteenth-century copies survive at the Royal Academy and Edinburgh College of Art.[2]

At 10.30 a.m. his majesty arrived on Blackheath to review the 3rd regiment of dragoon guards, having travelled at the rate of fifteen miles an hour in a post chariot and four. He was dressed in the uniform of the regiment, mounted on a fine bay horse to inspect the troops, and appeared in health and high spirits. The roads and fields leading from town were crowded with such multitudes going to attend as was hardly ever remembered. A woman was beat down during the review, and was so trampled on, that she died before any assistance could be given her.[3]

The king returned to the Queen's Palace and the royal family took coach to Kew for the summer. Among the crowds gathered to watch their departure was a group of American refugees including Samuel Curwen.[4]

The coroner's inquest sat on the body of Mr Cain and returned their verdict, *felo de se.*[5]

The body of a child, about six weeks old, with a cord round its neck, was taken out of the river near Westminster Bridge and taken to Lambeth bone-house to be owned.[6]

About dusk a woman attempted to drown an infant about a fortnight old in the ditch which conveys the water into Five Foot Lane in the Borough, but a man observing her take something out of her lap, went up and prevented her. The reason she gave was that the father of the child was gone to America, and she could not bear to see it want.[7]

Kew Palace from the lawn, by Joshua Kirby, 1763

From the *London Magazine* for March 1776, part of the Court Beauties series

At Drury Lane Theatre Garrick took the title role in *Richard the Third* for the first time in four years. Edward Gibbon was in the audience. Also there was Lady Granby, who, according to the *Morning Post*, 'is now become the very pink of the *ton*' and was wearing 'white and black plumes, which ... resembled those mournful ones which adorn the top of a hearse'.[8]

The Chevalier d'Éon wrote a long letter to the Comte de Vergennes in an attempt to undermine Beaumarchais. D'Éon believed himself still to be owed over £9,000 by the French government and was frustrated by lack of progress in negotiations with Beaumarchais to resolve the matter. He claimed that during his many visits to London the playwright had spent no more than five hours dealing directly with him. His celebrity, and the powerful support he had from great men in France, had given him 'the insolence of an upstart lackey, or of a boy watch-maker who, by chance, has discovered perpetual motion'. Believing himself 'too grand a seigneur to treat with me', he had delegated the task to his sidekick Morande, 'while he himself, wrapped in his dressing gown, has not left it except to run to his pleasures'. These included going with another Frenchman 'regularly three times a week among the brothels of Covent Garden, where they have gathered groups of street girls, whom they have undress in order to serve and dance totally naked, during their obscene and astonishing orgies. Knowledge of these nocturnal goings-on ... is public here.'*

D'Éon went on to express dismay at having to negotiate with Morande, 'who has neither morals, nor fortune, nor reputation to lose'. He attached various papers to support his case, including a statement signed by himself and three others regarding Morande's confession at dinner six weeks earlier [> 11 Apr]. The whole was enclosed in a folio box addressed to Vergennes and his fellow minister Maurepas. It was carried from London to Versailles by d'Éon's brother-in-law, the Chevalier O'Gorman.[9]

28th May, Tuesday A very bright warm day

At 7 a.m. many hundreds of servants assembled at Drury Lane stage-door to take places for the approaching benefit, in which it is said Mr Garrick will again play Richard the Third. Three-fourths were not able to succeed in their embassies.[1]

The Earl of Holdernesse, governor to the Prince of Wales and the Bishop of Osnaburgh, and the Bishop of Chester, preceptor to the princes, resigned their offices, as did their deputies. Next day (Wednesday) Lord Bruce was appointed governor and Richard Hurd, Bishop of Lichfield and Coventry, preceptor. Bruce shortly withdrew, to be replaced by the Duke of Montagu.[2]

Sir William Chambers, comptroller of the Board of Works, attended by the master tradesmen, laid the first stone of the intended new buildings at Somerset House, on which occasion he gave the workmen a handsome sum to drink his majesty's health, and success to the undertaking. Several Royal Academicians assisted at the ceremony.[3]

Common Sense and *Plain Truth*, an anonymous loyalist response, both first printed in Philadelphia, were published in one volume by John Almon in Piccadilly, price 1s. 6d. The most critical references in *Common Sense* were omitted, blank spaces being left where, for example, the king was referred to in the original as 'an inveterate enemy to liberty' and 'the royal brute'.

---

* This account is uncorroborated and may arise in part at least from d'Éon's rancour. The lack of newspaper reports concerning Beaumarchais's time in London suggests a relatively discreet way of life. In 1774 he had met Marie Thérèse de Willermawlaz, twenty-five years his junior, who would become his third wife. She may have accompanied him on at least some of his trips to London, and on 5th January 1777 would give birth to their daughter, Eugénie.

While later parts of the book discussed America, in the earlier parts Paine addressed perceived failings in the British constitution, which he saw as the fundamental cause of oppression on both sides of the Atlantic. Britons did indeed enjoy greater liberty than other peoples in Europe, but that was 'wholly owing to the constitution of the people, and not to the constitution of the government'. The country's treasured combination of monarchy, aristocracy, and democracy, each part supposedly checking and balancing the others, was 'farcical'. The people had no guarantee of liberty because the crown remained 'in possession of the key' to the door to absolute rule. Monarchy itself was 'a form of government which the word of God bears testimony against, and blood will attend it'.

The *Critical Review*, in its June edition, was unimpressed: 'We shall ... only observe, that under a specious title, it contains the most impudent, absurd, and erroneous doctrines, relative to the British government, that ever were suggested by the fervour of political fanaticism.'[4]

29th May, Wednesday A very bright warm day
Having taken a pilot on board on 6th May, but been delayed by the lack of a favourable wind, Captain Cook finally set sail from Deptford, arriving next day at Long Reach, near Erith, 'where our artillery, powder, shot, and other ordnance stores were received'.[1]

Near 100 soldiers lately arrived from America, after being at the Sick and Wounded Office on Tower Hill, marched through the city for Chelsea. It was a most shocking sight: some of them had no arms, some no legs, and most of them were under 30 years old and had wives and children.[2]

A woman was found hanging in her lodgings in East Smithfield with two small children sitting by her. Her husband being gone abroad and leaving her in great distress is said to be the cause of her committing so rash an act.[3]

30th May, Thursday Cloudy, with some gentle showers
Edmund Burke wrote from Westminster to a friend in Bristol: 'Our session is over, and I can hardly believe, by the tranquillity of every thing about me, that we are a people who have just lost an empire. But it is so. The present nursery revolution,* I think, engages as much of our attention.'[1]

At Drury Lane Theatre Mr Garrick performed Hamlet for the last time, to a crowded audience, for the benefit of a fund for the relief of those obliged by infirmities to retire from the stage.[2]

A rural masquerade was held at Carlisle House with tickets at the reduced prices of 1l. 6s. to admit one mask, or two and three guineas respectively to admit two or three. The rooms were decorated in the *al fresco* style, a collation of hams

---

* The changes in the household of the young princes: see under 28th May.

and chickens was laid out, and catches and glees were sung by performers from the theatres, to the great satisfaction of all who heard them.

The company was numerous considering the season and formed a motley medley of nobility and commoners. Turks, Indians, Nabobs, Mohawks, Watchmen, Chairmen, Nosegay Girls, &c. were innumerable as usual. Lady Grosvenor was a Milk Maid, as lascivious and bewitching in her looks and manner as ever; she kept it up till the very last. When unmasked she was rather impertinently accosted by a female mask, who told her that 'all her intrigues were found out'. Her lady-ship very prudently avoided entering into a conversation, and went away without returning an answer.

Roaring Jack Roper was more vociferous and troublesome than ever. He appeared in the character of an Old Bawd, and amused himself and the company all night with taking off Foote in the character of Mother Cole. However, the fifth bottle of port, luckily for the company, *took him off*, laying him face upwards about three in the morning.

Several incidents happened while the masks were withdrawing from Carlisle House. A Milk Maid, in too hastily stepping into her carriage, slipped and broke her pail to pieces. An Harlequin, in flourishing his wooden sword rather too briskly, struck a Nosegay Girl in the face, and set her mouth a-bleeding. An Old Woman, in leaning from the window of her carriage, and displaying her comic powers to the populace, lost both her mask and high-crowned hat. Another Old Woman, who affected much humour, but possessed none, had her gown and petticoat torn by the poles of a chair. The goddess Flora stumbled over the rake of an Irish Hay-maker, and bruised her forehead. Among the people outside there were some of the rudest and most vulgar of the community. The most foul-mouthed language was bestowed upon some of the characters, and one gentleman had his mask actually torn off his face.[3]

MP 'A few days since died at her house in Wimpole-street, Cavendish-square, Mrs Webb, a gentlewoman of large fortune, and by her will bequeathed a legacy to her footman to hang 14 favourite cats which she constantly kept. As soon as her will was known, the footman hanged the cats, and by her desire they were all buried in the garden of her dwelling-house.'[4]

31st May, Friday Cloudy morning, fine bright afternoon

A vast concourse of journeymen sawyers assembled, determined to have their wages raised, and to punish all who worked at a lower price. Accordingly they fixed on one Hawkins, a journeyman, whom they bound with cords, and put him on an ass, with his face to the tail, tied a saw on his back, and a label with these words, *Working under price*, and in that manner proceeded through Wapping and those parts. Notice being given to Justice Sherwood, he with the assistance of the high constable and other peace officers rescued the poor man, and apprehended four of the ringleaders, and sent them handcuffed to Newgate.[1]

June

1st June, Saturday Cloudy, with a good deal of rain

In the evening Frederika, Baroness Riedesel, 29-year-old wife of the commander of the Brunswick troops in Canada, arrived in London on her way to join him. She was accompanied by her three daughters, Gustava, Frederika, and Carolina, aged from four years to just three months old. As she later recalled in a memoir, an apparently obliging landlord at Calais, Monsieur Guilhaudin, had advised her to leave her carriage there because 'I should be obliged to pay a tax of thirty or sixty guineas if I entered England in a coach built in a foreign country'. He also advised travelling with 'some trusty man, because I should otherwise be exposed to great dangers', and produced 'a well-dressed man, whom he introduced to me as a nobleman, a friend of his'.

Arriving at the hotel in Suffolk Street, however, she 'could not help feeling some astonishment when ... I was ushered into a miserable room in the fourth storey, though I had asked for a good apartment'.

> On the following day, the landlord came with an abashed air, and the most reverential demeanour, to ask me, whether I knew the man with whom I had arrived, and whom I had so particularly desired him to provide with good lodgings? ... I answered, that he was a nobleman, who ... had been kind enough to accompany me on my journey. 'Ah!' cried the landlord, 'that is one of his tricks. The man is a footman, a *valet de place*, a rogue ... Seeing him sitting next to you in your carriage, when you arrived, I could not, I confess, believe that you were the lady you pretended to be, and thought that these rooms were

Frederika Riedesel at the age of 16, after a portrait painted shortly before her marriage good enough for you. But I see now, by the persons that visit you, how much I was mistaken, and I ask your pardon, madam, and beg that you will follow me into another apartment, for which you shall not pay more than for that which you now occupy, for I really wish to atone by all means for my error.' I thanked my host, and requested him to rid me of my companion as soon as possible. I was, however, obliged first to pay him four or six guineas (I do not remember the exact sum) for his company.

She also learned that Guilhaudin's advice about her carriage had been self-serving, enabling him 'to do with it what he had already done with other vehicles entrusted to him, namely, to hire it to travellers on their way to Germany'. She was not so easily bested, however, and wrote to Lord North for permission to bring it to England without duties, which he granted at once, and the carriage duly arrived a few days later.

During her brief stay in London she went twice to St James's Park, 'and had a near view of the king and queen, who were in their sedans'. She also found that being a foreigner had its hazards:

I had been advised to buy a short cloak and a hat, without which, I was told, I ought not to go into the street. One day, after a dinner at the Hanoverian envoy's, Mr de Hinüber, his lady proposed to me to take a walk into St James's, but forgot that our attire was not according to the English fashion. My Gustava, dressed in the French style, had a 'panier', and a neat little cap. I observed that some people stared, and almost pointed at us, and I inquired what it meant. Madame de Hinüber replied, that it was on account of my fan, which it was not the fashion to wear with a hat; that my little girl was too finely dressed; and that we were therefore taken for French women, who were generally of ill repute.

I went the next day to the same place, and as we were all dressed in the English fashion, I thought that nobody would notice us. Yet I heard some cry again, 'French women, pretty girl!' I asked our *valet de place* why ... and was told that it was because my children wore ribands. I immediately tore them off, and put them in my pocket; upon which I was the more stared at, and at last discovered that it was only on account of the form of the children's hats. I was thus led to know how important it is to conform to the manners of the country, in order to live peaceably, for the mob is soon gathered together, and if one ventures to dispute with them, it is at the risk of still greater insults.

On 10th June she left for Bristol, arriving next day and hoping to sail from there to Canada. 'When I stopped at the inn, the rabble stared and laughed at the German style of the steps of the carriage, and at the two guns which my servant had fastened under the driver's seat. They touched them, and lifted the oil-cloth with which the carriage was covered, to see how it was painted.' When her servant, who knew little English, began to scold them, 'the whole rabble ... fell upon him, and the story might have had a tragical end, had the mayor not arrived in time to prevent it'.[1]

2nd June, Sunday An exceeding bright warm day. Full moon
At 12.30 a.m. Morande wrote to Beaumarchais to warn him that O'Gorman was
on his way to Paris with the Chevalier d'Éon's damaging account [> 27 May].
When he was presented by Vergennes with the accusations, Beaumarchais, probably
forewarned by Morande's letter, responded equably, saying he pardoned d'Éon
'with all my heart. She is a woman. That word explains everything.' He and Morande
need not have worried: Vergennes had no intention of withdrawing his support
for Beaumarchais and his American plans at a critical time.[1]

In the morning, as Lord North's game-keeper was coming to town with venison
for his majesty's birth-day, he was watched out of Bushy Park by two Custom
House officers. They followed him as far as Downing Street, where they attacked
him, and a desperate battle ensued. The game-keeper, being upon a spot where
he was known, and with some assistance, gave the officers a severe drubbing and
sent them off.[2]

3rd June, Monday Flying clouds, very hot, thunder and lightning in evening
About 5 a.m. two fishermen brought the body of a man decently drest on shore
at Bell Dock, Wapping. A person from a window saw them strip the deceased
of his money, his watch, and his silver shoe-buckles, after which they immediately
put off again.[1]

According to Horace Walpole, 'The wind, which had long been easterly, turning
to the west, much intelligence came in from America that raised the desponding
spirits of the Court.' It was said that 'another attack on Quebec ... had been repulsed
with the loss of 1300 men'; that 'General Lee had been taken prisoner by General
Clinton in Carolina'; that 'General Howe was safely arrived at Halifax with his
army'; that General Washington was 'in disgrace with the Congress'; and that
'their Admiral Hopkins was ... beaten and disgraced with two or three frigates
by a single ship. The courtiers exulted extremely on this cargo of good news, and
the king behaved with great levity. Still the intelligence was so vague or dubious,
that not one of the above articles was mentioned in the *Gazette*'.[2]

After an excursion into the Borough, Governor Hutchinson returned to hear
similar reports. 'This is the only good news for some time,' he wrote in his diary,
'and everybody on the side of government is in high spirits. Lord Cranley, in his
phaeton, stopped me in Piccadilly, and seemed in an extasy. ... Exceeding hot for
this country all day.'[3]

At Drury Lane Theatre Garrick played Richard the Third for what was expected
to be the last time. 'It is vanity to endeavour to describe Mr G.'s merits,' noted
prompter Hopkins in his diary. 'They beggar all description. Sufficient to say he
was what he represented.'[4]

In the evening there was a private concert at the Queen's Palace, where Mrs
Sheridan had the honor to be received as the queen's visitor, and sung several
songs to their majesties.[5]

4th June, Tuesday Chiefly cloudy, cool pleasant day

Perhaps in retaliation for the Chevalier d'Éon's recent letter to Vergennes, Morande wrote to inform him that he was working on his biography. He said he was planning to make it sympathetic, but added ominously that d'Éon's shortcomings and history placed him in need of friendly treatment.[1]

This being his majesty's thirty-eighth birth-day, the morning was ushered in with ringing of bells at St Martin's Church and Westminster Abbey. At one o'clock the park and Tower guns were fired. At half past one their majesties came from the Queen's Palace to St James's. At twenty minutes past two his majesty went into the drawing-room, and upon his entrance the overture struck up, and afterwards an ode on the occasion was sung by the gentlemen and boys of the Chapel Royal. The king was drest in a plain blue frock suit with gold buttons. The queen did not appear, as it was apprehended attendance at both the drawing-room and the ball, planned for the evening, would have been too much for her so soon after her lying-in. Notwithstanding, there was a splendid appearance of the nobility, &c. To their honour the ladies, even the foreigners, wore our English manufacture. Amongst the rich dresses were those of the Duchess of Devonshire and Lady Granby, who seem'd to rival each other for grandeur and elegance.

Garrick was present and was so praised by everyone, from the Archbishop of Canterbury to the page of the back stairs, that he felt 'suffocated with compliments'.

The lord chancellor and lords North, Suffolk, and Weymouth gave great dinners to their friends on the occasion. On being asked about the good news from America, Lord North replied prudently, 'We have heard all this, but have no certain intelligence.' The attorney general asking if he had a plan ready on the submission of America, he answered, 'I believe we shall have time enough to form one ...'

The academicians, professors, and associates of the Royal Academy dined at Somerset House in honour of the birth-day.

The Spanish ambassador gave a grand dinner to a number of the nobility and foreigners of distinction, and in the evening fireworks were played off before his house.

The lord and lady mayoress were at Court to pay their compliments, and at night the portico of the Mansion House was illuminated with upwards of 300 glass lamps.

Illuminations were also displayed on the front of the opera house in the Haymarket, which was decorated with his majesty's arms and two other transparencies, emblematical figures of Liberty and Plenty, larger than life.

A band of music played in the apartments over the Great Piazza,* eight and thirty pieces of cannon were discharged, a variety of fireworks were played off, and plenty of strong beer was distributed among the populace.[2]

---

* The original report adds 'in the Haymarket', but 'the Great Piazza' was usually used in reference to Covent Garden.

At about 9 p.m. their majesties entered the ball-room at St James's and the ball was opened by the Duke of Dorset and the Duchess of Devonshire. Minuets were danced alternately till past eleven, when their majesties withdrew, and country dances followed till near one.[3]

Among those present at the ball were Governor Hutchinson's daughters. Fellow refugee Samuel Curwen had a characteristically less satisfactory day: 'Walkt out after dinner ... to the Mall, and St James, to see the king and queen, waited till I was tired and returned home, to which I arrived at 6 o'clock without seeing them. There were collected a very large croud from whom I received 2 or 3 mortifying affronts; no more mix in mobbs without absolute necessity.' Later he went with friends 'to the Tower to see fireworks, but was disappointed there being none, by the king's order at the request of the inhabitants. From thence with S. and Mr E. I went to Marybone [Gardens] but it was late, and the doorkeeper imposing, my companions refused to enter and we returned home meeting a very pretty town girl in high Holborn, who would fain have engaged us, which I prevented by telling my age.'[4]

At the King's Oak in Epping Forest the day was marked by a *fête champêtre* held by gentlemen from the wards of Farringdon Within and Without. To create mirth and promote festivity, a flitch of bacon was given to the best runner in sacks, and an elegant gold-laced hat to the best grinner. Many thousands attended, including gentlemen and ladies from almost all the neighbouring villas.[5]

M. Garnier wrote to the Comte de Vergennes in Paris:

The number of horses being embarked for America is thirteen hundred at the rate of 12 tons per horse. The cost of freight is 13 shillings and 6 pence per ton, and that for forage 5 pounds sterling per ton. You see, monseigneur, what expense there is for this item alone, the least important in this famous expedition. When one recalls that the original purpose of this enormous expense was to impose a small tax on America, we seem to see an Alchemist of a new kind throwing into the crucible all he can gather of gold and precious metals in order to turn it into lead, for this ruinous and mad war will be for England the reverse of the Philosopher's stone.[6]

5th June, Wednesday Cloudy, a good deal of gentle rain, frost in night

Notwithstanding his resolution to appear no more in the part, Garrick played Richard the Third at Drury Lane Theatre, their majesties having expressed an earnest desire to see him once more in the character before he quits the stage. Nearly as many persons crowded as would have filled the house had it been three times as large. The king and queen did not come till seven o'clock, and on entering were met by loud applause. The prince's box was fitted up for the Prince of Wales and the Bishop of Osnaburgh to sit there for the first time.

At the beginning of the play a violent tumult arose in the pit, occasioned by the extraordinary number of people crammed in it, many of whom were unable to

Samuel Curwen by Benjamin Blyth, 1772

sit down. This so offended the rest that they hooted and hissed off the performers, till Mr Reddish came forward and asked their pleasure. 'Open the pit door.' This being complied with, a fresh riot ensued, about who should go out, which did not terminate for some time. The king appeared much embarrassed at the uproar, and was heard to say he was very sorry to see his subjects so oppressed. 'During this time', noted prompter Hopkins, 'the king sent two messages to Mr G. to desire that he would not let this noise disconcert him and his majesty would take care that all should be quiet before the play began.' Order being restored, the piece went on. According to the *Morning Chronicle*, 'Mr Garrick was not quite so perfect in voice in the first two acts, as he was when he last played the character; in the third and fourth he grew clearer and clearer, and in the fifth he shone with the fulness of meridian splendor, and was honoured with most extravagant tokens of applause'.[1]

The OVERFLOWING of the PITT.

Oh had we staid & said our pray'rs at home. Popes Rape of the Lock.

Done from the ORIGINAL DRAWING by S.H. GRIMM.

Printed for S. Sledge, Printseller in Henrietta Street Covent Garden. Publish'd as the Act directs 25. June 1771.

Two views of the challenges involved in attending Drury Lane Theatre

1. Published by Mrs Sledge, Henrietta Street, Covent Garden, 25th June 1771.

The PIT DOOR.   La PORTE du PARTERRE.

2. Published by Carington Bowles, 69 St Paul's Churchyard, 9th November 1784.
The figure in the doorway at the back is thought to be Sheridan, one of the owners
of the theatre's patent since 1776, who is shown intent on the takings.

6th June, Thursday Cloudy, a great deal of hail and rain, frost in night
Between five and six o'clock in the morning a messenger arrived express at Lord
George Germain's office with dispatches. Among them may have been a sobering
private letter from General Howe, dated 26th April at Halifax:

> The scene here at present wears a lowering aspect, there not being the least
> prospect of conciliating this continent until its armies shall have been roughly
> dealt with; and I confess my apprehensions that such an event will not be readily
> brought about; the rebels get on apace, and knowing their advantages in having
> the whole country, as it were, at their disposal, they will not be readily brought
> into a situation where the king's troops can meet them upon equal terms. Their
> armies retiring a few miles back from the navigable rivers, ours cannot follow
> them from the difficulties I expect to meet with in procuring land carriage. It
> cannot be denied that there are many inhabitants in every province well affected
> to government, from whom no doubt we shall have assistance, but not until his
> majesty's arms have a clear superiority by a decisive victory.[1]

In the morning the legs and arms of four human bodies were taken up by a
waterman in a hamper, floating on the river amongst the shipping below bridge.
The bodies are supposed to be in the hands of some surgeons.[2]

Mary Griffiths, otherwise Davis, otherwise Richard, with many other *alia*,
stood on the pillory opposite Old Street Church for perjury, in swearing herself
an inhabitant of a great number of parishes, by which she obtained a weekly relief
from them all. She is to suffer six months imprisonment in Newgate and to stand
in the pillory twice more. Some rotten eggs were thrown at her by the populace.[3]

Near 500 persons attended a second rural masquerade at Carlisle House. His
holiness the Pope appeared in *pontificalibus*, and many masks took the opportunity
to apply for dispensations. Among other characters were a Bird-seller and his Girl,
a Wapping Landlady, and a Watchman who showed spirit and good humour in
a scuffle with three Bridewell Boys, who attempted to take his pole and lanthorn.
Mr W—ld of Covent Garden, and two very pretty women, figured the Three
Weird Sisters in *Macbeth*. Lady Grosvenor and Miss V— were *filles religieuses*,
veiled. The *Middlesex Journal* thought it in vain in the former's case, 'for her most
exquisite beauty will always shew itself, and proclaim the original'. About seven
in the morning some were dancing, some singing, some reeling, and some fighting,
but no material mischief ensued. About eight the rooms were pretty clear.[4]

MP 'Lord George Germaine, when he first came into office, spoke upon all
occasions with uncommon superiority, but of late he is strangely crest fallen. He
has not the king's ear so much since, as before he was minister, which has been
the case with some others before him.'[5]

7th June, Friday Cloudy
In the morning Lady Charlotte Burgoyne, wife of General Burgoyne, died of a
consumption at her apartments in Kensington Palace, where she had gone for
the benefit of the air.[1]

At Doctors' Commons a motion came on at the instance of the Earl of Bristol, that a decree be issued against his countess, lately Duchess of Kingston, to shew cause why the late sentence of jactitation should not be revoked, and she pronounced to be his wife (a necessary first step towards divorce). The judge refused, ruling that the countess should receive notice in order to raise her defence, such notice to be verified on oath, her ladyship being at Calais.[2]

8th June, Saturday Cloudy
General Richard Smith and Thomas Brand Hollis, convicted of bribing the electors of Hindon at the last general election, were brought from the King's Bench prison to Westminster Hall, where, at eleven o'clock, Sir Richard Aston passed sentence upon them, each to pay a fine of 1,000 marks (666l. 13s. 4d.) and to be imprisoned for six months. 'How crouded would the prisons be were every member to be treated as these culprits are!' noted Samuel Curwen in his journal after attending.[1]

In Long Reach, Lord Sandwich, Sir Hugh Palliser, and others members of the Board of Admiralty paid a farewell visit to Captain Cook. 'They, and several other noblemen and gentlemen their friends, honoured me with their company at dinner ...,' noted Cook, 'and, on their coming on board, and also on their going ashore, we saluted them with seventeen guns, and three cheers.' The dinner cost £12 2s. and included venison, chickens, Westmorland ham, pigeon pie, currant jelly, a turbot, trout, lobsters, stewed mushrooms, 'spinage toasts', sweetbreads, and strawberries.[2]

In the evening Garrick played King Lear at Drury Lane Theatre, his penultimate performance.[3]

9th June, Sunday Chiefly cloudy, a great deal of rain
John Wilkes dined at the house of Miles Peter Andrews with other guests including Andrews's lover, the runaway actress Ann Brown, and her aunt.[1]

10th June, Monday Chiefly cloudy, trifling rain
In the morning Lord George Germain received long-awaited news from General Carleton in a letter dated 14th May at Quebec.

> My lord, After this town had been closely invested by the rebels for five months, and had defeated all their attempts, the *Surprize* frigate, *Isis*, and sloop *Martin* came into the bason the 6th instant. | As soon as that part of the 29th they had on board with their marines, in all about two hundred, were landed, they, with the greatest part of the garrison, by this time much improved, and in high spirits, marched out of the ports of St Louis and St John's, to see what those mighty boasters were about; they were found very busy in their preparations for a retreat. A few shots being exchanged, the line marched forward, and the plains were soon cleared of those plunderers; all their artillery, military stores, scaling ladders, petards, &c., &c. were abandoned. ... | This ended our siege and blockade ...

Germain immediately wrote a short letter and dispatched it by messenger to the king. Another messenger was dispatched to Lord North at Bushy Park.[1]

At a few minutes after ten his majesty arrived at Blackheath to review the Horse Guards Blue. During the review his majesty received the account of the retreat of the provincials before Quebec. He gave it to General Hervey, who read it before all the officers present.[2]

A bull, two cows, two calves, and eighteen sheep, with hay and corn for their subsistence, were taken on board the *Resolution* in preparation for Captain Cook's voyage to the South Seas, the king having commanded useful animals be carried out to convey some permanent benefit to the inhabitants of Otaheite.[3]

Samuel Curwen spent much of the day reading *Common Sense* and *Plain Truth*. He also wrote to a friend in Antigua:

> It is surprising what little seeming effect the loss of American orders has on the manufactories; they have been in full employ ever since the dispute arose; stocks are not one jot lessened, the people in general little moved by it; business and amusement so totally engross all ranks and orders here that administration finds no difficulty on that score to pursue their plans. ...
>
> Six vessels laden with refugees are arrived from Halifax ... Those who bring property here may do well enough, but those who expect reimbursement for losses, or a supply for present support, will find to their cost the hand of charity very cold; the latter may be kept from starving, and beyond that their hopes are vain.[4]

At 3 p.m. a badger was baited for sport at the King's Head, Walworth.[5]

Drury Lane Theatre closed for the season with the comedy of *The Wonder*, in which Mr Garrick played Don Felix, his last theatrical appearance, generously giving the profits of the night to the theatrical fund.

The play being ended, he took leave of the town in his public capacity. Behind him, and between every scene, stood groups of mournful actors, tears speaking their sorrow. After a short pause, as soon as he recovered a little from the first shock, he addressed the audience:

> 'Ladies and gentlemen, It has been customary with persons under my circumstances, to address you in a farewell epilogue. I had the same intention, and turned my thoughts that way; but indeed I found myself *then*, as incapable of writing such an epilogue, as I should be *now* of speaking it. The jingle of rhime, and the language of fiction, would but ill suit my present feelings. This is to me a very awful moment; it is no less than parting for ever with those from whom I have received the greatest kindness and favours, and upon the spot where that kindness and those favours were enjoyed. (Here for a moment he was unable to proceed until relieved by a flood of tears.) Whatever may be the changes of my future life, the deep impression I have of your kindness, will always remain HERE, (putting his hand to his breast) fixed, and unalterable.
>
> 'I will very readily agree to my successors having more skill and ability for their station than I have; but I defy them all to take more sincere, and more

uninterrupted pains for your favour, or to be more truly sensible of it, than is, your most obedient and grateful servant.'

'Here he retired,' noted the *Morning Post*, 'crown'd with never-fading laurels, amidst the blendid tears and acclamations of the most brilliant theatre that was ever assembled, all ranks uniting in their invocations for the future happiness of a man, who has so repeatedly, and essentially contributed to theirs.'

Henry Angelo and his mother were with Mrs Garrick in her box. He later recalled the actor's taking his leave of the public:

More tears were shed when he had finished this touching part, and the curtain dropped, than he had ever excited, perhaps, mighty as his command might be over the passions of his audience, when acting a character in the most affecting tragedy. Mrs Garrick and my mother continued their sobbing after they quitted the theatre, which induced my father to observe, 'One should suppose you ladies had been following my honoured friend to the grave; whereas, it is his labours which are buried this night, that he may live the longer and the happier ...'

For my own part, being then a thoughtless young man, I witnessed this pathetic scene with little emotion.

The Laſt Time of the Company's performing this Seaſon.

At the Theatre Royal in Drury-Lane,
This preſent MONDAY, June 10, 1776,

The W O N D E R.
Don Felix by Mr. GARRICK,
Col. Briton by Mr. SMITH,
Don Lopez by Mr BADDELEY,
Don Pedro by Mr. PARSONS,
Liſſardo by Mr. KING,
Frederick by Mr. PACKER,
Gibby by Mr. MOODY,
Iſabella by Miſs HOPKINS,
Flora by Mrs. WRIGHTEN,
Inis by Mrs. BRADSHAW,
Violante by Mrs. YATES.
End of Aɛ I. The G-and GARLAND DANCE,
By Signor GIORGI, Mrs. SUTTON,
And Mr. SLINGSBY.
To which will be added a Muſical Entertainment, call'd

The W A T E R M A N.
The PRINCIPAL CHARACTERS by
Mr. BANNISTER,
Mr. DAVIES,
And Mr. DODD.
Mrs. WRIGHTEN,
And Mrs. JEWELL.
To conclude with the Grand Scene of The REGATTA.
Ladies are deſired to ſend their Servants a little after 5 to keep Places, to prevent Confuſion.
The Doors will be opened at HALF after FIVE o'Clock.
To begin at HALF after SIX o'Clock.   Vivant Rex & Regina.

The Profits of this Night being appropriated to the Benefit of The Theatrical Fund, the Uſual Addreſs upon that Occaſion
Will be ſpoken by Mr. GARRICK, before the Play.

Garrick himself recalled the occasion in a letter to Suzanne Necker:

It was indeed a sight very well worth seeing! Though I performed my part with as much, if not more spirit than I ever did, yet when I came to take the last farewell, I not only lost almost the use of my voice, but of my limbs too: it was indeed, as I said, *a most awful moment*. You would not have thought an English audience void of feeling if you had then seen and heard them. After I had left the stage, and was dead to them, they would not suffer the *petite piece* to go on; nor would the actors perform, they were so affected; in short, the public was very generous, and I am most grateful.[6]

In Paris, Beaumarchais received one million livres from the French treasury, enabling the house of Roderique Hortalez & Co. to commence business. On 27th June the Spanish government would add their support to the scheme with a letter of credit for the same amount.[7]

11th June, Tuesday Wet morning and evening, fair mid-day
In the morning a young lady of fashion, in the neighbourhood of St James's Park, made an elopement with her father's butler. It is said she has 20,000l. at her own disposal and that they are gone to France. The young man is an Hibernian, and lately engaged in the family.[1]

At the Court of King's Bench one of the Hindon voters, Benjamin Chosey, received sentence for perjury in his evidence to a House of Commons committee. His punishment is to stand in the pillory at Hindon with a paper on his forehead signifying his crime, 'Wilful and Corrupt Perjury', twice on market days between the hours of eleven and two.[2]

In Long Reach, Captain Cook 'received on board ... several astronomical and nautical instruments, which the Board of Longitude intrusted to me, and to Mr King, my second lieutenant ... to make all the necessary observations, during the voyage, for the improvement of astronomy and navigation'. He also received 'the same watch, or time-keeper, which I had carried out in my last voyage, and had performed its part so well. It was a copy of Mr Harrison's, constructed by Mr Kendall.'[3]

12th June, Wednesday Heavy wet morning, fine bright afternoon
Between two and three in the morning, checking the house of John Robinson, secretary to Lord North, in Parliament Street, a watchman found the area door open and saw two men run off. He alarmed two other watchmen and they went inside to rouse the maid, Sarah Wilkins, who was alone in the house, her master and the other servants having gone into the country. They found shutters, doors, and drawers broken open and cloaths scattered. Among items missing were twenty-five pair of silk stockings, twenty-three linen shirts, four waistcoats, of which two were laced with gold, a pair of silver shoe-buckles, and four silver tea-spoons.

Information was taken to Bow Street and about 10 a.m. William Barnett, Charles Jealous, and other officers went in pursuit of Daniel Hopkins, a noted burglar.* They found him in bed with two girls in a house of ill fame in Vine Street, Covent Garden. When Jealous entered, Hopkins said without scruple, 'Under the bed, you'll find my tools, Mr Jealous.' A cutlass, a dark lantern, a number of iron-crows, files, &c. were found there.

As they were leaving Barnett saw Henry Horner and George Todd, who had been coming in and who immediately ran away. 'We ran after them. They ran into a barber's shop in Chandos-street. We asked the barber if two men did not run in there; he denied them. We went through the passage, and found Horner and Todd in the necessary.' Todd was searched and a pair of silk stockings marked 'J. R.' was found hidden under his ham, next his skin, with his own stocking drawn over them, and his breeches buttoned at the knee.

Justice Wright went with Jealous to Mr Robinson's house to see if the implements found under the bed fitted the places which had been wrenched open. They corresponded exactly.

A servant of Mr Robinson's having sworn positively to the stockings, Hopkins, Horner, and Todd were charged with the burglary and committed to separate gaols for re-examination.[1]

Captain Cook took leave of his majesty, he being in a few days to sail in the *Resolution*.[2]

In the afternoon a number of butchers in Oxford Market procured a cart, which they hung with black matting, and placed in it the effigy of a man with a halter round his neck, who they said was an informer against butchers, bakers, barbers, green-grocers, &c. for exercising their trades on Sunday. The cart was attended by three men, one of whom, in a black coat, a large curled wig, a calf's tail hanging down his back, with a book in his hand, represented the ordinary of Newgate; the others represented Jack Ketch and his deputy. The cart was preceded by a man mounted on an ass, with a white wand in his hand, in imitation of the sheriff, and was followed by near fifty butchers with large clubs, who acted as constables. In this manner they paraded round the principal markets in Westminster before returning to Oxford Market, where they hung the effigy on a high gallows erected for that purpose.[3]

By command of their majesties *The Commissary* was performed at the theatre in the Haymarket, with Mr Foote in the title part. It was followed by a new comedy, *The Contract*, by Thomas Francklin, a royal chaplain.

The king was dressed in a suit of salmon coloured silk, the queen in silver tissue, and they sat under an elegant blue silk canopy, trimmed with white. Foote told friends that when he lighted the king to his chair he was asked who had written the after piece. 'One of your majesty's chaplains,' he had replied, 'but it is dull enough to have been written by a bishop.'

---

* While in prison for an earlier offence he gave evidence regarding the murder of Stubbings the coachman: see under 3rd January.

Their majesties were received with unusual plaudits from a very full house, which included Samuel Curwen. An observation in the after piece, that 'the most happy government is that enjoyed under a good king,' met with great applause.

Foote's own performance disappointed the *St James's Chronicle*, which next day observed with regret that he 'is not so alert, and has not so instantaneous a command of his muscles, as formerly. He seems to be sensible of it at times, by his bustle and exertion to ape that real spirit and drollery with which he has entertained us. He forces his voice into a very disagreeable harshness, and bustles into ridiculous motions.'[4]

13th June, Thursday Some flying clouds, but a fine day

Between seven and eight in the morning a bricklayer and two labourers entered the common sewer, between the end of Fenchurch Street and Aldgate, by the common grate, near the end of Fenchurch Buildings, in order to inspect it. They explored their way till one of them took a candle out of a lantern and it set fire to the foul air in the sewer, supposed replete with inflammable particles. The blast was so sudden that the poor fellows had not time to get away. The bricklayer saved himself by falling in the mud, but not without being burnt in the hands, face, &c. The labourers were likewise burnt, particularly one of them, whose hair, eyebrows, and clothes were much singed and scorched.[1]

The *Colebrooke* East Indiaman arrived safe at moorings in the river. On board are several curious birds and beasts including a leopard, a tyger, a tyger cat, and a monkey of a very extraordinary species.[2]

Captain Clerke wrote to Secretary Stephens at the Admiralty: 'His majestie's sloop *Discovery*, under my command, being in every particular equip'd for sea, I have receiv'd orders from Capt. Cook immediately to proceed for Plymouth, but some of my own private affairs of the utmost importance to me requiring my attention to them in town, I wou'd be highly oblig'd to their lordships if I cou'd be indulg'd in attending them, and sending the ship round under the command of Lieut. Burney.' Clerke was being pursued by the creditors of his brother Sir John, who had decamped to the East Indies and whose debts he had generously but unwisely guaranteed. By 18th June, if not before, he would be in the King's Bench prison.

Meanwhile James Burney, brother of Fanny, wrote from the *Discovery* in Long Reach to ask Cook what he should do. On 15th June Cook forwarded Burney's letter from Mile End to Stephens, suggesting that the Admiralty send the appropriate instruction as 'I have no authority to order the *Discovery* to proceed in the absence of her commander.'[3]

Peter Oliver, former chief justice of Massachusetts, headed towards London having arrived at Falmouth at the end of April. Coming over Hounslow Heath, 'infamous for robberies ... our eyes were saluted with 3 or 4 gibbets, the insignia of highwaymens exploits. They may possibly serve *in terrorem*, but they are disagreeable to travellers.' Pressing on he passed the king riding to Kew with his guards.

Arriving in town he took lodgings at a saddler's in Jermyn Street, paying 1½ guineas a week for three rooms. 'Thus ... I am set down in a city which appears to be a world of it self ... Thanks be to Heaven, I am now in a place where I can be protected from the Harpy claws of that rebellion which is now tearing out its own bowels in America, as well as destroying all, who in any degree oppose its progress.'⁴

A gibbet, by Rowlandson

14th June, Friday As yesterday
Four hundred horses were sent down from Whitechapel to Portsmouth, to be put on board some very large ships fitting up there with stalls, for carrying them to America.¹

A masquerade was given at Ranelagh by the members of the five fashionable clubs near St James's, Almack's, Boodle's, Saunderson's, the Savoir Vivre, and the Thatched House.

About nine o'clock upward of 1,600 masks, conveyed by land and water carriage, began to assemble. Almost all the people of fashion were there that had not yet set out for the watering-places, and most of the celebrated wits, authors, critics, &c. The company included the dukes and duchesses of Cumberland, Devonshire, Manchester, and Gordon; Lord and Lady Grosvenor; Lord Lyttelton; Lord George Gordon; Mr and Mrs Garrick; Mr Colman; and Mr Wilkes attending his daughter and Mrs Molyneux. Meanwhile large parties had been planned in barges and boats on the river opposite, with intent to have a view of the frolicks.

The masks were first admitted to an elegant covered colonade, erected on one side of the canal. In this was placed a band of twenty country-dance players habited in sylvan dress, and several females who served coffee, tea, &c. Clarinets, horns, and bassoons were stationed elsewhere about the garden to entertain the company, but these other parts were insufferably dark, and the bridge was without a single lamp.

About half after eleven a smart shower fell and there was a clamour for admission to the rotunda, and at last the doors were thrown open. The organ loft resembled a beautiful green-house, emitting fragrant odours from myrtles, orange trees, and other exotics. The sides of the rotunda were handsomely illuminated, and the Orchestra was filled with an excellent band of music, who played during

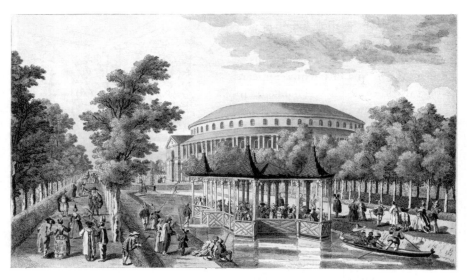

Looking broadly north to the canal and rotunda at Ranelagh.
After Canaletto. Published 1752. The Chinese pavilion had since
been removed from the canal and placed near its southern end.

supper. On the ground floor a range of tables were covered with almost every eatable
now in season, and various sorts of confectionary, all of them exceeding good,
except the jellies, which tasted as if they had been made in an untinned stewpan.
The burgundy was of the first growth, and the champagne was super-excellent.

About two o'clock a confusion arose between the many ladies of pleasure present
and certain female spirits, whom they call interlopers. One *fille de joie* was particularly smart upon Lady M—,* calling her a smuggler and an enemy to the fair
trader. At length, growing a little angry, she declared the lady ought to be ducked,
that it was a burning shame, and was proceeding with great vehemence, till Lord
E— stepped between them and made peace.

About five o'clock the company was annoyed by an irruption of strangers,
who had till then been with great difficulty kept out, and whose rank did not at
all correspond with that of the rest of the company. They rushed in, some in dirty
shirts, long beards, ragged coats, and other marks of dishabille, and used the wine
in a very plentiful manner. The *Middlesex Journal* felt that the managers should
have prevented the intrusion, 'and not allowed the first people of fortune and
fashion in this kingdom, to be thus insulted with the company of common whores,
bullies, sharpers, gamblers, and others, whose weekly incomes don't come near
what a person of fortune pays to his lacquey'.

---

* Possibly a reference to the celebrated Nancy Parsons. Her marriage to Viscount
Maynard was reported at about this time, although it did not take place until 24th
September.

According to the *Middlesex Journal* the admission ticket for the masquerade was
'not extremely *decent*, but very *inviting* ... The drawing was by Cipriani, the engraving
by Bartolozzi. We never saw a more finished production among the various excellent
works of the same great masters, but we object to its glaring indelicacy.'

Among very few characters the most remarkable was Sir Moses Sampson, a Jew broker, who, like Dogberry in the play, seemed 'too cunning to be understood'.* He wore a large oil-skin bag, about the size of a kitchen fire shovel, stuffed full of something, but he went off without 'letting the cat out of the bag'. On it his profession was inscribed in gold letters: 'Sir Moses Sampson, K.G., M.P. &c. &c. &c. Most Money for Old Places, and New Peerages. Wanted, several hundred Votes for a County Election. Ten thousand pounds ready for a good Government.'† Mr H. Bunbury was a Goose-driver, with his long stick and red streamer, and a couple of artificial geese under his arm.

The *Gazetteer* found the event 'dull and unentertaining, in proportion as it was splendid and magnificent ... | Dulness transferred her empire from the East,‡ and erected her standard in the very centre of Ranelagh-house. You might see sleepy dukes, yawning duchesses, stupid lords, drowsy ladies, snoring epicures, silent demireps, tongue-tied lechers, and dreaming *filles de joye*.' Soon after three the company began to break up, and about six the rotunda was deserted, except by a few bacchanals who had earlier drank themselves into a state of insensibility, and now waking were surprized to find themselves abandoned and forlorn.[2]

15th June, Saturday Chiefly cloudy, some slight showers
Governor Hutchinson and Peter Oliver breakfasted in Queen Street, Mayfair, with the wife of General Howe, who was presumably keen to hear from Oliver about the situation in America. Later the two refugees went to look round the Queen's Palace.[1]

At the Tower, 40,000 sacks for earth, 1,000 shirts for officers, 10,000 shirts for private men, &c. were put on board a transport to sail with all expedition to Quebec.[2]

The *Resolution* and the *Discovery* sailed from Long Reach and in the evening anchored at the Nore. Next day the *Discovery* continued on its way but the *Resolution* remained at the Nore waiting for Captain Cook, who was still in London.[3]

The *Morning Chronicle* reported that Mrs Siddons and her husband and about seventeen others had 'received notices of their discharge from Drury Lane Theatre'. The actress later recalled receiving the news in 'an official letter from the prompter' while at Birmingham to perform for the summer. She described it as 'a stunning and cruel blow' and felt betrayed by Garrick, who had promised to 'procure me a good engagement with the new managers'. She was later told by Sheridan, one of those new managers, that Garrick had in fact 'depreciated my talents' to them, although Sheridan had of course an interest in casting the blame onto Garrick.[4]

---

* *Much Ado About Nothing*, act 5 scene 1.
† The particular target of the satire was probably Sir Sampson Gideon. Next day, 15th June, two newspapers reported that a patent was being prepared to make him a peer, although this proved mistaken.
‡ In Pope's *Dunciad* 'Martinus Scriblerus' describes the poem's action as 'the removal of the Imperial seat of Dulness from the City to the polite world'.

Mrs Siddons in her later eminence

After a painting by Reynolds, 1783-1784, showing her as the Tragic Muse

MJ 'A new square is erecting between the Museum and Tottenham-Court Road, to be called Bedford-square, from the title of the noble owner, on whose ground it is built.'[5]

16th June, Sunday A very wet day, fair evening

His majesty went from Kew to Windsor Castle to give some instructions in respect of fitting up the royal library, which it is said will be the compleatest in Europe.[1]

17th June, Monday Chiefly cloudy, but fair

At 4 a.m. a duel was fought in Hyde Park between an officer of the navy and an Irish gentleman. The latter was mortally wounded and the officer immediately set out for France. The dispute was about the dress of a lady at the opera on Saturday night.[1]

In the morning a private soldier of the guards was found hanging in the new-erected untenanted house near Jenny's Whim Bridge, Chelsea.* He had often been heard to declare that he never would fight against his countrymen in America, and a dread of being draughted is supposed to have determined him on this fatal exit.[2]

A silver cup, value 20 guineas, given by his royal highness the Duke of Cumberland, was sailed for on the river from Blackfriars Bridge to Putney Bridge and back again. Bridges, wharfs, stairs, &c. were lined with spectators, thousands being assembled before noon. The river was crowded with barges, sailing boats, cutters, wherries, &c. with flags and streamers flying and filled with gay company.

Shortly before one o'clock the duke and his duchess arrived at Blackfriars Bridge in the Admiralty barge, attended by an open boat with a band of music. The duke then went into a sumptuous barge with twelve rowers and the royal standard at the prow, attended by two other barges. The sailing vessels were ranged in a line opposite Temple Stairs, all their sails close furled. At a quarter after one, on a firing gun, the sails were unfurled in a moment, and the vessels got under way, attended by an incredible number of barges, boats, &c. and saluted by music and the firing of cannon from shore to shore.

The weather proved very favourable, the sun shining the whole time, and the wind blowing a fine westerly breeze. At four o'clock the whole fleet returned thro' Westminster Bridge, very near each other. About ten minutes later the first boat, the *King's Fisher* sloop, preceded by the duke's barge, passed thro' the center arch of Blackfriars Bridge amidst the acclamations of many thousand spectators, and then loughed up alongside the barge. The duke took the silver cup filled with claret, drank to the successful gentleman, presented him with the cup, and invited him to dine at Smith's Tea Gardens, Vauxhall. After dinner there the duke's health and many loyal toasts were drank out of the prize cup by all present.

---

* A wooden structure crossing part of Chelsea Water-works, on a site now occupied by Ebury Bridge. It was named after Jenny's Whim, a nearby tavern and tea-garden.

Anne, Duchess of Cumberland, after a portrait by Reynolds, 1772-1773

Horace Walpole described the duchess as 'extremely pretty, not handsome, very well made, with the most amorous eyes in the world, and eyelashes a yard long. Coquette beyond measure, artful as Cleopatra, and completely mistress of all her passions and projects.'

At about 11 p.m., after other engagements, the duke and duchess went to Vauxhall Gardens, where crowds of all ranks were assembled in hopes of seeing them. After walking round and politely bowing to the company, they supped in a box publicly, a band of music playing before them. They left the gardens at one in the morning.[3]

18th June, Tuesday Bright morning and evening, cloudy mid-day
In the evening three fellows put a little boy into a house at Islington. He packed up a quantity of linen, and was going off, when a dog in the house ran after him, and seized him by the coat. The boy stripped off the coat and ran away, but the family being alarmed, the parties were pursued. Two of the men and the boy were taken and committed to Clerkenwell Bridewell. The boy is 11 years old, and has previously been sentenced to transportation.[1]

At night Elizabeth Caroline Perreau, aged two, youngest child of Daniel Perreau and Mrs Rudd, was buried in St James's Church, Piccadilly. She was one of three children buried there on this day.[2]

LC 'Omiah ... has made such good use of his time while in England, that he was able to write his sentiments in our language. The following is a copy of the card he sent to several of his friends. | "Omiah to take leave of good friend. He never forget England. He go on Sunday. God bless King George. He tell his people how kind English to him."'[3]

19th June, Wednesday Several flying clouds, but a fine warm day
Five men were executed at Tyburn, including Daniel Greenwood, for stealing 180 guineas, Robert Street, for possession of a dye on which was impressed the resemblance of a sixpence, and Christopher Saunders, for bestiality [> 18 Apr]. They came out of the prison at nine o'clock, as usual, but the sledge for the coiner had been forgot, which occasioned a delay of more than half an hour, and gave rise to a report that one of them had been reprieved; but at twenty minutes before ten the gloomy procession moved off.

The croud assembled in coaches, chaises, carts, and on horseback was immense, besides the prodigious numbers on foot. The prisoners were extremely penitent, and prayed and wept incessantly. A man in the croud called out to Greenwood, but he would not lift his eye from his book. Christopher Saunders had no book, and appeared unpitied. Having no friends to take care of his body, he was taken by the mob, who, after breaking every bone, to prevent his being taken up by the surgeons, dug a hole in the adjoining field, and there threw him in, with no more ceremony than a dog.[1]

In the morning it was strongly reported in the City that Commodore Hopkins, the American commander, with nine ships, had taken the island of Bermudas, and carried off all the valuable goods he could meet with whilst he staid, which was three days.[2]

COMMODORE HOPKINS,
COMMANDER in CHIEF of the AMERICAN FLEET.
Publish'd as the Act directs 22 Aug.r 1776 by Tho.s Hart.

Esek Hopkins, in a mezzotint published 22nd August 1776

In the background are two flags used by the American navy early in the war.
The one on the left shows a rattlesnake with the motto 'Dont tread upon me,'
while the one on the right bears the words 'Liberty Tree. An appeal to God'.

At the theatre in the Haymarket Mr Foote introduced a new scene into his comedy *The Cozeners*, founded on a well known story told of Mrs Rudd and a silk mercer. To avoid paying for silks Mrs Fleece'em (based on Rudd) engineers the bundling away of the mercer to a mad-house in Chelsea. This afforded a very comic situation and was received with universal applause, but the *London Magazine* detected double standards in the author. 'Can this gentleman reconcile it to his conscience to condemn a woman, in a court much more public than the Old Bailey, of a crime, of which she has not been legally accused, and for which if true, she would be liable to be taken up, prosecuted, and suffer capitally? ... We wish ... he may learn to keep that divine precept still in view which is, "to do unto others, as you wish they would do unto you".'[3]

LLEP 'By a gentleman who is just arrived from St Maloes we learn, that when he left that place, which was the 29th of May, "there were four American vessels just arrived there, deeply laden with wheat and flour; that the Americans take in return, arms, ammunition, and other goods they want; that the French are very fond of the Americans, or seem to be so; and that the American ships slip out in the night, when there is a fair wind."'[4]

20th June, Thursday As yesterday

Early in the morning the house of refugee Jonathan Sewall, No. 1 Brompton Row, was found to have been robbed of plate, linen, and other effects to a considerable amount. After being told, Sewall noticed 'that the bottom door, which opens into the area, had a hole cut in it, but it seemed rather to be meant as a colour for the manner in which the door was opened, for putting in your hand, you could not unfasten the door'. One of Sir John Fielding's men attended, took Richard Goodwell, the footman, into custody, and found four handkerchiefs concealed in his breeches. Finding things strong against him, Goodwell begged his mistress for mercy, to no avail, before admitting that he had let in another man who had carried the rest of the stolen items away.[1]

The cabinet met at the Admiralty to consider recent intelligence relative to armaments in the ports of France and Spain. It was agreed, *inter alia*, to prepare measures for a press with secrecy so that if necessary it might be carried suddenly and effectually into execution.[2]

At Guildhall a young woman who undertook duties at a house in Mitre Court, Gracechurch Street, for a servant that was gone into the country for a short time, gave an account to the lord mayor that when she went on the leads of the house to beat a carpet she found the head and bones of a human body, and imagined some murder had been committed. His lordship sent his officers to search the house, where they found everything according to the girl's description. Having heard of the affair, a surgeon who lived at the next door appeared, and declared upon oath that he reserved the upper part of the house to carry on his business. He said the head and bones were part of the body of a man executed lately for the murder of the Custom House officer [> 27 May], which he had obtained of the Surgeons' Company for experiments, whereupon the affair was dismissed.[3]

A match of cricket began playing in the Artillery Ground between five gentlemen of Surrey and five of Kent and Middlesex, for £50 each side. It was concluded next day in favour of the latter two counties, who won by fifty notches. A great deal of money was sported on the occasion.[4]

As the man that takes care of the queen's elephants was airing them, the young one pushed him down, and bruised him in so terrible a manner that his life is despaired of.[5]

21st June, Friday Chiefly cloudy, some trifling rain. Longest day
Orders were given for 4,000 head of oxen to be immediately delivered into the Victualling Office on Tower Hill, for the use of the navy.[1]

Peter Oliver, former chief justice of Massachusetts, went to view the Tower:

> The Foot Armory, of 60,000 arms, is very curious ... but I observed there were many vacancys, as a number of arms had been sent to America to quell the rebellion; where I hope they will be rendered more usefull than in their usual torpid state. ... From hence I went to view the Menagerie for birds and beasts, but here I saw none of them in so great perfection of nature as I had seen in America, some of the most curious having died in the severity of the preceeding winter. The lions seemed to have lost their natural ferocity; and I doubt not, that if the omnipotent American Congress were caged in the same manner, their diabolical ferocity would subside into the tameness of any of these Tower animals ...[2]

The Tower, after Joseph Farington. Published 1795.

22nd June, Saturday Cloudy morning, bright day

Sodom and Onan, an anonymous satire aimed at Samuel Foote, thought to have been written by William Jackson, was published at No. 23 Fleet Street, opposite St Dunstan's Church. Its title page featured a portrait of Foote with an illustration of a foot below in lieu of an identifying caption. The poem described the alleged assault on Sangster the footman:

> Boldly the man repell'd the vile essay,
> Judging it wrong in all things to obey,
> A master, so inflam'd with strange desires,
> And eyes betraying wrong directed fires.

It proceeded to threaten the lord chief justice in case he should take Foote's side:

> Mansfield beware, a cause like this is nice;
> No tongue hath dar'd to taint your name with vice
> Like this ...
> With honest candor, weigh in equal scale
> The pros and cons, and let the truth prevail.

It also alluded to the rumoured homosexuality of Lord George Germain, formerly Sackville:

> S—e, both coward, and catamite, commands
> Department hon'rable, and kisses hands,
> With lips that oft in blandishment obscene
> Have been employ'd ...

It concluded with a lurid vision of the fate awaiting 'Aristophanes', as Foote was known, 'rank corruption' consuming his vitals, chancres perforating his mouth and nose, 'plung'd in darkness for his lust'.[1]

23rd June, Sunday Many flying clouds, bright intervals, churlish and cold

Early in the morning, as some boys were looking after larks, they discovered in a field near Richmond a man dead, with his throat cut, supposed to have been robbed and murdered. The coroner's inquest later brought in a verdict wilful murder against persons unknown.[1]

24th June, Monday, Midsummer Day A cloudy, churlish, cold day

At 6 a.m. Captain Cook set out from London with Omai.

> We reached Chatham between ten and eleven o'clock; and, after dining with Commissioner Proby, he very obligingly ordered his yacht to carry us to Sheerness, where my boat was waiting to take us on board.
> Omai left London with a mixture of regret and satisfaction. When we talked about England, and about those who, during his stay, had honoured him with their protection or friendship, I could observe that his spirits were sensibly

affected, and that it was with difficulty he could refrain from tears. But, the instant the conversation turned to his own islands, his eyes began to sparkle with joy. He was deeply impressed with a sense of the good treatment he had met with in England, and entertained the highest ideas of the country and of the people. But the pleasing prospect he now had before him of returning home, loaded with what, he well knew, would be esteemed invaluable treasures there, and the flattering hope which the possession of these gave him, of attaining to a distinguished superiority amongst his countrymen ... operated, by degrees, to suppress every uneasy sensation; and he seemed to be quite happy when he got on board the ship.[1]

At 7 a.m. the 64th regiment of foot marched through Wandsworth with drums beating and colours flying, on their road to Portsmouth, where they are to embark for America with the Brunswick and Hessian troops. They appeared all very cheerful and in high spirits.[2]

The purchase of Mr Garrick's share of the patent of Drury Lane Theatre was compleated, £35,000 being paid into his hands. He afterwards gave the new proprietors possession of the theatre.[3]

Being Midsummer Day, the livery of London assembled in Guildhall to elect two sheriffs, a chamberlain, and other officers. Near 3,000 were present and there were two candidates for the chamberlainship, Benjamin Hopkins, the incumbent, and John Wilkes, alderman. Mr Wilkes's speech was repeatedly interrupted with tokens of disapprobation. Upon the first shew of hands, the sheriffs doubted which candidate had the majority. They therefore withdrew into a corner, and after a minute's confab, returned to the hustings, and desired that the friends of each candidate would hold up their hands, and not their hats. This being done, they declared the choice had fallen on Wilkes. A poll was immediately demanded, and the books were opened at 4 p.m.[4]

In the evening, as four of Mrs W—'s fillies were going in a hackney coach from King's Place Court to Ranelagh, they were stopped in Grosvenor Place by a highwayman, who demanded their money. The poor girls were unable to raise more than half a guinea, which they offered him, alledging their *occupation*, and the absence of their gallants from town at this season, as the cause of their present poverty. The highwayman refused it with a generous oath and bid them go home, be less constant, and more *industrious*.[5]

25th June, Tuesday Frosty in night, cloudy morning, bright afternoon
Having agreed not to work till their wages are advanced from 18s. to 20s. per week, about 4,000 journeymen carpenters met at Mother Red Cap's, the half-way house to Hampstead, and entered into articles for the support of their schemes. The most material was that no man, under the severest penalties, should work for less than 20s., and that those who entered upon those wages should allow three shillings a week for the support of their brethren who continued out of employ.[1]

At 10 a.m. John Robinson wrote to the king enclosing drafts of dispatches to generals Carleton, Howe, and Burgoyne. 'Mr Robinson finding that the Treasury has occasion to trouble his majesty often on the American business, and East India affairs, has presumed to have some boxes made in order to save his majesty the trouble of making up packets, and to send inclosed a key, in which he humbly hopes he shall not offend.' At 11.57 a.m. the king replied approving the dispatches and the innovation of the boxes, 'for the mode of sending sealed packets was rather inconvenient'.[2]

Lord North wrote from Bushy Park to General Howe:

> We expect before the end of August to have shipped from England and Ireland a sufficient quantity of provisions to feed your army (computed at 36,000 men) till May 1777. We will send out some more sour krout towards the end of the year, but I am afraid that there is some danger of your not being supplied with it in time, as the cabbages will not be ripe enough to make it till the month of September, and last year's experience has taught us the uncertainty of navigating the American seas after that time.[3]

At half past eleven at night American Edward Bancroft wrote from his house, No. 4 Downing Street, to his old tutor Silas Deane, who was on his way to Paris to try to open negotiations with the Court of France. The apparently rebel-supporting Bancroft accepted Deane's invitation to meet in Paris, and said he planned to set out 'on Monday or at farthest on Tuesday next'.[4]

26th June, Wednesday Clouds and sunshine at intervals all day

A great body of journeymen carpenters went to the house of Mr Matthews, a master carpenter in Marylebone, and forcibly took away near thirty men who were at work for 16s., and behaved in a very riotous manner. Another body of carpenters assembled at the new buildings, Brown's Gardens, in St Giles's, where several of their fellows were at work. They began to pull down the scaffolding and commit other outrages, but information being given at the office in Litchfield Street, peace officers were dispatched, and on their arrival the men dispersed.[1]

A very curious map of America was presented to the king, the largest and most compleat one ever drawn.[2]

Elsewhere, at 8 a.m. the *Resolution* anchored in the Downs. Captain Cook sent on shore for two boats that had been built at Deal. 'I was told that many people had assembled there to see Omai; but, to their great disappointment, he did not land.'[3]

27th June, Thursday A very wet day

At about 10 a.m. the trial began in the Court of Common Pleas in Westminster Hall of an action for damages brought by Stephen Sayre, an American banker, against Lord Rochford, formerly secretary of state for the southern department. In October 1775, believing Sayre to be involved in a plot to kidnap the king,

Rochford had issued a warrant to examine his papers and seize his person. On 23rd October three of his messengers had gone to Sayre's house, rummaged his cabinet, seized his papers, and taken him into custody. Sayre had afterwards been committed to the Tower in spite of an offer of bail, but was later released for lack of evidence.

The case for Sayre was opened by Arthur Lee, as junior counsel, who was followed by the recorder, Mr Serjeant Glynn. The attorney and solicitor generals appeared for Lord Rochford. About six in the evening the jury found for Sayre with £1,000 damages, subject to the opinion of the court upon two questions regarding the offer and refusal of bail. Samuel Curwen attended and found 'the crouds and noise too great ... to hear distinctly', but he did notice 'an hiss when the verdict was read'.

There followed long legal delay and new hearings in 1777. Sayre's case was ultimately thwarted and he did not receive any damages.[1]

In the morning, as a journeyman carpenter was going to work, with his tools on his back, he was met in Oxford Street by about twenty of his fellows who had left their work on account of the wages. After taking his tools they beat him in a most shameful manner and made off.[2]

At the East India Company's private trade warehouses in Lime Street a case was opened in which was a coffin containing the remains of Major Preston. This gallant officer was killed at the siege of Madura, on the coast of Coromandel, in 1761. It is said that an agreement existed between the deceased and General Smith, lately arrived from Madras in the *Colebrooke*, which brought the coffin, that if either of them should die in the service, the survivor should cause the remains of his deceased friend to be conveyed to England in the same ship with himself. According to the *Morning Chronicle*, 'The opening of the above coffin exhibited a very mortifying picture to the pride of human nature viz. dry bones and saw dust.'[3]

In the evening a young bear was baited in a field opposite Bancroft's almshouses in Mile End Road. A great number of human savages and their bull dogs attended and contributed to the horror of the diversion. The bear twice broke loose, but no person received any injury.[4]

About 10 p.m. Monsieur Rançonnet and Captain Fanshaw were talking together at the St James's Coffee-house, when the celebrated Baron de Linsing entered the coffee-room. As the subject of conversation was humorous, Rançonnet burst out a-laughing. The baron imagining the foreigner laughed at him, with a look of contempt uttered the words *Jean Foutre*, meaning a good-for-nothing or blackguard or worse. The Frenchman asked if he meant to apply that ignominious term to him. The baron replied, 'You may dispute it if you please.'

More words passed, and they both got into a coach and drove to Linsing's lodgings in Suffolk Street, from whence Rançonnet, a captain of hussars, went for his sword. On his return they drove to Hyde Park, where, dark as it was, they fought for some time. The baron, knowing his own superiority as a swordsman, at first only scratched his adversary, hoping he would desist from further trial of skill, but the Frenchman, not thinking the matter ought to end so slightly, urged him to push again. The baron presently perforated the fleshy side of the Frenchman's belly near his right hip, and again desired to know whether he had had enough. Being answered in the negative, he pushed with more violence, broke Rançonnet's sword, and gave him a much deeper wound than before.

Supposing he had killed his adversary, the baron posted away with great speed to his lodgings. On his way he met Capt. Fanshaw, who had followed them, and told him 'the affair was over'. Fanshaw soon afterwards saw Rançonnet and accompanied him to his lodgings. Mr Tomkins the surgeon was sent for, who, after dressing him, thought the wound so dangerous that he sent notice of the affair to Bow Street. Though it was a late hour, Justice Addington immediately went with some of his attendants in pursuit of the baron. After searching the house for some time, at last they found him naked and concealed in a closet. He was taken into custody and committed to Tothill Fields Bridewell.

Linsing had an erratic past marked by bouts of insanity. On one occasion he had killed his favourite dog by thrusting a rapier through its heart. In 1773 he had been sent to the Bastille after accusing a benefactress of attempted poisoning, but had escaped during a transfer between prisons and fled to London. According to the *Middlesex Journal*, 'He is said to be one of those characters, which Shakespeare calls "the very butcher of a silk button,"* having ... been obliged to leave Vienna, Brussels, Paris, and several other places upon the Continent abruptly, for what are called affairs of honour.'[5]

28th June, Friday Cloudy day, a deal of misling rain, cold and chilly
At 5 p.m. a great number of persons of distinction were at the public office in Bow Street to hear the Baron de Linsing examined before Sir John Fielding. Mr Tomkins the surgeon was not able to pronounce his patient out of danger, and the prisoner, who behaved in a most undaunted manner, was re-committed.[1]

29th June, Saturday Cloudy day, with some trifling rain
Early in the morning a fire broke out at Mr Booth's, one of the king's messengers, in Great Maddox Street, which destroyed the same and two houses adjoining, and greatly damaged several others. No water could be got for an hour after the fire broke out. Mr Booth, with his wife and family, were obliged to make their escape out of the garret windows, over the tops of several houses, and Mrs Whitwell, sister of Sir John Griffin Griffin, with her maid, perished in the flames. The lady had got down stairs in her shift, but unfortunately went up again to put some clothes on.

The fire was near the back of the lord mayor's house in New Burlington Street, and he attended the whole time, encouraging the people to work at the engine.

* Mercutio of Tybalt in *Romeo and Juliet*, act 2 scene 3.

Next day, Sunday, his wife was safely delivered of a daughter at the house in New Burlington Street.[1]

A woman was taken up as a vagrant for begging with counterfeit petitions. On examination several such petitions were found on her, one of which stated that her husband was killed at the foot of Bunker Hill, though it was proved that he died in the London Infirmary. By this petition she obtained two guineas from General Gage, and one guinea from a lady who happened to be at the general's house when she presented it.[2]

Edward Gibbon wrote to his friend J. B. Holroyd from Almack's, to which he had recently been elected:

> Town grows empty and this house, where I have passed very agreeable hours, is the only place which still unites the flower of the English youth. The style of living though *somewhat* expensive is exceedingly pleasant ... I am now deeply engaged in the reign of Constantine, and from the specimens which I have already seen, I can venture to promise that the second volume will not be less interesting than the first ... We are in expectation of American news.[3]

In the evening a set of ruffians seized a very beautiful dog belonging to a lady passing thro' Leicester Fields. Notwithstanding her threats and entreaties they held its hinder legs and beat each other with the carcase until it was dead. The *Morning Post* judged it 'an instance of cruelty which perhaps would not be met with in the most savage nation in the world'.[4]

MJ 'A correspondent informs us, that a lady not many miles from Grosvenor-square, has procured a small carriage, in which she places two lap-dogs, which the footman draws round the above square two hours every morning, for an airing.'[5]

30th June, Sunday Cloudy morning, fine bright day
The remains of Mrs Whitwell and the maid who were burnt in the fire at Mr Booth's in Great Maddox Street were found by the firemen digging in the ruins. On the following night, 1st July, their bones were interred in St George's burying-ground.[1]

In the evening a lady appeared in one of the publick gardens near Bagnigge Wells with her head dressed in the extreme of the modern taste, the enormity exactly resembling that which some of the print shops exhibit as a caricature. This so much attracted the eyes of all present that they left their tea, cake, wine, &c. and flocked from every part of the garden to satisfy their curiosity. Such were the crouds that although assisted by a gentleman, her friend, it was with great difficulty she made her escape.[2]

Meanwhile, at three o'clock in the afternoon, the *Resolution* under Captain Cook anchored in Plymouth Sound, where the *Discovery*, under Lieutenant Burney, had arrived four days earlier.[3]

July

1st July, Monday Chiefly cloudy, but fair. Full moon

A woman with a child in her arms took a boat at Westminster Bridge, but had not been rowed far before she threw the infant into the Thames. The waterman saved its life, and brought it and the woman safe back to shore. Her name is Dutton and she has been some time in a state of lunacy. She had stolen away from a house in Westminster where she is kept at the expence of a brother, and had taken with her the child of the mistress of the house, who was almost distracted till the infant was restored to her.[1]

At 3 p.m. the poll for chamberlain concluded at Guildhall, which was prodigiously crouded. There being 2,896 votes for Mr Hopkins and 1,673 for Mr Wilkes, it was declared the election had fallen on the former, whose name was received with extravagant joy. The bells were rung in his honour, and at every egress were men singing ballads abusive of Mr Wilkes, who a twelvemonth ago would have had their bones broken for such an attack.[2]

2nd July, Tuesday Cloudy morning, wet afternoon

LC 'The gentlemen lately arrived from Georgia have brought over some new dollars, as they are called, such as are now current all over America. They differ from the old dollars, the one being a good solid piece of silver, which would pass for 4s. 6d. or 5s. of sterling; the other, this new sort, is only a bit of paper, with a copper-plate line or two, and signed by order of the Congress.'[1]

3rd July, Wednesday Cloudy, with some trifling rain

In the morning, as the Okehampton coach was going out of town, one of the passengers on the roof, being in liquor, fell off in Piccadilly and fractured his skull. He was carried to St George's Hospital.[1]

At Doctors' Commons a further motion was made on the part of Lord Bristol against his countess, calling herself Duchess of Kingston. It asked the court to order a citation to be affixed on one of the pillars of the Royal Exchange for her to appear and shew cause why the previous sentence, which forbade the earl to boast himself her husband, should not be declared null and void.

A translation of a process drawn up by two French notaries was read to the court. It recorded that, with Monsieur Morlet, a wine merchant of Lisle Street, London, they had gone at 2.30 p.m. on 26th June to the house in the rue de l'Etoile in Calais where the countess was living. In a courtyard near the kitchen door they had found two servants wearing waistcoats with the lady's livery. Morlet asked them if he could deliver a letter to their mistress concerning Lord Bristol's law suit.

He was told that she was indisposed and still in bed and that it would not be possible to speak with her. After repeated abortive attempts to gain access, Morlet opened the letter and left it on the table in the middle of the kitchen, telling one of the servants to deliver it to her mistress. As the three visitors left they noticed the countess herself at an upstairs window, dressed in black, her curiosity having led her to show herself, but as soon as she saw them she retired from view.

The judge, hearing the arguments, ordered the citation to issue.[2]

4th July, Thursday Cloudy morning, fine bright afternoon
At Guildhall the common serjeant made formal declaration that the election for chamberlain had fallen on Benjamin Hopkins. Mr Wilkes made a speech saying that 'the same iniquitous and corrupt arts' had been practised in the present election as in the last. He was interrupted by hisses and groans, but went on: 'The Court nominated; the livery tamely acquiesced.' Later there were processions to the London Tavern headed by an ass decorated with ribbons, &c. with a droll fellow riding upon it. A numerous company of Mr Hopkins's friends followed with purple cockades, musick playing, and colours flying. An empty coach, its horses decorated with ribbons, closed the procession.[1]

A butcher and a baker ran in sacks twice round the Artillery Ground for a considerable wager, which the former won with ease in about ten minutes. The baker found the sacks but unfortunately the one he chose for himself was too narrow.[2]

At 7 p.m. a very numerous meeting of master carpenters and joiners was held at the Buffalo Tavern in Bloomsbury. It was unanimously resolved not to advance the wages of the journeymen, or to let any taskwork, or to comply with demands made by the sawyers.[3]

MP 'Baron L—g, the foreign gladiator, still holds his post in Tothill-fields Bridewell; his pride and savage valor are at least a little humbled on the occasion: his apprehensions induce him to send three times a day, to the lodgings of his wounded adversary, to enquire after the state of his health; where he regularly received for answer, "The captain is not *yet dead*!"'[4]

5th July, Friday A very heavy wet day
Captain Rançonnet having recovered, he went with his compatriot the Chevalier d'Éon to Tothill Fields Bridewell and delivered to Baron de Linsing a certificate from Mr Tomkins the surgeon confirming that he (Rançonnet) was out of danger. The baron received it with great joy.[1]

In the evening Richard Jarvis, a drayman, better known by the name of Eating Dick, undertook to eat seven mackrel, weighing a pound each, within an hour at a public-house in Old Street. He won a guinea for himself, and more than twenty for other people, by performing this feat of gluttony.[2]

6th July, Saturday Misling rain most part the day

Mrs Thrale wrote in her diary: 'This day is made remarkable by the departure of Mr Baretti, who has, since October 1773, been our almost constant inmate, companion, and, I vainly hoped, friend.' He had been employed to teach the Thrales' eldest daughter Hester, also known as Queeney, now aged 11. At the start of the year the Thrales had planned to visit Italy under his conduct, with Dr Johnson of the party, but following the death of their son on 23rd March they had abandoned the plan. To try to assuage Baretti's disappointment Mr Thrale had given him 100 guineas, but since that time, according to Mrs Thrale, he had grown 'sullen and captious'. On Friday 5th July 'he packed up his choke-bag, which he had not done for three years, and sent it to town; and while we were wondering what he would say about it at breakfast, he was walking to London himself, without taking leave of any one person, except it may be the girl, who owns they had much talk, in the course of which he expressed great aversion to me ... | I must sincerely rejoice at his departure, and hope that we shall never meet more but by chance.'

Baretti later gave a rather different account. He was not of 'so meek a temper' as to bear neglect, and when 'madam took it into her head to give herself airs, and treat me with some coldness and superciliousness, I did not hesitate to set down at breakfast my dish of tea not half drank, go for my hat and stick that lay in the corner of the room, turn my back to the house *insalutato hospite*, and walk away to London without uttering a syllable, fully resolved never to see her again'. They only met again four years later and by chance, on which occasion he was 'coaxed ... into a reconciliation, which, as almost all reconciliations prove, was not very sincere on her side or mine; so that there was a total end of it on Mr Thrale's demise, which happened about three years after'.[1]

The Admiralty issued secret instructions, signed by Lord Sandwich and two other Admiralty lords, for Captain Cook on his imminent voyage:

Upon your arrival at Otaheite, or the Society Isles, you are to land Omiah at such of them as he may choose, and to leave him there.

You are to distribute among the chiefs of those islands such part of the presents with which you have been supplied, as you shall judge proper, reserving the remainder to distribute among the natives of the countries you may discover in the northern hemisphere ...

You are also, in your way ... strictly enjoined not to touch upon any part of the Spanish dominions on the western continent of America, unless driven thither by some unavoidable accident; in which case you are to stay no longer there than shall be absolutely necessary, and to be very careful not to give any umbrage or offence to any of the inhabitants or subjects of his Catholic majesty. ...

In case you shall be satisfied that there is no passage through [from the west coast of North America to Hudson's Bay or Baffin's Bay] you are ... to proceed ... to the northward, as far as, in your prudence, you may think proper, in further search of a north east, or north west passage, from the Pacific Ocean

ABOVE Baretti, after a portrait by Reynolds painted for the Thrales in 1773 and exhibited at the Royal Academy in the following year. BELOW Streatham Park, from which he walked out on this day.

into the Atlantic Ocean, or the North Sea ... and, having discovered such passage, or failed in the attempt, make the best of your way back to England ... repairing to Spithead with both sloops ...

You are ... to observe the genius, temper, disposition, and number of the natives and inhabitants, where you find any; and to endeavour, by all proper means, to cultivate a friendship with them; making them presents of such trinkets as you may have on board, and they may like best; inviting them to traffic; and shewing them every kind of civility and regard; but taking care, nevertheless, not to suffer yourself to be surprized by them, but to be always on your guard against any accidents.

You are also, with the consent of the natives, to take possession, in the name of the King of Great Britain, of convenient situations in such countries as you may discover, that have not already been discovered or visited by any other European power; and to distribute among the inhabitants such things as will remain as traces and testimonies of your having been there; but if you find the countries so discovered are uninhabited, you are to take possession of them for his majesty, by setting up proper marks and inscriptions, as first discoverers and possessors.[2]

The Chevalier d'Éon and Monsieur Rançonnet attended Sir John Fielding at Brompton on behalf of Baron de Linsing. They procured his discharge, and directly went with it to the baron in prison, released him, and conducted him home. The three men afterwards dined together with several French and English officers and other gentlemen. In the evening they went to to pay their respects to Sir John at Brompton, where they were genteely entertained and that worthy magistrate gave the baron a proper reprimand, with some salutary advice.[3]

7th July, Sunday A great deal of rain, with bright intervals. Stormy

In the morning a man was found shot near the Bull in the Pound by Bagnigge Wells. He is supposed to have been killed about midnight, a person in the neighbourhood having heard the firing of pistols about that time.[1]

8th July, Monday Chiefly fair, a heavy shower or two

At the quarter sessions for Middlesex at Hicks's Hall, footman John Sangster, accompanied by the Rev. William Jackson, editor of the *Public Ledger*, preferred an indictment against Samuel Foote for an attempt on 1st May to commit 'that detestable and sodomitical crime, not to be named amongst Christians, called Buggery'. Having satisfied themselves respecting the testimony of the witness, the jury returned a true bill, and a bench warrant was granted for the apprehension of Mr Foote. Mr Naylor, solicitor for the prosecution, accompanied by Mr Chapman, a constable, repaired to Foote's house in Suffolk Street. Being informed that he was not at home, they waited for about half an hour.

Meanwhile Foote had heard of the matter by chance and went to Hicks's Hall with his attorney, Joseph Hickey, his treasurer, William Jewell, and William

Woodfall, printer of the *Morning Chronicle*. He obtained a *supersedeas*, or writ commanding the stay of legal proceedings, and they all entered into separate recognizances of bail for his appearance next day, Foote in 500l. and the others in 250l. each. Afterwards, as Foote was returning to his house in a hackney coach, Naylor and Chapman saw him and approached to execute the warrant. Hickey, who was with Foote, said to Naylor, 'By Jasus, you are Mr Jackson's brother-in-law.' Naylor replied, 'By Jasus, Hickey, if you was not old enough to be Foote's grandmother, I should suspect you to be his mistress.'[1]

At Plymouth, Captain Cook 'received, by express, my instructions for the voyage, and an order to proceed to the Cape of Good Hope with the *Resolution*. I was also directed to leave an order for Captain Clerke to follow us, as soon as he should join his ship; he being, at this time, detained in London.'[2]

9th July, Tuesday Chiefly fair, a very trifling shower or two
In the morning the lady of Governor Guy Carleton, and her sister, set out from their house in Lower Grosvenor Street for Quebec. The governor's lady took her husband's patent creating him Knight of the Bath. The honour had been bestowed against the advice of Germain: 'My wish was that such a mark of favour should have been deferred till the province of Canada had been regained. I then imagined it would have done the general more honour, but I suppose the king could not forbear granting so agreeable a commission to Lady Maria as the carrying such a mark of his royal approbation to her husband.'[1]

Samuel Foote returned to Hicks's Hall accompanied by Jewell and Hickey. A second bill was preferred against him by Sangster, this time for an assault at Foote's house at North End, Fulham, on 2nd May. The jury having found it a true bill, Hickey delivered a writ of *certiorari*, removing the cause into the Court of King's Bench. Counsel for the prosecution objected, but without success. The chairman informed Mr Foote that having appeared personally in court, agreeable to the recognizance, he might go about his business. He took the hint and decamped, Mr Jewell and Mr Hickey accompanying him.[2]

Meeting his would-be biographer Morande in King Street, Covent Garden, the Chevalier d'Éon told him that he would grant him an interview only in Hyde Park — that is, in the form of a duel. D'Éon was a celebrated swordsman and Morande did not take up the offer.[3]

10th July, Wednesday Cloudy close day, but no rain
At his theatre in the Haymarket, by command of their majesties, Mr Foote appeared in *The Orators* in the character of Lady Pentweazle. He wore a head-dress in the utmost extravagance of the fashion, the breadth of the tete, which was a yard wide, being stuck full of ostrich feathers. Even if the *tout ensemble* had not been of itself a sufficient satire on the absurd mode of decorating the head now prevalent among the ladies of *ton*, the modest and decent stile of the queen's

head-dress would have rendered it so. Her majesty laughed exceedingly when Mr Foote came on, and the whole fabrick of feathers, wool, and hair dropped from his head and remained on the stage as he went off, which continued the roar of the house.[1]

11th July, Thursday A very wet day

Early in the morning some milk folks discovered a fine girl, about five years old, in a field adjoining to the Foundling Hospital, stripped naked, and with her hands tied behind.[1]

This being the birth-day of Mr Wilkes, upwards of 300 freeholders of Middlesex dined with him at the George in Chiswick. There were present the aldermen Bull and Lee, Sir Watkin Lewes, Stephen Sayre, Esq., and several other patriotic gentlemen. Among many toasts one was, 'May the Americans have more courage in supporting their freedom, than the deluded citizens of London.'[2]

In Plymouth Sound, as Captain Cook noted, 'in the morning ... I delivered into the hands of Mr Burney, first lieutenant of the *Discovery*, Captain Clerke's sailing orders', and left a copy to be given to Clerke as soon as he arrived. 'In the afternoon, the wind moderating, we weighed with the ebb, and got farther out, beyond all the shipping in the Sound; where, after making an unsuccessful attempt to get to sea, we were detained most of the following day'. He also wrote to thank Lord Sandwich for 'the many favors confered upon me, and in particular for the very liberal allowance made to Mrs Cook during my absence'.[3]

12th July, Friday Cloudy, with a smart shower or two

Twenty-three prisoners were tried at the Old Bailey, one of whom was capitally convicted, viz. Richard Goodwell, for a burglary in the dwelling-house of Mr Jonathan Sewall [> 20 Jun]. Also tried were Daniel Hopkins, Thomas Horner, and George Todd for a burglary in the house of John Robinson, Esq., secretary to Lord North [> 12 Jun]. The jury acquitted Hopkins and Horner but found Todd guilty of stealing 39 shillings. He was sentenced to be kept to hard labour for three years upon the Thames.[1]

13th July, Saturday Much rain in the night, fine fair day

In the afternoon the body of a man came on shore near the church at Chelsea, and was laid in the engine-house of the water-works to be owned. He had only his breeches and stockings on, and a ribbon on the wrist of one hand. It appeared he had laid a long time in the water.[1]

Refugee Samuel Curwen may have been nearby at the time. He walked to Chelsea with a friend and visited Don Saltero's Coffee-house in Cheyne Walk, celebrated for its collection of natural curiosities. From there they took a view of Sir Hans Sloane's funeral monument in the churchyard before going over the bridge, 'which is a toll, and of wood covered with earth'.[2]

In the evening a Spitalfields weaver was seen throwing aqua fortis on a lady's gown in Henrietta Street. He pleaded for his excuse that he had a wife and five children without bread, and that she wore foreign silk, and he was suffered to depart.[3]

Also in the evening, as two girls, aged about 13 and 10, were going along the Minories, they were accosted by a man who, after walking with them a little way, called a coach and put them in. He ordered the man to drive to a house in Covent Garden, but just as they got opposite the New Church in the Strand the coachman was alarmed by the cries of one of the children, on which he stopped and took them out, and delivered the culprit into the custody of a watchman. Two days later the man appeared before the magistrates at Bow Street and was committed for trial on a charge of attempting a rape on a girl about 13 years of age.[4]

Two ladies from North America were met in Vauxhall Gardens by a gentleman relation who had been reported to have been killed in New England, and for whom they had been in mourning. The surprize and transport of happiness on this occasion were such as no words can express.[5]

At about 10 p.m. Charles Loraine Smith, a captain in the guards, arrived in a hackney coach at the house of a Mrs Hooper in Glanville Street, Rathbone Place, and enquired for lodgings for a single lady just come out of the country. He was shown the first floor, consisting of a dining room and bed chamber. Mrs Hooper insisted on seeing the woman, saying she did not like to let her lodging to a single lady, as many of them were bad, and might get a bad name to the house. Smith said she was of good character, and he would be answerable for her. He then handed a young woman out of the coach and she went up to inspect. Smith took the lodgings for a week certain, at a guinea and a half, and said the woman would return in about two hours, which she did, alone.

The mysterious lodger was Frances, Countess of Tyrconnel, daughter of the late Marquis of Granby. She had eloped from her husband's house in Hanover Square earlier in the day. When the rest of the servants were out she had sent the porter to fetch a chairman, but by the time he returned she was gone. Meanwhile her husband was at Randall's, his house in Surrey, expecting her to join him on that day or the next.

They had married four years earlier when she was 19 and he was 22. In 1773 she had given birth to a dead child, a girl, and in 1774 had suffered a miscarriage.

She had been conducting an affair with Smith for over a year. He would ride in front of the house in Hanover Square almost every day, and, seeing him pass, she would order her horse or carriage immediately and go out. They rode together, sometimes in Hyde Park, sometimes in the King's Road, and generally parted before they came near home, though Smith sometimes went with her to the stables at the back of the house. Almost every night she went to Ranelagh, Vauxhall, and other public places, where Smith would join her. Afterwards she would carry him back to his lodgings in Portland Street in her coach, sometimes going greatly out of her way to set down the rest of her company first, to have him the last in the coach with her. She was now about two months pregnant by him.

Lady Tyrconnel and Charles Loraine Smith,
from the *Town and Country Magazine* for February 1777

Over the following days Smith was often at the house in Glanville Street. Mary Mears, a servant there, heard the lady singing to him, and laughing, and telling him he took a great many liberties with her, and that he had the greatest assurance of any man she ever knew. One evening, going abruptly into the dining room, Mears saw the couple kissing on a sofa, and they started up in great confusion.[6]

14th July, Sunday Cloudy, with several showers
In the evening a man preached to above 2,000 people in a field behind the Middlesex Hospital.[1]

15th July, Monday, St Swithin Heavy cloudy day, with some showers
In the afternoon an immense croud assembled in St George's Fields, hand-bills having announced that there would be a race of asses, and there was more bye-sport than was produced by the race itself. Two men fought for a wager. Men ran, or rather hopped, races in sacks. There was a dog-fight and a cock-fight. About seven o'clock three asses started for the prize of a plate, which was won by a soot-coloured beast called Black and All Black. The riders were butchers, two of whom were thrown from their seats. Booths were erected, gin and gingerbread were plenty, and the whole scene furnished a perfect jubilee in low life.[1]

In the evening there was an ass race in Tothill Fields by some chimney-sweepers for a silver watch. The asses and riders were all nobly christened, started in full accoutrements, and caused much diversion among the ladies and gentlemen present.[2]

Lady Frances Manners, shortly before her marriage to Lord Tyrconnel
Mezzotint by David Martin after his own painting. Published 1772.

About 9 p.m. two of Sir John Fielding's men arrived at the public office in Bow Street in a post-coach and four from Portsmouth, with Robert Harley and Edward George, charged with the murder of revenue officer Joseph Pearson, for which two men have already been executed. They were committed to separate gaols.[3]

MP 'Captain Bromfield of the *Salisbury* East Indiaman, now in the river, has brought over one of the largest and most beautiful tygers ever beheld in this country, as a present to Lord North; he was so ferocious on his passage as to bite off a hand from each of his two feeders, but by being kept on the open deck in a large iron coop, he is become somewhat more tame.'[4]

MP 'His majesty has given orders for building a place for the elephants in the stable-yard at Kensington. It is to be large that they may have room to walk about, and plenty of air; it is to be begun this day, and carried on with all expedition.'[5]

MP 'Advice is received by the *London*, Hill, which is arrived at Brighthelmstone from Tobago, that the American privateers swarm about every island in order to intercept our homeward bound ships, and that many vessels which have been loaded for some time, are fearful of sailing till they can procure a convoy to England.'[6]

MP 'Notwithstanding the ill natured reports to the contrary, we are assured, the little differences between the managers of Covent-garden, and Miss Brown, are terminated to the satisfaction of all parties, and that she returns to her theatrical situation, with a considerable increase of salary. | Miss Catley is said to be engaged at the same theatre, the ensuing season, at the enormous salary of eighteen pounds a week, and a benefit.'[7]

16th July, Tuesday As yesterday

At 3 a.m. Samuel Curwen rose at lodgings he had taken in the Heralds' Office. An hour later, with his trunk, he boarded the Salisbury coach at the Belle Sauvage on nearby Ludgate Hill as the only passenger. At the Black Bear in Piccadilly he was joined by a woman and her parrot, and a little further on by four other passengers. On Hounslow Heath they passed three gibbets with the remains of hanging men in chains, as noted by Peter Oliver a month before. At seven in the evening Curwen alighted at the Red Lyon in Salisbury. He would be away from London for the rest of the year.[1]

In the morning two fellows attempted to pick a gentleman's pocket in Lombard Street. They were instantly seized to be taken before the lord mayor, but one of them proving refractory, and refusing to walk, the spectators tied his hands and legs and then called a porter, who carried him.[2]

Horace Walpole dined with Princess Amelia, presumably at Gunnersbury House, where she spent the summer. When he reached Twickenham on his way home, 'two footpads ... stepped up to my footman on horseback, damned him and bid him stop. Luckily [the footman] was ... the young fellow, who rode up to the coachman and bid him drive on ... I expected to hear a pistol calling after us, but the lad saw nothing but a large stick, which one of them held up at him.'[3]

About ten o'clock several young lads set on a girl in Catherine Street, Strand, and stripped her almost naked; and had it not been for the watch and some standers by they would have carried her to the water side, and thrown her into the Thames.[4]

About 500 persons, including the Duke and Duchess of Devonshire, Lady Grosvenor, and many ladies and gentlemen of the town, attended a masqued ball at Carlisle House. Papers were stuck up to inform the company that the difference between the master and journeymen carpenters had prevented Mrs Cornelys beautifying the rooms as she intended, and the provisions were not in such variety as usual.

Among the masks none attracted applause so much as two gentlemen in the characters of Boreas (for Lord North) and Minden (for Lord George Germain), evidently taken from the celebrated parody of *The Duenna* just published.* They were both in dress and persons exceedingly like the characters they represented, the first being a short, fat figure, not unlike a prime minister. They sung several of the parody's songs after supper with such humour, that they kept the company in one continual roar of laughing. There was also a little Chimney-sweeper, about five years of age, who supported his character well, though perhaps he had better been at home in bed. A French Frizeur broke a bottle of port with his curling irons and poured the contents into a Dutchman's breeches. He then caused a riot by taking a most impudent liberty with a modest lady, but was hunted down and severely chastised.

The celebrated Jack Roper made his last appearance for the season, in the character of Lady Pentweazle, with an enormous head-dress, led in by an Old Bawd. Her ladyship for some time conducted herself with decorum, but as the various liquors operated, she wound herself up into her usual spirits, when lo! about five o'clock she became outrageous, kicking up some of her old breeze. A little before six she was sick in a cypress grove.

The house was not clear till after eight. For the two last hours those who remained were chiefly free-hearted ladies and drunken gentlemen, with that vociferous Son of Frolick, Jack Roper, at their head, and were exceedingly noisy.

Great crouds assembled in Soho Square to see the company leave. Many appeared intoxicated with liquor and took extraordinary liberties with the masks as they went to their coaches. The light-fingered gentry were very busy, and eight or ten watches were missed by the company. Mr Cooper, of Gray's Inn Lane, returning home, was stopped in his chaise at the end of King Street, Holborn, by a single footpad and robbed of his watch and a few shillings. The footpad declared that he had made four considerable collections that morning.[5]

---

* Published anonymously but thought to have been written by Israel Pottinger. 'One hundred guineas have been offered to the ministerial scouts on a discovery of the author,' reported the *Morning Chronicle* on 10th July.

The *Middlesex Journal* published an extract of a letter from Shepton Mallet, dated 12th July, concerning a riot there by weavers and others, 'with intent to destroy, under cover of the night, a machine lately erected by the clothiers', called 'the spinning Jenny', which they believed would deprive them of labour. In the early hours of 11th July they had 'made an attack on the poor-house, where the machines were worked ... and not only destroyed ... the machines, but committed other injuries'. Soldiers had appeared, preceded by a magistrate, and secured five of the ringleaders, 'but in conveying them to the prison, they were attacked by the whole body with an intention to effect a rescue'. The rioters had refused to disperse until their companions were discharged and some began to stone the soldiers, badly wounding seven. 'The command to level their pieces was given, and one man fell, and six were wounded.' The mob then dispersed. That night the coroner sat on the body, 'and brought in a verdict, accidental death by the military, under the command of the civil power'.[6]

17th July, Wednesday Clouds and sunshine alternately
Seven men were executed at Tyburn. On their arrival, and at the instant of their being turned off, pigeons were thrown up to announce the fatal event. About ten minutes after they were turned off a man ran up Oxford Street with a written paper fixed on a pole, which occasioned a rumour that a reprieve was arrived for one of them. The croud flocked to see which should be cut down, but it proved only a rumour.[1]

About 6 p.m. a duel was fought in a field near Paddington between an officer of dragoons and another gentleman who was dangerously wounded in the side. He was immediately conveyed to his apartments in the Haymarket, where he was attended by an eminent surgeon. The quarrel arose from some liberties he had taken with a lady the night before at the masquerade.[2]

MC 'A correspondent cautions all persons who may go on board the *Salisbury* Indiaman, at Blackwall, from putting their hands too near the cage which contains the tiger, as several persons have been much hurt from not attending to such caution.'[3]

18th July, Thursday Clouds and sunshine alternately
The body of an infant, not many days old, was found on the starlings of London Bridge, with its throat cut in a shocking manner.[1]

Governor Hutchinson attended the drawing-room at St James's. 'The king said more to me upon America than ever before, it not being his custom to say anything of public affairs at Court.'[2]

From Brighthelmstone, where he had arrived five days earlier, John Wilkes sent his daughter 'a little present of rabbits and chickens, both which are remarkably good here. ... | This place begins to be pestered on account of the races with the vilest vermin, called at Newmarket the black-legs, a despicable set of gamblers, whom I abhor'.[3]

19th July, Friday Clouds and sunshine alternately

In the evening a lady and gentleman of the west end of the town were robbed of upwards of 30l. upon Clapham Common. The robber was masked and uttered not a single word except 'Deliver.' It is thought he was their own servant, who has not been heard of since.[1]

Having heard that Lady Tyrconnel was lodging at a house in Glanville Street, Samuel Dickweed, porter to Lord Tyrconnel, went to see if it was true. He saw her in a front room, looking out of a window, and Mr Smith with her. She put the window shutters to, took up a candle, and went into a back room. About a quarter of an hour later she threw up the sash and looked out of the window again. Dickweed stayed watching the couple from eight till eleven at night, and then left.

It seems Lord Tyrconnel himself had already learnt of his wife's whereabouts and had visited the house, offering to forgive her and trying to persuade her to return home, but in vain. The *Middlesex Journal* of 20th July reported that he had made a 'most diligent search' with his brother-in-law, the Marquis of Granby, and finally found her 'in lodgings at a private house, where she was denied; but the unhappy noblemen insisted on seeing her, forced their way to her apartments, and after some vain expostulations, retired, taking a final, yet affecting leave of a woman, who has plunged a good husband, an affectionate brother, and an honourable family, into the utmost shame and disgrace'.[2]

MC 'Wednesday night a waggon loaded with specie set out from the White Hart, in the Borough, for Portsmouth, to pay the troops in North America. This freight makes above a million sterling in specie, that government have sent thither from hence since the first of last December.'[3]

MP 'There never was so remarkable a season as the present, both for the number, and the quality of turtle, arriving in every ship from the West Indies.'[4]

20th July, Saturday Clouds and sunshine alternately

Omiah's Farewell, an anonymous poem 'inscribed to the Ladies of London', was published for G. Kearsly in Fleet Street. The preface noted of Omai that 'his address is uncommonly courteous and polite, and even carries with it the air of some breeding', but lamented that the attention shown him had not been truly benevolent: 'instead of dressing him out in a bag and sword, and leading him forth to all public spectacles', it would have been better 'to have instructed him in such things as might have rendered him useful to his uninformed fellow creatures upon his return', not least because of 'the injustice done to these innocent mortals ... by introducing some dreadful diseases among them'. It also regretted that the intimate familiarity bestowed upon Omai by 'women of quality' had had 'such illiberal insinuations put upon it; but scandal will be predominant, if a dove and a raven of the blackest hue publicly appear together'. It concluded that he was 'now returning to his native isle, fraught by royal order with squibs, crackers, and a various assortment of fireworks, to show to the wild untutored Indian the great superiority of an enlightened Christian prince'.[1]

In the afternoon the king and queen came from Kew to the Queen's Palace and viewed the new sets of horses just brought over from Hanover for his majesty's stud. Next day, Sunday, their majesties went from Kew to Windsor.[2]

Edward Gibbon went with his stepmother to stay at Sheffield Place in Sussex. While there he continued to work on his history and had an excursion to Lewes races, where he lost two guineas.[3]

21st July, Sunday A very wet day

At night a highwayman, who has long infested the road between Kennington turnpike and Clapham, robbed several carriages near Vauxhall, which he stopped in a most insolent and daring manner. He told the passengers he wanted nothing but their money, neither watches nor rings, but 'money! money!' on pain of instant destruction. His audacity was so great that he attacked some gentlemen before dark, while several foot passengers were near him on the causeway. He is a tall man, in a brown short riding-coat, with a round gold-laced buck hat, and rode a spirited black horse with a swish tail.*[1]

Also at night, a messenger arrived express from Dover at Lord George Germain's office with dispatches from General Howe, and was sent on to his lordship at Richmond. Germain set out directly from there for Windsor Lodge, and messengers were sent to Lord North at Bushy Park and to Lady Howe at Fulham, with an account of Lord Howe's being safe arrived in the harbour of Halifax.[2]

William Hickey, future memoirist, arrived in London from Erith. Following early waywardness and scandal he been had sent abroad to seek his fortune, first to India and more recently to Jamaica, in both cases without success. Now 27 years old, he was anxious for reconciliation with his father Joseph, a successful lawyer whose clients included Samuel Foote, but was wary of calling at the family home in St Alban's Street, Pall Mall.

His first step, probably taken late in the day or next day, Monday, was to go to the Jerusalem Coffee-house, off Cornhill, a common resort of those with interests in India.

> I there heard that my old friend and shipmate, Mr Jacob Rider, was returned to England with an ample fortune, residing in Upper Harley Street. I immediately went in search of him, and found him in a capital good house, splendidly furnished. ... He received me with the most affectionate regard, said he had lately made many enquiries about me in St Albans Street, and was sorry to see I was in disgrace with my father, who seemed greatly offended with me. 'However,' added he, 'I, and the rest of your numerous friends and well-wishers, must exert our influence to bring about a reconciliation, and that once effected, away with you to Bengal as fast as you can. In the new court established at Calcutta, I am certain you will succeed, nature having intended you for the profession of the Law.'[3]

* A long flowing tail that can be swished about. (*OED*)

22nd July, Monday Many flying clouds, but a fine day

Early in the morning a soldier was found shot through the head on Clapham Common.[1]

In the morning the body of a young woman, decently dressed and big with child, was taken up drowned in the horse-pond in the King's Mews near Charing Cross. She was owned on Wednesday, and appeared to have been a servant to a tradesman's family in the Haymarket. The coroner's inquest sat on her body that night, and returned their verdict *felo de se*.[2]

On about this day, having established that his father had gone to Bath, William Hickey 'called in St Albans Street to see my sisters, from whom I grieved to hear that he continued inexorable respecting me, and was resolved to interest himself no further about me'. Hickey passed the rest of the week in town and then returned to Erith.[3]

23rd July, Tuesday A very bright fine day, cloudy evening

The orange regiment, one of six which made up the City militia, exercised in the Artillery Ground. To the great annoyance of the citizens its heroes amused themselves with firing their muskets in the open streets, and seemed highly entertained when they terrified any women or children. In the morning, before they assembled, the journeyman of an eminent peruke-maker fired a gun which had been overcharged. The explosion broke five panes of glass, and laid him sprawling on the floor in such a manner that it was much ado before he could be persuaded he was not himself shot.[1]

'A March of the Train Bands' by Edward Topham
Published by Matthew Darly in the Strand, 10th April 1777

About noon a woman stood in the pillory on the other side of Westminster Bridge, in the publick road near the Asylum, for keeping a disorderly house in nearby Britannia Row. She was severely pelted by the populace, on account, it is said, of having received money for the prostitution of her own daughter.[2]

In the evening an extraordinary masked ball was given at a well known roll and butter shop near Lambeth, at which most of the middling order of demi-reps and their admirers were present. The celebrated S. P., Esq., a Marshalsea court officer, acted as master of ceremonies, and kept tolerable order till the masks, from frequent potations, were rather too full of spirits, and riot and disorder took the place of mirth and raillery. One gentleman, in the character of a Hussar, grew suddenly valiant, and to shew his courage gave a lady a dreadful cut across her arm with his sabre. At length the meeting broke up, and those who could keep their legs reeled home. The rest were carried in coaches and carts.[3]

About 1,000 persons attended Marybone Gardens, including many of the *ton* and an Arcadian Shepherd accompanied by two men disguised as Shepherdesses. The gardens were newly and whimsically disposed. The ball-room was illuminated with coloured lamps, and women attended at one end to sell orgeat, lemonade, and other cooling liquors. In the large circular space fronting the saloon were compact little shops occupied by different trades: milliners, perruquiers, fruiterers, toy-men, jewellers, print sellers, and musick sellers. A band of music played all night in the Orchestra, and another in the saloon. Mr Astley's pupils exhibited on the rope and in the Temple of Apollo. In a booth eight men exhibited a dance called the Egyptian Pyramids, standing on the backs, arms, and shoulders of each other, to an astonishing height. In one corner near the booth were drummers and fifers. Fastened to trees on the opposite side were two very sagacious monkies, making wry faces at their two-legged fellow creatures, while in front were boys swinging on ropes decorated with flowers.

At ten o'clock fireworks were played off, and were truely capital and much applauded. At about the same time a little *fracas* happened in the saloon between an officer and a gentleman, which terminated in an agreement to settle the matter next morning.[4]

24th July, Wednesday A good deal of rain, bright fine evening

In the morning a man, very richly dressed in woman's apparel, with a head in the present *ton*, was brought before the magistrates in Litchfield Street on a charge of wandering the streets at an unseasonable time of night. It appeared on examination that he was a footman to a gentleman in Cavendish Square. The family being out of town, he had taken the opportunity to put on his lady's clothes, and went to Marybone Gardens, where he got so intoxicated with liquor that he could not find his way home, but fell into the hands of the watchman. As several gentlemen of reputation appeared to his character he was discharged, having first made some acknowledgement to the watchman for assaulting him.[1]

About half past twelve o'clock their majesties arrived from Windsor at St James's, when there was a levee. Afterwards the king had conferences with lords North, Weymouth, and Barrington. Lord Sandwich made a report on the condition of the dock-yards, having returned in the morning from making a review of those at Chatham and Sheerness.[2]

His majesty in council ordered that parliament, which stood prorogued to 1st August, should be further prorogued to 5th September. On 28th August it would be prorogued again and it did not reassemble until 31st October.[3]

Died at its apartments near St James's Park, the elder of the queen's two elephants. The king made a present of the body to Dr Hunter for dissection.

According to the *Middlesex Journal*, a short time earlier the elephant had 'received a violent blow from a soldier on duty' while it was drinking, and had 'by the strength of its trunk flung the bucket and water upon the soldier, which so enraged him, that he took a pitch-fork and stuck it several times on its trunk, which, it is thought, was the occasion of its death. He has frequently treated the other beast in the like barbarous manner.'[4]

In the evening the body of James Barret, coachman to Mr Thomas Hill, master of the Fulham stages, was buried in that place. During the funeral service a person present imagined that he heard a noise within the coffin, just as it was let down into the grave. The lid was instantly wrenched off, and luckily at that juncture Mr Parry, a surgeon, was passing through the churchyard. He jumped into the grave, ripped the shroud open with a knife, and examined the corpse carefully

From the *Gentleman's Magazine* for October 1763. This may be the elephant which died on this day. A petition from the two elephants, printed in the *Public Advertiser* in February, referred to their having 'resided for the space of twelve years in this metropolis'.

but did not find the least signs of the body having struggled or any blood in the coffin. Several papers nonetheless reported that 'there were evident proofs that the unhappy man ... had revived, as there was a quantity of blood in the coffin; the body was very much bruised in several places, some of which were then bleeding.'[5]

Also in the evening, a horse took fright and ran away with a gentleman at Kentish Town. In the man's endeavouring to get off, one of his legs became entangled in the stirrup, by which he was dragged a considerable distance, and was taken up with his brains beat out. About eight o'clock the beast came full speed down Tottenham Court Road, going clean over the turnpike, threw down and greatly hurt a lamplighter, and dismounted a post-chaise boy, who was much bruised by the fall. It afterwards continued its career till it came to Little St Martin's Lane, where it was stopped by running against and breaking a shop window.[6]

Their majesties went again to Mr Foote's theatre to see a comedy called *The Devil upon Two Sticks*. Several ladies had their pockets cut in the entrance of the theatre. One young lady lost a fine gold watch, purchased that morning at a cost of £30.[7]

25th July, Thursday A very bright fine day

Early in the morning two fresh water pirates were detected in plundering a ship in the river. The crew caught them, tied them to the shrouds for four hours, and between every hour gave them fifty lashes on their bare backs with a cat-o'-nine-tails, after which they put them into the ship's boat and set them on shore.[1]

Dr Hunter, attended by six of his pupils, began to anatomize the queen's dead elephant.[2]

In Paris, Beaumarchais met Silas Deane. 'He has informed me of his needs,' Beaumarchais wrote to the Comte de Vergennes, 'and I will do my best to satisfy them.'[3]

26th July, Friday An exceeding bright, warm day

In lowering the floor of a cellar at a house in Great Garden Street, Whitechapel, the remains of three children were discovered. It was recollected that a woman who took in lying-in women formerly lived there, which gave rise to some conclusions not much to her credit.[1]

The French chargé d'affaires M. Garnier wrote to Vergennes:

> If we proceed ... to our political interests, we will probably find that it is essential for us to weaken a power which claims sovereignty over three parts of the world and, after appropriating the empire of the sea to itself, applies tyrannical methods to trade. It is no less than a matter of breaking the British power in half. M. de Montesquieu believed that making Ireland independent was the only way to achieve this. He could not have foreseen what is about to happen. Never perhaps has a more important event offered itself to the speculations of France. ...

ABOVE Looking south towards the turnpike near the north end of Tottenham Court Road. Aquatint, published 1798, after Thomas Rowlandson.

BELOW Foote as the title character in *The Devil upon Two Sticks*. Print published 1769.

N[ote]. To give you an idea, my lord, of the manner in which these people think and express themselves, it might be useful to offer you quite a recent example. The other day, Lord North was speaking of the Dutch in front of me and was turning their ambition into ridicule as they place themselves on the same footing with England and say 'we maritime powers'. It is, Lord North added, like the story of the shoemaker who lived next door to the lord mayor and said 'my neighbour and I'.[2]

27th July, Saturday An exceeding bright, warm day

In the afternoon Dr Burney set out from his house in St Martin's Street on a trip to Bristol with his second wife Elizabeth and his 14-year-old daughter Charlotte. According to Fanny Burney, writing to a family friend, 'That dear little girl went so much *à contre coeur*, that I was quite sorry and concerned for her. I believe she would willingly and literally have parted with a little finger to have been left behind with me ... And so I am now quite alone — at large and at liberty!' She added that with two other sisters at Worcester until September, she had been left in charge of her three-year-old stepsister Sarah, or Sally. 'I have nobody but little Sally for a companion. But I have no dread of ennui, nor fear of idleness or listlessness. I am going (as soon as I have finished this letter) to study Italian, which I can do alone at least as easily as I did French.' It seems likely that she also took advantage of the comparative freedom to work on *Evelina*, the novel which would make her famous and which she would submit to a bookseller on Christmas Day.[1]

In the evening James Walley, who worked for a coach-master in Cripplegate, went as instructed to an address in Glanville Street. At about eight o'clock he took up Lady Tyrconnel and Captain Smith, who were strangers to him, and drove them to a ready-furnished house at Stamford Brook, arriving at around midnight. Smith had been to the house earlier in the day with an upholsterer who knew the servant looking after it. At Smith's request the upholsterer had taken the house for a month, being told it was for a lady of fashion.

Lady Tyrconnel's identity had been rumbled in Glanville Street a few days earlier. Perhaps as a result of boredom, she had sent the servant Mary Mears to fetch an old woman who lived in Pitt Street and used to tell her fortune. The old woman called that day and the next, and coming down into the kitchen asked Mears if she knew who the lady was. On her saying No, the old woman told her she was the Marquis of Granby's daughter, and wife to Lord Tyrconnel, and that the gentleman was Captain Smith. Mears told her mistress, Ann Hooper, who had guessed as much from reading the newspapers. The mysterious lady's identity had also been deduced by a Dr Watson, who lodged on the second floor.

At Stamford Brook, notwithstanding the late hour, Smith asked if there was anything in the house for supper. There being nothing but bread and cheese, they ate of that, and drank part of a bottle of red wine. Ann Pearce, the servant looking after the house, asked if they would want dinner next day, as the butcher would

Fanny Burney
After a portrait by her cousin Edward Francis Burney, 1782

not call in the morning and she must go to market. With great chearfulness Lady Tyrconnel ordered ribs of lamb and a fowl, as they should both dine there. She then told Pearce to go to bed, as she was not wanted, but Pearce insisted that she must attend to the fire and candle and lock the doors. At about one o'clock they all retired to separate rooms for the night. Pearce heard Smith and the lady talking together, but could not understand them, and thought they spoke French. In the morning she found the bed in one of their rooms undisturbed, but that in the other 'very much tumbled'.

Smith returned on the next night, Sunday, but thereafter did not come again. Lady Tyrconnel remained, using the name Mrs Porter, adopted from her maid, Ann Porter, who attended her along with a newly hired cook. Five weeks later she moved to another ready-furnished house, at Hammersmith, but by early December, big with child, had moved back into town.[2]

Lady Tyrconnel by Reynolds, *circa* 1775-1776

Probably exhibited at the Royal Academy in April 1776. The sitter's brother, Lord Granby, paid Reynolds 70 guineas for it in September.

28th July, Sunday Clouds and sunshine alternately, cooler
Arthur Lee wrote to Silas Deane in Paris:

> It seems necessary to me that we shoud have an interview to settle a plan with
> more safety than can be done by letter, even in cypher. For this purpose I woud
> come to you immediately, but that it being now in the middle of our law circuit,
> my quitting it abruptly woud be remarkd. That will be over the 10th of next
> month, when I will set out to meet you, unless you shoud think it improper.
> I have inclosed you a cypher for greater safety, and beg you will answer me as
> soon as possible inclosing it to Mr Alderman Lee, No. 33 Great Tower Hill,
> London. If you have no objection to my coming, be so good as to hire for me
> a convenient private lodging near you, to be enterd the 15th of the month and
> continued in weekly. Let me know the house, street and quarter, that I may
> drive to it immediately because enquiries are always made about those who
> come to the hotels. I woud have it taken in the name of Mr Jackson. I beg too
> that you will mention precisely where you lodge, that I may find you without
> inquiries which are dangerous.[1]

In the evening the queen's surviving elephant attacked his keeper and two
other men. He beat them all down, and the keeper narrowly escaped with his life.
According to the *London Chronicle*, the elephant 'is grown quite unmanageable'
in consequence of the death of his companion.[2]

29th July, Monday A fine grey pleasant day
In the morning the body of a child about seven years old was drove ashore by the
tide near the Adelphi. It proves to belong to a tradesman in Charles's Court in
the Strand.[1]

In the afternoon a decent-looking elderly man went about Tothill Fields, and
several parts of Westminster, declaring the wickedness of the times had justly
incensed the Almighty against us, and that he would give a striking proof of his
resentment next night during the eclipse. He even mentioned the names of some
great men, whom, he said, Heaven had marked out as objects of punishment.
His discourse greatly interested the lower ranks of the people, who crowded round
him in prodigious numbers; but on his being questioned by some gentlemen in
the Almonry, and threatened with Bridewell, he was found to be a poor unhappy
creature disordered in his senses, and was directly after conveyed to his friends
in Fetter Lane.[2]

30th July, Tuesday Bright warm day. Full moon at midnight. Dog Days begin
At 10.10 p.m. an eclipse of the moon, many years since prognosticated by Sir Isaac
Newton, began to be observable. The moon's face, which was uncommonly bright
and luminous, commenced gradually to be obscured by the shadow of the earth;
it was wholly covered at half after twelve, and from that period recovered its lustre.
Great numbers of people assembled to see the event, on the banks of the river,
in the various squares, and on every rising ground. In Covent Garden market the

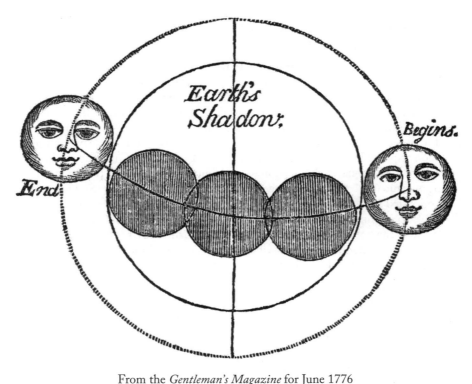

From the *Gentleman's Magazine* for June 1776

mob grew rather impatient at ten o'clock. Upon a wag's declaring that the eclipse was put off for a fortnight they began to grumble and separate, and the well-dressed part of the assemblage discovered that the pickpockets had been expertly at work.[1]

While the family of Mr Crew were on the top of his house in Berners Street to see the eclipse, some villains, by means of false keys, entered the lower part and stole plate and other effects to a large amount.[2]

Also this night a young fellow near Exeter Exchange in the Strand, known by the name of Ned the Shaver, inlisted into the Coldstream Guards. He came home to his master's house about nine o'clock, and invited the other journeymen in the shop to a public-house in the neighbourhood, when he acquainted them with what he had done. One of his companions reflected very severely on his conduct, as he could have lived so well by his business. Another told him he would be obliged to go to America in two or three weeks at farthest, and being but in a poor state of health, it would be almost certain death to him. After spending most of his inlisting money, and being very much intoxicated, he wished them good night, assuring them he should never see them more. He happened to have a great coat belonging to one of the young men, who went for it about half an hour after he was gone, when he found him hanging in his room, and cut him down, but to no effect, as there were no signs of life.[3]

Meanwhile Captain Cook observed the moon totally eclipsed through a night telescope at six minutes and thirty-eight seconds past ten o'clock. The *Resolution* was by now heading for Tenerife to restock with hay and corn for the animals on board.[4]

The *Discovery* was still in Plymouth Sound but on this night, having gained release from the King's Bench prison, Captain Clerke finally arrived. The long wait to sail seems to have undermined discipline. On 29th July Moses Smith, a marine, was given '12 lashes for absenting himself from the ship and selling his cloaths', and two days later Jeremiah Holloway, marine drummer, received the same punishment 'for striking the serjeant'. On 1st August, perhaps with relief, Lieutenant James Burney would write in his log book: 'At 1 afternoon hove up our anchors and sailed out of Plymouth Sound with a fine breeze from the E. Left from England towards the Cape of Good Hope.'[5]

GA 'In the latter end of the month of May, and the beginning of the month of June, the transports sailed that had on board the waggons for the use of the English army in America. This 29th of July the horses designed to draw those waggons are lying in the harbour of Plymouth. Thus, by a perspicuity peculiar to themselves, the ministry have reduced to practice the old aphorism of putting the cart before the horse.'[6]

31st July, Wednesday An exceeding fine, bright, warm day
A new lighter, fitted up for the convicts who are to be employed in clearing the Thames, was launched from Mr Mott's yard at Limehouse. She is to be stationed at Barking Shelf.[1]

Former chief justice Peter Oliver attended the public office in Bow Street. He noted that Sir John Fielding, although 'quite blind', seemed 'to know persons and turns his face to those he speaks to', and was impressed by the way he examined and determined cases.

> He executed one piece of justice, which had a New England justice have executed, he would have been exposed to the tar and feathers: vizt. a master was complained of for a piece of hardship on his prentice boy, who was small and about a dozen years old. He had ordered his boy to carry buckets and other things, of a porters burden, to the distance of 2 miles. The boy was found in the street at night, sunk under his burden. Sir John, after first dismissing the boy from his master's service, and reprimanding the master for his cruelty, ordered the man to be loaded with the boys burden in open court, and carry it off, to the great diversion of [those attending].[2]

'Yesterday and to-day the weather has been hot, the air stagnated,' noted Governor Hutchinson in his diary, 'much like the Dog-days weather in America.'[3]

Lord North gave a grand dinner of turtle to the secretaries of state, and several other noblemen, at his house in Downing Street.[4]

Meanwhile in America

2nd July. Congress resolved, 'That these united colonies are, and of right ought to be, free and independent states'.[1]

4th July. A declaration to the same effect was read in Congress.

We hold these truths to be self-evident; that all men are created equal; that they are endowed, by their creator, with certain unalienable rights; that among these are life, liberty, and the pursuit of happiness. That to secure these rights, governments are instituted among men, deriving their just powers from the consent of the governed; that whenever any form of government becomes destructive of these ends, it is the right of the people to alter or to abolish it, and to institute new government, laying its foundation on such principles, and organizing its powers in such form, as to them shall seem most likely to effect their safety and happiness. Prudence, indeed, will dictate, that governments long established, should not be changed for light and transient causes ... But when a long train of abuses and usurpations, pursuing invariably the same object, evinces a design to reduce them under absolute despotism, it is their right, it is their duty, to throw off such government, and to provide new guards for their future security. Such has been the patient sufferance of these colonies; and such is now the necessity which constrains them to alter their former systems of government. The history of the present king of Great-Britain is a history of repeated injuries and usurpations, all having in direct object the establishment of an absolute tyranny over these states. ...

We, therefore, the representatives of the United States of America, in General Congress assembled ... do, in the name, and by authority of the good people of these colonies, solemnly publish and declare, That these united colonies are, and of right ought to be, free and independent states; that they are absolved from all allegiance to the British crown, and that all political connexion between them and the state of Great Britain, is, and ought to be, totally dissolved; and that as free and independent states, they have full power to levy war, conclude peace, contract alliances, establish commerce, and to do all other acts and things which independent states may of right do.[2]

9th July. At 6 p.m. the declaration was read at the head of each brigade of Washington's army in New York and received by three huzzas. The statue of the king on Bowling Green was pulled down by a crowd of soldiers and civilians and its head was hacked off. According to a letter dated 11th July at New York, 'the equestrian statue of George III, with Tory pride and folly raised in the year 1770, was by the Sons of Freedom laid prostrate in the dust, the just desert of an ungrateful tyrant. The lead wherewith this monument is made is to be run into bullets, to assimilate with the brains of our infatuated adversaries, who to gain a peppercorn, have lost an empire.'[3]

15th July. Having arrived at Staten Island three days earlier, Lord Howe sent a flag of truce with a letter addressed to George Washington, Esq. The officer who carried the letter was told that it could not be received as it was not addressed to Mr Washington in his public capacity as a general of the American army.[4]

ABOVE The declaration being read in public, from a history of England published in 1783.
BELOW A fanciful view, published at Paris, of the pulling down of the statue of George III.
The statue was equestrian and there is no record of slaves having been involved in its toppling.

August

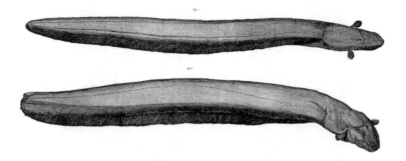

1st August, Thursday, Lammas Day A very bright warm day
The president and many gentlemen of the Royal Society attended an exhibition
of the wonderful powers of the Gymnotus Electricus, commonly called the Electrical Eel. As the *Gazetteer* explained, 'Mr George Baker, mariner, who last year
made an unsuccessful attempt to bring some alive from the equinoctial parts of
America ... has now succeeded in landing here five living Gymnoti, all taken by
himself 150 miles up the river of Surinam: he is probably the first who has landed
any of the kind alive in Europe'. The exhibition probably took place at the former
Ford's Auction Room in the Haymarket, where from about this time the eels
were on public display, 9 a.m. till 8 p.m. each day, admission five shillings.[1]

In the afternoon immense numbers of people assembled on the banks of the
Thames, and in vessels on the river, to see the annual rowing match for Doggett's
coat and badge, from the Old Swan near London Bridge to the Swan at Chelsea.
The candidates assembled at five o'clock, pushed off at six, and passed under
Blackfriars Bridge in about eleven minutes. In their progress they were saluted
by the firing of guns and the music of drums, violins, French horns, salt-boxes,
&c. The fineness of the evening, the number of barges, sailing boats, cutters, &c.
with gay company and flying colours, rendered the scene abundantly agreeable.
The taverns and public-houses on the river banks were crouded with company,
drinking to 'the merry memory of Old Doggett'.

In the hurry of people getting into boats at the Old Swan to see the match, a
boat was overset, and several persons were drowned.[2]

ABOVE The Gymnotus Electricus, from an article by John Hunter in the Royal Society's
Philosophical Transactions for 1775.

FACING PAGE The Doggett race as depicted by Rowlandson some thirty years later.
In 1715 Thomas Doggett, a well known actor and a supporter of the house of Hanover,
had established a prize of a waterman's coat and silver badge to be rowed for each year on
this date, the anniversary of the accession of George I. The race survives to the present day.

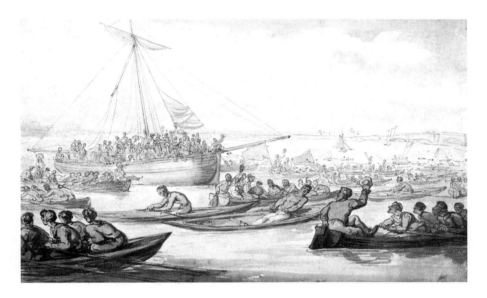

2nd August, Friday Exceeding bright hot day, thunder and lightning in evening
At 3 a.m. the queen's surviving elephant was moved to Kensington.[1]

By Fahrenheit's thermometer it was the hottest day by four degrees these seven
years. No less than five persons were drowned bathing in the Thames, including
a shoemaker of Fetter Lane, who was found about 8 p.m. among the coal barges
lying off Whitefriars. As he was an excellent swimmer, it is not known how this
accident happened. Some of the medical society for assisting drowned persons
attended, but to no purpose.[2]

At night a group of ruffians, stript naked and armed with thick twisted ropes,
ran through streets in the city, assaulting every one, particularly females, who fell
in their way. On Ludgate Hill one of them struck a lady so violent a blow on her
back that she fainted. She was carried in a sedan chair to her home, where she
continues dangerously ill. Two of the men were taken in Fleet Market and secured
in the watch-house.[3]

Also at night, an elderly woman, seemingly an enthusiast, and disordered in
her senses, drew together a vast crowd in Lincoln's Inn Fields, where she held
forth in a most blasphemous and indecent manner.[4]

3rd August, Saturday Many flying clouds, but a fine day, cooler
In the morning the beautiful daughter of a rich Jew merchant, not far from
Crutched Friars, eloped with a clerk in the counting-house of a West India merchant in the neighbourhood. The frantic father immediately dispatched two peace
officers in pursuit. The fugitives were overtaken in a chaise and four a few miles
on the other side of Dartford, but the hero clerk jumping out of the chaise, armed
with pistols, and seconded by one of the post-boys, also armed, swore he would

protect the girl at the expence of his life. Upon this the officers retreated, comforting themselves by dining and getting drunk on their return to London, while the lovers pursued their amorous journey.[1]

In the afternoon Morande sent or delivered a draft of his planned biography of the Chevalier d'Éon to its subject. The manuscript has not survived, but, from a later newspaper report probably written by Morande, it seems clear that it revived the old accusation that d'Éon had taken an 'underhand part ... in that scandalous business of the policies, respecting the gender of her sex'.

The recipient was not impressed and wrote in reply from Brewer Street the same day:

> Mademoiselle d'Éon has this evening read, with as much disgust as contempt, the miserable epistle of thirty-eight pages in folio that the wretched author of the *Gazetier Cuirassé* ..., slaving for six weeks like an ox, has taken the trouble to forge, write, transcribe, and address to her this afternoon. He can do what he wishes with it. ...
>
> All Europe knows that M. Morande only lives in London on the foul proceeds of his libels ... No one in the world will be surprised at this atrocious proceeding, but he can be sure that it will gain him only contempt ...

He repeated his previous statement that he would grant Morande an interview only in Hyde Park, and in the meantime asked him 'either to keep quiet or go to the Devil'.[2]

MP 'So general is the taste for pleasure, and the indulgence for luxury become, that we are well assured the person who appeared at Mrs Cornelys' last masquerade, in the character of a Highlander, was neither more nor less than a barber from the town of Margate. That in order to experience the festivity of that night he purchased the dress in which he exhibited, and went to the expence of a post journey to London and home again, and paid the full price for his admittance.'[3]

4th August, Sunday A very fine summer's day

At noon two young men, who went in to bathe at Somerset Stairs, were carried down by the tide and drowned. The body of one of them was soon found, and delivered up to his aged parents; the other could not be recovered.[1]

In the afternoon John Wesley, recently returned from a tour to Scotland and the north, preached to thousands in Moorfields on Acts chapter 2 verse 31: 'Him hath God raised up, whereof ye are all witnesses.'[2]

5th August, Monday Chiefly cloudy, a little rain in the evening

The felons, sentenced under what is called the Convict Act [> 9 May], began to clear the bed of the river about two miles below Barking Creek. They are chained by the leg, two and two, and are to be employed in as much labour as they can sustain; to be fed with legs and shins of beef, ox-cheek, and such other coarse food; to have nothing for drink, but water or small beer; to be clad in some squalid uniform; never to be visited without the consent of the overseers; and whoever gives them the smallest relief incurs a penalty of 40 shillings.[1]

A very large body of journeymen carpenters assembled in Stepney fields for the purpose of raising their wages. Justice Sherwood and two other magistrates, attended by the high constable and peace officers, met them near Bow Common, where the men drew up in a ring, and received the justices with great respect, acquainted them with their grievances, &c. The justices told them, if they would leave at Mr Sherwood's office their case, or any plan they wished to have put in force, they would give any assistance, but feared nothing but a bill in parliament to regulate their wages would do, as in the case of the weavers.* In the meantime they recommended to them to have no more of these large meetings abroad, as, notwithstanding the carpenters' pacific intentions, they tended to many mischiefs. They insisted on their dispersing, which the carpenters complied with chearfully, without the least indecent or irregular behaviour.[2]

MP 'Administration are in hourly expectation of advices respecting the event of the motion concerning a general *Independency*, which was agitated in the American Congress on the 1st of July last, and which it was imagined was lost by a very considerable majority.'[3]

6th August, Tuesday Clouds and sunshine at intervals, much cooler
Workmen began to pull down two houses in St James's Street and two in Park Place adjoining, in order to make another gaming house. It is to be built on a more elegant plan than the Savoir Vivre, and is said to be for Mr Brooks, one of the partners at Almack's.[1]

GEP 'A letter received from an officer on board of his majesty's ship *Antelope*, at Jamaica, says, "An extraordinary discovery has been made on board of our ship; a person who went by the name of Phillips, who came out in a vessel from England, has been discovered to be a young woman; she was stationed as a boy in the foretop, and discharged her duty extremely well. A desire of seeing the world, she says, induced her to take the above method."'[2]

7th August, Wednesday Some smart showers, with a little thunder
John Robinson wrote from the Treasury to William Knox, under secretary in the American department, reporting that seven American ships had been seen at Bordeaux, discharging flour, biscuits, deer-skin, and other goods, loading arms, gunpowder, and ammunition, and making no secret of their trade.[1]

On this day or shortly before, the Chevalier d'Éon sent his brother-in-law Thomas O'Gorman and the Chevalier de Piennes, a French captain of dragoons, to Morande's house in Duke Street to demand that he choose the day, hour, and

---

* The Spitalfields Act, 1773, had regulated the prices of silk-weaving in Spitalfields and the vicinity of London.

weapons for a duel. Morande responded by writing on this day to d'Éon to excuse himself: 'M. de Morande ... does not have the hand sufficiently vile, nor the heart sufficiently base, to test himself against a woman who has lifted her chemise to him, has shown him what she has beneath, and, in order to establish the fact more certainly, has made him touch it!'[2]

Between eight and nine in the evening, some unknown persons threw stones and broke the windows of the house in Brewer Street in which the Chevalier d'Éon lived.[3]

MP 'Among the *nymphs in training* in King's-place, is one not more than nine years old; who a few weeks ago was actually sold to the Priestess of the Temple, to which she is dedicated, by her own mother, for a trifling sum of money, to answer the laudable purpose of gin drinking.'[4]

8th August, Thursday Turbulent morning, fine bright day

In the morning, as the marriage of a young couple was beginning at Bishopsgate Church, a young man, genteelly dressed, came in and was astonished to see his intended bride marrying to another person. He took hold of her hand, said, 'My dear, you are certainly mistaken!', and desired the curate to stop, for she had promised to marry him some time ago, and had appointed that morning to meet him there, and he took out of his pocket a ring and a licence. This astonished the intended bridegroom and the curate, but the lady replied with a smile, 'You may go on with the ceremony, for I am determined to marry the man I like best.'[1]

Two girls of the town were brought before the magistrates in Litchfield Street, charged by a watchman of St Giles's in the Fields as being found in the streets at an unseasonable hour of the night. It appeared that he had several times had connections with the prisoners, and given them a certain disease; and on their refusing him any further favors, he took them into custody. The girls were released and the watchman, after a severe reprimand, was ordered to be reported to the parish watch board, that he might be discharged.[2]

Enraged by Morande's letter of the previous day, and probably assuming he was behind the subsequent stone-throwing, the Chevalier d'Éon wrote in reply: 'Your speech and your conduct towards me for several months, monsieur; the letters, or rather libels, that you send; combined with your repeated refusal to fight against me, whether with pistol or with sword, proves to me, and will prove to all the world, that you are nothing but a vile libeller ... and the most cowardly poltroon who has ever existed in the kingdom of rascals.' He went on to claim that Morande had been imprisoned in France, had caused his own father's death, and had wanted to bring his own mother to the gallows. As for his career as a libel writer:

> Never forget that you have been compelled to burn, in the furnace of Sodom and Gomorrah, near Marybone, all the noble productions of your infernal brain. It was but the harbinger of the fate that awaits your infected corpse. If you have any honour and conscience, before going to rejoin your grandfather

the cloven-footed Devil, you will repay me ... the money that I lent you gratis, last winter, to keep you out of prison.

Farewell, for the last time, cowardly scoundrel, before you give your blessing to the London mob with your dangling feet at Tyburn ...

P.S. *Jean Foutre*, do not send me any more paper smeared with your cloven hoof. Keep it for filling your pistols, if you have any courage. What does it matter to you whether I have a cock or not? You are not being asked to fight against a cock. Fight against my pistol, my sabre, or my sword. That should be sufficient, if you have any guts.[3]

9th August, Friday Cloudy, with a good deal of rain
A floating engine, for the use of the London Insurance Fire Office, was launched at Morris's Causeway, Lambeth, and brought to its moorings off the Tower. It is esteemed one of the most capital pieces of mechanism of its kind ever finished, is said to have cost upwards of £1,000, and will be of the utmost utility in cases of fire among the shipping, as well as in buildings, timber-yards, &c. contiguous to the river.[1]

A woman was committed to the New Gaol in the Borough on a charge of stripping divers children for their clothes in St George's Fields, where she inticed them under pretence of giving them fruit.[2]

Mr Burt, a carpenter near Lambeth, was bit by a mad dog. Three days later, on Monday morning, he died raving mad, as he was conveying to the salt water to be dipped.*[3]

In the evening stones were again thrown at the windows of the house in Brewer Street where the Chevalier d'Éon lived. In addition, on this night or the next, two iron bars at the front of the house were wrenched off, one of which was carried away.[4]

10th August, Saturday Turbulent wet morning, fine bright day
Lord George Germain received letters from General Howe dated 7th and 8th July at Staten Island. In the 8th July letter Howe reported that 'several men have come over to this island ... and by a newspaper of the 6th, I learn that the Continental Congress, on the Tuesday preceding, had declared the United Colonies free and independent states.' This seems to have been the first news of independence to have reached government. Adjusted extracts from the letters, including this news, were printed in the *London Gazette* later in the day. The news was also noted briefly in the *London Evening Post*: 'Advice is received that the Congress resolved upon independence the 4th of July; and have declared war against Great Britain in form.'[1]

---

* 'Bathing will always act the part of a diuretic, and plunging over head in cold water, especially in that of the sea, will do more in the cure of melancholy, madness, and particularly that occasioned by the bite of a mad dog, than any other medicine.' (*Complete Dictionary of Arts and Sciences*, 1766)

On Wimbledon Common some experiments were made before the king of a method of securing houses from fire. For the purpose of the experiments Mr Hartley had built a house three stories high, with two large rooms on a floor. Various tests were made with such degrees of fire as far exceeded all that accident or even malice could effect. The lower room on one side of the house was filled with faggots, pitch, tar, and other combustibles, which burnt with the utmost fury without doing any harm to the room over. His majesty was in all parts of the house, and in the room over the magazine of combustibles during the violence of the fire below.

A visitor who inspected the ruined 'fire house' many years later noted Hartley's method: 'Parts of the floors having been taken up, it appeared that they were double, and that his contrivance consisted in interposing between the two boards, sheets of laminated iron or copper ... not thicker than tinfoil or stout paper.'[2]

The *Westminster Gazette*, to which Morande seems to have had close links, reported that the Chevalier d'Éon had 'sent him a challenge; but Mr de Morand very properly replied, *that it was impossible for him to meet d'Éon any where but on a bed*'. It added, presumably at Morande's behest, that the paper's publisher had been promised 'a full, genuine, minute and authentic account of the epicœne d'Éon, containing the principal anecdotes of *its* life, and a full detail of *its* artful behaviour in regard of the policies which were done on *its* sex, to the amount of several hundred thousand pounds'.[3]

11th August, Sunday An exceeding wet day

Horace Walpole wrote from Strawberry Hill to Sir Horace Mann in Florence: 'The Congress has declared all the provinces independent ... They seem to be very determined, and that makes the prospect very melancholy.' He added that his friend General Conway was uneasy about his daughter Anne, who had married John Damer, eldest son of Lord Milton. 'Her husband and his two brothers have contracted a debt – one can scarcely expect to be believed out of England – of seventy thousand pounds! ... She does not only not complain, but desires her very own jewels may be sold. The young men of this age seem to have made a law amongst themselves for declaring their fathers superannuated at fifty, and then dispose of the estates, as if already their own.'[1]

12th August, Monday Cloudy morning, very wet afternoon

Thomas O'Gorman wrote to Morande about his 'scandalous libel' on Gorman's brother-in-law, the Chevalier d'Éon:

> Seeing your repeated refusal to give him satisfaction, under the vain pretext of his female sex, I should consider myself unworthy of living if I did not avenge his honour, which is so closely connected with mine and that of my children. I flatter myself, monsieur, that you will make no objection against my sex ... I have chosen, for the field of battle, a spot far removed from London

Anne Damer by Reynolds, *circa* 1771

and very isolated, so as not to be interrupted in an affair which cannot be other than very serious. Choose yourself a second at once, and be armed with pistols and a sword, because I wish to give you the choice of arms for the first attack.

With the letter in hand, O'Gorman's second, the Chevalier de Piennes, sought out Morande at his home in Duke Street and at his other accustomed haunts, but to no avail.[1]

In the evening George Samba, a black servant, of No. 35 Bird Street, Wapping, ran away. An advertisement four days later offered 'a handsome reward' for his recovery and gave a description: 'slender made, very likely in the face, talks good English, aged about fourteen, a native of the Pool nation in Senegal; had on a brown suit of cloaths, with black horn buttons, cocked up hat, a solid gold grape ear-ring in his right ear'.[2]

At Windsor, it being the fourteenth birth-day of the Prince of Wales, their majesties received the compliments of the nobility and foreign ministers, &c. Afterwards upwards of 100 of the young nobility, aged 12 to 15, complimented the prince, and the evening concluded with a grand ball.[3]

13th August, Tuesday Fair morning and evening, wet mid-day
At about 8 a.m. the Chevalier de Piennes returned to Morande's house in Duke Street and read him O'Gorman's letter of challenge. Morande replied that he was content to fight against any man, and indeed needed to for the sake of his reputation, but not against d'Éon, whom he knew to be a woman. He said he needed some time to put his affairs in order but agreed to a duel early in the morning of Saturday the 17th. He promised to indicate the precise hour and place on the day before.[1]

14th August, Wednesday Chiefly cloudy, but no rain
Richard Goodwell was executed at Tyburn for robbing the house of his master, Mr Sewall, of Brompton Row [> 20 Jun]. When he came out of Newgate his sister, who had come too late to see him in prison, got into the cart to take a last sad leave. She wept, knelt, clinged round, and embraced him, then left and looked at him with features expressive of unutterable woe, before returning to take one more fond farewell. Her distress drew tears from the surrounding multitude. She had a young woman with her, to whom, in her anguish she exclaimed, 'He would never have come to this untimely end but on your account.'

About nine o'clock the procession moved off, the cart hung with black. The prisoner seemed half dead with the horrors of his situation, and when the bell-man repeated the words, 'All good Christians are desired to pray,' &c. he seemed insensible of what passed. When he came to the place of execution he desired that his fellow servant be called, and having presented him with his breast-buckle, by way of remembrance, said, 'Avoid bad women — they have been my ruin'. He was soon afterwards turned off, and died with seeming composure.

The Prince of Wales and his brother the Bishop of Osnaburgh

Mezzotint published 1779, after a painting by Benjamin West, 1777

Three days later Sewall wrote of the affair to a friend in America:

I petitioned his majesty for the poor fellow's life, but the crime being of so dangerous a kind, burglary by a servant, my prayer could not be granted. I believe he was drawn into it by a bad woman, who nevertheless had art enough to manage matters so as to save her own neck, and leave poor Richard, as the Devil also did, in the lurch. I hope and believe Heaven makes all the allowance for him that I do; if it does, the worst is over with him.[1]

A boy who got up behind a hackney coach in Oxford Road to see Goodwell go by was whipped severely by the coachman, who afterwards ducked the boy's head in a pail of water. This led to a desperate battle, a drayman beating the coachman severely. It is thought he would have killed him had not the drayman's wife interfered.[2]

A great match of cricket was played behind Bedford House, between the City of Westminster and the parish of Marylebone. It began about 10 a.m. and concluded in the evening in favour of Westminster. Great bets were depending.[3]

Having returned to London at the end of July after visiting Silas Deane in Paris, Edward Bancroft had somehow been persuaded to provide information to the British government, and on this day he wrote a narrative of his activities for its use.

Cricket as played in 1784 by members of the White Conduit Club, a forerunner of the MCC, at White Conduit House, a popular tavern and tea garden near Islington. One of the men seated in the foreground is marking the notches or runs scored.

He had met with Deane on 8th July. Two days later Deane had had an interview of over three hours with the Comte de Vergennes, 'at which he communicated his letter of credence, and acquainted the count that the Congress, expecting a publick declaration of independency would soon become expedient, had determined, among all the powers of Europe, first to sollicit the friendship and alliance of France'. Bancroft had not been present but understood that Vergennes had 'appear'd very sollicitous to conceal the intercourse began with Mr Deane, from the knowledge of the British government'.

Bancroft added that subsequently Vergennes had 'recommended (by letter) a Mr Beaumarchais to Mr Deane, as one who would with great secrecy, and on the best terms supply the Congress with such other goods and commodities as they might want, and Mr Beaumarchais offered to credit them with merchandise, &c. to the amount of three millions of livres. But being known as a man of more Genius than Property, Mr Deane for this and other reasons objected against this recommendation ... but the count and his secretary assured Mr Deane that Beaumarchais would be properly supported and enabled to fulfill his engagements ... to the Congress, and Mr Deane therefore proposed to obtain from him a quantity of ammunition and other articles'.[4]

MC 'Yesterday a ship arrived from Quebec which brings letters dated the 6th of July from thence, and of the 4th from Montreal; they inform us that General Carleton had left one thousand of the foreign troops to garrison Quebeck, and as many at Montreal, and that the main army, consisting of 8000 regulars, and 2000 Canadians, with a large body of Indians, making 12 tribes, were getting and assembling the vessels and batteaux as fast as possible upon Lake Champlain ... towards embarking the army, and proceeding to Crown Point in pursuit of the rebels, and from thence to enter the province of New York, &c. Meanwhile nothing could exceed the eagerness of the British army in general to come up with the enemy, and ... several parties of Indians had already made excursions through the woods and swamps as far as Crown Point, and slain many of the scattered provincials, and were frequently bringing in scalps (although against General Carleton's orders)'.[5]

15th August, Thursday Rain early, day chiefly cloudy
At 3 a.m. the Hon. John Damer, aged 32, eldest son of Lord Milton and heir to an estate of over £20,000 per annum, shot himself through the head at the Bedford Arms tavern in Covent Garden. Shortly before he was in company with four women of the town, and Burnet, a blind fiddler. He drank hard, but did not express, either by words or actions, the least degree of despondency. After the women were dismissed he ordered Burnet to go down for about twenty minutes. Returning after that time to the apartment, the fiddler was the first who discovered the dreadful event, by the strong smell of gunpowder.

It is conjectured that Mr Damer held the pistol close to his temple in order to prevent a loud explosion, and in case the first attempt should fail he had another pistol ready charged and laid within reach. When the waiters entered the deceased was discovered sitting, and in the same attitude in which it is supposed he committed the fact. The ball had not gone through his head, nor made any report. On the table lay a scrap of paper with these words: 'The people of the house are not to blame for what has happened, which was my own act.'

The melancholy circumstance was first intimated to Mrs Damer by Mr Charles Fox, who met her in her phaeton as she was driving up Park Lane, in return from her seat in Buckinghamshire. He enquired was Lady Ailesbury in town? 'No.' Is the Duchess of Richmond? 'No. Mr Fox, your questions alarm me!' After the most tender consolations, he bad her prepare for the worst event, and left her. She immediately drove home. Mr George Damer received her at the door, conducted her to her apartment, and made a discovery of the catastrophe in the presence of Lady Harrington, Lady Harriot Foley, and Mr Thomas Foley. She remained in the utmost agony of mind for some time.

In the evening the coroner's jury sat upon the body at the Bedford Arms, and at ten o'clock, after a very deliberate enquiry, brought in their verdict lunacy. The ball lodging in Mr Damer's brain proves clearly that he must have loaded the pistol but with a very small quantity of powder, as the surest means of producing a certain and speedy dissolution.[1]

Johann Wilhelm von Archenholz, a Prussian who was in London at this time, later gave a more colourful account of Damer's end:

> Having repaired to a bagnio, he commanded twelve of the most handsome women of the town to be brought to him, and gave orders that they should be supplied with all manner of delicacies. Having afterwards bolted the door, he made them undress one another, and, when naked, requested them to amuse him with the most voluptuous attitudes. About an hour afterwards he dismissed them, loaded with presents, and then, drawing a pistol from his pocket, immediately put an end to his existence.[2]

On the same morning Mr Ball, pawn-broker, in Cheshire Court, Oxford Street, also shot himself through the head with a pistol. The reason for his committing this rash action is not known.[3]

16th August, Friday A great deal of rain, some thunder and lightning
The new floating engine, built for the London Insurance Fire Office, was tried in the river off the Tower, to the satisfaction of some of the proprietors and a croud of spectators. Upwards of forty men were employed to work her on board, besides several others who held the hose, &c.[1]

Under the heading 'Most secret and most confidential' Lord Weymouth wrote from St James's to Lord Stormont in Paris, relaying much of the information provided by Bancroft two days earlier but not naming him as the source. 'About the middle of July Deane asked from the French ministry in behalf of the Congress, arms and clothing for 25000 men, together with 200 light brass field canon.' As a result, a Monsieur de Chaumont had taken military clothing patterns to Deane at the Hôtel du Grand Villars. As for the cannon, a problem had arisen because those available were 'stamped with the arms of France, and it being doubtful whether the mark could be effaced without too much weakening the canon', one Dubourg had been commissioned 'to look out for a foundery'. Weymouth asked Stormont to ascertain the facts with 'the greatest secrecy and circumspection'.[2]

At Strawberry Hill Horace Walpole heard the news of Mr Damer's death and wrote to Lady Ossory:

> It is almost impossible to refrain from bursting out into commonplace reflections on this occasion; but can the walls of Almack's help moralizing, when 5,000l. a year in present and 22,000l. in reversion are not sufficient for happiness, and cannot check a pistol! ...
>
> What a distracted nation! I do not wonder Dr Battie died worth 100,000l.* Will anybody be worth a shilling but mad doctors? I could write volumes; but recollect that you are not alone as I am, given up to melancholy ideas, with the rain beating on the skylight, and gusts of wind. On other nights, if I heard a noise, I should think it was some desperate gamester breaking open my house; now, every flap of a door is a pistol. I have often said, this world is a comedy to those that think, a tragedy to those that feel; but when I thought so first, I was more disposed to smile than to feel; and besides, England was not arrived at its present pitch of frenzy.[3]

Morande went with his English wife Eliza to Lord Mansfield's house in Bloomsbury Square to testify jointly with her that his life was in danger and that he had no wish to fight against either the Chevalier d'Éon or the Chevalier O'Gorman. Meanwhile, expecting to be given details of the duel planned for next day, the Chevalier de Piennes spent five hours in vain search after Morande. Finally, at 10.30 p.m., he received a note summoning him to Duke Street. On his arrival there, however, rather than set a time and place as previously agreed, Morande told him 'that he was firmly resolved neither to accept nor to indicate any place of rendezvous, and he would not fight unless he was attacked in the streets of London, which he had no intention of leaving'.[4]

17th August, Saturday Chiefly cloudy, with several showers
Charles Fox wrote to Edmund Burke: 'The declaration of independency seems to be an event which we ought not surely to pass over in silence. I have seen the Duke of Portland who agrees with me upon this subject, and who has written to Lord Rockingham to settle a meeting at Wentworth for Monday Aug. 26. For God's sake endeavour to be there by that day as there is no time to be lost. Parliament certainly meets Octr. 24.' He added that he would travel via the Duke

---

* William Battie, a well known 'mad doctor', had died at his house in Great Russell Street on 13th June leaving a considerable estate.

of Grafton's seat, Wakefield Lodge in Northamptonshire, and bring either the duke himself or 'full powers' from him. This gathering of opposition leaders duly took place, Burke arriving at Wentworth on 25th August and Fox and others over the following days, but little was achieved.[1]

In the evening Gibbon wrote to J. B. Holroyd:

> You have ere this heard of the shocking accident which takes up the attention of the town. Our old acquaintance poor John Damer shot himself, last Wednesday night, at the Bedford Arms, his usual place of resort, where he had passed several hours with four ladies and a blind fidler. By his own indolence rather than extravagance, his circumstances were embarrassed, and he had frequently declared himself tired of life.
>
> No public news, nor any material expected till the end of this or beginning of the next month when Howe will probably have collected his whole force. A tough business indeed; you see by their declaration that they have now passed the Rubicon and rendered the work of a treaty infinitely more difficult. You will perhaps say, so much the better; but I do assure you that the thinking friends of government are by no means sanguine.

He added a reference to his stepmother, who had been staying with him for over a month. 'I am pretty much a prisoner except about one hour in the evening: but as she dines to-morrow with Mrs Ashby, I take the opportunity of eating turtle with Garrick at Hampton.'[2]

18th August, Sunday Fair morning, misling afternoon
William Hickey was taken by a friend to see an East India Company director, who 'promised to obtain leave from the court for me to proceed to Bengal in one of their ships'. In the evening he dined with his old shipmate, Jacob Rider. 'He told me he had spoken to General Richard Smith, Mr Leicester, and others of his India connections, from all of whom he should get very powerful and useful recommendations for me.' Later he went to the Bedford Coffee-house and met 'Major Nugent, Jack Tethrington, and some others of the old set', and agreed to dine with them next day at the Shakespeare tavern.[1]

At Bagnigge Wells a gentleman dropped his watch down the necessary and offered a reward of a crown to any person who would get it up: upon which a lad stripped himself naked, and jumped down, where he was up to the middle, and in a short time found it.[2]

In Paris, Beaumarchais wrote to the Chevalier d'Éon, asking why, if he was indifferent about returning to France, he didn't just stay in England with the money the king had already given him? Alternatively, if he did wish to return, why did he keep making impossible demands for the settlement of his debts? His attitude was alienating Vergennes, who felt he was behaving not like 'a modest and unhappy woman who asks for favours, but a potentate who treats with his equal'. Beaumarchais advised, 'Sweeten your tone, and above all resolve wisely.'[3]

19th August, Monday An exceeding wet day

As John Heley, a servant at Whitbread's brew-house, was cleaning out a vat, he fell into it and was smothered. He had but just made his will, saying he should not live many days.[1]

A mad dog ran up Dyot Street and bit Mr Square of that street in a shocking manner, tearing his nose almost off. The dog was pursued as far as Brooke's Market, Holborn, where he was killed.[2]

William Hickey dined at the Shakespeare as agreed, 'and there once more fell in with the choice female spirits, Pris. Vincent, Newton, Sally Hudson, Kit Frederick, &c. The two first-named sang a number of delightful songs, and proved themselves in as fine voice as I had left them before my India voyage. The women all expressed great satisfaction at thus unexpectedly meeting me. This convivial party brought to my recollection many former scenes of dissipation, which, though highly gratifying at the time, ultimately occasioned me acute suffering and remorse.' Next day he returned to Erith.[3]

Mr Foote's new comedy called *The Capuchin* was performed for the first time at his theatre in the Haymarket, to a very crouded audience. It was formerly *A Trip to Calais*, but much altered in order to pass muster at the lord chamberlain's office.* The character of Kitty Crocodile, representing the Duchess of Kingston, was removed and replaced as the main target of the satire by the new character of Dr Viper, representing Mr Jackson of the *Public Ledger*, the duchess's agent in her feud with Foote. As the title character, Father O'Donnovan, played by Foote, says to Viper, 'You became doer of the *Scandalous Chronicle*,' and 'mow'd down reputations like muck.' John Palmer, the actor playing Viper, imitated Jackson's manner and copied the peculiarities of his dress with black frogs on his coat. The *St James's Chronicle* considered the play 'a continuation of the warfare between Mr Foote and the D—ss of K—n', while the *Morning Post* observed that Foote and Jackson 'seem inclined to butcher the reputation of each other, for the amusement of the town'.

In the prologue Foote compared himself to an itinerant painter, who suited all faces by altering portraits ready painted, and to a shoe-maker in Cranbourn Alley, who had to make several shoes from the same last. 'It was comic throughout,' according to the *Morning Post*, 'and universally relished.' The play itself was pretty favourably received, but not without marks of disapprobation owing to a situation or two, in particular when, in the dark, an attempt was made to deceive the character of Sir Harry Hamper that Father O'Donnovan was in fact his beloved Jenny Minnikin. According to the papers, this 'disgusting chamber scene' roused the audience, 'and it was with difficulty that the play went on'. The *Morning Chronicle* judged that 'Mr Foote never played worse in his life'.

The same night an express was sent off to the Duchess of Kingston, with an account of the contents of the play.[4]

* For the background see pp62-63.

Mary Wilkes may have been among the audience. In a letter to her father, dated simply 'August', she wrote that she had just returned 'from a party at Foote's' where 'his new piece, called the *Capuchin* ... was performed to a full and candid audience. There was great applause, but rather more disapprobation. Our party agreed that there were some good strokes, particularly in the first act; but, on the whole, that it is an indifferent piece. Great part of it runs on the stale jokes occasioned by Irish blunders. Foote spoke a good prologue.'[5]

MP 'No less than 46,000 of the pamphlet called *Common Sense* have been printed and dispersed in different parts of America, which has been attended with a greater effect than any other public performance of the kind that ever appeared in any country, and gave the decisive spirit for independency. | The queen once found the Prince of Wales reading Dr Franklin's pamphlet *Common Sense*.* She expressed her disapprobation, and asked him who put it into his hands. He answered *Nobody*. Where did you get it? *I don't know*. When did you see it first? *I can't tell*. Who has seen you reading it? *I know nothing at all of the matter*. It seems clearly from hence, no easy task to get anything out of his royal highness, that he does not wish to communicate.'[6]

20th August, Tuesday Bright morning, cloudy afternoon

In the morning, at a coffee-house behind the Royal Exchange, a gentleman betted 50 guineas that the provincials would not come to a general engagement with Lord Howe, and, if they did, he betted 100 guineas to 80 they were defeated.[1]

The weather being moderately cool, orders were sent to the Victualling Office to begin to kill again, in order that a sufficient quantity of salt provisions may be ready within a month to put on board some men of war ordered for the American service.[2]

Heroic games were celebrated in Tothill Fields consisting of ass races, cudgel playing, boxing, running for a Holland smock, and dog-fighting. The activity of the contestants afforded no small delight to a concourse of butchers, drovers, and pickpockets. According to the *Morning Chronicle*, 'Each class of these worthies was accompanied by a great number of their nymphs, whose language and behaviour were ... grossly obscene'.[3]

Horace Walpole wrote from Strawberry Hill to Sir Horace Mann in Florence relating the 'dismal story' of Mr Damer's demise.

> We are persuaded lunacy, not distress, was the sole cause of his fate. He has often, and even at supper that night, hinted at such an exploit — the very reason why one should not expect it. His brothers have gamed — he never did. He was grave, cool, reasonable, and reserved; but passed his life as he died, with troops of women and the blind fiddler — an odd companion in such scenes! ...

* Franklin was one of several writers to whom Paine's anonymous work was wrongly attributed at this time.

Lord Milton, whom anything can petrify and nothing soften, will not only not see his remaining sons, but wreaks his fury on Mrs Damer, though she deserves only pity, and shows no resentment. He insists on selling her jewels, which are magnificent, for discharge of just debts. This is all the hurt he can do her; she must have her jointure of 2,500l. a year.[4]

In the evening a new-born infant was taken up smothered out of the necessary of the milk-shop in Little Russell Street, Covent Garden. A woman heard it cry a short time before, and from the information of a midwife in the neighbourhood it is thought the mother will be apprehended. Next night, Wednesday, the coroner's inquest sat on the body at the Unicorn in Henrietta Street, and brought in their verdict wilful murder by a person or persons unknown.[5]

At night, as the Hon. Miss Boscawen, one of the maids of honour to her majesty, was coming from the country to her apartments in St James's Palace, her trunk, which contained jewels and wearing apparel to the value of 300l., was

'An Holland Smock to be run for, by any woman born in this county ...'
Published 1770, after a painting by John Collet

cut from behind the carriage between St James's and the palace gate. It was found the next morning in Moorfields, stripped of every thing except a pocket-book, by which means it was brought home to the owner by three mean looking men.[6]

21st August, Wednesday Chiefly gloomy, with some bright intervals
As a result of the appeal to Lord Mansfield by Morande and his wife five days earlier, the Chevalier d'Éon appeared before his lordship at his house in Bloomsbury Square. He entered into a recognizance to keep the peace and to appear the first day of next term in the Court of King's Bench.[1]

Mr Foote's new piece *The Capuchin*, having undergone several judicious cuttings, was performed for the second time, and received with general approbation.[2]

In the evening Captain Hope arrived with dispatches from Commodore Sir Peter Parker and Lieutenant General Clinton informing government of the failure of an attempt on Charles Town, South Carolina, on 28th June. Having received intelligence that the fortress erected by the rebels on Sulivan's Island (the key to Charles Town harbour) was in an unfinished state, they had resolved to attempt the reduction thereof by a coup de main. That the army might co-operate with the fleet, the general landed his troops on Long Island, represented to him as communicating with Sulivan's Island by a passable ford, 18 inches deep at low water. To his mortification he found the channel to be seven feet deep, which rendered it impossible for the army to give the intended assistance.

The sorry result was described in a letter from Parker to Philip Stephens at the Admiralty, a long extract from which would be published in the *London Gazette* on 24th August.

> During the time of our being a-breast of the fort, which was near ten hours, a brisk fire was kept up by the ships ... We drove large parties several times out of the fort, which were replaced by others from the main. About half an hour after three, a considerable reinforcement from Mount Pleasant hung a man on a tree at the back of the fort, and we imagine that the same party ran away about an hour after, for the fort was then totally silenced, and evacuated for near one hour and an half; but the rebels finding that our army could not take possession, about six o'clock a considerable body of people re-entered the fort, and renewed the firing ... About nine o'clock, it being very dark, great part of of our ammunition expended, the people fatigued, the tide of ebb almost done, no prospect from the eastward, and no possibility of our being of any farther service, I ordered the ships to withdraw to their former moorings. ...
>
> The *Bristol* had 40 men killed and 71 wounded; the *Experiment* 23 killed and 56 wounded, and both of them suffered much in their hulls, masts, and rigging; the *Active* had Lieutenant Pike killed, and 6 men wounded; and the *Solebay* 8 men wounded. Not one man who was quartered at the beginning of the action on the *Bristol*'s quarter-deck escaped being killed or wounded. Captain Morris lost his right arm, and received other wounds, and is since dead; the master is wounded in his right arm, but will recover the use of it ... Captain

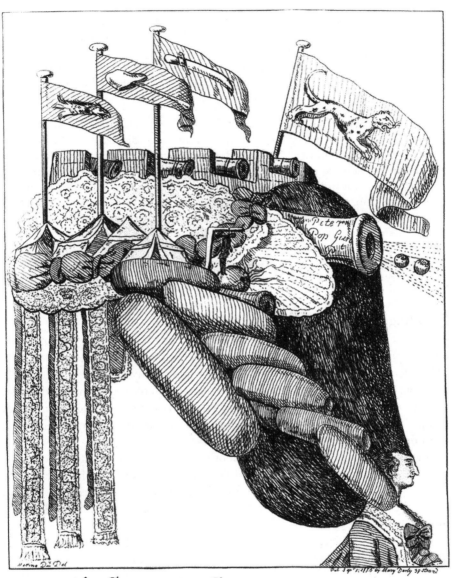

Miss CAROLINA · SULIVAN ·
one of the obstinate daughters of America. 1776

Satire upon the British failure at Charleston, published by Mary Darly, 39 Strand, 1st September 1776. The cannon is inscribed 'To Peter Pop Gun', referring to Sir Peter Parker, and the balls it fires are inscribed 'Red' and 'Hot'. The hanged man mentioned in Parker's letter appears near the centre of the image.

Scott, of the *Experiment*, lost his left arm, and is otherwise so much wounded, that I fear he will not recover. I cannot conclude this letter without remarking, that when it was known that we had many men too weak to come to quarters, almost all the seamen belonging to the transports offered their service with a truly British spirit, and a just sense of the cause we are engaged in.

According to Horace Walpole:

The ministers were exceedingly dismayed at the failure at Charles Town, which was much worse than they had owned, and thoroughly disgraceful. The Duke of Newcastle went to Lord North at Bushy Park, to lament the miscarriage ... but finding Lord North treat the affair with his usual indifference and jollity, took notice of it to him. 'Faith, my lord,' said Lord North, 'if fretting would make me thin, I would be as sorry as your grace; but since it will not have that effect, I bear it as well as I can.' Clinton and Parker were much blamed; but it was seen now that there was little prospect of finishing the war this year, and the expense was so enormous that it could not be borne for another. It was now in their own mouths that, unless Howe succeeded at New York, the ministry must be changed.[3]

22nd August, Thursday As yesterday

About one o'clock in the morning a hair-dresser hung himself at his lodgings near Aldgate pump, but the nail to which he had fastened the rope gave way and he fell on the floor. The noise awaked a man and his wife who lay in the room underneath. They ran up stairs, and found the hair-dresser's wife in the next room, ready drest, sitting without the least concern, otherwise than an exprest disappointment at not being a widow, and cursing her unhappy fate in being married to a fellow who from first to last did his work by halves.[1]

In the morning a chimney-sweeper's boy being sent up to sweep a stove chimney in a counting house at Mr Freer's, distiller, in Ratcliff Highway, he stuck in the narrow part. Trying all his might to disengage himself, he missed his hold, and fell to the bottom, by which he was so terribly bruised that he expired almost immediately.[2]

Considering his lodgings in St James's Street 'scarcely habitable' as a result of the pulling down of nearby houses to create a new gaming club, Governor Hutchinson removed to No. 147 New Bond Street. Meanwhile, having heard the news from Carolina, Edward Oxnard visited fellow Americans in Highgate and found them 'much dejected from the present appearance of things'.[3]

Lord George Germain wrote from Whitehall to General Carleton: 'The rapid success of his majesty's arms in driving the rebels out of Canada does great honour to your conduct, and I hope soon to hear that you have been able to pursue them across the Lakes'. In a separate letter he underlined the importance of gaining the support of the Indians, to which end 'a considerable supply of goods, suitable for presents to them' was being sent.[4]

The king came from Kew to St James's, where there was a grand drawing-room followed by a council. Afterwards Lord North held a conference with his majesty.

As soon as the drawing-room broke up many of the nobility and foreign ministers set out to see a regatta held at Richmond in honour of the Prince of Wales.[5]

Long before noon, numbers of people had assembled on the banks of the Thames near Richmond Bridge, uncertain at what hour the regatta would begin. The race was to be from the center of the river opposite Sir Charles Asgill's house to the Royal Nursery at Kew, and back to the farthest extremity of Lady Cowper's Island, on which a standard was affixed to mark the end. On the island were also placed above twenty other standards, a fine band of music, and a guard of six soldiers and a corporal. A similar guard was placed on the Richmond side of the water.

By two o'clock the town was amazingly crowded and every house filled with people. At three o'clock a band of music belonging to the train of artillery came up the river, and now arrived immense numbers of sailing boats, barges, cutters, wherries, bum-boats,* &c. many of them distinguished by elegant awnings and the fine women who sat under them. Not a few of the vessels were from the east of Temple Bar, as was evident from the depth of their lading in the culinary way. Strong beer was sold without licence in boats on the water, and fruit was eaten from baskets on the land.

The candidates assembled at the Roe Buck to receive instructions. There were two rowers for each of six boats. Their dresses were striped linen waistcoats and trowsers, white stockings and pumps, and caps painted with stripes.

Soon after four o'clock several guns were fired, understood as a signal that their majesties were coming from Kew, and about an hour afterwards other guns followed. Near half past five o'clock, neither king nor queen having appeared, the prize boats put off on the firing of a pistol. A rocket was fired at the same time as a signal for other boats as far as Kew Bridge to keep clear of the channel. About a quarter of an hour later their majesties arrived in a low four-wheel'd chaise, the king driving a pair of small ponies. He was dressed in a white coat and blue waistcoat trimmed with silver, the queen in white silk.

Their majesties took their stations in an octagon summer-house erected for the occasion in a nursery ground adjacent to Sir Charles Asgill's house, and the Prince of Wales stood on the opposite shore. The king joined with the queen in saluting the company, who received them with loud marks of loyalty, several audibly repeating, 'God bless our king and queen!' The king asked if the procession had passed, and seemed chagrined that it had, but waited patiently for the return of the boats. They came in so as to afford no sport, the first being full 100 yards before the second and winning the prize of five guineas.

---

* Originally scavengers' boats, employed to remove human sewage from ships in the Thames. They were also used to carry vegetables and other provisions out to ships. (*OED*)

When the race was ended the band of music on Lady Cowper's Island struck up 'God save the King', in which they were seconded by several bands on the river. A flight of sky-rockets was played off from the island, followed by other fireworks from the surface of the water, and a discharge of twenty-one guns placed round the island.

One of the rowers did himself a material mischief by endeavouring to outdo his competitors. He was taken to a surgeon's on the Green, where proper applications were put to his loins, which he had violently strained.

A boat in which were a gentleman and two ladies was crushed to pieces between two barges opposite Sir Charles Asgill's, but happily the company escaped by climbing into larger vessels. Another boat was overset, in which were seven persons, by which accident one man and a boy were drowned. The only other accident was that of a noble lord, who had been on board a barge which could not come close enough to shore to land the company without a plank. In crossing the plank his foot slipped and he fell into the river. He seemed very much frightened, but received no other damage than dawbing his cloaths.

One pleasing part of the scene was several boarding schools of young ladies and gentlemen standing in rows on either side the water.

Their majesties retired amidst the applauses of the company, and drove at a very slow rate through Richmond Gardens to Kew.

Among those present was Horace Walpole, who thought it 'the prettiest and foolishest sight in the world, as all regattas are. The scene ... is so beautiful, that, with its shores covered with multitudes, and the river with boats, in the finest of all evenings, nothing could be more delightful.'

At eight o'clock those of the company who had tickets went to the theatre, where the day closed with a magnificent ball.

At night, as a coach was returning to town with three gentlemen and their ladies, they were attacked near Shepherd's Bush by two highwaymen, who made a collection of near 13l. Several other robberies were committed upon the Richmond road.[6]

Meanwhile in Paris, Silas Deane wrote anxiously to the Comte de Vergennes:

> I was this morning informed of the arrival of Mr Arthur Lee, and that he would be in Paris to-morrow. This was surprising to me, as I knew of no particular affair that might call him here, and, considering the extreme jealousy of the British minister at this time, and that Mr Lee was the agent of the United Colonies in Great Britain and known to be such, I could wish, unless he had received some particular intelligence from the United Colonies, that he had suspended his visit ...[7]

23rd August, Friday Clouds and sunshine alternately

Lord George Germain wrote from a house he had taken in Kew Lane, Richmond, to General Burgoyne in Canada: 'I hope every precaution has been taken to secure the Indians to our interest. The Congress is exerting all their influence to debauch them from you, presents are preparing, deputies appointing and all arts practised to gain their affections. The dread the people of New England, &c. have of a war with the savages, proves the expediency of our holding that scourge over them.'[1]

24th August, Saturday Cloudy, little or no sun

In the morning a girl about 16 years of age was found dead in her bed at her lodgings in Goodman's Fields. It is imagined she had taken poison on account of being deserted by a gentleman who had seduced her a few months ago.[1]

MC 'So astonishing is the rage for gaming, that at present a new house is building in St James's street, which will cost 16,000l. Two new rooms are building at the Cocoa Tree, which will cost 1100l. and one at the Star and Garter 600l. for the Dillettanti Club.'[2]

25th August, Sunday A very bright fine day

In Brentford, between one and two o'clock in the morning, the house of Mr Bean, gardener, near 80 years of age, was broken into by five ruffians. Bean laid hold of a pistol but was overpowered and knocked down with it, severely cut in several parts of his head, and tied up. The search for money took above an hour, the intruders breaking every lock and opening every piece of paper they found. They told Bean's niece and a maid that if they put their heads out of the window they would blow their brains out. Finally they left, washing their bloody hands at the pump. The effusion of blood was so great that every thing they handled was marked with it, and their footsteps traced through the house and garden.[1]

The same morning, a little after two o'clock, three villains attempted to break into the house of Justice Penleaze in Hackney Road. They were thought to be part of the gang who robbed the same house at about the same hour on 21st April, for they broke the window and endeavoured to force the shutters through which the others entered. The shutters being fastened on the inside with strong bars, and bells fixed to them, the noise awakened a maid. Throwing up the sash, she saw two villains breaking their way through the window, and a third keeping watch at the garden gate. Her cries alarmed her young master and a man servant, who lay on the same floor with him, who were both well armed. The young gentleman fired a blunderbuss at one of the villains, but it seems the balls missed, for the men immediately walked off, cursing the maid for alarming the family.[2]

In Edinburgh, David Hume died at his house in St David's Street. The funeral took place four days later in pouring rain.[3]

26th August, Monday Chiefly cloudy, but little sun

By express from Dover Lord Weymouth received a letter from Lord Stormont in Paris, dated 21st August and headed 'Very secret'. Acknowledging Weymouth's letter of the 16th, Stormont said he suspected that Silas Deane might plan to return to America on a ship 'now waiting at Bordeaux ... which perhaps may deserve to be watched as it would I think be of some importance to seize Mr Deane'. He added that he was at a loss to comprehend one part of Weymouth's intelligence:

> That Beaumarchais should be recommended as an active hustling man, and ready for this or any similar business I can easily conceive, but I do not understand how he who has neither money nor credit could offer to credit the Americans to the amount of three millions of livres unless this Court have secretly engaged some merchants or adventurers here to risk that sum.
>
> I shall not fail to give this important object all the attention it deserves. At the same time, my lord, I am but too sensible how much circumspection it requires ... I must not appear to have the least suspicion since it is evidently wise to dissemble our knowledge of the duplicity of France as this is not the time to resent it. Complaints would avail little, and if she was pushed home, and saw she was discoverd, she might at once throw off the mask which in the present conjunction might have dangerous consequences.[1]

MC 'It is said that the Chevalier d'Éon has sent a message to the under-writers at Lloyd's, who have thought proper impertinently to gamble about his sex, that he cannot persuade himself to gratify their curiosity; but if the under-writers wives are fit to be seen, he will give them proofs of his manhood whenever they please.'[2]

MP 'It is incredible the alarm and confusion that the threatened discovery of the Chevalier d'Éon's sex has occasioned amongst the sporting gentry, who have *done him*, or rather done *her* so much: the premium received by them was 25 to pay 100 if *it* proved a woman: no less than 200,000 is said to be depending on the issue, which it is hoped will at last take place, if it be only to strike at the root of that infamous spirit of *policy gambling*.'[3]

27th August, Tuesday As yesterday, with some trifling rain

GA 'Lieutenant Caulfield, now captain of the *Bristol*,* in his letters, makes the most honourable mention of the extraordinary gallant behaviour of his late commander, Capt. Morris, who was wounded five times before he was carried from the deck to have his arm cut off. After the amputation, he ordered them to bring him on the quarter deck again, where he shewed a coolness and resolution not to be equalled by any page in history. After his return upon deck, he was twice more wounded, but notwithstanding kept his station, until a red hot ball took him in the belly, and put an end to his existence.'[1]

28th August, Wednesday Chiefly bright, a very fine day

MP 'The produce of the corn harvest this year, upon an average through Great Britain, is expected to turn out a full third more than any other for this century past; a very favourable circumstance to throw in the opposite scale to that of national calamities.'[1]

---

* Involved in the recent action at Charleston: see under 21st August.

MADEMOISELLE de BEAUMONT, or the
CHEVALIER D'EON.

Female Minister Plenipo. Capt. of Dragoons &c. &c.

From the *London Magazine* for September 1777

29th August, Thursday Very wet till eleven, bright day after. Full moon
More than 7,000 people, as appears by the doors receipt, attended the last night at Vauxhall. Soon after six o'clock great numbers had assembled, and seemed determined to be as happy as a fine evening, gay company, good wine, and an inclination to jollity could make them. According to the *Morning Chronicle* it was rather like Margate, 'a receptacle for all orders, having the bulk of its summer visitors conveyed there in the hoys, the waggons, and the stage coaches; a few in post-chaises, and fewer still in their own carriages. ... There was indeed among the multitude a small number of persons of fashion', but the company seemed largely 'collected from Cheapside, Gutter-lane, Whitechapel market, King's Place, Newman Street, and St Giles's'.

A boat was overset at the landing at Vauxhall Stairs, in which were five ladies and two gentlemen, but luckily they were all saved.

The gardens were much crowded, the boxes bespoke early, and the tables placed among the trees soon filled. The music began soon after seven, but the songs not till about eight. Mr Vernon was excellent in his Laughing Song, and the glees were also well received. 'Lord! Lord!' cried a simple countryman, on the humour of the women turning to the men in these pieces, 'I never *seed* such an impudent song in my life!'

Billy Riggle, the little macaroni of Little Britain, who for several years past has been distinguished for *keeping it up* on the last night of the season, made a prodigious appearance in a coat down to his heels. A female companion, who knew he was more famous for mischief than generosity, contrived while he was in amorous parley with her in a box, to pin one of his enormous long flaps to the table cloth, and then starting forward, drew Billy, plates, glasses, &c. after her, leaving him amidst the general wreck, for the amusement of the company. Billy damn'd her for a *wixen*, and wished he might never break a lamp again, if he ever had a whore to supper any more.

Order was tolerably preserved till near twelve. Between twelve and one, two macaronies in low life, who appeared to be drunk, attacked two ladies of *ton*, whose heads were enormously high, and with their sticks poked the extravagant incumbrances. Some more manly-minded persons called them to account for their rudeness. A fray ensued, but it was soon quelled, with only a dozen or two of thwacks on the bones, and the demolition of nine earthenware plates, one dish, six stone mugs, three mustard-pots, a salt-seller, and an oil cruet.

About one o'clock the annual *nocturnal fun* took place and the bloods began to *kick up a dust* and do *mischief*. From two till four the whole place was a scene of drunkenness and riot. The women of the town gave rein to their appetites, drank burnt hock, and reeled about in the full wantonness of inebriety. The *filles* from King's Place, and the district of Soho, &c. were all let loose, and became exceedingly wild towards the approach of daylight.

A SCENE at VAUXHALL STAIRS.

London *Printed for* R.Sayer *and* J.Bennett *Map & Printsellers* N.º 53. Fleet Street, as the Act directs 1 Jan.ʸ 1779.

The VAUXHALL DEMI-REP.

Publish'd according to Act Aug.r 20 1772, by MDarly N.o 39 Strand.

A certain amorous apothecary from Bishopsgate, dressed in a suit of orange silk, was assaulted by a demi-rep, and lost an antiquated hair bag in the scuffle. A lamplighter got fuddled with champaign, and insisted upon exercising his profession. Two macaroni shopmen from the City, who had spent the first part of the night in perfect good fellowship, quarrel'd about a town lady, and one of them fell down and broke his arm; a surgeon who happened to be present immediately set it. A gentleman had his pocket picked of a valuable snuff box, and a number of people lost watches and handkerchiefs. The night concluded with the demolition of 100 lamps. A lady who was passing by just as one was broke unluckily looked up, a piece of glass fell into one of her eyes, and it is thought she will lose it.

The gardens were not wholly clear till seven in the morning.

Three young women returning from Vauxhall were assaulted by a set of ruffians in Lambeth, and treated with great indecency. A gentleman who interposed had like to have been killed by one of the fellows, who wounded him in the head with a slater's hammer.

Edward Oxnard attended with some fellow Americans, as he noted in his diary:

A pickpocket was detected and taken into custody. Two ladys were oblig'd to leave the gardens for their preposterous headresses, or the people would have used them roughly. A barber who had taken the freedom to personate an officer was severely handled.

The young bucks behav'd extreamly riatous — broke the lamps, kick'd the waiters, bully'd every [body] — till some were committed into the hands of the constable — which being near day, we returnd home.[1]

30th August, Friday Chiefly cloudy, some little rain

Seven persons concerned in the riot at Vauxhall appeared at the rotation office in the Borough, and the fact of breaking lamps was clearly proved against five of them. As that was their only crime the justices appealed to Mr Potter, who attended for the proprietors, whether paying for the damage would not be sufficient. He replied that that was not the object the proprietors aimed at. They wished the delinquents to acknowledge their error, ask pardon of the public and the proprietors, and promise never to be guilty of the like in the future, and the same to be published in some of the daily papers. The clerk wrote a paper to that effect, which the culprits signed. They also paid for their discharge and fees at Bridewell, and half a guinea each to the constables who secured them, and there the matter ended.[1]

A great number of common prostitutes were carried before Alderman Bull at Guildhall. He committed seventeen of the most abandoned to Bridewell, till St Bartholomew Fair is over, that they may not have the opportunity of seducing apprentices and other young fellows. They were put into a cart to be carried to Bridewell, but one of them jumped out and got off.[2]

31st August, Saturday An exceeding fine bright day

LC 'A correspondent asks, "What idea must any foreigner present at Vauxhall last Thursday night form of the manners of this *polished* nation as we call ourselves, from the behaviour of a parcel of silly mischievous young rascals who call themselves *gentlemen*, in destroying the lamps, glasses, &c. and violently assaulting inoffensive, unarmed men, or defenceless women?"'[1]

Meanwhile in America

27th August. At the battle of Long Island the Americans under General Washington were routed by the British under General Howe. Six days later Major General Earl Cornwallis wrote home to his mother, the dowager countess: 'On the 27th we gained a great and important victory; we killed and took prisoners about 3,000 of the rebels, the loss on our side does not exceed 250. They have abandoned all their works on this island, and I believe in a short time their army will disperse and the war will be over.'[1]

September

1st September, Sunday Several smart showers, but a fine day

In the morning an elderly man, a Jew, was found tied to a post by the beard in St George's Fields, with his hands tied behind him. He said three drunken men met him late on Saturday night, and after abusing him, used him in this cruel manner.[1]

In the afternoon a sailing boat overset near Hungerford Stairs with five persons on board, two of whom were drowned. One of those lost was Master Colvill, 18 years old, apprentice to some proctors in Doctors' Commons. After dining at Lambeth with his mother and sister, he would cross the water, contrary to their entreaties, the wind being very boisterous. The man that drowned with him was to return with the boat, which the mother and sister waited for at the water side. Instead some strange men appeared and presented the hat and cane of a favourite son. Every means has been made to find the body, but to no purpose.[2]

2nd September, Monday A great deal of heavy rain, bright intervals. Stormy

It being illegal to kill partridge between 12th February and 1st September, Tothill and St George's Fields, and Chelsea and Islington, were this day overspread with gunners. Those living nearby had their repose disturbed at half past four in the morning by the discharge of all sorts of small arms, and the bellowing of a variety

CITY FOULERS.— MARK!—

Etching by Thomas Rowlandson, after Henry Bunbury

of four-footed animals. The heavy shower which fell about ten o'clock drove the motley sportsmen into town, loaded with cocks, hens, ducks, geese, owls, crows, and sparrows, which were consumed in the lower parts of Westminster and the neighbourhood of St Giles's. A farmer near Highgate had a cow much wounded by a Monmouth Street popper.[1]

The waggoner who drove the Gloucester waggon was found dead in the road near Acton. The waggon went on a considerable distance before he was missed.[2]

Another newspaper attack on the Chevalier d'Éon appeared, this time in the *Public Ledger*. Perhaps spurred by it to further searching, at about 10 p.m. Thomas O'Gorman entered the Spring Garden Coffee-house, near Charing Cross, where he found his prey.

According to newspaper accounts favourable to Morande, O'Gorman cried out, 'There you are sir, I have met with you at last,' to which Morande replied, 'Yes, I am here, what are your commands with me?' 'No hesitating,' replied O'Gorman, and drew his sword. Morande at once drew and defended himself, upon which O'Gorman stepped back and put up his sword, and some gentlemen interposed, saying that a coffee-house was not a proper place for such a rencounter. O'Gorman then roared out, 'By Jasus, we will both set off together this moment in a post chaise for the country,' at which Morande laughed and said he would walk in St James's Square until twelve o'clock. He went at once, and continuing walking there until one, but O'Gorman did not appear.

Duellists in a coffee-house, *circa* 1770

According to another account, however, 'when the vapouring "Gazetier Cuirassé", the hero of his own tales,' was attacked in an open coffee room, the gentlemen present 'lamented that Mr O'Gorman had not knocked him down with his cane, instead of putting his hand to his sword'. Morande then 'had the impudence, with a pale face and trembling joints,' to claim friendship with one of the spectators, but his appeal was rejected. 'Whereupon, report says, Mons. Cuirassé got to the door and ran out, crying out lustily, Watch! Watch! and so ran as fast as his trembling age would permit him, perhaps to St James's-square, or God knows where.'[3]

3rd September, Tuesday Many sharp showers, with fair intervals
At about 6 a.m. Captain Charles Horneck of the foot guards, accompanied by a French lad, with a cockade in his hat, knocked at Morande's door in Duke Street to deliver an invitation to breakfast with O'Gorman four miles from town. From his window Morande told Horneck that he was determined not to make any country parties, but that he walked in and near London every day, and carried a sword by his side. A mob having gathered as a result of the noise, Morande added that if Horneck did not leave his door, and no longer frighten his wife, who was seven months gone with child, he would amuse them at his expense. This had the desired effect and Horneck retreated.

Later, at about 11 a.m., Horneck met Morande by chance at the Mount Coffee-house in Grosvenor Street. Morande claimed that 'a motion Captain Horneck made, induced me to believe that he would draw his sword. I was ... laying my hand on my sword, when I heard Captain Horneck say, *that he would fight me with pistols*, on which, reproaching him for his inconsistency, in very severe terms, I saw this young officer in his regimentals ... retire to his house'.[1]

Horneck had come to public notice through his short-lived marriage to Sarah Keppel. Early in 1774, less than a year after their wedding, she had begun an affair with Horneck's fellow officer and close friend John Scawen, giving rise to a trial for adultery and a divorce. According to Edward Gibbon, Scawen was only one on a long list which included 'both the Storers, Hodges, a steward of Lady Albemarle's, her first love, and half the town besides'. Horneck may not have provided the most robust counter attraction: Goldsmith dubbed him 'Captain-in-Lace' and he is thought to have inspired the caricature opposite, published by M. Darly in 1771.[2]

In Smithfield the mob assembled long before noon to hear the lord mayor proclaim Bartholomew Fair. On account of the old gate being pulling down in Newgate Street, his lordship went round St Paul's churchyard and up the Old Bailey, which delayed his arrival. On his way he stopped at Newgate where, according to annual custom, Mr Akerman the keeper regaled him with a cool tankard.

While they waited the mob were entertained by pulling off and throwing about each others hats and slinging dirt in faces. When their patience was almost

Pray Srs do You Laugh at me

THE MARTIAL MACARONI.

Pubd according to Act of Parlt Nov. 6th 1771 by MDarly 39 Strand.

exhausted, and their indignation wholly excited at the delay, a man exalted himself among them and said, 'Ladies and gentlemen! My lord mayor desires his compliments to you, and will wait on you as soon as he is shaved.' This created a laugh that no words can describe. About one o'clock the mayor arrived in state and the Fair was proclaimed. His lordship gave particular direction to the City marshal not to suffer any shews or interludes, and to take all persons so offending into custody.[3]

Among the amusements of the Fair is the grand Temple of Minerva, with a Sultan and Sultana from the East, displayed by Mr Astley near the George inn. Near the end of Hosier Lane is a curious Eastern Monarch mounted on his elephant. The amazing little horse, who plays a variety of tricks with cards and dice, is nearby. On the same pavement is the wonderful and surprising tall woman, who exposes her lovely person at a penny per head. On the side of Smithfield next Bartholomew Hospital may be found the celebrated Mr Bateman with his Prussian dog, named *Petite Merveille,* who is a master of figures, tells ladies fortunes, and dances in a manner not to be conceived. His prices are: gentry at their own discretion; middling people sixpence; working people and children three pence; chimney-sweepers and cattle drovers one penny each. There is also Mother Rossi, who plays tricks with her snakes, puts their heads in her mouth, &c.[4]

Bartholomew Fair earlier in the century: detail from a design for a painted fan, 1721

In the evening the *Westminster Gazette* reported the ongoing d'Éon-Morande feud, as usual from Morande's point of view, and cast aspersions on Horneck: 'The public are at a loss how to account for the *valiant* Captain Horneck's friendship to Miss d'Éon, as it [is] well known this brave officer has given various proofs of his aversion to her sex.'

Late in the evening, returning to his house in Duke Street, Morande found two letters from Horneck waiting. The first was a simple demand that he appoint a time for a duel. The second, delivered later in the day by Horneck's adjutant Captain Douglass, was as follows:

> I have given you, sir, the choice of the place and hour to give me satisfaction for the language you have had the insolence to hold out to me. As you have not as yet answered as you should, I appoint you myself to meet me to-morrow morning, at six o'clock precisely, in Hyde Park Ring. If you fail, I'll proclaim you to be the greatest JEAN FOUTRE in the universe.
>
> I inform you I have a second worthy of me; it is the adjutant of my regiment. Choose one of suitable appearance. I acquaint you that I carry pistols; if that is not sufficient, I have my sword by my side.

Morande replied that night:

> I will not accept a stated rendezvous from, or permit the weapons to be appointed by, any body. ... After having refused to go out with Mr O'Gorman, I will not have it laid to my charge, that I have chosen for an adversary a child, who calls for pistols when he has his sword by his side, and when arrived at the field of battle would very likely faint away.
>
> My answer to Mr Horneck is such as I have given to Mr O'Gorman. I wear a sword, and am out every day. If Mr Horneck is willing to find me, *that is his business*. As to myself, I shall never think of him but when I may happen to see him ...[5]

4th September, Wednesday Thunder, lightning, hail and rain, smart showers, fair intervals

As a gentleman who was a lunatick was conveyed to a private mad-house at Hoxton, he found means to open the coach door in Old Street and fell to the ground. The wheel went over his neck and killed him on the spot.[1]

Some further experiments were tried upon Wimbledon Common, before the lord mayor, the gentlemen of the corporation, and the committee of City lands, upon the method of securing buildings against fire. The party, which included John Wilkes, was first taken round the house to see the marks of twenty-five fires lighted upon former days. Afterwards a number of severe trials were made upon the floors, stairs, wainscot, &c. In one fire, made upon the bare boards of the floor, a smith forged a horse-shoe and nails, which were presented to the mayor. The experiments concluded by lighting a room filled with faggots, pitch and tar, and other combustibles while the mayor and his company were in the room immediately above.

After returning to town his lordship gave the company an elegant dinner at the Mansion House. Besides plenty of venison, &c. there was a fine turtle which weighed 139 pounds.[2]

At his lodgings in Bread Street, Edward Oxnard packed up his things ready for a move to Brompton, where a number of other American refugees had already settled. He then went with an American friend to Bartholomew Fair, but found it 'wretched and miserable. Whores and rogues entireley.' Afterwards he set out for Brompton. 'At 8 arriv'd at my new lodgeings. My landlady rather plain, very talkative and strangely misapplys words.'[3]

Several persons were taken into custody at Bartholomew Fair for exhibiting shews, &c. and were lodged in the compters for examination. Late at night the Fair exhibited a scene of confusion, with fighting, drinking, swearing, picking of pockets, and demolishing gingerbread stalls, several of which were levelled to the ground. A number of drunken people were rolled in the kennel. One in particular, genteelly dressed in a new suit of mourning, was first kennelled, and then rolled in a heap of lime and mortar, so that his coat was literally dyed white.[4]

In the evening *The Capuchin* was performed at Foote's theatre by command of their majesties. Woollen draper William Mawhood tried in vain to gain admission but did see the king returning home in his coach.[5]

At night some villains again got over Justice Penleaze's garden wall in Hackney Road, removed a stone roller from one of the gates that opens into the field, unbolted the gate, and left it wide open. They likewise opened a gate that leads from the garden into the back yard, and unbolted a door which separates the yard from the court before the house, leaving both open. 'The repeated attempts of these villains are singular,' noted the *Gazetteer*, 'for since the late atrocious robbery, the justice keeps every portable thing of value at his banker's.'[6]

The *Public Ledger* carried three letters, probably written by Morande or at his behest, which accused d'Éon of various deceptions. One said he was in cahoots with the underwriters in order to prevent the policies on his sex ever being finally adjusted. Another added that it was a mistake to think he had 'a capital stake depending on the policies'. Rather, 'she received her share of the first policy as one of the projectors of the plan', and was now being paid an 'annual bounty' of £400 by the underwriters to use 'every artifice' to keep matters unresolved.[7]

MP 'Gaming among the females at Chatsworth, has been carried to such a pitch, that the phlegmatic duke has been provoked to express at it; and has spoken to the duchess in the severest terms, against a conduct which has driven many from the house, who could not afford to partake of amusements, carried on at an expence of 500l. or 1000l. a night.'[8]

5th September, Thursday Chiefly bright, some showers at times

A boy not 12 years of age was detected in picking a gentleman's pocket at Bartholomew Fair. On his being searched thirteen handkerchiefs and two pocket-books were found concealed in different places about him. He was carried before William Blackbrow, Esq., who committed him to Clerkenwell Bridewell.[1]

The paper war between d'Éon and Morande continued with an article in the *Public Advertiser* attacking Morande and outlining his history of extorting money by threatening to publish scandalous memoirs. It said that, after being paid not to publish the memoirs 'of a certain lady' (Madame du Barry), he 'commenced fine gentleman here, figured away about town in a chariot at the theatres, and in coffee-houses as a Man of Fortune, Critic and Writer of Paragraphs, &c. and ... formed a scheme for taking in and duping alike the gallant Chevalier'.[2]

6th September, Friday Clouds and sunshine at intervals, a fine day
The bodies of the two gentlemen who were drowned on Sunday last off Hungerford Stairs were taken up, the one at Chelsea, the other at Limehouse.[1]

Governor Hutchinson went to the levee at St James's but found 'the smallest attendance I ever saw there, everybody being out of town'.[2]

At night Bartholomew Fair ended as usual by the throwing down stalls, picking of pockets, blowing up sausage pans, &c.[3]

Between eight and nine in the evening, as the lord mayor, Mr Sawbridge, was coming from Staines in his post-chaise and four, just on the other side of Turnham Green, a well mounted highwayman stopped his footman, examined if he had any fire-arms, and with many oaths and imprecations threatened that if he made the least noise he would blow his brains out. Finding no fire-arms he rode on to the mayor's gentleman and robbed him of three guineas. He then rode up to Dick the coachman, saying, 'Damn your eyes, you bloody bouger, stop.' When Dick drove on a little way the highwayman followed, repeating his demand and putting a pistol close up to him, which at last caused him to stop. The highwayman then rode up to the door of the chaise, but it was several minutes before the window was put down, apparently because Sawbridge was asleep. He called out to him, 'Your money, you bouger, your money,' several times, and swore that if he did not immediately deliver he was a dead man, upon which the mayor gave him his green silk purse. 'Two guineas will not do for me,' he said. 'Damn your eyes, you bouger, give me your watch.' This was done, and the mayor also gave up a steel watch chain and two cornelian seals set in gold. The highwayman then rode off with his loot and a few parting words: 'Good night, catch me, hang me, and be damned.'

The *London Chronicle* reported that the assailant was 'known by a person who was behind the lord mayor's chaise, and it is thought he will soon be taken'. The witness was Thomas Barrett, one of Sawbridge's servants. He claimed the culprit was one William Davis, whom he had previously seen at the Maidstone assizes and who would be brought to trial on 5th December.[4]

MC 'A few days since a master baker, near Tower-hill, having bought six very curious tulip roots, at five shillings a root, at an auction, brought them home and laid them near his oven to dry; at night his journeyman having some bread and cheese for supper, not being informed of the tulip roots or their value, and being very fond of onions, mistook them for such, and eat them every one, declaring that they were the mildest onions he had ever eaten in all his life.'[5]

7th September, Saturday Cloudy day, but fair. Dog Days end
In the evening Mr Bliss, mealman, near Uxbridge, walking too near the sails of his windmill, was struck by one of the wings, and killed on the spot.[1]

8th September, Sunday A great many smart showers
In the afternoon, as Mr Robert Williamson was sitting in the parlour at his house in Macclesfield Street, Soho, he heard the cries of a child, but could not tell from whence they came. Looking outside, he saw a girl of about seven years old hanging by her hands at a three pair of stairs window. He ran into the house in order to take her in, but before he could break open the chamber door she fell into a stone yard, fortunately without the least hurt. After she had been examined by a gentleman of the faculty, and had recovered from the fright of the fall, she gave an account, that her grandmother and her mother used to beat her in a most cruel manner with a large cord, and lock her up in a room for days together without a morsel of bread, which caused her to get out of the window to escape. Her bones were ready to break through her skin, and she was almost mortified from head to foot by the stripes and kicks she had received. She was sent to Middlesex Hospital and a constable went to apprehend the mother, whom he found with her throat cut from ear to ear. The wound was immediately sewed up by a surgeon, but the woman has since torn it open. Next day, Monday, the grandmother, Ann Adams, was put to the bar at the rotation office in Litchfield Street and committed for re-examination.[1]

9th September, Monday A very fine bright day
On Saturday last, in consequence of the great number of robberies lately committed about Turnham Green and Brentford, Mr Bond, with three of Sir John Fielding's people, rode in the neighbourhood of Gunnersbury Lane, &c. for four hours in the dark, without obtaining any information; but on going to Richmond and Chiswick on Sunday morning, they obtained intelligence that several suspected persons lived in a house on the Strand near Kew bridge. At eleven on Sunday night they viewed the house, and after returning to London for assistance, beset it this morning about five o'clock.

Mr Bond and his friends broke open the back yard door. One of them got in at the back kitchen window and let the rest in. After bursting open a door they ran up to the first floor and forced the chambers on each side of the landing place. In one they found John Harding, and in the other Thomas Harrison. Notwithstanding the noise Sir John's people made, the villains were but just awaked when they entered, which probably prevented much bloodshed, as Harrison was armed with three large loaded pistols and Harding with a brace. When Harrison, who is 6 feet 2 inches high, was first seized he behaved very quietly, but soon after fiercely attacked those about him. It was some time before he could be secured, which was not done until he was severely wounded in the head.

These desperate ruffians, with an accomplice, are supposed to have committed most of the robberies in the area for some time past. Four pistols, and two bags containing pick-lock keys, chisels, iron-crows, and other instruments for house-breaking, were found in the garden. Two fine bay horses were in the stables and are said to be well known by some gentlemen lately robbed.

Harding is 55 years of age, has a wife and six children, and some years since rented a farm of 400 acres. At that time he was esteemed a sober, honest, industrious man.

At noon both men were examined before Sir John Fielding and committed to New Prison.[1]

10th September, Tuesday Thick fog till noon, very bright after
Sarah Metcalf, Jane Metcalf, and Mary Metcalf, all infants, were buried at St Mary le Bow, Cheapside.[1]

The *Public Ledger* published a long letter from Morande in which he claimed he had proof that the Chevalier d'Éon was a woman and of the various allegations he had made against her. He issued a challenge: 'I repeat that Miss d'Éon is an impostor of the first magnitude; and, if she doth not, in defence of herself, convict me of falshood she must be a reptile of the most contemptible class.' The letter would be reprinted four days later in the *Westminster Gazette*, which meanwhile reported that a gentleman was prepared to bet any sum up to 5,000 guineas that d'Éon was a woman. Alternatively, if anyone would deposit 500 guineas with his banker, he would 'pay ten thousand pounds if d'Éon proves herself either a MAN, an HERMAPHRODITE, or any other animal than a WOMAN'.[2]

After this the paper war seems to have fallen silent. D'Éon was prompted by Morande's letter to sue for libel, but he had to wait for the Michaelmas law term to begin in November before bringing the matter to court.

11th September, Wednesday Hazy morning, fine bright day
Bartholomew Coote Purdon, Esq. and some other gentlemen lately robbed near Acton, Brentford, &c. went to Bow Street to view Harding and Harrison, the reputed highwaymen, and their supposed accomplice, one Charles Frime, but the croud was so great that they could not get into the office during their examination. Afterwards, however, they saw the men in the room at the Brown Bear in Bow Street. Most believed they were the offenders, yet they could not positively swear to them, the robberies being committed in the dark, and so they declined prosecuting.

The *Gazetteer* thought it 'highly probable, from the artful manner in which these fellows have conducted themselves, in never robbing by daylight, nor taking watches, pocket-books, or any remarkable coins, they will escape from justice'. In fact, one of nine shillings found on Harding at the time of his arrest was marked and was later identified as having been taken in the robbery at the house of Mr Bean in Brentford on 25th August. As a result, on 17th October, Harding was convicted and sentenced to death. He was also found guilty of an earlier robbery on the Uxbridge Road, having been recognised, but Harrison, tried with him for the earlier robbery, was acquitted.[1]

MP '*Anecdote of a new made Peer.* In the midst of Mr Foote's late malicious persecution, a great many people of fashion waited upon him daily, forming a kind of morning levee. Amongst the polite throng, who should step forth on this occasion, to offer his protection, but the sapient Mr Ons—w (now Lord Cranl—y),* who entering Mr Foote's apartments the morning that he had received his patent of peerage, (the wax of which was warm in his pocket) with the true air of a man of fashion, shook hands with Aristophanes, and thus addressed him: "Take comfort my dear Foote; you have nothing to fear, when a peer of Great-Britain takes you by the hand!"'[2]

12th September, Thursday As yesterday

At 2 a.m. a fire broke out at the Goat alehouse in Great Shire Lane, Temple Bar. It began in the bar, and that and the tap-room were in a blaze before the family were alarmed. Mrs Davis, wife of the landlord, lay in the one pair of stairs room, and was not alerted till the staircase was burnt so as to prevent any escape that way. She is within a few days of being brought to bed, and was with her child who is about nineteen months old. She delivered the child to a maid and they, with others of the household, made their escape onto the top of the adjoining house. Mrs Davis herself, by the assistance of a long bench, came out of the one pair of stairs window, and falling on the stones, cut her face in a terrible manner. She lay for a few minutes in the general confusion with only her shift on, and all over blood, till conveyed to a house a good way up the lane, where she now lies in a fair way of recovery.

Mr Tudor, clerk to an attorney in Clifford's Inn, who lodged in the house, had the misfortune of being very hard of hearing, and going to bed a little intoxicated with liquor, was not alarmed so soon as the rest of the household. After the maid had secured the child, she went into his room, and with difficulty waked him. When made sensible of his danger, he ran down stairs in great haste, tho' Mr Davis called to him to come back, as there was no possibility of escaping that way. Either his deafness prevented his hearing, or he had got so far down that a return was impracticable, and he perished. His body has not yet been found.

* George Onslow (1731-1814), created Baron Cranley on 20th May.

The flames were uncommonly rapid, and threatened devastation to the whole lane, but by the vigilance of the turncock, and the Lincoln's Inn engineer, they were entirely got under.[1]

At night a hat finisher killed his wife in Snow Fields in the Borough by stabbing her in three places in the belly, and afterwards cleaving her down the skull with a poker. He was immediately secured and sent to the New Gaol.[2]

The *Morning Post* reported that 'certain young gentlemen of landed property' had made 'considerable falls' of timber to pay off gambling debts from last season or 'to put themselves in cash, in order to open the ensuing campaign at the new house ... with some *eclat*!' After a further paragraph about the effect of 'the extravagance of the age' on landed estates, it added: 'The public is more nearly concerned in this than may be at first imagined; for no sooner has a nobleman run out, or gamed away his fortune, than he sells himself, body and soul, to the Court, to be supported out of the public revenue. If every instance of this were given, it would take away all surprise at the majorities there are in parliament.'[3]

13th September, Friday As yesterday

In the morning an attempt was made to carry off Thomas Slop, a clerk aged about 18, as he was going to Hicks's Hall to give evidence against his master William Davis, accused of a capital forgery.

According to one report, Slop received a message which it was pretended came from the prosecutor's attorney, who wanted him upon business relating to the trial. As he was going along the Strand he was accosted by two persons, who, after some strange conversation, forced him into a hackney coach. He made great outcry which collected a mob, and they took him out of the coach and set him at liberty, his assailants escaping in the confusion. According to another report, he was seized by three ruffians who carried him to a house in Suffolk Street. There they locked him in a back room for over two hours, threatening murder if he should make the least noise. A post-chaise was brought to the door to take him off, but he escaped out of a back window and ran to the house of a magistrate, who sent his servant with him to Hicks's Hall. Slop himself later identified James Ogilvie, a highwayman, as one of the assailants, saying Ogilvie had held a pistol to his head and threatened to blow his brains out if he stirred.[1]

Thirteen prisoners were tried at the Old Bailey, four of whom were capitally convicted, including Edward George and Robert Harley for the murder of Customs officer Joseph Pearson at Deptford [> 12 Apr]. The trial lasted over four hours and a half. Every circumstance of the murder was proved by the clearest evidence, but the identity of the culprits only by the testimony of Samuel Whiting, an accomplice. After the verdict both men persisted in declaring their innocence. When sentence of death was pronouncing, and the recorder came to the part mentioning that they were to be dissected and anatomized, Harley burst into tears. It is said that George was lately married, and that his wife is big with child.[2]

Lord Shelburne
by James Sayers
1782

At 1 p.m. his majesty came to St James's for a levee, at which were present lords Weymouth and Germain, Sir William Hamilton (recently arrived from Naples), Mr Burke, &c. His majesty conversed some time with Lord Shelburne upon his improvements at Bowood, and at last asked him somewhat suddenly, what he thought of the Americans? This was so much out of the common turn of the king's conversation with minority lords, that Lord Shelburne hesitated for a moment, but quickly recovering his surprize, replied, 'I think your majesty's troops will not be able to effect what a little condescension would do at once.' 'Why, what is that, my lord?' 'Conquer them, sir. A little mildness would do the business, force never will.' 'Do you use mildness with your tenants, my lord, when they refuse to pay your rents, but threaten to burn their houses down?' And then he turned the conversation, with a laugh, to Dr Priestley's experiments.

After the levee Lord Barrington had a conference with the king and reminded him of his longstanding wish to resign. He confided that his role in the House of Commons created difficulties 'of the most serious kind, as they affected my conscience and my character'.

> 'I have', said I, 'my own opinions in respect to the disputes with America. I give them, such as they are, to ministers in conversation or in writing; I am summoned to meetings, where I sometimes think it my duty to declare them openly, before perhaps twenty or thirty persons; and the next day, I am forced either to vote contrary to them, or to vote with an opposition which I abhor.

I know the use and necessity of practicability, but it may be carried too far.' ... After some pause the king said, 'Why should you not remain for the present in the War Office, and quit the House of Commons; can it be done so as to carry on the parliamentary business of that department?' I said I thought it might, and that, if he pleased, I would open the matter to Lord North. This he approved ...

In the event Lord North took the view that a secretary at war had to sit in the Commons, and Barrington was persuaded to remain in office for another two years.[3]

A youth, the son of a worthy inhabitant of Hoxton, standing to see a cricket match in the Artillery Ground, was struck by the ball on one of his temples. It stunned him, and although he was taken up and so well recovered as to walk home, he died next morning in great agonies, in consequence of the blow.[4]

14th September, Saturday An exceeding bright fine day
At the Old Bailey the trial of William Davis, for a forgery, was put off on the affidavit of himself and two witnesses that a principal evidence of his was out of town. The prosecutor opposed the petition, and acquainted the bench that the day before a most daring attempt had been made at Davis's instigation to kidnap Thomas Slop, who is to be a principal witness against him. Slop was in court and gave the bench an account of the incident.[1]

Mrs Smith, of Queen Ann Street, Cavendish Square, a widow lady near 60 years of age, with a jointure of 3,000l. a year, eloped with her footman, and was married at Marylebone Church. She has left three daughters in her house, all marriageable, and gone into the country with her new husband.[2]

In the evening the season of the Theatre Royal in the Haymarket closed. As soon as the entertainment was over, Mr Foote came forward, bowed respectfully to the audience, and addressed them to the following effect: 'Ladies and gentlemen, as this is the last night that I am permitted to have the honour of appearing before you, 'till the next season, suffer me to make my most grateful acknowledgements for the indulgence you have shewn me, and the protection you have granted to my little theatre.'[3]

15th September, Sunday Heavy morning, very wet afternoon
In the morning, at the George inn in Drury Lane, Mr Pritchard, book-maker, of Russell Court, called to the waiter for a glass of brandy, which having drank, he shot himself with a pistol and died immediately. A second pistol, loaded, was found in his coat pocket. The coroner's inquest sat on the body next day, Monday, and brought in a verdict of lunacy.

This unfortunate young man was one of the most eminent in his business in this metropolis. He began a few years since with a capital of about 1,500l., which was so much increased by his success, and a considerable sum left him by his uncle, that he was shortly after worth as many thousands; but falling into the company of gamblers, and neglecting his business for the amusements of the Garden, his finances were reduced so low as to throw him into fits of despondency. He was in very good spirits on Saturday night at a club of convivial friends, where he was president, from which he went with a female companion.[1]

16th September, Monday Cloudy morning, fine bright afternoon

In the morning Edward George and Robert Harley were executed at Tyburn for the murder of Customs officer Joseph Pearson. About five minutes before they were turned off they declared that Gypsy George, the principal in the murder, paid them a visit in Newgate the Monday before in disguise. The reason they did not discover him at the time was the hopes they had of getting off, for they had been hired by him and had struck Pearson, yet had no intention to commit murder.

A few minutes before eleven they each gave the executioner an handkerchief, which being tied over their faces, they were launched into eternity amidst the lamentations of the crowd. When they had hung a few minutes a young woman got upon a ladder to be stroaked by the hand of a dead man, as a remedy for a wen on her breast. A few minutes before noon the bodies were cut down and conveyed in a coach to Surgeons' Hall for dissection.[1]

Also in the morning, the skull and some of the bones of Mr Tudor, who was missing, and supposed to be burnt at the Goat alehouse in Shire Lane [> 12th], were found among the rubbish.[2]

At the rotation office in Litchfield Street, Ann Adams was re-examined touching the beating, wounding and almost starving to death of her granddaughter Sophia Jane Wilson, a child about seven years old [> 8th]. It appeared that the girl used to work from four in the morning till ten at night. When she was unable to continue it, owing to her cruel treatment, the mother used to send her up stairs with the prisoner, who stripped her naked, and flogged her with a five-string cord tied in knots, till she lay for dead. The cord was produced in court. The child would then be left, sometimes for three days, without any thing to eat. Another girl, almost 10 years old, was produced, whom the women had likewise used in a cruel manner. The life of Sophia Wilson was declared by a surgeon to be still in danger and the grandmother was remanded to prison. The mother will also be remanded in a few days, being nearly recovered of the wound in her throat.[3]

17th September, Tuesday An exceeding wet day

At night, in consequence of an information being given at the office in Litchfield Street, of a great number of pickpockets infesting Leicester Fields, the Haymarket, and parts adjacent, several officers were sent to apprehend them. Five were taken, the eldest of whom was not 14 years of age. One was a boy not seven years old, who has been twice sentenced to transportation, but received his majesty's pardon on account of his youth. Another, about 10 years of age, has been tried eight times at the Old Bailey. They were all committed for one month to hard labour in Clerkenwell Bridewell.[1]

Edward Shuter as Lovegold in Henry Fielding's adaptation of *The Miser*
Published 20th October 1776

18th September, Wednesday Wet morning, fair afternoon
Lord North arrived in town having been absent for several weeks on visits into
Staffordshire, Warwickshire, and Worcestershire.[1]

About twelve o'clock a coach and four, full of goods seized by Customs officers
a few miles from Hyde Park Corner, passed through the city to the Custom House.
It was guarded by ten men, who walked on each side of it with blunderbusses,
carbines, pistols, and other arms.[2]

In the evening *The Miser* was performed at the theatre in the Haymarket for the
benefit of Mr Shuter.* Afterwards he performed the Cries of London, and the whole
concluded with Joe Haines's epilogue, spoken by Mr Shuter riding on an ass.†[3]

GA 'The date of General Howe's last letter (hitherto made public) was the
8th of July from Staten Island, being seventy-two days, within which time we
might have received news from the Cape of Good Hope. Adverse winds cannot
be pleaded for this negligence, as Governor Eden, from Maryland, and several
ships from Quebec, are lately arrived in less than thirty days.'[4]

* While Foote's patent did not allow performances after 15th September, several
actors obtained licences to have benefits after that date.
† Actor Joseph Haines (*d.* 1701) was celebrated for his delivery of prologues and
epilogues, including one epilogue spoken while sitting on an ass.

19th September, Thursday Bright morning and evening, very wet mid-day
A painter was whipped at the cart's tail from the end of Denmark Street to the end of Hog Lane for stealing a quantity of Prussian blue, the property of his employer.[1]

20th September, Friday Clouds and sunshine at intervals, one smart shower
MP 'When good news comes from America it is laid at once before the public, and numerous anecdotes favourable to the ministry circulated with all imaginable industry. When bad news arrives, it is some days before the accounts are sufficiently garbled, to be laid before the public; and it is generally some weeks before half the truth is really known. ... | The following instance will suffice. Sir P. Parker's letter from Charlestown [> 21 Aug] contained the following passage: "It is proper to inform their lordships, that the batteries of the rebels were served with a skill that surprised me, insomuch that they certainly have very experienced engineers among them." This passage administration did not chuse should see the light; for what reason may easily be conjectured.'[1]

    MP 'Lord George Germaine read the declaration of the Congress of independency to the king, who betrayed not the least emotion till he came to that passage, "A prince whose character is thus marked by every act which may define a tyrant, is unfit to be the ruler of a people!" when he changed colour, and cried out, *It is possible, my lord! — and will my kingdoms hear this and not persist till such flagitious rebellion and licentiousness is punished?*'[2]

21st September, Saturday Clouds and sunshine at intervals, one smart shower
In the evening Drury Lane Theatre opened under its new managers, Messrs. Lacy, Sheridan, Ford, and Linley, with a prelude called *New Brooms!* written for the purpose by George Colman. After some compliments to Mr Garrick, the theatre was compared to a stage coach, driven by a new coachman, who has purchased the machine, and promises every possible accommodation to his customers, although he laments that like his brethren of the road, he can't ensure their watches and their purses. Hopkins the prompter noted in his diary that it 'went off with tolerable applause' but was 'much too long'. Afterwards *Twelfth Night* was performed to general applause. Samuel Foote attended and placed himself in the side boxes behind a young gentleman, who no sooner perceived him than desired him to advance, which piece of civility put the wit out of countenance.[1]

22nd September, Sunday Clouds and sunshine at intervals
At 2 a.m. a fire broke out at the house of Messrs. Williams and Co., saddler and harness makers to her majesty, in Great Queen Street, Lincoln's Inn Fields, which entirely destroyed the same, together with the stock in trade, household furniture, wearing apparel, &c. A fellow who attempted to run away with two saddles was detected by a soldier and delivered into the hands of the mob, who tore all his clothes off his back, and dragged him through the kennel till he was almost

suffocated with mud and dirt. A gentleman who was very assiduous in encouraging the firemen had his pocket picked of a gold repeating watch, which cost upwards of 50 guineas, as it is supposed by a decent looking woman who had begged his protection. The young William Blake, serving his apprenticeship, was working and probably living in the street and perhaps witnessed the scene.[1]

23rd September, Monday Clouds and sunshine at intervals
Between two and three o'clock in the morning some villains again endeavoured to break into the house of Justice Penleaze in Hackney Road. They broke the glass of the kitchen window and forced the bolts of the casement, but their entrance was prevented by iron bars and inside shutters. They also tried to break the kitchen door, but this being likewise secured, the noise alarmed the family, guns were immediately fired, the alarm-bell was rung, and the neighbours kindly assembled, but the villains escaped. 'As there is but very little more in the house than books and furniture,' noted the *Morning Chronicle*, 'and this is the third attempt since the robbery, it is to be feared their execrable design was nothing less than murder. The several anonymous letters threatening vengeance against the family plainly evince the probability of this conjecture.'[1]

In the morning, as Lord North was taking an airing in Bushy Park, he was flung from his horse and his arm was broke. Mr Strudwick of Richmond set the broken arm while two other eminent surgeons stood by.[2]

Near 200 invalids home from America were disembarked from transports in the river and marched into quarters about Chelsea, to be examined for admission into that hospital.[3]

Having returned from Paris, Arthur Lee wrote to Charles Dumas, a Swiss based in Holland who was acting there for Congress's committee of secret correspondence:

> By our latest and best accounts from America, the die is now cast, and we may every day expect to hear of a decisive action at New York; decisive I mean as to the fate of General Howe and New York, but not of America, which depends very little upon the event of New York being taken or saved.
>
> There is a public torpor here, which, without being superstitious, one may regard as a visitation from Heaven. The people in general think [of] the Declaration of Independence as a thing of course, and do not seem to feel themselves at all interested in the vast consequences which that event must inevitably draw after it. The ministry have by certain manoeuvres contrived to keep up the demand for and price of manufactures; and while trade and manufactures apparently prosper, the people are so deaf, that wisdom may cry out in the streets and not be heard.[4]

At 7.05 p.m. the king wrote from Windsor to John Robinson, one of Lord North's secretaries at the Treasury: 'I am sincerely affected at the accident that has befallen Lord North, whom I love as well as esteem. I know I can rely on the punctuality of Mr Robinson and therefore desire he will send early enough to Bushy tomorrow morning to know how Lord North has rested that he may send an account for me to Kew by ten o'clock in the morning when one of my servants will as usual bring that and any other parcels for me.' This letter initiated a daily routine for Robinson whereby, during North's convalescence, he visited him first thing each day and then reported on progress to the anxious king.[5]

Marybone Gardens closed for the season with a benefit night for the waiters. According to an advertisement in the *Morning Chronicle*, the entertainments included vaulting on the slack rope, 'Mad Tom by a gentleman', and 'an address to the town, with imitations'. They concluded with 'a magnificent fire work, in twelve divisions, by Sieur Masteaus'. The divisions included a grand salute of maroons;* a capital windmill, 30 feet in diameter; a grand discharge of Roman candles; and a pigeon taking flight and alighting to set fire to 'a most capital erection, called The Palace, which appears beautifully illuminated in slow fire'.[6]

GA 'It is remarkable that there have been more highway robberies committed within the last three weeks, than in any equal space of time for twenty-six years past. However amiable the exercise of mercy, says a correspondent, there can be little doubt but the too frequent pardoning of offenders operates as an encouragement to others.'[7]

24th September, Tuesday A very fine bright day, cloudy evening

Nancy Parsons, one of the most notorious beauties of the age, married Charles, Viscount Maynard at Marylebone Church. He was 25 and she was probably a little over 40. Her other lovers, past and future, included three dukes and two prime ministers.[1]

In the morning the king took the diversion of stag-hunting in Windsor Forest.[2]

25th September, Wednesday A very fine bright day

At 11.07 a.m. John Robinson wrote to inform the king that he had seen Lord North between eight and nine o'clock at Bushy and had found him 'refreshed with a good sleep ... He is quite free from fever and chearful and lively.' He passed on North's 'most humble acknowledgements' for the king's 'kind inquiries after him'.[1]

A protest from the father of errant actress Ann Brown was delivered to the managers of Covent Garden Theatre:

> Gentlemen, My daughter's name being printed in your public bills for performing the part of Leonora in the musical entertainment of *The Padlock* this evening ... without my privity, consent, or approbation, is an unjustifiable proceeding: and I do hereby give you notice, that any engagement entered into between you and my daughter, or any person on her behalf, for performing at your theatre, will not be countenanced by me: and I do hereby forbid and enjoin you, not to permit or suffer her to perform the character aforesaid, or any other

---

* Fireworks designed to make a single loud report like the noise of a cannon, often with a bright flash of light. (*OED*)

R. Ronold pinx.t   *Miss Nancy Parsons.*   R. Housman fecit.

character whatsoever: and I do demand of you my said daughter, and expect, and I insist, that you do not detain her from me on any pretence whatsoever.

In the evening Miss Brown nonetheless appeared as Leonora. When she came on stage she was received with most uncommon applause, which affected her so much she was obliged to be supported by Mr Reinhold, but after a short palpitation she recovered.

She was not alone in being moved. According to the *Morning Post*, 'a gentleman, said to be a captain in the army, was so very much agitated on Miss Brown's appearance ... that it was imagined it would be necessary to convey him out of the house; but a sudden burst of tears released him, and he sat out the farce with tolerable calmness and composure. The gentleman is said to have entertained a passion for that lady last winter, and meant to have asked her hand as a man of honour; but — !'[2]

26th September, Thursday Very wet night, chiefly fair in the day
About 10 a.m. William Eden, Esq., of Downing Street, principal secretary to Lord Suffolk, married Miss Eleanor Elliot, of Great George Street, youngest daughter of Sir Gilbert Elliot, at St Margaret's Church, Westminster. Miss Elliot and the two eldest daughters of Lord North were bridesmaids, and several young people of fashion were likewise present. After the ceremony was over, and the new-married couple had got into their coach, Mr Eden threw a handful of silver among the crowd who surrounded the door in Margaret Street. This created much confusion for a time, several old women being pushed down and trampled under foot.[1]

At 11.25 a.m. John Robinson wrote from Sion Hill to inform the king that he had found Lord North 'in a fine sleep' and that on waking he had been 'chearful, lively, without fever, and in a most hopeful way'. At 11.56 a.m. the king replied from Kew, asking for another account next day as he found the favourable news 'a real cordial'.[2]

27th September, Friday A very bright fine day. Full moon
At 9 a.m. the king and queen, with the Prince of Wales, the Bishop of Osnaburgh, the princess royal, and the Princess Augusta went to Mr Hartley's house upon Wimbledon Common to see a repetition of the experiments for securing houses from fire. They first breakfasted in one of the rooms, the tea-kettle being boiled on a fire made on the floor of the opposite room, which the king and queen afterwards went into, and saw the bed set on fire. Their majesties gave the greatest attention to every experiment, and expressed the utmost satisfaction. The whole was concluded by lighting a large magazine of faggots, pitch, and tar, in the same room which had undergone this trial twice before. It burnt out with an amazing fury, but had no effect at all upon the room over. Their majesties, the princes, and the princesses went up there while the room below was burning with the greatest violence.[1]

Miss Catley being announced in the bills for the part of Polly in *The Beggar's Opera*, after two years' absence, all the avenues to Covent Garden Theatre were filled some time before the doors were opened, and the house was much crouded before the curtain drew. She was received with repeated bursts of applause and warbled all her songs away with a peculiar taste and strict musical precision. In the song of which the line 'All the night we'll kiss and play' is a part, she gave a specimen of her old wantonness, which was highly relished by the majority of the audience, but received with disapprobation by the more serious and solid. A gentleman who sat in the king's box, seeing the house extremely crowded, said that Miss Catley had certainly found the philosophical stone, since it was in her power to change her *brass* into gold.

Mrs Green, in the part of Mrs Slammekin, had her head ornamented in the fullest extravagance of the modern fashion, and the audience applauded so fair a piece of ridicule. Mrs Mattocks was well received as Lucy, but, according to the *Morning Chronicle*, erred in having her cry. 'Lucy is (if we may borrow a word from the Newgate *Vade Mecum* ...) a wench of too much *spunk* to shed tears for a fellow; she'd rather have made Macheath cry by giving him a smart dowse in the chops, than have cried herself.'[2]

MP 'They write from Worcester, that the mobility of that *truly patriotic* city, in compliment to their unsuccessful candidate,* treated Lord North upon his arrival there, at the late music meeting, with an audacity not to be paralleled. They threw dirt at his carriage, and some say, carried a halter before it, uttering the most insulting invectives that malice, or modern *patriotism* could invent. His lordship, however, received their insolence with that firmness and composure which strongly mark his character, and defeated their intent, not even expressing the least surprize, or disapprobation of their extraordinary conduct.'[3]

28th September, Saturday Wet morning, fine bright day

At Guildhall Sir Thomas Halifax was elected lord mayor for the year ensuing.[1]

Lord George Germain received several letters from America. In one, dated 6th August at Staten Island, General Howe reported that 'we are in force sufficient to enter upon offensive operations; but I am detained by the want of camp-equipage, particularly kettles and canteens, so essential in the field, and without which too much is to be apprehended on the score of health'. He added that, as expected, he had found 'the principal force of the rebels assembled at New-York, from whence to dislodge them, it will require our collected strength'. A second letter, dated 11th August, from Howe and his brother, was accompanied by a printed copy of the Declaration of Independence, and concluded with their frank assessment that they saw 'no prospect of a disposition in those who now hold the

* Sir Watkin Lewes. For the disputed Worcester election see 30th January and 4th April.

supreme authority over the colonies to make any advances towards a reconciliation with Great Britain'.[2]

In the evening lamps placed along the road from the end of Gray's Inn Lane, through Kentish Town to Highgate, were lit for the first time. The posts are twenty-five yards apart, and at every eighth post a watch-box is to be erected, where a guard, armed with a blunderbuss and cutlass, is to stand. According to the *Morning Chronicle*, 'This road may therefore now be travelled at all hours in safety.'[3]

29th September, Sunday Exceeding bright morning, cloudy afternoon
By express from Dover, Lord Weymouth received a letter written by Lord Stormont in Paris four days earlier:

> Mr Cyrus Deane ... is certainly in constant intercourse with Beaumarchais who was lately not worth a shilling but has now millions at his command. He keeps a table and entertains Deane and other Americans, and friends to their cause. He is likewise, as I am well assured, in regular correspondence with Mr Wilkes. Their letters are not trusted to the post but sent by private hands. When I learnt this I immediately suspected that Wilkes is not the only person in England with whom Beaumarchais corresponds. My suspicion is right, there are several other persons. I do not yet know their names, but hope to get them soon.

He added that Deane was trying to recruit former French officers to join the rebel army. 'He bribes high and has engaged several. Some have refused. This Court cannot be a stranger to these manoeuvres of Deane, and no doubt is glad to wink at them.'[1]

This being the tenth birth-day of Charlotte, the princess royal, their majesties received the compliments of the nobility, &c. at Windsor. In honour of the occasion a grand ball was held at Kew next day for the young nobility of both sexes.[2]

30th September, Monday Very fine bright day
The Beggar's Opera was performed again at Covent Garden Theatre to an over-flowing house. Miss Catley now played Lucy. Ann Brown joined the cast as Polly and was highly praised. 'The amazing progress which this little Syren has made ... may serve as a proof to confute the impertinence of those whimsical connoisseurs, who pretend that an English pipe cannot attain the perfection of an Italian singer' (*Gazetteer*). 'We confess ourselves so highly pleased with her last night's perform-ance, that we could almost venture to pronounce her, not only a complete woman, but an accomplished actress' (*Morning Chronicle*). The *London Magazine* was not so impressed: 'Miss Brown ... filled the cells of Newgate with all the affected quavers and warblings of a first serious signora at the opera-house.'

Mrs Green dressed Mrs Slammekin more *outré* about the head than ever, having six large pink streamers flowing from her enormous head-dress down to the ground. Her *entrée* caused a roar of some minutes through every part of the house.[1]

Queen Charlotte and her eldest daughter the princess royal,
after a painting by Benjamin West, 1776

Meanwhile in America

11th September. A polite but fruitless peace conference took place on Staten Island between representatives of Congress, including Benjamin Franklin and John Adams, and Lord Howe.[1]

15th September. British troops landed at Kipp's Bay and took possession of New York.[2]

16th September. The American army defeated the British at the battle of Harlem Heights. In a letter four days later Washington downplayed it as 'a pretty sharp skirmish', but added that it had 'inspirited our troops prodigiously'.[3]

19th September. The Howe brothers issued a declaration designed to impress upon Americans that their own leaders were the main obstacle to peace.[4]

21st September. Shortly after midnight a fire broke out in New York, destroying about a quarter of the town.[5]

22nd September. Nathaniel Hale, an American spy, was hanged in New York by the British.[6]

26th September. Benjamin Franklin, Thomas Jefferson, and Silas Deane were chosen as commissioners from Congress to the Court of France.[7]

30th September. General Howe issued a proclamation of pardon for all 'deserters from his majesty's service' who should surrender on or before 31st October.[8]

October

1st October, Tuesday A heavy dull day, no sun appeared

Part of the common sewer fell in of a sudden in Titchfield Street, Oxford Road. A cart which was passing at the time fell in, but luckily the horses were taken out without much damage.[1]

At 3.20 p.m. the king wrote from Windsor to John Robinson: 'Words cannot be found of force enough to express the joy I feel at the opinion of the surgeons on changing the bandage upon Lord North's arm. ... I desire to have a letter on the same interesting subject tomorrow at Kew.'[2]

The *Morning Post* printed an enquiry from 'an old correspondent' casting doubt on the morals and motives of the father of actress Ann Brown. Referring to Mr Brown's recent notice to the managers of Covent Garden Theatre [> 25 Sep], the writer asked whether his intention was 'to procure a larger share of the fruits of her labour than the 100l. a year which he asked, and she dutifully agreed to give last winter? Or does paternal piety *just now* prompt him to desire his daughter's company in his own house, that her morals may improve under the excellent example set her there? — How many maid servants does this virtuous gentleman keep?'[3]

2nd October, Wednesday A fine bright pleasant day

In the morning, a journeyman apothecary not coming down stairs at his usual hour, the servant maid went up to call him. She found him hanging in his bed-chamber, with a slip of paper on a table, on which was written in very large letters, 'Not a lunatic.'[1]

In the afternoon Mr Cutler, butler to the dowager Duchess of Portland in Privy Gardens, went out at the garden to the water side. He set himself down at the side of a barge, discharged a pistol underneath his right ear, and fell backward into the Thames, from whence he was taken out dead by a waterman, who heard the pistol and saw him fall. Two letters were found in his pockets, but they did not assign any reason for this rash action. He died worth upwards of 950l. A large box of insects he left to her grace, in which he said she was very curious. At night the jury sat on the body at the King's Arms in Cannon Row, and brought in a verdict of lunacy.

In a letter four days later Mrs Delany wrote that the 'sad accident' had been 'a great shock' to the dowager duchess, adding, 'No cause can be asign'd but insanity. He was a sober honest man, but of a melancholly turn.'[2]

3rd October, Thursday A heavy dull day

LEP 'The letters received in town by the *Sandwich* packet from the officers of the detachment of the guards, dated from Staten Island, inveigh most bitterly against the infamy of the contractors, who victualled the transports; all kinds of animal provisions being in a state of putrefaction before they made Halifax, after a voyage of two months, and their biscuit being almost eaten up by the maggots.'[1]

4th October, Friday A heavy dull day, bright evening

About half past five o'clock an uproar was created in Bow Street, in consequence of Mr Brown's attempting to seize his daughter at the end of the play-house passage. The little syren came in a hackney coach, accompanied by her aunt, and was dressed for the part of Polly. Her father, attended by one Mr Stacey, insisted on her going home with him, but on the runaway crying 'Murder,' and the aunt saying Mr Brown was mad, the mob came to their rescue. The alarm presently reached the play-house, and the theatrical garrison sallied out in great numbers. The thieves in *The Beggar's Opera*, armed with pistols, &c. made a formidable appearance, and the crowd was so numerous that for a time the street was impassable. At length the lady was handed into the theatre in triumph.

The moment she came on stage during the play she burst into a flood of tears, and fell into Mr Wilson's arms in a swoon. After she was taken off, Mr Hull came on, and acquainted the audience, 'that the young lady's sudden illness arose from an alarm she had met with about an hour before, but that she was nearly recovered, and would appear in a few minutes to go through her part,' which she accordingly did. Notwithstanding her agitation, she performed to the satisfaction of the audience, who received her with repeated shouts of applause.[1]

5th October, Saturday A heavy dull day, moist evening

At 2.43 p.m. the king wrote from Kew to tell John Robinson that he could 'discontinue his daily accounts of Lord North's health as he is now so far recovered. I intend about Tuesday to call on Lord North at Bushy as I trust by that time he will not suffer by a visit.'[1]

6th October, Sunday An exceeding fine bright day

Westminster Abbey was opened for divine service, having been shut up sixteen months and fourteen days in order to erect a new choir and make other necessary repairs.[1]

In the afternoon, as a gentleman of Fleet Street was coming with friends from Canonbury House, he picked up a paper by the side of the New River, on which the following was written in red chalk: 'I hope the world will excuse me for this rash act. I cannot live under the aspersions wickedly thrown upon me. My wife has accused me with the most abominable of all crimes, which, as I am shortly to appear in the presence of the Almighty, I declare I am innocent of.' From a man's hat having been found near the spot by a cow-keeper the same morning, it is presumed the unhappy writer had put a period to his existence.[2]

7th October, Monday Frost early, bright morning, coarse wet afternoon
The *Morning Post* published a long letter to the editor from G. Stacey in response
to its report of the attempted abduction of Ann Brown near Covent Garden Theatre.
The paper had named Stacey as assisting Mr Brown and he now gave his side of
the story.

> Mr Brown and myself were overtaken by Miss B. in a coach in Hart-street,
> where we were confessedly waiting for her coming to the theatre. She was
> attended by the most infamous of her own sex, and the just contempt of ours
> (O! shocking to relate) her own aunt! who, dead, to all the ties of consanguinity
> and humanity, personally sacrificed the innocence of her own niece to a v—.
> Mr B. very tenderly desired her to go with him, which she refused in such
> language, as would disgrace the most abandoned prostitute.
>
> He then (with my assistance) forcibly took her into the fishmonger's shop
> the corner of Bow-street, where we were soon surrounded by an impertinent
> mob, several of whom, I verily believe, were suborn'd for that purpose ... So
> circumstanc'd, Mr B. was prevailed on to accompany his daughter to the theatre,
> where he left her to impose on the credulity of the public ...
>
> No man is more sensible of the honours his daughter has received from an
> indulgent public, and it would be his greatest happiness would she still deserve
> it, but he is determined not to see her perform in public, whilst she lives in a
> state of prostitution with Andrews; neither will a British audience ever receive
> any pleasure from a performer (however excellent) when they know it is at the
> expence of a parent.
>
> That I assisted Mr B. in the recovery of his daughter last night, as well as
> the time she eloped before, is most true. I boast it, proclaim it to the world ...[1]

MP 'Mrs Abington has at length signed and sealed a theatrical engagement
with the new managers of Drury-lane, after the extraordinary promises, and transactions of the last season. *Frailty, thy name is* WOMAN!'[2]

8th October, Tuesday Dull morning, coarse wet afternoon
At Bushy Park, according to his wife Anne, Lord North 'was a good deal fatigued ...
as he got up earlier than usual expecting the king to come about ten o'clock, but
he did not come till one when the queen came with him and they stay'd here till
half an hour after four. The king insisted on Lord North's sitting in his great chair;
indeed it wou'd have been quite impossible for him to have stood all the time.'
According to Horace Walpole, 'It was thought that Lord North had a mind to
resign; and at the beginning of the month the king and queen went to him at Bushy,
and staid with him three hours, as it was supposed, to prevail on him not to quit.'[1]
    The king wrote from Kew to John Robinson with guidance as to the drafting
of the speech for the opening of parliament at the end of the month. 'Some delicacy
may be necessary in stating the foreign article of the speech, but as to the American,
[what is needed is] a firm and manly determination of a thorough exertion of every
nerf to bring the rebellious collonies to submission, and some spirited expressions

to draw forth the resolution of the landed interest to make them chearfully contribute to what so nearly concerns them.'[2]

Having decided to sell his theatre patent, Samuel Foote had a meeting with an intermediary, John Colborne, not yet knowing the identity of the intended purchaser. Afterwards Colborne wrote to George Colman, who had previously managed Covent Garden Theatre and for whom he was acting. 'It is now near ten o'clock, and I am but just come from Mr Foote, with whom I think we shall soon settle this business, should the proceedings of the day meet your approbation.' The plan, subsequently agreed, was that Foote should receive £1,600 each year during his life.[3]

The word war over Miss Brown continued in the *Morning Post*:

> A correspondent who was an accidental spectator of the brutal violence exercised in Hart-street, on Friday last, wonders how any one can assert so many falsities as the writer of a letter in yesterday's paper ventured to do. The unhappy young lady therein mention'd instead of the Billingsgate language ascribed to her, did indeed with tears resent the unnatural and unmanly treatment of her father, in thus dragging her a second time like a criminal thro' the streets, taxed him with his conduct at home, and roundly charged him with the various methods he had made use of to obtain money for her talents, her inexperience and her errors; and convinced an astonished and compassionate multitude, that the steps then taken proceeded from motives that disgrace humanity.[4]

9th October, Wednesday Very bright morning, cloudy afternoon

A bull was baited in Tottenham Court Road. The beast was no sooner chained, and the dogs let loose at him, than he pulled up the stake, which was but slightly put in the ground, and set off amongst the numerous spectators, several of whom were run over, and some much hurt.[1]

At the public office in Bow Street a boy was ordered to be publickly whipped for stealing pears out of an orchard at Fulham.[2]

William Hopkins, prompter at Drury Lane Theatre, was told by actor George Mattocks that one of the owners, Willoughby Lacy, 'had sold half his share of the patent' to a Mr Langford and a Captain Thomson. 'I acquainted Mr Sheridan of it,' noted Hopkins in his diary. 'He had not heard.' In fact a sale was planned but had not yet come to pass.[3]

10th October, Thursday Heavy dull day

By 3 a.m. Major Cuyler, first aide-de-camp to General Howe, arrived at Lord George Germain's bearing a letter from Howe dated 3rd September at Newtown, Long Island. It told of the unopposed landing of British and Hessian troops on 22nd August and of the subsequent rout of the rebels at the battle of Long Island. 'The enemy is still in possession of the town and island of New York, in force,' Howe noted, 'and making demonstration of opposing us in their works on both sides of King's Bridge. | The inhabitants of this island, many of whom had been

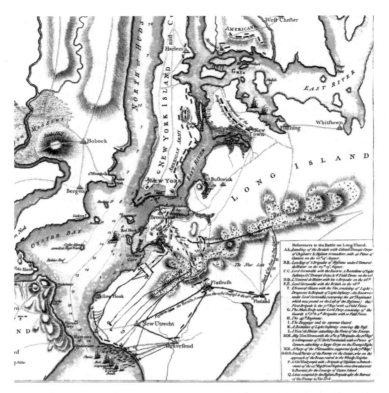

Plan of New York and the surrounding area, showing the recent action on Long Island. Published by William Faden, Charing Cross, 19th October 1776.

forced into rebellion, have all submitted, and are ready to take the oaths of allegiance.' Losses on the American side were computed to be 'about 3300 killed, wounded, prisoners, and drowned; with five field pieces, and one howitzer taken'. Among the king's troops 61 had been killed, 257 wounded, and 'one officer and twenty grenadiers of the marines taken by mistaking the enemy for the Hessians'.

According to the *Morning Post*, 'The moment the happy tidings ... was confirmed ... on 'Change, it is impossible to express the joy that beamed on every countenance'. The *Morning Chronicle* added: 'Nothing could equal the buz and hurry ... Some forgot their appointments, some their dinners, and some almost themselves. In short, Cornhill, from the many groups of male gossips, was for some time utterly impassable to persons on foot.'

Writing to a friend, Edmund Burke was not so sanguine: 'Here is terrible news in town for the poor Americans. It would be a consolation if I could call it good for this country.'

Howe's letter was published in a *London Gazette Extraordinary* the same day. According to Walpole, it 'much changed the state of affairs, and filled the Court with an extravagance of joy, which they displayed with the utmost ostentation'.[1]

*News from America, or the Patriots
in the Dumps.*

The Court's ostentatious joy as referred to by Horace Walpole. With Lord
Mansfield beside him, and Lord Bute and the king behind, Lord North shows
off news of British victory. In the foreground on the right Lord Sandwich points
to his nose as he looks across to the dismayed 'patriots', among whom, in the
foreground, is John Wilkes. From the *London Magazine* for November 1776.

In the evening a genteelly dressed woman applied to the driver of one of the Bath stages, which stopped at Brentford, to bring her to town. She got into the carriage, in which was a gentleman, his wife and child; but pretending to recollect some business she had to transact at Kensington, she was set down there, and took leave of her companions with great ceremony. A short time after, however, the gentleman discovered she had picked his pocket of a silver watch, and the lady that she had lost her pocket case and a gold snuff box. The description of the culprit sent to Bow Street corresponds with the noted Miss West.[2]

11th October, Friday Heavy dull day, with some bright intervals
In the morning a council was held at Lord North's, Bushy Park, at which all the cabinet ministers near town assisted.[1]

In the afternoon a bullock, maddened by the brutality of his drivers, broke away from them in Oxford Street. Taking towards the fields he went over hedges and ditches until he reached Hampstead, where his pursuers overtook him, shackled him with cords, and brought him to town again, no less than twelve men guiding him with ropes affixed to his horns, and eight others with ropes to his tail and legs. Notwithstanding these incumbrances, he tossed and threw down upwards of twenty persons during his rural excursion. In Poland Street he ran into a coachmaker's shop, where, assisted by the mob, he is said to have broke glasses worth upwards of £50. He likewise broke the glasses of a hackney coach which was going by, and tossed several barrows and baskets of fruit before he reached Carnaby Market.[2]

In the evening Edward Oxnard and two fellow Americans went to see *Love in a Village* at Covent Garden Theatre, with Ann Catley in the part of Rosetta. 'She is by far the best singer that I have as yet seen on the stage,' he noted in his diary. 'She has a most melodious voice united with great judgement. Her person is genteel, her manner the most wanton I ever beheld. Notwithstanding her behaviour is so disgusting, the audience are exceeding fond of her and always receive her with marks of applause.'[3]

During the performance several persons in the gallery had their pockets picked. Henry Smallwood, the constable, soon after discovered the notorious Miss West upon the stairs. Saying 'You must come along with me,' he took her to Bow Street, where, on searching her, a guinea, a half guinea, and a cornelian stone were found. John Wilson, seal-maker, who had been robbed in the play-house, swore to the stone and Miss West was committed to Tothill Fields Bridewell. Several guineas and a watch were found on the gallery stairs at the theatre, which it is supposed this ingenious lady dropped for fear of detection. Re-examined next morning at Bow Street, she denied the charge, but desired to be committed to Newgate so that her innocence might the sooner appear from her being tried at the approaching sessions.[4]

At Drury Lane Theatre, Sheridan was convinced that everything had been done with respect to the sale of part of Lacy's share of the patent, 'except the actually

'The Unwelcome Customer'. After a painting by John Collet. Published 1772.

having executed the deeds'. Expecting that to occur next day, Saturday, he decided that his only recourse 'was to convince those who were to find the money, that they were going to embark their property on a vessel that was on flames, and at the same time to let Lacy see that, by thus dividing his share, he would ruin the whole of it'.

Lacy appeared at the morning rehearsal to tell Sheridan he could not be put off from the sale. Sheridan replied that if it went ahead he would withdraw from the management of the theatre. Later, after consulting Garrick, he wrote a long letter to the intended purchasers, Langford and Thompson, 'stating the injustice and illegality of the business, and informing them of my determination if they persisted in it'. His solicitor, Albany Wallis, delivered the letter to Langford before five o'clock.

At eight o'clock Sheridan sent prompter Hopkins to Lacy with formal written notice 'to provide for the business and management by himself. He scarcely believed till then that I would actually do this, and sent Hopkins back to me, &c., but as I would not talk even relative to the theatre, he returned to L. who was in great confusion.' Sheridan told Hopkins that from now on he was to take his orders from Lacy and that he was withdrawing his adaptation of a farce, *The Christmas Tale*, due to be performed next day, it being his property. As Hopkins noted in his diary, 'This put us all into confusion.' He 'sent to Mrs Abington to know if she would play in *The Hypocrite*', the other piece planned for Saturday. 'Her answer was that she had made her agreement with Mr Sheridan only, and would play under no other manager.' Only at midnight was a replacement main piece, *Richard the Third*, settled on and advertising bills sent accordingly.[5]

12th October, Saturday A fine grey day

At Drury Lane Theatre, Sheridan continued to play his hand well in the conflict with Lacy, Langford, and Thompson:

> Hopkins found them all three in great confusion and perturbation, Mr Langford particularly, on hearing from H. that he did not think he could keep the house open a week. However, T. spirited them as much as possible to stand to the business; but (as I suppose Langford began to have qualms about advancing the money) it was determined to try what a civil letter to me would do, which they sent hoping to be friendly, with a compliment to my abilities and so forth; and at night, and again on Sunday morning, Lacy sent by Hopkins to entreat I would return to the management ... As I ... felt on what secure ground I stood, I still declined hearing any thing on the subject ...[1]

LC 'One Mary Barnes has, for some time past, robbed on the highway. She rides a bay mare of the race breed, and dresses in a green coat and waistcoat and leather breeches.'[2]

13th October, Sunday A fine grey day

The leading actors at Drury Lane Theatre demonstrated their support for Sheridan, as Hopkins noted in his diary: 'On Sunday morning Mrs Yates sent word that she was ill and could not play. Sent to Miss Younge and she sent word that she was ill in bed. Mr King sent word he had a sore throat and could not play — so that we could do no play but *The Committee* and *Rival Candidates*.' Even this proved optimistic, for at noon on Monday 'Mrs Baddeley sent word she had a sore throat and could not play in *The Rival Candidates*.'[1]

14th October, Monday Cloudy heavy day

A woman was whipped round Covent Garden for stealing walnuts from several persons in that market. Another woman was whipped at the cart's tail through Petty France for stripping several children for their clothes.[1]

His majesty took an airing on horseback in the vicinity of Richmond and Kew, and afterwards paid a visit to Lord North at Bushy, where he staid upwards of two hours.[2]

About 3 p.m. John Colborne presented Samuel Foote with amended articles for the purchase of his theatre patent. It was agreed that Colborne would bring the mystery purchaser to dine with Foote on Friday at four.[3]

In the evening a man locked up his wife and two children in a room in a house in Spitalfields and set the house on fire. The cries of the woman alarmed the neighbours, and the flames were happily extinguished in time. The man was later taken into custody in Brewer Street.[4]

15th October, Tuesday Bright morning, cloudy afternoon, with a little rain

Sheridan wrote to Garrick about the troubles at Drury Lane Theatre, noting that he and his fellow purchasers of Garrick's share of the patent 'were to-day very friendly together, and received ... Mr Lacy's word that he would never part with his share, or any part of it, but to us'. He went on:

> I have seen none of the performers (purposely) except Mr Smith and Mr King, who called on me in Orchard-street, since the affair happened. King has acted particularly well. However, from one motive or other, almost all the principal performers declined playing, on various pretences; even one or two, who I believe he [Lacy] thought would stand forward, have been taken ill: indeed there never was known such an uncommonly epidemic disorder as has raged among our unfortunate company; it differs from the plague by attacking the better sort first; the manner too in which they are seized, I am told, is very extraordinary; many who were in perfect health at one moment, on receiving a billet from the prompter to summon them to their business, are seized with sudden qualms, and, before they can get through the contents, are absolutely unfit to leave their rooms; so that Hopkins's notes seem to operate like what we hear of Italian poisoned letters, which strike with sickness those to whom they are addressed.[1]

Meanwhile Hopkins himself noted in his diary: 'All the business of the theatre is at a stand and no rehearsal call'd.'[2]

16th October, Wednesday Thick fog in the morning, moist misling day

At about 9 p.m. Lacy met with Sheridan and two of the other Drury Lane patent owners. According to prompter Hopkins, 'everything was settled' to their mutual satisfaction 'and a paragraph sent to the papers'.[1]

17th October, Thursday Constant rain almost all day

Twenty-one prisoners were tried at the Old Bailey, six of whom were capitally convicted, including John Harding for a burglary in the dwelling house of Peter Bean at Brentford [> 25 Aug, 9 Sep]. At about ten o'clock Elizabeth West was tried for stealing several items at Covent Garden Theatre [> 11th]. After a trial of four hours the judge, Mr Baron Eyre, in his charge told the jury that the possession was merely a circumstantial evidence, and leaned with great tenderness in the prisoner's favour. The jury, after consulting a few minutes, pronounced her not guilty, a verdict at which she seemed equally surprized and delighted. She was decently dressed with her high head in a plain cap, a black silk cloak, and light blue silk gown, and behaved with modesty and resolution, curtseying both on entering the court and leaving it.[1]

18th October, Friday A very bright fine day
In the morning a duel was fought in Hyde Park between a gentleman of Doctors' Commons and an officer. After a few passes the former was dangerously wounded in the arm, but insisted on deciding the affair on the spot with pistols. The officer complied, and in his turn was wounded also, which finished the combat. The dispute concerned American affairs.[1]

Also in the morning, the Countess of Derby was safely delivered of a daughter at his lordship's house in Grosvenor Square.[2]

At 10 a.m., before Sir William Blackstone at the Old Bailey, William Davis was tried for the forgery of a warrant with intent to defraud Samuel Drybutter. Thomas Slop, the young clerk violently seized to prevent his appearance against Davis last sessions, declared that Davis had desired him to copy the name of Benjamin Barbaud, and indorse it on the back of several East India Company warrants, telling him that Barbaud had gone to America without indorsing the warrants, and that the writing his name on them was a mere matter of form. In his defence the prisoner declared he had long dealt as a purchaser of drugs, spices, &c. and was entirely innocent of any intention to defraud. Upwards of twenty witnesses were called to his character. All of them spoke highly in his favour, and one, Josiah Dornford, wine merchant, declared he heard Slop say upon 'Change that he would hang the prisoner if he could. Nonetheless the jury brought in their verdict guilty.[3]

Lord George Germain wrote from Pall Mall to Lord Howe in America:

> The Congress is using every possible means to induce France to espouse their cause, and the naval preparations making there must raise suspicions here ... What effect the late victory will have upon the French councils, we have not yet heard; what we perceived here was that the Spanish ambassador shewed the greatest satisfaction at our success, whilst the French minister looked disappointed and dejected.
>
> The Declaration of Independency has staggered many of the former advocates for America. Among others I hear Lord Camden says there is no supporting the Americans upon their present ground. Indeed the leaders of the rebellion have acted as I could have wished, and I trust that the deluded people will soon have recourse to your lordship for mercy and protection, leaving their chiefs to receive the punishment they deserve.[4]

George Colman
after a portrait
by Reynolds
circa 1770

George Colman wrote from his house in Soho Square to Samuel Foote, finally revealing that he was the intended purchaser of the theatre patent:

> My dear Foote, When I quitted Covent Garden, I never thought of attending to a theatre any more ... But having been told by several of our acquaintance that you had lately signified your wish to find a purchaser, and even gone so far as to name your price, I ... thought I might, without indelicacy or impertinence, inquire if you were serious. For this purpose I sent Mr Colborne to you; and though I am not so playhouse mad as not to feel the largeness of the sum he has agreed to on my behalf, nor so vain as to be unconscious of the many superior advantages you possessed, yet I shall, without much fear and trembling, put the last hand to the bargain ...

Colborne and the two principals later dined together at Foote's villa at North End.[5]

At Drury Lane the restoration of theatrical order was celebrated with Mrs Abington's first appearance of the season, playing Charlotte in *The Hypocrite*. According to the *Morning Post*, 'She was received with the warmest, and we may add, most deserved applause, as she is confessedly, in the comic line, the principal ornament of the British stage.'[6]

Meanwhile at Brighthelmstone, Dr Johnson ventured into the sea for the first time during a stay of some six weeks. He wrote to a friend in London that he planned to go in again most of the following week, 'though I know not that it does me any good'.[7]

19th October, Saturday Some showers, but a fine day

About 4 p.m. came on before Mr Baron Eyre at the Old Bailey the trial of Richard Arnold, wine cooper, of St Dunstan's Court, St Dunstan's Hill, for assaulting and ravishing Elizabeth Russ, his maid servant, on 14th September. The prosecutrix was led into court between two of her friends, and not being able to support herself standing, was permitted to sit while she gave a very circumstantial account of the transaction.

> 'I met my master in the landing-place of the stairs. He took me in his arms. I said, "What be you going to do with me?" He said, "No harm." Upon that I cried out "Murder." He carried me up stairs into the second room, my mistress's bed-room. I struggled with him from one bed-post to the other. I told him I would die or lose my life before I would yield to him, and I would cry out again. I struggled as long as I had any strength in me. He took me by the two shoulders with my hands behind me, and threw me down upon the bed. After he laid me on the bed, I cried "Murder," and struggled as long as I could, till I went into a fainting fit; and then he lay with me. ... I felt him in my body, and felt something come from him, but I know not what. ... After he had lain with me, he violently ran his hand up my body. I felt his hand and fingers in my body. He hurt me very much. I shrieked out, and said I was almost dead. After that he went down stairs, and I went into my own bed-room ... I was obliged to pull my linen off ... because it was so bad with blood.'

She told of her subsequent accusation against Arnold and of being examined by a doctor. As she remained weak, on the following Thursday 'another strange doctor ... grown out a little in his back' arrived.

> 'I never saw him before. He said I must go, and dragged me down three pair of stairs to the lower pair of stairs. I said he would kill me. My legs were under me, sometimes before me, and sometimes behind. The coach was standing at the door. They put me into the coach and carried me to Walworth, and my mistress went in the coach to see where I was. I was there a week, and the doctor that took me there attended me twice or three times a day.'

Parts of her testimony were confirmed by several witnesses, and upon the close of her narration she fell into a convulsion. Her account was, however, contradicted by other witnesses including two surgeons. Mr Thomas Smith, of St Thomas's Hospital, said he had examined her on 26th September and found 'not the least inflammation, extension, or laceration; so far from the hand entering, there was scarce room to enter my little finger into her private parts'. When the judge had finished his charge, the lord mayor read a paper to the jury listing several contradictions between the prosecutrix's then testimony and that which she had delivered upon her examination before him at Guildhall. Upon this, and the depositions of the surgeons, the jury found the prisoner not guilty. The trial lasted four hours.[1]

In the evening a boy about 12 years of age was found dead in the cow-house in Park Lane, near Hyde Park Corner. He belonged to the owner of the cows.[2]

20th October, Sunday Fair morning, wet afternoon

In the morning Lord Sandwich met with Sir Hugh Palliser to consider alarming reports of French armaments. Afterwards he wrote to Lord North: 'I must tell your lordship that every hour is precious, as the French are certainly greatly ahead in their preparations, and I dread the consequence of their being at sea before us.' He asked if he and Palliser might wait on North 'to talk the matter over and to consider what is advisable to be done'.[1]

21st October, Monday Moist heavy morning, bright afternoon

At night upwards of 400 persons attended the Robin Hood Society for a debate concerning John Molesworth, a well known 'lottery calculator' who claimed to have invented a mathematical method for selecting ticket numbers which had a greater than average chance of winning prizes (see Plate 22). The question was, 'Whether Mr Molesworth's calculations upon lotteries were of advantage to adventurers, or an imposition upon the credulity of the public.' It was almost unanimously resolved that the calculations were beneficial to the public, a decision which was received with loud applause.[1]

22nd October, Tuesday Cloudy day, with a good deal of rain

MC 'The difference between the managers of Covent Garden Theatre, and Miss Brown's father, is, we hear, happily adjusted. The town therefore may expect to see their favourite again in a night or two.'[1]

23rd October, Wednesday A very heavy moist day

Three convicts were executed at Tyburn, viz. William Wood and Charles Pipkins for housebreaking, and Robert Walker for coining. Walker was drawn on a hurdle. Wood was dressed in his best cloaths, viz. a plain chocolate-coloured coat, white cloth waistcoat, white silk stockings, &c., his linen clean, and his hair powdered. Pipkins wore an old soldier's coat and was otherwise in a wretched plight.[1]

Reports circulated that news had arrived of the taking of New York. 'Heard that Genl. Howe landed at York on the 15th Sept.,' noted Edward Oxnard in his diary. 'The provincials endeavouring to gain a retreat met with great slaughter.' Later he shared the news with several fellow refugees, prompting 'great joy'. *Lloyd's Evening Post* reported the story, wrongly saying New York had been taken on 18th September. Official advice of the event would not arrive for another ten days.[2]

Lord North was visited at Bushy by a cousin, John St John, who found him 'perfectly well and indeed I think the better for his accident, for it has reduced him very much and made him look a great deal better than usual'.[3]

As Mr Jolly, pump-maker, was repairing a pump at the Peacock brew-house in Whitecross Street, he fell into a copper of boiling wort, and was scalded in so miserable a manner that he died soon after in great agonies.[4]

The mask of *Comus* and the entertainment of *The Golden Pippin* were performed at Covent Garden Theatre for the benefit of Miss Catley. The demand for box places being uncommonly great, most part of the pit was laid into the boxes. This manoeuvre not having been advertised occasioned a riot, which was however appeased by Miss Catley making an apology in the handsomest manner.[5]

In the evening the Marquis de Noailles, ambassador extraordinary from the Court of Versailles, arrived at the French ambassador's house in Whitehall.[6]

MP 'A French war is now talked of with an air of confidence, that has converted many unbelievers. Mr Charles Fox, the other day, offered a bet of 5000 pounds, that war was formally declared between Great Britain and that nation, before the expiration of six months.'[7]

24th October, Thursday Chiefly cloudy, but fair

Rumours of the capture of New York continued. The *Morning Chronicle* reported that an express from General Howe had arrived the morning before and been taken to the king at St James's. In the evening a letter was read out at New Lloyd's Coffee-house, purporting to be from Joseph Cheeseman, master of his majesty's ship *Galatea*. It gave the correct date of 15th September for the taking of the city, but was wrong about more or less everything else, including saying that General Washington had lost an arm. On the 28th it was reported that the letter's handwriting had been found to agree exactly with that in other letters from Cheeseman, but by the 30th the letter was being attributed to 'a certain Middlesex justice'.[1]

MP 'The rebels have spies in all the coffee-houses, where they procure intelligence of ships fitting out, destination, time of sailing, value of cargo, number of men and guns; the same with respect to ships homeward bound; they insinuate themselves into the company of insurance brokers clerks, who unguardedly furnish these spies with every particular.'[2]

25th October, Friday Chiefly bright, dry air

This being the anniversary of the king's accession to the throne, the morning was ushered in with the ringing of bells. At one o'clock the guns in the park and at the Tower were fired, at which their majesties came from the Queen's Palace to St James's, where there was a brilliant levee attended by many nobility of the first rank and all the foreign ministers. The Marquis de Noailles was introduced to the king by the master of the ceremonies. In the evening there were illuminations and other public demonstrations of joy in London and Westminster.[1]

Edward Oxnard went with two other refugees to see the park guns fired. They proceeded to the guard room of St James's Palace 'to see the company go to the levee', among whom were 'some of the handsomest women I have seen in England'. Heading home an hour or so later, just as they entered St James's Park they noticed a coach in which were the Prince of Wales and the Bishop of Osnaburgh. 'Went back and got so near the door as to have an exceeding fine view. The Prince

Ann Catley as Euphrosyne in *Comus*, a role for which she was celebrated

After a painting by William Lawranson. Published by the engraver, Robert Dunkarton, 452 Strand, 'opposite Villers Street', 15th April 1777.

of Wales has a full countenance like his father, his height the middle size. The bishop rather thin favourd but a sprightly countenance.'[2]

A proclamation was issued at St James's 'for encouraging seamen to enter themselves on board his majesty's ships of war'. Able seamen between the ages of 18 and 50 who voluntarily enter themselves to serve before 31st December shall receive £5 as royal bounty, ordinary seamen £2 10s.[3]

In the evening *The Jovial Crew* was performed at Covent Garden Theatre with Miss Catley and Miss Brown both performing. Miss Catley's footman had his pocket picked of his watch as he was taking two of her children out of the boxes at the theatre.[4]

DA '*Extract of a Letter from Port-Royal, Jamaica, dated Aug. 16, 1776, brought by the* John and Mary, *Capt. Jenkins, arrived at Falmouth, from Jamaica.* "Our present situation is very deplorable. We have been now under arms ever since the beginning of August, on account of an insurrection of the negroes, who have been exceedingly troublesome for some time past, occasioned by the scarcity of provisions, our supplies from America being long since cut off. We were in great hopes the execution of about 30 of their ringleaders would have quelled the sedition, but it has not had the desired effect, as they still continue very outrageous, and have laid waste many plantations. A party of the Royal Americans attacked a large body of them, killed 76, and took 84 prisoners, who are under close confinement."'[5]

LLEP 'A tradesman at Wapping has received an order from government to furnish 10,000 deal boxes for the purpose of exporting shot to America, each box to contain 100 weight.'[6]

26th October, Saturday Heavy grey day, but fair

In the morning Mr Akerman, keeper of Newgate, with the proper officers, conveyed a person from that gaol to Enfield, where he was sentenced to stand on the pillory for deer-stealing. He was so much pitied by the populace that they collected a sum of money for him, on which he entertained them with several songs, which produced repeated plaudits from the merry multitude.[1]

All the cabinet ministers met at Lord North's house, and after a long debate there they went to Kew to settle the king's speech for the opening of parliament. At 6.55 p.m. the king wrote from Kew to John Robinson: 'The draught of the speech is in the proper tone for the present position of affairs. Notes of triumph would not have been proper when the successes are against subjects not a foreign foe'.[2]

27th October, Sunday Hazy morning, fine bright day

As a boy was riding out of the Horse and Groom stable-yard, on the Surry side of Blackfriars Bridge, the horse started and threw him on the spiked rail of an adjacent house. The rail pierced the boy's skull, and he was carried home dying.[1]

Edward Oxnard went with Jonathan Sewall to inspect the new choir in Westminster Abbey, finding it 'in the Gothic taste and neat in the highest degree'.

At 5 p.m. he went into the City and drank tea with a friend. 'The citizens much alarm'd from the stocks falling,' he noted in his diary. 'Great fears of a French war.'[2]

28th October, Monday Thick fog early, very bright fine day
Warrants were issued for pressing seamen in all the out ports of the kingdom, the government being afraid of a war with France, and hoping to prevent it by these preparations.

At night, upon the flood time, about twenty boats, properly manned and officered, came up the river from Deptford and Woolwich, when the press began, and every man was taken from on board the ships they boarded, except the master, mate, and boys.

A lieutenant and press gang having boarded an outward bound Grenada ship lying off Wapping, the sailors immediately ran to the arms chest, broke it open, and fired several times at the gang. The lieutenant persisting that he would go down the hatchway, one of the ship's crew swore if he attempted it he would shoot him. On his proceeding the sailor fired, lodging the whole of his charge in his body. The lieutenant lingered a short time and then expired.

On a gang boarding another merchant ship, the sailors behaved with great courage, and refused to go unless they would pay them the bounty money, which was refused. A battle ensued, in which two men were killed, and in attempting to swim ashore three more were drowned.

The LIBERTY of the SUBJECT.

A press gang at work, with St Paul's Cathedral in the background
By James Gillray. Published by William Humphrey, 227 Strand, 15th October 1779.

The captain of a press gang, attempting to gain admission up stairs at a public-house not far from Darkhouse Lane, Billingsgate, was resolutely withstood by the mistress of the house, who insisted he had no authority, unless his warrant was backed by the lord mayor, on which he very imprudently drew his sword. The woman, unterrified, kept her ground, till at length the officer and his crew were obliged to sheer off.

As a poor slip-shod taylor, whose wife was in labour, was running for a midwife, he was picked up by a press gang. Notwithstanding his piteous plea they carried him off, but he was later set at liberty by a humane regulating officer.

According to the *Morning Chronicle*, the press 'was so exceedingly rapid, that it is computed 1500 men were picked up' and 'no less than 16 men are supposed to have been drowned, on their retreat from the colliers and other ships'.[1]

PA 'A correspondent says that for several days past the Bears in the Alley have been extremely busy, fabricating reports in order to lower the price of stocks ... War between Spain and Portugal; Lord Stormont quitting Paris without taking leave; an inevitable rupture with France; and all the king's troops blown up at New York, were among the public calamities announced by the Bears; and on Saturday to compleat the catalogue, they circulated a report that a Spanish fleet with a powerful army on board, had invaded the island of Jamaica.'[2]

29th October, Tuesday Foggy morning, heavy day, with a good deal of rain
In the morning about 200 East India sailors, armed with broomsticks, bludgeons, and cutlasses, went in a body from Wapping to India House in Leadenhall Street, declaring they would be killed to a man sooner than be impressed. They presented a petition to the directors, praying for the protection of the company, that they may be reserved for its service.

By the press gangs taking out the men belonging to the fishing vessels, a very small quantity of fish was brought to market. The gangs took several persons from Billingsgate within the lord mayor's jurisdiction, which occasioned his lordship to issue out his order for apprehending the officers of all press gangs, unless they have legal warrants.

In the afternoon upwards of 150 journeymen carpenters were impressed and sent on board tenders for examination. Forty-eight watermen, who plied about Blackfriars Bridge, were also impressed. In the evening, there being no ships in the river to receive the impressed men, they were put on board the king's yacht and sent down to the Nore.

At night the press was as warm as on Monday, but did not meet with any great success, as most of the sailors of the outward bound fleet have secreted themselves till their captains can procure their protection; but none, it is said, will be granted, till his majesty's squadron has got its full complement.[1]

Writing to a friend in India, John Bourke, a London merchant and distant kinsman of Edmund Burke, noted, 'This moment I hear there was a hot press in the river last night. *Bella, horrida bella.*' In a postscript on the cost of the war he added: 'One of these German princes from whom we have hired subsidiary troops, I am told wrote to his agent in Paris, in the following words, *"Envoyez moi la meilleure danseuse et la meilleure chanteuse qu'il y ait à Paris. Ce sont Messieurs les Anglois qui payeront tout ça."*'*[2]

PA 'A gentleman just returned from a tour through Cornwall, Somersetshire, Worcestershire and Cheshire, says, that no language can describe the discontent of the people on account of the American war. At Birmingham alone are the townsmen pleased — for at Birmingham they make muskets. | The same gentleman says, that the head-dresses of the Bristol ladies exceed those of the London dames, in the full proportion of three to two; so that it is no uncommon thing to see a head-dress 26 inches above the parent skull, and in the breadth at the top from 16 to 22. *Risum teneatis, amici?*'†[3]

MP 'The *black legged* gentry at Jonathan's‡ who fabricated the *manoeuvre* of the French war, have no little reason to *crow* at the success of their ingenuity, as it is said that by the reduction of the stocks they obtained upwards of 200000l. A correspondent observes, that any thing which bears the complexion of novelty is swallowed by the wise citizens of London'.[4]

30th October, Wednesday An exceeding bright fine day
In the morning three poor fellows who had escaped the most diligent search of the press gangs were found hid under the coals in a collier near Shadwell, almost perished with cold and hunger, having lain there since Monday evening.

The body of one of the sailors drowned on Monday night was taken up near the Tower.

There was another hot press from Gravesend to Rotherhithe, and a gang armed with cutlasses pressed a number of men in Shoreditch. There was a fray between a number of Irish sailors and a press gang in Petticoat Lane. The former, having large bludgeons, knocked down six of the latter and got off.

The lord mayor ordered his officers to make search after the leaders of the two press gangs who violated the liberties of the City by impressing near fifty hands at Billingsgate, which put a stop to the fish being unloaded. They are now a-spoiling on board the different vessels, to the great loss of many people.

Lord Sandwich presided over a full board at the Admiralty Office. The returns of the number of men pressed on Monday, as near as could be made out, were laid before the board, and proved to be 1,100. Two hundred fresh impress warrants were signed.

---

* 'Send me the best dancers and singers at Paris. It is the English who will pay.'
† 'Can you refrain from laughter, friends?' (Horace)
‡ A well known coffee-house in Exchange Alley, Cornhill, described in the *Tatler* (no. 38, 7th July 1709) as 'the general mart of stock-jobbers'.

In the evening six notorious pickpockets, long in confederacy with the prostitutes who nightly infest London Bridge, were swept off by a press gang, to the relief of all persons who pass and repass that thoroughfare.

At night an officer belonging to a press gang was shot through the head near Tower Hill by a taylor whom he was attempting to press.[1]

Meanwhile, at St James's the king issued a proclamation for a general fast:

> We, taking into our most serious consideration the just and necessary measures of force which we are obliged to use against our rebellious subjects in our colonies and provinces in North America; and putting our trust in Almighty God, that he will vouchsafe a special blessing on our arms, both by sea and land, have resolved ... that a public fast and humiliation be observed throughout England, our dominion of Wales, and town of Berwick upon Tweed, on Friday the thirteenth day of December next ...

A separate order was issued regarding Ireland. In Scotland the fast was to be held on 12th December, the *London Chronicle* noting that 'the kirk ... never hold their fasts on Friday'.[2]

The following advertisement appeared on the front page of the *Morning Chronicle*:

DROWNED,

> A gentleman who left his house on Friday night last at nine o'clock; and there is great reason to believe he was drowned near Westminster-bridge. Had on a great coat, a mix'd coloured frock coat, white waistcoat, leather breeches, and grey silk stockings. Whoever finds the body, secures the same, and gives immediate notice at No. 160, in Oxford-street, shall receive Twenty Guineas reward.

A later appeal would add that he 'wore his own hair, had large scars under his chin, and was not more than five feet two inches high'.

A great number of watermen and fishermen searched for the body above and below Westminster Bridge, without effect.[3]

The missing man was Bartholomew Coote Purdon, a nephew of General Sir Eyre Coote. He had been a banker in partnership with American Stephen Sayre, but on 18th June the *London Gazette* had carried notice of the partnership's dissolution, and in late November the pair will be declared bankrupt. Sayre subsequently blamed Purdon, claiming that he 'had been too deeply involved in debt, from the very commencement of their co-partnership, to be extricated', and that 'his necessities had drawn a very large sum out of the house'. According to another account, Purdon had kept 'a splendid establishment' and been 'visited by personages of the highest rank and talent', including the Duchess of Devonshire and Sheridan.[4]

In the evening Lord North gave an elegant entertainment at the Treasury to the principal officers under government who are members of the House of Commons. About eight o'clock they went to the chamber in the Treasury to hear the king's speech read a first and second time, after which the company retired.[5]

MC 'The French ambassador's coming over here is merely to save appearances, till some secret, hostile manoeuvres are prepared: his lady and family do not come, because the countess [*sic*] is reported to be big with child, and cannot travel.'[6]

MP '*Extract of a letter from Portsmouth, Oct. 28.* "Last night press warrants were sent down here and it is expected there will be a warm press to night for sailors. We are informed that there are 10,000 wanted for immediate service. Every one imagines here we are upon the eve of a war with France, if not with Spain."'[7]

31st October, Thursday Foggy heavy morning, bright afternoon
In the morning Mr William Craven, messenger to the Admiralty, was found dead in the horse-pond in the King's Mews. He was heard to say the preceding evening he would drown himself that night.[1]

About two o'clock his majesty went in state to the House of Lords, and opened both Houses of parliament with the following speech:

'My lords and gentlemen. Nothing could have afforded me so much satisfaction as to have been able to inform you, at the opening of this session, that the troubles, which have so long distracted my colonies in North America, were at an end, and that my unhappy people, recovered from their delusion, had delivered themselves from the oppression of their leaders, and returned to their duty: but so daring and desperate is the spirit of those leaders, whose object has always been dominion and power, that they have now openly renounced allegiance to the crown ... and have presumed to set up their rebellious con-federacies for independent states.

'If their treason be suffered to take root, much mischief must grow from it ... One great advantage, however, will be derived from the object of the rebels being openly avowed, and clearly understood; we shall have unanimity at home, founded in the general conviction of the justice and necessity of our measures.'

He added that 'by the blessing of divine providence' Canada was recovered, that operations in the province of New York gave strong hopes of success, and that he continued to receive 'assurances of amity from the several Courts of Europe', but that it was nonetheless expedient to place the country 'in a respectable state of defence'. He closed by expressing his desire to restore to his American subjects 'the blessings of law and liberty ... which they have fatally and desperately exchanged for all the calamities of war, and the arbitrary tyranny of their chiefs'.

As soon as the speech was read in the Commons, Mr Neville moved that an humble address be presented to his majesty. Lord John Cavendish proposed an amendment lamenting 'a bloody and expensive civil war'. He criticised government for 'considerable errors' including its failure to provide parliament with sufficient information, neglecting the complaints and petitions of the colonies, delay in sending commissioners for peace, and failing to furnish them with sufficient powers.

In the debate that followed Governor Johnstone arraigned the conduct of administration in very severe terms. He said he did not entirely approve of the Declaration of Independence, but the Americans were driven to it by our persecution of them. We had hired foreign troops to fight against them, and they had no other way of putting themselves on a footing with us, than by throwing off the yoke, declaring themselves independent, and inviting foreign aid to defend them. As for the declaration itself, it was exceedingly rude and ill written; the language was more unmannerly and abusive than even worse treatment would have justified; but then it must be considered as written merely to captivate the common people, and therefore a polished stile, and very scrupulous decency, were probably but trifling objects with the writer.

Mr Wilkes said that since their last meeting the scene had totally changed. 'Instead of negociations with colonies, or provincial assemblies, we have a war to carry on against the free and independent states of America; a wicked war, which has been occasioned solely by a spirit of violence, injustice, and obstinacy in our ministers, unparalleled in history.' Regarding Governor Johnstone's criticism of the declaration of independency as ill written and drawn up to captivate the people, he said that that was 'the very reason why I approve it most as a composition, as well as a wise, political measure, for the people are to decide this great controversy. If they are captivated by it, the end is attained. The polished periods, the harmonious, happy expressions, with all the grace, ease, and elegance of a beautiful diction, which we chiefly admire, captivate the people of America very little; but manly, nervous sense they relish, even in the most awkward and uncouth dress of language.'

In his speech Thomas Townshend referred to 'that humorous paragraph, which the ministers have thought proper to insert in his majesty's speech, calling for the unanimity of this House, and of the nation a large ... We have, thank God, a very witty minister, and he has thought proper at this time, when the generality of the world think this country in a situation, that ought to make the boldest man among you tremble, to treat us with a joke.'

Lord North defended the speech and Lord George Germain answered some points as to the conduct of the campaign.

Charles Fox said opposition had been right last session in every one of their prophecies regarding America. It seemed that law and liberty were to be restored there 'by the bayonets of disciplined Germans'. If America was conquered, it could only be secured by a very considerable standing army accustomed 'to bow down and break the spirits of men, to trample on the rights, and to live on the spoils cruelly wrung from the sweat and labour of their fellow subjects'.

According to Horace Walpole, 'Mr Gibbon ... a very good judge, and, being on the Court side, an impartial one, told me he never heard a more masterly speech than Fox's in his life; and he said he observed Thurlow and Wedderburn, the attorney and solicitor generals, complimenting which should answer it, and, at last, both declining it.' Edmund Burke, who had the beginnings of a bad cold,

'A View of the House of Peers. The king sitting on the throne, the Commons attending him.' From the *Gentleman's Magazine*, 1769.

agreed: 'I never knew Charles Fox better, or indeed any one, on any occasion. His speech was a noble performance. To my surprise, none of the ministry attempted an answer to it. I did not speak, though up twice. ... I waited for the crown lawyers, expecting some of them would follow Charles Fox; but none spoke, and the debate could not lie better than he left it.'

At half after eleven the House divided. The amendment was rejected by 242 to 87 and the humble address was carried by 232 to 83. The House rose at midnight.[2]

Among those attending the opening of parliament was former chief justice of Massachusetts, Peter Oliver:

> The procession was grand, his majesty being in the elegant state coach, which is glazed all around, and the body elegantly gilt, with a gilt crown on the top, with other decorations, drawn by 8 dun horses, the finest I ever saw, and kept in such order that their skin and hair appeared like a rich velvet. The amazing string of coaches, and the vast crowd of spectators in the streets and in the windows of the houses, of ladies richly dressed, and the groupe of figures from the first gentleman to the lowest link boy, was very picturesque and was a true representation of the chequered state of mankind ...

He noted that after the speech the king 'returned to his palace in grand procession, the populace hanging upon his chariot wheels, and filling the air with their acclamations'.

Earlier, as the coach had come into the court-yard at St James's on its way to parliament, the crowd had been so great that a boy, about eight years of age, was thrown down and had his leg broke by one of the wheels going over it. Later, when his majesty was returning back in at St James's Palace gate, a black boy, about 17 years of age, servant to a gentleman in Charles Street, St James's Square, was also beat down by the croud, by which accident the state coach went over his thigh and broke it to pieces.

Both boys were carried to the Middlesex Hospital. His majesty gave orders that the greatest care should be taken of them and that each should receive a handsome present.[3]

MC 'A correspondent says, he hopes Miss West will, the first time she visits the playhouse, deprive the ladies in the pit and gallery of one part of their property, viz. their wigs. The writer went on Tuesday to see *Medea*, and it was his misfortune to sit behind a female with an enormous wig; he being not a very tall man, could only have every now and then an accidental glance of that incomparable actress, Mrs Yates.'[4]

FACING PAGE. UPPER The state coach, built for George III in 1762 at a cost of nearly £7,600. Cipriani was paid £315 for the painted panels.

LOWER Mrs Yates as Calista in *The Fair Penitent*. Published 16th July 1776.

November

1st November, Friday Bright frosty morning, cloudy mid-day, wet evening
A large hospital ship from Deptford arrived off the Tower for the reception of
impressed seamen and others.[1]

A press gang attempted to board a Greenland whaling vessel a little below
bridge. The captain took up a harpoon, declaring that he would put the first man
to death who came on deck, upon which one of the gang boarded. The captain
struck the harpoon into his head, and shattered his scull to pieces.[2]

The celebrated Mr Edward Shuter died, aged 47, at the house of a medical
gentleman in Windmill Street where he had been humanely placed by the managers
of Covent Garden Theatre. The *Morning Chronicle* described him as 'without a
doubt, the first comedian of the age he lived in, extraordinarily gifted by nature
to please the publick'.[3]

MC 'The unfortunate gentleman* who was supposed to drown himself on
Friday last ... has left a most amiable wife, with two girls, and a boy of thirteen, with
whom, till his late unhappy connections, he lived in a state of the greatest felicity.
His lady had prevailed on her father, a gentleman of great fortune in Ireland,† to
advance her husband a considerable sum to extract him from his difficulties; and
the very night the deceased left his house, in O— street, a messenger arrived a
few hours after his departure from his relation, Sir E— C—, who had allowed him
to draw for 10,000l. The house originally stopped for 80,000l. but, in consequence
of great sums of money having been paid, we are assured the unhappy gentleman
in question might have satisfied all his creditors for about 13,000l.'[4]

2nd November, Saturday Bright frosty morning, a few showers in the day
In the morning a man was found dead in a chimney at Peckham. It is imagined
he attempted to descend into the house in order to rob it, but stuck by the way.[1]

The *Morning Chronicle* reported that on the preceding day the body of Mr
Coote Purdon had been 'taken up by two watermen above London bridge, and
carried home to his disconsolate family'. The report appeared again in the *Morning
Post* two days later, but was not true.[2]

At night upwards of 100 journeymen carpenters, who refused to work at the
usual wages, were pressed, on information given by their masters.[3]

Having recovered the use of his arm sufficiently, Lord North wrote a long
letter from Downing Street to his father Lord Guilford at Waldershare Park near
Canterbury. He recounted a visit he had received at about eleven o'clock that

---

* Bartholomew Coote Purdon: see under 30th October.
† Purdon had married Mary, daughter of Henry Wrixon, of Glenfield, county Cork,
in 1762.

Edward Shuter
Mezzotint by Philip Dawe, originally published 12th June 1773

morning from Samuel Egerton of Tatton Park, Cheshire, a rich elderly member
of parliament, who told him 'in direct terms' that he wished his daughter and
only child Beatrix, aged 22, to marry the Norths' eldest son, George Augustus,
aged 19, whom neither Egerton nor his daughter had ever met. Egerton said 'his
daughter was sound in body, and sound in mind', and that she 'had always been
a most obedient child to him, and would therefore, he hoped, prove a good wife'.
He would 'give with her £100,000 down' and 'leave the rest of his estate to his

son in law and not to his daughter exclusively'. He added that he 'would never think of obliging her to marry any man against her will', but 'if she approved of Mr North, and if Mr North approved of her, he wish'd that this marriage might take place as soon as possible, and that she would be in town about Christmas'.

North had responded enthusiastically, saying he was 'made extremely happy' at the thought of such an alliance. Having told his father that 'the old gentleman took leave of me very well pleased, and is to dine with me on Tuesday,' he went on:

> Whether the young people will like one another is as yet uncertain, but all that I know to the disadvantage of the young lady is, that she has a bad complexion, and is rather inclin'd to be fat but that she is not deform'd, and has nothing disgusting in her appearance. That she is sensible, prudent, good temper'd, and well educated seems to be the opinion of all that have any acquaintance with her. To be sure, on our side, we are rather too young, but so great an establishment, if it can be acquired with a good and virtuous wife, who has no defect in character, temper, and understanding is an advantage not to be lost ...
>
> To add a word of public news to this important private concern, an officer is just arrived here, Sir Wm. Howe confirming the account of his having landed with very little loss, on the island of New York on the 15 of [September] and that the rebels had evacuated that place leaving many cannon and other stores there. The account of their having lost many men does not appear to be true. Sir Wm. Howe is now encamped near their entrenchments, within which they have an army from 25 to 30,000 men.

Signing himself 'your most dutiful son, North', he added in a postscript: 'Excuse the hurry and the trembling hand with which I write.'[4]

He was writing late in the day, for it seems not to have been until about 10.30 p.m. that Captain Balfour, second aide-de-camp to General Howe, arrived at Lord George Germain's office with the long awaited news from America.[5]

He brought three letters from Howe. The first, dated 21st September at York Island, began: 'I have the satisfaction to inform your lordship of his majesty's troops being in possession of the city of New York.' The second, dated two days later, had less welcome tidings:

> Between the 20th and 21st instant at midnight, a most horrid attempt was made by a number of wretches to burn the town of New York, in which they succeeded too well, having set it on fire in several places, with matches and combustibles that had been prepared with great art and ingenuity. Many were detected in the fact, and some killed upon the spot by the enraged troops in garrison ... | The destruction is computed to be about one quarter of the town; and we have reason to suspect there are villains still lurking there, ready to finish the work they have begun ...

The third letter, dated 25th September, cast an uncertain eye to the future:

> I look upon the farther progress of this army for the campaign to be rather precarious ... | The enemy is too strongly posted to be attacked in front, and innumerable difficulties are in our way of turning him on either side, tho' his

An inventive depiction of the New York fire, published at Paris and Augsburg

army is much dispirited from the late successes of his majesty's arms; yet have I not the smallest prospect of finishing the contest this campaign, nor until the rebels see preparations in the spring that may preclude all thoughts of farther resistance. To this end I would propose eight or ten line of battle ships to be with us in February ... We must also have recruits from Europe, not finding the Americans disposed to serve with arms ...[6]

At the same time, or very shortly afterwards, Germain received two further dispatches from the Howes, marked as received on 3rd November.

On 20th September Lord Howe had written from on board the *Eagle* with an account of a fruitless meeting on Staten Island nine days earlier with three representatives of Congress, Benjamin Franklin, John Adams, and Edward Rutledge, who had insisted that they would accept any peace or alliance only as free and independent states.

On the same day the Howe brothers had written with regret that they had so far found it impossible to make any progress with their civil commission for restoring peace, not least because the rebel leaders had made much of the limited nature of their powers as commissioners. As a result the brothers had published a declaration, dated 19th September at New York, of which they enclosed a copy. It was calculated to impress upon the rebels that their own leaders were the main obstacle to peace, and announced that the king had been 'graciously disposed to direct a revision of such of his royal instructions as may be construed to lay an improper restraint on the freedom of legislation in any of his colonies, and to concur in the revisal of all Acts by which his subjects there may think themselves aggrieved'. It urged Americans 'to reflect seriously ... and to judge for themselves' whether it was better to risk their lives in an 'unjust and precarious cause' or to 'return to their allegiance' and 'accept the blessings of peace'.[7]

3rd November, Sunday Smart frost in the night, foggy morning and evening
At 8 a.m. Lord George Germain set out to his majesty at Kew with the dispatches from New York.[1]

As a Methodist preacher was holding forth to a numerous audience he was seized by a press gang, and carried on board a tender.[2]

In the evening the wife of a tradesman in Fleet Street dogged her husband to a house of ill fame in one of the courts leading from Dean Street to Wardour Street. A quarrel ensuing, she snatched up a fork and stabbed him in the side of the neck, but it is hoped the wounds are not mortal.[3]

4th November, Monday Smart frost in the night, a very fine bright day
Early in the morning General Howe's letters of 21st and 23rd September, reporting the capture of New York and the fire there, were published in a *London Gazette Extraordinary*.[1]

At a levee at St James's his majesty was congratulated by many of the nobility and foreign ministers on the success of his arms against the rebel forces. Captain Balfour, who brought the dispatches, was introduced by Lord George Germain and had an audience with his majesty.[2]

Balfour had arrived home to melancholy family news. A few weeks earlier his elder brother, Major Henry Balfour, and a younger brother had been out shooting near Fort George, Inverness, 'when unluckily the major stept forward before the muzzle of his brother's gun, which went off, and lodged the shot in the major's head, who expired a few hours after'.[3]

Anne North wrote to Lord Guilford, following up her husband's letter of two days earlier:

> Lord North is afraid you must have found it very difficult to read the letter which he wrote to you Saturday as he has not yet quite recover'd the use of his hand. However, I dare say you made out enough to rejoice with us, at the prospect we now have of seeing our dear George happily settled. As for the fortune it certainly exceeds any in England, but the thing that pleases us (if possible) still more is the accounts which I hear of the amiable disposition and the good sense of the young lady. I don't remember to have ever seen her, but I hear she is short, and not handsome, but at the same time not at all ugly or disgusting, but rather agreable. Our young man has too much good sense to insist upon Beauty and seems to be very well inclin'd to like the young lady, but his only fear is that she may not like him, but my partiality makes me inclin'd to think that there is no great fear of that. The old gentleman dines here tomorrow.[4]

Gibbon wrote to his friend J. B. Holroyd:

> I send you the *Gazette* and have scarcely any thing to add ... Lord G[eorge] G[ermain] with whom I had a long conversation last night was in high spirits

and hopes to reconquer Germany and America.* On the side of Canada he only fears Carleton's *slowness*, but entertains great expectations that the light troops and Indians ... will oblige the provincials to give up the defence of the lakes for fear of being cut off. The report of a foreign war subsides. House of Commons dull; and opposition talk of suspending hostilities from despair.[5]

The *Morning Post* warned its readers that hawkers had 'entered into a combination' to print an impostor paper under the same name and with the assistance of a former servant of the *Post*, R. Haswell, 'who for his negligence and incapacity has been discharged'. The hawkers had even appointed someone to attend at the corner of Blake Court, Catherine Street, Strand, where the *Post* had its offices, 'to publish it, and take in advertisements, (in order to deceive advertisers) and hope by this artifice to substitute a paltry publication, in the room of one so long well received'. Customers were advised to 'enjoin their news carrier to bring the particular paper they order'.[6]

5th November, Tuesday No frost, chiefly cloudy, a little sunshine at times

In consequence of New York being taken by the king's troops, together with the anniversary of the gunpowder plot's discovery, a sheep of twelve stone weight was roasted in the open ground of the Marshalsea prison, paid for by subscription of the debtors there confined. There was, tho' not intended, exactly 45 subscribers, 45 gallons of beer drank, and 45 papers of tobacco smoked, and the day was spent with great good humour and mirth. Among the rest the following toasts were drank: The King — The Queen, and Royal Family — Success to the Two Brothers in America — Wilkes and Liberty.[1]

In the evening the remains of Mr Shuter were interred in the burying-ground of St Paul's, Covent Garden. The funeral was rather decent than splendid. The body was brought from Windmill Street, where he died, in a hearse attended by two mourning coaches, filled by eight of the performers of Covent Garden Theatre, who supported the pall to the grave, and retired pensively exclaiming, 'Alas! poor Ned!'[2]

6th November, Wednesday An exceeding thick fog all day

Lord George Germain wrote three letters to General Howe for a packet to be dispatched this night. The first reported that the news of the taking of New York had been greeted with 'general satisfaction' and the king approved Howe's conduct 'in the strongest terms'. The second touched on 'the great importance of engaging the Southern Indians in our interest'. The third accompanied 500 copies of a printed response to the Declaration of Independence which were being sent for circulation among troops and Americans.[1]

---

* i.e. hopes success in America will have the added advantage of repairing the damage done to his reputation by his apparent cowardice at the battle of Minden in 1759.

In the House of Commons the business was expected to be short and dry, but at around 4 p.m. Mr Fox begged the House would not adjourn as an honourable friend of his was coming down to move something of the first consequence, and seeing none of the ministers in the House, he desired they might be sent for. A few minutes later Lord North and Lord George George Germain were in attendance to hear Lord John Cavendish draw the House's attention to the Howes' declaration of 19th September, printed in the morning newspapers. Lord John called upon the ministers to say whether it was genuine or not, and on North and Germain admitting that it was, he moved, 'That this House will resolve itself into a committee, to consider of the revisal of all Acts of parliament, by which his majesty's subjects in America think themselves aggrieved.'

In the debate that followed Mr Fox observed that however absurd and inconsistent administration had shewed themselves in other respects, in their contempt for parliament they had been perfectly consistent. The account from New York was received late on Saturday night; an extraordinary *Gazette*, announcing the retreat of the provincials, was published early on Monday morning; another *Gazette* followed it the succeeding evening; and yet a syllable of the declaration never transpired. He first heard of it at the opera the preceding evening, and read it that morning in a newspaper.

Mr Wedderburn, solicitor general, did not consider the declaration's offer to be of immediate importance because if the Americans adhered to independency, as he was sure they would, 'there can be no discussion of other points. It is in vain to think of it.' He hoped that 'the difference of the troops on both sides' would resolve the problem, and deprecated the 'very sudden and unexpected' way of bringing the debate, a manoeuvre he said had been planned at the opera the night before.

Mr Burke remarked that Wedderburn had now called to his assistance the bayonets of 12,000 Hessians. 'It was well said, on another occasion, that your speech demands an army! And I may say, that the learned gentleman demands blood; reasoning he says is vain; the *sword* must *convince* America, and clear up their clouded apprehensions.'

Later in his speech, which lasted more than an hour, he mentioned the recent proclamation for a fast, saying it was indeed high time for this country to humble herself before God, for her sins were many. However, we were being called upon to go to the altar 'with war and vengeance in our hearts, instead of the peace of our blessed saviour. ... Till our churches are purified from this abominable service, I shall consider them, not as the temples of the Almighty, but the synagogues of Satan.' The House groaned at this part of his speech, and some called out *Order, Order*.

When the House divided there were 47 for the motion and 109 against it.

In a letter next day Gibbon noted: 'Yesterday we had a surprize in the House from a proclamation of the Howes which made its first appearance in the *Morning Post*, and which nobody seems to understand.'[2]

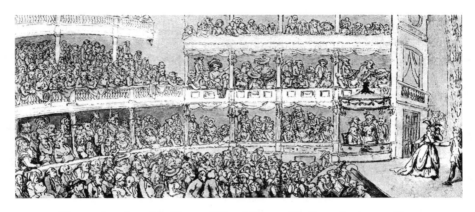

Theatre interior with George III and Queen Charlotte in the royal box

At Covent Garden Theatre *The Conscious Lovers*, a comedy by Sir Richard Steele, was performed by royal command. According to refugee Samuel Quincy, who was there, 'The parts of young Bevil by Mr Lewis, and of Indiana by Mrs Hartley, were admirably executed, insomuch that their majesties ... and the whole audience were in tears.'

At Drury Lane *The Gamesters*, a comedy by Garrick, with Mrs Abington as Penelope, was received with great applause. It was followed by *A Christmas Tale*, a dramatic entertainment with music, with Mrs Baddeley as Camilla and Mr Vernon as Floridor. Unfortunately, according to prompter Hopkins, 'Mr Vernon was so very drunk ... that he could scarcely stand, a man in the gallery cry'd out *Hold him up*,' and there were 'a few hisses at the end of the trio'.[3]

MC 'A correspondent says, that administration having appointed a fast, reminds him of an observation which has been made respecting sailors — that they never pray till near their last gasp.'[4]

GA 'Coals are now sold at the enormous price of 48s. per chaldron in the Pool, owing to the scarcity of hands to navigate the colliers, occasioned by the press.'[5]

7th November, Thursday Fog continues without intermission

Eight of the convicts employed in raising ballast in the river seized the arms chest, presented pistols at the heads of their keepers, and threatened to blow their brains out if they did not go down into the hold, which they were obliged to do. The villains then jumped into a boat, which had been brought alongside by some of their friends, and got clear off.[1]

In the evening most of the inhabitants of the Savoy were alarmed at a woman, who lives in Savoy Alley, firing a gun, and illuminating her house from the cellar to the garret. On enquiry being made into the cause, it was found she had that day received a letter from her husband, who is in his majesty's service, and with General Howe in possession of New York.[2]

8th November, Friday Fog continues, sun burst out a little about noon, little effect At Guildhall, Sir Thomas Halifax, lord mayor elect, was sworn into his office, the chair and other ensigns of mayoralty being surrendered to him in the accustomed manner.[1]

A motion was made in the Court of King's Bench, to shew cause why an information should not be filed against Charles Claude de Morande for a libel published in the *Public Ledger* of 10th September [>] in which it was said that the Chevalier d'Éon was a common cheat who had secretly connived with those taking out insurance policies on his or her sex. The affidavits having been read, Lord Mansfield directed the motion to be granted.[2]

In the House of Commons, about half past three o'clock, the Speaker left the chair and the House went into a committee to discuss a motion that 45,000 seamen be employed for the year 1777. The Hon. Mr Luttrell said that the nation's naval strength was by no means equal to the account publicly given, and spoke very severely regarding Lord Sandwich:

'If there was a ray of hope ... that such specious falsehoods of government could impose upon the clear-sighted statesmen on the other side of the Channel, or upon their ministers or emissaries on this side, we might allow that we had in the noble earl the best commissioner of the Admiralty that ever presided at that board; I mean so long as the safety of the nation depends upon concealing or disguising the truth; for I verily believe him to be the only man of his rank and education in these realms, I am sure he is the only professed moralist, who, after reiterated detection in the grossest impositions, and deep-laid fictions, can rally again, and return to the charge with so sanctimonious a composure, so dauntless an effrontery, that the rarity and perfection of the vice almost constitutes it a virtue.'

Mr Attorney General called Mr Luttrell to order, appealing to the committee whether such language, and so personal an attack, ought to be suffered, but Mr Luttrell persevered, observing that to give Lord Sandwich the palm of specious falsehoods, while he had so many competitors in the ministerial fraternity, was indeed no trifling compliment.

Mr Wombwell warmly defended Lord Sandwich, and gave a long panegyric upon his private virtues, public talents, and industry. He said he was the best minister, and perhaps the worthiest man, in this country, at which the House laughed heartily.*

Lord North also spoke in behalf of Lord Sandwich, saying he ought not to be thus attacked in his absence with a collection of loose surmises and low newspaper abuse.

---

* George Wombwell represented Huntingdon, and Sandwich was his patron. Since April he had been joint holder of a government contract for victualling 12,000 men in America.

The motion being put was agreed to and the House was resumed, Mr Speaker taking the chair.

Mr Luttrell then moved, as a first step towards displacing Lord Sandwich, that the latest accounts for the navy be laid on the table of the House. He said he would shew by them that the information given on the first day of the session as to the country's naval strength was a dangerous, wicked, and wilful imposition on parliament and the whole nation.

The attorney general and the friends of administration were for throwing his motion out without further discussion, but it was supported by Thomas Townshend and Mr Hartley. Mr Luttrell insisted that the absolute management of the maritime power of the British empire was too arduous, too solid, too important a trust, to be committed to a *bon vivant* of Lord Sandwich's levity of disposition and known depravity of conduct, 'especially now the piping hours of jubilee and dalliance are at an end;

Lord Sandwich by James Sayers, 1782

and we ought to prepare for naval operations of the most substantial and critical import to the safety of these islands'.

The question being put, the motion was negatived without a division.[3]

In the evening Edward Oxnard tried to get into the House of Commons but found the doors shut and went home. 'So foggy that a man lost his way in the park,' he noted in his diary.[4]

About 7 p.m., owing to the very thick fog, the coach of the outgoing lord mayor, John Sawbridge MP, was overturned at Charing Cross by one of the Chelsea stages. The coach was coming from the House of Commons and was also carrying his brother, Rev. Mr Sawbridge, and two other MPs. Happily they received no hurt.[5]

Frederick Montagu, a well connected politician, wrote from Hanover Square to Mrs Delany with news that 'the Duchess of Devonshire carries her plumes higher than ever' and that 'Mr North, Lord North's son, is going to be married to Miss Egerton, the great Cheshire heiress. Old Sam Egerton gives her *one hundred thousand pounds down*. I don't write in figures, for fear you should think I put an 0 too much.'[6]

9th November, Saturday, Lord Mayor's Day Fog till noon, then began to disperse, clear afternoon

PUBLIC OFFICE, Bow-street.
A CAUTION.

All persons whose business or curiosity may occasion their mixing with the crowd which will probably be assembled on this day, are cautioned to leave their pocket books, purses, watches, and matters of value at home, as numbers of pickpockets always make it a practice to take advantage of such public opportunities of exercising their dexterity.

Gazetteer[1]

The new lord mayor, accompanied by the late lord mayor, went from Guildhall, preceded by the City marshals on horseback, and six of his lordship's footmen in blue livery. At the Three Cranes they took water in the City barge and proceeded to Westminster Hall, attended by the several livery companies in their barges, adorned with streamers and pendants. After his lordship had been sworn into his office before the barons in the Court of Exchequer, he walked round the Hall, and with the usual ceremony invited the judges in the several courts to his feast and ball. He then returned in the same form, landed at Blackfriars, and went in procession to Guildhall, where a magnificent entertainment was provided, at which were present the lord chancellor and many other persons of quality and distinction.

Samuel Quincy was at the London Coffee-house on Ludgate Hill with other Americans to see the returning procession, and thought it 'a scene only of mock majesty, confusion, nonsense, and noise'. Edward Oxnard agreed, describing it as 'farcical enough'. According to the *Gazetteer*, 'the state coach, which was reported to have been new varnished and gilt, at a great expence, made a very shabby appearance.' The *Public Advertiser* judged that 'the most agreeable sight of the day ... was the faces of our British beauties from the windows of Cheapside; and the most shocking spectacle was the head dresses belonging to those very faces.'[2]

George North wrote from Downing Street to his grandfather Lord Guilford:

I am to set out for Cheshire on Monday. Mr Egerton is already gone down and will be there ready to receive me. From the character I hear universally given to the young lady, I can hardly entertain a doubt of my happiness, if she should but honour me with the same approbation that her father has already expressed for me. But she is so suspicious that her money is the pursuit of all her admirers, that I own I can not help entertaining the greatest doubts of success. You shall hear from me soon after my arrival.[3]

In the evening *The Duenna* was revived at Covent Garden Theatre with Miss Brown in the part of Clara. It would be performed nine times more before the end of the year.[4]

At night, whilst a labouring man was carrying home a leg of mutton and a bunch of turnips to his family, he was picked up by a press gang, which was for hurrying him away immediately to a house of rendezvous. The man for a long while remonstrated, urging his situation and the dependence of his family on his labours. At last he begged the lieutenant's permission to carry home their Sunday's dinner, before he was separated from them. The lieutenant consented, and sent two of his men with him to ensure his return; but the man no sooner came within sight of his dwelling, than taking his leg of mutton in one hand, and his bunch of turnips in the other, he aimed two blows so successfully at his kidnappers as brought them to the ground. He then raised the hue and cry and left them in the hands of the mob, who paid the usual civilities on such occasions, whilst he made his escape.[5]

MP 'His majesty's visits to Lord North, except one, which was expressly on business, were the strongest proof of his politeness, and good education as a gentleman; he never mentioned business; expressed his concern at the accident; advised him to be careful of cold; asked him what breed of sheep they were upon the lawn; said that Welch mutton was the best; in a word, trifled away the time, without mentioning America; and upon the minister's beginning to say something upon the subject, the king put it by, and desired him to think of nothing but the recovery of his health, as anxiety was a very bad attendant upon a broken limb. ... Yet is our king represented in the public prints, as a driveller; and in American declarations, as a brute.'[6]

10th November, Sunday A heavy, moist, misling day
About two o'clock in the morning the youngest daughter of a wealthy inhabitant of this city eloped with her father's footman, and before ten o'clock seven different persons were dispatched after them. The lovers had been at the lord mayor's ball the preceding evening.[1]

Meanwhile Captain Clerke and the *Discovery* arrived in Table Bay, Cape of Good Hope, joining Captain Cook and the *Resolution*.[2]

11th November, Monday A hazy moist day
David Hartley, MP for Kingston upon Hull, accompanied by other members of both Houses, exhibited on Wimbledon Common his sixth and last experiment for preventing the destruction of houses by fire. A great number of gentlemen and ladies attended.[1]

Lord Weymouth received a series of letters from Lord Stormont dated 6th November at Fontainebleau.

The first reported that the French had assembled between 15,000 and 16,000 sailors at Brest and Rochfort, and twenty ships of the line at Brest.

The second noted Stormont's belief 'that Beaumarchais and a M. Morand, well known in England, carry on a constant correspondence', Beaumarchais's letters being directed to an address in Crutched Friars. 'This correspondence, which is trusted to the common post, would be worth looking into, but it is essential that the letters should not be stopped, nor opened in such a way as to beget the least suspicion.' Meanwhile Dr Bancroft had arrived in Paris, and, if Stormont was correctly informed, 'the most important and confidential letters that Deane and Bancroft receive come to them through Monsieur Garnier's courier to M. de Vergennes. Their principal correspondents are Mr Thomas Walpole of Carshalton, Mr Saml. Wharton of Lisle street, Leicester fields and Hammersmith, and Mr Arthur Lee, Garden Court, Temple.'* Adding a series of other names in England and Paris, he noted that the interception of letters to and from any of them might 'lead to very useful discoveries'.

In the final letter he reported that Beaumarchais had hired L'Hôtel de la Tour du Pin, in vieille rue du Temple, 'to establish his bureaux there for what is called *le commerce des piastres*', or currency trading in piastres, to be opened on New Year's Day.

> Three millions of livres have been advanced him to carry on this commerce. I mean, my lord, that that is the pretence. The secret reason is to enable him to execute his American commission. He has actually agreed with a great cloth merchant at Paris for cloth, lining, buttons &c. for *ten thousand* men, and he is now in treaty with a M. Gerard ... to freight two vessels for America loaded with *twenty thousand* stand of arms, and a large quantity of warlike stores. ...
>
> Beaumarchais intends soon to return to England. One of the objects of his journey is to purchase for the navy of France a large forest in the neighbourhood of Colchester that is exposed to public sale. This his intention being known I hope, my lord, that it will be easy to find means to defeat it.[2]

12th November, Tuesday An exceeding fine bright day

The campaign against the spurious *Morning Post* moved to the streets. Horace Walpole described the scene in a letter to Lady Ossory written from Arlington Street next day.

> I heard drums and trumpets in Piccadilly: I looked out of the window and saw a procession with streamers flying. At first I thought it a press gang, but seeing the corps so well drest, like hussars, in yellow with blue waistcoats and breeches, and high caps, I concluded it was some new body of our allies, or a regiment newly raised ... This was a procession set forth by Mr Bate ... author of the old *Morning Post*, and meant as an appeal to the town against his antagonist, the new one. I did not perceive it, but the musicians had masks; on their caps was written *The Morning Post*, and they distributed hand-bills. I am sure there were at least between thirty and forty, and this mummery must have cost a great deal of money.

---

* Thomas Walpole, a cousin of Horace, was a banker, merchant, and opposition MP. He had been involved with Wharton, an American, along with Benjamin Franklin and others, in the Grand Ohio Company. The company's plan to establish a colony on a large tract of land on the borders of Virginia had been interrupted by the outbreak of the war and came to nothing.

Are not we quite distracted, reprobate, absurd, beyond all people that ever lived? The new *Morning Post* I am told, for I never take in either, exceeds all the outrageous Billingsgate that ever was heard of. What a country! Does it signify what happens to it? Is there any sense, integrity, decency, taste, left? Are not we the most despicable nation upon earth, in every light? A solemn and expensive masquerade exhibited by a clergyman, in defence of daily scandal against women of the first rank, in the midst of a civil war! and while the labouring poor are torn from their families by press gangs! and a foreign war is hanging over our heads! And everybody was diverted with this! Do you think, madam, that anything can save such a sottish and stupid nation? Does it deserve to be saved? You that have children will wish for miracles; as I have none ... I can almost wish we may be scourged.[1]

The lottery wheels, escorted by a party of horse guards, were moved from the office at Whitehall to Guildhall, previous to the drawing.[2]

At night a new born boy was laid at Lord Suffolk's door in Duke Street, Westminster, wrapped up in a couple of blankets. His lordship ordered it to be taken in, and sent for the parish officers, to whom he gave a strict charge to take care of it.[3]

The Chevalier d'Éon replied belatedly to Beaumarchais's last letter, sent from Paris nearly three months earlier.

Naturally I did not reply to the letter you took the trouble to write to me on 18th August [>], because, while you were writing sweet things to me in order to renew our little negotiation, you were at the same time writing to your fine protégé Morande, so as to shake the phial, or rather the pitcher, of venom that he carries always in his heart. That seemed to me neither loyal nor fair. Finally you incited him to write libels against me in the newspapers. He not only told me as much, but he showed various passages on this subject in your letters to several people of my acquaintance. He even had the stupidity to write it to me in the heat of his rages. When he was pressed to fight by me and then by my brother-in-law he retreated into his poltroonery, and used as an excuse the importance of staying alive for the sake of his wife and children and his lying correspondence with you. I regarded it as far beneath my dignity to reply in the newspapers to all the calumnies and impertinences of this escaped criminal. I have preferred silence, and have waited with patience for the Court of King's Bench to resume in order to bring this infamous libellist to trial. He is there now, and all honest people think that this calumniator of the late king, of princes, princesses, lords and ladies of the Court, will only leave it to lose his ears in the pillory. ...

Goodnight, too dear Monsieur Beaumarchais. It is two o'clock in the morning. I am very tired and am going to bed, cursing and berating all men who have so maltreated me, and above all you, whom I truly loved and esteemed, and who troubled my heart excessively, on your own and through your Jean Foutre de Morande.[4]

13th November, Wednesday An exceeding fine bright day

At 9 a.m. the lottery began drawing at Guildhall. No. 57470 (a prize of 20l.) was the first drawn ticket, and as such was entitled to 1,000l. besides the 20l. A great number of persons of all ranks attended and several had their watches *drawn* from their pockets, unperceived by themselves.[1]

A press gang stopped a man in Whitechapel, but he told them they would detain him at their peril, for that he was one of the members of parliament for Guzzledown, and should certainly move the House against the whole party. This threw the gang into consternation, being doubtful whether such a place existed, but the member, with great presence of mind, persisting in the affirmative, the lieutenant sagaciously observed, *It might, for any thing he knew, be some Cornish borough, and under the influence of his employers*, and the man was permitted to go about his business.*[2]

14th November, Thursday A heavy misling day

In the morning an excise officer had an information of four men, each with a basket containing contraband goods, being at a public-house in the Minories. On arrival he insisted on searching the baskets, which not being immediately complied with, whetted his expectation. He produced his warrant, but on examining the baskets found, to his mortification, that they were filled with hogs entrails, which the men had a little before bought at the Victualling Office.[1]

At the Royal Exchange gate the common cryer read the king's proclamation for the encouragement of sailors to enter his service, and encouragement to persons to give information where sailors are secreted.[2]

Lady North wrote to her father-in-law Lord Guilford: 'Lady George Germaine is to have a great ball this evening. Lord North, Kitty,† and I are the only people in town not invited to it, which is something odd. ... Nothing is now talk'd of but George and Miss E., which is very distressing to us, for while things are in this uncertain state we don't know what to say. As the old gentleman told it we think it wou'd appear odd in us absolutely to deny it.'[3]

In the evening, during the performance of *A Christmas Tale* at Drury Lane Theatre, one of the scene-shifters fell from the upper loft, or flies, upon the stage, broke one of his thighs, and was bruised in a terrible manner. He was immediately carried to the Middlesex Hospital.[4]

About 8 p.m. their majesties went from the Queen's Palace in procession, attended by officers of state and ladies of the bedchamber, to the Earl of Derby's

---

* 'Guzzledown' had been used as a satirical name for a corrupt borough at least since Vanbrugh and Cibber's *The Provok'd Husband*, first performed in 1728, and was adopted by Hogarth for his Election series in the 1750s. Cornwall was a good guess by the lieutenant as it had no fewer than 44 MPs, Edward Gibbon among them — more than the combined representation for Essex (8), Kent (10), Middlesex, including Westminster (8), and Surrey, including Southwark (14).

† Catherine, the North's eldest daughter, aged 16 and recently presented at Court.

house in Grosvenor Square, where they were sponsors for his lordship's daughter, who was christened about nine o'clock by the name of Charlotte. According to the *Morning Post*, 'Their majesties were charmed with the reception they met with ... The entertainment was served up in the most sumptuous style ... and even the meanest attendant in their majesties suite, as well as in his lordship's family, partook of cake and caudle'.[5]

15th November, Friday A fair day, and sometimes bright
Lord Derby waited on his majesty at St James's to return him thanks for the honour of the evening before. He also sent four large christening cakes to the Queen's Palace, which were sent on to Kew for the royal children.[1]

The Duke of Devonshire, the Marquis of Rockingham, the president and about thirty members of the Royal Society, many members of parliament, and other gentlemen of note, met at Mr Baker's exhibition in the Haymarket to see the astonishing phænomena of the Gymnotus Electricus. Pleasure and surprize were expressed at the vivid flashes produced by that animal, and above seventy of the company joined hands, all feeling its electrical stroke at the same instant of time.

Garrick wrote to Countess Spencer and, coincidentally, mentioned the eels, which he had evidently been to see. One of them, he said, had died and been dissected by Dr Hunter, and Lady Strathmore, putting her hands into the water to touch the live ones, had received such a shock that she threw water over the surrounding company.[2]

The Marquis de Noailles, French ambassador, wrote to the Comte de Vergennes in Paris:

> Impressment continues in the interior with the greatest animation, but all of the seamen are hiding, and they are abandoning the ships to the point where they are obliged to make use of French seamen for the navigation of the Dover-Calais packets. Last night they impressed a kitchen helper of the Spanish ambassador, to whom they had already given a choice of serving as a sailor or as a soldier. You can well imagine that this man was given up only with difficulty, and I only make mention of this incident to show you that they are seizing without exception anyone whom they can find.[3]

In the House of Commons a series of grants for military expenditure, totalling over £2.8 million, were agreed without debate. According to the *Parliamentary Register*:

> The gentlemen in opposition had repeatedly said to their friends, that it was in vain to oppose the measures of the Court in parliament; the ministry had a regular and fixed majority; accordingly they seldom attended, except upon private business. This day gave a signal proof of this opinion. Sir George Savile, Mr Burke, &c. who attended the House ... upon a private bill, as soon as Lord Barrington stood up to move the first resolution, they quitted their places, made their bows to the chair, and went away.[4]

At 6.49 p.m. the king wrote to Lord North from Kew:

I sincerely congratulate you on having been so little detained in the House of Commons this day. Indeed I had learnt from Lord Weymouth that Charles Fox had declared at Arthur's last night that he should attend the business of the House this day, and either tomorrow or Sunday should set out for Paris, and not return till after the recess. I think therefore you cannot do better than bring as much forward during the time parliament shall be assembled as can with propriety be done, as real business is never so well considered as when the attention of the House is not taken up by noisy declamations.[5]

Lady North wrote again to Lord Guilford:

I have just receiv'd a letter from George, in which he says that he arriv'd at Tatton Tuesday night, that he likes the lady extremely, her face is not handsome, nor disagreable, she has good dark eyes, a sensible look, a very pretty white hand and arm, and was very well dress'd. She appears to be very sensible and is very lively, and talkative and agreable in her conversation. I think by her appearing so lively and in good spirits we may flatter ourselves, that she did not disapprove of her visitor. Lord North has had a letter from ye old man in which he tells him that he was very happy in receiving Mr N. and that he shou'd do every thing in his power to promote the match which if it took place wou'd make him the happiest of men. He also wrote a letter to Sir G. Cooper in which he says his only apprehension now is for fear Mr N. may not approve of his daughter, so I think things appear now to be in *an admirable way*.[6]

About 10 p.m. a lawless press gang, consisting of about twenty ruffians, ran through Cheapside, up the Poultry, through Cornhill, and Leadenhall Street, &c. dragging and maltreating all persons in their way. In the Minories they cut off a poor man's ear, and committed other violences, after which they ran off towards Wapping. It was well they did, as the Whitechapel butchers, hearing of these outrages, began to assemble in great numbers.[7]

LLEP 'On account of the present fashionable taste for small horses, little Welch ponies, which formerly were purchased for two guineas each, are now sold for from twelve to twenty guineas a pair, and strings of them are daily arriving from Wales.'[8]

16th November, Saturday Heavy misling morning, fine bright day

In the evening the cabinet met at Lord Suffolk's house on affairs of great importance. They were together near five hours, and no other person was permitted to enter the room the whole time.[1]

17th November, Sunday An exceeding bright fine day

Died, Mr Hollingbury, taylor, in Cannon Street. About two months ago, as he was playing with a favourite parrot, it bit him in the fleshy part of his thumb. The inflammation from the bite was so violent as to produce a mortification, for which his arm was amputated, and occasioned his death.[1]

PHAETONA OR MODERN
FEMALE TASTE

Published by M. Darly in the Strand, 6th November 1776

18th November, Monday Fine morning, cloudy heavy afternoon
The *Morning Post* published a new advertisement for the missing banker, Mr Coote Purdon, which raised the reward to 30 guineas.[1]

The cabinet met at the Admiralty. With the advice of the attorney and solicitor generals, who were present, it was decided 'that the Admiralty be directed to proceed in the execution of press warrants within the City of London though the lord mayor should continue to refuse backing the warrants'.[2]

Lord Weymouth received a letter from Lord Stormont, dated 13th November at Fontainebleau, in which he said he had heard that Silas Deane had engaged 400 discharged French officers to go to North America. 'As I think it of importance to raise in M. de Vergennes a suspicion and mistrust of Deane,' he added, 'I contrived this morning to drop some obscure hints of a negotiation begun by Lord Howe. I did it in such a way as carried no appearance of design and made such an impression as I wished upon M. de Vergennes who began with eagerness to ask me questions to which I avoided giving a direct answer.'[3]

Very many people attended Westminster Hall expecting the case of the Chevalier d'Éon to come on in the Court of King's Bench, so that it was impossible to gain admittance after ten o'clock. Among those gathered were Edward Oxnard and two American friends. 'Its not coming on disappointed great numbers,' he noted in his diary. The court would continue to be crowded over following days by those hoping to hear the case.[4]

Meanwhile at Serjeants' Inn three affidavits were sworn to the effect that d'Éon had refused large sums offered to him to become involved in policies on his sex. His landlord, Joseph Lautem, swore that 'during the course of last year, and the foregoing year, two persons possessed of considerable wealth, severally intreated him' to tell d'Éon that they were ready to give him £7,000 and £8,000 respectively. Domenico Angelo, fencing master, swore that in 1772 'a rich merchant of the City of London' had asked him several times to offer d'Éon £10,000 on condition that he 'should suffer himself to be examined by two surgeons and two midwives, in order to ascertain his sex'. D'Éon's response had been that while £10,000 was 'a considerable sum ... the persons that propose it must wait till I am dead, and then, if they please, they shall be welcome to make their examination, and to kiss my backside'. Jean de Vignoles swore that he had been approached several times in 1771 and 1772, on one occasion being asked to pass on an offer of £7,000 in bank notes, with £2,000 for himself should it be accepted. A fourth affidavit to the same effect, by the Chevalier de Piennes, had been sworn on 9th November. It seems likely that when the case came to trial [> 27th] all four affidavits were read out to counter Morande's accusation of collusion in the policies, although reports of the trial do not mention them.[5]

19th November, Tuesday A very foggy misling day
Having been purged of many of its obscenities, and undergone other cuttings by Mr Sheridan, Congreve's *Old Batchelor* was performed at Drury Lane Theatre. A humorous prologue upon the cutting of the play, said to be written by Mr Sheridan, was spoke by Mr Dodd and received with applause. According to the *Morning Post*, it included 'two or three good strokes at our hypocritical prudes, who exclaim against the obscenity of Congreve, and at the same time conceal themselves muffled up with their maids in a corner of the two shilling gallery, to enjoy his luscious banquets'.

The general idea that the world entertain of *Gazette* intelligence may be collected from the manner in which the audience received the words of Captain Bluff in the play itself: 'Why, sir, there are not three words of truth, the year round, put into the *Gazette!*' The house burst out immediately into a violent clapping, and a roar of *Bravo! Bravo! That's true enough*, &c. That enormous head-dresses were the *ton* in the days of Congreve, as well as the present, was evident from a speech of Belinda's, where she orders her servant to 'see that he gets a chair with a high roof, or a very low seat'.

The effect of the piece was marred, however, by two of the actors, as Hopkins the prompter noted in his diary:

Miss Essex made her first appearance upon this stage in Silvia — a small mean figure and a shocking actress, so bad that she is to play no more. ... Mr Reddish was very imperfect in Vainlove from the beginning, but was so very much so in the last act, that the audience hiss'd very much and cry'd out, 'Off, Reddish,

The Cork Rump   or Chloe's Cushion.

Pub.ᵈ Nov.ʳ 19. 1776. by J. Walker N.₁₃. Parliament St.

Published 19th November 1776. The fashionable 'cork rump' encircled
the hips and extended the dress at the back. Actress Ann Brown was
reported as adopting 'the *cork-rumped* stile' on stage on 27th December.

Off!' He went forward, and addressed them as follows: 'Ladies and gentlemen. I have been honour'd with your favour and protection for these ten years past and am very sorry to give any cause for your displeasure now, but having undertaken the part at a very short warning, in order to strengthen the bill, and having had but two rehearsals for it, put it out of my power to do justice to the part or my self.' The play then went on. So great a lye was never delivered to an audience by any actor or actress before. He had the part at least six weeks in his possession and repeated notice to be ready in it and six rehearsals was called for it. Indeed he attended but three. Mr Vernon undertook to study the part at eleven o'clock to-night and to perform it to-morrow.

The replacement in the part of Silvia would be Priscilla Hopkins, the prompter's younger daughter.[1]

At night George North wrote from Downing Street to his grandfather in Kent:

I arrived here last night, after having been refused at Tatton, though I can not say that I entirely despair of succeeding, and especially as the old gentleman thinks it still in a very good way. But these hopes are a profound secret, as I am convinced nothing would obstruct my success more than the young lady's knowing that I entertained them. I hope soon to hear from Mr E. when I shall be able to give you a more satisfactory account. As to the young lady herself, she is not handsome, but not disagreable to look at, and has an exceeding good heart with an excellent understanding. She comes to London after Christmas when I shall renew my acquaintance with her.[2]

This night and the two following days there blew the greatest storm for some time past, in the Low Countries, some part of France, and all over England. On the night of the 20th it demolished the vane of Ely Cathedral, with part of the turret upon which it was fixed.[3]

20th November, Wednesday A very coarse day, some heavy showers. Stormy In the morning the body of a barber was found in Tower Ditch, with his head cut open in two places. It is supposed he was murdered in resisting a press gang.[1]

A press gang seized several persons in St Giles's including, it is said, Jack Ketch. He pleaded his office, and public service to community, but they hawled him away.[2]

Their majesties and all the young princes and princesses came from Kew to the Queen's Palace for the winter season. A little after six their majesties went to *The Duenna* at Covent Garden Theatre, Ann Brown playing the part of Clara.[3]

MP 'Signora Agujari,* we are informed, is engaged at the Pantheon for twelve nights the present winter, at 100 guineas a night; she sings but two songs in the course of the evening, so that she has fifty guineas a song. She has bound herself not to sing a passage in private or public, except at the above place, under the penalty of 5,000l.'[4]

* Lucrezia Aguiari (1743-1783), a celebrated Italian soprano. For Fanny Burney's account see under 1st December.

LP 'A poor sailor, just arrived from Barbary, where he had been a slave five years, (being taken on board a Danish ship in the year 1771) going on shore at Shadwell to look after his wife and family, was laid hold on by a press gang, and will, in all likelihood, remain in slavery five years longer.'[5]

21st November, Thursday Very churlish and cold, strong shower of hail, rain and sleet

In the morning a large stack of chimnies were blown down by the violence of the wind in Park Lane. A gentleman's servant, passing at the time, was killed on the spot.[1]

A 5,000*l.* prize was drawn in the lottery. The ticket was owned by Mr Hooper of America, a deserving young gentleman who is come from thence on account of the present troubles.[2]

Governor Hutchinson attended 'a very full drawing room, ladies especially,' at St James's. 'The queen never spoke with more freedom and condescension at any time of my being at Court; lamented the burning of the city of New York, &c. | Lord Talbot was very polite; said he hoped ministry consulted me, but it is certain they do not.'[3]

Another refugee, clergyman Jonathan Boucher, wrote from Paddington to an old friend in Cumberland:

> I told you of my despairing now to obtain an establishment in England ...
> When I first came I was caress'd and attended to by men who, I knew, had the
> power to serve me, and who said they had the inclination. This still continues.
> But after more than a year's experience of nothing being done, or nothing of
> any considerable moment ... what shou'd a man less sanguin, and more patient
> than I pretend to be, infer from it? ... At present I am busy on a very laborious
> and most difficult enquiry: an attempt to delineate a plan for the future govern-
> ment of ye colonies. ... If ever I get it lick'd into any decent form I intend it
> for administration, as my last arrow: and, if they will then do any thing for
> me, so, if not, 'tis high time I knew it.[4]

At night a press gang entered a public-house in New Street, Covent Garden, and took a chairman, but intelligence being given to some of his brethren in the Garden, a large body of them repaired immediately to the place, armed with various weapons. A battle ensued, wherein one of the gang was killed and several others much bruised. The chairmen then broke all the windows in the front of the house, and having released the pressed man went off in triumph.[5]

22nd November, Friday Bright morning, cloudy mid-day, very wet evening

A woman in Duck Lane, Westminster, was found hanging in her room. By a paper which she left on the table, it appeared that her husband having been pressed, and her being left with five small children, was the cause of her committing this rash act.[1]

Writing to Vergennes in Paris, the Marquis de Noailles noted that 'the impress-ment is at the point where it is beginning to snatch away servants from behind their masters' carriages. Not since the reign of Queen Anne has the commission of such excesses been witnessed.'[2]

Early news of British success in Canada arrived, although according to the *London Gazette* the official dispatches did not reach the Admiralty until next morning. *Lloyd's Evening Post* carried a brief report, and in the evening Gibbon wrote in a letter to J. B. Holroyd: 'News from the Lakes. A naval combat in which the provincials were repulsed with considerable loss. They burnt and abandoned Crown point. Carleton is besieging Ticonderoga.' According to Horace Walpole it was also reported that General Burgoyne was coming home, 'on pretence of his own affairs, but it was supposed on disagreement with Carleton'.[3]

23rd November, Saturday An exceeding heavy moist day

Early in the morning, according to the *London Gazette*, Lieutenant James Dacres of the royal navy arrived at the Admiralty with dispatches from Quebec. They included a letter from Sir Guy Carleton to Lord George Germain, written on board the *Maria*, off Crown Point, on 14th October. Carleton reported that 'the rebel fleet upon Lake Champlain has been intirely defeated in two actions', that their second in command, Mr Waterburg, had been captured along with two of their vessels, and ten other vessels had been 'burnt and destroyed'. On hearing news of the defeat the rebels had 'set fire to all the buildings and houses in and near Crown Point, and retired to Ticonderoga'. For further particulars Germain was referred to Lieutenant Dacres, 'who will be the bearer of this letter, and had a share in both actions'. Carleton concluded: 'The season is so far advanced, that I cannot yet pretend to inform your lordship whether any thing farther can be done this year.'

About ten o'clock Lieutenant Dacres was sent for to the Queen's Palace. He was introduced by Germain, and was in conference with his majesty upwards of two hours.[1]

In the evening, before the performance of *Jane Shore* at Drury Lane Theatre, Mr Reddish came on and read an address drawn up by Mr Sheridan:

> 'Ladies and gentlemen. Having ... on Tuesday night last accounted for my omission in the part of Vainlove in a manner which appear'd to reflect highly on the managers, I now beg permission to ascribe it to the confusion I was in from the displeasure of the audience; and as the managers are satisfied with my assurance that this was the case, I humbly hope for the indulgence of the public, whom I never meant to offend and whom I will ever study to please.'

This was received with approbation and the play was afterwards performed without interruption.

Reddish's conduct in this affair may have been related to the insanity which had been afflicting him at intervals since about 1774. This would be his last season at Drury Lane. He died in the York Asylum in December 1785.[2]

Samuel Reddish as Posthumus in *Cymbeline*

Mezzotint by Valentine Green, after Robert Edge Pine, published 1771

MP 'Nothing can exceed the vigor with which the present preparations in all the dock-yards are carrying on; but there is not a doubt of its being at present a race with France, who is straining every nerve to have a great fleet at sea before us; it is likewise true, that she had the start of us, and can, from the nature of her government, be more expeditious than we can.'[3]

24th November, Sunday Chiefly bright, some flying clouds, cutting wind. Stormy
Horace Walpole wrote from Strawberry Hill to Sir Horace Mann in Florence with news of the victory on Lake Champlain and the 'great naval preparations' being made by France. 'If you should ask what the opposition says, I answer, nothing. They have abandoned parliament, and some are gone into the country, and some to Paris: not to confer with Mr Deane, but to see horse-races — of which we have none here!'[1]

25th November, Monday Frost in the night, exceeding fine bright day. Full
moon
In the morning a tender, with above 300 impressed men, sailed from off the Tower for the Downs. Two men jumped out of a boat into the river, as they were going from the Tower to the tender, and were unfortunately drowned.[1]

By express from Dover, Lord Weymouth received several letters from Lord Stormont dated 20th November at Paris. 'War is now the general topic of conversation here,' reported Stormont in one. 'Not only the public at large look upon it as highly probable, but persons of the first rank and who have many opportunities of information consider it in the same light.' A further letter, marked 'Most confidential', brought more striking news:

> I am very secretly and, I am afraid, authentically informed that a treaty or convention is not only agreed upon by M. de Vergennes and Mr Deane, but is actually drawn out article by article. ...
>
> Indeed, my lord, after all we know of the present insidious policy of this Court it is impossible to place the least dependance upon their friendship or good faith. We can operate upon nothing but their fears, and trust to nothing but our own vigilance and superior naval strength.[2]

26th November, Tuesday Hard frost, foggy morning, bright day, very cold
Early in the morning a woman undressed herself entirely at the old watch-house, Blackfriars Bridge, got upon the top of the balustrades, and flung herself into the Thames.[1]

At noon, although the lord mayor has given strict orders to the contrary, two young men were seized by a press gang at the gate of the Mansion House, and were carried on board a tender, before any of the City officers could be procured to their assistance.[2]

At the Cape of Good Hope, Captain Cook wrote to Lord Sandwich, saying that they were to proceed on their voyage shortly and had provisions for over two years, having increased considerably the number of animals on board since leaving England. 'Nothing is wanting but a few females of our own species to make the *Resolution* a compleate ark'. He added that 'the takeing on board some horses has made Omai compleatly happy. He consented with raptures to give up his cabbin to make room for them'.[3]

27th November, Wednesday Hard frost, foggy till nine, fine bright day

The *Morning Post* carried another advertisement for Bartholomew Coote Purdon:

> A reward of 30 guineas having been offered for the discovery of his body, which has not yet been found, and several reports having been circulated that he is still alive, the family of the above unfortunate person, in order to do all the justice in their power to his bona fide creditors, do hereby offer the sum of 100 guineas to any person who shall in two months from the 23d of this instant November, give proof of his being now alive ...[1]

At 11.30 a.m. the long expected suit between the Chevalier d'Éon and M. de Morande came on before Lord Mansfield in the Court of King's Bench.* The court was greatly crowded, with refugee Edward Oxnard among those present. Morande was to show cause why the rule for an information to be filed against him as the author of a libel in the *Public Ledger* of 10th September should not be made absolute. The libel had imported that d'Éon was a woman and concerned in imposing upon the public in the matter of insurance policies on her sex.

Mr Bearcroft, leading counsel for Morande, observed that it had been a rule in that court never to grant informations where the parties applying could be proved guilty of the same offence. The chevalier, however, had written two letters to Morande in which he abused him in the most scurrilous language. Mr Bearcroft read out several passages from the letters, which contained so many out of the way and ridiculous expressions that he was repeatedly interrupted by the loud and hearty laughs of the whole court. He ended by expressing confidence that their lordships would agree that the wisest path for both parties would be to drop all animosities, and not only shake hands, but kiss and be friends.

The clerk then read Morande's affidavit. To support his assertion that d'Éon was a woman he gave a long account of the transactions involving Beaumarchais and the purchase of secret papers. As part of this a permission granted by Louis XVI for d'Éon to return to France as a woman was read out. Morande also sought

---

* Among earlier entries related to these proceedings are: 21st May (the Swinton episode may well be the brief departure from London mentioned by Morande); 3rd and 8th August (d'Éon's letters to Morande); 10th September (alleged libel in the *Public Ledger*); and 18th November (affidavits on behalf of d'Éon which may have been read at the trial but which are not mentioned in reports of it).

to support his claim that d'Éon had been privy to plans to make money on policies on her sex. He said she had been offered £10,000 and the negotiation had only foundered when she insisted on cash rather than a share in the policies equal to that sum. She had, however, received a smaller sum in return for leaving London for a time.

The affidavit also related Morande's quarrels with d'Éon, O'Gorman, and Horneck, and his receipt of the two letters from d'Éon, which were read out verbatim in French and then in translation. As with the extracts recited earlier by Mr Bearcroft, they were met with great laughter in court. Morande claimed that these letters had been the cause of his writing his own letter to the *Ledger*, which he thought a justifiable measure, since he knew the chevalier's sex, and disdained to fight a woman, and yet could not let her attacks pass in silence. He swore that to the best of his information and belief d'Éon had caused her letters to be read out publickly in several coffee-houses in town.

Mr Lee followed as second counsel for Morande. Referring to d'Éon as 'this animal of the doubtful gender', he observed that the whole matter had excited universal laughter in court, so that it was evident every person who heard it thought it a ridiculous affair. He hoped their lordships would dismiss the case and not countenance a serious prosecution.

For d'Éon, Mr Wallace argued that there was an essential difference between a private letter, however warm, and a publick newspaper attack. Mr Dunning followed and created considerable laughter by pointing out that Morande had, to prove his courage, bound over to keep the peace a person whom he declared to be a woman, and then had attacked her in a newspaper libel, knowing that she could have no redress but what the laws afforded.

Counsel having concluded, the students and short-hand writers were preparing to take notes, as it was expected that the judges would give a solemn opinion upon the case, when, to their great mortification, Lord Mansfield confined himself to the following words: 'Let the rule be discharged.' The *Morning Post* felt he had 'never pronounced a decision more to the honour of his understanding, as the whole business was of too ridiculous a nature for his more serious attention'.[2]

28th November, Thursday Cloudy heavy day
In the morning the press was very hot about the 'Change. Two fellows with asses, crying potatoes in Bishopsgate Street, were pressed, as were three Irish fruit-men who were standing by their baskets in Cornhill.[1]

Upwards of forty deserters lately brought from America were escorted, under a strong guard, to the Savoy gaol.[2]

In the evening Thomas Farmer, one of the convicts who escaped from the ship near Woolwich on 7th November, was examined before the magistrates in Litchfield Street. From the evidence of the mate of the ship it appeared that Farmer had, while on board, behaved so exceeding well that he was entrusted to have his irons off, and had the care of the keys to lock and unlock the convicts when they went to and from work. In his defence Farmer said that they were almost starved, having no more than half a pound of bread each man every day; that the meat they had was full of maggots before dressed; that the soup had the above vermin taken out by spoonfuls; that liberty was sweet, and finding a good opportunity to escape, they agreed to get off. He was committed for trial at the Old Bailey, where, in early December, he was sentenced to serve double the time, six years instead of three.[3]

29th November, Friday Heavy foggy morning, bright afternoon

In the morning a desperate battle took place between a press gang and the butchers in Oxford Market, in which the latter came off victorious. It happened about the impressing two black men, who were well respected, and lived servants in that neighbourhood.[1]

Near the Victualling Office, Tower Hill, a press gang got two smart girls to sing ballads, who soon drew a great concourse of people about them. The press gang then popped out, secured several useful hands, and carried them on board a tender. The girls narrowly escaped being thrown into Tower Ditch.[2]

Lord Weymouth replied from St James's to the letters received four days earlier from Lord Stormont in Paris. He confirmed a previous instruction that Stormont should pay for 'any important secret information whenever such an opportunity may offer. | In the present instance, if such a treaty has really been entered into by the Court of France with the Congress ... a copy should be purchased, if possible, at any price.' Even a draft treaty would be worth 'considerable expence'.[3]

In the evening Congreve's *Love for Love* was revived at Drury Lane Theatre, with minor alterations by Mr Sheridan to omit passages which the delicacy of the present times would not admit. According to the *Morning Post*, 'The comedy was admirably played throughout,' and 'Mrs Abington was the true natural *hoy ti! toy ti* in Miss Prue.'[4]

Mrs Abington as Miss Prue
Published 1st January 1777

GA 'A young lady of Parliament-street, Westminster, who is, on the death of her mother, entitled to a large fortune, a few days since set off for Paris with a clerk belonging to a public office, dressed in woman's cloaths, where they celebrated their nuptials. They returned to the bride's mother on Tuesday last, who refused them admittance. They are at present in lodgings, and the young lady is almost in a state of insanity.'[5]

30th November, Saturday A fine bright day, wet evening
The Royal Society held their anniversary meeting at their house in Crane Court, Fleet Street. The president, Sir John Pringle, presented the gold medal *in absentia* to James Cook, Esq., captain in his majesty's navy, for his useful discoveries in the South Seas. The society's members dined together as usual at the Crown and Anchor in the Strand, with John Wilkes among the guests.[1]

At night the press was very smart in the vicinity of Billingsgate. A gang appeared suddenly, attended with music and several girls of the town, which manoeuvre proved remarkably successful, a great number of useful hands being picked up by the attraction, who were conducted on board the *Nightingale*, lying off the Tower.[2]

Meanwhile in America

16th November. Fort Washington was surrendered to the British and some 2,700 prisoners were taken.[1]

30th November. At New York the Howe brothers issued another, more generous proclamation. It offered 'a full and free pardon' to all those taking an oath of 'peaceable obedience to his majesty' within sixty days.[2]

... and in Paris

Probably in early November, although possibly in late October, an unprepossessing 24-year-old Scotsman called James Aitken visited Silas Deane at the Hôtel d'Entragues in the Faubourg St Germain.

Born in Edinburgh, Aitken, later known as 'John the Painter', had drifted into a life of petty crime before setting out in hope of a new life in America. Not finding one he came back, arriving at Liverpool in May 1775. Unkempt and restless, he spent the next few months travelling around the country, enlisting twice in the army for the bounty money before deserting, returning to petty crime, and working as a jobbing painter. At the end of the year he was in London, 'where I got connexion with some women of the town, which led me to commit a number of street robberies for my support. I also broke open a house at Kensington, and committed several robberies upon the outskirts of London.'

Fearing arrest, in March 1776 he left for Cambridge, and then wandered the country, robbing to support himself, and enlisting and deserting for a third time. After raping a girl he had found watching sheep near Basingstoke he fled to

Oxford. There, 'one night in conversation, concerning the American war, the importance of his majesty's fleet and dock-yards was the favourite argument ... | It is amasing with what force this conversation kept possession of my mind. ... In the night I had a thousand ideas, and all tended to shew how important would be the event in favour of America, provided these dock-yards and shipping could be destroyed.' He spent two days 'in the contemplation of this malicious design', persuading himself 'it would entitle me to the first rank in America'. He set off for Portsmouth and gathered information about the dock-yard, proceeding to Plymouth, Chatham, Woolwich, and Deptford for the same purpose. Having discounted the idea of laying his scheme before Congress directly, he remembered that their representative Deane was at Paris, headed for Dover, and hired a small sailing boat. From Calais he proceeded to Paris and located the Hôtel d'Entragues.

The two men left different accounts of the encounter that followed. According to Aitken, he told Deane 'I was an utter enemy to Great Britain, as I understood he was, and had the interest of America so much at heart, that I would readily undertake any expedition, though ever so dangerous, in its behalf.' He added that he had it in his power, by 'an invention of my own', to destroy all the British dock-yards and 'the greatest part of the shipping'. He showed Deane plans he had made of yards and fortifications and explained the knowledge he had acquired 'of every particular storehouse and magazine in the different docks, the free access which strangers of all kinds had into them, and the facility with which the whole might be set on fire'. He had no objection to undertake the task himself, 'provided I was assured of being countenanced by America, and properly rewarded'. Deane raised some practical objections and expressed concern 'should it come out that America was privy to it', but asked him 'to attend at the same hour in the morning, to leave the drawings and observations for his consideration in the mean time, and on no account to drop a hint of my business at Paris, or my knowledge of him, or even to speak a word concerning the affairs of America'.

At the next meeting Deane apparently approved the plan and gave Aitken the name and address of Edward Bancroft in London, saying he should not call upon him 'till I had effected the business at Portsmouth, after which I should immediately make the best of my way to London, and he would secrete me till the rumour of the fire was abated'. Aitken would later be able to return to France, 'where I should meet with every reward which the greatness of my services would entitle me to expect'. Deane also gave him 'about three pounds English money' and offered 'to procure a pass from under the hand of the King of France', in case Aitken should have any difficulty in his journey back to England.

The pass was dated 13th November at Fontainebleau. As soon as it was procured Aitken set off for Calais and thence to Dover.[3]

December

1st December, Advent Sunday Many flying clouds, with bright intervals. Stormy
On or about this day James Aitken arrived at Chatham.

> Here I spent two days, in making some fresh observations on the shipping
> and dock-yard, after which I set out for London, in order to take the road for
> Portsmouth. When in London, I thought it adviseable to provide myself with
> such further articles, as were likely to be wanted in the perpetration of this infer-
> nal business. I purchased a pair of screw-barrel pistols, resolving, if any man
> should detect or molest me, to kill him on the spot. I also procured a pistol-
> tinder-box, a quantity of tinder, a gallon of the spirits of turpentine, and a
> quantity of nitre. These I packed up in the most careful manner, and the next
> day began my journey.
>
> I arrived at Portsmouth on Thursday evening the 5th of December, 1776,
> and immediately began to lay down a plan of operations.[1]

In the evening Lucrezia Aguiari sang at a private concert at Dr Burney's house
in St Martin's Street. Fanny Burney described the scene in a letter written next
day to a retiring and ailing family friend, Samuel Crisp. Aguiari had been 'invited
without the least thought of her singing, and merely as an auditor herself. She
looked charmingly, though horribly ill dressed, in old Court mourning'. Also among
the party were sculptor Joseph Nollekens and his wife, and a 'Miss B. ... a young
lady quite *à la mode*, every part of her dress, the very pink and extreme of the fashion;
her head erect and stiff as any statue; her voice low, and delicate, and mincing; her
head higher than twelve wigs stuck one on the other ... and her conversation very
much *the thing*.' To the delight of Fanny and the rest of the company, Aguiari
offered to sing.

> O, sir, what words can I use? Could I write what she deserves, you would come
> to hear her, let what would be the consequence. O, Mr Crisp, she would heal
> all your complaints, her voice would restore you to health and spirits. I think
> it is almost greater than ever — and then, when softened, so sweet, so mellow,
> so affecting! She has every thing, every requisite to accomplish a singer, in
> every style and manner, the sublime and the beautiful equally at command ...
> I die to have you enjoy the greatest luxury the world can offer; such to me,
> such, I am sure, to you, would be the singing of Agujari![2]

2nd December, Monday Hazy misling morning, fair afternoon, but cloudy
On about this day William Hickey returned to London and settled in Berners
Street. Still on the hunt for a position in India, he went 'at least twice a week to
the India House and Jerusalem Coffee House'. A few days before Christmas he
would learn that his efforts had borne fruit, John Roberts, a senior East India
director, having 'obtained the permission of his brother directors for my going
out to Bengal'.[1]

Further troubling news arrived for Lord Weymouth in a letter from Lord Stormont dated 27th November at Paris.

I am very secretly informed that Spain who, as your lordship knows, has long favoured the American rebels underhand, is now preparing to assist them more than ever. It is even not improbable that she will take an open and decided part in their favour. She likewise meditates an attack upon Portugal. All this is done in concert with this Court who chuses to keep behind the curtain for the present but has agreed to assist Spain with eleven millions of livres. ...

Mr Deane was at Versailles all Monday and yesterday. He has, I am told, obtained a promise of a French vessel to carry to America a number of officers, ammunition, clothes, &c. but from what port that vessel is to sail I have not yet been able to learn.[2]

Mrs Cornelys gave the town to know that she was still in the land of the living with the first masquerade of the season at Carlisle House. As the notice was sudden only some 400 masquers were present. Tickets were a guinea and a half. According to the *Morning Chronicle*, 'The smallness of the price ... afforded the middling rank of people an opportunity of sharing in the sports of the evening, but kept away the *beau monde*, who disdain to come to any entertainment within the reach of the vulgar.' Among the masks was a Lieutenant of the Navy with a number of Sailors as a Gang. They were pressing all night, as many ladies could testify.[3]

3rd December, Tuesday Foggy heavy day
Two chimney-sweepers were carried before the lord mayor having been found concealed in a chimney in Bishopsgate Street. They were told they could serve in the navy, which they refused, and were committed to the Poultry Compter for further examination.[1]

In the evening a press gang of fifteen persons, armed as usual, went to a public-house in Ratcliff Highway on the information of a woman that thirteen India sailors were in a room up stairs. When the gang arrived a dreadful conflict began. Having no arms, the Indiamen defended themselves for a considerable time with bottles, bowls, glasses, &c. but one of them receiving a stab in the body, a surgeon was sent for, who pronounced it mortal, on which two of the gang were taken into custody.[2]

4th December, Wednesday Cloudy mild day
A deserter belonging to the 14th regiment of foot hanged himself in the Savoy.[1]

A tradesman in Westminster shot himself through the head in his bed-chamber. It is said he had lost a considerable sum of money in the lottery.[2]

Nathaniel Wraxall, subsequently known for his indiscreet memoirs, dined at the house of the bookselling Dilly brothers in the Poultry. Among the company were John Wilkes, judge and orientalist William (later Sir William) Jones, and Dr Dodd. 'Before we parted Dodd invited us to a dinner at his residence in Argyle

Street. A day was named and all promised to attend. When we broke up, Dr Dodd ... offered to set me down at the west end of the town, adding that his own carriage was waiting at the door. I readily accepted the proposal, and he carried me back to the St James's Coffee-house.' As agreed the company met again at Dodd's on 24th January 1777, when, according to Wraxall, 'a very elegant repast was served, with French wines of various kinds'. Two weeks later Dodd would be arrested for the forgery which led him to the gallows.[3]

Elsewhere, Benjamin Franklin wrote from Auray in Brittany to inform Silas Deane of his arrival. He added that Congress had named the two of them plus Thomas Jefferson 'to negotiate a treaty of commerce and friendship with the Court of France'. Jefferson having declined, 'Mr Arthur Lee, at present in London, was named in his place'. In a postscript he added: 'If you could find some means to notify Mr Lee of his nomination, it would be well to do so. Perhaps the best way would be through the department of foreign affairs and the French ambassador. The regular post would not be safe.'[4]

5th December, Thursday Foggy heavy day, very warm

At the Old Bailey Thomas Burrows was indicted for assaulting one William Brooks on 28th November and committing with him that abominable crime (among Christians not to be named) called buggary.

Anthony Loame, a cabinet and chair maker, said he had met the prisoner in the public tap-room at the Harlequin in Drury Lane on the night of 27th November. After a drink of beer Burrows asked 'if I would go home and eat part of a piece of turkey and a piece of goose he had got'. Loame went with him to a house in Nag's Head Court, Drury Lane, where five gentlemen were waiting to sup. He told the court that Burrows 'washes and irons and cooks ... for these sodomites, and picks up young fellows for them'.

After drinking wine Loame had gone home, but next day Burrows came to him and said 'a gentleman would be glad to speak to me concerning some business out of the country. Accordingly I went along with him to his house. They took me up stairs. There were, I believe, about fourteen of them in all, gentlemen and gentlemen's servants together. By and by there was a rug hung up ... in one corner of the room. Brooks, who is a gentleman's servant, and the prisoner, went behind it. Brooks is not yet taken. And there they had connections together.' Told that he must be very particular in his account, Loame said he saw 'Brooks leaning his head against the wall: they had both their breeches down; he [Burrows] pulled out his — and put it into Brooks's —. ... Afterwards they sat down and began kissing and slavering over me, and wanted to do the same with me. They began kissing me, and used me very ill; a gentleman offered me three guineas if I would go and lie with him at an inn; and afterwards he offered to make it up [to] ten. ... This was about nine o'clock at night; they kept me till between twelve and one.'

In his defence Burrows said it was all 'as false as God is true', but he was found guilty and sentenced to death. He was executed at Tyburn on 29th January 1777.[1]

William Davis was tried for robbing a servant belonging to the then lord mayor, John Sawbridge, on the night of 6th September [>]. Five persons swore to a direct alibi but the jury, after retiring and considering for more than an hour, found Davis guilty. According to the *Morning Post*, 'The court and auditory all thought it a very severe verdict.' Davis was tried a second time for an assault on Sawbridge on the same occasion and was again found guilty. He was sentenced to death, but in the following March received a royal pardon on condition of leaving the kingdom for the rest of his life.[2]

In the evening died Elizabeth, Duchess of Northumberland, having just compleated her sixtieth year. She was the only daughter of Algernon Seymour, the last Duke of Somerset of his branch, and through him descended from the illustrious family of Percy, ancient earls of Northumberland. By marriage with the present duke she has left two sons, the elder being Hugh, Earl Percy, one of the members for Westminster and at present a lieutenant general in his majesty's service in America. According to the *Morning Chronicle*, 'With a most princely fortune, devolved to her from her ancestors, her grace sustained her exalted rank through her whole life with the greatest dignity, generosity, and spirit, and will ever be considered as one of the first characters of the present age.'[3]

The Duchess of Northumberland
After a portrait by Reynolds painted in the late 1750s

6th December, Friday Heavy foggy morning, bright afternoon
In the morning an express was sent to Lord Percy in America to acquaint him
with the death of his mother.[1]

7th December, Saturday As yesterday
The corpse of the Duchess of Northumberland was embalmed and put into lead.
It is to be interred in the family vault in Westminster Abbey.[1]

In Portsmouth dock-yard James Aitken lit two incendiary devices, the first
(which failed) in the hemp-house, and the second in the rope-house. Having left
the yard he was unnerved by meeting someone he knew and who looked at him
'very stedfastly'. He abandoned his plan to set fire to his lodgings and 'ran very
precipitately out of town, without giving myself time to call for my bundle'. At
around 4 p.m. he prevailed upon a woman driving a cart from market 'to give me
a lift, telling her I had to go to Petersfield that night, and would make her any
satisfaction'. At his request she drove with great speed for the first part of the
journey. A little further on, 'her horse getting weary, she said he wanted water,
and drove to a pond at the road-side. At this instant I looked round towards
Portsmouth, and saw the dock in a blaze, upon which I jumped out of the cart
without saying a word, and run for near four miles on the road to Petersfield ... |
I travelled all night without intermission, and arrived at Kingston upon Thames
about eleven o'clock on Sunday morning'.[2]

8th December, Sunday Foggy heavy day
In the morning, as soon as news of the fire at Portsmouth arrived at the Admiralty,
a messenger was sent off to Lord Sandwich, who was at Hampton Court. His
lordship went from thence to Kew, to inform his majesty, and immediately after
came to town.[1]

Having stayed in Kingston upon Thames for several hours, Aitken stirred,
setting out for London on foot at about 3 p.m. and boarding a hackney stage for
the later part of the journey.

> On my arrival in London, I concluded myself out of danger. I refreshed myself
> at a little public-house in Westminster, and then made it my business to find
> out Dr Bancroft, the gentleman to whom I was directed by Mr Deane, who
> lives in Downing Street, Westminster. I was taken into a parlour, and Dr
> Bancroft in a few minutes came to me. I told him my name was Actzen, that
> I was the person sent by Mr Deane from Paris, to burn and destroy the dock-
> yards and shipping belonging to government. That I had set Portsmouth dock
> on fire, which was then in flames, and that Mr Deane had directed me to apply
> to him, who he said he should communicate the secret to, and direct to supply
> me with what money I wanted, and to secrete me till suspicion was over. He
> appeared somewhat surprised at this information, said he knew Mr Deane
> perfectly well, but had never heard from him concerning this matter, and

ABOVE Hugh, Earl Percy, after a painting by Pompeo Batoni. Published 1st January 1777. BELOW Aitken's incendiary tin case, from an account of his trial published in 1777. 'A little wooden box is made to fit the case, which having a hole through the centre, admits the bottom of a candle into it ... The box is filled with combustibles of different kinds, which, when the candle is nearly burnt out, take fire ...'

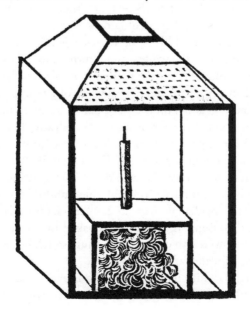

therefore should have nothing to do with it. That at present he had company in the house, and not time to talk with me, but if I would go to the Salopian Coffee-house, he would come to me in about half an hour.

About seven o'clock, or some little time after, Dr Bancroft came and sat down with me. I related to him my whole conversation with Mr Deane, my success at Portsmouth, which he would see confirmed in the papers of to-morrow, and my reliance on him for money, and such other assistance as I should want in the continuance of this scheme. After a short conversation, Dr Bancroft told me, that though he wished Mr Deane very well, and entertained a great friendship for him, yet he would not have to do with any of his schemes. That he lived and got his bread under this government, and must therefore be excused from meddling in this affair; nor would he encourage me in my proceedings, and desired me not to call at his house, or trouble him any more. I answered, that I would not; but was sorry to find Mr Deane was so much deceived in him; and that though he was such a friend to Great Britain, I declared myself an utter enemy to it, and told him he would soon hear more of my works at Plymouth to convince him of it, and wished him a good night.

Highly disconcerted at this treatment, and vexed at the disappointment of receiving a sum of money, I could not sleep the whole night.[2]

9th December, Monday An exceeding fine bright day

At a quarter after nine o'clock, before Lord Mansfield and a special jury in the Court of King's Bench, came on the trial of Samuel Foote, Esq., who was not required to attend and chose not to do so. He was charged by his former footman John Sangster with having attempted to commit buggery upon his person, first at Mr Foote's town house in Suffolk Street, and then next morning in the stables of his country house at North End, Fulham.

Sangster gave an account of his being hired by Mr Foote in November 1775, going with him to Dublin in the winter, and returning in February. He swore that he went into town with Foote on the morning of Wednesday 1st May. Foote's business was to meet his performers in advance of the opening of his theatre, and he spent an hour and a half on the stage before going to his adjoining house. There, a little after noon, Sangster being in the hallway, Foote rang for him to come up stairs, led him into a back room, locked the door, and behaved to him in a shockingly indecent manner. He told Foote that 'had he imagined or heard he had been a man of such a sort he would not have continued a second day in his service, even if he would have given him one hundred guineas a year'.

Sangster related the incident with great minuteness. He said that on his escaping down stairs Foote's housemaid, Nanny, had asked him what kept him so long above, to which he answered that he did not chuse to tell her now, but she would probably hear more of it hereafter.

Later Foote spoke to him in the ground floor parlour and persuaded him to stay in his service till next morning, when he would pay him his wages and give him a character. In consequence he accompanied Foote that afternoon to North End. Next morning Foote saw him in the little grove or orchard in the grounds, and desired him to go into the stable to shew him a new horse, and there Foote again attempted indecencies with him, but he gave him a hearty blow and quit the stable.

Next day, Friday, he came to town early and returned to Fulham in the evening, when a severe altercation happened between him and Foote. He gave Foote the grossest and foulest language and insisted he should settle with him that evening, but to no avail. He swore that Foote made him several friendly and advantageous offers, mixed with threats, on condition that he would not reveal what had happened. Foote warned Sangster that any story he might tell would have little effect: he had all the men of fashion and the nobility to protect and support him, and Sangster would not be believed.

On the Saturday morning Sangster went up stairs for the key of his box, and while there heard his master's voice in the kitchen. Listening at the head of the stairs, he heard himself being abused in violent terms. On this he went to the kitchen where Foote accosted him with 'Johnny, what is the matter? Can't you rest satisfied, stay in your place, and mind your business?' He said he would not, and called Foote 'an old buggering scoundrel, rascal, &c.' Foote called him a whoremonger, on which Sangster replied *he* could not be hanged for it. Later Foote sent up for him to pay his wages, and divided his cast cloaths into two lots, one for Sangster and the other for Louis Vallet, the butler.

That evening Sangster returned to town and acquainted his former employer Dr Fordyce with what had passed. Fordyce advised him to go to Sir John Fielding, as the most proper person to direct him what to do.

On cross examination Sangster admitted that his prosecution had been supported by a Mr Harvey, who had previously been a stranger to him. Harvey was a friend and patron of William Jackson, who had acted for the former Duchess of Kingston, now Countess of Bristol, in her long-running conflict with Foote.

Sangster also said that he had been indecently assaulted by Foote in January in Dublin, and had complained of the matter to his fellow servant Vallet at that time. Later, back in England, he had additionally complained to John Williams, the coachman.

He was questioned respecting his having changed the day of the week in his first allegation from 'Monday last', 29th April, to Wednesday, 1st May. He said it was a mere mistake, that he had not signed his information made before Sir John Fielding at Bow Street, and that it was not read over to him.

Mr Bond, one of Sir John's clerks, swore that when Sangster presented himself at Bow Street he had introduced him to Sir John Fielding in an inner apartment. After conversing with Sir John, Sangster had dictated the words of his information and had said nothing about 1st May, only saying 'Monday last'. Mr Bond produced the original information, with Sangster's name signed in his own handwriting.

Mr Bond said he saw him write his name and that the information was read over to him. On this, Sir John Fielding was sent for.

John Williams corroborated Sangster's claim that he had complained to him of their master's conduct.

Dr Fordyce said that Sangster had come to him one morning in May and informed him, with tears in his eyes, of what had happened, and that he had, as related, referred him to Sir John Fielding.

As Mr Wallace was opening the case for the defendant, Sir John came into court. He said he did not entirely recollect all that had passed at the time of making the information, but on being pressed said he thought Sangster had mentioned something of the day on which Mr Foote met his theatre company, and talked of the 1st of May. This piece of evidence was much to the satisfaction of the prosecution counsel, who asked Sir John no more questions, and he therefore made his bow and walked out of court.

Resuming, Mr Wallace drew attention to the characters of Sangster and Williams, both of whom had been discharged by Foote, the former for being an idle, drunken, saucy fellow, and the latter for being seen in Sangster's company soon after his discharge. He insisted that Sangster had been discharged on the Friday for drunkenness, and that three days before the trial Williams had offered not to testify if Foote would be reconciled to him, and give him a good character.

Wallace added that so far from Foote being at his Suffolk Street house on 1st May, he had not been in town the whole of the week in question. He then produced the *Morning Chronicle* of Friday 3rd May, in which there was a paragraph dated from Mr Foote's theatre acquainting the performers of the company that the customary meeting would be held on Monday the 6th instant. Two actors were called to confirm this. The first, Jeffery Pearce, said that 1st May was the day on which Mr Foote had met his performers for twenty years past; that they assembled as usual on that day, but he did not come, instead sending a message by Wilde, the prompter, that he could not attend, but would meet them on the ensuing Monday. Thomas Davis, another actor, confirmed this and added that he went up into Foote's dining room at a quarter after two o'clock to see if he had come, but he was not there.

The prosecution does not seem to have thought it worth enquiring why Foote had deferred the usual 1st May meeting and given such belated notice of the change, perhaps because they knew the case was lost: Sangster had claimed the assault took place on the day Foote met the company, but it was now clear that that meeting had not taken place until some two hours after Sangster had gone to the Bow Street office to make his allegation.

William Jewell, Foote's treasurer and confidant, deposed that on Friday 3rd May Sangster came drunk from town to North End. He heard him calling both Mr Foote and himself names in the kitchen. He informed Foote, who put down his cup of tea and instantly discharged Sangster his service. Next morning Sangster had gone to Mr Jewell's house at Brompton, asked his pardon, wept bitterly, and lamented having lost the best of masters through his own folly. Mr Jewell positively declared to the court that Foote was not in town on 1st May, and his account was corroborated in every particular by Mrs Jewell.

The prosecution recalled Williams the coachman to ask whether he had not driven his master to town on 1st May. He said he had, and recollected it was that day because he saw a garland in Piccadilly, but he could not tell whether Mr Foote dined in town that day or not, or at what hour he returned to North End.

The butler Louis Vallet directly contradicted Sangster's claim of having complained to him about Mr Foote's conduct, and concurred with Mr Jewell in declaring that his master was not in town on 1st May.

In summing up, Lord Mansfield pointed out the inconsistencies in Sangster's story and cast doubt on the evidence of Williams. The indictments appeared founded on conspiracy, he said, and the prosecution supported by perjury. He also drew attention to the curious involvement of Mr Harvey: 'And here a man takes up the prosecution, who is a stranger to the prosecutor, does not know him, and never meddled with the affair till the 23rd of May. Who is that man? Is he a friend to justice, or an enemy to Mr Foote? I expected to have heard of the real person who acts behind the curtain,' he added, presumably alluding to the Countess of Bristol or her agent William Jackson.

The jury, without quitting the box, in about two minutes returned their verdict of not guilty. The trial lasted nearly seven hours, Sangster's evidence over two hours, and the court did not rise till near four o'clock.[1]

Foote's counsel included his friend Arthur Murphy and Joseph Hickey. As soon as the trial was over, Murphy took a coach to Suffolk Street to be the first messenger of the good tidings. Foote had been looking out of a first floor window in anxious expectation. Murphy, as soon as he perceived him, waved his hat in token of victory, jumped out of the coach, and ran up stairs, but instead of meeting his old friend in all the exultation of high spirits, he saw him extended on the floor, in strong hysterics, in which state he continued near an hour before he could be recovered.[2]

In the evening a messenger was dispatched to the Countess of Bristol in Germany,* with an account of the result of the trial; it was intimated to the messenger that he need not distress himself on the score of expedition, as the tidings were not of a nature to import the least satisfaction to the countess.[3]

---

* She had set out from Calais in October on an intended journey to Rome. She reached Munich on 9th November but was by now in Vienna, where she would remain for the rest of the year.

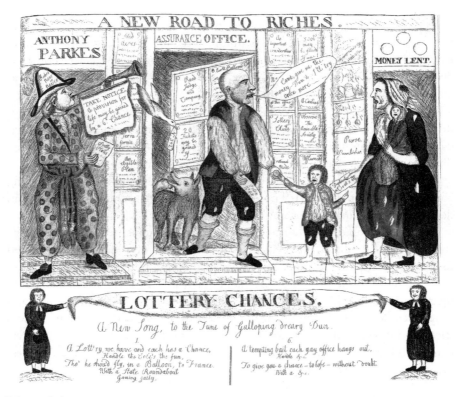

Meanwhile:

In the morning a young woman in Goodman's Fields was found hanging in her bed-chamber. A note was left on the table, declaring that the present lottery was her ruin. Meanwhile a young lady, daughter to a capital tradesman in Holborn, who was so fortunate as to get one of the 5,000l. prizes, eloped with one of her father's journeymen.[4]

James Aitken 'got up early, and walked to Hammersmith, scarcely knowing which road I had taken'.

> I supposed that a discovery would now most likely to be made, particularly as Dr Bancroft expressed himself in favour of government, and knew of my intention to proceed in the same way at Plymouth, as I had just done in the dock at Portsmouth. I went into an ale-house, I believe the sign of the Light Horseman, called for pen, ink, and paper, and wrote to Dr Bancroft on the occasion, requesting him not to disclose the circumstances I had related to him, as it would greatly injure his friend Mr Silas Deane, and the cause of America, and do himself no service. Whether this had any weight with him or not, I can't say, but believe he never discovered the transaction to the public.
>
> I began my journey to Plymouth, sometimes walking, and sometimes taking advantage of the stages; but I never rode far at a time, for fear of being taken notice of by the passengers.[5]

Two views of the lottery

ABOVE 'The Lottery Contrast', after Robert Dighton, published 1794.

FACING PAGE 'A New Road to Riches', published 1784.
'A tempting bait each gay office hangs out …'

Several of Sir John Fielding's men were dispatched to Portsmouth to apprehend some suspicious persons imagined to have had a hand in setting fire to the dock-yard.[6]

Sir James Porter, former ambassador to Constantinople, died at his house in Great Marlborough Street. According to his daughter Anna, after 'decaying some months' he had fallen 'dangerously ill' on 12th November. From that day she lived 'between hope and fear 'till ye 6th of December when O! my God! my father was dying. I felt the first stroke of grief at 3 o'clock in ye afternoon on ye 9th when I lost him.'[7]

A dead male child, supposed to have been but a few hours old, whose skull appeared to have been fractured, was found nailed up in a box in a field near Tottenham Court Road. Two days later, Wednesday, the coroner's inquest sat on the body and returned their verdict wilful murder against some person or persons unknown.[8]

At night General Burgoyne arrived in town from Quebec. According to Horace Walpole:

> He now pretended grief for his wife's death, which was laughed at. The king scarce spoke to him, and he was forced to ask for an audience. Some thought he had quarrelled with Carleton; but he was exceedingly disappointed at finding the opposition had quitted parliament, having probably hoped, as he had done last year, to be bribed from making complaints. He brought news that Carleton had caused his army to recross the lakes, had abandoned Crown Point, and not attempted Ticonderoga ...[9]

10th December, Tuesday A dark, heavy, black day

In the evening, being the anniversary of the institution of the Royal Academy, the academicians met at Somerset House. After the medals were given the president, Sir Joshua Reynolds, read a discourse to the students as usual. His subject was what is fixed and what is fluctuating in taste.[1]

Romeo and Juliet was performed at Drury Lane Theatre. Mary Robinson, née Darby, known to posterity as 'Perdita' and as a mistress of the Prince of Wales, played the part of Juliet in her first stage performance. Expectations were high: she had been hired by Sheridan, coached by Garrick, and encouraged by the Duchess of Devonshire. In her autobiography she recalled her nervousness, the theatre being 'crowded with fashionable spectators' and her mentor Garrick sitting in the centre of the Orchestra.

'When I approached the side wing my heart throbbed convulsively: I then began to fear that my resolution would fail, and I leaned upon the Nurse's arm, almost fainting. Mr Sheridan and several other friends encouraged me to proceed; and at length, with trembling limbs and fearful apprehension, I approached the audience.' Before she had uttered a word she was met with 'thundering applause that ... nearly overpowered all my faculties. I stood mute and bending with alarm, which did not subside till I had feebly articulated the few sentences of the first short scene,

Mrs Robinson

After a portrait by Gainsborough, 1781

during the whole of which I had never once ventured to look at the audience.' As the performance progressed 'I found the applause augment, and the night was concluded with peals of clamorous approbation'.

Hopkins the prompter noted 'a genteel figure — a very tolerable first appearance and may do in time'. The *Gazetteer* was more effusive: 'She distinguished herself throughout the character in such a manner, as would do honour to any capital actress. She reunites the advantages of a clear, melodious voice, of an engaging figure, and of an artless, graceful delivery, and cannot fail to prove a valuable acquisition to the public.'[2]

At night rioters assembled before the house of Messrs. Bailey, Jaques and Co., lottery office keepers, at No. 29 Ludgate Hill, near the Old Bailey, and broke the windows and did other considerable damage. The attack was prompted by the distribution of hand-bills claiming that 'an anonymous gentleman' had been refused a sum of money due to him upon the drawing of No. 8 in the present lottery.[3]

11th December, Wednesday Bright fine morning, cloudy afternoon
About 4 a.m. the Liverpool diligence was going out of town when it was stopped by three footpads in Goswell Street, opposite Coker's Yard. One man went on each side of the coach and the other stopped the horses, on which the guard fired and wounded him. His accomplices carried him over an adjacent field and escaped in the dark. A great deal of blood was found. It is supposed the wounded man was shot through the head as his hat, afterwards found by some milk people, had several shot holes in it.[1]

Eight men were executed at Tyburn including William Davis, for forging and uttering a warrant of the East India Company [> 18 Oct], and John Harding, for breaking into the house of Mr Bean, gardener, at Brentford [> 25 Aug]. John and Joseph White, two brothers, coiners, were drawn on a sledge. They all behaved with a penitence becoming their unhappy situation.

One report claimed that as they 'were conveying to the place of execution ... Doctor H. [William Hunter] bespoke four of them from the undertakers'.

As the convicts were passing by St Giles's, a man ran out of a public-house with a knife in his hand, and cut his throat in a shocking manner.

About ten minutes after the procession, five press gangs went up Holborn, and picked up several useful hands.

According to the *Morning Chronicle*, Davis, who went to Tyburn in a mourning coach, 'had more powerful interest made for him than any convict ... these seven years past'. After conversing with the ordinary, praying, and joining the other convicts in a psalm, he requested silence, and addressed the multitude for near a quarter of an hour, acknowledging the justice of his doom and imploring them to take example by his unhappy exit. After this he addressed his fellow sufferers with chearfulness and resolution. The ordinary put the rope over his head, and at parting kissed him with great affection.

The *Morning Post* noted that the crowd did not behave so well: 'While the unfortunate convicts were preparing for the tremendous expiation of their crimes, little was to be seen or heard but indecency and profanation, common prostitutes in hackney coaches singing, and pick-pockets employed busily in every quarter; from whence it is evident that public executions serve only to harden the minds of the common people, and to promote idleness and dissipation.' This prompted one spectator to write to the paper to say that he 'was much less shock'd at the indecent behaviour of the lower class of people, than at the City marshal's, who ... exulting in the dignity of his office in leading the procession, suffer'd a grin of self-consequence to pervade his countenance, and seem'd pleased with exhibiting his ape's face, and chalky white teeth, to the view of the spectators on each side the road'.[2]

General Burgoyne attended the levee at St James's and afterwards had a conference with the king.[3]

12th December, Thursday Clear air, but no sun, misling evening

In Paris, Silas Deane wrote to Congress's committee of secret correspondence to say that he had heard from Benjamin Franklin of his safe arrival in France.

> I sent an express instantly to Mr Lee to join us here without delay, for the news of Mr Franklin's arrival may occasion his friends being forbid coming from London to France. Nothing has for a long time occasioned greater speculation than this event, and our friends here are elated beyond measure, as this confirms them you will not negotiate with England; and for me I will not attempt to express the pleasure I feel on this occasion, as it removes at once difficulties under which I have been constantly in danger of sinking.[1]

MC 'There will be no play at either theatre, nor any other publick entertainment, tomorrow, on account of the fast ordered by the royal proclamation. | On the same account the lottery will not be drawn in Guildhall till Saturday.'[2]

13th December, Friday A very foggy, heavy, moist day

On the occasion of the general fast their majesties attended divine service at the Chapel Royal, where there was a greater number of the nobility than for some years past.

The House of Lords attended at Westminster Abbey. It is said that in his sermon Dr Hurd, Bishop of Lichfield and Coventry, paid his brother peers off pretty warmly, pointing out those traits of infidelity and debauchery in the higher orders which spread dissipation like a torrent through all the inferior ranks of the people.

The House of Commons attended at St Margaret's, Westminster, where there was a very large congregation including the Speaker (Sir Fletcher Norton), Lord North, Lord George Germain, and about fifty other members. In his sermon the Rev. Dr John Butler, Archdeacon of Surry, lamented the unhappy defection of the Americans and the necessity this country was under to oblige them to return to allegiance. 'The greatest empires have had their fall. Some of them have disappeared so totally, that no more than their names and their history remain; and, in the case of most of them, intestine divisions have brought on their dissolution. The British empire has sustained a shock ... "The hands and the feet have said to the head, we have no need of thee."'*

Guilty as the Americans might be in so rebelling, he added, there was no need to cross the Atlantic to find sins.

'We are as sinful a nation, as a fruitful land and a flourishing commerce can make us. The natural effects of such abundance as ours, let loose upon the human heart, when it is unguarded by good principles, are Pride and Sensuality.

'"Pride goeth before destruction, and an haughty spirit before a fall,"† in the case of nations as well as individuals. In America, it affects independency of legal government. Among us, it seems to aim at a yet more ruinous independency of God ...'

After the service the Speaker and most of the members returned to the House of Commons, which was then adjourned until 21st January next.

The lord mayor, aldermen, and other City officers attended divine service at St Paul's Cathedral. The lord mayor and his suite appeared in mourning, and the sword of state was carried in a sable scabbard.

The solemnity of the day was observed by all ranks of people, churches being crowded with congregations who seemed to join with great fervency in the prayers offered up for a speedy termination of the unhappy contest between the mother country and her rebellious colonies.[1]

Near Lancaster Court in the Strand a hawker was crying the new form of prayer, and sold a great number to the good people who were going up that court in their way to St Martin's Church. At the time of divine service, when the prayer was going to be read, they took their form out of their prayer books, where they had placed it as soon as purchased; but to their great surprise, instead of 'A new form of prayer appointed to be read in all churches and chapels throughout England', they read 'The last dying speech and confession, birth, parentage, and education, of the eight malefactors, who were executed this morning at Tyburn'. It appears that the hawker had made use of this expedient to get off the remainder of his dying speeches, which had stuck on hand the day before. He held open a real form of prayer in one hand, and by means of the purple cover, passed off the dying speeches without the least suspicion.[2]

During service at St Paul's, Covent Garden, while the Rev. Mr Rous, curate, was preaching on the solemn subject of the day, a decent dressed man got up in the middle of his discourse and bawled out, 'Don't you tell so many lies in your

---

* 1 Corinthians xii 21: 'And the eye cannot say unto the hand, I have no need of thee: nor again the head to the feet, I have no need of you.'
† Proverbs xvi 18.

sermon, Mr Parson!', which naturally threw both the minister and his congregation into confusion. Sir John Fielding being present ordered the man to be taken into custody. He made his escape out of church but was apprehended in Bedfordbury and lodged in the watch-house. After the service he was brought to the public office in Bow Street and committed to Tothill Fields Bridewell. He was lately a broker and housekeeper near Drury Lane.[3]

Governor Hutchinson noted in his diary that the fast was 'observed with strictness and great external devotion, the churches crowded more than ever known on Sundays, and shops everywhere shut, and few people to be seen in the streets'. Edward Oxnard agreed: 'The day has been keept more sacredly than I hardly ever see a Sunday.' Their fellow American Edward Bancroft claimed not to be so impressed, writing to Silas Deane in Paris that 'in defiance of the royal proclamation' he had 'been dining at Mr Walpoles with some well disposed friends and making merry'. Others, too, refused to comply with the proclamation, shops belonging to the Quakers being open as usual.[4]

Meanwhile the high bailiff, with his attendants, rode through the streets of Westminster, and at the usual places proclaimed the vacant seat for a member to serve in parliament in the room of Lord Percy, who is become a peer by the death of his mother the Duchess of Northumberland. Notice was given for electors to attend at Covent Garden on Tuesday 17th December, when the election will begin.[5]

14th December, Saturday Heavy dull day

A lottery office keeper in the neighbourhood of Smithfield decamped after a ticket which he had sold ten times over in shares came up a capital prize.[1]

At one o'clock a full board of Admiralty was held relative to the late fire at Portsmouth. After it broke up messengers were dispatched to the commissioners of the dock-yards of Portsmouth, Plymouth, Chatham, &c.[2]

At night a man servant belonging to Mr Stephenson at Mile End, being very much fatigued with his day's labour, unknown to any of the family went into an outhouse, where he laid himself down and fell fast asleep. Late in the night a drove of hogs were put into the place, and before morning they had devoured him. There were no remains but his head and bones, on which the hogs were feeding, when this unfortunate affair was discovered.[3]

15th December, Sunday Heavy dull day

In the morning upwards of forty sailors were impressed from a house in Bethnal Green, where they had been sheltered ever since the press began. A sailor belonging to a press gang observing several gallons of beer ordered by one person at a public-house, took an opportunity of watching where it went to, which led to discovery of their haunt.[1]

Lord Weymouth received several letters from Lord Stormont in Paris dated 11th December. In the first Stormont wrote:

I learnt yesterday evening, that the famous Doctor Franklin is arrived at Nantes, with his two grandchildren. They came on board an American privateer, which took several English vessels in her passage. Some people think that either some private dissatisfaction or despair of success have brought him into this country. I cannot but suspect that he comes charged with a secret commission from the Congress, and as he is a subtle artful man, and void of all truth, he will in that case use every means to deceive, will avail himself of the general ignorance of the French, to paint the situation of the rebels in the falsest colours, and hold out every lure to the ministers, to draw them into an open support of that cause. He has the advantage of several intimate connexions here, and stands high in the general opinion. In a word my lord, I look upon him as a dangerous engine, and am very sorry that some English frigate did not meet with him by the way.

In another letter he confirmed that as instructed he would try to purchase a copy of any treaty between France and America, but noted that, as it would necessarily come 'from a person of high quality', it 'must cost dear'. He added that he had heard from an apparently reliable source that a few days earlier the French king, talking to his brother the Comte d'Artois, 'made use of this expression, *Je vois que je ne pourrai pas eviter de faire la guerre à l'Angleterre.*'*[2]

At night a well-dressed man made an attempt of a detestable nature on one of the centinels at the Cockpit Stairs in St James's Park. The soldier threatened to take him into custody if he did not desist, upon which the wretch pulled a pistol out of his pocket and shot him thro' the hand, and then made his escape through the Keeper's Grove, notwithstanding he was fired at by other centinels. It is said the man was an Italian, brother to a cardinal.[3]

16th December, Monday Heavy rains in the night, fine bright day
The workmen began to erect a hustings under the portico of St Paul's, Covent Garden, for electing a member for Westminster in the room of Lord Percy.[1]

At a full board of Admiralty the commissioners of the navy reported that they had made a survey of the damages sustained by the late fire in the dock-yard at Portsmouth, and the loss was very inconsiderable.[2]

17th December, Tuesday Smart frost in the night, foggy thick day
The election of a member came on before St Paul's, Covent Garden. About half past eleven o'clock the high bailiff, attended by military officers, justices, constables, and others, came upon the hustings. He ordered the door to be shut against all who did not produce sealed tickets, and declared the vacancy by the common cryer, who added, that a gentleman present had nominated Lord Petersham, eldest son of the Earl of Harrington and now in the king's service in America. Lady Harrington and her daughters, attended by Colonel Craggs, were at a window of

---

* 'I see that I cannot avoid going to war with England.'

St Paul's, Covent Garden, from the east

Mr Low's Hotel to see the ceremony. Sir John Fielding arose to address the voters, but General Burgoyne getting up nearly at the same time, the magistrate deferred to the military officer and sat down. Burgoyne proceeded to harangue the populace in favour of the absent candidate, who was favoured by the ministry.

When the high bailiff put up Lord Petersham, there was a shew of several hands on the hustings, but very few among the many hundreds of electors assembled without. On the second proclamation, the cryer demanded whether there was any other candidate? Several electors in the front, near the rails, proposed aloud *Sir Watkin Lewes*, in which they were supported by several on the hustings and by a vast majority of the crowd without, who gave three huzzas upon his nomination. Soon after the second proclamation, a third was made, when almost every man in the crowd cried out *Sir Watkin Lewes — A poll! — A poll for Sir Watkin Lewes!*

Notwithstanding all this, the high bailiff would not put him up. Several electors then endeavoured to get through the door upon the hustings, to demand a shew of hands, but were refused. Being asked where Sir Watkin was, they answered, near at hand, they would fetch him, which they did in a few minutes, Sir Watkin having declined to come forward unless called upon by a majority of the electors.

During this absence a declaration was made that Lord Petersham was elected, and his friends were signing the indenture in great haste when Sir Watkin arrived. It was then seven minutes past twelve. He demanded admission and entered, but the constables drove the electors who were with him back. Sir Watkin insisted that the electors should enter, advanced to the high bailiff, and demanded a poll, which was refused by the returning officer on account of his not appearing at the declaration. A warm dispute arose in respect of the time allowed by Act of Parliament before they proceed to election. Indignation was expressed by the electors, whereupon the returning officer with his assistants precipitately retreated into the church, with the partizans of Lord Petersham.

Sir Watkin afterwards invited those electors who wished to bring this business before the House of Commons to attend him to the Swan in New Street, to draw up and sign a protest against the proceedings of the day, but any efforts they made came to nothing.[1]

MP 'Droll Cross-Readings [i.e. readings across columns] of the *Morning Post*. | Friday last a man stood an hour in the pillory — *after which he had a long conference with his majesty.* ... | To-morrow morning a charity sermon will be preached at St Paul's Covent Garden — *in the course of which there will be variety of tumbling, and rope-dancing, as usual.* ... | Yesterday morning a duel was fought behind Montague-House — *between the kings of Spain and Portugal.* | Her majesty is said to be again pregnant — *by most of the crowned heads in Europe.'*[2]

18th December, Wednesday Hard frost, foggy thick day
About ten o'clock the wooden funnel which runs up the side of Lincoln's Inn Hall, and conveys the smoke from the large stove there, took fire, and from the extreme foulness thereof, was soon consumed, much endangering the Hall. An engine being at hand, and immediate assistance given by the officers belonging to the court, porters of the inn, &c. it was put out without doing any further damage. Meanwhile, according to the *Gazetteer*, the scene was 'rather laughable', a large number of black gowns and large wigs, all in the utmost confusion, running about with their bags and briefs, pleading with porters and firemen to use diligence and activity in suppressing the fire.[1]

At the public office in Bow Street, the man taken into custody for misbehaving last Friday during divine service in St Paul's, Covent Garden, was brought up to give bail. Some reputable neighbours of his swore that he had intervals of insanity, which they believed was owing to some considerable disappointments he had met with, and he was discharged.[2]

On or about this day Edward Bancroft left London for Paris, arriving there on 21st December.[3]

Died suddenly, aged 27, at his lodgings in White Friars, Joseph Atkins, a pewterer. It is said that during the last three years of his life he drank on an average half a gallon of Geneva per day, and porter in proportion.[4]

At night the remains of Elizabeth, Duchess of Northumberland, were interred in Westminster Abbey, in apparel said to have cost 1,500l.

About ten o'clock the procession moved off from Northumberland House. First, a gentleman on horseback, then four conductors on horseback, with staves, and four horsemen in cloaks. Next a gentleman carried a banner on which were emblazoned the principal quarterings of her grace's arms: if they had all been displayed, they would have amounted to 156 quarters. Four further horsemen followed in cloaks, two and two. A gentleman of the household, on a grey horse, led by two pages, bore her grace's coronet on a cushion of crimson velvet. Then came the hearse, ornamented with 'scutcheons, penons, &c. followed by six coaches and six, in which were two chaplains, and ten gentlemen in cloaks, as deep mourners. Her grace's own chariot followed, empty, drawn by six horses, attended by her footmen, &c.

A little before eleven o'clock the corpse was met at the west door of the Abbey by the Bishop of Rochester, as Dean of Westminster, attended by the chapter and the gentlemen and boys of the choir. The crowd was so great, however, that they could not for a long time perform the service. It is said there were not less than 3,000 people gathered.

Many had earlier gained admittance to the Abbey and several had placed themselves upon monuments and other parts, the better to see the procession as it passed. A number of men and boys had climbed up and seated themselves over the front of St Edmund's Chapel, which joins to that of St Nicholas, where her grace was to be interred. The dean and attendants had not passed this place above three minutes before the old gothic skreen, or front, belonging to St Edmund's Chapel, supposed to have been built between four and five hundred years ago, fell down, consisting of thick heavy oak, with iron bars, and part of the stone work. Many people were carried out very much bruised.

In the confusion the corpse was rested in St Edmund's Chapel, and the dean returned to the deanery. Thinking the ceremony over, many of the populace dispersed. The bishop and the gentlemen choristers and boys then returned, and between one and two o'clock in the morning the corpse was interred in St Nicholas's Chapel, with as much solemnity as was possible amidst so much distraction, the cries of the wounded being heard almost the whole time.[5]

19th December, Thursday Rain early, fine bright day
Lord Weymouth received a hurriedly written letter from Lord Stormont dated Sunday morning, 15th December, at Paris:

> I have this moment received authentic information that ... above a hundred French officers of artillery and light troops sailed from Havre de Grace the 12th instant on board a French frigate called *L'Amphitrite* mounting eighteen guns. ...
>
> As there seems to me a possibility of this ship being intercepted I thought it my duty, my lord, not to lose a moment in giving you this authentic information

and have therefore dispatched this messenger and have orderd him to make the greatest haste and take an extraordinary packet.

I am persuaded that all the papers of this frigate will shew that her destination is for St Domingo, but think it very probable that she will make directly for some port in North America.

The *Amphitrite*'s cargo included, among other things, 52 brass cannons, 32,840 cannon balls, 129 barrels of gunpowder, 219 chests of arms, 237 boxes of musket balls, 8,877 grenadoes, 925 tents, and 3,330 spades. It was one of three vessels gathered at Le Havre by Beaumarchais, who was now working closely with Silas Deane. Stormont had been alerted because, unable to resist becoming involved in a production of *Le Barbier de Séville* at Le Havre, Beaumarchais had set aside his usual incognito to encourage the actors. Stormont protested to Vergennes and the other two vessels were delayed for a while, but it was too late to stop the *Amphitrite*, and all three ships would arrive in the roads of Portsmouth, New Hampshire, in time for the next campaign.

Stormont added: 'I am assured that Franklin, who offers France the exclusive trade of North America, is much listend to and there are indeed but too many indications of the insidious designs of this Court and too much reason to apprehend that in a few months they will pull off the mask and change these secret succours to the rebels into open assistance.'[1]

In the evening refugee Samuel Quincy went to Drury Lane Theatre to see *The Provok'd Husband*, 'which was extremely well performed ... Lord North and Sir Grey Cooper, who were in the stage box with their families, appeared much pleased with the part where Sir Francis Wronghead boasts of being a member of parliament, and the promises made him by the minister.'[2]

At night died, at her house in Great Russell Street, whilst she was kneeling down to her prayers, Mrs Lyon, whose husband is at present in America.[3]

20th December, Friday Frost in the night, foggy rainy day
In the morning the daughter of an eminent tradesman in the City was found dead in her bed, with her throat cut in a shocking manner. This rash action is attributed to her sister's being married, a few days since, to a young gentleman by whom the deceased was pregnant.[1]

Replying to the latest letter from Lord Stormont, Lord Weymouth said that the sailing of the French officers could not be prevented, 'unless we had sufficient proofs to produce that their destination is for the continent of America. The taking of a frigate of war would be such an act of hostility, as nothing could justify, but the most irrefragable evidence of the want of truth in the professions of the French king's ministers'. He did, nonetheless, suggest undermining Franklin in French eyes by suggesting that the true motive for his visit was not to negotiate but for his own safety, it being likely that after a series of defeats the American people would turn violently upon their leaders. The fact that Franklin was accompanied by family members 'would seemingly give some corroboration to this idea. ... These conjectures may perhaps not be well grounded, but the success of his majesty's arms ... gives you full ground for this representation of the cause of his arrival.'[2]

PA 'General Carleton's great and laborious expedition in crossing the Lakes, in hopes of compleating the conquest of America by a junction with the Howes, and his retreating back to his old quarters without effecting any thing of consequence, reminds us of the old remark on the King of France, who, "with forty thousand men | March'd up a hill — and then came down again."'[3]

21st December, Saturday An exceeding moist wet day
Eight beautiful horses from Westphalia were landed at the Tower, being a present from the Prince of Hesse to his majesty.[1]

At night a young woman, genteelly dressed, was getting up on the balustrade of Blackfriars Bridge in order to drown herself, but was hindered by the toll watch. She told him the cause was a love affair, and that it was the third time of her attempting to make away with herself.[2]

22nd December, Sunday Wet night, cloudy day, but fair. Stormy
In the morning Lord George Germain set out for his seat at Drayton, Northants, for a fortnight.[1]

As a farmer's cart was coming over Finchley Common it ran foul of the gibbet on which Stretton the grocer hung, for robbing the mail, by which accident he fell down. A bird's nest was found in the skull.*[2]

This day and Monday, near one hundred sail of transports from New York came up the river to refit, in order to their going out again early in the spring.[3]

23rd December, Monday Foggy morning and evening, bright mid-day
The Archbishop of Canterbury ordered 200l. to be distributed among the poor housekeepers in Lambeth and gave victuals at his palace to a great number of poor persons.[1]

Workmen began fixing a new front to St Edmund's Chapel in Westminster Abbey, in the room of that demolished by the mob on the burial night of the Duchess of Northumberland. It will be some time before it is compleated, as it is to be put up after the old gothic manner, to answer the building of the chapel.[2]

Edward Oxnard heard that an answer was likely to be received soon to a petition on behalf of himself and other refugees for financial support from government. 'May it never be my lot again to be dependant,' he noted in his diary. 'It is by no means a pleasing situation – to be fawning to the understrappers of a Court – which every one must do that expects any favors.'[3]

* John Stretton had robbed the post-boy carrying the Chester mail in March 1770. He was executed at Tyburn on 1st August the same year, after which his body was hung in chains on the Common, near the scene of his crime.

24th December, Tuesday Churlish day, heavy shower of rain and sleet about noon

About 10 a.m. a lieutenant of a press gang had an information against one of the waiters at Almack's in Pall Mall, and went to demand him, but the chairmen on the stand at the door seized the lieutenant and several of his companions, and after giving them a severe drubbing, sent them off without their prize.[*1]

In the morning a council, attended by lords North, Sandwich, and Weymouth, sat near three hours at the Queen's Palace on the subject of private foreign dispatches received the day before. Afterwards Lord North set out for his house at Bushy for the Christmas holidays, and Lord Sandwich set out for his seat at Hinchingbrooke.[2]

Her majesty's annual bounty of 500l. was distributed among the poor at Kew.[3]

The lord mayor, attended by the two sheriffs, went round all the markets in the City, the India House, the Bank, and all the bankers, and made a very considerable collection of money, meat, bread, and vegetables, which he divided equally, and sent to different gaols for the relief of the poor prisoners confined there.[4]

It being Christmas Eve, the gentlemen belonging to the Queen's Arms Concert in Newgate Street had their annual supper, which consisted of several haunches of mutton, drest *à la venaison*, and minced pies. The grace was said in recitative.[5]

At night a press gang of seven men, headed by two officers, having searched many houses in the neighbourhood of Covent Garden, took a notorious fighting man, well known at Sir John Fielding's, from the Genoa Arms, a house of ill fame, despite great opposition. On their passing a public-house of the same stamp in Bridges Street, an attempt was made to rescue the man by about forty of his companions, who sallied forth assisted by a mob of some hundreds, many of whom were chairmen. In a contest of near an hour the gang was severely handled, but finally they prevailed and lodged their prize, with three cheers, in Covent Garden watch-house.[6]

MC 'A vessel is daily expected from New-York with accounts from General Howe, with the result of his expedition against the provincials ... | All intelligence from General Carleton is entirely closed till the latter end of next May, or the beginning of June; for when the last ships came from Quebec, the ice was become troublesome in the navigation of the river St Lawrence, and would soon put a stop to it.'[7]

GEP 'The spirit of duelling appears lately to have prevailed more in this kingdom than it has done for a considerable time past; and, however ludicrous it may appear, there are now two clubs established at the west end of the town, for which no gentleman is qualified to be a member who has not *wounded* or *killed* his man. ... Strange infatuation, that men in a polished nation should value themselves upon destroying their fellow-creatures!'[8]

---

* In a letter of 25th January 1777 Gainsborough noted that his footman at nearby Schomberg House was afraid to venture into Pall Mall for fear of being pressed.

'Christmas Gambols'. Published 1785.

25th December, Wednesday, Christmas Day Smart frost, fine bright day. Full moon

The day was observed at Court as a high festival. There was a numerous and splendid appearance of the nobility and gentry, the knights companions of the several orders appearing in their respective collars. At noon their majesties, preceded by the heralds and pursuivants at arms, went to the Chapel Royal, where they received the sacrament from the Bishop of London, and the lord chamberlain in behalf of his majesty made the usual offering.[1]

'A fine, clear, soft day; many people in the park,' noted Samuel Quincy in his diary. 'Little did I expect to see a return of this day in England,' noted his fellow refugee Edward Oxnard. 'It is kept very decently by all sects but the Quakers, who open their shops and do the ordinary business of another day.'[2]

Among others at work was George Romney, who had a Mr Foster sit to him at noon.[3]

Also at work was bookseller and publisher Thomas Lowndes at No. 77 Fleet Street, who received an unexpected and unsigned letter:

Sir, As business, with those who understand it makes its own apology, I will not take up your time with reading excuses for this address, but proceed immediately to the motives which have induced me to give you this trouble.

I have in my possession a MS. novel which has never yet been seen but by myself; I am desirous of having the two first volumes printed immediately — and the publication of the rest shall depend wholly on their success.

But, sir, such is my situation in life that I have objections unconquerable to being known in this transaction, and I, therefore, must solicit the favour of you to answer me the following queries, which I hope you will not think impertinent.

First, whether you will give a candid and impartial reading to a book that has no recommendation to previously prejudice you in its favour?

Secondly, whether, if, upon perusal the work should meet with your approbation, you will buy the copy, of a friend whom I shall commission to wait upon you, without ever seeing or knowing the editor?

I shall be obliged to you to direct your answer to Mr King to be left at the Orange Coffee House, to be called for, in the Haymarket.

The writer was Fanny Burney and the novel was *Evelina*. She had written the letter that morning in a feigned hand, fearing that her own might be recognised as she had acted as amanuensis for her father's *History of Music*. She had previously approached another publisher, James Dodsley, but he had declined to consider anything anonymous. 'Mr King' was her younger brother Charles, who had recently left Charterhouse and was to enter Gonville and Caius, Cambridge, in January.

Lowndes replied encouragingly the same day: 'Sir, I've not the least objection to what you propose, and if you favour me with sight of your MS. I'll lay aside other business to read it and tell you my thoughts of it. With two presses I can soon make it appear in print, for now is the time for a Novel.'[4]

GA 'One of the richest transports sent to America this year, is taken and carried into Boston. She was commanded by Capt. Bell, and was laden with 16,000 suits of cloaths for the army in Canada; 30,000 shirts, 30,000 pairs of shoes, 30,000 pairs of stockings, &c. &c. all for the same; valued at upwards of 80,000l. sterling. This loss will be severely felt by the army in Canada; but it is a lucky circumstance for the contractors.'[5]

PA 'A lady of family and fortune at the west end of the town was a short time since robbed on the highway by her own butler, masked. She knew his voice, and readily gave him fifteen guineas; but next day requiring a restitution of the sum, the man immediately ran away, and was never heard of till last week, when he was seen in Paris in a very shabby condition. He had been in the service of the lady almost from his childhood, and bore an unexceptionable character.'[6]

26th December, Thursday, St Stephen   Smart frost, bright morning, heavy day, with some snow

On or about this day Fanny Burney received Thomas Lowndes's reply with 'no small delight' and 'a certain pride ... that the answer opened by "Sir", which gave [me] an elevation to manly consequence'. Her brother Charles 'was muffled up now by the laughing committee' of Fanny and her sisters 'in an old great coat, and a large old hat, to give him a somewhat antique as well as vulgar disguise; and was

EVELINA

or

A

Young Lady's

ENTRANCE

into

LIFE

VOLUME I

ABOVE Fanny Burney's first sketch for the title page of *Evelina*.
BELOW Her letters to Thomas Lowndes:
left, a draft in her usual handwriting; right, a subsequent letter in the feigned hand.

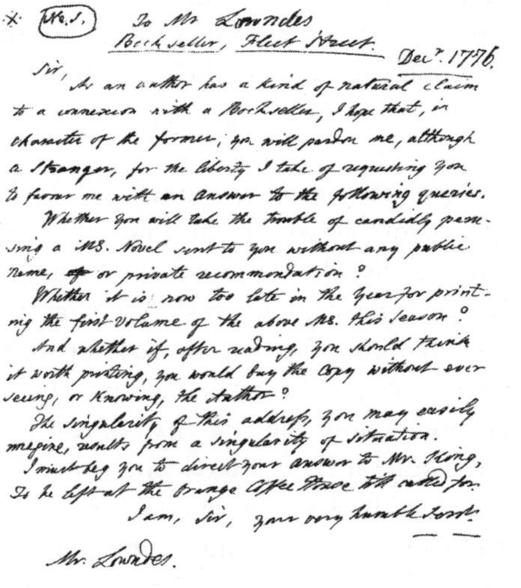

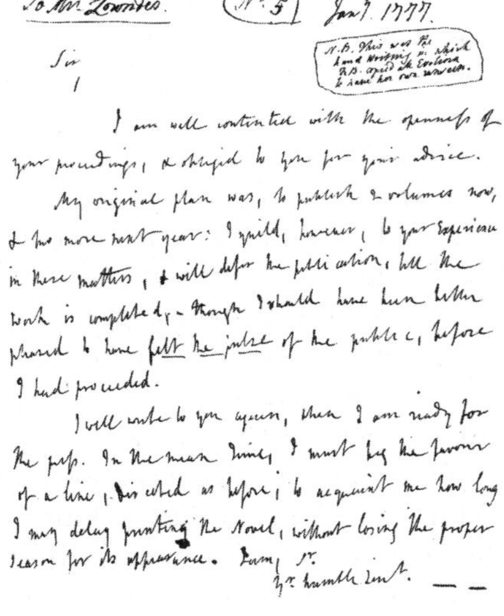

sent forth in the dark of the evening' with the first volume to Fleet Street, where he left it to its fate. To protect her identity Fanny had laboriously copied out the manuscript in her feigned handwriting, which was also used for the accompanying letter.

> Sir, The frankness with which you favoured me with an answer to my letter induces me to send you the MS. with the firmest reliance upon your candour.
>
> The plan of the first volume is the introduction of a well educated but inexperienced young woman into public company, and a round of the most fashionable spring diversions of London. I believe it has not before been executed, though it seems a fair field open for the novelist ...
>
> I shall send you the second volume with all the expedition in my power, if that which is now under your examination makes you desirous of seeing it.[1]

27th December, Friday Smart frost in the night, foggy moist day, some snow Lord Weymouth received several letters from Lord Stormont dated 23rd December at Paris. One reported that Benjamin Franklin 'arrived here on Friday night, and is at present in the same *Hôtel Garni* with Mr Deane ... | I am privately informed that he has already had a number of visitors, but most of them low people, *des aventuriers* [adventurers], who are, as your lordship well knows, in this country a very numerous band.' In another letter Stormont added that he had been told Franklin and Deane 'were at Versailles on Saturday morning ... | Franklin press'd to be admitted to an audience of the most Christian majesty which was flatly refused, and came back from Versailles much out of humour ... | Beaumarchais is returned from Havre, and has given great offence to the French ministers by his indiscretion there and the very open and public manner in which he conducted the business intrusted to him.'[1]

A Methodist preacher hanged himself at his lodgings in Blackfriars. A pocketbook was found in his coat pocket, in which were the following lines: 'Some moments on this faithful guide bestow, | I'll point the way a Christian ought to go, | To seek a Saviour in the realms above, | Whose looks are glory, and whose words are love.'[2]

Shakespeare's *Tempest*, altered into an opera with music by Purcell, Dr Arne, J. C. Smith, and Mr Fisher, was performed at Covent Garden Theatre. The *Morning Post* judged it 'an operatical mutilation ... Mr Dunstall was horrible in Caliban; he dressed it like an old mangy bear ... Miss Brown was much easier in Miranda than we expected to find her; but she was habited, for what reason we know not, like a mountain huntress!' The *Morning Chronicle* thought she 'looked prettily ... although her dress rather made her appear too much in the *cork-rumped* stile'.[3]

John Wilkes and Samuel Foote, who were both at Bath, dined with others at a Mr Plunkett's in the Circus. Both men remained in the town into the new year, dining on New Year's Day at the Bear with George Colman and Joseph Hickey. On 2nd January the *Morning Post* reported that Foote had been received at Bath

The FASHIONABLE DRESSES for the YEAR 1776.

Printed for Carington Bowles, at his Map & Print Warehouse, N°.69 in S.^tPauls Church Yard, London. Published as the Act directs 26.Dec^r1776.

Published by Carington Bowles at his Map and Print Warehouse,
69 St Paul's Churchyard, 26th December 1776

'with the warmest tokens of friendship by all the people of rank there, who one and all congratulate him on his providential escape from the snares of premeditated villainy'.[4]

GA 'By accounts received from Paris, people are forbid to talk openly upon American affairs. Franklin and the other American deputies from the Congress, are received with the utmost cordiality and politeness. Every thing is kept a profound secret, though it is generally conjectured a treaty of assistance is concluded.'[5]

28th December, Saturday Smart frost in the night, moist day, cutting wind
In the morning one of the watchmen belonging to the Custom House was found burnt to death at his lodgings in Bear Lane, Tower Street. About 1 a.m., being much intoxicated with liquor, he had taken a candle from his landlady to go to bed, and it is supposed it set light to his shirt.[1]

In a fit of jealousy a fishmonger in Clement's Lane, Clare Market, bit off one of his wife's fingers and cut his own throat with a razor. A surgeon was sent for, who sewed up the man's wound, but he now lies without hope of recovery.[2]

29th December, Sunday Smart frost in the night, cloudy morning, rainy afternoon
Thomas Lowndes sent a reply 'To Mr King at the Orange Coffee House. To be left till called for.' It read, 'Sir, I've read and like the manuscript, and if you'll send the rest I'll soon run it over.'[1]

Lord Weymouth received several letters written by Lord Stormont in Paris on Christmas Day. In one he said he thought Benjamin Franklin had not yet seen the foreign minister Vergennes, and that 'if I am not greatly misinformed Franklin and Beaumarchais, tho so much together, are very suspicious and mistrustful of each other'. Stormont understood that Franklin was saying different things to different people, telling some that the Americans would never surrender and others that General Howe would bring about an accommodation.

> This weak conduct, which will soon be known in such a prating town as this, will confirm the general suspicion of his duplicity. Many of the French are already persuaded that he comes here not only as a fugitive, but as one who is watching an opportunity to obtain his pardon, and who will correspond openly with the Congress, and secretly with the English ministry. It matters not whether this has any foundation in truth, the very suspicion will sink him.[2]

30th December, Monday Hard frost, a great deal of snow
In the morning Captain Gardner, an aide-de-camp to General Howe, arrived at Lord George Germain's office with dispatches from New York. They included a letter from Howe dated 30th November and reporting a series of military engagements including the capture of Fort Washington two weeks earlier:

> The importance of this post, which, with Fort Lee on the opposite shore of Jersey, kept the enemy in command of the navigation of the north river, while

it barred the communication with York by land, made the possession of it absolutely necessary. Preparations were therefore made for a general attack, and thirty flat boats under the directions of captains Wilkinson and Molloy passed up the north river on the night of the 14th, undiscovered by the enemy.

Every thing being prepared, and the attack fixed for the morning of the 16th, Lieutenant Colonel Patterson, adjutant general, was sent the 15th to summon the commanding officer to surrender, and to warn him of the consequences that must attend a general attack; to which he replied, he would defend himself to the last extremity.

There followed details of a four-pronged attack and the capture of the fort along with over 2,700 prisoners of war. Within days Fort Lee had also fallen into British hands, having been abandoned by the rebels, who 'escaped in the utmost confusion, leaving all their artillery, and a large quantity of stores and provisions; their tents standing, and kettle upon the fire'.

A messenger was sent off to Germain at Drayton, and, the news being good, Howe's letter was published in the evening in a *London Gazette Extraordinary*. Lord Weymouth sent a copy of the *Gazette* at once to Lord Stormont in Paris, with a note saying he would know how to make proper use of it.[1]

A second letter from Howe to Germain, of the same date, not published in the *Gazette*, outlined a plan for the next campaign, 'in order, if possible, to finish the war in one year'. It involved an army of 10,000 men to take Providence and if possible Boston; another army of similar size 'to move up the north river to Albany'; 5,000 men 'for the defence of New-York and adjacent posts'; and 8,000 men 'to cover Jersey, and to keep the southern army in check'. The plan would require at least ten ships of the line 'and a reinforcement of ... 15,000 rank and file, which I should hope may be had from Russia, or from Hanover, and other German states, particularly some Hanoverian chasseurs, who, I am well informed, are exceeding good troops'. He calculated that the army in the southern district would then consist of 35,000 effective men, to oppose 50,000 that Congress had voted for the next campaign.

> The enemy, though much depressed at the success of his majesty's arms, are encouraged by the strongest assurances from their leaders of procuring assistance from foreign powers, for which end it is understood that Dr Franklin is gone to France, to solicit aid from that Court. I do not presume to point out a way of counteracting him; but were that effected, and the force I have mentioned sent out, it would strike such terror through the country that little resistance would be made to the progress of his majesty's arms ...[2]

The Howe brothers, as commissioners for restoring peace, also sent a printed copy of a proclamation they had issued on 30th November offering 'full and free pardon' to all who took an oath of obedience within sixty days. It was accompanied by a letter in which they anticipated Germain's response to such clemency: 'Notwithstanding the atrocious delinquency of some of the leaders and instigators of the war, we were unwilling in the present situation of affairs to exclude any of them from the benefit of the king's mercy'.[3]

Among others letters arriving for Germain was one from Colonel Guy Johnson, dated 25th November at New York, which included news of Joseph Brant:

> I have the pleasure to assure your lordship that the Indians have faithfully observed the promises they made to me, rejected all the proposals of the rebels, and a considerable number of them proceeded on service. ...
>
> To pave the way for their future operations, I have, with the approbation of General Howe, lately dispatched (in disguise) one of my officers with Joseph the Indian chief (who desired this service), to get across the country to the Six Nations; and from their activity and knowledge of the way, I have hopes of their getting through undiscovered, and of their preparing the Indians to cooperate with our military movements ...

Brant had been dispatched on 16th November. The accompanying officer was Gilbert Tice, who had looked after him during his stay in London.[4]

The *Morning Post* reported that 'Mr Garrick is laid up with a severe fit of the gout at his house upon the Adelphi terrace.' Mrs Garrick attributed the attack to his having dined out every day for a week. Garrick himself bridled at his doctor's insistence that he drink only barley water in order to recover.[5]

At his villa at Sunning Hill, in the county of Berks, 'the neat houshold furniture, china, linen, wines, live and dead stock, garden utensils, post coach and phaeton, and other valuable effects of | Bartholomew Coote Purdon, Esq. | A Bankrupt' were auctioned by Mr Christie.[6]

31st December, Tuesday Hard frost, bright at times, a little scattering snow
At 11 a.m. Lord North sent from Bushy Park to the king letters received the previous day from General Howe and the commissary general, 'by which his majesty will see that the army is amply supplied with provisions for a long time although the complaints about the bread and flour continue'.[1]

About 2 p.m. their majesties came from Kew to the Queen's Palace. They were afterwards visited by the Princess Amelia, who also visited the royal children. In consequence of the important news from America, Lady Howe was at Court, and was received by their majesties in the most affable and cordial manner.[2]

French ambassador the Marquis de Noailles wrote to Vergennes in Paris that the news of the capture of Fort Washington had made London wild with joy. This delirious people, he said, were ready to defy all the powers of the world, and 'they talk loftily of attacking France'.[3]

George Romney was at work again in Cavendish Square, his diary recording the sitting of 'A lady at 1.'[4]

Edward Gibbon called on Horace Walpole, who was recovering from the gout at his house in Arlington Street. Next day Gibbon left town to spend a fortnight at Sheffield Place in Sussex.[5]

John Wesley, who had returned to London on 20th December after a preaching tour, noted in his journal: 'We concluded the year with solemn praise to God, for continuing his great work in our land; it has never been intermitted one year or one month since the year 1738, in which my brother and I began to preach that strange doctrine of salvation by faith.'[6]

At Covent Garden Theatre the musical *Tempest* was performed again with Ann Brown as Miranda. At Drury Lane, Congreve's *Way of the World* was revived with Mrs Abington as Millamant, Mrs Hopkins, the prompter's wife, as Lady Wishfort, and Mr Reddish as Fainall. According to the *Morning Chronicle*, 'Mrs Abington's dress was one of the most fashionable and becoming' ever conceived.[7]

As darkness came, petty crime continued in its usual course. Two fellows attempted to steal some lead off the top of a house in Upper Brook Street, Grosvenor Square, but one of them fell over the parapet onto the iron rails of the area, and was wounded in so shocking a manner that he died in great agonies within an hour afterwards.[8]

Lord George Germain was still at Drayton and wrote from there to William Knox, under secretary in his department, about the news from America. General Howe had, he noted, finished the campaign 'honourably and advantageously', but he could not approve the issuing of a general pardon: 'It is poor encouragement for the friends of government, who have been suffering under the tyranny of the rebels, to see their oppressors without distinction put upon the same footing with themselves. ... This sentimental manner of making war will, I fear, not have the desired effect.'[9]

In Paris, Arthur Lee wrote to Congress's committee of secret correspondence to report that he had joined Dr Franklin and Mr Deane. 'We have employed every moment in preparing the way for fulfilling the purport of our mission. It is impossible to say yet in what degree we shall be able to accomplish our instructions and our wishes. The politics of Europe are in a state of trembling hesitation.'[10]

Meanwhile in America

13th December. General Charles Lee was captured by British soldiers while staying at a tavern on Basking Ridge, New Jersey.[1]

14th December. British troops under Lord Cornwallis returned to their quarters, having been unable to cross the Delaware in pursuit of Washington's retreating army. General Howe later wrote to Germain that the weather had become 'too severe to keep the field', and at about this time he called off the campaign for the winter. He gave Cornwallis permission to return to England, left garrisons at Trenton and elsewhere to defend New Jersey, and retired to the comparative comfort of New York.[2]

19th December. The first issue of Thomas Paine's *The American Crisis* was published in the *Pennsylvania Journal* in Philadelphia:

These are the times that try men's souls. The summer soldier and the sunshine patriot will, in this crisis, shrink from the service of their country; but he that stands it *now*, deserves the love and thanks of man and woman. Tyranny, like hell, is not easily conquered; yet we have this consolation with us, that the harder the conflict, the more glorious the triumph.[3]

26th December. In the early hours Washington's troops crossed the icy Delaware river nine miles above Trenton. At about eight o'clock, after a night march through wind, rain and hail, they attacked the garrison town, which was largely manned by Hessians. Realising they were surrounded, the previously fearsome mercenaries laid down their arms with little resistance. Their commanding officer, Colonel Rall, was fatally wounded, and 918 prisoners were taken.

Washington after victory at Trenton, by Charles Willson Peale, *circa* 1780

James Wilkinson, present at the capture of General Lee two weeks earlier, happened to ride up to Washington at the moment Rall was presenting his sword in surrender. Apprehending the significance of this first American success after a string of dispiriting defeats, Washington took him by the hand and observed, 'Major Wilkinson, this is a glorious day for our country.' Wilkinson himself recalled:

> The joy diffused throughout the union by the successful attack against Trenton, reanimated the timid friends of the revolution, and invigorated the confidence of the resolute. Perils and sufferings still in prospect, were considered the price of independence, and every faithful citizen was willing to make the sacrifice. ... The American community began to feel and act like a nation determined to be free.[4]

An emblem of America, published 23rd November 1776

W. Cave ad viv. del. Winton.

JOHN AITKEN.
Commonly called *JOHN the PAINTER*.

Convicted of setting Fire to Portsmouth Dock.

Publifhed as the Act directs by I.Wilkes Winchefter. March 22.1777.

ABOVE An improbably dapper Aitken, from a contemporary Life.
FACING PAGE A perhaps more realistic depiction,
from the *London Magazine* for March 1777.

Afterwards

A: War, politics, peace

Having started several fires at Bristol, the first in the early hours of 16th January 1777, **James Aitken** headed for Paris 'to acquaint Mr Deane with my success'. On the way he was arrested in Hampshire and transferred to the New Prison, Clerkenwell. On 4th February he was questioned for nearly three hours at the public office in Bow Street by Sir John Fielding and several lords of the Admiralty, behaving 'in a most artful and reserved manner' throughout. Despite further questioning three days later, Fielding drew a blank, but while in prison Aitken confided much of his story to John Baldwin, a fellow painter who visited him day after day, gained his trust, and reported everything to government.

JAMES AITKEN.
Alias, John the Painter.

As a result Aitken was tried and convicted at Winchester Castle on 6th March, Lord Sandwich reportedly sitting on the bench throughout. Four days later Aitken was taken under a strong guard to Portsmouth dockyard, 'drawn round the remains of the rope-house ... and desired by the public to cast his eyes upon the destruction his mischievous hands had wrought'. He was executed on Portsmouth Common, being 'drawn up by pulleys to the top of the gibbet, which was made of the mizen mast of the *Arethusa* frigate ... He hung one hour, and was then taken down, and hung in chains on Block-house Point, at the mouth of Portsmouth harbour.'[1]

News of General Washington's success at Trenton reached London in February 1777. At the end of the same month **General Burgoyne** submitted his 'Thoughts for conducting the War from the side of Canada', proposing that a force advance south to join General Howe and cut off rebel-heavy New England from the rest of the colonies. The plan provided the basis for the next campaign.[2]

On 3rd April Burgoyne set sail from Plymouth for Quebec. Once in Canada his advance southward met with early success, Ticonderoga being captured without a shot fired, but thereafter the plan unravelled, and on 17th October he surrendered at Saratoga with his entire army of nearly 6,000 men. 'Thus ended all our hopes of victory, honour, glory &c. &c. &c.' noted one officer in his journal. Blame would be cast upon Burgoyne for pressing on after retreat had become preferable; upon

Germain for failing to provide effective instructions; and above all upon General Howe for taking his army to Philadelphia rather than heading north to assist Burgoyne.[3]

The news reached Germain's office late in the evening on Tuesday 2nd December. According to Horace Walpole, upon hearing it 'the king fell into agonies ... but the next morning, at his levee, to disguise his concern, affected to laugh and to be so indecently merry, that Lord North endeavoured to stop him'. On the same day, Wednesday, stocks fell two and a half per cent and in a heated Commons debate Germain admitted that 'powerful as this nation was, and great as her resources might be, he did not think it was in the power of Great Britain long to support a war carried on like the present'. A few days later Governor Hutchinson reflected the views of loyalist refugees in his diary: 'Everybody in a gloom: most of us expect to lay our bones here.'[4]

The news from Saratoga emboldened France and on 6th February 1778 it entered into a defensive treaty of alliance with the former colonies, recognising their independence. The American signatories in Paris included Benjamin Franklin, Silas Deane and Arthur Lee.

On Friday 13th March the French ambassador, the Marquis de Noailles, delivered a declaration to Lord Weymouth informing the British government of the treaty. Lord Stormont was recalled from Paris and at 6 a.m. on the 20th de Noailles set off for France, 'not without some slight expressions of ill humour from John Bull', according to Gibbon. The two countries were now effectively at war.[5]

The faltering effort in America was soon reflected by the return of several commanders to England, Burgoyne arriving in May, General Howe in July, and Admiral Lord Howe in October.

In 1779 Spain joined France in siding with America, declaring war on Britain on 16th June. Five days later communication between Spain and Gibraltar was closed and on 16th July Spanish ships began a blockade of the peninsula which would last until 1783.

On 19th October 1781 British forces under Lord Cornwallis surrendered at Yorktown, bringing any lingering hopes of British victory to an end. The news reached London on Sunday 25th November. According to Germain, Lord North received it 'as he would have taken a ball in his breast ... For he opened his arms, exclaiming wildly, as he paced up and down the apartment during a few minutes, "O God! it is all over!" Words which he repeated many times under emotions of the deepest consternation and distress.'

On 20th March 1782, facing a no confidence vote in the Commons, North resigned. 'A successor of greater abilities, of better judgment, and more qualified for his situation, was easy to be found,' he told the House, but not one 'more zealous for the interests of his country' or 'more loyal to his sovereign'.[6]

On 30th November preliminary articles of peace with America were signed in Paris. On 3rd September 1783 final treaties with both France and America were signed in the same city. Benjamin Franklin was among the signatories for America. The British signatory of the American treaty, who arrived home with it on 11th September, was inventor David Hartley, appointed his majesty's plenipotentiary for the purpose. The fire had finally been put out.[7]

Six years later France was ablaze with its own revolution, brought on in part by the vast cost – estimated at some 1.3 billion livres – of supporting America. As historians have noted, France was more debilitated by its victory than Britain was by its defeat.

Since achieving independence America has of course not looked back. As for Britain, it recovered from the loss of its first empire remarkably quickly, expanding its dominion in India, Australasia, and parts of Africa, and remaining the pre-eminent imperial power into the twentieth century. Perhaps more importantly, the English language and parliamentary institutions continued to spread, both through the enduring empire and through the one which had been lost.[8]

Peace sees America and her allies celebrate on the far side of the Atlantic while in the foreground the king is beset by divided and self-serving politicians. 'I thought to have had America at our feet,' says the rotund Lord North, 'but I see tis otherwise.' Above the print's title is a line from *Macbeth*: 'Alas poor country, almost afraid to know itself,' and in the distance England's sun is, rather prematurely, setting. Published 16th April 1783.

Mrs Abington
as Roxalana in
The Sultan,
after a
painting by
Reynolds,
1782-1783

B: Some people

Having thought better of retirement, **Mrs Abington** had the greatest triumph of her career as Lady Teazle in Sheridan's *The School for Scandal*, first performed at Drury Lane Theatre on 8th May 1777. She continued to perform for over twenty years. She died on 4th March 1815, 'at her apartments in Pall Mall, in good circumstances', although it was said she had by then lost a good deal of money gambling at cards.[9]

Edward Bancroft returned to London from Paris on 20th January 1777. In February he formalised his spying arrangement with the British government whereby he was to receive £200 a year for life, rising to £500 if the rebellion ended or France entered the war openly. During February and early March he became an object of public suspicion because of his contacts with Aitken, who was then in prison awaiting trial. At about the same time Bancroft was himself arrested, or at least was reported to have been, or himself claimed to have been. The purpose seems to have been to convince the Americans that he was on their side, and to provide a plausible explanation for a planned move to Paris which would enable him to spy on Benjamin Franklin and Silas Deane. The ploy worked, Deane writing on 16th March that 'this worthy man is confined in the Bastile of England ... | He deserves much from us; consequently will be pursued with the utmost rigour by them'.

On 26th March, after being 'released', Bancroft headed for Paris. As he later recalled, during the first year there he 'resided in the same house with Dr Franklin, Mr Deane etc, and regularly informed this government of every transaction of the American commissioners' and 'of every step and vessel taken to supply the revolted colonies'. His methods of passing information included placing messages in a sealed bottle in a hollow tree in the Tuileries gardens. It seems he played the stock market on the side, making lucrative use of early intelligence of events in America, so that, in the words of Arthur Lee, 'Dr Bancroft ... from being penniless, keeps his —, his house, and his carriage.' He returned to England in 1783 and in later life pursued scientific interests in dyeing and printing. He died at home in Margate on 8th September 1821. The double role he had played during the American war remained largely unknown until the 1890s.[10]

Beaumarchais remained energetically active in organising aid for the Americans for the rest of the war, and to great effect: by one estimate ninety per cent of the guns and ammunition used on the rebel side at Saratoga were obtained through French channels. In 1781 he completed *Le Mariage de Figaro*, his sequel to *Le Barbier de Séville*. Unfortunately Louis XVI found it '*detestable*' and it was not performed until 27th April 1784, when it enjoyed immense success.

Less successful were his post-war efforts to secure reimbursement from the American Congress for the work of Roderique Hortalez and Company. The matter remained unresolved until 1835, when his heirs, faced with a choice of receiving 800,000 francs or nothing, chose the 800,000 francs.

Having fallen foul of the French Revolution in its later stages, Beaumarchais himself died in comparative poverty on 18th May 1799 at the age of 67. Engraved on his tomb at his request were the words '*Tandem quiesco*' (I rest at last). In a note about his life he claimed, with some justification, that 'of all Frenchmen, whoever they may be, I am the one who has done the most for the liberty of America, the begetter of our own'.[11]

Joseph Brant did his utmost on the opposing side, leading Mohawks and other loyalists into battle for 'the great king' during the remainder of the war. He received little immediate reward: his opponents dubbed him 'Monster Brant' and the terms of the peace ignored Britain's Indian allies, the new boundary leaving many of them under American jurisdiction. As a result, in 1785 Brant led nearly 2,000 Mohawks and others to a new settlement on the Grand River. At the end of the same year he travelled to London once more to seek compensation for Mohawk losses, a pension for himself in lieu of his position in the department of Indian affairs, and a commitment to provide military support in the event of conflict with the United States. He succeeded on the first two counts but not the third. As in 1776 he received a warm welcome, being presented to the queen and visiting Windsor Castle. He sat for another portrait, was presented with a snuff box by Charles Fox, and attended a masquerade 'dressed in the costume of his nation, wearing no mask, but' (perhaps aptly) 'painting one half of his face'.

After returning home he pursued a controversial policy of selling off surplus land to white loyalists and migrants. In 1795 he acquired land in what is now Burlington, Ontario, where he built a large house and lived in comfort, reportedly employing some twenty servants and sleeping in an English bed under fine English blankets. He died there in November 1807, aged 64.[12]

Ann Brown continued to enjoy success as an actress and serial eloper. She married a Mr Cargill in 1780 and gave birth to a child, but her restlessness persisted. In September 1781 she played the male part of Macheath in *The Beggar's Opera* at Foote's former theatre in the Haymarket, but eloped to Bath before the end of the run, taking her stage costume with her.

A year later the *Morning Herald* reported that one of her lovers had pursued her to the Isle of Wight, only to discover her '*à la couché* with the captain of an Indiaman, with whom she has since actually shipped herself — *Eastward, ho!*' In January 1783 the *Public Advertiser* noted that her voyage 'is said to have given great offence' to the East India Company in Leadenhall Street, who presumably feared her distracting effect. 'Some people go so far as to say, there is a direction gone out for her not to be landed, but to be returned, like damaged goods, on the hands of the exporter.' In fact she was warmly received in India. 'She played all her applauded opera characters at immense prices' and 'her benefit at Bengal amounted to the astonishing sum of 12,000 rupees'.

By now she was attached to a Captain Haldane – probably the Indiaman captain – but he doubted her fidelity and employed 'a trusty servant to watch her motions'. One day at Madras, as he was sitting down to dine with a large party, the servant brought news 'that an elopement was in agitation'. Haldane left at once and found her 'just stepping into a post chaise that had been prepared to receive her by Mr Lechmore, a writer in the Company's service. She promised penitence — and he forgave her. He placed her with a confidential friend at some little distance from the town, and a few days afterwards sailed in the *Nancy* packet for Europe'.

In March 1784 it was reported that the *Nancy*, captained by Haldane, had been 'unfortunately lost on the rocks of Scilly ... It was five days after her immersion before she broke to pieces. Mrs Cargill's body was one of the first that came on shore, which looked extremely well, except that one of her breasts was shockingly torn.' Reports of the details differed: one said 'she was found floating in her shift, and her infant in her arms'; another that the infant 'was not her own'; and yet another that she and the captain 'were found together in the cabin'. Her body was 'buried at Scilly, by a private gentleman, at his own expence'. She was about 24 years old.[13]

After surrendering at Saratoga, **John Burgoyne** arrived back in London on 14th May 1778. He requested a court martial but it was refused because he was still officially a prisoner of war. A year later a House of Commons committee finally met to examine his conduct but produced no report. That October, still at loggerheads with government in general and Lord George Germain in particular, he was stripped of military offices worth some £3,500 a year. He was left with the bare rank of lieutenant general in order to fulfil his commitment to Congress, whose prisoner he formally remained until 1782.

In his later years he became an embittered figure in parliament, but enjoyed success as a playwright with *The Heiress*, first performed in 1786, and had an enduring affair with a married actress, Susan Caulfield, by whom he had four children. He died at his house in Hertford Street on 4th August 1792, aged 70, from 'a violent fit of the gout in his stomach'. He was buried nine days later next to his wife and daughter in the cloisters of Westminster Abbey, no name being placed on his grave. He had wanted a private funeral and so it was. 'Of the gay, the witty, and the fashionable, who earnestly sought his acquaintance ... not one was present to drop the tear of reminiscence ... | One coach only attended with four gentlemen; a lady was likewise present, whose convulsive agitations proved her to "have that within which passeth shew".'*[14]

In 1777 **Charles Burney**, carrier of the first *Evelina* manuscript to Lowndes the publisher, went up to Gonville and Caius College, Cambridge. His stay there was brief, however, for in October he was found to have stolen valuable classical books from the university library and to have sent them to booksellers in London to be sold as his own. He was dismissed in disgrace and his family did all they could to suppress the scandal. Over the following decades he achieved slow rehabilitation, working as a schoolmaster and classical scholar. Thirty years on from the theft he was reinstated at Caius, granted a degree, and ordained into the priesthood. He also turned his acquisitive bibliophilia to good purpose, amassing a vast private library which was sold to the British Museum for £13,500 after his death. He died at Deptford on 28th December

Charles Burney, after a portrait by Sir Thomas Lawrence, 1802

1817 from a stroke. The library included an extensive collection of early newspapers that he had begun by gathering old issues at Gregg's Coffee-house in York Street, Covent Garden, run by his maiden aunts. A large part of the material in this book is drawn from this Burney Collection of Early English Newspapers, now held by the British Library.[15]

Her brother's disgrace probably added to **Fanny Burney**'s desire that *Evelina, or A Young Lady's Entrance into the World*, be published with strict anonymity. She dispatched the second volume to Thomas Lowndes early in 1777. On 17th January he responded by saying he would publish once the work was completed by a third volume. Reluctantly she agreed. As she later explained:

* *Hamlet*, act 1 scene 2.

This man, knowing nothing of my situation, supposed, in all probability, that I could seat myself quietly at my bureau, and write on with all expedition and ease, till the work was finished. But so different was the case, that I had hardly time to write half a page in a day; and neither my health nor inclination would allow me to continue my *nocturnal* scribbling for so long a time, as to write first, and then copy, a whole volume. I was therefore obliged to give the attempt and affair entirely over for the present.

In November 1777 Lowndes finally had the completed manuscript, for which he paid 20 guineas. The novel was published at the end of January 1778 and sold well, Lowndes writing to Fanny a few months later: 'The great world send here to buy *Evelina*. A polite lady said, "Do, Mr Lowndes, give me *Evelina*. I'm treated as unfashionable for not having read it."' Dr Johnson declared that 'Fielding never wrote so well', Burke sat up all night to read it, and Reynolds 'left it neither for sleep nor food' and offered £50 to discover the author.

Between 1786 and 1791 she served as second keeper of the robes to Queen Charlotte and witnessed episodes in the king's madness, including one occasion when he chased her round Kew Gardens. In 1793, having escaped from Court tedium, she married Alexandre-Jean-Baptiste Piochard d'Arblay, a soldier, and had a son by him in the following year. She died at her house in Lower Grosvenor Street on 6th January 1840, aged 87.[16]

Fanny Burney's brother James was among those voyaging to the Pacific with **Captain James Cook**. Having carried Omai home, in January 1778 they became the first Europeans to land on the Hawaiian islands, which Cook named the Sandwich Islands. They then made an extensive survey of the north-west coast of North America, their aim being to discover a passage around the north of the continent to the Atlantic. Finding the way blocked by ice, Cook decided to turn back and winter in the Sandwich Islands before renewing the attempt in the spring.

Initially their return was well received by the islanders, but on 14th February 1779, in a dispute about the *Discovery*'s cutter, which had been stolen by the natives, Cook and a handful of marines became isolated on a beach on Hawaii. Cook fired in self-defence and, on being pelted with stones, the marines also opened fire. According to David Samwell, the *Discovery*'s surgeon, the natives or 'Indians' then 'rushed among them, and forced them into the water, where four of them were killed'. Left without support, Cook made in the direction of a pinnace lying a short way offshore, but as he did so one of the natives advanced from behind with a large club and 'gave him a blow on the back of the head'. Cook 'staggered a few paces, then fell on his hand and one knee, and dropped his musket. As he was rising, and before he could recover his feet, another Indian stabbed him in the back of the neck with an iron dagger. He then fell into a bite of water about knee deep, where others crowded upon him, and endeavoured to keep him under'. As he tried to use a rock for support, 'a savage gave him a blow with a club, and he was seen alive no more. They hauled him up lifeless on the rocks, where they

The death of Captain Cook, after a painting by George Carter, 1781

seemed to take a savage pleasure in using every barbarity to his dead body, snatching the daggers out of each other's hands, to have the horrid satisfaction of piercing the fallen victim of their barbarous rage.'

Cook's men were unable to recover the body, but, according to Captain James King, on 20th February the natives returned a bundle 'covered with a spotted cloak of black and white feathers'. It contained 'both the hands of Captain Cook entire ... the skull, but with the scalp separated from it, and the bones of the face wanting; the scalp, with the ears adhering to it, and the hair upon it cut short; the bones of both the arms ... the bones of the thighs and legs joined together, but without the feet'. The remaining bones followed next morning along with 'the barrels of his gun, his shoes, and some other trifles ... | In the afternoon, the bones having been deposited in a coffin, the funeral service was read over them, and they were committed to the deep with the usual military honours. Our feelings, on this mournful occasion, are more easy to be conceived than expressed.' **Captain Charles Clerke** took over command of the expedition but died six months later, from tuberculosis contracted while in the King's Bench prison in the summer of 1776. The *Resolution* and the *Discovery* arrived home in October 1780, to a subdued welcome, after an absence of over four years.[17]

Teresa Cornelys continued to preside over occasional masquerades at Carlisle House until at least January 1778, but the fashion for such entertainments was on the wane. She continued to be pursued by creditors and in October 1779 the *Morning Chronicle* reported that she had died in the Marshalsea prison, only to correct itself next day: 'Mrs Cornelys is not dead ... but now lies extremely ill in the Marshalsea.' A letter in the same paper in July 1781 remarked on her decline: 'that empress of mock splendor and intrigue, Mrs Cornelys, late of Carlisle House, has sunk into a state of poverty and oblivion; from which, neither her ill-judged waste of wax-candles, her glare of tinsel and painted-paper ornaments, her grove of ever-greens ... nor her convenient stair-cases and rooms of accommodation, could save her'.

She remained in obscurity under the name Mrs Smith for some years, only to re-emerge in the 1790s keeping a house at Knightsbridge and selling asses' milk. Arrested for debt, she ended up in the Fleet prison. Apparently still dreaming of fashionable projects, she died there on 19th August 1797, 'at a great age, and in a distressed situation,' according to the *General Evening Post*. 'She was formerly the soul of fashion, and the envy of the gay; she closed her existence in the most wretched part of the prison, viz. the hospital room, which the warden had permitted her to reside in.' A friend recalled being sent for in her last moments and finding her 'sitting up in her bed, with a large crucifix before her, exclaiming, in a voice that denoted the most dreadful horror, "The devil is dragging me down!" which she kept constantly repeating, and expired in the most shocking agonies. Her body was committed to its mother earth at the expense of the parish ... as her daughter sent word it was a burial good enough for a woman who had led such an improper life.'[18]

Following the suicide of **the Hon. John Damer**, in February 1777 Messrs. Christie and Ansell sold his 'superb household furniture, magnificent jewels, beautiful Sèvres china, an extensive wardrobe of rich, elegant, and fashionable wearing apparel, stock of domestic linen, wines, and select library in neat bindings, and other valuable effects ... | At his late mansion in Tilney Street, Mayfair.' The *London Evening Post* reported that the sale 'is allowed by even connoisseurs in *ton*, to afford one of the greatest instances of modern luxury for some time. That part of his wardrobe which has never yet been used, is said to consist of above ninety suits of the most superb cloaths; nor is any article of dress, equipage, or furniture, inferior in point of elegance or expence'.

The clothes sold at extravagant prices, the *Morning Chronicle* noting that 'there will scarcely be seen a Jessamy in the park, or at the Cocoa-Tree, for some time, who will not owe his *pretty* appearance to the late Mr D.'s taste.' It added a few days later that since the auction 'a considerable party of the young men of fashion, at the west end of the town ... have resolved to *scout* every man who owes his finery to Mr D.'s sale; and whenever they meet a jay so peacock-feathered, they run up to him, seize him by the lappell, and roar out, *a Damer! a Damer!* The consequence will be, that if the wearers have any sense of shame, they'll no longer strut in borrowed plumes.' Other items were apparently bought by the managers of the Theatres Royal for use as costumes. Receiving less attention was the sale of the dead man's 'neat library of books', including, perhaps unread, 'Hogarth Moralized'.[19]

Elizabeth, Countess of Derby, who had been at the centre of the *ton* in 1776, later began an affair with John Sackville, 3rd Duke of Dorset, cricket lover,

The Countess of Derby

After a painting by Reynolds probably begun in 1776. Exhibited at the Royal Academy, 1777. The original picture is lost, apparently destroyed by Lord Derby after she left him.

philanderer, and nephew of Lord George Germain. In February 1779 Lady Sarah Lennox wrote to her sister:

> It is immagined the D. of Dorset will marry Lady Derby, who is now in the country keeping quiet and out of the way. There is a sort of party in town of who is to visit her and who is not, which creates great squabbles ... I'm told she has been and is still most thoroughly attached to the D. of Dorset, and if so I should supose she will be very happy ... [but] what with giving up her children, sorrow for a fault, dread of not preserving his affection, I think she is much to be pitied.

This proved prescient, for Dorset's affections soon moved on and Lord Derby, while taking actress Elizabeth Farren as his own new companion, would not divorce his wife, consigning her to a social ostracism which persisted to a degree for the rest of her life. She died of tuberculosis at the house of a relative in Gloucester Place, Portman Square, on 14th March 1797, aged 44. Her remains were placed in the family vault at Bromley in Kent 'with great funeral pomp'. Less than two months later Lord Derby married Elizabeth Farren.[20]

On 7th February 1777 **Dr William Dodd** was arrested at his house in Argyle Street for forging a bond for £4,200 in the name of his former pupil the Earl of Chesterfield. Asked what had induced him to do such a thing, he pleaded 'urgent necessity'. As a biography published later in the year noted, 'At no period of Dr Dodd's life was he influenced by the rules of œconomy. A mode of living far above the bounds of his income, a fondness for splendor and gaiety, and a total inattention to all the maxims of worldly prudence, united together, had contributed to embarrass his circumstances'. On 22nd February he was convicted at the Old Bailey. In the evening the jury presented a petition recommending him to the royal mercy, and over the following months further efforts were made to secure a pardon, including letters written by Dr Johnson and a petition signed by some 23,000 people. The king would not relent, however, reportedly saying, under the influence of Lord Mansfield, 'If I pardon Dodd, I shall have murdered the Perreaus.'

Meanwhile escape plans were afoot, as Boswell was later informed by Johnson:

> Dodd's city friends stood by him so, that a thousand pounds were ready to be given to the gaoler, if he would let him escape. He added, that he knew a friend of Dodd's, who walked about Newgate for some time on the evening before the day of his execution, with five hundred pounds in his pocket, ready to be paid to any of the turnkeys who could get him out: but it was too late; for he was watched with much circumspection. He said, Dodd's friends had an image of him made of wax, which was to have been left in his place; and he believed it was carried into the prison.

According to another account, Patience Wright fashioned a head of Dodd – presumably the 'image' referred to by Johnson – and 'carried it to him under her pettycoats, in order to favor his escape', but 'Dodd had not courage to attempt it'.

On 6th June an address written by Johnson was delivered by Dodd to his fellow prisoners in Newgate chapel. When it was later put to Johnson that he,

THE REV.^D DR DODD.

Taken from the Life in Newgate the Morning of his Execution.

From the *Town and Country Magazine* for July 1777

not Dodd, was the author, the address being beyond the clergyman's abilities, Johnson replied disingenuously: 'Depend upon it, sir, when a man knows he is to be hanged in a fortnight, it concentrates his mind wonderfully.'

The execution took place at Tyburn on 27th June. Dodd ascended the executioner's cart 'with his arms tied, dressed in a suit of black, and a full-bottomed wig, over which he wore a flapped hat'. It was reported that half a million people were either at Tyburn or lining the route from Newgate, and that 'even Jack Ketch himself shed tears'. After hanging for an hour the body was carried 'to the house of Mr Davies, undertaker in Goodge-street; where a hot bath was ready prepared, and many efforts were used by his medical friends to revive him'. The friends included surgeon John Hunter, and it was thought that 'if the excessive curiosity of the crowd had not occasioned great delay, the attempt would have been successful.'[21]

Mercy Draper, the blind foundling whose performances at fashionable oratorios attracted attention in 1776, later left the Foundling Hospital and had a singing career under the direction of composer John Stanley. By 1783, however, she was refusing to sing in his oratorios and was allowed to return to the Hospital as a singer in the chapel. Mental disorder soon became apparent, and on 1st February 1785 she was removed to Dr Perfect's private asylum at Malling, Kent, where she remained until her death in 1818.[22]

Wanting to return to France, but unable to do so without paying off his English creditors, the **Chevalier d'Éon** remained in limbo in London into 1777. On the night of 1st/2nd March his friend Captain Horneck became involved in a violent scuffle at the Mount Coffee-house in Grosvenor Street with their old antagonist **Charles-Claude de Morande**. As a result Horneck and Morande met in Hyde Park early in the morning on 7th March to fight their long-pending duel, but the day before Morande's wife Eliza, perhaps prompted by her husband, had asked Justice Addington to intervene, and before shots could be fired the high constable of Westminster arrived and took the would-be duellists into custody. Morande was mocked in the newspapers for his wife's role, but the incident seems to have marked the end of his feud with Horneck.[23]

Meanwhile several actions were begun regarding the insurance policies on d'Éon's sex, one of which came to trial before Lord Mansfield at Guildhall on 1st July. The plaintiff was Mr Hayes, a surgeon, who in about 1771 had paid £100 to the defendant, Mr Jacques, an underwriter, for a signed guarantee or insurance policy to pay Hayes £700 whenever he could prove that the chevalier was a woman. Three witnesses, including Morande, gave perjurious evidence that d'Éon was indeed a woman. 'She one day shewed me her woman's cloaths, ear-rings, and shewed me her breasts,' he claimed, adding that on a subsequent occasion, in her bedchamber, 'I put my hand into bed, and was fully convinced that she was a woman.'

The defence countered that as the claim arose from a gambling wager it was unfit to be brought into a court, but no attempt was made to prove that d'Éon was a man and d'Éon himself did not attend. Lord Mansfield said he wished both sides could lose, but, as the law did not expressly prohibit such wagers, he thought the jury would find for the plaintiff, which they promptly did, to the amount of £700. According to the *Gentleman's Magazine*, it was perhaps 'the most extraordinary' cause that 'ever happened in this or any other country', and 'immense sums on policies' were depending upon it.[24]

On 13th August d'Éon set out from Brewer Street to return to France, in a 'neat post-chaise, drawn by four horses, with proper attendance, leaving great part of her valuable effects behind her in England'. In a letter published in the *Morning Chronicle* a few days later he claimed that his departure had been caused by the recent court judgement and advised those 'interested, and losing, in those policies ... not to pay any thing yet ... because I will oppose myself to that judgment when the tribunal of the King's Bench shall have resumed their sittings'. In fact it seems the real cause of his return was that, with further funds from the French government, he had cleared enough of his debts to feel he could travel without his goods in England being at risk from his creditors. In particular he was concerned for his fine wines and his library of some 6,000 volumes, which was too large to take with him and which he was anxious not to see plundered.[25]

Once at Versailles he was ordered to assume female dress, which he would wear for the rest of his life. He did not return to London to challenge the court's decision. However, following a further trial relating to the policies in December (da Costa versus Jones), which was also won by the plaintiff, on 31st January 1778 Lord Mansfield effectively went back on his previous rulings. Having noted the danger of courts of justice becoming 'subservient to the ridiculous whims of gamblers', he proceeded to grant arrest of judgement on the grounds that such cases tended to produce indecent evidence and to have a negative effect on a third person not concerned in the outcome. According to the *Gazetteer*, 'In consequence of this decision, above one hundred thousand pounds that was won by different people will remain in the pockets of the right owners, who must return the premiums they received when the wagers were laid.' When the news reached d'Éon in Paris he wrote: 'Victory!'[26]

He returned to London in November 1785, when his Brewer Street landlord was threatening to sell his library to cover unpaid rent. He would stay for the rest of his life, in spite of straitening finances. To raise funds he began to perform in exhibition fencing matches at venues ranging from Ranelagh to the theatre at Margate, but the payments he received from France came to an end as a result of the country's revolution, and in 1791 his 'capital and extensive library' was auctioned by Mr Christie, to be followed in 1792 by 'a valuable and elegant assortment of jewels, trinkets, plate, and ... prints'. In 1793 he gave up his lodgings in Brewer Street and later moved in with a French-born widow, Mary Cole. In 1796, at the age of 68, while fencing 'before a crowded and genteel company in the rooms at Southampton', the opponent's foil 'entered four inches above the right breast', bringing to an end this final career.[27]

Fencing match between the Chevalier d'Éon and Monsieur de Saint George
at Carlton House on 9th April 1787, with the Prince of Wales looking on

By 1804 his finances were such that he spent five months in prison for debt. He was forced to sell his cherished Cross of St Louis. Having been more or less bedridden for two years, he died on 21st May 1810, aged 81, at No. 26 New Milman Street, near the Foundling Hospital.

For over thirty years he had worn female attire and been assumed to be female. On laying out the corpse, however, Mrs Cole was dismayed to find that her companion of some fourteen years had been a man. It was several hours before she recovered from the shock. Next morning she informed some of his close friends, 'who judged that it would be proper to ascertain all points relative to so singular an occurrence'. Accordingly, on 23rd May a well known surgeon, Thomas Copeland, 'inspected and dissected the body ... in the presence of Mr Adair, Mr Wilson, and Le Pere Elizee, and ... found the male organs in every respect perfectly formed'.[28]

According to the *St James's Chronicle*, while lying at the house in New Milman Street the body was visited by 'many hundreds of the most distinguished *Curiosi* of the metropolis. Strange to say, the female visitants have exceeded those of the other sex as three to one. His highness the Duke of Gloucester, and several other persons of distinction, were among the latter. It lies in a handsome oak coffin, covered with black cloth, and a black velvet cross on the lid'. The paper also reported that the discovery of the chevalier's true sex 'is likely to give rise to several actions, for the recovery of sums unjustly paid by various underwriters ... about 30 years ago, several of these duped paymasters being still alive to reclaim such sums'.[29]

The body was interred in St Pancras churchyard on 28th May, a crucifix and a copy of the *Imitation of Christ* being placed between the chevalier's hands. Within a month 'a cast of the face ... made in the presence of a surgeon and physician of the highest respectability', along with 'an engraving from the body, which is signed by gentlemen of the faculty, testifying its correctness', were on sale. 'There has not been on the theatre of life a more distinguished character than the chevalier,' noted the *Morning Post*, 'and the attestations of the gender of [his] sex ... is not more astonishing than the variations of fortune which he encountered.' In 1868 his burial stone was one of many lost or destroyed when the Midland Railway Company made a cutting through St Pancras churchyard.[30]

After 1776 d'Éon's former *bête noire* **Morande** remained in London acting as Beaumarchais's agent. However, in August 1778, with Britain and France at war, he was 'smoaked' by a series of articles in the *Morning Post* which accused him of spying. In response he wrote a characteristically vituperative letter to the *General Advertiser* accusing the *Post*'s editor, the Rev. Henry Bate, of being 'a coward ... a knave and a scoundrel'. The letter was accompanied by a long list of 'queries' addressed to Bate which insinuated, among other things, that his wife worked in a brothel; that he received £600 a year to keep scandalous stories out of his paper; and that in a duel he had agreed with the seconds that no lead bullets should be used, his pistols instead being 'only loaded with powder and bran'.[31]

If this last accusation led Morande to assume that Bate was duel averse, he was soon undeceived. A challenge was issued and the parties met in Hyde Park Ring at about 5 a.m. on 28th August. This time Eliza Morande did not intervene. Each man fired two pistols at close quarters without effect. The report of the pistols having drawn a small crowd, the combatants set off in post-chaises to find a more private spot. In a field about a mile along the Edgware Road they each fired again without effect. Morande then snapped his fourth pistol. Bate shot again, and the ball pierced Morande's hat, giving him 'a slight contusion on the head'. At this point the seconds intervened, they all returned to town, and the affair was adjusted 'to the satisfaction of all parties'.

Nonetheless, by the end of the year suspicions about Morande had led to his being asked by government to leave London for the duration of the war. He removed with his family to Great Stanmore, Middlesex, remaining there until 1783. After returning to London, from 1784 to 1791 he edited the *Courier de l'Europe* newspaper while continuing to act as a spy for France. He also enjoyed a surprising rapprochement with d'Éon, dining with him several times. Morande returned to France in May 1791 and died there in July 1805, apparently still believing that the chevalier was a woman.[32]

After the scandal of 1776 **Samuel Foote** was deserted by his health and high-ranking friends. His lawyers pursued the libel case against the *Public Ledger*, securing evidence that William Jackson was the author of the offending paragraphs, but Jackson fled to France and it seems the suit came to nothing.

Having sold his Haymarket theatre patent to George Colman in return for an annuity, Foote returned to perform at the theatre half a dozen times in the summer of 1777. On 6th June, however, appearing in *The Devil upon Two Sticks*, he was 'obliged immediately to retire to his chamber' after the second act. Appearing again three days later he had 'another relapse ... which was attended with fainting fits of a very alarming nature'. Advised to bathe, he spent the end of the summer at Brighthelmstone, 'where he apparently recovered his former health and spirits'. Nonetheless, after he had returned to London his physicians advised warmer climes and he set out, attended only by his valet, 'to spend the winter at Paris, and in the South of France. He had got no farther than Dover, when he was suddenly attacked by another stroke of the palsy, which in a few hours terminated his existence.' He died at the Ship Inn, Dover, on 21st October. His faithful former treasurer William Jewell, one of his executors and beneficiaries, travelled thither to bring the body back to town, and on the evening of 3rd November it was interred in the cloisters of Westminster Abbey. According to the *London Evening Post*:

> The procession (if such a funeral for so great a genius, could be called a procession) began at about nine o'clock, from the deceased's house in Suffolk-street, consisting of three mourning coaches and two hacks. In the former were Dr Foote, Messrs. Hunter and Atkinson (the surgeon and apothecary), Messrs. Hamilton, Woodfall, Toozen, and Jewel. In one of the latter, Mr Dibble Davis, and Lewis, the deceased's footman; and in the other, two gentleman volunteers.
>
> The body was covered in three coffins; one which brought it to town from Dover, the other lead, and the outside oak, covered with black cloth, and gilt escutcheons. On the lid of the outside coffin was the following plain inscription:

> SAMUEL FOOTE, Esq;
> Died October the 21st, 1777,
> Aged 55 years.

> Thus ended the career of one of the first geniuses in the country, carried to the grave without the attendance of one lord, or man of fashion, out of the many he entertained for these twenty years past ... Alas! poor Foote!

His furniture and effects were sold by Christie and Ansell at the Suffolk Street house on 26th January 1778 and following days. They included 'capital jewels ... excellent gold repeaters, two fine pictures, by Zoffani ... fire arms, an air pump ... rich wearing apparel' and 'his neat crane-neck town coach and chariot, brought from his late villa at North-End'.[33]

Among the most notable absentees from Foote's funeral was **David Garrick,** who was himself to enjoy only a brief retirement, dying on 20th January 1779, aged 62, at his house in Adelphi Terrace. The *Morning Chronicle* noted the cause of death as 'that dreadful malady the stone, with which he had been occasionally afflicted for a great number of years'.

On 1st February his remains were carried to Westminster Abbey and interred at the foot of Shakespeare's monument. 'The procession from the Adelphi to the

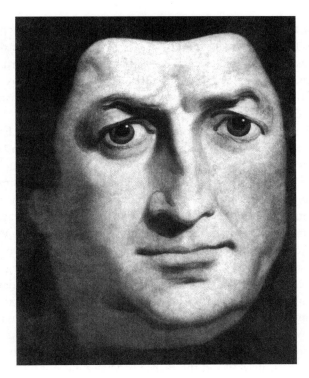

Garrick's death mask. Mezzotint by R. E. Pine, published 4th April 1779.

Abbey was one of the most grand ... that has lately been seen in this kingdom,' observed the same paper. 'There were upwards of thirty mourning coaches, followed by twice the number of gentlemens carriages. ... | The coaches were covered with eschutcheons, and the horses loaded with mournful plumes'. The pall bearers included the Duke of Devonshire, Lord Camden, Richard Rigby, and Albany Wallis. Sheridan walked as chief mourner. Among those following in the mourning coaches were Colonel Barré, the Rev. Henry Bate, Edmund Burke, Dr Burney, Charles Fox, Edward Gibbon, Dr Johnson, and Sir Joshua Reynolds. 'Many of the comedians of both theatres, housekeepers, &c. &c. joined in the procession.' The crowd 'was enormous, there being more people present in the windows, and on the tops of houses, in the streets and the avenues of the Abbey, than were ever remembered to have been collected since the coronation'.

Garrick's widow Eva lived on in the house in Adelphi Terrace for over forty years, dying there in October 1822, aged 98. The Terrace was demolished in 1936 to make way for an office block.[34]

George III remained resolute in the conflict with America and felt betrayed by Lord North's resignation in March 1782. According to Horace Walpole, when North went to take formal leave, 'the king parted with him rudely without thanking him, adding, "Remember, my lord, that it is you who desert me, not I you."' During the following crisis he drafted an abdication message: 'His majesty therefore with much sorrow finds he can be of no further utility to his native country which drives him to the painful step of quitting it for ever.' It was never delivered. He was also increasingly troubled by the wayward behaviour of the Prince of Wales, who in 1781 had to be extracted from the first of many indiscretions by a payment of £5,000 to the actress Mary Robinson, who had become his mistress and was in possession of compromising correspondence.

In 1788 the king suffered a first and prolonged bout of insanity. Fanny Burney, now a keeper of the robes to Queen Charlotte, noted in her diary on 1st November that 'he grows so weak that he walks like a gouty man, yet has such spirits that he has talked away his voice, and is so hoarse it is painful to hear him. The queen is evidently in great uneasiness. ... | The king is very sensible of the great change there is in himself, and of her disturbance at it. It seems, but Heaven avert it, a threat of a total breaking up of the constitution.' In December Dr Willis, a 'mad doctor', was brought in and the king was subjected to the indignities of a straitjacket and a restraining chair. On 17th February 1789, shortly before a regency was due to come into effect, the physicians reported to general relief that, having been 'in a state of amendment for some time', the king was 'now in a state of convalescence'. Next day Fanny Burney saw him walking arm in arm with the queen in Richmond Gardens. 'It was a pleasure that quite melted me, after a separation so bitter, scenes so distressful — to witness such harmony and security.' He did not have a serious relapse until 1801 and the Prince of Wales did not take over as regent until February 1811.

Blind and increasingly deaf, the king passed his last decade in darkness, talking to people who were not there and playing on a harpsichord which he struggled to hear. In October 1814 he was declared King of Hanover but was never aware of the fact. Queen Charlotte died in November 1818. He followed on 29th January 1820, aged 81, and was buried beside her in St George's Chapel, Windsor.[35]

George III's mind may have proved ultimately irrecoverable but **the head of his statue**, toppled in New York in July 1776, did not. Captain John Montresor, chief engineer in America during the war, later recalled hearing reports as follows:

That the rebels had cut the king's head off the equestrian statue ... and that they had cut the nose off, clipt the laurels that were wreathed round his head, and drove a musket bullet part of the way through his head, and otherwise disfigured it, and that it was carried to Moore's tavern, adjoining Fort Washington, on New York Island, in order to be fixed on a spike on the truck of that flagstaff as soon as it could be got ready. I immediately sent Corby through the rebel camp in the beginning of September 1776, to Cox, who kept the tavern at King's Bridge, to steal it from thence, and to bury it, which was effected, and [it] was dug up on our arrival, and I rewarded the men, and sent the head by the Lady Gage to Lord Townshend, in order to convince them at home of the infamous disposition of the ungrateful people of this distressed country.

George III in old age

Mezzotint by S. W. Reynolds, published 24th February 1820. Earlier versions show the king looking more Lear-like and dishevelled, with long hair and a long beard. Permission to publish was granted only after adjustments had made him appear more dignified.

On 22nd November 1777 Governor Hutchinson visited Lord Townshend's house in Portman Square. 'Lady Townshend asked me if I had a mind to see an instance of American loyalty, and going to the sopha, uncovered a large gilt head, which at once appeared to be that of the king ... By some means or other ... Montresor took it into his possession, and sent it to Lord T., which he received last night. The nose is wounded and defaced, but the gilding remains fair; and as it was well executed, it retains a striking likeness.'[36]

As the war slipped beyond recall the hawkish **Lord George Germain** became increasingly isolated in cabinet. On 12th December 1781 he declared in the House of Commons that 'from the instant when American independence should be acknowledged, the British empire was ruined'. In February 1782 he agreed to resign in return for elevation to the peerage as Viscount Sackville, recovering his natal name. According to Horace Walpole, 'When Lord North told Lord George Germaine that he must go out, he replied, shrewdly, "And pray, my lord, why are you to stay?"' He died at Stoneland Lodge in Sussex on 26th August 1785, aged 69, with the old charge of cowardice at the battle of Minden apparently still on his mind. According to one report, he called his friend Richard Cumberland to his bedside and said to him: 'I have seen much of life, and have experienced its vicissitudes; but in no one situation throughout my life did I ever feel a failure in my fortitude, any more than I do at the present moment.'[37]

William Hickey's planned departure for India was delayed, first by difficulty arranging passage and then by the recurrence of a throat infection. Advised to undergo 'the very unpleasant process of salivation', on 1st February 1777 he took lodgings directly opposite his father's house in St Alban's Street, 'which I was induced to do that I might have the use of his kitchen, of servants, &c., in supplying me with the requisite broths and articles I should want during my confinement'. On 10th March he was pronounced fit to embark. Five days later, at a dinner arranged by a friend, among guests including Edmund Burke, Hickey was surprised to find his father Joseph, 'who rose and received me with the utmost affection'. The next day 'I had the supreme felicity once more openly to enter my father's house. He behaved with his accustomed goodness, only remarking that as my own judgment must bespeak the necessity of a steady and decorous conduct in future, he would not distress me by a word more upon the subject of what had passed. He then presented me with fifty pounds, adding, too, his blessing and ardent prayers for my success.'

After delays at Portsmouth Hickey finally set sail on 1st May and arrived in the Bay of Bengal in October. Apart from a two year return to London he remained in India for the next thirty years, enjoying a successful career as an attorney. On retiring in 1808 he returned to England, and he died in London in 1827.[38]

The exile of **Thomas Hutchinson** grew progressively melancholy, the news from America offering no prospect of a return. Ill health took its toll on himself and his family. His daughter Peggy died of consumption in September 1777 at the age of 22, followed by a son in February 1780. Hutchinson himself died a few months later, on 3rd June, aged 68, at lodgings at Brompton Park where he was living with another daughter, Sarah, who was seriously ill.

A surviving son, Elisha, recalled the governor's last morning. Having talked about the Gordon riots then convulsing London, he expressed 'his expectations of dying very soon, repeating texts of Scripture, with short ejaculations to Heaven. He called for a shirt, telling Ryley his servant, that he must die clean.' As he walked the few yards from the front door to his coach he held out his hands to Ryley, 'and caught hold of him, to whom he said "Help me!" and appeared to be fainting'. He was brought back into the hallway and laid on a bed, 'after which, with one or two gasps, he resigned his soul to God who gave it. I was unhappy in being so near. The scene was too affecting, and I could scarce support myself from falling.' The governor was buried at Croydon where he had reserved a resting place near Peggy, and within a month the remains of Sarah would also be interred there.[39]

Among other refugees, former chief justice **Peter Oliver** moved to Birmingham in 1778 and died there in 1791. **Edward Oxnard** returned to America in 1786 and died at Portland on 2nd July 1803, 'as he was on the eve of moving into a large three-story house which he had built'. **Jonathan Sewall** left London for Bristol in 1777. Ten years later he recrossed the Atlantic to take up an appointment as admiralty judge for Nova Scotia and New Brunswick, dying at St John, New Brunswick, in 1796. He never returned to Massachusetts.

Jonathan Boucher finished his plan for the future government of the American colonies but it did not bring him satisfaction. 'There are so many people, of so many opinions, to be consulted, that it is endless ...,' he wrote in January 1777. 'It is now in the hands of Sir Grey Cooper, whose judgment on it is to be decisive. God help the poor man that is dependent on Great Men. I am weary of it.' What became of the plan is not known. Boucher remained at Paddington until 1785, when he was appointed vicar of Epsom. He died in his native Cumberland in 1804 and was buried in Epsom churchyard.[40]

From July 1776 **Samuel Curwen** travelled extensively through England before returning to London to wait in the hope that events would allow him to go home to America. On 29th July 1784 he bid what he assumed was 'an everlasting farewell to London', to the sound of '80 or 100' guns discharged at the Tower, 'this being the day appointed ... as a thanksgiving for the general peace'. He arrived at Boston on 25th September, 'and at 20 minutes after 3 o'clock set my foot on the end of Long Wharff' after an absence of over nine years, 'occasioned by an execrable and never enough to be lamented civil war'. To his dismay he found that he was among those who had 'to lament over the wrecks of their departed wealth and estates', his affairs 'being sunk into irretrievable ruin' as a result of 'folly, vice, wickedness'.

His situation was later described by the pastor of Salem, William Bentley:

When he left our country he possessed a convenient house in Essex Street ... and he had a good assortment of goods. His wife ... was left behind with the property, and being not too well acquainted with business and deluded by a nephew ... there was almost an entire sacrifice of the property. The remains of a valuable library were sold just before his return ... A rich collection of coins was robbed of its best pieces, and indeed things were in such a state as must have been disagreable to a less irritable man than Mr Curwin.

Curwen's wife Abigail had 'an hysterick fit' on hearing of his return and further fits when he arrived at their home and discovered what had happened. In the following summer, resigned to separation and spending the remainder of his days in foreign parts, Curwen returned to London. In September 1785 he wrote from lodgings off Fleet Street to a Salem friend to say that, while he expected Abigail to outlive him, whenever she died his heirs were on no account to allow her body to 'be entombed with my late niece or any of my family ... I should not be a little deranged in the Resurrection morning to find A. C. starting up by my side, for I am very sure, however I may forgive, I cannot wholly forget the wrongs she has done me'.

In the event she died first, in 1792, and two years later Curwen returned to Salem. William Bentley recalled that he 'was much of a gentleman, and had a good address. He appeared in our streets, much like a patriarch. The English tye wig, the long scarlet cloak, the heavy rings, and the golden headed cane, attracted notice after the war, tho' it was the best dress before it, for persons of condition.' He died on 9th April 1802, aged 86, and was buried four days later, his funeral pall being supported by the six ministers of the town.[41]

At some uncertain date the **Rev. William Jackson**, antagonist of Samuel Foote, followed the former Duchess of Kingston to the Continent, before reportedly returning to England 'in his bag and sword, *toute francoise* having thrown aside his *canonicals*, with a considerable sum of money, as the final reward of his services'. Between 1784 and 1786 he edited the *Morning Post*, and then dabbled unsuccessfully in theatre management in collaboration with John Palmer, the actor who in 1776 had lampooned him as Dr Viper in *The Capuchin*. In late 1788 and early 1789 he was in Paris helping one of the claimants to the duchess's estate (see below).

In the early 1790s he was living in France and became involved in French plans for an invasion of Britain. Seeking to advance these he travelled to London early in 1794, but 'finding that he was not likely to succeed in his object against Great Britain', he went to Ireland 'to see what could be effected there'. While in London he renewed an old acquaintance with John Cokayne, an attorney of Lyon's Inn, and they travelled together to Dublin, arriving early in April. Cokayne was playing a double game, however, and within weeks Jackson had been arrested and charged with high treason. He remained in prison for a year until tried at the Court of King's Bench, Dublin, on 23rd April 1795. After a trial lasting eighteen hours the jury returned at 4 a.m. to give their verdict of guilty, with a recommendation to mercy on account of Jackson's age and long imprisonment.

A week later the court reconvened to hear a plea by Jackson's counsel for arrest of judgement, but it soon became clear that the prisoner was severely indisposed. According to the *Morning Post*:

> During the argument, he dropped from his seat, and after labouring for some minutes under the strongest convulsions, he expired. Previous to his death he foamed at the mouth, and immediately on the breath leaving him, he swelled to a considerable size. The court seemed awfully affected, and instantly adjourned. The body of this wretched man lies in the dock [and] is to be opened by a jury of surgeons. There are many conjectures ... It was thought he would make discoveries to save himself from being executed, if poison had not been administered to him by some of his *former friends*.

The body remained in the dock overnight under a guard of soldiers. The inquest next morning found that he had died as a result of 'some acrid and mortal matter taken into his stomach; but how or by whom administered, is to the jury unknown'. One report noted that in the dead man's pocket were found 'an handkerchief, one of his pamphlets, and a very elegant short prayer, written by himself, praying to God to deliver him from his enemies, who were great and violent'. The report added: 'The business, altogether, is so dark, that scarcely three people have the same sentiments.'[42]

Jackson's former mentor the **Duchess of Kingston*** travelled back from Vienna to France early in 1777 to consult her lawyers about the continuing efforts of her husband, Lord Bristol, to secure a divorce. In August she sailed from Calais to Petersburg in her own 'most superbly decorated' yacht, which was reported to have cost £14,000. To avoid the depredations of American privateers it sailed under French colours and was manned by French sailors. It arrived safely but in late September was severely damaged when a hurricane ravaged Petersburg. According to one report, 'the yacht not only lost its rudder, but all her masts and sails; the organ, which cost her grace 1500l. is entirely broke to pieces, and the elegant coach which lay in the hold, totally destroyed.'[43]

The duchess herself received a gratifyingly warm welcome from Catherine the Great, but, temporarily yachtless, she had to journey back to France overland and in winter, prompting her to lament in a letter to Lord Barrington that she was 'a wanderer'. In another letter she recalled: 'Evelyn Meadows declared on the day of tryal I should have no rest while on the face of the earth, and minds guided by superstition might be led to believe that he could influence my destiny.' Over the following years her restlessness continued, with a trip to Rome in the summer of 1778 followed by shuttlings between Calais, Paris, and Russia. Wherever she went her wealth and susceptibility to flattery saw her falling prey to adventurers,

---

* Correctly Countess of Bristol, but she continued to go under the higher title and it persisted in general use.

including a noted swindler, James Semple, and one John Worta, who claimed to be an Albanian prince.[44]

Her troubles back in England began to recede. At the end of 1779 Lord Bristol died, removing the prospect of a humiliating divorce. In April 1780 a renewed challenge to the Duke of Kingston's will by the Meadows family ran aground in the Court of King's Bench, 'the validity of the will being fully established by the concurrent testimony of the duke's apothecary, and attorney'.

The impecunious Evelyn Meadows seems subsequently to have adopted a more direct approach in seeking to mitigate the loss of his anticipated inheritance. In November 1780 an English traveller in Bonn noted the presence of 'Mr Meadows, who is come in search of the Duchess of Kingston, to compromise matters with her; but he has not yet traced her out'. Whether as a result of his solicitations or not, she shortly began paying him an allowance of £400 a year, later raised to £600, and was to leave him £15,000 in her will. When this rapprochement later became known it prompted a marked raising of eyebrows, one newspaper noting that Meadows had brought the duchess 'to a trial, and would have had her hanged, if it had been in his power, and the laws would have suffered it,' and now, 'after ten years violent abuse of each other, they are become the best friends in the world'.[45]

Having returned to Russia, the duchess bought an estate near Petersburg in the spring of 1781, naming it 'Chudleigh' and reportedly becoming the proud owner of a brandy distillery. A year later she bought a house in Montmartre, Paris, before returning to Russia once more. By 1786 she was back in France and in the following year crowned her acquisitive career with the purchase of a chateau and small estate near Fontainebleau. She had not long to enjoy them, dying suddenly on 26th August 1788 at the age of 67. 'As in life, so in death, this lady was eccentric,' noted an early biography. 'The day before her demise she ate a brace of partridges, and some other game; she expired having scarcely swallowed two large bumpers of Madeira.'

The Duke of Kingston's vast English estates now passed as planned to Charles Meadows, who took the duke's family name Pierrepont, but things did not proceed so smoothly with regard to the duchess's personal estate. Although she owned a range of houses she died at the Hôtel du Parlement d'Angleterre in rue Coq-Héron, Paris, where she had been staying for some months. The French authorities placed the customary seals on her apartments but it was too late, many of her effects having already been bundled away to the lodgings of Evelyn Meadows, who was perching conveniently nearby.

Shortly after death the duchess's body was embalmed but it remained unburied for over two months. On 9th October the *Whitehall Evening Post* reported that it was still at the hotel, 'to the no small satisfaction of the master ... for he declares he never had so quiet a lodger, nor one who pays so well; her apartments are at 30 guineas a month, and the *Garde Robe* [wardrobe] is now large enough for all her greatness'. Her mortal remains were not left entirely unmolested, however. 'Yesterday Dr Freeman returned from Paris,' reported *The Times* on 25th October, 'where he had been to try the effects of his *Animal Magnetism* on the body of the Duchess of Kingston, but without success, which he says was owing to the surgeons who embowelled her grace, having cut the right ventricle of the heart'.[46]

On 27th October Colonel Phillips Glover, a distant relative of the duchess and one of a field of claimants to her estate, arrived in Paris. He arranged for her remains to be 'deposited in Belleville, a place appropriated by the government for the purpose', which was done on the night of 1st November.

On 6th November, galvanised by Glover, Commissaire Guiyot and other officials went to the hotel and questioned the duchess's servants. Initially her young steward, John Lilly, refused to co-operate, but on prison being mentioned he claimed that 'about one o'clock of the morning, preceding the day on which the duchess died, she called him to her bed-side, took him by the hand, and said, *My dear child, I do not know whether I am in danger or not, but carry whatever you can of my effects to Mr Meadows.* Thus ... between four and five o'clock in the morning, a *fiacre* [hackney carriage] was sent for, and ... three large cases, containing, among other effects, a large box of jewels, were put into the carriage.' Lilly added that the duchess's physician, Dr Gem, and her coachman 'got into the *fiacre*, which drove to the apartments of Mr Evelyn Meadows, on the Boulevards, where the cases were delivered,' and that between eleven and twelve on the same day 'a cart and horse had been hired of the master of the hotel, and ... two large coffers were put into it, and the cart was driven to the apartments of Mr Meadows'.[47]

This convenient tale of the effects having been given away while the duchess was still alive was corroborated by the other servants, but Glover was not to be so easily thwarted and he prevailed upon the officials to visit Meadows a few days later. Meadows claimed he had already sent all the loot to England but refused to provide any details. On 22nd December he was ordered to surrender the duchess's effects within twenty-four hours. Just as the time for doing so was up he sent a single large case to a legal repository, not only showing that he had previously lied but also begging further questions about the other cases and coffers mentioned in Lilly's confession.

By this time Glover had been joined in Paris by William Jackson, who wrote long letters to the newspapers setting out the case against Meadows. Eventually Glover prevailed, becoming the duchess's officially accepted heir in France, but as he also became responsible for her debts it proved a pyrrhic victory. His relentless pursuit prompted Meadows to flee Paris. In July 1789 it was reported that Meadows was in Picardy with his wife and 'always travels with arms'. The duchess, his fellow wayward spirit and belated mentor, would have understood. In later life 'she had always a brace of loaded pistols by the side of her bed, and her injunctions to her female domestics were, never to enter her chamber unless the bell rang, as, by sudden surprize she might be induced to fire at them.'[48]

In another improbable rapprochement between antagonists of 1776, **Lord North** returned to office in coalition with Charles Fox in April 1783, just over a year after stepping down. The Duke of Portland presided in name as first minister and North held the then recently created post of home secretary, with his eldest son George as under secretary. Holding a dim view of Fox, and feeling further let down by North, in December the king intervened, causing the House of Lords to reject an important India bill by making it known that whoever voted for it would be considered his enemy. On 17th December North told the Commons that such interference threatened 'all the privileges of parliament, and the rights of the people'. At around midnight on the 18th/19th he and Fox were separately visited by a special messenger with advice that the king 'had no longer occasion for their services'.

North continued to sit in the Commons until he succeeded his father as Earl of Guilford in 1790, by which time his poor eyesight had deteriorated into blindness. Horace Walpole, dining at Bushy in October 1787, noted that his 'spirits, good humour, wit, sense, drollery, are as perfect as ever — the unremitting attention of Lady North and his children, most touching. Mr North leads him about, Miss North sits constantly by him, carves meat, watches his every motion, scarce puts a bit into her own lips ... If ever loss of sight could be compensated, it is by so affectionate a family.'

According to his eldest daughter Katherine, as death approached North 'expressed considerable anxiety on the subject of his character and fame — that he should have wished to know how he stood and would stand with the world. That this might be a weakness, but he could not help it.' He died at his house in Grosvenor

Satire on the Fox-North coalition, with the king under their
feet but looking to recover. Published 8th March 1784.

Square on 5th August 1792, surrounded by his family. According to the *Gentleman's Magazine*, 'their grief did not suffer them to leave the room for some time after the event', and his daughter Caroline had at last to be forced away. Even his physician and friend Dr Warren, used to such scenes, ran from the room 'convulsed with sorrow ... for, perhaps, no man was ever more generally beloved by all who had access to him'. Considering his public life, however, the notice concluded that, having been 'fatally wedded to the destructive plan of subduing the republican spirit of the Americans, his administration will not only stand marked in the page of history with an immense waste of public treasure, but it will appear besprinkled with the kindred blood of thousands of British subjects'.[49]

The mooted match between North's eldest son **George North** and Beatrix Egerton was kept alive into the spring of 1777, but on 5th April Samuel Egerton wrote to Lord Guilford to indicate that it was at an end: 'I find I am disappointed by Mr North not having made himself agreable to my daughter ...' George did in time succeed in the marital stakes. In 1785 he married the dowerless Maria Hobart, causing concern to his parents. She died in 1795 and in the following year, now 4th Earl of Guilford, he took as his second wife Susan, daughter of banker Thomas Coutts, who brought a dowry of £150,000. Beatrix Egerton married a Westmorland landowner in 1778 but died in childbed at the end of the following year. Her father survived her by less than two months and his alluring estates passed to his sister.[50]

According to Captain Cook, in returning home **Omai** 'vainly flattered himself, that I meant to use force' to restore to him lands his father had lost over a decade earlier on Ulietea, one of the Society Islands. Instead Cook decided to leave him on nearby Hualhine, where the *Resolution* and the *Discovery* arrived on 12th October 1777. Cook negotiated with the local chiefs for a tract of land, and, as he recorded, 'the carpenters of both ships were ... set to work, to build a small house for Omai in which he might secure the European commodities that were his property. At the same time, some hands were employed in making a garden for his use, planting shaddocks, vines, pine-apples, melons, and the seeds of several other vegetable articles; all of which I had the satisfaction of observing to be in a flourishing state before I left the island.' According to George Gilbert of the *Resolution*, Omai's 'principal furniture was a bed in the English fashion, several tin pots and kettles, and a hand organ, on which he used to play and divert the natives'.

On 26th October, the house being nearly finished, 'many of his moveables were carried ashore', including 'a box of toys, which, when exposed to public view, seemed greatly to please the gazing multitude'. Two days later some fireworks given to Omai in England were set off 'before a great concourse of people, who beheld them with a mixture of pleasure and fear'.

On 30th October, readying to leave, Cook had his men return their animals to the ships, 'except the horse and mare, and a goat big with kid, which were left in the possession of our friend'.

I also gave him a boar and two sows of the English breed; and he had got a sow or two of his own. ... | His European weapons consisted of a musket, bayonet, and cartouch-box; a fowling-piece; two pair of pistols; and two or three swords or cutlasses. The possession of these made him quite happy [but] I was always of opinion, that he would have been happier without fire-arms ... as such implements of war, in the hands of one, whose prudent use of them I had some grounds for mistrusting, would rather encrease his dangers than establish his superiority.

Cook also feared that Omai retained hopes of revenge on those who had taken his father's lands. 'To this, I guess, he is not a little spurred by the coat of mail he brought from England, clothed in which, and in possession of some fire-arms, he fancies that he shall be invincible.'

At 4 p.m. on 2nd November, taking advantage of a breeze, Cook and his men sailed out of the harbour. Cook noted that Omai remained with them till they were at sea, at which point he returned to land in a boat, 'after taking a very affectionate farewel of all the officers. He sustained himself with a manly resolution, till he came to me. Then his utmost efforts to conceal his tears failed; and Mr King, who went in the boat, told me, that he wept all the time in going ashore.'

Cook feared that they had probably left him 'in a less desirable situation, than he was in before his connexion with us', not because he might hanker after 'the sweets of civilized life', but because 'the advantages he received from us, have placed him in a more hazardous situation, with respect to his personal safety'. Cook had, however, taken the precaution of telling the islanders that he intended to return, 'and that, if I did not find Omai in the same state of security in which I was now to leave him, all those whom I should then discover to have been his enemies, might expect to feel the weight of my resentment'. He thought this threat would probably be effective, 'for our successive visits of late years have taught these people to believe, that our ships are to return at certain periods'.

According to Gilbert, just before sailing Cook 'particularly desired Omai, after we had been gone about three weeks, to send a canoe to us, to the island we were going to; and if the natives treated him ill, to send a black bead, if moderate a blue one, and if well a white one'. A few weeks later, now on Ulietea, Cook received two people in a canoe sent by Omai. They brought a white bead and, as Cook noted, 'the satisfactory intelligence, that he remained undisturbed by the people of the island, and that every thing went well with him, except that his goat had died in kidding. He accompanied this intelligence, with a request, that I would send him another goat and two axes.' The axes were sent, along with two kids, male and female. What became of Omai thereafter is uncertain, but it is thought he died two years or so later from natural causes.[51]

It appears that **Henrietta Perreau**, widow of **Robert Perreau**, stayed on in their house in Golden Square until 1798. She died in September 1809 in Upper

Marylebone Street, aged 76, and was interred in vault no. 4 beneath St Martin in the Fields, next to her husband.

Fifty years later their remains, along with those of **Daniel Perreau** and other family members, were disturbed. In November 1858, in the interests of public health, an order in council was made that the coffins in the 'vaults and catacombs of Saint Martin-in-the-Fields, be imbedded with soil mixed with charcoal, or McDougal's disinfecting powder, and entombed in an airtight manner'. On 10th January 1859 a notice in *The Times* advised those with relatives or friends deposited 'in any of the vaults under the church, or in any of the catacombs under the church-yard', to remove them before 1st February if they so desired.

Believing surgeon John Hunter to be buried there, and hoping to retrieve his remains and have them re-interred in Westminster Abbey, naturalist Francis Buckland hurried to the church. Among the series of vaults in the crypt he concentrated on no. 3, where Hunter was supposed to lie, stationing himself at its entrance for fifteen days and examining 'every coffin as it came sliding down the plank, occasionally climbing on to the top of them – dangerous work by the way – and looking about among them with my policeman's lamp to see if I could find the much-wished-for name'. He noted that in total 3,260 coffins were removed 'to the catacombs outside the church'. Eventually he found Hunter's coffin, and in the meantime also came across the coffins of the Perreaus, which were removed from vault no. 4 and deposited in catacomb D. Before this was done Buckland managed to retrieve some grisly mementoes, now held by the Science Museum: 'the skin of the neck of one of the brothers' with 'the rope mark plainly visible', and 'the vertebrae of both of them which were not dislocated'.[52]

In an apparent act of kindness **Robert Samuel Perreau**, eldest son of Robert and Henrietta, was appointed a writer for the East India Company in 1777. According to William Hickey, who knew him in India, 'after remaining at Bencoolen about three years he obtained permission to visit Calcutta, where he established himself as a merchant and agent'. All was not well, however:

> The first cause of his character's being called in question was upon the discovery of a very considerable deficiency in his cash account as secretary to an insurance company ... The amount was made up and paid by his private friends. He nevertheless was soon afterwards so embarrassed in his circumstances as to make it necessary for him suddenly to abscond, and he secretly embarked for his original situation at Bencoolen, leaving a multitude of creditors completely in the lurch, amongst whom I was a sufferer to the amount of more than five hundred pounds ... not a sixpence of which shall I ever receive, he having lately died at Bencoolen without leaving any property ...

Hickey had previously written to him from Bengal requesting reimbursement but received 'a pert and insolent answer. ... I had only the poor satisfaction of telling him by letter he was a despicable scoundrel, and deserved a halter quite as much if not more than his father and uncle.'[53]

The fate of missing banker **Bartholomew Coote Purdon** is cloaked in uncertainty. At the beginning of 1777 it was still generally believed that he had taken his own life. In June, however, the *Morning Post* reported that 'it is now said to be past a doubt, that Bartholomew Coote Purdon, Esq. late of Oxford-street, who was supposed to be drowned, is now living abroad.' In July 1781 the directors of the Perpetual Assurance Office gave notice in the *Morning Chronicle* that they were ready 'to pay claims due by the deaths of ... several persons' including 'Bartholomew Coote Purdon, heretofore of Portman-square, but late of Bergus, in French Flanders, Esq.'[54]

In his memoirs playwright Frederick Reynolds recalled that his father had insured Purdon's life for £5,000 but his claim foundered through lack of a burial certificate. When the family heard that Purdon had died somewhere in France, the young Reynolds was dispatched with an aunt to investigate. Having drawn a blank in Paris they were advised to seek out Sir Francis Vincent in Berne. Vincent seems to have thought Purdon was still alive, although he had not seen him or heard of him 'for some years'. Reynolds completes the story by saying: 'We heard some years afterwards, that Mr Purdon died a natural death in the East Indies.' If this was true he had perhaps been helped in finding refuge by his uncle, Sir Eyre Coote, who returned to India in 1778 for the last of several spells as commander-in-chief of British forces there.[55]

After a frustrating failure to sail for Canada, first from Bristol and then from Portsmouth, **Frederika Riedesel** arrived back in London at the end of September 1776. She wrote to Lord George Germain for advice, but was still in London at the end of the year, and was warmly received at Court on New Year's Day. It was not until 16th April 1777 that she sailed from Spithead with her young children. Having reaching Quebec in mid June, they joined General Riedesel and embarked with him on the Saratoga campaign, in which he commanded the German forces. Frederika was not impressed by the overall command of Burgoyne, noting that he 'liked to make himself easy, and ... spent half his nights in singing and drinking, and diverting himself with the wife of a commissary, who was his mistress, and who was as fond of Champaign as himself'.

She herself seems to have shown considerable courage and resourcefulness, protecting her daughters and tending the wounded. On one occasion, a British general coming to see how she was, she asked him why the retreat had paused given that her husband's troops were providing the necessary cover. 'What a pity it is that you are not our commanding general!' came the reply. After the surrender, riding through the American camp, she was 'gratified to observe that no body looked at us with disrespect, but, on the contrary, greeted us, and seemed touched at the sight of a captive mother with three children'.

After travelling to Boston with the rest of the prisoners, she and her husband moved to New York, where, in March 1780, she gave birth to a daughter whom they named America. In the following year, after Riedesel had been released from his parole as part of an exchange of prisoners, they returned to Canada. The house they occupied there was so near the outposts that 'for fear of a surprise' the general 'had six men always watching in the entrance hall during the night'.

In August 1783, with the war effectively over, the family embarked for Europe. Once in London they were summoned to Court, where Frederika found herself seated between the queen and one of the princesses, 'and was obliged to relate a great deal'. Meanwhile the king and General Riedesel 'conversed a long time respecting America, and always in German, which his majesty spoke with great fluency'. By the autumn the Riedesels were back in Germany, where Frederika gave birth to four more children and later published the journals in which she recounted her experience of the American war.[56]

Captain Jack Roper, who kicked up such a dust at masquerades in 1776, continued in his merry way for at least another year or so. In November 1777 the *Morning Chronicle* reported the presence of 'noisy Jack R—' and two friends at Carlisle House. 'It is needless to observe, that these three made more fun before supper than all the rest of the company, that they drank more wine afterwards, and were, as the morning increased, exceedingly riotous and ridiculous.' By the time of a masquerade at the Pantheon in April 1778, however, it seems he was in marked decline. Among the masks was 'Captain Roper, for the last time (if the legs be any symptom) in the character of Fluellen; not being able to speak, he discharged one universal manual joke, and thrust his leek in the mouths of every one he met.'

In the following March the *Town and Country Magazine* mentioned 'one of his mad freaks', of unspecified date, when he broke a chandelier at Carlisle House and refused to pay for the damage: 'a constable was called up, when the captain meeting him upon the stairs, knocked the officer down, and with the assistance of his trusty chairman, (whom he kept in constant pay to promote his escape whenever he got into a scrape) made his retreat'. This seems to be the last report of his revels, and by the time of a masked ball at the Pantheon in May 1781 he was dead. The *London Courant* reported that 'Capt. H. of the guards, the pristine associator of the famous masquerade hero, the ever memorable Capt. Roper, was amongst the most conspicuous contributors to the lively tumult of this merry assemblage, and bids fair to be a very adequate successor to his deceased friend'.

According to the *Town and Country Magazine* of March 1783, before he died Roper had been obliged by his finances to go abroad. It added:

In so high esteem did he consider the bottle, that to him it was the only *summum bonum*: besides, he drank for spirits and a colour, and he was successful in both respects; for it is the general opinion of his acquaintance, that he was in a state of incessant inebriation for the last six years of his life; and with respect to colouring, he seemed as great a master of it as Sir Joshua; for when he lay in his coffin at Antwerp, he possessed as fine a bloom, as he ever had done at Cornelys's or the Pantheon in the zenith of frolic at five in the morning.[57]

After 1776 **Mrs Rudd** lived her life in the shadows, reports of her progress being sporadic and not always reliable. In July 1777 the *Morning Post* alluded to her apparently continuing connection with Lord Lyttelton and the reappearance of her impecunious and long forgotten husband, Valentine Rudd. 'There is no foundation for the report of Mrs R— having forged a bond in the name of Lord L—n for 3000l. She absconded abruptly the other day, but that was, it seems, to avoid the unwelcome visits of her husband, who has lately obtained his liberty by an insolvent Act.' In April 1778 Boswell heard from Lord Pembroke that he had come across her 'at a certain house', possibly a brothel, suggesting that she had by then fallen on hard times. In June 1779 it was reported that she had died in Ireland, 'in very distressed circumstances'. In October the *St James's Chronicle* assured its readers that 'notwithstanding the repeated assertions of the death of Mrs Rudd ... she is now living, at a small village in Wiltshire, called Imber on the Down'. Another premature notice appeared in the summer of 1782, when she was said to have died at Hampstead under the name 'Mrs Palmer'.[58]

In fact it seems that from about 1779 she was living with an unknown admirer, a successor to Lord Lyttelton, who had died in that year. This new connection came to an end in 1785, when, according to her own account, 'I voluntarily relinquished a dependence, which, consistent with my better feelings, I could no longer retain.' A short time later, on 9th August, she sent a card to Boswell, who was then in London. Using the alias 'Mrs Stewart', the maiden name of her mother, through whom she claimed aristocratic connections, she asked him to visit her at No. 47 Devonshire Street, Bloomsbury. He went the same day and found her looking well.

Once reintroduced he could not stay away for long and at some point an affair began. It seems to have ended on 23rd April 1786, on which day they went to the popular Sunday service at the Magdalen Hospital for penitent prostitutes in St George's Fields. Mrs Rudd mentioned that she had heard the preacher before at St Martin in the Fields, but that she didn't go to St Martin's any more because of who was buried there. This allusion to the Perreaus may have unsettled Boswell, as perhaps had an earlier joking suggestion by a friend that he might *leave* Mrs Rudd at the Magdalen. Having walked her home he felt unease at 'this *low* association', and his journals mention no further meeting with her.

Over a year later, on 29th May 1787, after dreaming of her the night before, he called at the house to which she had removed, only to learn that she was in the Fleet prison. According to her own account, 'unable to appease the importunity of creditors, I was arrested in February 1787, and thrown into prison. In this gulph of wretchedness I suffered, upwards of eleven months, the extremes of penury, sorrow, and sickness'.[59]

Both before and after her time in the Fleet she sought assistance from Lord Rawdon and other Scottish aristocrats to whom she claimed kinship. Feeling slighted by them, and incensed after Rawdon maligned her to one of her creditors, she wrote *Mrs Stewart's Case, written by herself.* It is dated December 1788, with a postscript added in February 1789. Thereafter she slips from view, but in February 1793 she was reported to be in Newgate. She was still there that December, when a newspaper noted that 'Mrs Rudd, of Perreau memory, whose adventures have so often been the subject of public curiosity, seems fated to end her career in Newgate. She is now absolutely living in that wretched prison with a man whose appearance bespeaks misery in the extreme! He is confined on the debtors' side and she seldom stirs out of the place in which they sleep.'

On 4th February 1797 the *Morning Chronicle* and other papers reported that 'the once celebrated Mrs Rudd died a short time since in an obscure apartment near Moorfields.' This time the reports do not seem to have been exaggerated and they were not corrected. One writer later noted that, in contemplating death, she had 'requested to be placed near the coffins of the Perreaus' in the vaults of St Martin in the Fields, but it seems unlikely this was done, and her place of burial is unknown.[60]

In the spring of 1779, when **Lord Sandwich** was under mounting pressure for his management of the navy, his mistress **Martha Ray** was murdered.

On the evening of Wednesday 7th April she went to see a comic opera, *Love in a Village*, at Covent Garden Theatre, in company with Caterina Galli, a celebrated mezzo-soprano whom Sandwich had employed as her companion and singing teacher. The performance did not end until after eleven. Seeing them struggle to make their way through the departing crowd, John McNamara, a dashing lawyer who knew Ray slightly, came to their assistance and escorted them to the piazza. 'Lady Sandwich's carriage' was called and Signora Galli entered it first. As Ray was making to join her a man in black approached, pulled at her gown, and shot her in the forehead. He proceeded to try to shoot himself in the head with a second pistol but only grazed his temple. Falling to the ground beside her, he tried to club himself, crying out, 'Oh! kill me! kill me! for God's sake kill me!' Not realising the seriousness of Ray's injuries, McNamara reached down to help her only to find that 'his hands were in blood'. According to Mary Anderson, a fruit-seller who was standing nearby, 'The lady bled like a cock with his throat cut.'

With the help of a link boy McNamara carried the corpse into the Shakespeare tavern, to which the culprit was also taken. Sir John Fielding was summoned from Brompton and arrived at about three in the morning. He ordered the culprit to be held in Tothill Fields Bridewell for the rest of the night. Word had meanwhile been sent to the Admiralty. According to one report, 'When Lord S— was first acquainted with the fatal catastrophe ... he seemed not to credit it; however he sent a servant to the Shakespeare, with whom a surgeon returned to his lordship. When informed that she was really dead ... he wrung his hands and cried, exclaiming, "I could have borne any thing but this; but this unmans me."'

The murderer turned out to be James Hackman, a former army officer, recently ordained, 'about 30 years of age, five feet nine inches, very genteelly made, and

The Rev.ᵈ JAMES HACKMAN

Published by G. Kearsly in Fleet Street, April 24.1779.

of a most polite address'. He had first met Ray when, as part of a recruiting party at Huntingdon, he had been invited to Sandwich's house at Hinchingbrooke, probably in the summer of 1775. The nature and extent of his subsequent relationship with her is uncertain, accounts varying from a few chaste meetings followed by distant pining to a passionate affair and plans to marry.[61]

Three weeks after the murder the *Gazetteer* reported 'the most current account':

The lady had actually engaged to marry him; in consequence of which he quitted the army, and entered into the church. That Signora G— served them as a go-between, but when the affair was on the point of being accomplished, dreading the effects of Lord S—h's resentment, should he discover her to have been concerned in it, she disclosed the secret to his lordship, and delivered to him a letter with which she had been entrusted by Mr Hackman for Miss Ray: this his lordship, after having opened and read, ordered the signora to return to Mr Hackman with a verbal message as from Miss Ray, that she would never more have any connection with him. Frantic with the disappointment, the unhappy man, it seems, had formed the desperate resolution of putting an end to his life in the presence of his supposed faithless mistress; but seeing her with Mr McNamara, and imagining she had quitted him for that gentleman, in a transport of jealousy he determined she should not survive him to make a rival happy. This is said to be the true cause of the tragical scene that ensued; whether it be so or not we will not pretend to say ...

That Galli had played a central and equivocal role in the tragedy was widely believed at the time and led to her being spurned by polite society.[62]

Martha Ray, after a painting by Nathaniel Dance, 1777

Mezzotint by Valentine Green, published 24th May 1779

'I have frequently enjoyed the pleasure of hearing her sing at Hinchinbroke,' wrote R. D. Cumberland shortly after her death, 'and … always thought her the most accomplished woman I have seen. … I look upon her as a second Cleopatra — a woman of thousands, and capable of producing those effects on the heart which the poets talk so much of and which we are apt to think Chimerical.'

On the evening after the murder Ray's body was 'wrapped up in a sheet' and removed from the Shakespeare to an undertaker's near Leicester Fields to be prepared for interment. It was reported that Sandwich had 'ordered the corpse of Miss Ray to be buried in the cloaths she died in, and that not a jewel she then wore shall be taken away; so that property to the amount of near 2000l. will be deposited in her coffin'. She was buried on 14th April in the chancel at Elstree, Hertfordshire, near the remains of her mother. She left five children by Sandwich, the eldest of whom, 'a fine youth of sixteen, is now a lieutenant in the navy'.[63]

Hackman was convicted at the Old Bailey on 16th April and executed three days later. On the day of the execution Charles Fox moved in the Commons for an address to the king, 'that he would ... remove John Earl of Sandwich, from his presence and councils, on account of the general ill state of the navy'. The motion was defeated by 224 votes to 118, and in spite of continuing criticism Sandwich remained in office until the fall of North's government in March 1782.

In private life he proved consolable. Within a year of Ray's death he had taken a new mistress, Nelly Gordon, who was to remain with him for the rest of his life. He died on 30th April 1792 at his house in Hertford Street.[64]

On 24th March 1777 the eloping **Frances, Countess of Tyrconnel** gave birth to a son, but it died within twenty-four hours. Six weeks earlier her husband had gained a judgement in the Court of King's Bench against Charles Loraine Smith of Enderby, Leicestershire, for criminal conversation with her, and on 16th May an Act of Parliament was passed dissolving the Tyrconnel marriage. On 28th October she remarried, not to Smith but to a third man, Philip Anstruther. She died in 1786, aged 33.[65]

Pickpocket **Elizabeth West** finally came unstuck on 14th February 1777 when she robbed a man as he was leaving Drury Lane Theatre. A constable arrived and took hold of her, saying to her victim, 'O sir! Don't you know her? It is the famous Miss West.' At the resulting trial she claimed that she had been innocently on her way 'from my Lord Mansfield's chambers to my own house in Berkeley Square', and that the constable had seized her simply because he recognised her, but this time the jury were not to be won over and she was found guilty.[66]

The *Morning Chronicle* reported that on 16th June she was 'safely delivered of a fine boy, at her apartments in Newgate', adding that the keeper, Mr Akerman, 'in order to give her an easier couch than the common barrack, with which every room in Newgate is furnished, last week bought a little snug bedstead, and sent it up for the use of the poor woman ... Mrs Thomas, the respited convict for forgery, is in the same room with her, and assists her as a nurse.' In the apartment directly opposite was Dr Dodd, shortly to be executed. It seems West did not repay Akerman's kindness. During a riot in August she was said to have been 'encouraging the riotous prisoners during the whole procedure', and she was perhaps the female prisoner who 'repeatedly called out to the insurgents, "Go it, lads, go it, dash away, don't spare them! Liberty! Liberty! Liberty!"'[67]

She regained her own liberty in the following spring but within two months was arrested again, this time for picking the pocket of a glover's wife who had gone to view the remains of the Earl of Chatham, then lying in state at Westminster. She was tried and convicted at the Old Bailey on 16th July 1778 under the name Mary West, otherwise Groves. 'She was dressed very genteely, and held in her arms the child of which she was delivered in Newgate'.

Over the following years she was in and out of jail. In September 1781, noting that she was at large again, the *Public Advertiser* observed that 'the history of this woman, at a proper period, will be more extraordinary than that of the famous Jenny Diver, of Cutpurse memory.' On 3rd April 1783 the same paper noted her death, 'last week at Hampstead'. The *Gentleman's Magazine* added: 'She has bequeathed to her two children near 3000l.'[68]

In June 1777 **John Wilkes** stood in vain again for the post of City chamberlain in the hope of repairing his finances, one broadside announcing, 'Your vote poll and interest are desired for John Wilkes ... he having more creditors than anyone else.' He failed once more in 1778, but in November 1779 the incumbent Hopkins died, opening the way for Wilkes finally to be elected to the post, which he held for the rest of his life.

He proved less tenacious regarding his mistress Marianne de Charpillon. The rift between them seems to have begun with a quarrel at supper in May 1777, when her parting shot was that he had become as odious to her as her mother. By November the affair was over and before long Wilkes had a new, younger, plainer, and more enduring mistress, Amelia Arnold, by whom he had a daughter, Harriet, born in 1778.[69]

In later life he became increasingly conservative, supporting the king and deploring the barbarities of the French Revolution. In 1791 he removed from Prince's Court to a grander house in the south-west corner of Grosvenor Square. He died there on 26th December 1797, aged 72. In his will he left the lease of the house and the household contents 'to my beloved daughter Mary Wilkes', who was still living with him. He added: 'I desire to be buried in the parish where I die, in great privacy; and carried to the grave by six of the poorest men of the said parish, to each of whom I give a suit of coarse brown cloth and one guinea. I wish that a plain marble may be erected near the place where I shall be buried, with this inscription: "The remains of John Wilkes, a friend of liberty ..."' His wishes were followed and he was interred in Grosvenor Chapel, South Audley Street, on 4th January.[70]

THE *PROMENADE AT CARLISLE HOUSE.*

ABOVE Carlisle House during its sedate later years. Published 1st December 1781.

BELOW On the left, the old theatre in the Haymarket, formerly Foote's, prior to demolition, and on the right the new theatre. Published 1822.

C: Some places of diversion: Closing time in the gardens

As the years passed **Bagnigge Wells** became less fashionable, and by the early nineteenth century it was 'much resorted to by the lower sort of tradesmen'. In December 1813 it was put up for auction, the lots including 200 drinking tables, the bake-house, summer-house, water-organ, grotto, fountains, and all the gold and silver fish. Having resumed on a reduced site and under new management in the following year, it continued under various owners until 1841, when a final performance on 26th March featured glees, farces, and comic songs. The site was soon built upon and now lies broadly south-east of King's Cross railway station, King's Cross Road having formerly been Bagnigge Wells Road.[71]

Carlisle House, scene of Mrs Cornelys's masquerades, remained in use for concerts and other entertainments for several years. In November 1780 Samuel Curwen attended a 'Sunday evening entertainment, called the promenade ... The employment of the company is meer simple walking through the rooms'. In June 1782 a 'grand rural masque ball' was held, but that December the property was offered to let, 'with all the elegant furniture, on very advantageous terms'.[72]

By March 1784 part at least of the building was housing Jos. Jacob's manufactory for 'coach wheels of superior quality', and he was still manufacturing there two years later. Meanwhile in June 1785 Carlisle House had been offered for sale and Mr Christie had auctioned 'all the valuable household furniture, china, and other effects ... consisting of superb pier glasses of distinguished magnitude, rich girandoles, cut glass lustres, blue sattin and mixed damask window curtains, crimson silk damask, do. elegant cabriole chairs, sophas, &c.'[73]

In January 1788 the property was offered for let again, in two parts: the house on Soho Square and 'the large rooms in Sutton-street, adjoining ... recently built by Mrs Cornelys for a ball-room and supper-room'. In 1791 the part fronting Soho Square was demolished. 'Where the luxurious orgies of Carlisle House were once held,' noted *The World*, 'and where the *bon vivants* of those days, the Jack Ropers, and the Rohan Hamiltons, once indulged themselves in every riotous excess, there a quiet private mansion is now rising over the ruins of the former, and Soho-Square will soon have to remember Carlisle House only by its name.' Part of the site is now occupied by St Patrick's Catholic church.[74]

The **theatre** in the **Haymarket** formerly managed by Samuel Foote closed for good in October 1820. The new and grander Haymarket Theatre, designed by John Nash, was built on an adjoining site to the south and opened in the following year.[75]

It seems that after closing for the season on 23rd September 1776 **Marylebone** or **Marybone Gardens** never re-opened. On 3rd April 1777 and following days an auction on the premises offered 'the materials of many substantial buildings, the boxes, tables, and benches,' along with 'the remarkably fine-ton'd and well seasoned organ ... several elegant glass chandeliers ... the stock of excellent wines, and several hundred globe and other lamps, &c.' On the final day were sold 'the scenes, musick, lamps, and about 40 puppets belonging to the favourite entertainment called the Comick Mirror,' along with 'an excellent harpsichord' and 'a collection of printed and manuscript musick'. Another auction a month later offered 'about four hundred elm and lime trees, the materials of a large dwelling-house, the Orchestra, saloon, theatre, and sundry other brick and timber buildings'. In June the *Morning Chronicle* described the ensuing upheaval:

> The Gardens at Marybone, that so lately were the seat of diversion and entertainment, where Vulcan chose to erect his forge,* and the gods of etherial fire resided, is now become like a volcano, where the eruptions have overturned the fine Orchestra, beautiful temples, and pleasant walks, that used to be grandly illuminated with transparent lamps of various colours, and left nothing but a mere chaos of confusion and desolation, which in a short time will undergo another transmutation, and be formed into spacious streets.

The site is now occupied by Beaumont Street, Devonshire Street, and part of Devonshire Place.[76]

The Pantheon suffered as a result of the waning appeal of masquerades. In 1791 it re-opened as an opera house, but in January 1792, amid 'extreme hurry' in preparing a new opera for the king and queen to attend, 'a great fire' was made to dry a piece of scenery, 'which being attracted by the fire, the turpentine blazed up with great violence, and put the whole room in flames'. The fire soon spread and in the early hours of 14th January 'the finest rotunda in England' was 'burnt to ashes, while an unfeeling mob ... seemed to exult in the conflagration'. A second, less splendid Pantheon soon took its place but was demolished in 1812. A third Pantheon opened in the following year but did not meet with success. In the 1830s it was converted into a bazaar. In the 1860s it was taken over by wine merchants and in 1937 it was sold to Marks and Spencer, who demolished it and built the present shop in its place.[77]

The rotunda at **Ranelagh** opened for the last time as a place of public entertainment on 8th July 1803. In September 1805 the directors ordered the demolition of Ranelagh House and the rotunda. Shortly afterwards the 'capital finger organ', with 'thirteen stops and a powerful swell', was advertised for sale. In June 1807 the *Gentleman's Magazine* published a poetic lament:

> You see where clouds of dust ascend the sky,
> See where the scatter'd ruins load the plain ...
> On that same spot once stood fam'd Ranelagh!
> That haunt of fashion, and once gay resort
> Of England's beauteous dames ...

The site is now occupied by the eastern part of the grounds of the Royal Hospital, Chelsea.[78]

---

* One of Marybone's attractions had been a firework display which ended with 'a representation of the Forge of Vulcan, and the Cavern of the Cyclops, under Mount Etna', with 'the Eruption of the Volcano, and the Flowing of the Lava'.

The last public execution at **Tyburn** occurred on 7th November 1783, after which 'the gallows was purchased by a carpenter and converted into stands for beer butts, in the cellars of a public-house in the neighbourhood, viz. the Carpenter's Arms in Adams Street'. Thereafter the condemned met their ends outside Newgate prison, the aim being to avoid the long procession through the city and the air of riot and festivity.[79]

Vauxhall Gardens outlived its rivals but went through many changes. Fireworks were introduced in 1798 and it later became known for balloon ascents in the afternoon — although, as Charles Dickens noted, Vauxhall by daylight was 'a porter-pot without porter, the House of Commons without the Speaker, a gas-lamp without the gas'. It closed in 1840 but was revived in the following year. Finally, in 1859, it was announced that 'this celebrated place of amusement, after an existence of nearly a century and a half, is doomed to be destroyed.' The last night was set for Monday 25th July, when it would 'positively close for ever'. As the *Morning Post* reported:

> The attendance of visitors was enormous ... The hand-bills circulated profusely among the company made frequent and pathetic allusion to the last grand concert — the last time of Miss Lizzie Harris — the last performance on the ballet stage — the last horsemanship — the last dancing on the monster platform — the last *al fresco* entertainment — the last suppers (including the last ham-wafers) — the last punch — and the last fireworks. Everything, in fact, was ultimate. Yet this reflection did not appear to detract from the merriment of the audience, who, on the contrary, seemed to think that they were acting in the true spirit of the occasion by enjoying themselves to the full extremity ...

According to another report, the evening closed with 'the customary display of fireworks, signalised on this evening by the introduction of two concluding tableaux, in which the devices appeared of "Thanks, kind friends," and "Farewell for ever." The dancing on the large platform was then prolonged till some time after midnight, and with the national anthem and a hearty parting cheer from the crowd, that lingered to the last, Vauxhall rendered up the ghost.'

Next day the builders moved in to clear the ground, and on 22nd and 29th August the fixtures, fittings and building materials were auctioned on the premises. They included fountains, statues, vases, and grotto work; figures of Neptune and sea horses; the firework gallery; '10,000 illumination lamps'; 'a transparency of the queen on horseback, 10 ft. square'; the 'monster platform for dancing', which sold for £53; and 'the entire erection of the elegant circular Orchestra, with minarets, leaded cupola, roof, and gallery, American, stout, and oyster bars', which sold for £99. Before long 'the once famous scene of so many pleasant revels' was covered with streets and houses, the site bounded by Goding Street on the west and St Oswald's Place on the east. More recently part of it has been been cleared to form a small public park which railway trains trundle past on their way to Waterloo.[80]

Extended notes: Some vexed questions

For details of works referred to please see the Bibliography

i. How many Mohawks came to London?

A doubt about 'Colonel Guy Johnson and Karonghyontye (Captain David Hill)' by Benjamin West, 1776, in the National Gallery of Art, Washington

See Chronicle 29th March and Plate 8

The picture's history and the arguments for its current dating and titling are set out in Miles et al. pp321-328 (1995) and Reinhardt (1998).

The picture was first documented only in 1927, when it was sold at Sotheby's as a portrait of Joseph Banks. In 1938 and again in 1967 it was exhibited as a portrait of Colonel Guy Johnson and Joseph Brant.

The identity of both figures was doubted, however, particularly that of the Indian, and in 1975 and 1984 the painting was exhibited simply as a portrait of Guy Johnson. Milton Hamilton (1958, p123) thought it very unlikely that the painting's Indian was Brant, not least because 'Joseph was never one to appear in the background'. He suggested that it might instead be John Hill, Brant's companion in London, or simply an idealised, generic figure symbolic of Johnson's position as superintendent of Indian affairs. More recently Thomas Abler et al. (2008, p193) have noted that the Indian has had the upper part of his ears pierced, whereas portraits of Brant show only modest lobe piercings. In the standard work on West, Helmut von Erffa and Allen Staley listed the picture as '[?] Sir William Johnson, bt., c. 1767-70' (1986, pp523-524). They considered the identity of both figures highly uncertain and argued on stylistic grounds that the painting was 'unlikely' to date from as late as 1776.

In 1988 attention was drawn to a letter from David Hill (Karonghyontye), brother of John, in which he referred to a double portrait of Guy Johnson and himself. The letter was dated 6th November 1784 and was sent to Daniel Claus, an Indian department official who is thought to have been in London at the time. It asked him to bring back a copy of the double portrait but gave no details of its date, size, medium, or where or by whom it was painted.

The current identification of the second figure in the National Gallery of Art painting arises from this 1784 letter and rests on four propositions: i) the NGA portrait was painted by West in 1776; ii) its white sitter is Guy Johnson; iii) David Hill's letter must refer to the NGA painting because there is no record of any other double portrait of Johnson and an Indian; iv) David Hill must have been in London in 1776.

All four propositions could be true, but von Erffa and Staley considered the first two unlikely. Regarding the third it is worth noting that the NGA painting, by an eminent artist, went apparently unrecorded for the first 150 years of its existence, suggesting that one or more additional double portraits may well have been painted without any documentary trace having come to light.

Unhelpfully for the fourth proposition, not only do the contemporary accounts not mention David Hill's presence in London in 1775-1776, but they are also more or less consistent in indicating that only two Indians accompanied Guy Johnson on the trip.

It is worth noting in passing that a third member of the party, Peter Johnson, a son of Sir William Johnson and Molly Brant, had Indian blood, but he seems to have been treated very much as Sir William's son. The *Public Advertiser* (1 April 1776 3a) reported that 'his majesty has been pleased to present Mr Peter Johnson, son of the late Sir William Johnson, bart., to a pair of colours in the 26th regiment,' and went on to refer to him as a 'young gentleman'. He was only 16 or 17 years old at this time and it seems safe to say he is not the Indian in the portrait.

The following are the references found to Indian visitors in London in 1776 which give, or may be taken to imply, information as to their names and/or number.

i.   Guy Johnson to Lord George Germain, 26 January 1776: 'The Indian chief who accompanied me, with his companion, are persons of character and influence in their country'. (DCHNY vol. 8 p657)

ii. Note by Guy Johnson in front endpapers of his diary for 1776: 'To get some thing warm for 2 Indians'. (Beinecke GJD)

iii. Newspaper reports in 1776 (e.g. *Morning Post* 1 March 2b / *Gazetteer* 2 March 3b / *London Chronicle* 5 March 223a / *Gazetteer* 20 March 2d / *Gazetteer* 30 May 2b) refer repeatedly to there being two Indian 'chiefs' in London and make no reference to any further Indian(s).

iv. 'The Speech of Thayendenegeh a chief, accompanied by Oterough-yanento a warrior, both of the Six Nations, 14 March, 1776.' Delivered to Lord George Germain. (DCHNY vol. 8 pp670-671)

v.   'The Answer of Thayendanagea a sachem, and of Ohrante a warrior of the Mohocks to the Right Honourable Lord George Germaine.' Dated 7th May 1776. (DCHNY vol. 8 p678). This is the one contemporary reference which may indicate the presence of a third Mohawk. William Beauchamp (p62) says Ohrante is Oteroughyanento, 'Indians often having two names', but Leslie Reinhardt (p302 n.26) cites expert advice that Ohrante is not Oteroughyanento. The speech in question was written down by Joseph Chew, secretary of Indian affairs, and it seems plausible that for practical ease he might have used a short form for Oterough-yanento. Whether he did so or not, there appears to be no suggestion that David Hill was ever known as 'Ohrante' or anything similar.

vi. Lord George Germain to Guy Johnson, 14 January 1777: 'I was very glad to find by your letter of the 9th August that you were safe arrived at New York with the two Indians that accompanied you'. (DCHNY vol. 8 p695)

vii. Daniel Claus, in anecdotes of Brant written in September 1778, regard-ing his return voyage to America: 'Joseph and his companion, John of the lower Mohawk town who attended him, having brass rifle guns ... were so dexterous and good marksmen as to pick off those on board the rebel ship whom by their dress they took to be officers'. (Bryant p14)

viii. Anna Larpent, writing in 1787, recalled seeing Brant often in London in 1776 and refers only to 'another Indian with him'. (HM 31201 vol. 17 f49v)

In addition, Isabel Kelsay, in the most authoritative biography of Brant, appears to be in no doubt that only two Indians came to London (see for example pp158, 159, 162, 170, 174).

There seem to be two main possibilities: either there were two (or more) double portraits painted at around this time of a British official and an Indian warrior, or a third Mohawk, of striking and impressive appearance, came to London in 1776 and went not only unrecorded but also apparently unnoticed.

If the NGA portrait was painted by West in 1776, but, as seems almost certain, David Hill did not come to London, Milton Hamilton's 1958 suggestions seem plausible: either the Indian warrior is John Hill or it is a generic, idealised figure in the vein of those depicted by West in earlier works such as 'The Death of General Wolfe' (1770). Perhaps, indeed, it is both: an idealised figure based upon John Hill.

ii. Who was 'Smugglerius'?

See Chronicle 27th May

The earliest printed reference to the cast seems to be the description quoted in the Chronicle from Baretti's *Guide through the Royal Academy* (p24), published on 30th April 1781.

Also quoted in the Chronicle is an extract from a letter written by sculptor John Deare as a young man in which he refers to a cast. The extract was included in *Nollekens and his Times* by J. T. Smith (1828, vol. 2 pp305-306) with the heading: 'To his Father, dated London, May 1st, 1776.'

While it is possible that two similar figures were cast in this period, it seems likely that Baretti and Deare were referring to the same figure, although their accounts appear to differ slightly as to how the cast came about: Deare suggests that the fineness of the corpse led to its being taken to the Royal Academy where it was covered with plaster of Paris; Baretti says Dr Hunter was going to dissect the body at the Academy for one of his lectures and at that point it was considered 'very fine and worth preserving'.

Two double hangings occurred within a few weeks of Deare's letter:

12th April. James Langar, for robbery in Hyde Park, and Samuel Whitlow, for burglary. 'The prisoners were both very well-looking young men' (*Middlesex Journal* 13 April 3c).

27th May. Benjamin Harley and Thomas Henman, smugglers, for the murder of Customs officer Joseph Pearson. 'They received sentence immediately (this being Friday) to be hanged at Tyburn the Monday following, and their bodies to be afterwards dissected and anatomized; which sentence was executed upon them' (OBP May p277). 'Great numbers returned to see them dissected at Surgeons Hall' (*Morning Chronicle* 28 May 3a).

Regarding Langar and Whitlow:

i.   They were not smugglers, so it is hard to see why a cast made from the body of one of them should have been dubbed 'Smugglerius'.

ii. Their crimes were comparatively minor and there is nothing to suggest that either man was sentenced to dissection.

iii. On 14th April the body of a Samuel Whitlow, presumably the executed man, received a non-conformist burial in Deadman's Place, Southwark (NA RG 4/4358).

Regarding Harley and Henman:

i.   The date ascribed to Deare's letter would seem to rule out either of them as the model for the cast, but it could be wrong, either as a result of Deare himself misdating the letter or of Smith transcribing or assuming incorrectly. Alternatively the letter may have been started on 1st May but added to over a period, a fairly common practice at the time.

ii. The *Morning Chronicle* report quoted above indicates that the bodies of both men were dissected at Surgeons' Hall in the usual way, whereas it appears the 'Smugglerius' corpse was taken intact to the Royal Academy and then kept there while the cast was made.

iii. As noted in the Chronicle, one of the Harley and Henman corpses subsequently came to public attention in another context. On 20th June a female servant went before the lord mayor at Guildhall having been alarmed to find human remains on a rooftop, and it turned out that they had been acquired innocently by a surgeon. Accounts differ as to some details but agree about the identity and source of the remains: they were 'part of the body of a man executed lately for the murder of the Custom-house officer, which he [the surgeon] had obtained of the Surgeons' Company by a petition, for surgical experiments' (*London Chronicle* 22 June 599b); 'the corpse was one of the two murderers lately executed at Tyburn ... he obtained it of the master of the Surgeons Company by a petition' (*Middlesex Journal* 22 June 1d).

The evidence is therefore awkward and appears contradictory, but the bodies of Harley and Henman seem the likelier candidates to have served as the model for Carlini's cast.

iii. Supposed wagers at Almack's (later Brooks's) relating to America

> First wager in the betting book in Brooks's club, dated Christmas Day, 1776: Gen. George Burgoyne wagers Charles Fox one pony (fifty guineas) that he will be home victorious from America by Christmas Day, 1777. This is a significant record of Burgoyne's overconfidence.
>
> Thomas G. Frothingham, *Washington, Commander in Chief*, 1930, p179 note 2

This striking wager has been referred to in several subsequent works: for example, Alan Valentine (*Lord George Germain*, 1962, pp163-164) discusses its implications while pointing out that Burgoyne's Christian name was John, not George. However, a search of the original betting book at the London Metropolitan Archives (ACC/2371/BC/04/073) found no such entry. Folio 28 verso has a bet dated 14th November 1776, then, at the bottom of the page, an undated bet about the lord lieutenancy of Ireland. The next bet, at the top of folio 29 recto, is dated 24th January 1777.

The wager is not mentioned by G. S. Street in 'The Betting Book at Brooks's' (*North American Review*, vol. 173, no. 156, 1901, pp44-55), in which he referred to and quoted a series of notable entries relating to America.

Moreover, and rather importantly, Fox was in Paris at the time. As quoted in the Chronicle, on 15th November the king wrote to Lord North saying he had heard Fox was about to set off for Paris 'and not return till after the recess'. In his *Memorials and Correspondence* of Fox (1853, vol. 1 p148) Lord John Russell notes that this plan 'was carried into execution'. This is confirmed by letters to Horace Walpole from Madame du Deffand, who between 1st December and 13th January refers repeatedly to Fox's presence in Paris (Walpole Correspondence, Yale edition, vol. 6 pp376-389).

Regarding another entry in the betting book, Street (p51) quotes: 'Aug. 19th 1776. Mr Fox bets Ld. Bolingbroke five guineas that America does not belong to the King of Great Britain this day two years.' While the handwriting in the original (folio 26 verso) appears partly overwritten, it seems clear that the subject of the bet was not 'America' but 'Jamaica', about which there was much concern at the time.

Acknowledgements

I am grateful to the following for permission to quote from manuscripts in their collections or from previously published material of which they own the copyright: Beinecke Rare Book and Manuscript Library, Yale University (Hannah More letter and Guy Johnson journal); Bodleian Libraries, University of Oxford (North papers); Irish Academic Press, Dublin (*Documents of the American Revolution 1770–1783*, volumes 10 and 12, ed. K. G. Davies); Lewis Walpole Library, Yale University (Anna Porter accounts of the trial of the Duchess of Kingston); London Metropolitan Archives (City of London sessions papers); Maine Historical Society, Portland (Edward Oxnard diary); the McGraw-Hill Companies, Inc., New York (*Boswell: The Ominous Years, 1774–1776* ed. Charles Ryskamp and Frederick A. Pottle); Morgan Library and Museum, New York (Edward Gibbon pocket-book); Phillips Library, Peabody Essex Museum, Salem (*The Journal of Samuel Curwen, Loyalist* ed. Andrew Oliver); the Royal Academy (James Northcote letters).

This book is additionally indebted to a number of institutions which have made illustrations available and, where applicable, granted permission to reproduce them, including: Birmingham Museums and Art Gallery; Folger Shakespeare Library, Washington DC; Garrick Club, London; Huntington Art Collections, San Marino, California; Lehigh University Art Galleries, Bethlehem, Pennsylvania; Library of Congress, Washington; Metropolitan Museum of Art, New York; National Gallery of Art, Washington; New York Public Library; Peabody Essex Museum, Salem; Rijksmuseum, Amsterdam. As a quick glance at the illustration sources list will show, the greatest debts are to two outstanding Yale University institutions, the Lewis Walpole Library and the Yale Center for British Art.

I would also like to thank Ian Faul, secretary of Brooks's, for permission to inspect the club's betting book; the Huntington Library, San Marino, California, for providing images of Anna Porter's diary; Kristen McDonald at the Lewis Walpole Library, for particular help in providing illustrations; Mark Pomeroy at the Royal Academy archives; Stewart Emmens of the Science Museum; and Rory Lalwan of City of Westminster Archives. I am also grateful for a great deal of other help received from staff at the various institutions listed above and at the British Library, the London Library, and the National Archives at Kew.

Source Notes

Sources are cited by author name or by a short title or abbreviation, under which they are listed alphabetically in the Bibliography. Additional brief information is included where needed to identify a particular work.

Newspaper references include page and column details, 'a' indicating the left-hand column and so on. The *London Chronicle* (LC) and *Lloyd's Evening Post* (LLEP) have continuous page numbering by half-yearly volume (January to June, July to December). In the case of other newspapers, which lack printed page numbers, the numbers given are derived from the page's position in the relevant day's sequence. In most cases the source is digital (usually the Burney Collection database) and missing pages and duplicate scans sometimes complicate the sequence. The page numbers given should therefore be regarded as fallible.

Months are given as Jan, Feb, etc. Unless otherwise indicated the year in all date references is 1776.

In newspaper references, secondary dates in square brackets (e.g. 'LC 5 Sep [4 Sep]') refer to internal subheadings in issues published on the later date.

Basic biographical information, including dates of birth, and hence ages, has been drawn largely from the *Oxford Dictionary of National Biography*, which is not separately noted as a source below except in a few particular cases.

Sources of quotations are identified where necessary by (q) or (qs), for single and multiple quotations respectively; by the opening word or words of the quotation; or by an indicative word or phrase.

In the notes relating to the Chronicle the day in question is listed numerically: 1st March, for example, is 03.01.

Other abbreviations used:

ad	advertisement. In most cases these relate to future events and it is of course worth bearing in mind that what was planned may not have happened.
C	cross reference to a Chronicle entry e.g. C 10 Aug
Fr.	translated from French original
MIA	Meanwhile in America (section at end of some Chronicle months)
orig.	indicates a variant spelling in the source.

Glossary and Introduction

1 Boswell LJ ii 348 (7 Apr 1775).
2 C 10 Aug / Burke ed. Fitzwilliam ii 107 (to Richard Champion, 30 May).
3 MC 19 Jun 2b-c / MC 12 Jul 2a-b.
4 BD iv (q) / White 3, 79-80.
5 MP 16 Nov 2b / Buckle i 194 ('probably').
6 Walpole Letters ix 392 (to Sir Horace Mann, 17 Jul addition to letter of 16 Jul) / Boucher Reminiscences 143 (Oct 1775, busy streets) / Moritz 28 (5 Jun 1782, lighting; phrasing of translation adjusted slightly) / Boswell LJ ii 337 (2 Apr 1775, tide), iii 178 (20 Sep 1777, tired).
7 Price, Civil Liberty, 76-77.
8 Lawson and Phillips 228 / MP 30 Jul 2a.
9 Harrison 567.
10 Johnsonian Miscellanies ii 251 / Archenholz 179 ('that the crowds').

11 Critical Review 1774 p41 / Lichtenberg's Visits 122 ('as never') / Curwen 1864 p33 (to Rev. Thomas Barnard at Salem, 22 Jul 1775) / Lichtenbergs Briefe i 244 (letter dated 12 Nov 1775).
12 C 10 Feb, 9 Mar, 21 Mar, 28 May.
13 History of North America 68-69.
14 Hutchinson i 447 (18 May 1775).
15 They appeared eleven months in arrears. The January diary is in GM 1776 (supplement) p609. Other months follow at intervals ending with December in GM (Nov) 1777 p510. Diary entries fairly often just read 'ditto'. Where there is a single 'ditto' below an entry containing several elements this has usually been converted to 'As yesterday', although it should be borne in mind that it is not always clear whether 'ditto' applies to the first part of the previous day's entry or to all of it. In cases where it seems clear that 'ditto' applies to the entire preceding entry, that entry has been repeated in full. The GM diaries broadly accord with the single word notes of conditions, observed at two set points in the day, in the meteorological journal kept at the house of the Royal Society in Crane Court, Fleet Street, and published in the *Philosophical Transactions* for 1777 (lxvii [67] pt. 1 pp358-381). In the case of a few dates, however, the diaries and the journal appear starkly at odds.
16 'Squire Randal 13.

Briefing Notes

In Briefing Notes and the Tour ages are given as at the start of 1776.
1 Wraxall Memoirs i 283-284.
2 MHS Oxnard 13 Sep 1775 (countenance), 11 Dec 1775 (small).
3 CCR 79.
4 CCR 92 / Wraxall Mem. v 387.
5 CCR 70-85, 87-89.
6 Oxford History British Empire ii 327 (debt) / Johnson, Taxation, 6 / LLEP 29 Nov [28 Nov] 1775 516b.
7 Coll. Massachusetts Hist. Soc., 4th series, x 561 (effigy), 571 (Justice W. Smith, Jr. to General Monckton, 30 May 1765, New York, q).
8 Hutchinson 1828 p439.
9 SJC 22 Jan [21 Jan] 1774 1a (Tea Party news) / AA 4th series i 913-916 (Association of 20 Oct 1774) / Adams 40-41 (dated 20 Sep 1774, Philadelphia).
10 Parl. Reg. Lords ii 5-17 (p7, q).
11 Parl. Reg. Commons i 195-215 (p195, North q, orig. 'rights'; p211, Burke qs).
12 Parl. Reg. Lords ii 84-85, 89-90.
13 LC 28 Mar 1775 294b.
14 Parl. Reg. Commons i 363-369 / Burke 1775 pp23, 67 (qs).
15 MP 11 Apr 1775 2b-c (q) / MC 11 Apr 1775 2d.
16 MP 24 Apr 1775 2b (*Cerberus*) / Kingsford v 405.
17 AA 4th series ii 1848 (Washington) / Gage Correspondence ii 686 (to Lord Barrington, 26 Jun 1775).
18 AA 4th series ii 1870-1871, 1899-1902.
19 DAR x 51-52 (nos. 165, 168, Lord Dartmouth to Gage and to Howe) / Fortescue iii 237 (no. 1685, to Lord North, 28 Jul 1775, q).
20 MC 25 Aug 1775 2b / PA 5 Sep 1775 2a-b / DAR x 74 (no. 274).
21 GA 24 Oct 1775 2c / LC 24 Oct 1775 399b-c / MC 30 Oct 1775 2d.

22 Wilkes Diaries 86.
23 Parl. Reg. Commons iii 2-3 (king's speech) / AA 4th series iv 710-711 (captain of an English transport to its owners in London, 17 Jan, Boston, rebel reaction).
24 LG 11 Nov 1775 5a-b.
25 DCHNY viii 662 / DAR x 118 (no. 487).
26 Kingsford v 471 / Walpole LJ i 493.
27 AA 4th series iii 1936 (Congress) / Kingsford vi 15.
28 Journals, Lords, xxxiv 542.
29 DAR x 163 (no. 702), 166 (nos. 716, 717).
30 DAR x 133-134 (no. 548, addressed to Lord Dartmouth).
31 MC 28 Dec 2a / DAR x 138, 142-144 (nos. 575, 599, 602, all Howe to Dartmouth, 26 Nov, 2 Dec, 3 Dec 1775).
32 Brougham i 392 (letter from North's daughter, Charlotte Lindsay, 18 Feb 1839, title of prime minister).
33 Wraxall Mem. i 374 / SOL xl 164-66 (Grosvenor Square).
34 Lucas i 355 (to his father, 16 May 1772) / Glenbervie 231 (Pay Office).
35 Fortescue iii 279 (no. 1742, to Lord North, 7 Nov 1775, anchor), 479 (no. 2059, to Lord North, 19 Sep 1777, debts).
36 Cavendish Debates ii 85 (22 Nov 1770, Burke) / Gibbon PL i 255 (to his step-mother, 2 May 1775).
37 Wraxall Mem. iv 217 / Sackville Trial 342 (unfit) / Hutchinson ii 184, 289, 339 (rumours).
38 Memoirs of Dr Burney ii 64 (tall) / Cradock iv 166 (dancing master) / Parl. Hist. xv 1346-1347 (15 Nov 1763, Essay).
39 Hutchinson i 309 (28 Nov 1774, plum pudding) / Barrington 158-159 (to king, 31 Jul 1775; to Lord North, 8 Aug 1775), 170.
40 Wraxall Mem. i 415-416 (Jenkinson), 428 (Robinson), iv 228-229 (Eden) / HMC Abergavenny 10 (no. 59, king to Robinson, 4 Aug 1775).
41 Parliamentary Papers, Robinson, 12-17, gives long lists of offices held by lords and MPs in 1774.
42 Wraxall Mem. ii 2 (Fox, features etc), 35 (Burke), 38 (Barré), 58 (Rockingham) / Parl. Reg. Commons iii 41-42 (26 Oct 1775, pilot).
43 ODNB (Wilkes, nephew) / Bleackley, Wilkes, 339-347 / Bleackley, Casanova, 184 (parrot).
44 Angelo i 55 / Wraxall Mem. ii 48-49.
45 LEP 10 Jan 1778 4c (contract rumour) / LG 15 Oct 1a (knighted) / Valentine, Germain, 145 ('Awake'). No date found for ditty but probably *c.* 1777.
46 Walpole LJ i 501-502 / Wraxall Mem. ii 42.
47 Walpole Letters x 158 (to Lady Ossory, 13 Nov 1777, Swagger) / Walpole LJ i 433 (vain) / Letters of Junius 1894 i 250-255 (letter 34, to Duke of Grafton, 12 Dec 1769) / Fonblanque 117 ('I look'), 142-205 (letters to ministers) / Fortescue iii 203-204 (no. 1642, king to Lord North, 14 Apr 1775, return approved).
48 MJ 25 Jul [24 Jul] 1775 2c.
49 Oxford History British Empire ii 337. The difficulty of assessing public opinion regarding the war is discussed by James E. Bradley in an essay in *Britain and the American Revolution* (pp124-154).
50 Fortescue iii 276 (no. 1737, 'a clear refusal'), 289 (no. 1760, North to king, 12 Nov 1775, German states).

51 Beinecke GJD Jan, recto (arrival etc) / LEP 30 Dec 1775 4d / Kelsay 157-159.

52 HMC Dartmouth ii 348 (William Knox to Lord Dartmouth, 5 Aug 1775), 349 (John Pownall to Dartmouth, 5 Aug 1775, 'pumped'), 366 (undated paper, received 6 Aug 1775, 'there are' etc).

53 Deane Papers i 100-108 (Fr.). Beaumarchais's letter is undated and may have been written later. Shewmake p38 dates it to Oct or Nov 1775; Morton and Spinelli p41 suggest mid Nov; Wharton i 369 suggests it was among papers presented to the king by Vergennes on 22 Jan 1776; Deane Papers says it was submitted in Feb 1776.

54 Gaillardet 1836 ii 232. The date given by d'Éon for Beaumarchais's return conflicts with a letter from Beaumarchais to Vergennes dated 1 Jan 1776 at Paris, but the letter may well have been post-dated: Beaumarchais's dating was often awry, and a letter from him to d'Éon dated 9 Jan 1776 refers back to another of 31 Dec 1775 which was presumably written in London (Beaumarchais Correspondance ii 162-163, nos. 336, 338).

55 Wharton ii 63 ('the disposition'), iii 119 (Arthur Lee to Secret Committee, 20 Apr 1779, Wilkes) / Riggs 273 / CHOP iv 398 (no. 1125, Aug to 2 Sep 1775, ship-wrights), 506 (no. 1340, 22 and 23 Dec 1775, mail).

56 Dunlap i 135 (scolding) / Sellers 38, 69, 81-85, 218-220 / Thicknesse 140 ('crazy').

57 Schaeper 45.

58 Hutchinson i 477 (26 Jun 1775, rabble), 557 (14 Nov 1775, coach).

59 Boucher Letters vii 2 ('As long'), viii 343-344.

60 Curwen 1842 pp463-464 (Sewall) / Quincy 211 / Curwen 1972 i 26 / MHS Oxnard 29 Aug, 13 Oct 1775. Oxnard's wife was 'safely delivered' but 'the child was dead'.

61 Weitzman 12, 35-36 (q), 46, 221-247, 263-264.

62 Secret History of Green-Room i 41-56 / Taylor i 410-411 ('more profligate') / BDA i 12-20 / Harris's List for 1773 pp43-45 / Abington Life 72-83 (letters from Southampton Street, 14 Jul to 27 Nov 1775; Leicester Fields, 4 Mar and 7 Apr 1776) / MP 26 Apr 3c (ad, house sale) / Boswell LJ ii 349 (8 Apr 1775, jelly) / Lichtenberg's Visits 33 (small book) / Lichtenberg trans. Noel i 253 ('She has', slightly adjusted).

63 O'Keeffe ii 22 / Boaden i 114-115 ('It was') / GA 7 Feb 2d (Dublin) / MJ 30 Apr [29 Apr] 1d / C 27 Sep.

64 SOL xxxiii 73-79 / Walpole Letters viii 13 (to Mann, 22 Feb 1771) / PA 2 Aug 1775 3d and PA 9 Dec 1775 4d (ads) / MC 28 Nov 1775 2b / MP 11 Dec 1775 2c / MP 20 Dec 1775 2d / PA 30 Dec 1775 1b (ad).

65 Walpole Letters ix 161 (to Lady Ossory, 1 Feb 1775) / MP 7 Apr 1775 2b.

66 Curwen 1972 i 52 (23 Aug 1775).

67 Nigh 77-100 / Foote Memoirs 44 ('wooden') / O'Keeffe i 328 / Archenholz 240 ('His productions') / SJC 28 Dec 1775 1a (Dublin). Foote's date of birth is not known. ODNB says he was baptised Jan 1721 but other sources (e.g. Kelly 22; Fitzgerald, Foote, 3) say Jan 1720.

68 Brydone ii 319-325 / Wraxall Tour 205 / MP 6 Nov 1775 1a (ad) / Memoirs of Dr Burney ii 35-43 ('Nothing' etc), 48 (Edgcumbe) / MC 13 Nov 1775 2a / MP 3 Jan 1776 2c ('At the opera').

69 Garrick Private Corres. ii 169-170 (Fielding to Garrick, 23 Jul) / Lichtenberg trans. Noel i 161-163 (slightly adjusted).

70 LM (Aug) 1774 pp363-364 (letter dated 11 Aug, signed 'Apyrexia') / MJ 25 Jul 1775 4c / Burney Early Diary i 321-326 (1st visit, 29 Nov 1774), ii 131-135 (2nd visit; James Burney's return).

71 Knight i 9 (accent) / Reynolds Works i lxxvii-lxxxi (Malone).

72 MC 18 Jan 1775 2b ('insufferably') / MC 30 Jan 1775 2c ('encourages') / MC 23 Nov 1775 2b (applause) / MC 16 Dec 1775 3a (royalty) / MC 26 Dec 1775 2d (managers) / Moore 48-82 / Walpole Letters viii 255 (to Lady Ossory, 16 Mar 1773) / Burney Early Diary i 201-203 (April 1773).

73 Walpole Letters ix 299 (to Mann).

74 TCM (Jan) 9-11 / MP 6 Dec 1775 2b / MP 7 Dec 1775 2a (qs).

75 MP 15 Dec 1775 2c.

76 SJC 30 Dec 1775 3b / PA 19 May 1775 1b and GA 27 Mar 1776 1c (ads, Sal Pietro addresses) / NA KB 21/41 (unpaginated; Hilary Term 1776, first page, reference to writ 'lately issued out') / C 25 Jan, 1 Oct (alleged motives). LC 2 Jan 8c has 'The affair of Miss Brown, it is said, will terminate in Westminster-hall,' suggesting the writ had been issued or at least mooted by that date.

77 Rudd, Facts, 58-77 / MJ 14 Mar 1775 4d ('blow-up').

78 MP 21 Mar 1775 2c / PA 28 Mar 1775 2b / MP 2 Jun 1775 1d ('there was' etc).

79 Perreau Trials 112 ('according') / LC 9 Dec 1775 559c.

80 MC 8 Jun 1775 2d ('the cause') / GA 1 Jan 3d.

81 General sources for Duchess of Kingston section: Gervat, Melville, ODNB.

82 Walpole Letters ii 371-372 (to Mann, 3 May 1749) / General Advertiser 3 May 1749 1c / Gervat 43-44 / BM Sat. iii pt. 1 p745 (quotes LEP 3 Aug 1749 2c; original not seen). Horace Walpole, who attended both the Ranelagh ball on 26 Apr and the King's Theatre masquerade on 1 May, says she appeared as Iphigenia at the latter. However, on 3 Aug LEP advertised a print of the Ranelagh ball 'in which is introduced Miss —, in the actual habit she appear'd in the character of Iphigenia', and the year also saw publication of an anonymous *Poetical Epistle to Miss C—h—y, occasioned by her appearing in the character of Iphigenia at the late Jubilee Ball at Ranelagh*. It seems unlikely that Walpole, writing only two days after the masquerade, would have erred. Moreover, the comparatively select masquerade, taking place entirely inside, seems the more likely occasion for the wearing of a revealing costume. Perhaps the two striking events – the jubilee ball and the wearing of the costume – became conflated in public memory.

83 Grenville Papers iv 343 (Hervey to Grenville, 13 Aug 1768), 394 (Hervey to Grenville, 31 Oct 1768) / Walpole Letters vii 256 (to Mann, 28 Feb 1769) / Hutchinson ii 33 (entry dated 16 Apr 1776) / Melville 68-78 (ecclesiastical court documents, 'totally' etc).

84 Gervat 91, 109 / LC 11 Mar 1769 238c / Melville 22 (will) / Collins's Peerage v 721-725 (Meadows family).

85 Walpole Letters viii 338-339 (to Lady Ossory, 1 Oct 1773) / Gervat 108-109.

86 HMC Rutland iv 237 (Duchess of Kingston to Capt. Harden, 30 Jun 1774, Lille) / Gervat 118 / NA C 12/1051/2 f1 ('imposition') / Walpole Letters ix 23 (to Mann, 3 Aug 1774).

87 MC 9 Dec 1774 3b / Gervat 127 (citing order dated 9 Feb, NA C 33/442 f160) / Kingston Detail 33-34 (pistols).

88 DA 23 May 1775 1b / MP 25 May 1775 2a.

89 SJC 29 Jun 1775 3b.

90 Foote, Trip, 57, 67, 69, 84.

91 PL 16 Aug 1775 2c.

92 MC 17 Aug 1775 2a.

93 LC 19 Aug 1775 176a / Posthumous Letters 313 (Garrick letter, dated 29 Aug 1775, orig. 'Foster').
94 Journals, Lords, xxxiv 497 (3 Nov) / Parl. Reg. Lords v 101-104 (qs).
95 LC 5 Dec [4 Dec] 1775 538c.
96 CHOP iv 498-499 (no. 1315, petition to king) / Parl. Reg. Lords v 107.
97 Journals, Lords, xxxiv 531 (doctor qs) / Parl. Reg. Lords v 108-128 / PA 13 Dec 1775 2d.
98 Journals, Lords, xxxiv 539 (20 Dec) / Gervat 139 / LC 23 Dec 608c.
99 Walpole Letters ix 298-299 (to Mann) / HMC Carlisle 313 (Selwyn).
100 CHOP i 328 (no. 1087) / Telfer 103, 106, 122, 127-128 / Gaillardet 1866 pp377-381 (Vergy's account) / Political Register for 1767 pp369-377 (d'Éon to Guerchy, 5 Aug 1767).
101 Walpole Letters vi 40 (to Charles Churchill, 27 Mar 1764) / Gaillardet 1866 pp167-170 (d'Éon to Tercier, 23 Mar 1764).
102 AR 1764 pp85-86 (9 Jul) / AR 1765 pp71 (1 Mar), 99 (13 Jun, d'Éon outlawed) / Telfer 161-163, 185-188, 248-249.
103 LM 1777 p445 / BM Add. Ms. 11341 ff193-194 ('Account of Insurance on the Sex of Monsieur Le Chevalier d'Éon', 1770) / Burrows, Morande, 225 n.29 / Gaillardet 1866 pp191-192 (d'Éon to Comte de Broglie, 25 Mar and 16 Apr 1771, '*Anglais*'). On the left hand side of the 'Account', under the year '1770', are entries dated 28 and 30 Mar and 10 and 30 Apr listing purchases of policies at long odds. On the right hand side, also under '1770', is the single date 19 Jun with four entries for sales of the same policies at much shorter odds. The resulting profit is calculated and a note reads: 'Whereof your 1/4th of the profit is £164: 13: 4'. Slightly oddly, the earliest other known references to uncertainty as to d'Éon's sex do not appear until 28 Oct and 14 Dec 1770, in both cases in letters written in France, the first from Louis XV to one of his generals (Boutaric i 411) and the second from Madame du Deffand to Horace Walpole (Walpole Correspondence, Yale edition, iv 494). If the 'Account' were to date from a year later than stated, '1770' having been written for '1771' either in error or as some kind of precaution, it would therefore better accord with the other available information. In addition, its dates would tie in suggestively with those of d'Éon's disappearance and return: between 28 Mar and 30 Apr policies were purchased; on 7 May d'Éon disappeared, stirring speculation and shifting the odds; on 19 Jun the policies were sold at a healthy profit; late in the evening of the next day, 20 Jun, he returned.
104 LEP 9 May 1771 4b (ad), 4c.
105 LEP 14 May 1771 3b / MJ 16 May 1771 4c / LEP 8 Jun 1771 4c.
106 LEP 22 Jun 1771 3b / Gaillardet 1866 p194 (to Broglie, 5 Jul 1771) / PA 1 Jul 1771 2d-3a (q).
107 Burrows, Morande, 59-68.
108 Lever 2009 pp4-18, 39-41, 63, 80 / Loménie 55, 60-61, 78 ('initiated'), 132, 134, 147-164, 172-173, 201.
109 BCE i 112-113 (Beaumarchais to unknown correspondent, 24 Jan 1781), 221 (doc. 1, Morande to d'Éon, [1774], Fr., 'adorable'), 225-226 (doc. 5, Beaumarchais to Sartine, 11 Jun 1775, Fr.) / Gaillardet 1836 ii 180-188 / Burrows, Morande, 70.
110 Loménie 210-211 / Burrows, Morande, 76, 79.
111 Gaillardet 1836 ii 187 (Fr., 'and we') / Lever 2003 ii 114 (Fr., 'like a') / Brenellerie 166-169 (Beaumarchais to Louis XVI, 27 Apr 1775, Fr., 'this astonishing' etc) / Lever 2009 p111 n.

112 Lever 2003 ii 117 / Loménie 233 (Vergennes to Beaumarchais, 21 Jun 1775, 'all reasonable') / Gaillardet 1836 ii 191 (Fr., 'I hold') / Telfer 238.

113 Gaillardet 1866 p399 (no. 16, Fr., q) / Wilkes Diaries 85.

114 Lever 2009 p113 / Loménie 262-264 ('crisis', 'badly') / BCE i 231-235 (docs. 8 to 11), 233 n.1 (Fr., 'trivial'; this part of letter omitted by Loménie).

115 Gaillardet 1836 ii 199-211 (Fr.).

116 Gaillardet 1866 p209 (d'Éon to Beaumarchais, 7 Jan 1776, Guerchy challenge).

117 Pieces Rélatives 57-58 (d'Éon to Vergennes, 27 May 1776, Fr.).

118 MP 10 Nov 1775 2a / MP 11 Nov 1775 2c.

119 MP 13 Nov 1775 2a / MP 14 Nov 1775 1c-d.

120 Gaillardet 1836 ii 230 (Fr.).

121 Beaumarchais Correspondance ii 150-157 (nos. 328 and 329, to the king, 7 Dec and 13 Dec 1775) / Gaillardet 1836 ii 232-234 (Fr., 'relight'), 241 / Gaillardet 1866 p419 (no. 21) / Burrows, Morande, 83 / BM Add. Ms. 11339 f215r (d'Éon to Joseph Lautem, 6 Jan, Fr., 'the good'). D'Éon says (Gaillardet 1836) he was invited to dine at Morande's house but then that he arrived 'chez Beaumarchais'.

122 Spinelli 64 ('We do not have proof positive') / Kates 231 (£100,000).

TOUR
Preamble and North route

1 A to Z Georgian London v-vii (Rocque dates) / A to Z Regency London vi-vii (Horwood dates).

2 LWG 15 (wall, deer) / PA 4 Oct 1759 2b ('new moving') / GM 1783 ii 714 (29 Aug, 'The gallows was fixed about 50 yards nearer the park wall than usual') / MGL 259, 261-262. MGL notes that a drawing of 1785 shows a gallery for spectators about fifty yards up Edgware Road on the west side and facing east, and a house on the corner of Bryanston Street is said to have had 'curious iron balconies' used by the sheriffs for surveying the scene (Smith, St Mary-le-bone, 153). A letter in the *Antiquary* in 1873 (iv 205-206, 239) gave a slightly confusing account which seems to suggest the site was roughly where Connaught Place meets Edgware Road.

3 'Squire 41-42 ('All').

4 Desc. Mid. 107 ('reckoned', 'an equestrian') / MHS Oxnard 10 Oct 1775 ('many trees') / CCR 19-20 / SOL xl 117-166 / Wraxall Mem. i 374 (North) / HMC Carlisle 312 (Anthony Storer to Lord Carlisle, 14 Dec 1775, 'makes'; George Selwyn to Lord Carlisle, 19 Dec 1775, 'Their').

5 CCR 10 (Townshend) / C 4 Mar, 11 Mar, 26 Mar / Graves vii 296 (Stubbs) / MC 8 Apr 1788 1b (ad, Stubbs) / Burrows, Morande, 49 / GA 27 Aug 1778 2b (Morande) / BCE i 608 (doc. 249, letter from Morande, 'No. 40 New Duke Street', 8 Aug 1780) / Harrison map ('N. Duke Street' for portion north of Oxford Street) / MHS Oxnard 20 Sep 1775 ('rather') / Gibbon Autobiographies 306-307.

6 Harrison 536 ('evening') / MC 23 Sep 1c (ad, 'vaulting') / Wroth 93-110.

7 Desc. Mid. 109 (q) / CCR 215 / C 27 Jun, 30 Oct. LD has 'Gillouse'.

8 Wheatley ii 620 / Noorthouck 732 ('a superb') / Desc. Mid. 110 ('are chiefly') / Gibbon Misc. Works ii 74 (to J. B. Holroyd, 3 Feb 1772).

9 MC 9 Aug 2c (pillory) / DA 1 Jan 1b (q).

10 MGL 248, 302-303 / MC 27 May 2b (Gunnersbury) / Cross 65-66 / Whitley, Artists, i 312 / Ward and Roberts i 43, 47 / Kidson i 16 / Reynolds ed. Penny 58.

11 Cunningham v 40 (Ramsay qs) / MP 13 Mar 4d (ad, 'an elegant').

12 Graves v 381 (Nollekens) / Wilkes Letters ii 34 (dated 11 Aug) / Collison-Morley 291 / C 6 Jul.

13 Weber 33-35 / Wilkes Diaries 99 (22 Sep, Andrews) / C 13 Jul.

14 C 28 Mar, 29 Mar, 15 Jun / MC 18 Jul 3a (labourers).

15 Wheatley i 3 (Adam and Eve) / GA 4 Apr 3a (ad, Brookes) / MHS Oxnard 17 Dec (orig. 'beast') / DA 10 Jul 1c (ad, Sampson). Rocque shows turnpike location.

16 Stuart 12 ('carriages') / MHS Oxnard 14 Mar / Carter 126, 141 / CWA RB 1776 ff28-29 (Banks, Sawbridge).

17 C 4 Dec / Fitzgerald, Dodd, 98, 101 / CWA RB 1776 f32 (Dodd) / MC 28 Feb 1c (ad, Sheridan) / Beinecke GJD Feb recto (Johnson). **Fn. Porter** HM 31201 vol. 17 ff49r-56v (Anna Porter).

18 HMC Abergavenny 16 (no. 121, Wentworth) / MP 11 Jan 2b ('Logins') / MC 3 Feb 3c ('To prevent').

19 MGL 239, 299-301 / SOL xxxi 138-145 / Memoirs of Dr Burney ii 35 (q).

20 HMC Dartmouth ii 368-369 / GA 27 Mar 3b (ad, bird-shop) / DA 1 Jan 1c (ad, Welcker) / Boswell OY 260 / Boswell Club 249 / LMA MJ/SP/1776/05/018 (orig. 'Tallner').

21 LLEP 8 May [7 May] 444c (ad, Smith) / MGL 296-298 / Wheatley i 123.

22 GA 24 May 1c (ad, 'the finest' etc) / MP 14 Sep 2a ('an action') / PA 15 Jun 1772 1a (ad, 'with a') / LLEP 21 Apr 1773 383a / BDA xvi 89 (Wildman).

23 New Present State 204 ('one of') / LWG 25 ('The curious') / Altick 26 (delay, no source cited) / MHS Oxnard 17 Jul (staircase) / CCR 18-19 / LC 16 Jan 54c (Battie) / MGL 295 / TCM 1773 p509 ('Behind').

24 C 24 Mar / MGL 293 (Harrison listed to 1773 but gap follows until 1782) / Stuart 13 (q).

25 Harrison 363-364 ('two large', 'by one') / LG 245-246 ('a fine').

26 LWG 140 (Gray's Inn) / MC 30 Sep 3a ('be travelled').

27 LG 11 ('Hither') / GA 23 Mar 3c (ad).

28 Trusler 139.

29 LD 15, 59, 66, 89, 107, 117, 122, 138, 183 (coach-makers).

30 Harrison 524 (market) / LWG xxviii-xxix ('There').

31 TCM 1773 p507 (church) / SJC 15 Mar 1774 4a (ad, Low) / SOL xxxvi 166-169 / MC 10 Feb 4b (ad, Martyn).

32 MP 24 Jun 2a / MC 25 Mar 1775 4c ('in the highest', 'neatly') / MC 1 Jul 1775 3c ('most of') / MC 19 Jun 1773 3a ('fine' etc). Several advertisements (e.g. PA 30 Dec 1773 1a) refer to the shop as 'near Southampton Street'. A late notice (The World 11 Aug 1788 1b) is headed 'Sledge and Wellings, The Original Shop, No. 1, Henrietta-street'. Horwood's 1790s map places No. 1 on the corner with Southampton Street. Jeffares ('Sledge, Susanna') suggests that, notwithstanding her moniker, Mrs Sledge was a Susanna Sledge who never married.

33 DA 2 Jan 1c (ad, Burgess) / Abington Life 72-83.

34 LS pt. 4 iii 1908-1909 (*Duenna*) / MHS Oxnard 20 Oct 1775 (q, orig. 'appology').

35 MGL 145-148 / C 25 May, 15 Aug / SOL xxxvi 222-223 (Dance).

36 MP 30 Aug 2b (q). Public office is not indicated by Rocque or Horwood but it is on a site plan of *c.* 1760 (SOL xxxv plate 39) and on William Faden's 1813 revision of Horwood.

37 MJ 23 Sep 1775 2a / PA 3 Oct 1775 2b / MHS Oxnard 29 Nov 1775.

38 BDA vii 409-411. The Hopkins daughters were quite young (born 1756 and 1758), unmarried, and acted occasionally at Drury Lane Theatre, so it seems fairly likely they were still living with their parents.

39 PA 10 Jan 3b (ad, Partridge) / Gilchrist i 22 / LC 2 May 1775 416c / C 23 May / CCR 133 ('are impowered').

40 MP 10 Aug 4c (ad).

41 TCM 1773 p508 (q) / CCR 93 / SOL iii 53, 66, 79, 86 / Bentham Corres. i 290.

42 GA 9 Nov 4b (ad, Earle) / Harrison 522 ('It consists') / Oracle 6 May 1795 2c ('elegantly').

43 MC 31 May 4a (ad, Tiffin) / CWA RB 1776 f29 (Linley) / Wheatley i 480 / C 13 Apr.

44 GA 13 Jun 4c (ad, Cooke) / DA 2 Jan 1c (ad, Stone).

45 KD 11 (Atterbury) / Wheatley i 431-433 (Cock Lane).

46 PA 17 Aug 1775 3b / PA 28 Jun 1777 3a / Harrison 482 / Noorthouck 616-617 (qs), 654. Noorthouck says passing bell tolled from 6 a.m., Harrison and PA 28 Jun say from 7 a.m.

47 LWG 156 (ventilator) / MC 26 Mar 3c ('to pull') / GA 18 Jul 4a (timber) / GA 4 Sep 2d (detour).

48 MC 5 Nov 4c (ad, 'This day is published') / Smith, Gaols, 39-40 / Boswell LJ iii 431-433 / LG 166-167.

49 Harrison 483 [printed 473 in error] ('It has', 'a convenient') / BM Egerton Ms. 2672 f50r (Oliver, 13 Jul).

50 Villette, title page / MHS Oxnard 1 Sep 1775, 17 Jan, 24 Jun, 4 Sep 1776 / GA 6 Dec 1b (ad, q) / Noorthouck 545 / Wheatley ii 486-488.

51 MP 21 Feb 1d (ad, Long) / Noorthouck 598 ('obtained') / Desc. Mid. 43-44 ('spiring') / TCM 1773 p399 ('Though').

52 Harrison 480 / LG 115 ('serve') / DA 30 May 1c (ad, '30').

53 Bell 539 / Altick 55 / MC 13 Mar 4c (ad, 'celebrated', whale, woman) / DA 13 Jul 2a (ad).

54 Companion 1767 pp60-62 / GA 28 Aug 1767 2d (ad, Brownrigg) / LG 116-117 ('who fired'). Mrs Salmon's date of death is often given as 1760 (e.g. Bell p537, Altick p53) but see death notices in LEP 11 Mar 1740 2b and LM 1740 p153.

55 LD 186-187 (bankers); 11, 36, 58, 95, 106, 118, 123, 132, 152, 174, 176, 179 (book-sellers); 1, 20, 27, 87, 100, 155 (cutlers) / MC 1 Jan p4 footer (Murray) / C 25 Dec.

56 MC 6 Nov 3b (ad, Sharp) / MP 21 Mar 3a (ad, Green).

57 Burke ed. Fitzwilliam ii 42 (Lee) / MC 1 Jan p4 footer (MC address).

58 CCR 222 / C 16 Mar, 18 Apr / Knight i 12 (pain) / Hawkins 530 (garden etc).

59 DA 3 Jan 1c (ad, Ferguson) / MC 18 Nov 3b (Ferguson death) / CCR 65 / C 17 Feb, 9 Mar.

60 Wheatley ii 56 / GA 5 Feb 3a (Payne).

61 TCM 1773 p452 ('allotted') / Smith, Gaols, 41-43.

62 Howard 156-160 (qs) / Wheatley ii 58.

63 TCM 1773 p452 / LG 229-230 ('a house', 'wear') / Howard 178-179 ('by a').

64 C 10 Dec / MHS Oxnard 19 Aug / LWG 113-114 / Trusler 159 / Desc. Mid. 54 / KD 114 (Long).

65 Desc. Mid. 48 ('the spiritual', 'ordination') / TCM 1773 p451 (wills) / Harrison 449-451 / MC 28 Sep 3a (ad, Morris). In September Morris moves to No. 3 Paul's Chain, the northern section of the same north-south road.

66 Harrison 566 ('formerly') / Curwen 1972 i 81 (he removed to there on 24 Oct 1775).

67 MC 8 Apr 1b (ad, 'diversions') / Companion 1767 p182 ('many') / Harrison 567 ('Great') / MC 29 Apr 3a (Chandos) / BM Egerton Ms. 2672 f40v (Oliver, 24 Jun, 'some very') / MC 12 Aug 3a (Rossignol).

68 Wroth 15-21 / MC 7 Mar 1a (ad, *The Spleen, or, Islington Spa*).
69 SOL xlvii 55-57 / Noorthouck 752 / Wroth 27 / PA 28 Aug 3c (ad, auction, orig. 'Buzzaglo') / Harrison 541.
70 Wheatley i 420-421 / Smith, Gaols, 33.
71 MC 11 Jan 2d (ad).
72 LG 141-142 (qs) / Wheatley ii 213.
73 LWG 158 ('the greatest' etc) / MJ 3 Sep [2 Sep] 1d.
74 Curwen 1972 ii 663 (2 Sep 1780).
75 Desc. Mid. 61 ('the sick') / LWG 122-124 (Christ's Hospital).
76 Smith, Gaols, 31 / Howard 174 (12 Mar, 10 May).
77 Wheatley iii 342 / C 20 Apr, 13 May / MC 21 May 3b (ad, qs).
78 C 15 Mar, 15 May / Howard 170 (12 Mar) / Smith, Gaols, 32-33.
79 LWG 3 (qs) / MP 29 Mar 2c / LD 28 (Cahill, coffee-house).
80 TCM 1773 p398 (arcades) / MC 3 Jan 1c (ad, *Betsey*) / MC 10 Oct 1778 3d (ad, New Lloyd's) / Noorthouck 603 (vaults) / Companion 1767 p39 (clock).
81 KD 47 (Crawley) / LD 15, 17, 30 (coffee-houses, under Bicknell, Blew, Catmur) / Wheatley ii 85-87 / KD 5 (Adam, George, at Garraway's) / GA 3 Feb 1c (plantation) / GA 22 Aug 4a (theatre).
82 CCR 121-122 / DAR x 100 (no. 397, Todd to John Pownall, 11 Oct 1775).
83 GA 13 Aug 3c (ad, Whitworth) / LD 186 (bankers) / MP 3 Jul 4b (ad, turtle).
84 LWG 151-152 (q) / CCR 211-212.
85 MC 6 Nov 3c (ad, Ryder). Rocque shows Axe inn location.
86 Companion 1767 p47 ('for feasting') / C 3 Jan / King 46-48 / MHS Oxnard 15 Nov 1775 ('There are') / LEP 7 Dec 1775 1d ('he was prevailed') / PA 13 Dec 1775 3b ('but confined') / Ewen 202, 238, 250-252 (orders to prevent abuses).
87 KD 25 (Bosanquet) / Harrison 459 (q) / MC 9 Apr 2d.
88 MC 28 Dec 3c (ad, Parkes) / MP 6 Feb 2c (Linch) / KD 181 (Walford). KD p37 has Caslon at No. 62.
89 Wheatley ii 73-74 / ODNB (Wesley).
90 Noorthouck 554-556 (qs) / KD 40 (Clark).
91 LWG xv / KD 174 (Thorpe; orig. 'Widegate-alley' but LD has 'Street'). Elder Street runs north off White Lion Street, between 'Lion' and 'Str' on the 1772 map. Vine Court lies west of Vine Street.
92 GA 6 Jun 3c (ad, Wilson's).
93 Noorthouck 664 (qs) / LMA MJ/SP/1776/10/059 (Scourfield) / LD 4, 40, 87 (Anderson, Creed, Hufton).
94 LWG 127 (q) / Beaglehole 1974 p75 / C 22 Apr. Horwood shows Assembly Row.
95 Harrison 564 (q) / C 21 Apr, 25 Aug, 4 Sep.

South route

1 Kielmansegge 280.
2 Wheatley ii 345-346.
3 TCM 1773 p512 ('pleasant') / Desc. Mid. 195-196 (bridge) / Catalogue of the Rarities 5, 11, 14 (stockings etc).
4 Desc. Mid. 197 (qs) / CCR 167-168 / C 29 May.
5 Desc. Mid. 197 ('a place' etc) / Companion 1767 p181 (chimney) / Boswell LJ iii 199 / Gibbon PL i 90 (letter to his stepmother, 18 Apr 1768) / MC 14 Mar 1a (ad) / LWG 29 (band) / Ambulator 138-147 (lamps) / GA 28 Jun 1b (ad, patrol).

6 Desc. Mid. 106 ('gentlemen') / C 19 Jan, 31 Jan / GA 6 Jun 2d (bathing) / GA 13 Jun 2c (hand-bills) / GA 26 Jun 2d (punishment) / TCM 1773 p512 (reservoir).

7 Harrison 531 (q) / BCE i 223 (Morande to d'Éon, May 1774).

8 CCR 55 / CWA RB 1774 f27, 1775 f27, 1779 f27 / C 7 Jun, 15 Aug. Rocque shows turnpike location.

9 CCR 19, 64 / ODNB (Selwyn) / More ed. Roberts i 39 (letter dated 1775). Boswell (OY 90, 120) mentions Hill Street as Paoli's address in March and April 1775 and does not indicate any change in 1776. City of Westminster green plaque report by Gillian Dawson dated 1 Oct 2007 lists Paoli's London addresses with Hill Street in 1773 followed by South Audley Street in 1778.

10 LC 6 Jan 23c (ad, Berry) / DA 6 Jan 3a (ad, van Butchell) / MP 12 May 1775 4a (embalming).

11 LWG 17 (q) / LC 14 Mar 255a.

12 MGL 254-255, 303-304 / Schofield 8 / Wraxall ii 61 / C 26 Mar, 14 Apr / Critical Review 1783 p191 (q).

13 CCR 20 / Harrison 532 ('is fenced') / Stuart 24 ('How many').

14 C 28 May / MP 13 Mar 1b (ad, Mackay) / CCR 58 / Jesse i 19 / LMA MJ/SP/1776/12/003 (Quick). **Fn. pie** Briggs 417. No record found as to when Fox, with his friend Richard Fitzgerald, lodged with Mackay, who moved to Piccadilly in 1773 (PA 8 Jun 1773 1a, ad).

15 Hume, Strahan, 321-322 (to William Strahan, 2 May) / MP 3 Sep 3a (ad, d'Éon) / LC 14 Aug 1777 160c / LMA MJ/SP/1776/07/024 (Sangster). Horwood shows No. 38 on the south side of Brewer Street, the third house east of Sherard Street excluding the corner house.

16 GA 22 Jan 3a (ad, Hunter).

17 Harrison 531 ('so called') / MP 29 Feb 4b (ad, Valle) / GA 12 Aug 1b (ad, 'Electrical') / GA 25 Oct 3c (ad, 'are now') / MP 25 Dec 3b ('the approbation') / GA 26 Nov 2d (ad, apartments) / C 1 Aug, 15 Nov.

18 LG 170.

19 Harrison 532 ('in which') / Nigh 66-67 (patent) / Gibbon PL i 262 (to his step-mother, 3 Jul 1775) / GA 10 Dec 2b (Sangster trial evidence, 'a communication between the dwelling-house and the theatre') / Walford vi 526-527 (Fulham house). Writing after a new theatre had been built by John Nash *c.* 1820 a short way south of the theatre Foote knew, Timbs 1829 p54 refers to Foote incorporating 'a house in Little Suffolk-street with the theatre', an error repeated by some later writers. A deed of conveyance dated 25 Dec 1776 between Foote and George Colman includes 'all that messuage or tenement standing and being on the west side of Great Suffolk Street' (Nigh 592) and the 1776 rate books (CWA RB 1776 f82) list Foote twice in Great Suffolk Street, suggesting he was responsible for contiguous properties there. The 1778 Foote Memoirs say (p21) that 'a house was taken at the back of the theatre in Suffolk-street, where Mr Foote resided, part of which he converted into a green room, wardrobe, and other necessary conveniences'. Horwood's 1790s map shows the pre-Nash theatre as seven houses adrift from Little Suffolk Street to the south but extending east so as to be close to the houses at the north end of the west side of Great Suffolk Street.

20 MC 4 May 3b (Sestini).

21 MP 31 Jan 1c (ad, fires) / Burney Early Diary ii 249 (to Fanny Burney, 16 Jul 1778).

22 MGL 86, 288-289 / Prown ii 259, 262 / C 1 Apr / Reynolds ed. Penny 58 (prices) / Whitley, Artists, ii 303 (pupils) / Leslie and Taylor ii 636 (Kirkley) / Northcote,

Reynolds, i 252 (macaw), ii 27 (painting room) / Graves and Cronin i 181-182, 242-243 (macaw present in portraits of 1773 and 1777) / McIntyre, Reynolds, 233-236 (Wick House).

23 Abington Life 82-83 (letters dated 4 Mar, 7 Apr) / GA 2 Mar 3b (Bruce).

24 SOL xx 107-108 / Hill, House, 1-2 (q).

25 ODNB (Cipriani) / LG 169 (mews).

26 MP 8 Feb 1a (ad, Breslaw) / MHS Oxnard 8 Feb / ODNB (Pinchbeck family, 'to my') / MC 18 Mar 3b (patent; orig. 'circumstances') / GA 16 Apr 4d (ad, Hebb) / GA 4 Oct 2d (Catley) / Rae 267.

27 Sandby i 125, 139-140, 151-156 / SOL xxix 346-348.

28 MC 7 May 3a / HM 31201 vol. 17 f54v (Anna Porter).

29 MC 6 Sep 2d (q) / Wheatley i 332 / ODNB (George IV).

30 Hickey ii 80 / CWA RB 1776 f20 (Joseph Hickey listed twice, apparently for contiguous properties) / MC 24 Aug 4c / TCM 1773 p456 (q) / Dasent 218-254.

31 SOL xxx 547 (Hunter) / C 13 Jun / MP 13 Mar 3c (ad, Pilton).

32 CCR 63, 148. SOL xxix pp326-327 says, citing rate books, that Palliser occupied from 1777 but as CCR lists him in Pall Mall in 1776 it seems likely he was here earlier.

33 SOL xxix 327 and pocket plan. MGL pp60-61 indicates that it was the twentieth house east from St James's Street.

34 SOL xxix 327-331 (p328 plan places it three doors east of King's Place) / Morgan PML 19089 (Gibbon) / MP 24 Jun 2a / HM 31201 vol. 17 f53v (Anna Porter) / Malmesbury Letters i 342 (Mrs Harris to her son, 26 Mar, Duchess of Devonshire).

35 SOL xxix 328, 332-333 (p328 plan places it two doors east of King's Place).

36 Archenholz 193-194.

37 MGL 60-61 ('the seventh house east' from St James's Street) / SOL xxix 338 ('east side of Crown Court (now Passage)'). SOL says that the Smyrna's life in Pall Mall probably ended in 1772, but see GA 18 Apr 2c ('Debates at the Smyrna were never higher than at this present time') and MC 6 Jun 3d (ad, seeking replies to 'Smyrna coffee-house, Pall-mall').

38 SOL xxx 547. SOL xxix pp335-336 says that having taken over No. 52 (Horwood numbering) from his brother Robert, James Dodsley continued the business 'on the same side ... but further towards St James's Street'.

39 SOL xxix 364-367.

40 SOL xxix 367-368 / MP 9 Aug 3b (ad, next Cumberland House) / PA 26 Oct 4b (ad, Royal Academy).

41 SOL xxix 368-377 / Whitley, Gainsborough, 108-124 (q) / Gainsborough ed. Hayes 127 (no. 74, 15 Nov 1775, servants), 133 (no. 79, 25 Jan 1777, footman), 134 (no. 80, 12 Sep 1777, coach). Fischer married Mary Gainsborough in 1780 but separated from her soon afterwards. Her sister Margaret never married.

42 CCR 2, 19.

43 SOL xxx 548 / LC 23 Jul [22 Jul] 75a / HMC Various vi 123-126 (letters from 'Kew Lane', 27 Jul to 23 Oct).

44 SJC 18 Jan 2c (ad, Scarbrough) / MP 15 Feb 1b (ad, Dalmain).

45 Noorthouck 718 ('an irregular') / Companion 1767 pp172-173 ('In the front') / Ambulator xvi ('is like') / Curwen 1972 i 101.

46 SOL xxx 437.

47 SOL xxx 441-443 / C 4 Mar.

48 Hutchinson i 303, ii 89-91 (q) / MP 7 Aug 2a.

49 SOL xxx 450.

50 Wheatley i 62 (Walpole) / CCR 20 / SOL xxx 487-489 / CWA RB 1776 f42 (secretary of state offices).
51 MC 12 Dec 2d (q) / Delany ii 193.
52 LWG xxviii ('The park') / Moritz 16-17 ('towards' etc) / Grosley i 80-81 ('Most of') / BM Egerton Ms. 2672 f33v (Oliver, 15 Jun, 'at one') / Hutchinson ii 59 (28 May) / Curwen 1842 p567 (Quincy, 1 Jan 1777).
53 CHOP iv 550-552 (permission lists dated 14 Mar and 23 May 1775).
54 Holt 63.
55 Curwen 1972 i 42-43 (3 Aug 1775) / LC 28 Jun [27 Jun] 1777 611a.
56 Ambulator xvii ('and it began') / Wheatley i 293 / LWG 6 ('a fine') / C 15 Jul, 24 Jul, 2 Aug / Hutchinson i 440 (8 May 1775) / Curwen 1972 i 32 (14 Jul 1775), 166-167 (8 Jun 1776) / MHS Oxnard 4 Dec 1775 / PA 9 Feb 2c ('there was'; remark attributed to 'a nobleman in a blue ribbon', a phrase customarily used to refer to North, a member of the Order of the Garter) / C 24 Feb. A petition from the elephants (PA 9 Feb 2b-c) and an account of a visit by a well-wisher (PA 16 Feb 2b) give further details of their plight.
57 Howson 72, 106.
58 Noorthouck 715 ('a house') / Smith, Gaols, 25-26. Howard p193 notes 86 prisoners on 6 Mar, 75 on 3 May.
59 C 22 Apr / MC 20 Jun 2a (ad).
60 Walcott 73 / KD 190 / Wilkes Correspondence iv 31 (11 May 1770, 'the last') / Angelo i 55 / CCR 20 (Suffolk).
61 CCR 93 / MC 1 Feb 3a (danger) / MC 5 Jun 2c (fireworks) / PA 29 Oct 2c (gout).
62 LC 13 Jan [12 Jan] 43b (ad, Reid) / CCR 55.
63 MC 13 Apr 3c ('superb') / MC 3 Oct 4c / Trusler 160 ('the wax-work') / Desc. Mid. 102 ('formerly') / Gilchrist i 17-18 (Blake).
64 Desc. Mid. 103.
65 Harrison 517 ('is reckoned', 'from a') / CCR 101-104 / C 9 Dec / MHS Oxnard 8 Dec 1775 / Desc. Mid. 78.
66 MGL 20 / Vardy plate 48 (Kent screen) / London Daily Post 28 Jun 1739 1c ('After the sittings in Trinity (the present) term ... there is to be erected a screen, with a large Gothick arch in the middle') / Gerhold 44-47 / C 15 Apr, 16 Apr. A French visitor in 1765 (Grosley ii 167) describes all four courts as adjoining the Hall and refers to the use of a curtain: 'The court of Chancery, the King's-Bench, the Common-Pleas, and the Exchequer ... have each of them a tribunal upon the same floor, and joining with Westminster-hall, from which they are separated by a large curtain, which supplies the place of a door.' A footnote adds: 'When the chancellor passes through Westminster-hall, he stops opposite to each court, the curtain is undrawn, and he salutes the judges, who rise and pay him the same compliment.'
67 Companion 1767 p114 ('to which') / Harrison 518-519 ('having been') / MHS Oxnard 18 Mar / Moritz 51 (1782).
68 Curwen 1972 i 90 / C 20, 29 Feb / MHS Oxnard 8 Nov.
69 Harrison 518 (q) / CCR 67.
70 CCR 54, 56, 64 / C 12 Jun / ODNB (Sancho).
71 CCR 57, 95-96 / ST xx 1365 / C 8 Dec.
72 SOL xiv 79-80 / CCR 109 / Hutchinson i 309 (29 Nov 1774).
73 MP 2 Jul 1777 2b / GEP 4 Jun 1778 4c (bet) / SOL xiv 42-45.
74 LC 27 Jan 96b (North) / MC 7 Feb 2c (Germain) / SOL xiv 77-78 / CCR 95.

75 MC 19 Jan 2a ('adjoining', 'remarkably') / MP 22 Feb 2a / SJC 27 Feb 1b ('with a very') / MP 25 Oct 1d / SOL xiv 65 / NA SP 78/299 f107 (Garnier to Lord Weymouth, 17 May) / Wharton ii 80 (committee of secret correspondence to Silas Deane, 3 Mar, 'extremely'). PA 29 Oct 2c says de Noailles 'resides at the house next the Horse-guards, which was occupied by the last minister from France, and not in Great George-street, where the French ambassadors have lived for several years past,' but MC 19 Jan 2a indicates that de Guines used the Whitehall house.

76 SOL xvi 17-27, 75-81 / CCR 134 / TCM 1773 p455 (q, orig. 'Adams') / Cradock i 132-133, 146 / C 9 Feb.

77 LWG 4 ('has been') / MHS Oxnard 28 Jan ('painted') / SOL xiii 128 (26 Apr, 'at leisure') / PA 8 Oct 2b / MC 2 Dec 2a. SOL also notes a board inspection of Cipriani's completed work on 28 Nov 1777; an inspection a year earlier would sit more happily with the newspaper reports.

78 SOL xiii 221-222, quoting *The Lottery display'd, or the Adventurer's Guide*, 1771, pp 18-20 (wheels) / C 12 Nov / TCM 1773 p453 ('to Whitehall').

79 DA 4 Jul 1b (ad) / Quincy xix 214.

80 TCM 1773 p455 / CCR 85-86.

81 Boswell LJ ii 337 (2 Apr 1775) / LWG 25-26 ('one of') / GA 1 Mar 3b (ad, servants).

82 Harrison 526 (qs) / ODNB (Chippendale) / Gilbert i 9 / Wheatley iii 252-253.

83 PA 8 Feb 3d (ad, Leake) / Harrison 525-526 (qs) / C 13 Jan.

84 Moritz 11 ('countless') / SOL xxiii 58-61 / GA 24 May 1c (ad, Coade).

85 LWG 159-160 / Companion 1767 pp109-113 / Maitland i 682 (q).

86 SOL xxiii 70-71 / MC 22 Apr 3c (ad, 'instructed', 'carefully', 'the company') / MC 4 Apr 1a (ad, 'Mr', 'feats') / MC 11 Jul 1775 1d (ad, 'well known') / MC 28 Aug 1b (ad) / MC 13 Sep 1b (ad, 'Madam') / MP 30 Sep 3a (ad, 'besides'). Horwood shows location.

87 Noorthouck 693 (admission, 'When') / LG 6-7 ('In very') / LWG 33 ('Vauxhall') / Ambulator 193 (prices) / Wheatley iii 426-430.

88 CCR 232-233 / SOL xxiii 41-42, 72-73 / Harrison 510-511 ('employed') / LWG 116 ('the forlorn').

89 SOL xviii 99-108 / Desc. Mid. 68-69 (q; first part occurs last in original).

90 Harrison 524 / TCM 1773 p508 ('here') / C 27 Feb, 2 Mar / MC 4 Mar 3b-c / MP 9 Mar 2c / Howard 192 (15 Mar, 25 May).

91 Desc. Mid. 67 ('a large') / Noorthouck 735-736 ('so far') / Whitley, Artists, i 273 / Smith, Nollekens, ii 306 (John Deare to his father, 24 Mar 1777, 'There') / GA 5 Feb 3a / Angelo i 254-255 ('"What are"'), 262.

92 MP 9 Mar 2c (q) / C 28 May.

93 LWG xxix ('To observe') / PA 26 Jan 1c (ad, Darly) / KD 15 (Barnes), 98 (Jaffray) / MC 30 Sep 3d (ad, Lund).

94 Harrison 524 ('erected') / MC 16 Jan 3a (pillory) / MP 1 Jan p4 footer (address) / Elmes 67 (Blake Court) / GA 1 Feb 1b (ad, Buzaglo). Blake Court is not shown by Rocque. Horwood shows an unnamed court on the west side of Catherine Street, with five houses and the corner house between its entrance and the Strand, which tallies with the location later given by Elmes.

95 LG 137 ('is lighted') / MC 25 Jan 2d ('as adjusted') / GA 18 Jan 3a ('and refusing') / Vincent 35.

96 CCR 232 / Harrison 510 ('for the reception', 'making') / PA 9 Dec 1775 3b / LG 158-159 ('The windows', etc) / Carlyle 503 (1769 visit, 'the unfortunate').

97 TCM 1773 p567 ('a mineral') / MHS Oxnard 12 Nov 1775 ('for women').
98 Harrison 509 ('for the') / Archenholz 164-168 ('existing' etc) / Smith, Gaols, 49 / Howard 198.
99 SOL xxii 78-82 / Boswell LJ i 493 (q). LD lists Thrale's address as 'Park Street', the name given in Horwood's plan to the southern part of Deadman's Place.
100 Noorthouck 680 (q) / CCR 229.
101 Harrison 509 ('persons') / Smith, Gaols, 27-29 / Howard 205-206.
102 Smith, Gaols, 27.
103 LWG 152.
104 Desc. Mid. 22-24 (orig. uses words for numbers).
105 Noorthouck 551-552 ('the only') / Trusler 31 ('live' etc).
106 Desc. Mid. 19-20.
107 KD 12 (Baker) / Noorthouck 546 (q) / CCR 135-137.
108 Harrison 82, 84-86 ('the offices' etc) / CCR 134 / LC 24 Dec 608c.
109 Moritz 266.
110 Harrison 489 (q) / CCR 141-142.
111 Noorthouck 760.
112 MHS Oxnard 13 Nov 1775 / LC 23 Mar 286c / C 29 May.

CHRONICLE

January

01.01 1 GA 1 Jan 2c / MC 1 Jan 2b / HMC Dartmouth ii 405 (Suffolk to Dartmouth, 30 Dec 1775) / LLEP 1 Jan 7a / Fortescue iii 327 (no. 1805, dated 'Jany 1st 1776. m/18pt P.M.', q). **2** MC 2 Jan 2b / MP 2 Jan 2a / GEP 2 Jan 3a / LC 1 Jan 2a (ode) / PA 1 Jan 2b (alternative ode) / Beinecke GJD Jan recto. **3** Wesley iv 65 / Johnson Works 1823 ix 535 / Wilkes Diaries 89. **4** GA 3 Jan 3a / MC 2 Jan 2d. **5** HM 31201 f60r-60v (Anna Porter; 'let' is a best guess). **6** MHS Oxnard 1 Jan. **7** LS pt. 4 iii 1941 / MC 3 Jan 3a. **8** MC 1 Jan 1a (ad) / MC 2 Jan 2d / GA 2 Jan 2d (q). **9** MC 3 Jan 3c. **10** LC 9 Jan [8 Jan] 27a. **11** GA 1 Jan 2c-d. **12** GA 1 Jan 2d. **13** GA 1 Jan 2d.

01.02 1 GA 3 Jan 2d. **2** GA 3 Jan 2d-3a / MP 3 Jan 2c / MP 5 Jan 2b. **3** LLEP 3 Jan 15c. **4** MC 2 Jan 1a (ads) / MJ 30 Dec 1775 3d / LC 30 Dec 1775 632b. **5** MC 2 Jan 2c (orig. 'Corke', 'twenty-second'). **6** MC 2 Jan 2c.

01.03 1 MC 4 Jan 2a. **2** LC 4 Jan 14c / MC 4 Jan 4a-b / MP 4 Jan 2c (q). **3** MC 4 Jan 3a / MP 4 Jan 2d / MC 3 Jan 3a. **4** MP 5 Jan 2a. **5** Gibbon PL i 275-276. **6** MP 5 Jan 2a. **7** Moore 134-137 (Sheridan to Thomas Linley, 31 Dec 1775, 4 Jan 1776). **8** MP 6 Jan 2c.

01.04 1 Moore 136-138. **2** MC 4 Jan 3a (orig. 'joice' for 'joist').

01.05 1 DAR xii 33-35. **2** MC 6 Jan 2a / GA 6 Jan 3a / LC 6 Jan 22c-23a / MP 8 Jan 2b / GA 10 Jan 2d. **3** MP 11 Jan 2c-d. **4** MC 5 Jan 2b.

01.06 1 GA 8 Jan 2d. **2** PA 5 Jan 2b / LC 6 Jan 24b. **3** Wesley iv 62, 65. **4** PA 6 Jan 2c. **5** PA 6 Jan 2c. **6** MP 6 Jan 2b.

01.07 1 LC 9 Jan 26c-27a. **2** Gaillardet 1866 pp403-410 (no. 19, Fr.). **3** GM (Jan) 44. GM tended to copy its 'Historical Chronicle' items from daily newspapers and this comment may have been a paraphrase of MC 15 Jan 3b: 'The fall of snow has not been so great in the memory of the oldest man in the liberty of Westminster'.

01.08 1 MJ 11 Jan 4c. **2** Hutchinson ii 4. **3** Boucher Letters viii 343-346 (to Rev. John James of Arthuret). **4** GA 11 Jan 4c. **5** MC 8 Jan 1b (ad) / MC 10 Jan 2c-d / LC 11 Jan 36b-c / GA 11 Jan 2a-b. **6** Allen 71, 77.

01.09 1 GA 10 Jan 2d. **2** Fortescue iii 328 (no. 1808, Sandwich to king, 10 Jan) / MP 12 Jan 2c / HMC Various vi 315 (Capt. J. Leveson Gower to Capt. the Hon. William Cornwallis, 27 Feb, q). MP says 'messenger arrived on Wednesday at the Earl of Sandwich's house in the Admiralty' but Sandwich's letter seems to indicate Tuesday. A satirical letter signed 'The Friend of Twitcher' in PA 16 Feb 2a gives a similar account to the later Leveson Gower letter, saying Sandwich 'can revel in the joys of mirth, though Death should snatch a son; nor did his eye, that index of the soul, betray the fatal news, but, Roman-like, he smiled at grief, and mocked all woe'. **3** Gaillardet 1866 pp271-272 (Fr.). **4** MP 11 Jan 2a (orig. 'Capt. R—'). It seems likely he was the Grand Turk mentioned in the masquerade report under 8 Jan in the Chronicle. **5** GA 9 Jan 4b. **6** MC 9 Jan 3a. **7** GA 9 Jan 2c.

01.10 1 Fortescue iii 328 (no. 1808) / Sandwich i 97 (Sir Hugh Palliser to Sandwich, 6 Jan). From Sandwich's letter it seems clear that the flag he sent is the one referred to in Palliser's letter, from which the description is taken. **2** MC 11 Jan 2c-d / GA 13 Jan 4c. **3** BM Egerton Ms. 2180 f3. **4** MC 17 Jan 2d ('Extract of a letter from Cambridge, Jan. 12'). **5** MC 10 Jan 3c.

01.11 1 Fortescue iii 331-332 (no. 1810). **2** Wilkes Diaries 89 (MPs were Governor Johnstone and Temple Luttrell) / Beaumarchais Correspondance ii 164 (no. 339, Fr.). **3** MP 11 Jan 2a. **4** GA 11 Jan 2b. **5** LC 11 Jan [10 Jan] 34b.

01.12 1 MP 13 Jan 2c / MC 15 Jan 3b / Lichtenberg trans. Noel i 159. There is uncertainty as to the date of death. It was reported as having occurred as early as New Year's Eve (MC 1 Jan 3a) but most papers (e.g. MC 15 Jan, LC 16 Jan [15 Jan] 51c) dated it to the 12th. He was not buried until 21 Jan. **2** GA 13 Jan 2d. **3** MC 15 Jan 3a. **4** MC 13 Jan 2c / MJ 13 Jan 3b. **5** MC 16 Jan 2b. **6** GA 15 Jan 2d. **7** LC 13 Jan 46c-47a. **8** MJ 16 Jan 4c. **9** GA 12 Jan 3a.

01.13 1 MJ 16 Jan 4d. **2** LC 18 Jan 58c. **3** Villette 11 / LC 16 Jan 56a (q). **4** Curwen 1972 i 106. **5** LC 16 Jan [15 Jan] 51c, 53a-c / MP 15 Jan 2c-d ('Joe, my dear') / MC 15 Jan 3c / DA 16 Jan 1b / OBP Jan 132-140 (no. 191, Joseph Bull, all other qs). Reports differ regarding several details. **6** GA 13 Jan 4b. **7** LEP 13 Jan 4b. **8** LC 13 Jan 48b (orig. 'Corke').

01.14 1 Villette 11. **2** MC 16 Jan 3a.

01.15 1 MC 16 Jan 2d. **2** MJ 18 Jan 1c / MC 17 Jan 3a. **3** MC 22 Jan 2a / Rudd, Genuine Letter, 5-10. **4** MJ 16 Jan 4b. **5** Villette 11-12. **6** LC 16 Jan 56c. **7** LC 16 Jan 56c. **8** MC 16 Jan 2b-c (Newcastle) / MC 17 Jan 2b (Kingston, lord chancellor) / MC 22 Jan 2c (Garrick) / MC 24 Jan 2b (Walpole) / MC 26 Jan 2c (Johnson) / MC 29 Jan 2a (Wilkes). **9** MJ 16 Jan 4c / GA 17 Jan 3b-c (dates to 'yesterday' in error). **10** MC 16 Jan 3a. **11** DAR x 186-187 (no. 805). **12** MC 15 Jan 3a.

01.16 1 MC 18 Jan 2d. **2** PA 18 Jan 2d / LLEP 17 Jan 61c. **3** GA 16 Jan 2c / MP 18 Jan 2c. **4** MC 18 Jan 3a. **5** LC 18 Jan 63a. **6** MJ 16 Jan 4c. **7** LLEP 17 Jan 63b. **8** MC 16 Jan 4d (ad, q) / MC 23 Jan 3d (ad, price). **9** MC 16 Jan 3b. **10** GA 16 Jan 2c.

01.17 1 Villette 12-20 (orig. 'opprobious') / MC 18 Jan 3a-b / MP 18 Jan 2b-c / MP 24 Jan 4b (letter signed 'A.B.', re Lee) / GA 18 Jan 2d / GA 19 Jan 2d / GA 20 Jan 4b / LC 18 Jan 63a-b, 64c / LC 20 Jan 67a / PA 18 Jan 2d-3a / PA 20 Jan 2d / TCM (Jan) 53. MC 20 Jan 3a has an alternative back story for Lee: he 'was a footman, but upon receiving a sum of money, set up for a gentleman, and frequented the turf ... but having met with great losses, took to the road to repair them'.

2 RA NOR/16 f1v (letter dated 25 Jan; orig. 'the' for 'they' twice, 'to near'). **3** MHS Oxnard 17 Jan / Hutchinson ii 6-7. **4** GA 18 Jan 3a. **5** MC 18 Jan 3a. **6** MC 18 Jan 3a. **7** MC 18 Jan 3a / MJ 18 Jan 3c. **8** MC 19 Jan 2d. **9** MP 17 Jan 2b. **10** MC 17 Jan 2c.

01.18 1 MP 19 Jan 1d / MP 20 Jan 2a / MC 19 Jan 2a / MC 20 Jan 2a / MJ 18 Jan 4b / SJC 20 Jan 3a / Hutchinson ii 7 / MHS Oxnard 18 Jan. **2** MP 22 Jan 2a / GA 22 Jan 2c. Walpole records a similar theft of 'a diamond order' at the same event a year later (Walpole Letters x 6, to Lady Ossory, 19 Jan 1777). **3** MJ 20 Jan [19 Jan] 1b / SJC 20 Jan 3a / GA 20 Jan 4b / MC 19 Jan 2a. **4** Gibbon PL i 277. **5** Gaillardet 1866 p411 (no. 20, Fr.). **6** PA 22 Jan 2d. **7** MP 19 Jan 2a. **8** More ed. Roberts i 45. The letter, from London, is undated but it seems likely that this part of it at least was written on this day. **9** MC 25 Jan 2c. **10** MP 20 Jan 2a / MC 20 Jan 2a.

01.19 1 GA 20 Jan 2c. **2** LC 25 Jan [24 Jan] 83a. **3** PA 19 Jan 2d. **4** MC 19 Jan 2c. The contract of sale was signed on the night of 18 Jan (LS pt. 4, iii 1945).

01.20 1 Winslow Papers 13-14. Letter dated 10 Jan but see text for date of writing of this part. **2** MC 22 Jan 2a / LC 23 Jan 79b / GA 22 Jan 1d / Folger W.a.104 (13) f5r (Hopkins). **3** MC 20 Jan 2c. **4** MC 20 Jan 3a.

01.21 1 LC 23 Jan 78c-79a / CWA Acc 419/253 (q). LC reported that the coffins of four of Robert Perreau's deceased children were laid over his. CWA F6102, which dates from 1859, lists only two earlier Perreau coffins: those of Esther, *d.* 1758, in vault no. 3, and of Master Spencer, *d.* 1766, in vault no. 4. It is of course possible there were other earlier coffins which were no longer intact by 1859. **2** MP 22 Jan 2d. Church location not specified. BDA xvi 7 suggests Clerkenwell.

01.22 1 GA 23 Jan 3b. **2** Boswell OY 223.

01.23 1 MC 25 Jan 2b. **2** MP 23 Jan 2c.

01.24 1 MC 25 Jan 2d-3a. **2** MP 24 Jan 2a / MC 26 Jan 3b. **3** MC 26 Jan 3b. **4** MC 20 Jan 1b (ad) / MC 26 Jan 2a-b / MP 27 Jan 1d-2a (letter signed 'M.O.B.'), 2b (q) / MP 30 Jan 2b.

01.25 1 MC 26 Jan 2c, 2d / MP 27 Jan 1b (ad) / Burney, Music, 1776, i, list of subscribers / Scholes i 293-294 (857). **2** MC 26 Jan 2c / LC 27 Jan 96a. **3** MC 25 Jan 3a. **4** MP 25 Jan 2a (orig. 'Sal Peitro'). **5** LC 25 Jan 85a. The letter was originally dictated by Boswell on 16 Jan (Boswell OY 221).

01.26 1 LC 27 Jan 96c / GA 29 Jan 2c. **2** LC 27 Jan 95a / GA 29 Jan 2b. **3** Beinecke GJD Jan recto ('seized' etc) / DCHNY viii 654-657 ('Without' etc). From a note in Beinecke GJD (Jan verso) it seems Johnson delivered his letter in person to Germain on 1 Feb 'and had a conference'. **4** NDAR iii 535-536.

01.27 1 MC 31 Jan 4b. **2** MP 27 Jan 2a.

01.28 1 MC 31 Jan 3c. **2** LC 30 Jan 102c. **3** Howard 196 / LC 15 May [14 May] 1777 460b (ad). **4** Walpole Letters ix 320-322 ('red hat' quoted p321 n.3 from *Description of Strawberry Hill*).

01.29 1 GA 31 Jan 3b. **2** GA 30 Jan 2c / MP 30 Jan 2c / PA 31 Jan 2d. **3** Gibbon PL i 278. **4** LP 31 Jan 3d. **5** PA 1 Feb 2d. **6** PA 29 Jan 2b / SJC 30 Jan 4c-d (q).

01.30 1 Lawson and Phillips 234 / MC 31 Jan 2c-d. **2** Gaillardet 1866 pp414-420 (no. 21, Fr.). **3** SJC 30 Jan 4d.

01.31 1 GA 3 Feb 4d / SJC 1 Feb 4d (Wilson, carpenter) / MC 31 Jan 3c (future tense, coal porters) / LC 3 Feb 114c (skaters). **2** MC 31 Jan 1a (ad) / GA 5 Feb 2d (no performance date indicated but 31 Jan is only one possible). **3** MC 31 Jan 4b. **4** GA 31 Jan 3a. **5** LP 31 Jan 4b.

MIA 1 AR Chronicle 113. **2** Paine, Common Sense, 2nd edition, 43, 57.

February

02.01 **1** GA 2 Feb 3a / MC 2 Feb 3b / LC 3 Feb [2 Feb] 114b. **2** LC 3 Feb [2 Feb] 114a-b. **3** AA 4th series iv 902-903. **4** MC 1 Feb 1b (ad) / Gibbon, Decline, 1776, i v. **5** MC 2 Feb 2a, 3a (orig. 'Captain R—r') / Folger W.a.104 (13) f5v (Hopkins) / LM (Feb) 70.

02.02 **1** GM (Feb) 92 / Hutchinson ii 15. **2** MC 3 Feb 2d. **3** Fortescue iii 335-336 (nos. 1816, 1817). **4** MC 3 Feb 2a. **5** GA 2 Feb 2c.

02.03 **1** DA 5 Feb 1b. **2** Fortescue iii 337 (no. 1820). **3** LLEP 5 Feb 127c / MP 5 Feb 2b / Folger W.a.104 (13) f6r (Hopkins). **4** MP 3 Feb 2d / MJ 27 Jul [26 Jul] 1c. **5** LC 3 Feb 118c.

02.04 **1** MP 7 Feb 2c (orig. 'Captain R—'). **2** GA 7 Feb 4d. **3** MC 6 Feb 3b / MP 9 Feb 2b.

02.05 **1** MP 7 Feb 2d. **2** Wilkes Diaries 90. **3** MC 8 Feb 3a / GA 8 Feb 2c / Fortescue iii 338 (no. 1823, addressed from Grosvenor Street). The newspapers say a Lt. Col. Julian arrived and Germain went with him to the Queen's Palace, but Germain says dispatches were brought by 'a lieutenant of the Welch Fusileers' and his forwarding them with a letter suggests he did not attend the king in person. **4** MC 6 Feb 3b / Folger W.a.104 (13) f6r-6v (Hopkins). Hopkins's account is less detailed than that in MC but broadly corroborates it, although he says it was Mr King who told the audience 'that the author had taken the copy from the prompter and was gone away with it'. **5** MP 7 Feb 2c. **6** Angelo i 165-166, ii 253-255. Angelo gives two similar accounts. The text follows the first except for the wording of the reference to Dumergue. Angelo's evidently mistaken reference to Captain Roper being of Bate's party has been omitted.

02.06 **1** MC 7 Feb 3c. **2** MC 7 Feb 3a. **3** GA 6 Feb 2d. **4** MC 6 Feb 3c.

02.07 **1** MP 10 Feb 3a.

02.08 **1** MC 10 Feb 2c-d. **2** GA 8 Feb 2c.

02.09 **1** Kippis 324-325. Cook's formal letter of appointment was dated 10 Feb. If Kippis is speaking literally in saying 'no time was lost', 9 Feb seems the most likely date for the dinner. Cook 1784 i p1 refers to receiving commission on the 9th, which is either a slip for the 10th or refers to a verbal agreement the day before, perhaps at the dinner. Cook ed. Beaglehole iii pt. 1 xxix places the dinner 'probably a day or two before the 10th'. It should be noted that some modern authorities are sceptical of Kippis's account. Beaglehole 1974 pp472-473 says he may have 'dramatised into one famous dinner party' a decision arrived at over a period, but adds that 'it is not impossible that they brought him to a final, spoken, decision' at the dinner.

02.10 **1** Cook 1784 i 1-2 ('hoisted') / Cook ed. Beaglehole iii pt. 2 pp1486-1487 (exchange of letters dated 10 Feb confirming Cook's appointment; 'Lieut.'). **2** Price Correspondence i 248-250 (to William Adams, 14 Aug, 'sink') / Priestley i 289-290 n. (Rev. Theophilus Lindsey to Dr John Jebb, 17 Feb, Bank threat, 'without fear') / MC 18 Mar 1a (ad) / Frame 109-111 / Aitken Life 14, 21. **3** Price, Civil Liberty, 8-10. **4** Price, Civil Liberty, 54-56. **5** Price, Civil Liberty, 74-77, 113 (debt). **6** Price, Civil Liberty, 94-96, 98. **7** Walpole LJ i 529-530 / Priestley i 288-290 (to Rev. C. Rotheram, 9 Feb) / GM (Feb) 82 / TCM (Mar) 156 / Wesley iv 68 (4 Apr). **8** Wilkes Diaries 90 / NDAR iv 931 n.1 (Lauraguais). **9** PA 10 Feb 1a (ad) / HM 31201 f53v (Anna Porter). **10** MC 10 Feb 3c.

02.11 **1** MC 13 Feb 3a. **2** MJ 15 Feb 4d.

02.12 1 Sharp 147-148.

02.13 1 MC 2 Feb 3d (ad). **2** Franklin ed. Sparks viii 171-172. **3** Wharton ii 71-74.

02.14 1 Wilkes Diaries 90. **2** Hist. Records NSW i pt. 1 p386. **3** LLEP 16 Feb [15 Feb] 164a / GA 15 Feb 2b / Parl. Reg. Commons iii 311-313. **4** Walpole Letters ix 324. **5** MP 14 Feb 1d-2a (signed 'Benevolus').

02.15 1 MC 16 Feb 2d-3b / MP 16 Feb 2b-c / LM (Feb) 71-72 (under 16 Feb in error). **2** MC 17 Feb 3c (orig. 'Baumgarton').

02.16 1 Hutchinson ii 40. **2** GA 16 Feb 1c (ad).

02.17 1 GA 19 Feb 3a. **2** AA 4th series v 939-940. **3** MP 17 Feb 1d (ad, 'elegantly') / Gibbon Autobiographies 310-311. **4** LM (Mar) 154 (orig. 'any historian who have'). **5** GM (Jul) 365-367 (orig. 'wave'). Gibbon quote is from Decline, 1776, i 449.

02.18 1 MC 20 Feb 3d (orig. 'Chinirey') / MJ 20 Feb 3c.

02.19 1 GA 20 Feb 3b. **2** MC 20 Feb 3b. **3** NA SP 78/298 ff117v-118r (SF xiii no. 1314). **4** MP 22 Feb 2c-d (orig. 'Daw—n', 'Ken—y', 'Mah—n') / MP 26 Feb 3a / MC 21 Feb 2c-d / MC 22 Feb 2d / LC 22 Feb 183a / GA 19 Feb 3c-d. Reports vary as to numbers attending: MP 22 Feb 'about 800', MC 21 Feb 'upward of twelve hundred', LC 'not less than fifteen hundred'. **5** MC 19 Feb 2d-3a.

02.20 1 MC 21 Feb 2d-3b / MP 21 Feb 2c. **2** SJC 22 Feb 4a / LC 22 Feb 184a / Parl. Reg. Commons iii 328-341 / Fortescue iii 339 (no. 1825). **3** MP 20 Feb 2b.

02.21 1 DA 16 Feb 1a / MP 22 Feb 2a / BCE i 233 n.1 (memoir to king, 21 Sep 1775). The background to the recall is outlined in Price, *Preserving the Monarchy*, pp30-41.

02.22 1 AA 4th series iv 836 (q) / DAR x 192-193 (no. 846). **2** MHS Oxnard 22 Feb.

02.23 1 MC 24 Feb 3b. MP 26 Feb 2c concurs but MP 27 Feb 3a says it was begun on 26 Feb. **2** Registers of St Paul's Covent Garden ii 78. **3** MP 24 Feb 2d (Miss Draper is referred to but not named) / MHS Oxnard 23 Feb.

02.24 1 SJC 27 Feb [26 Feb] 1b. **2** MJ 27 Feb [26 Feb] 1d. **3** MP 24 Feb 2c. **4** MJ 24 Feb 4c.

02.25 1 GA 26 Feb 3d. **2** Doniol i 402-406 (Fr.). Doniol i 369 n.2 says the original bears a note by Beaumarchais: '*Remis à M. le Cte de Vergennes, cachet volant, le 29 février 1776.*' i.e. sent, submitted or delivered to Vergennes, under a loose seal, on 29 Feb. It seems clear from the letter's reference to conversing with Lee 'today' that Beaumarchais wrote it in London and it seems unlikely that he would have sent it from London under a loose seal by a third party. D'Éon (Gaillardet 1836 ii 248) noted that Beaumarchais travelled to Paris *circa* late February and Lever 2009 p127 refers to 'one of his lightning trips to Paris' in relation to the letter. It seems likely, therefore, that it was written on or about 25 Feb and carried by Beaumarchais to Paris, where he submitted it to Vergennes on 29 Feb. **3** Gaillardet 1836 ii 248-249 (Fr.). **4** MC 27 Feb 3d / LC 27 Feb 199a / GA 27 Feb 3c (orig. 'Chester') / MJ 29 Feb 4d (orig. 'Charter').

02.26 1 Hutchinson ii 20-21 / Curwen 1972 i 117-118. **2** MP 26 Feb 2b-c.

02.27 1 MJ 29 Feb 3c, 4d / MP 28 Feb 2c (says 'about eleven o'clock' and that 'near sixty' escaped). **2** Curwen 1972 i 118 / MC 28 Feb 2d / LC 29 Feb 206b / LC 2 Mar [1 Mar] 210b. **3** GA 27 Feb 3a-b.

02.28 1 LMA DL/C/0177 ff358r-359r (q) / SJC 29 Feb 4d (says in error that hearing took place 'this day' i.e. 29 Feb) / GA 1 Mar 3a / ODNB (Tenducci) / Berry 170, 173, 190-191, 273 n.99, n.101. **2** GA 1 Mar 3a.

02.29 1 MP 1 Mar 2b / GA 2 Mar 3b / Beinecke GJD Feb recto (Johnson) / Kelsay 165 (quoting Brant to Samuel Kirkland, 4 Feb 1792, q). **2** Hutchinson ii 21. **3** GA 1 Mar 2d / GA 2 Mar 2c-d / Parl. Reg. Commons iii 341-360.

March

03.01 1 MC 4 Mar 3a-b / GA 2 Mar 2d. **2** Malmesbury Letters i 340-341. **3** GA 1 Mar 3a.

03.02 1 MC 4 Mar 3a / MP 27 Mar 2a. **2** MC 4 Mar 3b-c.

03.03 1 MC 4 Mar 3a. **2** HMC Stopford-Sackville ii 23 (qs) / Burke's Peerage 1869 p328. Burke's says Lady Margaret died 9 Mar, conflicting with HMC date for Burgoyne's letter, and that Lady Mary lived until 1795.

03.04 1 MJ 7 Mar [6 Mar] 1c. **2** MJ 5 Mar 3a. **3** Abington Life 81-82. **4** MP 5 Mar 2b / More ed. Roberts i 52 (letter dated only '1776' but evidently written 5 Mar) / Walpole LJ i 545-546 (17 May entry).

03.05 1 GA 6 Mar 3a. **2** MHS Oxnard 5 Mar. **3** Boswell LJ ii 423. **4** Parl. Reg. Lords v 174-214 / MP 7 Mar 2a-c. **5** GA 8 Mar 3c. **6** MJ 5 Mar [4 Mar] 1c.

03.06 1 LLEP 8 Mar [7 Mar] 236a-b. **2** MP 7 Mar 2d. **3** Hist. Records NSW i pt. 1 p388. **4** MP 6 Mar 2b.

03.07 1 Abington Life 83. **2** MC 8 Mar 2d / LLEP 8 Mar 237a / MJ 9 Mar 3c. **3** Hutchinson ii 23. **4** HMC Stopford-Sackville ii 23-25. **5** Kippis 314 / Phil. Trans. Royal Society lxvi pt. 2 pp402-406.

03.08 1 Sharp 148-152 (speech on polygamy delivered 13 Nov 1800). **2** Gibbon Misc. Works ii 153 (dated 9 Mar; date adjusted by reference to Garrick ed. Little iii 1080 no. 991). **3** Parl. Reg. Commons iii 401-402 / MP 9 Mar 2a-b (q).

03.09 1 MP 9 Mar 1c (ad, 'elegantly') / WN ii 277 ('not in'), i 411 ('the annual'), ii 35 ('Every individual'). **2** WN ii 245 ('Every derangement'), i 160 ('People'), ii 82 ('that their'), ii 84 ('A nation'). **3** WN ii 366 ('as stupid'), i 17 ('It is not'). **4** WN ii 235-236 ('The discovery'), 243 (East India Company). **5** WN ii 178 ('the more advanced'), ii 182 ('exclusive'), ii 222 ('the sole', 'the principal'), ii 223 ('in reality'), ii 179-180 ('from making', 'in a more advanced'). **6** WN ii 224 ('give up' etc). **7** WN ii 231 ('The leading'). **8** WN ii 231-232 ('each colony' etc). **9** WN ii 586 ('a sort of splendid'), ii 587 ('The rulers'). **10** MC 11 Mar 2d / GA 12 Mar 2d.

03.10 1 GA 11 Mar 3a. **2** MC 12 Mar 2d. **3** MC 1 Mar 1d (ad) / MC 11 Mar 2d-3a / GM (Mar) 139. **4** MC 12 Mar 3a.

03.11 1 MJ 12 Mar 3c. **2** LC 12 Mar 246b. **3** MC 13 Mar 3a. **4** Parl. Reg. Commons iii 402-404. **5** Walpole Letters ix 336 (to the Rev. William Mason). **6** Hutchinson ii 24. **7** MC 11 Mar 3b. **8** MP 11 Mar 2c.

03.12 1 MP 13 Mar 2c / GA 13 Mar 3a / PA 3 Sep 2d. PA says she was tried 'at a late sessions at the Old Bailey' but a search of OBP found no record. **2** MHS Oxnard 12 Mar / MC 12 Mar 1a (ad). **3** MC 13 Mar 2d. **4** Malmesbury Letters i 341 (dated 15 Mar; orig. 'Cowper'). It seems likely that the ball was at 10 Downing Street but the letter does not specify. **5** GA 14 Mar 3b (Bow Street public office ad dated 13 Mar). **6** ST xx 1226-1286. **7** MP 12 Mar 2a. **8** LC 12 Mar 246a.

03.13 1 MP 13 Mar 4d (ad).

03.14 1 DCHNY viii 670-671, 678. Johnson's diary (Beinecke GJD Mar recto) has: 'Thursday 14th to take the Indians to Lord Germaines levee.' Perhaps there was a more formal meeting earlier. **2** MP 15 Mar 2a-b / MP 16 Mar 2a / Parl. Reg. Lords v 216-256 / Journals, Lords, xxxiv 593-594. **3** GA 16 Mar 3c.

03.15 1 GA 22 Mar 2d. **2** MC 16 Mar 3c. **3** Boswell OY 253-255. **4** MC 15 Mar 1a (ad) / GA 15 Mar 2b / GA 18 Mar 2d. **5** LLEP 18 Mar 270a. **6** MP 15 Mar 2d.

03.16 1 Boswell LJ ii 427-435 (qs) / Boswell OY 255-262.

03.17 1 MC 18 Mar 3b / MJ 19 Mar [18 Mar] 1b. **2** Rutter 29-31 / Australian Dict. Biog. i 118.

03.18 1 MC 19 Mar 3b. **2** MC 20 Mar 3b. **3** MC 18 Mar 3b (future event) / PA 18 Mar 3a (future event). **4** GA 20 Mar 2d-3a. **5** PA 18 Mar 3c (ad). **6** Boswell LJ ii 438. **7** Boswell OY 272-275. **8** MP 18 Mar 4a-b.

03.19 1 Boswell LJ ii 438 (q) / Boswell OY 275-276. **2** MC 20 Mar 2d, 3a / MP 20 Mar 2b-c / MP 21 Mar 2b / GA 20 Mar 2d / LC 21 Mar [20 Mar] 274c. Accounts differ as to details. **3** MP 20 Mar 2c.

03.20 1 MP 20 Mar 2c.

03.21 1 LC 23 Mar 288b / Parl. Reg. Commons iii 432-442 (qs; orig. 'unbiassed'). **2** MJ 23 Mar 4d. **3** LC 23 Mar 286c-287a.

03.22 1 MC 25 Mar 2d. **2** AR Chronicle 127-128 / MC 23 Mar 2d-3a (qs) / LC 23 Mar 286b. **3** LC 23 Mar 288b / MJ 23 Mar 3a. **4** MJ 23 Mar 4c. **5** Walpole Letters ix 337-339.

03.23 1 MP 27 Mar 2c / Baretti European Mag. xiii 314. **2** MJ 23 Mar 4c. **3** LC 23 Mar 286c.

03.24 1 GA 26 Mar 2d / AR Chronicle 129. ODNB says his death reputedly occurred on his 83rd birthday.

03.25 1 MP 29 Mar 2a. **2** MC 26 Mar 3c. **3** LC 26 Mar 294b. **4** GA 28 Mar 2d-3a.

03.26 1 MJ 24 Feb 4c. **2** LLEP 27 Mar 302a. **3** MC 28 Mar 2d. **4** Gibbon PL i 280. **5** Malmesbury Letters i 342. **6** HMC Stopford-Sackville ii 25-26 (Howe) / Fortescue iii 345-346 (no. 1836, Germain).

03.27 1 MJ 28 Mar 3b. **2** MP 28 Mar 2a-b.

03.28 1 MC 29 Mar 3b / MP 29 Mar 2b / LC 30 Mar [29 Mar] 306b-c / GA 29 Mar 3a / GA 1 Apr 1c (ad, reward) / AR Chronicle 128-129 (dated 26 Mar in error). Accounts differ as to details. **2** MC 2 Apr 3c. **3** MP 30 Mar 2c-d. MC 30 Mar 3c and LC 2 Apr 319a say one (LC) or two (MC) carts was/were stopped on Friday morning. LC adds that the mob found the stables in Black Horse Yard and discovered 'upwards of 100 dead bodies'.

03.29 1 Ward and Roberts i 81, ii 155. **2** Graves vi 283. **3** MC 30 Mar 3c. **4** CR 6 Apr [1 Apr] 2a. **5** MP 30 Mar 2c-d. See note 3 under 28 Mar re differing accounts. **6** CR 6 Apr [1 Apr] 2a. **7** NDAR iv 1007. **8** Boswell LJ ii 468, iii 5-6 (q). **9** Baretti European Mag. xiii 314-315. In error he places the departure for Bath 'on the fourth day' after the death of Harry Thrale. **10** MP 30 Mar 2d / MC 1 Apr 3c / GA 6 Apr 3a / GEP 2 Apr [1 Apr] 1b ('In attempting') / MC 20 Apr 3b / Registers, Westminster Abbey, 421 n.2 / Garrick Private Corres. ii 146 (to the Bishop of London). **11** LC 2 Apr [1 Apr] 314c / MC 30 Mar 3c-d / GEP 2 Apr [1 Apr] 1b. **12** Boswell OY 304.

03.30 1 Johnson Letters ed. Hill i 382-384. First quote ('was made ...') is from letter to Mrs Thrale dated 1 Apr. **2** Boswell OY 304-305. **3** Fortescue iii 346, 348 (nos. 1838, 1841). **4** MP 30 Mar 2b / MC 2 Apr 3a.

03.31 1 Fortescue iii 348-349 (no. 1843) / Complete Peerage iv 430. **2** Burney Early Diary ii 139-140 (orig. 'Chesington'). Letter is undated but was probably written in first few days of April: Crisp endorsed it 'Ap. 5, 1776', presumably the date of receipt. **3** Boswell OY 306.

MIA 1 Deane Papers i 123-127. **2** C 2 May.

April

04.01 1 LC 2 Apr 318b. **2** HMC Stopford-Sackville ii 26-27. **3** Boswell OY 307. **4** Curwen 1972 i 132-133 (orig. 'wether', 'Copely').

04.02 1 Ward and Roberts i 81, ii 22 / Kidson i 105-106. Kidson outlines uncertainties concerning the 1776 portrait and suggests that the engraving reproduced in the text may derive not from it, as traditionally assumed, but from another portrait painted ten years later. **2** MC 3 Apr 2d. **3** HMC Stopford-Sackville ii 28. **4** MP 3 Apr 2c / MC 3 Apr 3a. **5** Boswell OY 308-311 (latter part under 3 Apr). **6** MC 2 Apr 2b (ad).

04.03 1 MJ 4 Apr 3b. **2** Boswell LJ iii 7-8. **3** Morgan PML 19089 (Gibbon pocket-book) / Craddock 74. The windfall's timing appears surprising as the 1775 lottery had finished drawing on 3 Jan and the 1776 one did not begin until 13 Nov.

04.04 1 Ward and Roberts i 81. **2** MC 4 Apr 2c (future event). **3** GA 5 Apr 2a / MC 8 Apr 2d.

04.05 1 MJ 6 Apr 4d. Report does not indicate a.m. or p.m. but former seems likely. **2** Curwen 1972 i 134. **3** MJ 6 Apr 4d. **4** GA 5 Apr 2c.

04.06 1 MC 9 Apr 3c / LC 9 Apr 343a / MJ 6 Apr 4d. **2** Sharp 148. **3** Turgot ii 571 (Fr., q) / Wendel 283.

04.07 1 Walpole Letters ix 344 (to Rev. William Mason, 8 Apr). **2** MC 8 Apr 2c / MP 8 Apr 2a. **3** Boswell OY 320-321 ('received') / Boswell LJ iii 24-26 ('After'). **4** Johnson Works 1823 ix 535-536.

04.08 1 MJ 9 Apr 4d / GA 8 Apr 3a (prediction: road 'will be lined' etc). **2** Hutchinson ii 32 / PA 8 Apr 2c. **3** LLEP 8 Apr 343b / MJ 9 Apr 4d / AR Chronicle 132. **4** MC 8 Apr 1b (ad) / MC 9 Apr 2b-d (q). **5** MJ 9 Apr 4d / GA 10 Apr 3a. MJ says arms and legs were broken 'but we do not hear of any lives being lost'.

04.09 1 MJ 11 Apr 4b. **2** Hist. Records NSW i pt. 1 p393 (orig. 'anemals'). **3** MJ 11 Apr [10 Apr] 2c. **4** MJ 11 Apr 3b. **5** MP 10 Apr 2b. **6** MC 9 Apr 3a. **7** MJ 9 Apr 4c.

04.10 1 MP 11 Apr 1d / MP 10 Apr 2c (q).

04.11 1 Boswell OY 327-329 / Boswell LJ iii 34-36 (qs). **2** MP 12 Apr 2c. **3** Gaillardet 1866 pp425-426 (no. 23, signed by Jacques Dupré, Francois de la Chèvre, Jean de Vignolles, and the Chevalier d'Éon, 8 May, Fr.). **4** MC 11 Apr 2c-d (q, orig. 'Nantz') / MC 13 Apr 3c / NA SP 78/299 f11 ('Further information given by John Sands'). **5** Hutchinson ii 32 / More ed. Roberts i 58 (undated letter) / MP 12 Apr 2c / Garrick ed. Little iii 1092 (no. 1005).

04.12 1 OBP May 269-277 (nos. 462, 463, 464, Joseph Blann, otherwise Bland, Benjamin Harley, and Thomas Henman) / OBP Sep 386-397 (nos. 664, 665, Robert Harley and Edward George). The account given is selective and combines testimony from the various trial reports, which are lengthy and in places contradictory. Different witnesses refer to the attack as occurring at different times and on different dates, 10-13 Apr, but it seems clear it occurred in the early hours of 12 Apr. OBP has 'Pierson' but 'Pearson' is the form used in almost all other reports. **2** MJ 13 Apr 3c (orig. 'William Whitlow') / MC 13 Apr 3d. **3** MC 13 Apr 3a. **4** NDAR iv 1033-1034. **5** Hume, Strahan, 314-315, 318 n.7. **6** MP 12 Apr 2b / MP 16 Apr 2c / Foreman 42. **7** MC 12 Apr 3a.

04.13 1 MJ 16 Apr [15 Apr] 1d. **2** Boswell LJ iii 41 (where dated 12 Apr in error, qs) / Boswell OY 334.

04.14 1 MP 15 Apr 2a / MC 15 Apr 2d / Boswell OY 338. **2** Doniol i 407-410 (letter of 16 Apr, dated 12 Apr in error by Beaumarchais; Fr.). **3** GA 16 Apr 3b.

04.15 1 LWL Larpent ff1r-2v (Anna Porter Account, for this and following Porter qs under this day). **2** Newspaper sources for this 1st day of Kingston trial: DA 16 Apr 1a / GA 16 Apr 2c-d (met by Newcastle's coach) / GEP 16 Apr 4c / LC 16 Apr 368b, 368c / MC 15 Apr 3a / MC 16 Apr 2d-3b / MC 19 Apr 3a ('on hearing a noise') / MJ 16 Apr 3d-4c / MP 16 Apr 2a-c / MP 17 Apr 2c / PA 16 Apr 2c-d. **3** Curwen 1972 i 141. **4** Walpole Letters ix 348 (to Mann, 17 Apr, Castiglione). **5** Hutchinson ii 33 / Boswell OY 338-339 / BCE i 255 n.2 (Beaumarchais) / C 14 Apr. **6** Kingston Detail 67 (Harrington). Anna Porter refers to 'three chambermaids in white'. **7** ST xx 358-359 (charge). **8** Malmesbury Letters i 343-344 (Mrs Harris to her son at Berlin, 16 Apr). PA 16 Apr 2d says queen arrived 'about eleven o'clock ... but did not stay more than three hours'. In contrast MP 16 Apr 2c says she 'withdrew at half after six'. **9** Walpole Letters ix 346 (to Mason, letter headed 'Eve of St Elizabeth of Kingston, Strawberry Hill', but relevant part under sub-date 16 Apr). **10** Delany ii 206-208. **11** MP 15 Apr 2a.

04.16 1 HM 31201 f55r (Anna Porter diary, 'in the gallery') / LWL Larpent ff5v-7v (Anna Porter Account, 'To an exceeding') / Boswell OY 339 / Hutchinson ii 33 / More ed. Roberts i 54-56 (no date or recipient indicated; 'were in full', 'we had only'; orig. 'villanous') / Beinecke Gen Mss file 457 ff1r-4v (More to Theophila Gwatkin, 17 Apr [1776], 'impossible to describe' and subsequent qs). Newspaper sources for this 2nd day: GA 17 Apr 2a-c / MP 17 Apr 2a-b (Talbot). Various phrases and passages occur in both the More letter as printed by Roberts and the Beinecke letter, but even allowing for possible editorial intervention by Roberts they differ sufficiently for it to seem clear that they are distinct documents. **2** MC 16 Apr 1a (ad) / Boswell OY 340 / Beinecke Gen Mss file 457 f4r (More to Gwatkin, 17 Apr, 'drove' etc).

04.17 1 Walpole Letters ix 348. **2** Tayler and Tayler 95. **3** MC 18 Apr 3a. **4** GA 17 Apr 1d (ad). **5** GA 17 Apr 3b.

04.18 1 LC 20 Apr [19 Apr] 378b. **2** OBP Apr 211-212 (no. 324, Christopher Saunders, q) / MP 19 Apr 2c. **3** MP 19 Apr 2c. **4** MC 20 Apr 3b / MP 19 Apr 2c. MC says first that body was found 'Thursday evening' but two paragraphs later 'Wednesday afternoon'. MP says 'yesterday afternoon'. **5** GEP 16 Apr 3d (ad) / Bentham, Fragment, xiv ('a system'), xviii ('abject'), 62 ('the principle', 'the sole'), 149 ('the only'). **6** Boswell OY 341-342 / Phil. Trans. Royal Society lxvi pt. 2 p447. **7** MC 18 Apr 2c. **8** MJ 18 Apr 4c (orig. 'so extravagant a pitch of extravagance', presumably in error).

04.19 1 Boswell OY 343. **2** Boswell 1931 pp259-261 / LWL Larpent f8v (Anna Porter Account) / Wilkes Diaries 92. Newspaper sources for this 3rd day of Kingston trial: MJ 20 Apr 3b, 4a-d / LC 20 Apr 382b, 383b-384a / MC 20 Apr 2c-d. Some reports (e.g. MJ 4a) indicate an earlier start. **3** ST xx 540-568 (qs) / Whitehead 187 (Fozard). **4** DA 20 Apr 1a / MC 20 Apr 2d.

04.20 1 Hutchinson ii 34 / LWL Larpent f12r (Anna Porter Account) / ST xx 568-602 (trial qs). Newspaper sources for this 4th day of Kingston trial: MP 22 Apr 2a-d / MJ 23 Apr [22 Apr] 1c, 2a-3a / PA 22 Apr 2d. **2** MP 22 Apr 2d / MC 22 Apr 3b / Curwen 1972 i 144 / MC 2 Jan 1778 4b (Latin inscription) / Registers, Westminster Abbey, 421. **3** Boswell 1931 p261 / Boswell Club 248-249. **4** LM (Jul) 339.

04.21 1 MC 24 Apr 2d / LC 27 Apr 406c / MC 29 Apr 4d / OBP May 250-254 (no. 419, Benjamin Bates and John Green, 'between') / OBP Sep 364-376 (no. 643, James Grant). Testimony of Mrs Penleaze has been amalgamated and condensed from OBP reports. Her two accounts differ as to several details. **2** LC 23 Apr [22 Apr] 387b. **3** Malmesbury Letters i 347 (Mrs Harris from Salisbury to her son at Berlin, 9 Jun). Her source for the story was Mrs Egerton, who attended the duchess at the trial.

04.22 1 ST xx 602-652 (all qs unless otherwise indicated) / LWL Larpent ff3r, 14r-15v, 17r (Anna Porter Account) / Cradock iv 321-322. Porter refers to 'Mary Pritchard' in error. Account of duchess's fit combines qs from different Porter passages: f3r ('most horrid'), f17r ('Sensibility'). Newspaper sources: GA 23 Apr 2a-c / GA 24 Apr 1c-2d / MC 23 Apr 2a-d / MJ 23 Apr 4a-d ('the lady, whom': PA has same) / MP 23 Apr 2a-c / PA 23 Apr 2c ('the lady, whom': MJ has same). PA says duchess's speech 'consisted of upwards of thirty pages in folio, and took her upwards of two hours'. **2** Fortescue iii 352 (no. 1850, dated 'April 21' in error). **3** More ed. Roberts i 56 (letter undated but this part evidently written 22 Apr; no recipient indicated) / Burke ed. Guttridge iii 247 (currants), 260 (trial attendance) / Burke ed. Fitzwilliam ii 101-102 (to Richard Champion, 'The lady'). **4** Boswell 1931 p262 / Boswell OY 356 (letter to his wife, 23 Apr, q; n.3, Macqueen). **5** MC 23 Apr 3a. **6** MC 24 Apr 2d. **Fn. White** MP 27 May 2b / OBP May 297 (no. 495, Elizabeth Whites). **7** MP 23 Apr 2c. **8** MC 24 Apr 2d. **9** Boswell OY 356-361.

04.23 1 DA 23 Apr 1a / MC 24 Apr 2c / LLEP 1 May 422a / MJ 30 Jul 4b ('Yesterday the workmen began to pull down the scaffolding'). **2** Walpole Letters ix 353-354. **3** MC 3 Feb 3a / Walpole Letters ix 382-383 (letter apparently from Countess of Bristol to Marquise de los Balbasos, 26 Apr, Calais; recipient identified in Yale edition of Horace Walpole's correspondence xxxii 299 n.31) / Kingston Detail 72 / Whitehead 191-192 (q). **Date of Countess of Bristol's departure from England.** In the postscript of the letter to the Marquise de los Balbasos the countess says *'Aussitot que la sentance fut passée je me suis embarqué pour Calais'*. This is supported by the 1792 account of Thomas Whitehead, unreliable former valet to the Duke of Kingston, who says (p191) 'the instant Sir Francis [Molyneux, black rod] discharged his prisoner, she departed in Sir James Laroche's carriage to Dover, where her packet waited to take her to France.' (Laroche received a baronetcy in August 1776.) These two accounts suggest that she left London either late on Monday 22nd (the trial ending at around 7 p.m.) or at some point on Tuesday 23rd. An extract of a letter from Calais, dated 1 p.m. on Wednesday 24th and reporting her arrival an hour earlier, was printed in three newspapers on 27 Apr (MC 3a, GEP 1b, LC 402b-c). This letter would seem to accord with departure from London at some point on Tuesday and perhaps with embarkation from Dover early on Wednesday (in May Frederika Riedesel crossed from Calais to Dover in five hours (Riedesel p63)). One newspaper (PA 27 Apr 3a) printed the Calais letter extract but headed it Thursday 25th April, suggesting departure a day later. A brief report in MP 26 Apr 2c suggests a similar delay: 'Wednesday night last Lady Bristol set off for Rome. She embarked early yesterday [i.e. Thursday] morning at Dover, and as the wind has been fair, it is expected she is now at Calais.' The departure date is therefore uncertain, but the balance of evidence and probability suggests that she left London on Tuesday at the latest and reached Calais at noon on Wednesday. Given the well known threat of a writ of *Ne exeat regno*, it would have been oddly complacent of her to have delayed her flight further. **4** LLEP 24 Apr 399c (orig. 'Pens Common'). **5** MP 25 Apr 2b-c (orig. 'Brasore' for Henry Quirforth, 'Davison' for Dennison) / OBP Apr 246-248 (nos. 413, 414, 415, Henry Quirforth, John Dennison, and Jane Dennison, q). MP report has been adjusted by reference to OBP including re sentences received. **6** Boswell 1931 p263 / LC 27 Apr [26 Apr] 402b / Leslie and Taylor ii 154.

04.24 1 MP 27 Apr 4a-b (Reynolds, West; sequence changed in quote re Duke of Devonshire portrait) / MP 30 Apr 4a-b / MP 1 May 2a (Stubbs, Barry) / Leslie and Taylor ii 155-156 / Northcote ii 36 n. **2** Parl. Reg. Commons iii 499-487 [*sic*; pagination error; de facto 499-511] / Walpole LJ i 537 / MC 25 Apr 2a-d / GA 26 Apr 2a-d / LLEP 26 Apr 401a-402b. **Fn. Rigby** MP 17 Apr 2c. MC and GA have £1.4 million for vote of credit but LLEP has £1 million, the amount actually voted (C 6 May). **3** MC 27 Apr 3a / LLEP 24 Apr 399c (orig. omits names: 'the heirs at law of a late noble duke'). Yacht reference is contradicted by Kingston Detail p72 which says 'Mr Harding, the captain of her yacht ... conveyed her in the first open boat that could be procured'. On departure date see 23 Apr note 3. **4** MC 26 Apr 3b. **5** Hutchinson ii 36. **6** MC 26 Apr 2d. **7** MC 26 Apr 2c-d / MP 26 Apr 3a.

04.25 1 MC 26 Apr 2d / LG 27 Apr 1a / LC 27 Apr [26 Apr] 401c-402a / MJ 27 Apr [26 Apr] 1b. **2** GA 3 May 3a. **3** Parl. Reg. Commons iii 492-494 [pagination error; de facto 516-518].

04.26 1 MC 27 Apr 3a. **2** GA 27 Apr 3a. **3** Doniol i 413-416 (Fr.). Letter is dated 26 Apr but in a passage omitted here Beaumarchais refers to Lord North's speech in the Commons as happening yesterday, suggesting the letter was at least partly written on 25 Apr. **4** MP 29 Apr 2a.

04.27 1 MC 27 Apr 1a (ad) / MP 1 May 2b / Garrick Private Corres. ii 147 (from Grey Cooper, 29 Apr, q). **2** GA 27 Apr 3a.

04.28 1 LLEP 1 May 422a.

04.29 1 MC 1 May 3b. **2** MC 1 May 2c.

04.30 1 MP 2 May 2b / DAR x 282 (no. 1451). **2** MC 30 Apr 1a (ad) / Northcote ii 36 n. Presence of Norths assumed: see C 27 Apr. **3** MP 2 May 2b / MP 1 May 2d (q). According to Hopkins's diary (Folger W.a.104 (13) ff8v-9r), Garrick's words were, 'Come, Colonel, give us that song again for two very good reasons — the first, because your friends desire it, and secondly because I believe I shall never be in such good company again.'

May

05.01 1 MC 2 May 2c / GA 2 May 2c / Beinecke GJD May recto (Johnson diary). **2** MC 3 May 3c-d. **3** Hume, Strahan, 319-321. **4** MC 1 May 3b.

05.02 1 Parl. Reg. Commons iv 18-22. **2** MP 3 May 2c. **3** Hutchinson ii 41-42. **4** AA 4th series v 458-460 (Howe to Dartmouth), 1186-1187 (Germain to Howe, 3 May, 'Mr Brown'; Germain says Howe's dispatches arrived 'this afternoon' but see Fortescue and DAR) / DAR x 246 (no. 1231) / Fortescue iii 355-356 (no. 1859, Germain to king) / Hutchinson ii 41. **5** MC 1 May 1b (ad) / MJ 4 May 4c-d / MC 4 May 2c ('Mrs B—ly' of 'the theatrical world') / MP 4 May 2c ('Lady G—r' re fracas). **6** MJ 4 May 4d.

05.03 1 AA 4th series v 1186-1187. **2** Gaillardet 1866 pp345-347 (Fr., q) / BCE i 301 (doc. 43, to Vergennes, 18 Jul, 'Ogreman'). **3** Burton ii 491-492 (q) / Smith Correspondence 194-195. **4** MC 4 May 3b.

05.04 1 LG 4 May 1b. **2** MP 4 May 2c.

05.05 1 MC 6 May 2c / MP 6 May 2c / Burke's Peerage 1830 p500. **2** Boswell 1931 pp268-269 (q) / Johnson Works, Yale edition, i xviii. **3** MP 8 May 2a.

05.06 1 MC 3 May 3d (summons of performers) / MJ 9 May 4d / PL 11 May 2d / NA KB 1/20/4 (Foote's oath, 17 May) / Mansfield Manuscripts ii 1007-1008 (trial accounts of Bond, Jewell, Fielding, 9 Dec) / MC 10 Dec 2d (trial account, Bond,

9 Dec). **2** GA 7 May 2d. **3** MC 7 May 2d / LG 4 May 1b (q). **4** NA SP 78/299 ff66-69, marked 'No. 7' (SF xiii no. 1333). **5** MC 6 May 4b-d (letter dated 1 May, Fr.). **6** Morgan PML 19089 (Gibbon pocket-book). **7** MP 7 May 1d-2a / Parl. Reg. Commons iii 509-513 (q) / Walpole LJ i 540. **8** MJ 9 May [8 May] 2c / MP 8 May 2c / MC 8 May 2c-d.

05.07 1 DCHNY viii 678. **2** Folger W.a.104 (13) f9r (Hopkins) / MC 7 May 1a (ad) / Curwen 1972 i 155 / MP 9 May 2a.

05.08 1 Gaillardet 1866 pp348-351 (Fr.).

05.09 1 MJ 11 May [10 May] 1d. **2** Malmesbury Letters i 345-346 / Journals, Commons, xxxv 796-797 / Journals, Lords, xxxiv 749 / Statutes at Large viii 484 (An Act to authorise, for a limited time, the punishment by hard labour of offenders). **3** MC 9 May 1a (ad) / Folger W.a.104 (13) f9r (Hopkins).

05.10 1 PL 10 May 2c-d, 11 May 2d (12 paragraphs), 13 May 2d-3a (12), 14 May 2d (7). **2** Boswell 1931 pp275-276. Boswell's notes are fragmentary but the meaning seems clear. **3** LLEP 13 May [11 May] 458c. **4** PL 13 May 3a. **5** MC 10 May 1a (ad) / MC 11 May 3b / LLEP 13 May 462a. **6** Hume, Strahan, 323-328 / MC 8 May 2d (section headed 7 May in apparent error) / GEP 16 May 4b / MP 17 May 2a / NDAR iv 1053-1137 / Journals, Lords, xxxiv 645-749 / Fortescue iii 354-362 (nos. 1855, 1858, 1862, 1869) / NA ADM 51/4529 46. f117r (Rickman log, 27 Apr) / NA ADM 51/4557 191. f5r (Charlton log, 11 May) / NA ADM 51/4559 212. f4r (Watts log, 18 May). Possible jaunt gaps indicated allow for the possibility of Sandwich's name being appended to instructions in his absence.

05.11 1 MC 15 May 3a. **2** Johnson Letters ed. Hill i 393 (q) / Johnson Letters ed. Chapman ii 476 (Mrs Thrale to Johnson, 8 May). **3** MP 11 May 2d. **4** MC 11 May 3b (orig. 'will then').

05.12 1 RA NOR/18 ff1v-2r (letter to his brother, 28 Feb, 'never gave') / Northcote ii 36-37 (other qs). **2** Morgan PML 19089 (Gibbon pocket-book).

05.13 1 Boswell 1931 pp280-281. **2** NA KB 1/20/4 f1r (oath by Hamilton et al., 17 May; item A annexed is PL 13 May) / MC 12 Jul 1d ('On ... 11th of February, William Law Hamilton, clerk to the printer') / C 8 Jul. **3** MC 15 May 3a (orig. 'one B—d'). **4** MJ 14 May 4d. **5** Folger W.a.104 (13) f9r (Hopkins) / Morgan PML 19089 (Gibbon pocket-book). **6** Beinecke GJD May recto (Guy Johnson diary) / GA 14 May 3b / HM 31201 vol. 17 f49r-49v (Anna Porter) / Bryant 14 (Daniel Claus, 'Anecdotes of Capt. Joseph Brant', Niagara, Sep 1778, 'all the') / BM Add. Ms. 21784 f4v (Major John Ross to Captain Mathews, 26 Jun 1782, Oswego, 'An English') / PA 22 May 2c (Townshend) / Kelsay 170 (gifts from king). Brant told the masquerade story to Ross. Guy Johnson recorded the considerable sum of £148 for sundry expenses relating to Brant's time in London (Beinecke GJM f3r).

05.14 1 NA KB 1/20/4 f1r (oath by Hawkins et al., 17 May; item C annexed is PL 10 May on which Hickey has written above masthead: '14 May 1776, showed this paper to Thomas Brewman'). Hawkins is described in the oath as 'Thomas Hawkins the younger of Saint Albans Street Westminster', where Hickey had his offices. **2** MP 15 May 2b. **3** LLEP 17 May 479c. **4** Boswell OY 344.

05.15 1 Boswell LJ iii 64-80. **Fn. Americans** Boswell LJ ii 312, iii 290. **2** MC 17 May 2d-3a (q) / GEP 16 May 4b / MC 18 May 3b. Weitzman pp45-47 outlines the immediate background to this debate.

05.16 1 MC 17 May 3a. **2** Boswell 1931 pp287-289 / Boswell OY 351-352 (qs except last) / Boswell LJ iii 80 ('Sir'). **3** MC 16 May 1a (ad) / MC 18 May 3b / GA 18 May 3b. **4** GA 16 May 2d-3a.

05.17 1 MP 18 May 2b / HPHC i 415-416 (entry on Hindon by J. A. Cannon) / C 12 Mar. Smith's re-election was declared void in Jan 1777. **2** NA KB 1/20/4 (oath) / MC 18 May 3a. **3** More ed. Roberts i 59-60 (to Mrs Gwatkin, dated 12 May but this portion evidently added on 17 May).

05.18 1 MP 20 May 2c / SJC 21 May 4a.

05.19 1 MC 20 May 2c / Jackson v 289-292 (qs). **2** MP 20 May 2a / GA 20 May 2c. **3** Johnson Letters ed. Hill i 400 (to Mrs Thrale, 22 May). **4** MP 20 May 2a / MJ 21 May 4c / LC 23 May [22 May] 490a. **5** PA 22 May 2d.

05.20 1 MP 21 May 2a / MC 21 May 2d. **2** MJ 21 May 4c-d (Foote speech) / MC 21 May 2d / SJC 21 May 4a, 4c.

05.21 1 Gaillardet 1866 p356 (Beaumarchais to Vergennes, 17 May, Fr., 'I plan to leave on Tuesday morning') / BCE i 298-299 (no. 39, Beaumarchais to Vergennes, [12 Jul], Fr.; orig. 'Suinton', qs). Beaumarchais had arrived in Paris by 3 a.m. on Friday 24 May (NDAR iv 1141, letter to Vergennes). Ostensibly he related the story of d'Éon's visit in order to claim expenses but he was also taking the opportunity to undermine the pious account that the chevalier had given of his own role in his letter to Vergennes of 27 May (see Chronicle). While Beaumarchais could be referring to one of his earlier departures from London, the 'with all my papers' reference makes it unlikely. **2** SJC 21 May 4d.

05.22 1 MC 23 May 2c. **2** MC 23 May 2a / Parl. Reg. Commons iv 119-129 (qs).

05.23 1 MJ 23 May 4d. **2** Mansfield Manuscripts ii 1007 (Sangster's trial testimony, 9 Dec, q) / MC 10 Dec 2c (Sangster testimony, 9 Dec). The Oracle 6 May 1795 2c refers to William Jackson's chambers in Lyon's Inn having been 'elegantly furnished at the cost of S—l C—y H—y, Esq. then proprietor of the *Public Ledger*'. PL published a series of long anti-government articles by Harvey (e.g. PL 21 Jul 1775 1c-2a, PL 1 Dec 1778 1d-2a) indicating that he was already involved with it by this time. **3** LC 25 May 502c / Harrison 691 n. **4** MC 24 May 2a. **5** Wharton ii 94, 97 (qs) / Shewmake 134. **6** Beinecke GJD May recto, Jun recto, Jul verso (Guy Johnson diary) / GA 30 May 2b (says in error that Johnson left 'yesterday') / DCHNY viii 682 (Johnson to Germain, 9 Aug, 'much') / Bryant 14-15 (Daniel Claus, 'Anecdotes of Capt. Joseph Brant', 'Joseph'). In his diary Johnson dates the sea-fight to 17 Jul, names Dr Constable as the person shot through the leg, and says four others were slightly wounded.

05.24 1 MJ 25 May 4c. **2** GA 25 May 3a. **3** MJ 25 May 4c. **4** MC 27 May 4b-d / MP 25 May 2b-c.

05.25 1 Hist. Records NSW i pt. 1 p396 (Cook at Mile End to Banks, 24 May). Entry rests on assumption that Cook did as he planned. The painting is now at the National Maritime Museum, Greenwich. **2** NA SP 78/299 ff153-155.

05.26 1 MP 28 May 1d / MC 29 May 2d / GA 29 May 2d / LC 30 May 519a / GA 31 May 2b. Reports differ as to details e.g. dead man's name also appears as Cane and Kayne, and GA 29 May says he had been missing since Saturday morning and was found on Sunday night. **2** MC 27 May 2a-b.

05.27 1 MP 28 May 2a / MC 28 May 3a. **2** ODNB (Deare) / Smith, Nollekens, ii 305-306 (Deare q) / Baretti, Guide, 24. **3** MJ 28 May 4b, 4c / MC 28 May 2b. **4** MC 28 May 2b / Curwen 1972 i 160. Departure details are uncertain. MC says queen and children left for Kew at noon and, separately, that the king went to Kew after the review. Curwen refers to a crowd waiting to see the royal children 'take coach for Kew' and later says he saw the king and queen set off together.

5 MJ 28 May 4c. **6** MJ 28 May 4c. **7** GA 29 May 2d. **8** MP 28 May 2c / Morgan PML 19089 (Gibbon pocket-book) / MP 29 May 2a (q). **9** Pieces Rélatives 50-65 (qs). **Fn. rancour** BCE i 293 n.18 points out that Morande, who is not known to have left London during this period, wrote to Beaumarchais on 2 Jun in terms suggesting he had met de Willermawlaz.

05.28 1 MP 29 May 2a. **2** MC 30 May 2c / Fortescue iii 370 (no. 1884, king to Lord North, 2 Jun). **3** GA 30 May 2b-c / MC 29 May 2c. **4** GA 28 May 1d (ad) / MC 5 Jun 2d (blank spaces) / Paine, Common Sense, Almon's 4th edition, 4 ('farcical'), 6 ('wholly', 'in possession'), 14 ('a form'); 24, 28 (omissions) / Critical Review (Jun) 483. Almon reprinted the enlarged 'new edition' of *Common Sense* which has an introduction dated 'Philadelphia, February 14, 1776'.

05.29 1 Cook 1784 i 2. **2** LC 30 May 518c / GA 3 Jun 2b. **3** MP 30 May 2b.

05.30 1 Burke ed. Fitzwilliam ii 107 (to Richard Champion). **2** MP 31 May 2c / LS pt. 4 iii 1983. **3** MC 30 May 1b (ad) / MP 1 Jun 2b / MC 1 Jun 2d / MJ 1 Jun [31 May] 2a-b / GA 1 Jun 2d. Grosvenor and Roper names are dashed in some reports. **4** MP 30 May 2c.

05.31 1 GA 1 Jun 3a.

June

06.01 1 Riedesel 5, 58-71.

06.02 1 BCE i 289 (no. 35) / Gaillardet 1866 p282 (Fr., q). **2** MC 3 Jun 2d.

06.03 1 MC 4 Jun 3d. **2** Walpole LJ i 559. **3** Hutchinson ii 60. **4** MC 3 Jun 1a (ad) / Folger W.a.104 (13) f10r (Hopkins). **5** MC 6 Jun 2b.

06.04 1 Burrows, Morande, 86, 234 n.49 (citing Archives nationales, Paris, 277 AP/1, dossier Morande, f261) / MP 24 Aug 1d. **2** MC 4 Jun 3a / MP 4 Jun 2a / MC 5 Jun 2b-c / MP 5 Jun 2b (Great Piazza) / GA 5 Jun 2a-b ('upwards of 500 lamps' at Mansion House) / LLEP 5 Jun 541b / LC 6 Jun [5 Jun] 538b / Garrick Letters iii 1106 (no. 1022, to Hannah More, dated 'Tuesday almost 11', evidently 4 Jun) / Walpole LJ i 559 (North qs). **3** LC 6 Jun 542a. MC 6 Jun 2b-c differs re dances and says ball ended 'before twelve'. **4** Hutchinson ii 61 / Curwen 1972 i 164-165. **5** GA 6 Jun 2d. **6** SF ix no. 872 (Fr., q) / NDAR vi 401.

06.05 1 MP 4 Jun 2c / MC 6 Jun 2d (orig. 'two first acts') / MP 6 Jun 2b / LLEP 5 Jun 543c / MC 10 Jun 2d / Folger W.a.104 (13) f10r-10v (Hopkins).

06.06 1 MC 7 Jun 2b / HMC Stopford-Sackville ii 30 (q). MC says the dispatches 'brought a confirmation of General Carlton's conquest over the provincials at Quebeck' but DAR calendar does not corroborate and other sources show the Quebec news arriving on 10 Jun (see Chronicle). DAR x 275 no. 1420 is a letter from Howe at Halifax to Germain dated 26 Apr and received 6 Jun but the brief calendar entry does not correspond with HMC Stopford-Sackville text. Date of receipt of letter quoted is therefore uncertain. Perhaps there were two letters of 26 Apr, one official and one private, in which case it seems likely that they were sent together and arrived together on 6 Jun. **2** GA 7 Jun 2d. **3** LC 8 Jun [7 Jun] 546c-547a. **4** MC 8 Jun 2a-b / MJ 8 Jun 4c-d (orig. 'Lady G—r') / LC 8 Jun 552c. **5** MP 6 Jun 2a.

06.07 1 MC 8 Jun 2b / MP 10 Jun 2d. **2** LC 11 Jun [10 Jun] 554c-555a (orig. omits names Bristol and Kingston).

06.08 1 MC 10 Jun 2b / Curwen 1972 i 166. **2** Cook 1784 i 2-3 (q) / Beaglehole 1974 p504 n.2 (citing day book of Messrs. Birch, Birch and Co. of 15 Cornhill). Among the ships' logs (NA ADM 51), Charlton's (f6r) agrees with Cook in placing

Sandwich's visit on this day but those of Gilbert (136r), Rickman (f118v), Riou (f324v) and Watts (f7r) place it on Sunday 9 Jun. **3** MC 8 Jun 1a (ad).

06.09 1 Wilkes Diaries 94.

06.10 1 LGE 10 Jun 1a (q) / MC 11 Jun 2d / MC 12 Jun 2c. **2** LLEP 12 Jun [11 Jun] 562a. MC 12 Jun 2c says king gave letter to Lord Townshend but does not mention it being read out loud. **3** Cook 1784 i 3 / NA ADM 51/4557 191. f7r (Charlton) / NA ADM 51/4559 212. f136r (Gilbert). Gilbert dates to 11 Jun. **4** Curwen 1864 pp61-63 (to Dr Charles Russell). **5** DA 8 Jun 2a (ad). **6** MP 11 Jun 2c (Garrick speech etc) / Angelo i 37 / Garrick Private Corres. ii 161-162 (letter dated 18 Jun, Hampton). Gibbon was also in the audience (Morgan PML 19089). **7** Lever 2009 p135.

06.11 1 GA 12 Jun 2d. **2** LC 13 Jun 567a. **3** Cook 1784 i 4.

06.12 1 OBP Jul 324-325 (nos. 547, 548, 549, Daniel Hopkins, George Todd, and Thomas Horner, 'We ran') / MC 15 Jul 4d / MC 13 Jun 2d / MC 20 Jun 2d ('Under'). **2** LC 13 Jun 566b-c. **3** GA 14 Jun 2d. **4** GA 12 Jun 2d / GA 13 Jun 2b / LLEP 14 Jun [13 Jun] 569c / MJ 13 Jun 4d / SJC 13 Jun 4a / Curwen 1972 i 168 / Biographia Dramatica ii 125 (published 1812, earliest source found for 'bishop' exchange).

06.13 1 LLEP 14 Jun 575c. **2** MP 14 Jun 2b / MC 1 Jul 3b. **3** Hist. Records NSW i pt. 1 p397 (qs) / ODNB (Clerke) / LG 18 Jun 11a. **4** BM Egerton Ms. 2672 ff32v–33r (Oliver).

06.14 1 LLEP 17 Jun 581c. **2** MJ 18 Jun [17 Jun] 2a-c / MC 15 Jun 3c (future tense, parties on river opposite) / MC 17 Jun 2c-3a / MP 17 Jun 2b-c / MP 19 Jun 2a / GA 17 Jun 1d / Wilkes Diaries 95. **Fn. Parsons** MJ 15 Jun [14 Jun] 1c. **Fn. Gideon** MJ 15 Jun [14 Jun] 1a / GEP 15 Jun [14 Jun] 1a.

06.15 1 Hutchinson ii 69. **2** MJ 18 Jun [17 Jun] 1b. **3** Cook 1784 i 5-6. **4** MC 15 Jun 3c / Campbell i 62-63 ('an official' etc). **5** MJ 15 Jun [14 Jun] 1c.

06.16 1 GA 17 Jun 2b.

06.17 1 GA 18 Jun 2b-c. **2** MC 19 Jun 3a. **Fn. bridge** Wheatley ii 305-306. **3** MJ 18 Jun 4b / MC 18 Jun 3a / MP 18 Jun 2a.

06.18 1 MJ 20 Jun [19 Jun] 1d. **2** CWA St James's, Piccadilly, Burials, vol. 22 / MP 20 Jun 2c (says in apparent error that buried 'on Monday night' i.e. 17 Jun) / Bakewell 66, 163-167. Burial register and MP have 'Carolina' but she was christened Caroline. In the register the address 'Hungerford' is given in a subsequent note of arrears for burial fees, suggesting she had not been living with her mother at the time of her death. **3** LC 18 Jun 582c.

06.19 1 MJ 20 Jun 3c, 4d / MC 20 Jun 2d / GA 22 Jun 4b. MC says delay was 'full an hour' which 'kept them till ten o'clock'. **2** GA 20 Jun 2a. **3** MP 20 Jun 2b, 2c / LM (Jun) 287-288. **4** LLEP 19 Jun 589b.

06.20 1 MP 22 Jun 2d / OBP Jul 329-331(nos. 561, 562, Richard Goodwell and Margaret Glover, q). MP says, apparently in error, that the footman was taken in Piccadilly. **2** Sandwich Papers i 212-213. **3** LC 22 Jun 599b. MJ 22 Jun [21 Jun] 1d has a rather different account. **4** MJ 22 Jun 4c-d / LC 22 Jun 599b (says 50 guineas). **5** MP 22 Jun 2a.

06.21 1 MJ 22 Jun 4c. **2** BM Egerton Ms. 2672 ff39r-40r (Oliver).

06.22 1 MP 22 Jun 1a (ad) / Sodom 5, 7, 18, 27, 29. *Harris's List* (C 16 Jan) was published from the same address.

06.23 1 GA 27 Jun 4a.

06.24 1 Cook 1784 i 6. **2** MC 25 Jun 2d. **3** MC 25 Jun 3b. **4** MC 25 Jun 2b-d. **5** MP 29 Jun 2b.

06.25 **1** MP 24 Jun 2c / MP 27 Jun 2a. **2** BM Add. Ms. 37833 ff20-21. **3** HMC American i 47-48. **4** Deane Papers i 143.

06.26 **1** MJ 27 Jun 4b-c. **2** MC 27 Jun 2b. **3** Cook 1784 i 8.

06.27 **1** ST xx 1285-1316 / MC 28 Jun 1d-2d / MJ 29 Jun [28 Jun] 2a-3a / Curwen 1972 i 176. **2** MJ 27 Jun 4c. **3** MC 29 Jun 3a. **4** MC 29 Jun 3d. **5** MC 29 Jun 3c-d / MP 29 Jun 2b / MC 3 Jul 2d / MJ 29 Jun 3c-d / Burrows, Libellistes, 46-47 (gives spelling as 'Rauçonnet'). MP says source of quarrel was Rançonnet 'accidentally smiling' when Linsing was telling a tall tale.

06.28 **1** MC 29 Jun 3d / MJ 29 Jun 3c-d.

06.29 **1** LC 2 Jul [1 Jul] 3b / LLEP 1 Jul 6b. **2** MJ 4 Jul [3 Jul] 1d. **3** Gibbon PL i 284 (election), 285-286. **4** MP 1 Jul 2c. **5** MJ 29 Jun 4c.

06.30 **1** LC 2 Jul 7a. **2** MC 2 Jul 2c. **3** Cook 1784 i 8 / NA ADM 51/4528 f175r (Burney log). Cook says *Discovery* had arrived 'only three days before'.

July

07.01 **1** LC 6 Jul [5 Jul] 18c. **2** MJ 2 Jul 4b.

07.02 **1** LC 2 Jul 6b-c.

07.03 **1** MJ 4 Jul 3d / MP 4 Jul 2b (orig. 'Oakingham'). **2** GA 5 Jul 3a / GA 6 Jul 1d-2b / LMA DL/C/0558/12.

07.04 **1** GA 5 Jul 2a-c (q) / LLEP 5 Jul 21a-c. **2** LLEP 8 Jul [6 Jul] 26c. **3** MC 4 Jul 1b (ad) / MC 10 Jul 1c (ad, resolutions). **4** MP 4 Jul 2a.

07.05 **1** MC 8 Jul 2d-3a. **2** LC 9 Jul 31b.

07.06 **1** Collison-Morley 297-301 (Thrale diary entry) / Baretti European Mag. xiii (Jun 1788) p398. **2** Cook 1784 i xxxi-xxxv. **3** MC 8 Jul 2d-3a.

07.07 **1** GA 11 Jul 4a (orig. 'killed about twelve o'clock'; midnight seems likely given that body was found in morning).

07.08 **1** PL 9 Jul 2a-b (qs) / LC 9 Jul 32b-c [printed 23 in error] / MC 10 Jul 2b / Cooke i 224-225. **2** Cook 1784 i 9.

07.09 **1** MJ 11 Jul [10 Jul] 1c / HMC Stopford-Sackville ii 39 (Germain to Burgoyne, 23 Aug). **2** MC 10 Jul 2b / LC 11 Jul 39a-b (dates hearing 'yesterday' in error). **3** Gaillardet 1836 ii 258 (d'Éon to Morande, 3 Aug).

07.10 **1** MC 10 Jul 1a (ad) / MC 11 Jul 3a.

07.11 **1** MC 12 Jul 3a. **2** GA 13 Jul 2c (q) / Wilkes Diaries 96. **3** Cook 1784 i 12 (first two qs) / Cook ed. Beaglehole iii pt. 2 p1512 ('the many').

07.12 **1** MC 13 Jul 3a / MC 15 Jul 4d / OBP Jul 350 (sentences; orig. 'George Stodd').

07.13 **1** MC 15 Jul 3b. **2** Curwen 1972 i 184. **3** MC 16 Jul 3c. **4** MJ 16 Jul 4d. No report found of the upshot. **5** LLEP 15 Jul 54a. **6** Journal, Lords, xxxv 144-145 (17 Apr 1777, evidence on 2nd reading of bill to dissolve Tyrconnel marriage) / Trials for Adultery i 5-40, vii 3-9.

07.14 **1** MC 16 Jul 3b.

07.15 **1** MJ 20 Jul [19 Jul] 1d. **2** LLEP 17 Jul 62b. **3** MP 16 Jul 2a-b. **4** MP 15 Jul 2a. **5** MP 15 Jul 2c. **6** MP 15 Jul 2b. Hill was the captain of the ship. **7** MP 15 Jul 2a-b.

07.16 **1** Curwen 1972 i 185-186 / C 13 Jun. **2** MC 17 Jul 3a. **3** Walpole Letters ix 393-394 (to Lady Ossory, 17 Jul). **4** MC 18 Jul 2d. **5** MP 18 Jul 2b / MC 18 Jul 1d-2b, 2d / GA 18 Jul 2b-c / MJ 18 Jul 4b-d. **Fn.** *Duenna* MC 10 Jul 3a. **6** MP 15 Jul 2c ('the spinning Jenny') / MJ 16 Jul 3b-c (all other qs).

07.17 **1** MJ 18 Jul 3c. **2** MC 19 Jul 2c. **3** MC 17 Jul 2d.

07.18 **1** LLEP 19 Jul 70a. **2** Hutchinson ii 82 / MC 19 Jul 1d. **3** Wilkes Diaries 96 / Wilkes, Daughter, ii 19-20.

07.19 1 GA 24 Jul 4a. **2** Journal, Lords, xxxv 145 / Trials for Adultery i 6-7, 22-26 / MJ 20 Jul 4d (omits names). **3** MC 19 Jul 3a. **4** MP 19 Jul 1d.

07.20 1 MC 20 Jul 1b (ad) / Omiah's Farewell, title page, i-iii. **2** LC 23 Jul [22 Jul] 74c. **3** Morgan PML 19089 (Gibbon pocket-book).

07.21 1 GA 24 Jul 3a. **2** MC 23 Jul 1d. **3** Hickey ii 79.

07.22 1 GA 23 Jul 2d. **2** MP 25 Jul 2b. **3** Hickey ii 80. Seems to indicate visit was on Monday but it may have occurred a day or two later.

07.23 1 MP 24 Jul 2a / MP 25 Jul 2b. **2** MP 25 Jul 2c / MC 25 Jul 2d. **3** MC 25 Jul 2c. **4** MC 24 Jul 2a / MJ 25 Jul 4c-d.

07.24 1 GA 26 Jul 2d / MP 26 Jul 2c. **2** GA 25 Jul 2a / MP 25 Jul 1d. **3** LG 27 Jul 1b / MC 31 Aug 2c. **4** MJ 27 Jul 3c, 3d / MP 26 Jul 2a (says elephant died on Tuesday evening). **5** MC 6 Aug 2d-3a. Revival report: PA 1 Aug 2b / MP 2 Aug 4a / LC 3 Aug [2 Aug] 115b. **6** GA 27 Jul 4b. **7** MC 24 Jul 1a (ad) / MP 25 Jul 1d / MP 26 Jul 2a.

07.25 1 MP 26 Jul 2a. **2** MJ 27 Jul 3c / MP 26 Jul 2a. MP says Hunter was 'attended by near 20 of his pupils'. **3** BCE i 304 (no. 45, Beaumarchais to Vergennes, 25 Jul, Fr.).

07.26 1 MC 29 Jul 3b. **2** NDAR vi 505.

07.27 1 Burney Early Diary ii 142-143 (to Samuel Crisp, q) / Burney ed. Troide ii 207 (dates letter to 27 Jul). **2** Journal, Lords, xxxv 144-145 (orig. 'Warner' for 'Walley', q) / Trials for Adultery i 5-40.

07.28 1 NDAR vi 511. **2** LC 1 Aug [31 Jul] 107a.

07.29 1 MP 30 Jul 2a. **2** GA 2 Aug 2d.

07.30 1 MC 31 Jul 2d. **2** LC 3 Aug [2 Aug] 115b. **3** MP 31 Jul 2b-c. **4** Cook 1784 i 15-16. **5** Hist. Records NSW i pt. 1 p404 (Clerke letter dated 1 Aug) / NA ADM 51/4529 41. f326r (Riou log, '12 lashes', 'for striking') / NA ADM 51/4528 f175r-175v (Burney log). Burney says Clerke 'came down to the ship' on 1 Aug. **6** GA 30 Jul 3a.

07.31 1 GA 2 Aug 4a. **2** BM Egerton Ms. 2672 ff51r-52r (Oliver; orig. 'carry it of'). **3** Hutchinson ii 86. **4** MJ 1 Aug 3a.

MIA 1 Journals, Congress, ii 239 (orig. 'independant'). **2** Journals, Congress, ii 241-245. **3** Webb i 153 / Bangs viii 125 / Gibbs 171 (q). Gibbs says the letter was published in the *New Hampshire Gazette* of 20 Jul. It is also quoted in Wall (iv 50) where it is ascribed to the *Pennsylvania Journal* and the *Weekly Advertiser* of 17 Jul. **4** AA 5th series i 352-353 (Col. Joseph Reed to Charles Pettit, dated 15 Jul, New York).

August

08.01 1 GA 5 Aug 2c (q) / GA 12 Aug 1b (ad). **2** MJ 3 Aug [2 Aug] 1d / LC 3 Aug 118c.

08.02 1 MP 3 Aug 2c. **2** MC 6 Aug 2d / MP 5 Aug 2b / GA 6 Aug 4b. **3** MP 5 Aug 2b. **4** MP 3 Aug 2c.

08.03 1 MP 7 Aug 2a. **2** MP 24 Aug 1d ('underhand') / Gaillardet 1836 ii 257-259 (Fr., 'Mademoiselle'). **3** MP 3 Aug 2c.

08.04 1 GA 6 Aug 4b. **2** Wesley iv 80.

08.05 1 GA 7 Aug 3b / AR Chronicle 163-164. **2** MC 7 Aug 2c-d. **3** MP 5 Aug 1d.

08.06 1 MP 7 Aug 2a. **2** GEP 6 Aug 1b.

08.07 1 NA SP 78/299 f344 / DAR x 349 (no. 1941). **2** Gaillardet 1836 ii 259-260 (Fr.). **3** PA 31 Aug 3c (ad). **4** MP 7 Aug 1d.

08.08 1 MJ 10 Aug 4d. **2** MJ 10 Aug 4d. **3** Gaillardet 1836 ii 261-264 (Fr.).

08.09 1 MC 13 Aug 2d. **2** MP 10 Aug 2b (orig. does not specify 'for their clothes'). **3** GA 15 Aug 3a. **Fn. bathing** Unpaginated, entry for 'Bath'. **4** PA 31 Aug 3c (ad).

08.10 1 AA 5th series i 105, 121 (Howe q) / DAR x 334-335 (nos. 1825, 1830) / LG 10 Aug 1a-b / LEP 10 Aug 4c. Howe's reference was to the resolution of Tuesday 2 Jul. **2** MC 13 Aug 4d / AR, Appendix to Chronicle, 244-248 / Phillips, *Morning's Walk*, 136-137 (q). **3** WG 10 Aug (BM Add. Ms. 11340 f4, cutting).

08.11 1 Walpole Letters ix 398-401.

08.12 1 Gaillardet 1836 ii 264-266 (Fr.). **2** GA 16 Aug 3c (ad). **3** GA 13 Aug 2b.

08.13 1 Gaillardet 1836 ii 265-266 (account by de Piennes, 13 Aug).

08.14 1 LC 15 Aug 159b ('Avoid') / MJ 15 Aug 3b / GA 17 Aug 4c ('He would') / Sewall x 416 (to Thomas Robie, dated 17 Aug from No. 16 Knightsbridge). **2** GA 15 Aug 3a. **3** MC 16 Aug 3b. **4** Deane Papers i 177-184. **5** MC 14 Aug 2d.

08.15 1 MC 16 Aug 2d / GA 19 Aug 4a-b / MP 20 Aug 2b-c / PA 19 Aug 3c. Names are dashed in several reports. GA and PA say Damer was heir to an estate of £30,000 a year but Walpole says £22,000 (Walpole Letters ix 406, to Mann, 20 Aug). **2** Archenholz 112. **3** MC 17 Aug 3b.

08.16 1 MC 17 Aug 3b. **2** NA SP 78/299 ff359-361 (British Diplomatic Instructions vii 151-152). **3** Walpole Letters ix 402-403. **Fn. Battie** MC 15 Jun 3d. **4** Gaillardet 1836 ii 267 (statement signed by O'Gorman, de Piennes, d'Éon, and Captain Horneck, no date, Fr., q) / Burrows, Morande, 88. The signed statement says Morande went to Lord Mansfield 'on the eve of the day appointed by him' i.e. presumably the eve of the day (Saturday) previously appointed for the duel.

08.17 1 Burke ed. Guttridge iii 291. **2** Gibbon PL i 286-287 (headed 'Saturday evening'; date derived from Damer reference).

08.18 1 Hickey ii 89-90. **2** MJ 20 Aug 4c. **3** Beaumarchais Correspondance ii 239-241 (no. 383, Fr.).

08.19 1 MJ 22 Aug [21 Aug] 1d. **2** MJ 20 Aug 4c. **3** Hickey ii 90. **4** GA 20 Aug 2a / MP 20 Aug 2d-3a ('seem inclined', 'It was comic') / SJC 20 Aug 4c ('and it was with difficulty') / MC 20 Aug 1d-2b / MP 22 Aug 2c ('disgusting') / MP 21 Aug 1c / Foote, Trip, 114 / Taylor ii 325. **5** Wilkes Correspondence iv 253. **6** MP 19 Aug 2a.

08.20 1 GA 21 Aug 2c. **2** MC 22 Aug 2c. **3** MC 21 Aug 3c. **4** Walpole Letters ix 405-407. **5** GA 23 Aug 3a ('new-born male infant') / MP 22 Aug 2c ('fine female child about three days old') / GA 24 Aug 3b. **6** GA 22 Aug 3b (says men who brought trunk 'said they found it in Tottenham-court-road') / GA 24 Aug 4b.

08.21 1 PA 22 Aug 2c. **2** MP 22 Aug 2c. **3** LG 24 Aug 1b-2b / DAR xii 162-164 (Clinton letter) / Walpole LJ i 569. LG printed a long extract from Parker's letter, dated 9 Jul at Charles-town Bar, and summarised Clinton's, dated 8 Jul at Long Island, South Carolina.

08.22 1 MC 23 Aug 3b. **2** GA 23 Aug 3b. **3** Hutchinson ii 90-91 / MHS Oxnard 22 Aug. **4** AA 5th series i 1104-1105. **5** MC 23 Aug 2b. **6** LC 24 Aug [23 Aug] 188b-c / GA 23 Aug 2c / GA 24 Aug 3a / MC 23 Aug 2b-c / MJ 24 Aug [23 Aug] 2b / MP 23 Aug 2c / MP 24 Aug 2c-d / Walpole Letters ix 409 (to Lady Ossory, dated 22 Aug, Strawberry Hill). **7** Wharton ii 132-133.

08.23 1 HMC Stopford-Sackville ii 40.

08.24 1 GA 26 Aug 3b. **2** MC 24 Aug 3a.

08.25 1 MP 27 Aug 2c / MP 30 Aug 2b / OBP Oct 474-478 (no. 756, John Harding). **2** MC 28 Aug 3a. **3** MC 2 Sep 3a / Ross 301.

08.26 1 NA SP 78/299 ff401-402 (SF xiii no. 1350). **2** MC 26 Aug 3a. **3** MP 26 Aug 3a.

08.27 1 GA 27 Aug 2c.

08.28 1 MP 28 Aug 2a.

08.29 1 MC 30 Aug 2d ('a receptacle') / MC 31 Aug 2d / MP 31 Aug 2b, 2c / MP 4 Sep 2a / MJ 31 Aug 4c-d / MHS Oxnard 29 Aug.

08.30 1 LC 31 Aug 214c-215a. MP 31 Aug 2b differs, saying 'near 20 young bucks' appeared and those who could not find bail were committed for trial at the next Surrey quarter sessions. **2** MJ 31 Aug 3d.

08.31 1 LC 31 Aug 216b.

MIA 1 HMC Various vi 315 (letter dated 2 Sep).

September

09.01 1 GA 3 Sep 3a. **2** MJ 3 Sep [2 Sep] 1d / MJ 5 Sep 4c / MP 3 Sep 2b (says boat overset 'yesterday' i.e. 2 Sep).

09.02 1 Chitty 603 (Game Act, 1761) / MC 5 Sep 2d. **2** MJ 5 Sep 3c. **3** PL 2 Sep, WG 3 Sep (second paragraph qs), PL 5 Sep (BM Add. Ms. 11340 ff16, 17v, 20, cuttings) / PA 6 Sep 1c (third paragraph qs, orig. 'Gazettier').

09.03 1 WG 3 Sep, PL 5 Sep, WG 14 Sep (letter from Morande, 'a motion') (BM Add. Ms. 11340 ff17v, 20, 34, cuttings). Like other WG and PL reports these evidently favour Morande. **2** Trials for Adultery ii, 2nd case, 1-28 / Journals, Lords, xxxiv 587-588 / Gibbon PL i 207 (to Holroyd, 16 Mar 1774) / BM Satires iv 790 (no. 4711). **3** GA 4 Sep 2d / MJ 5 Sep 1d. **4** MC 5 Sep 3a / MC 17 Sep 3b (orig. 'Rossini', adjusted by reference to MC 13 Sep 1b (ad)). **5** WG 3 Sep, PL 5 Sep (letters, reprinted MC 6 Sep 4b), WG 14 Sep (BM Add. Ms. 11340 ff17v, 20, 34, cuttings).

09.04 1 GA 6 Sep 3b. **2** LC 7 Sep [6 Sep] 234c / MC 6 Sep 4d (incorrectly dating to 3 Sep) / Wilkes Diaries 99. **3** MHS Oxnard 4 Sep. **4** MJ 5 Sep 4c / MJ 7 Sep [6 Sep] 1c. **5** MC 3 Sep 1a (ad) / MP 5 Sep 2a / Mawhood 109. **6** GA 6 Sep 3c. **7** PL 4 Sep (BM Add. Ms. 11340 f19, cutting). **8** MP 4 Sep 2a.

09.05 1 MP 6 Sep 2d. **2** PA 5 Sep 2b.

09.06 1 MJ 7 Sep 3c. **2** Hutchinson ii 93. **3** MJ 7 Sep 4d. **4** LC 10 Sep 247b / OBP Dec 22-24, 28 (nos. 29, 40, William Davis, qs except LC). Accounts differ as to some details. Version given rests partly on Barrett's evidence at the trial. **5** MC 6 Sep 3b-c.

09.07 1 MJ 12 Sep 3d.

09.08 1 MJ 10 Sep 4c / MJ 12 Sep 4c.

09.09 1 LC 10 Sep 248c / MC 11 Sep 4c-d / GA 11 Sep 4a / GA 13 Sep 3b / OBP Oct 474-478 (no. 756, John Harding), 503-504 (nos. 812, 813, John Harding and Thomas Harrison).

09.10 1 Registers of St Mary Le Bowe i 246. **2** WG 10 Sep, WG 14 Sep (BM Add. Ms. 11340 ff30, 34, cuttings). PL 10 Sep not seen but MP 8 Nov 3b says 'the same libel' appeared in PL 10 Sep and WG 14 Sep. WG 10 Sep wording is unclear as to whether the wager was being made by 'an eminent banker' or a third party 'gentleman' acting through him.

09.11 1 GA 14 Sep 4a / OBP Oct 474-478 (no. 756, John Harding), 503-504 (nos. 812, 813, John Harding and Thomas Harrison) / C 25 Aug, 17 Oct. **2** MP 11 Sep 2b.

09.12 1 GA 13 Sep 3a / MJ 14 Sep 4d / GA 18 Sep 4b. **2** MP 14 Sep 2b. **3** MP 12 Sep 1d, 2a (orig. 'new house in St James's Place', presumably a reference to Brooks's, being built on the corner of St James's Street and Park Place).

09.13 1 MP 16 Sep 2d / MJ 14 Sep 4d (Suffolk Street version) / MC 3 Oct 4a (Bow Street hearing, 2 Oct, Ogilvie) / OBP Oct 440-453 (no. 736, William Davis). **2** MC 14 Sep 3b / MC 16 Sep 4c-d / MP 14 Sep 2b. **3** MP 14 Sep 1d-2a / Barrington 174-177. **4** MC 17 Sep 3b.

09.14 1 LLEP 16 Sep 270a. **2** MP 17 Sep 2a. **3** MC 16 Sep 3b.

09.15 1 GA 18 Sep 2d / LC 17 Sep 271a-b / MC 18 Sep 3a.

09.16 1 LC 17 Sep 271b / LC 19 Sep 277b [printed 275 in error] / MC 18 Sep 3a. **2** MP 17 Sep 2b. **3** GA 19 Sep 4b. No further report found relating to this case.

09.17 1 MP 20 Sep 2c.

09.18 1 LC 19 Sep 276a [printed 278 in error]. **2** MP 19 Sep 2c. **3** MC 18 Sep 1a (ad). **Fn. benefits** Nigh 67 / MC 16 Sep 3b. **Fn. Haines** Ass-sitting epilogue was to *The Unhappy Kindness*, a play by Thomas Scott performed at Drury Lane Theatre in 1697. **4** GA 18 Sep 2b.

09.19 1 MC 20 Sep 3b / MP 20 Sep 2c.

09.20 1 MP 20 Sep 2a-b. **2** MP 20 Sep 2a (orig. 'men' for 'may' and full stop in place of question mark). The end of the quotation from the Declaration of Independence should read 'of a free people'.

09.21 1 MC 23 Sep 2b-3a / GA 25 Sep 3d / Folger W.a.104 (14) f1r (Hopkins).

09.22 1 MC 23 Sep 3b / MC 24 Sep 3b / GA 24 Sep 4a.

09.23 1 MC 25 Sep 3c. **2** MC 25 Sep 3c / MC 28 Sep 2d. Early reports (e.g. LLEP 25 Sep 302b) say the operation was performed by 'Charles Hawkins, Esq., of Pall-mall ... (in the absence of his father who is now at Bath)', Charles being the son of Caesar Hawkins, sergeant surgeon to the king. MC 28 Sep says earlier reports are incorrect and names Strudwick, and it is hard to see why it should do so unless it is true. Caesar Hawkins does, however, seem to have attended to the prime ministerial arm later on: in a letter of 26 Oct the king refers to an assurance from 'Hawkins' regarding its likely progress (BM Add. Ms. 37833 f99r, to John Robinson). **3** MC 24 Sep 3a. **4** Wharton i 603, ii 148-149. **5** BM Add. Ms. 37833 f34r (orig. 'puntuality'). **6** MC 23 Sep 1c (ad). **7** GA 23 Sep 4a.

09.24 1 Registers of Marriages of St Mary le Bone iii 14. Grafton has been counted twice (dukes: Grafton, Dorset, Bedford; prime ministers: Grafton, Shelburne). **2** LC 24 Sep 296b.

09.25 1 BM Add. Ms. 37833 f40r (from Sion Hill). **2** MC 26 Sep 1d (letter) / MP 26 Sep 2b / MP 27 Sep 2b ('a gentleman').

09.26 1 MC 27 Sep 2a. **2** Fortescue iii 394 ('in a fine') / BM Add. Ms. 37833 f45r ('a real').

09.27 1 MP 28 Sep 2c. **2** MC 28 Sep 1d-2a (orig. 'Mackheath'), 2d / GA 28 Sep 2b / MP 28 Sep 2b. **3** MP 27 Sep 2a.

09.28 1 GA 30 Sep 2b. **2** AA 5th series i 788-789 (6 Aug letter) / DAR xii 182-183 (11 Aug letter, also from Staten Island) / DAR x 348, 352 (nos. 1931, 1961). **3** MC 30 Sep 3a.

09.29 1 NA SP 78/299 ff536-537, 'Most confidential' (SF xiii no. 1366). **2** MC 30 Sep 2c.

09.30 1 MP 1 Oct 2c / MC 1 Oct 1d-2a / GA 1 Oct 2a-b / LM (Oct) 511.

MIA 1 Wharton ii 139-145. **2** LGE 4 Nov 1a-b (General Howe to Germain, 21 Sep). **3** AA 5th series ii 417 (to General Schuyler). **4** AA 5th series ii 398. **5** LGE 4 Nov 1b-2a (General Howe to Germain, 23 Sep). **6** Mackenzie i 61-62. **7** AA 5th series ii 1379. **8** AA 5th series ii 603.

October

10.01 1 LLEP 4 Oct 334a. **2** BM Add. Ms. 37833 f63r. **3** MP 1 Oct 4b.

10.02 1 MC 8 Oct 4d. **2** LLEP 4 Oct 334a / MC 4 Oct 3b / MC 5 Oct 3a / MC 7 Oct 3b / GA 7 Oct 2d / Bod. North Papers d16 f154r (Delany letter, 6 Oct from Bulstrode, to Lord Guilford).

10.03 1 LEP 3 Oct 3c.

10.04 1 MC 7 Oct 3a / MP 5 Oct 2b / GA 7 Oct 2d.

10.05 1 BM Add. Ms. 37833 f75r.

10.06 1 MC 7 Oct 2c. **2** GA 9 Oct 2d.

10.07 1 MP 5 Oct 2b / MP 7 Oct 1d-2a (letter evidently written 5 Oct). **2** MP 7 Oct 2c.

10.08 1 Bod. North Papers d25 f92r (letter dated 9 Oct at Bushy, to Lord Guilford) / Walpole LJ i 574. **2** HMC Abergavenny 15. **3** Peake i 413. **4** MP 8 Oct 1d.

10.09 1 MC 11 Oct 3a. **2** MC 10 Oct 2d-3a. **3** Folger W.a.104 (14) f1r (Hopkins).

10.10 1 Walpole LJ i 574-576 / LGE 10 Oct 1a-2b (Howe letter) / MC 12 Oct 2b / MP 11 Oct 2b / Burke ed. Guttridge iii 293 (to Richard Champion). **2** GA 14 Oct 2d.

10.11 1 MC 12 Oct 2a. **2** MC 14 Oct 3a-b. **3** MHS Oxnard 11 Oct. **4** GA 14 Oct 2d / MC 12 Oct 3a / MC 14 Oct 3a / OBP Oct 499-500 (no. 792, Elizabeth West, q). **5** Garrick Private Corres. ii 180-181 (Sheridan to Garrick, 15 Oct, qs except final three) / Folger W.a.104 (14) f1v (Hopkins, 'This put' etc).

10.12 1 Garrick Private Corres. ii 181 (Sheridan to Garrick, 15 Oct). **2** LC 12 Oct [11 Oct] 355b.

10.13 1 Folger W.a.104 (14) f1v (Hopkins, orig. 'Young'; final 'word' is unclear but derived from sense).

10.14 1 MP 15 Oct 2c. Original report does not specify 'for their clothes'. **2** MC 15 Oct 2a. **3** Posthumous Letters 209-210. **4** LC 17 Oct [16 Oct] 371b.

10.15 1 Garrick Private Corres. ii 181-182. Identity of the 'we' who were 'very friendly together' is not stated but seems clear from the sense. **2** Folger W.a.104 (14) f2r (Hopkins).

10.16 1 Folger W.a.104 (14) f2r (Hopkins).

10.17 1 MC 18 Oct 3a-b / MP 18 Oct 2c / LC 17 Oct 376c.

10.18 1 GA 23 Oct 4a. **2** MC 19 Oct 3a. **3** MC 19 Oct 3b-d / OBP Oct 440-453 (no. 736, William Davis). **4** HMC Stopford-Sackville ii 44 (orig. 'Cambden'). **5** Peake i 414-415 (q) / Posthumous Letters 210-212. Dinner assumed from references in Colman and Foote letters of this date. **6** MP 19 Oct 2c. **7** Boswell LJ iii 92 (to Robert Levett, 21 Oct).

10.19 1 MP 21 Oct 2c / OBP Oct 457-466 (no. 747, Richard Arnold, qs) / LD (Arnold). **2** MP 22 Oct 2c.

10.20 1 Sandwich i 216-217.

10.21 1 LEP 24 Oct 4d / PA 29 Aug 1c-d.

10.22 1 MC 22 Oct 2c.

10.23 1 LLEP 23 Oct 399c / LLEP 25 Oct [24 Oct] 403a. **2** MHS Oxnard 23 Oct (orig. 'meet' for 'met') / LLEP 23 Oct 399a. **3** Bod. North Papers d17 f10r (letter dated 24 Oct from Arundel Street, to Lord Guilford). **4** MC 25 Oct 3b. **5** MP 24 Oct 2a / MC 24 Oct 2b. **6** MP 25 Oct 1d. **7** MP 23 Oct 1d.

10.24 1 MC 24 Oct 1d-2a / MC 26 Oct 2c / MC 28 Oct 3a / MC 29 Oct 4c-d / MC 30 Oct 2c. **2** MP 24 Oct 2a.

10.25 1 LG 26 Oct 2a / MP 26 Oct 2a / MC 26 Oct 2b. **2** MHS Oxnard 25 Oct.

3 LG 26 Oct 1a. **4** MC 25 Oct 1a (ad) / MC 28 Oct 3d. **5** DA 25 Oct 1a. **6** LLEP 25 Oct 406a.

10.26 1 MP 28 Oct 2c. **2** MC 28 Oct 3a / BM Add. Ms. 37833 f99r (q).

10.27 1 PA 28 Oct 2c. **2** MHS Oxnard 27 Oct.

10.28 1 Walpole LJ i 579 / MC 30 Oct 2b-c (q) / MP 30 Oct 2b / LLEP 30 Oct 421c / MC 31 Oct 2c. **2** PA 28 Oct 2a.

10.29 1 GA 30 Oct 3a / MP 30 Oct 2b / MC 30 Oct 2c / MC 31 Oct 2c, 4d / GA 31 Oct 3a. **2** Francis Letters i 270-274 (to Philip Francis). **3** PA 29 Oct 2c. **4** MP 29 Oct 2a.

10.30 1 MC 31 Oct 2b-c / MC 1 Nov 3a-b / LC 31 Oct 422a, 424b / MP 31 Oct 2d / GA 1 Nov 3a. **2** LC 2 Nov 432b-c ('We') / LC 5 Nov 438c ('the kirk') / LC 7 Nov [6 Nov] 441c. **3** MC 30 Oct 1c (ad) / MP 18 Nov 3b (ad, 'wore') / MC 1 Nov 3b. **4** LG 18 Jun 1b / MC 25 Nov 2b / MC 7 Jan 1777 2b-c ('had been') / Reynolds, Frederick, i 373 ('a splendid', 'visited'). Reynolds, born 1764, never met Purdon and was relating what he had heard from his own father. **5** MP 31 Oct 2b / MC 31 Oct 2a. **6** MC 30 Oct 2b. **7** MP 30 Oct 2c.

10.31 1 GA 1 Nov 3b. **2** MC 1 Nov 1c-2d / Parl. Reg. Commons vi 5-47 (speech and debate qs) / Walpole LJ i 580-585(orig. 'Wedderburne') / Burke ed. Fitzwilliam ii 129-130 (to Richard Champion, 2 Nov). **3** BM Egerton Ms. 2672 ff131r-133r (Oliver) / MC 1 Nov 3a / GA 1 Nov 3a-b (says first injured boy was 'about ten'). **4** MC 31 Oct 3a.

November

11.01 1 MC 4 Nov 2d. **2** LC 5 Nov 439a. **3** MC 4 Nov 3a-b. **4** MC 1 Nov 3b ('extract' and 'about' are uncertain). MP 4 Nov 4a-b has letter giving different account of Sir Eyre Coote's involvement.

11.02 1 GA 6 Nov 3b. **2** MC 2 Nov 3d / MP 4 Nov 2c. **3** GA 5 Nov 3b. **4** Bod. North Papers d25 ff98r-101r (orig. '15 of Novr.' in error). **5** MC 4 Nov 2c (says news arrived 'at half past ten o'clock') / MP 4 Nov 2b ('late on Saturday evening') / Parl. Reg. Commons vi 54 (Charles Fox in House of Commons, 6 Nov, 'late on Saturday night'). **6** LGE 4 Nov 1a-2a (letters of 21 and 23 Sep) / HMC Stopford-Sackville ii 41-42 (letter of 25 Sep) / DAR x 377-379 (nos. 2122, 2126, 2137). **7** DAR xii 225-227 / DAR x 376 (nos. 2113, 2114) / MC 6 Nov 2c (declaration).

11.03 1 MC 4 Nov 2c. **2** GA 7 Nov 3a. **3** PA 8 Oct 3a.

11.04 1 LGE 4 Nov 1a-2a / C 6 Nov. **2** GA 5 Nov 3b / MC 5 Nov 2d. **3** MC 16 Oct 3b (q) / LC 5 Nov 440b. **4** Bod. North Papers d25 f102r-102v. **5** Gibbon PL i 290-291. **6** MP 4 Nov 2b.

11.05 1 MC 8 Nov 3d. **2** MC 6 Nov 3a / MP 6 Nov 2c (indicates only six pall bearers).

11.06 1 AA 5th series iii 537-538 (qs) / DAR x 400 (nos. 2286, 2287, 2288). **2** Parl. Reg. Commons vi 48-66 (debate qs) / MC 7 Nov 2a-d / Gibbon PL i 291 (to Holroyd, from 'Almack's, Thursday evening'). The Howes' declaration appeared, for example, in MC 6 Nov 2c and MP 6 Nov 2d. **3** MC 6 Nov 1a (ads) / Quincy 215 (orig. 'part') / GA 7 Nov 3a / Folger W.a.104 (14) f3r (Hopkins). **4** MC 6 Nov 2c-d. **5** GA 6 Nov 3a.

11.07 1 LLEP 13 Nov [12 Nov] 466b. **2** MP 9 Nov 3a.

11.08 1 GA 9 Nov 3b. **2** MP 8 Nov 3b. **3** MC 9 Nov 2d / Parl. Reg. Commons vi 66-73 (qs). **Fn. Wombwell** HPHC iii 654-655. **4** MHS Oxnard 8 Nov. **5** LLEP 11 Nov [9 Nov] 458c / GA 14 Nov 3a. **6** Delany ii 275-277.

11.09 1 GA 9 Nov 3d. **2** GA 11 Nov 3a / MC 11 Nov 3a-b / LLEP 13 Nov [12 Nov] 466b / PA 11 Nov 2c / Quincy 215-216 / MHS Oxnard 9 Nov. Oxnard was not of Quincy's party. **3** Bod. North Papers d25 f105r-105v. **4** MC 9 Nov 1a (ad) / LS pt. 5 i 36-48. **5** GA 13 Nov 3b. **6** MP 9 Nov 2c.

11.10 1 PA 11 Nov 3c. **2** Cook 1784 i 39.

11.11 1 MC 13 Nov 3a. **2** NA SP 78/300 ff208-213, 'Most secret', 'Confidential', 'Most confidential'. **Fn. T. Walpole** HPHC iii 598-602.

11.12 1 Walpole Letters ix 439-440 (dated 13 Nov). Werkmeister 1963 pp25-32 gives a detailed account of the dispute. **2** MC 13 Nov 3a. **3** MC 14 Nov 2c. **4** Gaillardet 1836 ii 272-275 (dated 12 Nov; place in sequence rests on assumption that was started on 12 Nov and finished in early hours of 13 Nov; Fr.).

11.13 1 LC 14 Nov 471a / MC 14 Nov 2c. **2** MC 15 Nov 3a. **Fn. Guzzledown** CCR 23-42.

11.14 1 MC 15 Nov 3a. **2** LC 16 Nov [15 Nov] 474b. **3** Bod. North Papers d25 f113r-113v (undated; date derived from reference, not quoted, to Derby christening 'to night'). **4** GEP 16 Nov 3b. **5** MP 15 Nov 2a / MP 16 Nov 2b (q).

11.15 1 GEP 16 Nov 3a. **2** MP 18 Nov 2c / Letters of Garrick and Countess Spencer 51-53 (letter 23). **3** NDAR vii 742-743. **4** Parl. Reg. Commons vi 73-76. **5** Fortescue iii 402 (no. 1929). **6** Bod. North Papers d25 f107r-107v (dated 'Friday 4 oclock'; post stamp partly lost but clearly 15 Nov). **7** MC 18 Nov 3b. **8** LLEP 15 Nov [14 Nov] 474b.

11.16 1 LLEP 18 Nov 487a.

11.17 1 LLEP 22 Nov 502a / GA 22 Nov 4a.

11.18 1 MP 18 Nov 3b. **2** Sandwich Papers i 217. **3** NA SP 78/300 ff233-234, 'Confidential' (SF xiv no. 1373). **4** MP 19 Nov 2b / MHS Oxnard 18 Nov / MP 27 Nov 2c. **5** MC 15 Jul 1777 2a-b.

11.19 1 MP 20 Nov 2b ('two or three') / MP 21 Nov 2b / Congreve 12, 15 / Folger W.a.104 (14) ff3v-4r (Hopkins). **2** Bod. North Papers d25 ff110r-111r (undated but headed 'Tuesday night'; post stamp 19 Nov). **3** AR Chronicle 192.

11.20 1 MP 21 Nov 2c. **2** LLEP 25 Nov 509c. **3** MC 20 Nov 1a (ad) / MC 21 Nov 1d / MP 21 Nov 2a. **4** MP 20 Nov 2a. **5** LP 20 Nov 3d.

11.21 1 GA 22 Nov 3a. **2** LLEP 27 Nov [26 Nov] 514c. **3** Hutchinson ii 113-114. **4** Boucher Letters ix 235-237 (to the Rev. John James). **5** MP 23 Nov 2d.

11.22 1 MP 23 Nov 2d. **2** NDAR vii 755. **3** LLEP 22 Nov 503a / Gibbon PL i 294 / Walpole LJ i 591.

11.23 1 LG 23 Nov 1a-b (qs) / MC 25 Oct 2c. DAR x 387-388 (no. 2200) also gives 23 Nov as receipt date. PA 23 Nov 2c says 'yesterday at noon a messenger arrived at ... Germaine's office express from Sir Guy Carleton'. **2** MP 25 Nov 2d / Folger W.a.104 (14) f4r (Hopkins, q) / BDA xii 285-286. **3** MP 23 Nov 2b.

11.24 1 Walpole Letters ix 441-442.

11.25 1 MP 26 Nov 2d, 3a. **2** NA SP 78/300 ff249-254 (SF xiv nos. 1375, 1376).

11.26 1 GA 28 Nov 2c. **2** MP 27 Nov 2c. **3** Cook ed. Beaglehole iii pt. 2 p1520.

11.27 1 MP 27 Nov 3a. **2** MC 28 Nov 1d-2b / MP 28 Nov 2b / PL 28 Nov (BM Add. Ms. 11340 f48, cutting) / MHS Oxnard 27 Nov. It could be speculated that the second counsel for Morande was Arthur Lee, acting to defend Beaumarchais's protégé, but a Mr Lee also acted in the related Hayes v. Jacques trial on 1 Jul 1777 (GA 2 Jul 1777 2b), at which time Arthur Lee was in Berlin (Lee i 89-91).

11.28 1 LLEP 29 Nov 526a. **2** LLEP 2 Dec 533c. **3** GA 2 Dec 2d / OBP Dec 27-28 (no. 39, Thomas Farmer, otherwise Smith).

11.29 1 MC 30 Nov 2c. **2** GA 2 Dec 2c. **3** British Diplomatic Instructions vii 155. **4** MP 30 Nov 2d / LS pt. 5 i 40. **5** GA 29 Nov 3a.

11.30 1 LLEP 2 Dec 533c / Wilkes Diaries 101. **2** MC 3 Dec 2c-d.

MIA and Paris 1 LGE 30 Dec 3a-b (General Howe to Germain, New York, 30 Nov). **2** AA 5th series iii 927-928. **3** Aitken Life 21-36 (qs) / Deane Papers ii 6-11 (undated letter from Deane to Bancroft) / ST xx 1347 (date of pass). The few dates Aitken gives in the Life may not be reliable: for example he says his final army desertion was in August 1776 but that would have left scant time for all he then claims to have done before heading for Paris. Deane's letter refers to Rodney's defeat of de Grasse, 12 Apr 1782, and so must have been written after that date. His account of the first meeting is more cautious than Aitken's and his account of the second is missing, presumably removed because considered compromising. None of the accounts specify when the meetings occurred but early November seems likely.

December

12.01 1 Aitken Life 36-37. **2** Burney Early Diary ii 145-148 (qs) / Burney ed. Troide ii 209-212. Letter undated. Early Diary says it was endorsed by Crisp '2 Decr. 1776'. Troide gives bracketed date of 2 Dec for letter, plus Fanny Burney's annotation: 'on Agujari at a private concert at Dr Burney's. 2 Dec. 1776.' In the letter itself Burney refers to the concert occurring 'yesterday evening'. It seems likely that the letter was written on 2 Dec and the concert occurred on 1 Dec, but it is possible the dates were 3 Dec and 2 Dec respectively.

12.02 1 Hickey ii 97 (qs) / CCR 211. **2** NA SP 78/300 ff288-289 (orig. 'cloths') (SF xiv no. 1379). **3** MC 2 Dec 1b (ad) / MC 4 Dec 1d-2a (q) / GA 4 Dec 1d / SJC 3 Dec 4d (differs from MC and GA in saying 'near six hundred' were present).

12.03 1 GA 5 Dec 4a. **2** MC 5 Dec 2d.

12.04 1 MC 5 Dec 3b. **2** GA 5 Dec 3a. **3** Wraxall Mem. iv 248-249 (incorrectly dating Dilly dinner to Nov) / Wilkes Diaries 101, 104. **4** Deane Papers i 402-404.

12.05 1 OBP Dec 3-5 (no. 2, Thomas Burrows, qs) / PA 30 Jan 1777 3a. **2** MP 6 Dec 2d / OBP Dec 22-24, 28 (nos. 29, 40, William Davis) / SJC 27 Mar 1777 3b. **3** MC 7 Dec 2b-c.

12.06 1 MC 10 Dec 1d.

12.07 1 PA 9 Dec 2b. **2** Aitken Life 42-44 (qs) / ST xx 1343-1344.

12.08 1 GA 10 Dec 2d. **2** Aitken Life 44-46 (orig. 'Bencroft' repeatedly).

12.09 1 MC 10 Dec 2c-3b ('had he', 'And here') / GA 10 Dec 2b-d ('Johnny', 'an old'; orig. 'b—g s—l' for 'buggering scoundrel') / MC 3 May 3d (notice to performers) / Mansfield Manuscripts ii 1004-1009 (Mansfield's notes of the evidence). **2** Cooke, Foote, i 231-232. **3** MP 11 Dec 2a. **Fn. Germany** Gervat 161-163. **4** MP 10 Dec 2c / MC 11 Dec 3a. **5** Aitken Life 46-47 (orig. 'Bencroft'). **6** LC 10 Dec 559b. **7** GA 11 Dec 3a / HM 31201 f61r-61v (Anna Porter). **8** GA 12 Dec 3d (ad) / MP 13 Dec 2c. MP has 'its throat cut from ear to ear' but GA notice seems likely to be more reliable as it was placed by a solicitor acting for St Pancras parish. **9** MC 11 Dec 2b / Walpole LJ i 592.

12.10 1 LC 12 Dec 566b. **2** Robinson i 191-192, ii 1-2 / Folger W.a.104 (14) f4v (Hopkins) / GA 11 Dec 1d. **3** MC 11 Dec 3a / MC 14 Dec 2c-d (ad). MP 11 Dec 2c says 'near five hundred persons assembled'.

12.11 1 MC 12 Dec 2d / GA 13 Dec 3b / LC 14 Dec [13 Dec] 571b. **2** MC 12 Dec 2d ('had more') / MP 12 Dec 2d / MP 14 Dec 2c / MC 16 Dec 3b (Hunter) / GA 12 Dec 3a. **3** MC 12 Dec 1d.

12.12 1 Wharton ii 224. **2** MC 12 Dec 2a.

12.13 1 MC 14 Dec 1d-2a / SJC 14 Dec 3a / LLEP 16 Dec [14 Dec] 580a-c / MP 14 Dec 2a / MP 16 Dec 2a / Butler 6-14. **2** LC 17 Dec [16 Dec] 578b. **3** GA 16 Dec 2d-3a / MP 14 Dec 2a. MP says the man was reportedly 'a broker in Long-acre'. **4** Hutchinson ii 120 / MHS Oxnard 13 Dec / NDAR vii 789 (Bancroft) / MC 14 Dec 2a. Bancroft's account may of course have been tailored for Deane's consumption. NDAR has 'Mr [Horace] Walpoles' but the Mr Walpole referred to was probably Thomas Walpole: see C 11 Nov. **5** GA 16 Dec 2c / MC 17 Dec 1d.

12.14 1 GA 17 Dec 2d. **2** MC 16 Dec 2c. **3** MP 21 Dec 2b. MC 25 Dec 2d has variant in which 'a poor man went into a hog-stye, belonging to Mr John Stevens, a bacon butcher, at Mile-end,' and was found eaten away by rats.

12.15 1 GA 16 Dec 2d. **2** NA SP 78/300 ff382-385, 'Particular' ('I learnt'); ff390-391, 'Private' ('from a' etc) (SF xiv nos. 1386, 1388). **3** MP 20 Dec 2b, corrected by MP 26 Dec 2b / GA 30 Dec 2d.

12.16 1 MC 17 Dec 1d. **2** DA 17 Dec 1a.

12.17 1 MP 25 Dec 2c / LC 19 Dec [18 Dec] 585c-586a / MC 18 Dec 1d / LLEP 18 Dec 588c. Accounts differ. Text largely follows MP 25 Dec, which claims to correct earlier reports. **2** MP 17 Dec 2c.

12.18 1 MC 19 Dec 2d / GA 19 Dec 2c. **2** GA 19 Dec 2d. **3** Schaeper 80. **4** MP 21 Dec 2d. **5** MC 18 Dec 1d / MC 19 Dec 2b / PA 20 Dec 3a / MC 20 Dec 3b-c / MC 27 Dec 3a. PA and MC 20 Dec speak of legs and arms broken. MC 27 Dec says no major injuries resulted.

12.19 1 NA SP 78/300 ff399-400, 'Most confidential' (qs) (SF xiv no. 1391) / Loménie 291-294 / Lever 2009 pp152-154 / NDAR vii 735 n.2, viii 396-397 / Morton and Spinelli 82-90. The *Amphitrite* sailed on 14 Dec, slightly later than indicated by Stormont. Cargo items listed are derived from the manifest of what arrived at Portsmouth, New Hampshire, on 25 Apr 1777, one of several differing lists given by Morton and Spinelli. **2** Quincy 216-217. **3** MC 21 Dec 3b / GA 21 Dec 2d.

12.20 1 GA 21 Dec 2d. **2** NA SP 78/300 ff406-407 (SF xiv no. 1398). **3** PA 20 Dec 3a.

12.21 1 GEP 24 Dec 4c. **2** MC 24 Dec 3a.

12.22 1 MC 23 Dec 2b. Says he set out for 'Stone Land, in Sussex' but see C 31 Dec for his letter from Drayton. **2** MP 23 Dec 2b. **Fn. Stretton** OBP Jul 1770 280-287 (no. 453, John Stretton) / PA 2 Aug 1770 2d. **3** MC 24 Dec 2b.

12.23 1 GA 26 Dec 2c. **2** LLEP 25 Dec [24 Dec] 610b. **3** MHS Oxnard 23 Dec.

12.24 1 MP 25 Dec 2c. **Fn. Gainsborough** Gainsborough ed. Hayes 133 (no. 79, to William Jackson). **2** LLEP 25 Dec 612b / MC 25 Dec 1d. **3** GA 30 Dec 2c. **4** MP 25 Dec 2b. **5** MC 27 Dec 2d. **6** MC 26 Dec 3a. **7** MC 24 Dec 2b. **8** GEP 24 Dec 4c-d.

12.25 1 SJC 26 Dec 3a / GA 26 Dec 2b / MC 26 Dec 2a. **2** Quincy 217 / MHS Oxnard 25 Dec. **3** Ward and Roberts i 82. **4** Frith 454-457 (Burney letter) / Hill, House, 103 (Lowndes letter, misdated 23 Dec) / Memoirs of Dr Burney ii 121-129 / Burney ed. Troide ii 212-214 (letter dates). **5** GA 25 Dec 2c. **6** PA 25 Dec 2c.

12.26 1 Memoirs of Dr Burney ii 128-129 ('no small' etc) / Frith 457-458 (Burney letter) / Burney ed. Troide ii 214-215. Letter undated. Troide suggests '? 26 December'.

12.27 1 NA SP 78/300 ff445-447, 'No. 124' ('arrived' etc; orig. '*avanturiers*'); ff453-454, 'Most confidential' ('were at'). **2** LC 31 Dec [30 Dec] 627a. **3** MP 28 Dec 2b / MC 28 Dec 1d. **4** Wilkes Diaries 102-104 / MP 2 Jan 1777 2b. Wilkes and his daughter had set out for Bath on 7 Dec. **5** GA 27 Dec 2c.

12.28 1 LC 31 Dec [30 Dec] 627a. **2** MP 30 Dec 2c.

12.29 1 Hill, House, 104 (q) / Burney ed. Troide ii 215. **2** NA SP 78/300 ff477-478, 'Most confidential' (SF xiv no. 1402).

12.30 1 MC 31 Dec 1d (errs in saying Fort Washington was captured 25 Nov and that Germain was at Stoneland) / LGE 30 Dec 1a-3b (qs), 6a-7b / NA SP 78/300 f479 (Weymouth letter, dated 30 Dec at St James's). In placing the Howe dispatches under this date the text follows LGE which says (1a) 'this morning' Captain Gardner arrived in the *Tamar* from New York, and (6a-b) that Captain Mason, of the *Tamar*, 'arrived yesterday at Dartmouth, and came to town this morning with dispatches from Lord Viscount Howe'. However, early reports seem to have circulated on the Sunday: MC 30 Dec 2a says 'It was yesterday currently reported that Fort Washington was taken', and Walpole LJ i 595, written later, has 'Came accounts of the surrender ... of Fort Washington' under 29 Dec. There is also an apparent oddity in the DAR receipt dates: it gives 29 Dec as receipt date of Howe's letter of 30 Nov regarding the fort's capture (x 414 no. 2376), but 30 Dec as receipt date for numerous other dispatches from New York dated from 25 Nov to 3 Dec, including several from Howe and his brother (x 409-417, nos. 2355 etc). **2** AA 5th series iii 926-927 (qs) / DAR x 414 (no. 2377). **3** AA 5th series iii 927-928 (proclamation) / DAR x 414 (no. 2375), xii 257 (letter q). **4** AA 5th series iii 839-840 (q, orig. 'despatched') / DAR x 409 (no. 2355) / Beinecke GJD Nov verso. **5** MP 30 Dec 2b / Letters of Garrick and Countess Spencer 77-79 (Mrs Garrick to Lady Spencer, 28 Dec; Garrick to Lady Spencer, 6 Jan 1777). **6** MP 23 Dec 3c (ad).

12.31 1 Fortescue iii 410 (no. 1944). **2** MC 1 Jan 1777 3d. **3** Tyne 1916 p536 (citing Aff. Étr., Corres. Pol., Angleterre, vol. 519, no. 123). **4** Ward and Roberts i 82. **5** Walpole Letters x 1 (to Lady Ossory, 1 Jan 1777) / Gibbon PL i 299 (to his stepmother Dorothea Gibbon, 25 Dec). **6** Wesley iv 88. **7** MC 31 Dec 1a (ads) / MC 1 Jan 1777 3c. **8** GA 3 Jan 1777 2c. **9** HMC Various vi 128. **10** Wharton ii 242.

MIA 1 Wilkinson i 102-106. **2** AA 5th series iii 1316-1317 (Howe to Germain, dated 20 Dec, New York). **3** Paine 1894 i 169-170. **4** AA 5th series iii 1442-1445 (letter from unnamed officer in American army, and letter from General Washington to President of Congress, both dated 27 Dec, Newtown) / Wilkinson i 131-132.

Afterwards

1 Aitken Life 53-64 ('to acquaint', 'drawn round', 'drawn up'; orig. '*Arathusa*') / MC 5 Feb 1777 3a ('in a most') / ST xx 1333-1341 (Baldwin) / GA 8 Feb 1777 3a-b / MC 7 Mar 1777 2b (Sandwich) / MC 12 Mar 1777 2c.

2 GA 10 Feb 1777 2c / Burgoyne Appendix ii-vii ('Thoughts', dated 28 Feb 1777).

3 GA 9 Apr 1777 2d / Baxter 321 (William Digby journal, 'Thus').

4 Walpole LJ ii 80-81 / MP 4 Dec 1777 2a / MC 4 Dec 1777 2b, 2d ('powerful') / Hutchinson ii 171 (12 Dec 1777).

5 Parl. Hist. xix 913-914 (declaration) / MP 21 Mar 1778 2a / Gibbon PL i 333 (to Holroyd, [21 Mar 1778]).

6 Drinkwater 47, 55, 340 / MP 26 Nov 1781 2a-b / Wraxall Mem. ii 138-139 ('as he would') / MC 21 Mar 1782 2b ('A successor').

7 MP 4 Dec 1782 2a / LG 9 Sep 1783 1a / LG 13 Sep 1783 1a (Hartley).

8 Schama 62 (cost) / Britain and the American Revolution 233-257 (John Cannon, 'The Loss of America').

9 MC 9 May 1777 2c-d / Abington Life 103-104 (q).

10 ANB (Bancroft) / Schaeper 79-80 / Deane Papers ii 24 (to Robert Morris, 16 Mar 1777) / Bemis 476-495 (including Bancroft's memorial to Marquis of Carmarthen, Sep 1784, 'resided') / Lee i 163 (to Theodoric Bland, 13 Dec 1778, Paris, 'Dr').

11 Tyne 1925 p40 (Saratoga) / Loménie 335, 377-384, 452, 457 ('of all') / Lever 2009 p373 (*'Tandem'*).

12 C 14 Mar ('the great king') / ANB (Brant) / Stone ii 249-260 ('dressed') / WEP 24 Dec 1785 2a / GEP 31 Dec 1785 3a / Kelsay 652.

13 WEP 8 Aug 1780 4d (Cargill) / MH 14 Sep 1781 2c (Macheath) / MH 26 Sep 1782 2c (*'à la couche'*) / PA 31 Jan 1783 2c / LC 9 Mar [8 Mar] 1784 233b-c ('She played', 'she was found') / MP 20 Mar 1784 2c ('a trusty' etc) / SJC 11 Mar 1784 3a ('unfortunately', 'was not her own') / MP 13 Mar 1784 2d ('were found') / GEP 18 Mar 1784 2a ('buried').

14 MC 15 May 1778 2a / Fonblanque 375-387, 462-466 / O'Shaughnessy 161 (1782 exchange) / GM 1792 ii 771 / LC 11 Aug [10 Aug] 1792 138b ('a violent') / PA 16 Aug 1792 3d ('Of the gay').

15 ODNB (Charles Burney) / Walker and Oates 313-324.

16 Hill, House, 104-109, 117 ('The great'), 132 ('Fielding'), 138 ('left it') / Burney ed. Troide ii 216-217 / Burney Early Diary ii 163 (Prelude to the Worcester Journal, 'This man') / DA 30 Jan 1778 4c (ad, 'This day is published').

17 Samwell 14-16 ('rushed' etc) / Cook 1784 ii 191, 222; iii 241-242 ('covered' etc); iv 308.

18 GA 30 Jan 1778 3b / MC 8 Oct 1779 3a / MC 9 Oct 1779 2c / MC 27 Jul 1781 1c / GM 1797 ii 890-891 (asses' milk) / GEP 22 Aug 1797 4d ('at a great') / Sumbel iii 44-45 ('sitting').

19 MP 5 Feb 1777 3c (ads, 'superb', 'neat', 'Hogarth'; orig. 'Seve') / LEP 6 Feb 1777 4c / MC 14 Feb 1777 3a ('there will') / MC 19 Feb 1777 3a ('a considerable') / MP 3 Mar 1777 2c.

20 Lennox i 290-291 / SJC 30 Mar 1797 3b (Gloucester Place, house of G. J. Hamilton, Esq.) / LC 4 Apr 1797 320b ('with great'). Assumption made that G. J. Hamilton was a relative.

21 Dodd Trial 19 ('urgent') / Dodd Life 50-51 ('At no period'), 91 n. ('to the house', 'if the') / MP 24 Feb 1777 2d-3c / Fitzgerald, Dodd, 150 ('If I pardon') / Boswell LJ iii 166-167 (19 Sep 1777, 'Dodd's city', 'Depend') / Thicknesse 140 ('carried') / LC 28 Jun 1777 615c ('with his arms', 'even Jack') / MP 28 Jun 1777 2b / Newcastle Mag. i 127-128 (letter from Charles Hutton dated 4 Feb 1822, Hunter). No contemporary source found for king's reported remark linking Dodd and Perreau cases. Holliday (1797, p149) says it was generally reported that Mansfield's advice was to this effect.

22 McClure 238-239.

23 GA 4 Mar 1777 2b / MP 8 Mar 1777 2d / LEP 8 Mar 1777 2a / MP 10 Mar 1777 2b.

24 LC 6 May [5 May] 1777 426c / MC 2 Jul 1777 2a-b / GA 2 Jul 1777 2b-c (Morande qs) / GM (Jul) 1777 pp346-347 / WM (Jul) 1777 pp364-365.

25 LC 14 Aug 1777 160c ('neat') / MC 15 Aug 1777 2a-b (letter in French, dated 10 Aug 1777, Brewer Street) / MC 16 Aug 1777 2a (translation of 10 Aug letter) / Kates 250.

26 GA 2 Feb 1778 3b ('subservient') / Pieces Rélatives 47 (no. 8, dated 10 Feb 1778, d'Éon q, Fr.).

27 Telfer 307-308, 324-333 / Times 4 May 1791 4a (ad) / Times 11 Feb 1792 4b
     (ad) / Times 31 Aug 1796 3d ('before').
28 MP 25 May 1810 3e / MC 29 May 1810 3c-d ('who judged') / Times 25 May
     1810 3b (Copeland certificate, 'inspected').
29 SJC 29 May 1810 2c ('many') / SJC 26 May 1810 2d ('is likely').
30 ODNB (d'Éon) / Times 19 Jun 1810 2a (ad, 'a cast') / MP 25 May 1810 3e.
31 MP 24 Aug 1778 4a ('smoaked') / MP 25 Aug 1778 2b / MP 26 Aug1778 2d /
     General Advertiser 27 Aug 1778 2a-d.
32 GA 29 Aug 1778 3a (q) / MP 29 Aug 1778 2a / ODNB (Morande) / Burrows,
     Morande, 96. Duel accounts differ slightly and, deriving as they presumably do from
     those involved, may well overstate the bravery displayed. Morande's previous record
     rather belies the unflinching picture painted.
33 Kinservik 2007 pp193-195 / Nigh 543-549 / MC 7 Jun 1777 3c ('obliged') / MP
     11 Jun 1777 2b ('another relapse') / GEP 21 Aug 1777 3c (Foote to Brighton on
     18 Aug) / GM (Oct, Nov) 1777 pp508, 534-537 ('where he', 'to spend') / GEP
     25 Oct 1777 4b / LEP 4 Nov 1777 3c / MP 26 Jan 1778 3a (ad, 'capital') / DA
     15 Jan 1778 3c (ad, coach). LC 4 Nov 1777 439a refers to a 'long train of friends'
     at the funeral but this seems to have been an error or diplomatic lie. GA 5 Nov
     1777 3a noted that it 'was attended by very few of those who were his companions
     and admirers through life: an instance of ingratitude scarcely to be equalled. Not
     even the veterans of the stage accompanied our British Aristophanes to the grave.'
34 MC 21 Jan 1779 3a ('that dreadful') / MC 2 Feb 1779 4a ('The procession' etc) /
     MP 2 Feb 1779 2c / SOL xviii 103, 106.
35 ODNB (George III) / Walpole LJ ii 422 (20 Mar 1782) / Fortescue v 425 (no.
     3601, [March 1782], abdication message) / Burney ed. Barrett iv 274-275, 419 /
     MC 18 Feb 1789 3b ('in a state').
36 Montresor Journals 123-124 / Hutchinson ii 167.
37 Wraxall Mem. ii 440 ('from the instant') / Walpole Letters xii 162 (to Lady Ossory,
     9 Feb 1782) / MP 5 Sep 1785 2c ('I have seen').
38 Hickey ii 97-105 (qs), 112 / ODNB (Hickey).
39 Hutchinson ii 159-160, 342, 354 ('his expectations' etc; orig. 'gaspes'), 360.
40 ANB (Oliver, Sewall) / Oxnard 1872 xxvi 7-8 ('as he was') / Boucher Letters ix
     239-240 (to Rev. John James, 25 Jan 1777, q) / Zimmer 363 n.4.
41 Curwen 1972 i xix; ii 1019-1041 (first paragraph qs; letter to Richard Ward,
     16 Sep 1785) / Bentley ii 423-424 / Pynchon 195 ('an hysterick'), 213 / Holyoke
     Diaries 128, 141.
42 ODNB (Jackson) / Oracle 6 May 1795 2c-d ('in his bag') / Werkmeister, Jackson,
     45, 267 / Sampson 25-27 (attorney general's outline of case, 'finding'), 34, 92,
     93, 98-100 ('some acrid') / MP 5 May 1795 2d / Oracle 7 May 1795 3d ('an
     handkerchief').
43 MC 19 Apr 1777 3a ('most superbly') / GEP 25 Oct 1777 1c ('the yacht'). General
     sources for this and subsequent paragraphs: Gervat 161-244 / Kingston Detail 83-127.
44 BM Add. Ms. 73563 f11r (dated 25 Nov 1777 at Riga, 'a wanderer'), f17r (to
     Lord Barrington, Dec 1777, 'Evelyn').
45 MC 17 Apr 1780 2d (15 Apr 1780 trial, 'the validity') / Swinburne i 372 (letter
     dated 29 Nov 1780, 'Mr Meadows') / Kingston Detail 135 (E. Meadows bequest) /
     DUR 23 Jun 1787 3a ('to a trial').
46 Kingston Detail 117 ('As in life') / WEP 9 Oct 1788 2d / Times 25 Oct 1788 3a.

47 MP 22 Nov 1788 2a-2b (letter from William Jackson dated 16 Nov 1788 at Paris: 'deposited'; Lilly confession on 6 Nov 1788, 'about one'). It should be noted that the account given of events in Paris rests heavily on letters to the press from the partisan Jackson. Accounts differ as to duchess's final resting place. Gervat p244 leaves her remains 'in a vault in a Protestant burial ground waiting for a funeral that never happened'. ODNB says she was 'buried in Pierrepont, the ancestral village of the dukes of Kingston in the Île-de-France', a view supported by *Histoire de la vie*, 1789, p139.

48 MP 19 Jan 1789 3c (first part dated 5 Jan 1789, unsigned, probably by Jackson) / MP 22 Jan 1789 3a-b (letter from Jackson dated 5 Jan 1789) / The World 24 Jul 1789 3a ('always travels') / MP 8 Sep 1789 2d / Kingston Detail 116 ('she had always').

49 Lucas ii 254 / Parl. Hist. xxiv 204-205 ('all the privileges') / LC 20 Dec 1783 600a ('had no longer') / Walpole Letters xiv 27 (to Lady Ossory, 4-5 Oct 1787) / Glenbervie i 61 (as noted by her husband, 'expressed') / GM 1792 ii 771-772.

50 Bod. North papers d17 f44 (q) / ODNB (under Lord North) / Burke's Peerage 1869 pp396, 524 / LC 6 Jan [5 Jan] 1780 18c (death of 'the lady of Daniel Wilson', Beatrix Egerton).

51 Cook 1784 ii 91-116 (qs except the two indicated in text as being from Gilbert) / Besant, Cook, 128-132 (Gilbert's journal) / ODNB (Omai).

52 MGL 300 / GM 1809 ii 893 / CWA F6102 / LG 16 Nov 1858 p4851 ('vaults and') / Times 10 Jan 1859 3a / Buckland 215-227 / Labels by F. Buckland on Science Museum items A659629 ('the skin', 'the vertebrae') and A659630 ('the rope'). As a result of subsequent cataloguing by the Science Museum the original labels no longer match the contents, A659629 being skin only and A659630 being vertebrae only. I am grateful to Stewart Emmens of the Science Museum for this information.

53 Hickey iv 324, 447-449.

54 MC 7 Jan 1777 2b-c / MP 21 Jun 1777 2b / MC 18 Jul 1781 1c (ad). The 1781 notice seems consistent with the Oct 1780 death date given in Foster p142.

55 Reynolds, Frederick, i 332-373. Reynolds's account was not published until 1826 and parts of it invite scepticism. He says that Purdon's death was announced in the newspapers in 1787, but a search of the Burney Collection database found no such notice. He adds that his father had part of the Thames dragged, it being 'currently reported among his friends' that Purdon had drowned in the river. It seems unlikely this would have been done in 1787, not least because many people, including Reynolds senior, would have recalled Purdon's disappearance eleven years earlier.

56 Riedesel 75-90, 103, 120, 176 ('liked'; General Phillips, 'What a pity'), 188-189 ('gratified'), 194, 241, 248, 260-262 (Canada, 'for fear'), 282, 292-294 ('and was obliged'), 300.

57 MC 27 Nov 1777 2a-b / MP 2 May 1778 2b (30 Apr 1778 masquerade) / TCM (Mar) 1779 p124 / London Courant 4 May 1781 3d / TCM (Mar) 1783 pp122-123. Roper was also the subject of a tête-à-tête article in TCM (Jul) 1777 pp345-347.

58 MP 2 Jul 1777 2b / Boswell in Extremes 304 (21 Apr 1778) / GA 12 Jun 1779 3b / SJC 28 Oct 1779 4d / WEP 25 Jul 1782 2b.

59 Rudd, Mrs Stewart's Case, 8 ('I voluntarily'), 12-13 ('unable') / Boswell, Applause, 335-340 / Boswell, English, 44-61 ('this *low*'), 137.

60 PA 1 Feb 1793 3b / The Star 7 Dec 1793 3b (orig. 'Pereau') / MC 4 Feb 1797 4a / Smith, Nollekens, ii 233 ('requested').

61 Account given is largely based on: SJC 8 Apr 1779 4c / GEP 10 Apr 1779 1a-b ('Oh! kill me', 'When Lord S—'), 4c ('about 30 years') / MP 17 Apr 1779 3c-d / PA 17 Apr 1779 2b-c ('his hands', 'The lady'). Reports differ as to some details e.g. MC 9 Apr 1779 2c says Fielding did not get to town until 'about five'. Cradock (i 145-146), writing nearly fifty years after the event, gives a slightly different account of Sandwich hearing the news but echoes 'any thing but this'.

62 GA 28 Apr 1779 2d / Brewer 32-33.

63 SJC 10 Apr 1779 3b ('wrapped') / GA 12 Apr 1779 3a ('ordered') / LEP 15 Apr 1779 3a / SJC 8 Apr 1779 4c ('a fine').

64 GEP 20 Apr 1779 4a-b / MC 20 Apr 1779 2a-d (Fox motion) / Brewer 32.

65 Journals, Lords, xxxv 144 (King's Bench judgement, 10 Feb 1777), 213 (Act dissolving marriage) / Debrett's 1840 p636.

66 OBP Feb 1777 pp127-128 (no. 189, Elizabeth West).

67 MC 17 Jun 1777 3a / GEP 21 Aug 1777 3c.

68 GEP 9 Jun 1778 4d / MC 17 Jul 1778 3b ('She was dressed') / PA 21 Sep 1781 3d / PA 3 Apr 1783 4a / GM (Apr) 1783 i 364.

69 Treloar 196-204 (q) / Bleackley, Wilkes, 345-346.

70 Wilkes, Daughter, iv 36, 64 / Wilkes, Correspondence, v 88, 92 (qs) / LC 6 Jan 1798 24c.

71 Wroth 56-66 / Lysons iii 381 (q) / SOL xxiv 66-68.

72 Curwen 1972 ii 685 (12 Nov 1780) / Parker's General Advertiser 6 Jun 1782 1c (ad) / GA 21 Dec 1782 4c (ad).

73 GA 25 Mar 1784 1d (ad, Jacob) / SJC 16 Feb 1786 4b (ad, Jacob) / MP 14 Jun 1785 4c (ad, auction).

74 The World 16 Jan 1788 3d (ad, orig. 'Mr Cornelys') / The World 12 Aug 1791 2c / SOL xxxiii 78-79.

75 Wheatley ii 201.

76 Smith, St Mary-le-Bone, 162-169 / Sands 46, 123-126 / DA 27 Mar 1777 4b (ad, 'the materials') / DA 2 Apr 1777 3c (ad, 'the scenes') / MP 2 May 1777 4c (ad, 'about four') / MC 17 Jun 1777 2d-3a. **Fn. Vulcan** MC 18 May 1772 1b (ad, qs) / MC 10 May 1776 1b (ad).

77 MC 16 Jan 1792 4a (qs) / Wheatley iii 25.

78 Wroth 217 / MP 8 Oct 1805 1c (ad, 'capital') / GM (Jun) 1807 i 558.

79 GA 8 Nov 1783 4b / Smith, St Mary-le-Bone, 153 ('the gallows').

80 Wroth 312-326 / Dickens, Sketches, 211 / The Standard 14 Jul 1859 1e (ad, 'this celebrated') / MP 26 Jul 1859 5b ('The attendance', apparently superfluous 'the last dancing' omitted; 'the once famous') / The Era 31 Jul 1859 11c ('the customary') / Vauxhall sale catalogues, title page ('10,000'), no. 274 ('a transparency') / Times 23 Aug 1859 7f ('monster', 'the entire').

Illustration and caption Sources

Entries in this listing begin with the plate number or page location of the image in this book. For pages with several illustrations, 'a', 'b', et cetera indicate the particular image, the references working from top to bottom and from left to right. There follows a title or brief description and then a note of the source.

Some entries also include further information, for example artist and/or publication details (if these have not been provided in the relevant caption), sources of caption quotations and information, and references to listings in some standard works.

Book sources are listed in the Bibliography. Other images appear courtesy of a range of collections and institutions. Those listed most often are abbreviated as follows:

Folger   Folger Shakespeare Library, Washington DC
LOC   Library of Congress
LWL   Lewis Walpole Library, Yale University
Met.   Metropolitan Museum of Art, New York
NGAW   National Gallery of Art, Washington DC
NYPL   New York Public Library
PC   Private collections
RM   Rijksmuseum, Amsterdam
YCBA   Yale Center for British Art

Other abbreviations used:
eng.   engraved (by) / engraving
fp   facing page
frontis. frontispiece
n.d.   print lacks publication date
pl.   plate
pub.   published (by) / publication

Images from the Folger Shakespeare Library are used under a Creative Commons Attribution-ShareAlike 4.0 International Licence and those from the Wellcome Collection are used under a Creative Commons Attribution 4.0 International Licence.

Jacket

Front cover 'Noddle-Island or How are we decieved' [*sic*]. © The Trustees of the British Museum. All rights reserved. Pub. M. Darly, Strand, 12 May 1776. BM Sat. no. 5335. Satire on the evacuation of Boston, news of which had arrived ten days earlier. 'How' in title is a pun on 'Howe'.

The other jacket images also appear within the book and details can be found in the relevant entry in this listing as follows. *Front flap* Frontispiece. *Spine* p184 ('Boreas'). *Back cover* p53 (Ann Brown), Plate 22 (Molesworth), p435 (Lady Frances Manners), p297 (Joseph Brant), p323 (Duchess of Kingston). *Back flap* Plate 14 (Ranelagh), p262 (sedan chair).

Plates

1   'Can you forbear Laughing'. LWL. BM Sat. no. 5396 ('[P. Dawe?]').
2   Queen Charlotte by Benjamin West, 1777. YCBA. Erffa and Staley 468, 469 (no. 555), 473. A copy of a portrait probably painted in 1776.

3   The Duchess of Devonshire by Sir Joshua Reynolds, 1776. © Courtesy of the Huntington Art Collections, San Marino, California. Mannings i 124 (no. 327).
4   Elizabeth, Countess of Derby, by George Romney, 1776-1778. Met. Kidson i 185-186 (no. 366).
5   Earl and Countess of Derby and their son Edward, by Angelica Kauffman, *c.* 1776. Met.
6   'The Copley Family' by John Singleton Copley, 1776-1777. Courtesy NGAW. C 1 Apr.
7   Mrs Abington as Miss Prue, by Sir Joshua Reynolds, 1771. YCBA. C 29 Nov. Mannings i 55-56 (no. 29).
8   'Colonel Guy Johnson and Karonghyontye (Captain David Hill)' by Benjamin West, 1776. Courtesy NGAW. Erffa and Staley 523-524 (no. 647).
9   'A Sunday Concert' by Charles Loraine Smith. LWL. BM Sat. no. 6125.
—   Decorations below 'A Sunday Concert': History of North America, 1776, p75.
10 Carlini, Bartolozzi and Cipriani, after J. F. Rigaud. YCBA. Chaloner Smith iii 1253-1254.
11 'The Portraits of the Academicians of the Royal Academy', after a painting by Zoffany. YCBA. Chaloner Smith i 243-244. Webster 252-259.
12 'A General Prospect of Vaux Hall Gardens', 1751. YCBA. Eng. J. S. Muller after Samuel Wale. n.d. Later impression or state of a print pub. 1751. Coke and Borg 68-69.
13 Vauxhall by Thomas Rowlandson, *c.* 1784. YCBA. BM Sat. no. 6853 (print after a variant).
14 'Ranelagh House & Gardens with the Rotunda at the Time of the Jubilee Ball'. YCBA. Thomas Bowles after John Maurer. n.d. Probably a later impression or state of a print pub. 1751.
15 'The Bread and Butter Manufactory, or the Humors of Bagnigge Wells'. YCBA. John Raphael Smith after John Sanders. Pub. 15 Jan 1773. BM Sat. no. 5090 (earlier impression, pub. 15 Jun 1772).
16 'The Pantheon in Oxford Street', 1772. YCBA. William Humphrey after Edward Edwards.
17 'An Evenings Invitation; with a Wink from the Bagnio'. LWL. Date erased. BM Sat. no. 5219.
18 'A view of Kennington Common' by Samuel Hieronymus Grimm, 1776. YCBA.
19 'View at Chelsea on the 1st of August' by Edward Francis Burney. YCBA.
20 Blackfriars Bridge with St Paul's Cathedral beyond, by William Marlow, between 1770 and 1772. YCBA. It seems likely that Garrick owned this painting: the caption of a print apparently derived from it says it is 'from a picture in the possession of David Garrick Esqr.' For the print see p175.
21 Whitehall, looking north, by William Marlow, *c.* 1775. YCBA. PA 22 May 1776 2d.
22 'I. Calculator Esqr.' (John Molesworth), 1776. LWL. BM Sat. no. 5360. C 21 Oct.

Illustrations within the text

Frontis. 'The Female Combatants'. LWL. Publisher and place of publication unknown.
xii   Duchess of Devonshire. Lichtenbergs Briefe i 244 (letter dated 12 Nov 1775).
xiii Detail from 'Liberty Triumphant'. NYPL. n.d. Print's references to 'Poplicola' and 'Capt Lorings vessel' suggest publication in America early in 1774.

fp1 George III, after Zoffany. LOC. Pub. 1 Sep 1794. Webster 237-240.
2 Grosvenor-Cumberland Trial. LWL. n.d. BM Sat. no. 4845 ('probably from a magazine', [1770]).
3 Queen Charlotte and the royal children. Smith 1931 pl. 81. Erffa and Staley 469-471 (no. 556).
4 Map of European settlements. LOC.
6 Boston 'Massacre'. Met.
7 'The able Doctor'. LWL. LM (Apr) 1774 fp165. BM Sat. no. 5226.
8 'Bostonians paying the Excise-man'. Met. BM Sat. v 169.
9 'Society of Patriotic Ladies'. Met. BM Sat. v 197.
10 Lord North as Colossus. LWL. LM (Nov) 1774 fp520, p520 (q). BM Sat. no. 5242.
13a Political cartoon for 1775. LWL. WM (Apr) 1775 fp209. BM Sat. no. 5288.
13b Bunker Hill. Barnard fp687. 'Drawn by Mr Millar'.
17 Lord North, after Nathaniel Dance. NYPL. Eng. Thomas Burke. Pub. 1775. Wraxall Mem. i 361-362.
18 Lord Suffolk by Reynolds. Spielmann i pl. 49. Mannings i 267 (no. 950).
19 Lord George Germain, after Romney. YCBA. Eng. John Jacobé. Pub. 1 Nov 1780. Wraxall Mem. i 384-388. Kidson i 234-235 (no. 495).
21 Lord Sandwich, after Zoffany. NYPL. Webster 97.
22a William Eden. NYPL. Eng. T. Holloway. n.d.
22b Lord Mansfield. YCBA. Pub. David Martin, Dean Street, Soho, 1 Mar 1775.
24 Fox by James Sayers. LWL. Pub. 6 Apr 1782. BM Sat. no. 6054.
25 Burke by James Sayers. LWL. Pub. 6 Apr 1782. BM Sat. no. 6055.
27a Wilkes by Hogarth. YCBA. Pub. 16 May 1763. BM Sat. no. 4050.
27b Wilkes and daughter, by Zoffany. Bleackley, Wilkes, frontis. Webster 386-388.
27c Wilkes as lord mayor. LWL. Eng. William Dickinson. Pub. at Mrs Sledge's, Henrietta Street, 9 Nov 1774.
28 General Howe, 1777. NYPL. By fictional mezzotinter 'Charles Corbutt'. BM Sat. no. 5405.
30 'Lieut. Genl. John Burgoyne'. NYPL. n.d. Possibly from *Hibernian Magazine*, 1777. LG 26 Mar 1776 2b (promotion).
32 Vergennes. LOC. Eng. Edme Bodinet. n.d.
36 Mrs Abington as the Comic Muse. RM. Eng. James Watson *c.* 1769. Mannings i 55 (no. 28). Original painting is at Waddesdon Manor, with face and part of dress repainted 1772-1773.
38 Cornelys trial, 1771. OM (Mar) 1771 fp98. BM Sat. no. 4929.
39 'The Whimsical Duet' (Ann Catley and dog). OM (Mar) 1773 fp104. BM Sat. no. 5202.
40 Duchess of Devonshire by Jeremiah Meyer. Williamson fp24 (where attributed to Richard Cosway).
41 Sir John Fielding in robes. Leslie-Melville fp146.
43 Foote, after Reynolds. YCBA. Eng. T. Blackmore. Pub. 4 Jun 1771. Mannings i 198-99 (no. 656).
45a Gabrielli. LWL. TCM (Apr) 1776 fp177. BM Sat. no. 5349.
45b Garrick as Macbeth. PC. Printed for R. Sayer, 53 Fleet Street, and J. Smith, 35 Cheapside, 1769.
45c Garrick by Nathaniel Dance. Parsons fp154 (q on rather remote authority of a note by W. E. Image, who married a goddaughter of Garrick's niece Kitty).

47 Omai, after William Hodges. Cook, Voyage towards South Pole, i fp169. Eng. J. Caldwall (or Caldwell).
49a Reynolds self-portrait. Waterhouse pl. 160. Mannings i 50 (no. 18).
49b Sheridan. Armstrong fp64.
50 *Duenna* scene. Johnson's England ii fp184.
51 Elizabeth Sheridan as St Cecilia. YCBA. Mannings i 412-413 (no. 1614, Walpole q). Leslie and Taylor ii 552 (letter dated 20 Jan 1790, 'It is').
53 Ann Brown as Clara. YCBA. Pub. W. Humphrey. Chaloner Smith iii 1252-1253.
54a Robert Perreau. NYPL. LM (Jun) 1775 fp304.
54b Mrs Rudd and Daniel Perreau. LWL. LM (Jul) 1775 fp356.
56 Mrs Rudd on trial. Bleackley, Scaffold, fp61. Eng. Gaetano Bartolozzi (son of Francesco). Pub. 15 Dec 1775.
57 Perreaus on trial. Bleackley, Scaffold, fp39. Pub. 22 Jan 1776.
58 Elizabeth Chudleigh as Iphigenia. Melville fp8. BM Sat. no. 3030.
60 Elizabeth Chudleigh, after Reynolds. Walpole to Mann iii frontis. Eng. S. Bull. Mannings i 133-134 (no. 367) suggests date no earlier than late 1750s on basis of costume and hairstyle. Gervat, picture caption, gives date of 1740s.
65 'Married Maid of Honour'. LWL. BM Sat. no. 5319.
69a D'Éon and stockbrokers. LWL. OM (Aug) 1771 fp56. BM Sat. no. 4881.
69b Morande. Robiquet, frontis. n.d. Eng. Lenain. Pelleport 36 (q, Fr.).
71 'French Lawyer in London' (Morande). LWL. BM Sat. no. 5246.
72 Beaumarchais by Bosio. Met.
76 'A New Plan of London' &c., 1772; also the twelve subsequent sections derived from it, N1(p78) to S6 (p182). Noorthouck. Eng. Ashby.
79 Tyburn turnpike. YCBA. H. J. Schutz after Thomas Rowlandson. Pub. 1798.
81a Tyburn by Hogarth. Hogarth's Drawings pl. 48. MGL 259-261.
81b Marylebone Gardens. Photo © Birmingham Museums and Art Gallery. Wroth 98.
83 Pantheon exterior. Harrison fp533.
84a, b, c Pantheon interior plus two details. RM. Eng. Richard Earlom. Pub. 15 Aug 1772. BM Sat. no. 5091 (a later impression, pub. 30 Aug 1772).
85 Romney self-portrait. Ward and Roberts i frontis. Kidson ii 501-503 (no. 1119).
87 Dr Dodd by table. Fitzgerald, Dodd, frontis. n.d.
88 Angelica Kauffman. RM. Eng. Bartolozzi. Pub. 1780. Mannings i 284-285 (no. 1026).
89a Golden Square. LWL. By Sutton Nicholls. Pub. for Stow's Survey.
89b Cornelys masquerade characters. LWL. OM (Feb) 1771 fp64. PA 9 Feb 1771 2b. BM Sat. no. 4928.
91 British Museum. Harrison fp396.
93a Foundling Hospital. LWL.
93b Foundling Hospital chapel. YCBA. Pub. 7 Jan 1774.
94 Covent Garden from south. LWL.
95 'Humours of May Day'. LOC. Pub. Sayer and Bennett, 53 Fleet Street, 1 Aug 1778.
96 Covent Garden arches. YCBA. Eng. Edward Rooker. Pub. 1 Jan 1777 but an earlier impression is dated 1768. MGL 139 (where attributed to Paul Sandby).
97 Bow Street public office. Malefactor's Register iii frontis.
98 Drury Lane Theatre, auditorium. Adam Works ii no. 5 pl. vii.
99 Drury Lane Theatre, Bridges Street facade. Adam Works ii no. 5 pl. vi.

101a Lyon's Inn. Chancellor, Strand, fp253.
101b St Mary le Strand. YCBA. Detail.
103 St Sepulchre's. Harrison fp481.
104a Rocque detail (Newgate). LOC.
104b Newgate windmill. Gordon 171. n.d.
104c Mr Akerman. Griffiths, Newgate, i 307.
105 Newgate plan etc. Howard fp152. Spaces between title etc and images reduced.
106 Old Bailey Sessions House. Harrison fp484.
107a St Mary le Bow. YCBA. Detail. Pub. 1754 for Stow's Survey.
107b Surgeons' Hall. Harrison fp484.
109a Rocque detail (Fleet Street). LOC.
109b Temple Bar. Harrison fp536. Adjusted (traitors' heads removed).
109c The Wax Work. Chancellor, Fleet Street, fp33. After J. T. Smith. n.d.
111 Dr Johnson's house in Bolt Court. YCBA. n.d.
112a 'Humours of the Fleet'. LWL. Possibly 1760s. BM Sat. no. 3049 ([1749], an earlier impression).
112b Bridewell. Chancellor, Fleet Street, fp65 ('From a print by Sutton Nicholls, 1725').
113 Belle Sauvage. PC. Eng. Robert Laurie. Chaloner Smith ii 803. BM Sat. no. 5530. MGL 57. Accounts differ as to identity of some figures and BM Sat. places the scene at the Globe tavern in Fleet Street. However, London Metropolitan Archives has an impression pub. 1 Nov 1778 with printed title 'Court of Equity, Bell-Savage Ludgate-Hill'.
115a St Paul's School. YCBA.
115b Sadler's Wells. YCBA. Eng. William Wise, after a drawing by R. C. Andrews. Pub. 4 Jun 1814.
115c Smallpox Hospital. Harrison fp361.
117 Dancing Academy. LWL. BM Sat. no. 4250.
119a Rocque detail (Poultry etc). LOC.
119b Mansion House. Noorthouck fp588.
121a Royal Exchange walks plan. Harrison 214.
121b Royal Exchange arcades. Chancellor, XVIIIth Century, 175. Eng. Bartolozzi, 1788, after John Chapman and Philippe de Loutherbourg.
123 Lottery wheel, 1776. Ewen fp128.
124a Lottery drawing, 1780. Ewen fp204.
124b Bethlehem Hospital. RM. Thomas Bowles after John Maurer. Pub. 10 Sep 1747.
127 London Hospital. YCBA. J. B. C. Chatelain and W. H. Toms after William Bellers. Pub. 1 May 1753.
129a Kingston House. Country Life (20 Mar) 1937 p300.
129b Chelsea Bridge. Harrison fp557.
130 Rocque detail (Ranelagh). LOC.
131a Ranelagh rotunda (interior). LWL. Eng. Nathaniel Parr. n.d.
131b Chelsea Hospital from the river. LWL. n.d.
133a Elizabeth Montagu. YCBA. Mannings i 337 (no. 1270).
133b Lord Lyttelton. Chaloner Smith iii fp1386. Eng. Charles Townley. Pub. 28 Nov. 1781.
133c George Selwyn. Walpole Letters iii fp405.
133d General Paoli. RM. Eng. Jacob Houbraken, 1769.

135 Green Park reservoir. Chancellor, XVIIIth Century, 51. MGL 72.
136 Horwood detail (Berkeley Square). NYPL.
138 Opera house in Haymarket. Smith, Curiosities, pl. 97. Eng. Charles John Smith.
139a Leicester Square. YCBA.
139b Burney house. Hill, House, fp2. n.d. but appears as pl. 51 in Smith, Curiosities, 1840. Image adjusted to remove later addition of 'Orange Street Chapel' from facade.
140 The king's stables in the Mews. YCBA. Eng. Benjamin Cole. n.d.
141 Royal Academy exhibition, 1771. YCBA. Richard Earlom after Charles Brandoin. Pub. 20 May 1772. BM Sat. no. 5089.
143a Patience Wright. LM (Nov) 1775 fp556.
143b Horwood detail (Pall Mall etc). NYPL. Numbers added.
144 James Christie caricature. LWL. Pub. 1 Jan 1782. BM Sat. no. 6101.
145a Gainsborough by Zoffany. Whitley, Gainsborough, frontis. Webster 260.
145b Schomberg House. Whitley, Artists, ii fp114.
147 Pall Mall and St James's Palace. YCBA. By Thomas Bowles.
148 St James's Palace and the Mall. PC. Eng. Benjamin Cole. n.d.
149 Queen's Palace. YCBA. LM (Jul) 1762 fp352.
150 Queen's sedan chair. Bolton ii 302. Eng. P. Begbie. Pub. 1775.
153 Rocque detail (Westminster). LOC.
155a Westminster Hall interior, before 1739. LWL. C. Mosley after H. Gravelot. n.d.
155b Westminster Hall interior, 1809. YCBA. Pub. 1 Dec 1809.
156 House of Commons from river. YCBA. T. Simpson after Samuel Wale. n.d.
157a House of Commons interior. LWL. Eng. John Pine. Pub. 29 Sep 1749.
157b Westminster from the river. Smith, Antiquities, fp145. Etched by J. T. Smith after an earlier drawing. Pub. 1 Jan 1805.
159a Whitehall, 1793 plan. SOL xiv pl. 61.
159b Treasury. Noorthouck fp721. By B. Green.
160 Horse Guards by S. H. Grimm. YCBA. n.d.
161a Rocque detail (Whitehall). LOC. Adjusted (Holbein Gate, demolished 1759, removed).
161b Admiralty. Bolton i 37. Eng. D. Currego. Pub. 1775.
163a Banqueting House. YCBA. Detail from view of Whitehall.
163b Northumberland House and Charing Cross. YCBA. Attributed to William James, c. 1759.
165a St Martin in the Fields. YCBA. Pub. John Bowles. n.d.
165b York Buildings terrace. PC. Eng. for *The Modern Universal British Traveller*, 1779.
167a Astley's (exterior). YCBA. Eng. Charles John Smith. n.d.
167b Lambeth Palace. Maitland ii fp1386. Eng. Benjamin Cole. n.d.
167c Horwood detail (Vauxhall). NYPL.
168a Vauxhall, with the Grand Walk. GM (Aug) 1765 fp356.
168b 'Citizen at Vauxhall'. LWL. Gabriel Smith after Samuel Collings. Pub. 1 Jul 1784. BM Sat. no. 6741.
169 Adelphi. YCBA. Eng. Benedetto Pastorini. Caption quotation is from the print.
170 Savoy Prison. YCBA. Eng. J. T. Smith. Pub. 1 Jan 1793.
171a Somerset House, old north front. LWL. Francis Jukes after William Moss.
171b Somerset House, new north front. GM (Jan) 1779 fp1.

172 'Macaroni Print Shop'. LWL. By Edward Topham. Pub. 14 Jul 1772. BM Sat. no. 4701.

173a Somerset House, old river front. YCBA.

173b Somerset House, new river front. YCBA.

175 Blackfriars Bridge. YCBA. Eng. Valentine Green and Francis Jukes. Probably after the painting reproduced as Plate 20.

176a Dog and Duck sign. O'Donoghue 297. n.d.

176b Horwood detail (Magdalen Hospital). NYPL.

177a Magdalen Hospital. Compston fp72. n.d.

177b A Magdalen. Account of the Magdalen Hospital, 5th edition, 1776, frontis. Compston fp60 has earlier version from 3rd edition, 1766.

180 London Bridge. Harrison fp24.

181 Custom House. LWL. Thomas Bowles after John Maurer. Later state of print first pub. 1753.

183a Rag Fair. YCBA. n.d.

183b Thames to the east. Harrison fp577. Detail from 'A New and Correct Map of the Countries Twenty Miles round London' by Thomas Bowen.

184 'Boreas'. LWL. OM (Sep) 1774 fp276. BM Sat. no. 5231.

187 Mrs Yates as Lady Macbeth. Doran ii 126. Probably derived from print pub. J. Smith and R. Sayer, 1769.

189 Boston plan. GM (Oct) 1775 fp493. Title position altered.

191 Ann Brown tête-à-tête. LWL. TCM (Jan) 1776 fp9. BM Sat. no. 5346.

197 Captain Toper (Roper). LWL. TCM (Jul) 1777 fp345. BM Sat. no. 5417.

198 Struggle for rebel banner. LOC. Detail from *Carte du Port et Havre de Boston*, 1776.

200 Thomas Weston. LM (Feb) 1776 fp59. After a painting by Thomas Parkinson, 1772 (detail, in reverse, warts added).

213 Hannah More. Thompson frontis. Eng. E. Scriven. Pub. 4 Jun 1838.

214 Garrick as Abel Drugger, after Zoffany. RM. Eng. John Dixon. Pub. 12 Jan 1771. Webster 206-208.

218 'Lady Betty Bustle'. LWL. Pub. 13 May 1772. BM Sat. no. 5094.

219a Dr Burney. Burney, History of Music, 1789, i frontis. Mannings i 115-116 (no. 290).

219b Orpheus and Eurydice. Burney, History of Music, 1776, i pl. 3 (fp326).

221 Duel with pistols. LWL. *Macaroni and Theatrical Magazine* (Mar) 1773 fp265 ('A Scene in Islington Fields'). BM Sat. no. 5205.

223a Strawberry Hill. LWL.

223b John Howard. Field frontis. After a drawing by Thomas Holloway, *c.* 1788.

223c Horace Walpole. Walpole Letters xii frontis. After a drawing by Thomas Lawrence, 1795.

224 Night watchman. YCBA. Graves i 221.

227a Kew Bridge. Harrison fp569.

227b Skaters on Serpentine. YCBA.

227c London Bridge Water-works. Wellcome Collection. Eng. Benjamin Cole. From the *New Universal Magazine*. n.d.

228 *Common Sense* title page. LOC.

229 Garrick as Sir John Brute, with head-dress. Folger. After J. Roberts. Original frame and titling omitted.

231 Henry Bate. YCBA. Eng. Gainsborough Dupont.
233 Lord Howe. NYPL. By fictional mezzotinter 'Charles Corbutt'. Pub. John Morris, Rathbone Place, 10 Nov 1777. BM Sat. no. 5406.
234 'The Theatrical Dispute'. Folger. 'Garrick and his contemporaries', ART vol. d94 no. 80a. Note in an old hand above image in scrapbook says it shows the disturbance 'upon the 3rd night'.
237 Thomas King. RM. Eng. John Young. Pub. Nov 1803. Webster 414-415.
241a The *Resolution*. Kitson fp354. 'From a drawing in the possession of the Royal Geographical Society.' n.d.
241b Richard Price. LM (May) 1776 fp227.
248 Woman preparing for a ball. YCBA. Pub. Christopher Anstey, probably at Bath. Anstey 34-35 (q). LC 30 Jan [29 Jan] 1776 100b (ad). For other versions see BM Sat nos. 5385, 5386.
249 'Wise Men of Gotham'. LOC. BM Sat. v 216-217.
251 Gibbon. Gibbon, History, vol. 1, 1848, frontis. Eng. J. A. Dean. Mannings i 217-218 (no. 725).
255 'New Fashioned Phaeton'. LWL. Delany ii 197-198.
257a Thomas Linley. Sichel i 440.
257b Mary Linley. Armstrong fp92.
257c Maria Linley. Sichel i fp438. n.d. Black 10-11. ODNB (Thomas Linley and family). Maria was baptised 10 Oct 1763 and died 5 Sep 1784.
259 Lord Stormont. LWL. Pub. 14 Jul 1784. BM Sat. no. 6637.
262a 'The Ladies Ridicule'. LWL. Pub. 17 Jul 1772. BM Sat. no. 4653.
262b 'The Ladies Contrivance'. LWL. After 'Miss Bath'. Pub. 30 Apr 1777. BM Sat. no. 5440.
265 The Savoir Vivre. Country Life (24 Dec) 1932 p716. SOL xxx 441-442 (q).
266 Württemberg coin. PC.
271a Isaac Barré. Walpole ed. Barker iii fp172. Eng. Richard Houston. Pub. 2 Jul 1771.
271b *Wealth of Nations* title page. LOC.
273 Adam Smith. LWL. By John Kay, 1790.
277 River front of old Somerset House. RM. Detail from 'The south east prospect of Westminster' by Thomas Bowles. n.d.
279 Duke of Grafton. LWL. Pub. 14 May 1782. BM Sat. no. 6060.
281 Miss Draper. LM (Aug) 1776 fp400.
283 Boswell in profile. Roberts 1919 fp70. Reversed to accord with original portrait which is at Gunby Hall, Lincolnshire.
284 Cockpit. LWL. Pub. 5 Nov 1759. BM Sat. no. 3706.
287 'Preposterous Head Dress'. LWL. BM Sat. no. 5370.
291a Henry Thrale. LWL. Pub. Matthew Darly, 24 Aug 1772. BM Sat. no. 4691.
291b Mrs Thrale. YCBA. Eng. E. Finden, 1835. Mannings i 443-444 (no. 1750).
293a Old Somerset House, outer courtyard. LWL. Francis Jukes after William Moss. Pub. 31 Mar 1777.
293b Demolition of old Somerset House. YCBA. GM (Jan) 1798 fp9. Thomas Medland after Riley. GM p9 refers to the lead sheeting.
294 Macaroni Dress for 1776. LWL. Detail. 'Engrav'd for the New Lottery Magazine. Macaroni Dresses for 1740 and 1776'. n.d. but probably 1776. '*New Lottery Magazine*' not traced, so perhaps from *The Lottery Magazine, or compleat fund of literary, political, and commercial knowledge*, published from *c.* 1776 to *c.* 1777.

295 'Hint to the Ladies'. Paston pl. 22. BM Sat. no. 5395.

297 Joseph Brant, after Romney. Russell i pl. 37.

299 Bodysnatcher. LWL. Pub. 1 May 1773. BM Sat. no. 5119 (where attributed to William Austin).

301 Albany Charles Wallis. Courtesy Lehigh University Art Galleries, Teaching Museum. Not in Mannings.

303 Silas Deane. LOC. After Pierre Eugène du Simitière.

305 Edmund Burke, after Romney. Russell i pl. 32. Kidson i 105-106 (nos. 181, 182). See source note 1 for Chronicle 2 Apr.

309 Maundy service. YCBA. Eng. James Basire, 1777, after S. H. Grimm.

312 Grinning Match. LOC. Pub. 5 Sep 1775.

315 Garrick as Abel Drugger (boxing scene). BBT. J. Thornthwaite after J. Roberts.

320 Kingston trial, view framed by pillars. LWL. Detail. n. d.

321 Kingston trial layout. LC 18 Apr [17 Apr] 1776 p372.

322 'Iphigenia's late Procession'. YCBA. BM Sat. no. 5362 (where attributed to John Hamilton Mortimer). Bears pub. date 15 Apr but title suggests publication after trial's completion. Original caption misquotes MP 16 Apr 2a and cites 'May 16' issue in error.

323 Duchess of Kingston taken at the bar. LWL. Eng. Taylor. Pub. 20 May 1776.

325 Kingston trial ticket. Griffiths, Mysteries, ii 136.

334 Joseph Brant ('The Mohawk Chief'). LOC. LM (Jul) 1776 fp339.

335 Housebreakers. Met. 'Aquatinta by T. Malton'. Pub. 1 Aug 1791.

337 Molyneux and Quarme. LWL. Pub. 17 Jun 1782. BM Sat. no. 6074.

343 'Mrs Rudd. Drawn from the Life.' TCM (Sep) 1775 fp481.

346a Garrick (thumbs portrait). PC. Mannings i 211 (no. 705).

346b 'Tygers at Play'. YCBA.

347 Omai, after Reynolds. YCBA. Mannings i 357 (no. 1363).

349a Lord North by Sayers. LWL. Pub. 14 May 1782. BM Sat. no. 6063.

349b Richard Rigby. LWL. Pub. 6 Apr 1782. BM Sat. no. 6052.

353 Garrick as Sir John Brute, after Zoffany. YCBA. Eng. John Finlayson. Pub. 1 Nov 1768. Webster 190-191.

355 'May-Day in London'. NGAW. Pub. 1 Jun 1784. BM Sat. no. 6740.

357 Lady Grosvenor. YCBA. Eng. William Dickinson. Torpedo 5. Attribution to Cotes based on handwritten inscription on print at Fitzwilliam Museum, Cambridge, and style.

359 *London Gazette* read in coffee-house. LWL. BM Sat. no. 5923 (etching after this drawing, pub. 15 Oct. 1781).

361 Louisa Stormont. YCBA. Kidson ii 553 (no. 1245). Ward and Roberts i 82.

365 Bunkers Hill head-dress. LOC. BM Sat. no. 5330. Pub. date lacking from image as seen. BM Sat. suggests 1 Mar 1776 with the note, 'So dated in a contemporary hand.' LOC online listing says 19 Apr.

367 Edward Shuter as Falstaff. Folger. After Thomas Parkinson. Original frame and titling omitted.

375 Dr Johnson. Chaloner Smith i fp219. Mannings i 281-282 (no. 1014).

377 Warren Hastings. YCBA. Mannings i 247-248 (no. 861). Chaloner Smith iv 1558. YCBA version lacks date and is possibly a later impression.

378 'Vauxhall Syren'. LWL. TCM (Aug) 1776 fp401, 401-403 (q). BM Sat. no. 5353.
ODNB (Brent). Identified by Horace Bleackley as Charlotte Brent but apparently
in error as it is impossible to reconcile the facts of Brent's life as noted in the ODNB
with the account given in TCM. For example, TCM says the besotted envoy had
a taste for young girls and refers to him currently attending Vauxhall 'every night
whilst she sings', but in 1776 Brent was aged 42, married, decayed in her looks,
and living in Dublin. The envoy 'Count de B—' was presumably Ludovico, Count
de Belgioioso, who represented Habsburg Austria.

379 Vauxhall Orchestra. YCBA. Frontis. to J. Bew's *Vocal Magazine, or British Songster's
Miscellany*, 1778. Coke and Borg 210.

381 Wick House, Richmond. Dobson ii fp89.

382 Six of the royal children. RM. Erffa and Staley 476-477 (no. 570).

387 Captain Cook. Wellcome Collection. Samwell 27.

389 Kew Palace. Met.

390 Lady Granby. LM (Mar) 1776 fp128.

394 Frederika Riedesel. LOC. Detail. Original portrait usually attributed to Johann
Heinrich Wilhelm Tischbein, but he was born in 1751 and Riedesel married in 1762.
Tischbein's uncle, Johann Heinrich the elder (born 1722), is perhaps more likely.

399 Samuel Curwen. Peabody Essex Museum, Salem. Curwen 1972 i fp260.

400 'Overflowing of the Pitt'. LWL.

401 'The Pit Door'. Met. Pub. date erased on original print. Online listing describes
as 'after Robert Dighton the elder'. BM Sat. no. 6769. Sheridan identification is
from British Museum online listing.

405 *The Wonder* playbill. Hampden 288.

409 Gibbet. YCBA. Detail from 'Crowd by a Gibbet'. n.d.

410 Ranelagh, with canal. PC. Eng. C. Grignion. Pub. 28 Feb 1752. PA 7 Jul 1762
3b (pavilion).

411 Ranelagh masquerade ticket. LWL. MJ 18 Jun [17 Jun] 1776 2a-c.

413 Mrs Siddons as the Tragic Muse. YCBA. Eng. Francis Haward. Pub. 4 Jun 1787.
Mannings i 414-415 (no. 1619).

415 Duchess of Cumberland. YCBA. Eng. James Watson. Pub. 1 Dec 1773. Walpole
Letters viii 104 (to Sir Horace Mann, 7 Nov 1771). Mannings i 251 (no. 879).

417 'Commodore Hopkins'. NYPL. BM Sat. no. 5336.

419 Tower of London. YCBA. Eng. J. C. Stadler. Pub. 1 Jun 1795.

429a Baretti. Chaloner Smith iv fp1568. Eng. John Watts. Pub. 18 Jul 1780.
Mannings i 72-73 (no. 107).

429b Streatham Park. Broadley fp10. n.d.

434 Lady Tyrconnel tête-à-tête. LWL. TCM (Feb) 1777 fp65. BM Sat. no. 5412.

435 Lady Frances Manners with mask. LWL. Pub. 1 Feb 1772. Chaloner Smith
ii 917-918.

441 'March of the Train Bands'. LWL. BM Sat. no. 5438.

443 Elephant. GM (Oct) 1763 fp509. PA 9 Feb 1776 2b.

445a Tottenham Court Road turnpike. YCBA. H. J. Schutz after Rowlandson.

445b Foote in *The Devil upon Two Sticks*. PC. Pub. for J. Smith, 35 Cheapside, and
R. Sayer, 53 Fleet Street, 1 Oct 1769. Part of a series, *Dramatic Characters, or
Different Portraits of the English Stage*, published 1769-1773.

447 Fanny Burney. NYPL. Eng. C. Turner. Pub. 1840.

448 Lady Tyrconnel by Reynolds. Connoisseur vii (Sep-Dec 1903) 12. Mannings i 121 (no. 315).

450 Eclipse. GM (Jun) 1776 p269.

453a Declaration of Independence read. Barnard fp689. Noble after Hamilton.

453b George III statue pulled down. LOC. n.d.

454 Eels. Philosophical Transactions 1775 pt. 2 fp406 (pl. 1, figures 1 and 2).

455 Doggett race. YCBA. Thought to date from 1805-1810.

461 Anne Damer. YCBA. Mannings i 159 (no. 477).

463 Prince of Wales and brother. RM. Eng. Valentine Green. Erffa and Staley 474-475 (no. 564).

464 Cricket. YCBA. Watercolour by Robert Dighton.

471 Holland smock race. LWL. Detail. BM Sat. no. 4598.

473 'Miss Carolina Sulivan'. LOC.

479 Chevalier d'Éon in male and female attire. LWL. LM (Sep) 1777 fp443. BM Sat. no. 5427.

481 'Scene at Vauxhall Stairs'. LWL. Pub. 1 Jan 1779.

482 'Vauxhall Demi-rep'. LWL. Pub. 20 Aug 1772. BM Sat. no. 5027.

484 'City Foulers'. Met. n.d. BM Sat. no. 6883A. An earlier print version, by John Jones, was pub. 1785.

485 Duellists in coffee-house. LWL. Bears title 'The Duellists'. n.d.

487 'Martial Macaroni' (Horneck). LWL.

488 Bartholomew Fair (fan detail). YCBA.

496 Lord Shelburne. LWL. Pub. 14 May 1782. BM Sat. no. 6062.

499 Edward Shuter as Lovegold. BBT.

503 Nancy Parsons. YCBA. Bears apparently fictional creator names 'R. Renold' and 'R. Housman'. Mezzotint, probably by James Watson, after two portraits by Tilly Kettle, one of Nancy Parsons (face and hair), the other of Ann Elliot (dress, peacock, etc). n.d.

507 Queen Charlotte and her eldest daughter the princess royal. RM. Eng. Valentine Green. Pub. 25 Mar 1778. Erffa and Staley 473 (no. 562).

509 Hat. Harrison 499.

512 Plan of New York. LOC.

513 'News from America'. LWL. LM (Nov) 1776 fp599. BM Sat. no. 5340.

515 'Unwelcome Customer' (Bull in milliner's shop). Paston pl. 200. Eng. J. Caldwell. Pub. 17 Aug 1772. BM Sat. no. 4605.

519 George Colman. Peake i frontis. Eng. S. Fisher. Mannings i 140 (no. 396).

523 Ann Catley in *Comus*. YCBA. Chaloner Smith i 225.

525 Press gang. LWL. BM Sat. no. 5609.

531 House of Lords interior. LWL. GM (Jan) 1769 fp1.

533a State coach. Smith 1931 pl. 57.

533b Mrs Yates. BBT.

535 Edward Shuter, holding mask. Garrick Club (a later impression, pub. Baldwyn, Catherine Street, Strand, n.d.). Chaloner Smith i 156.

537 New York fire. NYPL. n.d.

541 Theatre interior. Parsons fp90. n.d.

543 Lord Sandwich by Sayers. LWL. Pub. 3 Jul 1782. BM Sat. no. 6076.

551 'Phaetona'. LWL. BM Sat. no 5375.

553 'Cork Rump'. LWL. BM Sat. no. 5381.

557 Samuel Reddish. RM.

561 Mrs Abington as Miss Prue (standing). BBT.

567 Duchess of Northumberland. YCBA. Eng. Edward Fisher, n.d. Mannings i 373 (no. 1431).

569a Lord Percy. YCBA. Eng. Valentine Green.

569b Aitken's fire box. Trial of James Hill 8.

574 'New Road to Riches'. YCBA. Pub. 29 Nov 1784.

575 'Lottery Contrast'. LWL. Pub. 17 Feb 1794. BM Sat. no. 3768 (an earlier state or impression).

577 Mrs Robinson. British Portrait Painters pl. 83. Eng. William Dickinson.

583 St Paul's, Covent Garden. Harrison fp524.

589 'Christmas Gambols'. LWL. Pub. 1 Jan 1785. BM Sat. vi 271.

591a *Evelina*, title page sketch. Hill, House, fp98.

591b and c Fanny Burney handwriting, usual and feigned. Hill, House, fp102, fp106.

593 'Fashionable Dresses'. YCBA.

598 Washington after Trenton. Met. One of several copies Peale painted after his own portrait of 1779. The original and other copies show Washington after the subsequent victory at Princeton on 3rd January 1777.

599 Emblem of America. LOC. George Richardson, *A Collection of Emblematical Figures*, chiefly composed from the iconology of Cesare Ripa, vol. 1, 1777, pl. 16, figure 60, bearing pub. date 23 Nov 1776.

600 Aitken in prison. Aitken Life frontis. Warner 206.

601 Aitken in the dock. LM (Mar) 1777 fp115.

603 'The Blessings of Peace'. LWL. BM Sat. no. 6212.

604 Mrs Abington as Roxalana. YCBA. Eng. J. K. Sherwin. Pub. 1 Feb. 1791. Mannings i 56 (no. 32). YCBA version lacks pub. details.

607 Charles Burney. Dobson iv fp406.

609 Death of Captain Cook. Kitson fp474.

611 Countess of Derby, after Reynolds. YCBA. Eng. William Dickinson. Pub. 1 May 1780. Mannings i 236-237 (no. 813).

613 Dr Dodd in Newgate. LWL. TCM (Jul) 1777 fp377. Title position adjusted.

616 Chevalier d'Éon fencing. LWL. [1787]. After Alexandre-Auguste (or possibly Charles Jean) Robineau. Print has been variously attributed including to Gillray and to Rowlandson.

619 Garrick's death mask. PC.

621 George III in old age. Wellcome Collection. Royal Collection Trust online catalogue entries for RCIN 604480 and RCIN 604483.

628 'Coalition Arms'. LOC. BM Sat. no. 6441.

636 James Hackman. NYPL. Space between image and caption reduced. Appeared as frontis. to *The Case and Memoirs of the late Rev. Mr James Hackman*, 8th edition, 1779.

637 Martha Ray. LWL. Cumberland Letters 228 (orig. 'allways').

640a 'Promenade at Carlisle House'. YCBA. By John Raphael Smith.

640b Old and new Haymarket theatres. YCBA. Dale after Schnebbelie. Pub. 1 Jun 1822.

751 'Noddle-Island'. LWL. Uncoloured version of image listed under Jacket above.

Bibliography

i. Manuscripts

Beinecke Rare Book and Manuscript Library, Yale University

Beinecke Gen Mss file 457 Hannah More letter to Theophila Gwatkin, Adelphi, 17 April [1776]. Describing attendance at trial of the Duchess of Kingston.

Beinecke GJD Guy Johnson Papers, Gen Mss 494, box 1, folder 28 Journal or diary written in Goldsmith's Almanac for 1776

Beinecke GJM Guy Johnson Papers, Gen Mss 494, box 1, folder 29 Memorandum and Account Book with government, officers &c., commencing in 1776

Bodleian Library, Oxford

Bod. North Papers, d16, d17, d25 North family letters

British Library

BM Add. Ms. 11339 Letters and papers relating to the affairs of the Chevalier d'Éon, 1763-1789

BM Add. Ms. 11340 Collection of printed paragraphs, cut out of English newspapers, relating to the Chevalier d'Éon etc, 1776-1777

BM Add. Ms. 11341 Notes and letters relating to the Chevalier d'Éon, Beaumarchais, etc, 1773-1789

BM Add. Ms. 21784 Haldimand Papers ff4-5 Letter from Major John Ross to Captain R. Mathews, 26 Jun 1782. Includes Joseph Brant reference.

BM Add. Ms. 37833 Letters between John Robinson and George III

BM Add. Ms. 73563 Letters from the Duchess of Kingston to Lord Barrington

BM Egerton Ms. 2180, ff1-18 Letters from James Cook to the Rev. John Douglas

BM Egerton Ms. 2672-2673 'Journal of a Voyage to England in 1776, and of a Tour through part of England', followed by accounts of other tours, by Peter Oliver, late chief justice of Massachusetts Bay

City of Westminster Archives

CWA St James's, Piccadilly, Burials, vol. 22

CWA Acc 419/253 St Martin in the Fields. Burial posting book

CWA F6102 St Martin in the Fields. Removal of coffins. Alphabetical list of names on coffins removed from Catacombs B, C, D, E, F, G, H, I, K, L, M, N, O and Vaults no. 1, 2, 3, 4, Vestry, Steeple, Chancel, Portico and various private vaults and deposited into Catacombs B, C and D. May 1859

CWA RB Westminster parish rate books

Folger Shakespeare Library, Washington DC

Folger W.a.104 (13) ff5-11 and W.a.104 (14) ff1-5 Diary of William Hopkins, prompter of Drury Lane Theatre

Huntington Library, San Marino, California

HM 31201, vol. 17 Anna Margaretta Larpent [née Porter] Diaries, 1773-1830. Entries relating to 1776 are from a 'Methodized Journal' which she compiled in 1787, after her marriage to John Larpent, from journals written between 1773 and 1783. Referred to as Anna Porter's diary.

LEWIS WALPOLE LIBRARY, YALE UNIVERSITY

LWL Larpent Anna Margaretta Larpent [née Porter], Account of the Bigamy Trial of the Duchess Dowager of Kingston. In two parts: i) ff1-3, a letter dated 15 April 1776 but added to on the 18th and the 23rd, written to 'Gertrude', presumably a friend; ii) ff4-19, 'A Short Account of the Proceedings on the Trial of the Duchess Dowager of Kingston for Bigamy', apparently written a short time later to be sent to the same recipient.

LONDON METROPOLITAN ARCHIVES

LMA ACC/2371/BC/04/073 Brooks's Betting Book

LMA CLA/047/LJ/13/1776/001 City of London Sessions Papers. Depositions made on 3, 4, 5 January 1776 on the murder of Henry Stubbings

LMA COL/RMD/CE/10/050 List of addresses of privy council members, for the lord mayor's banquet, 1776

LMA DL/C/0177 Consistory Court of London. Allegations, libels and sentence book, 1772-1777

LMA DL/C/0558/12 Consistory Court of London. Elizabeth Chudleigh against Augustus John Hervey. Testimony of Sieur Lazare Claude Morlet, merchant, regarding his visit to the Countess of Bristol in Calais on 26 June 1776

LMA MJ/SP/1776 Middlesex Sessions of the Peace, sessions papers for 1776

MAINE HISTORICAL SOCIETY, PORTLAND, MAINE

MHS Oxnard Edward Oxnard Diaries, 1775-1786. Coll. 1439. Vol. 1 (Journal 1), from 16 August 1775; vol. 2 (Journal 2), from 25 November 1775; vol. 3 (Journal 3), from 28 March 1776; vol. 4 (Journal 4), from 27 September 1776. Folios not numbered. Cited by date alone.

THE MORGAN LIBRARY AND MUSEUM, NEW YORK

Morgan PML 19089 *The Complete Pocket Book, or, Gentleman and Tradesman's Daily Journal, for the Year of our Lord 1776*, with autograph entries by Edward Gibbon

NATIONAL ARCHIVES, KEW

NA ADM 51/4528 Log kept on board the *Discovery* by Lieutenant James Burney, 10 February 1776 – 27 April 1778

NA ADM 51/4529 41. Log kept on board the *Discovery* by Edward Riou, midshipman, 22 February 1776 – 5 March 1778. | 46. Log kept on board the *Discovery* by Lieutenant John Rickman, 16 March 1776 – 29 November 1779.

NA ADM 51/4557 191. Log kept on board the *Resolution* by William Charlton, midshipman, 10 February 1776 – 22 November 1777. | 192. Continuation of the same, 23 November 1777 – 16 February 1779.

NA ADM 51/4559 212. Log kept on board the *Resolution* by John Watts, midshipman, 23 April 1776 – 29 November 1779. | 213. Log kept on board the *Resolution* by George Gilbert, midshipman, 9 April 1776 – 30 September 1777.

NA C 12/1051/2 Chancery. Bill dated 17 May 1774 on behalf of Philip Meadows and Lady Frances Meadows

NA KB 1/20/4 King's Bench Papers. Oath sworn by Samuel Foote and others on 17 May 1776. Annexed are copies of the *The Public Ledger*, 10, 11, 13 and 14 May.

NA KB 21/41 King's Bench. Crown side. Entry Book of Rules, 1774-1778

NA RG 4/4358 Burials, Union Street, Southwark, Deadman's Place
NA SP 78/298, 78/299, 78/300 State Papers. Stormont

ROYAL ACADEMY, LONDON
RA NOR/15 to NOR/22 Letters of James Northcote, 3 January to 4 May 1776

ii. Newspapers

In most cases these have been consulted via the British Library's Burney Collection database of 17th and 18th century newspapers.

Titles were published each morning, Monday to Saturday, unless indicated.

(E) indicates evening papers. These were published three evenings a week, Tuesday, Thursday, Saturday, except LLEP and LP, published Monday, Wednesday, Friday, and WG, published Tuesday and Saturday.

CR	*The Craftsman, or Say's Weekly Journal*
DA	*The Daily Advertiser*
GA	*The Gazetteer and New Daily Advertiser*
GEP	*The General Evening Post* (E)
LC	*The London Chronicle* (E)
LEP	*The London Evening-Post* (E)
LG	*The London Gazette* (government paper published each Tuesday and Saturday)
LGE	*The London Gazette Extraordinary* (occasional, usually for good news)
LLEP	*Lloyd's Evening Post* (E)
LP	*The London Packet, or, New Lloyd's Evening Post* (E)
MC	*The Morning Chronicle, and London Advertiser*
MJ	*The Middlesex Journal, and Evening Advertiser* (E)
MP	*The Morning Post, and Daily Advertiser*
PA	*The Public Advertiser*
PL	*The Public Ledger*
SJC	*The St James's Chronicle, or, British Evening-Post* (E)
WG	*The Westminster Gazette, or, Constitutional Evening-Post* (E)

Other newspapers of earlier and later date:

DUR	*The Daily Universal Register* (later *The Times*)
	The Era
	The General Advertiser (1744-1752)
	The General Advertiser, and Morning Intelligencer, latterly *Parker's General Advertiser, and Morning Intelligencer* (1777-1782)
	The London Courant and Westminster Chronicle
	The London Daily Post, and General Advertiser
MH	*The Morning Herald, and Daily Advertiser*
	The Oracle, Public Advertiser
	The Standard
	The Star
	The Times
WEP	*Whitehall Evening-Post*
	The World

iii. Periodicals

Apart from the *Annual Register* these were published monthly, usually on the first day of the month following (e.g. the June issue was published on 1 July).

Selected volumes and years drawn upon are detailed here but the notes also include occasional references to further volumes of some of these titles.

AR   *The Annual Register, or a View of the History, Politics, and Literature for the year 1776*. First published 25 September 1777. Text used: 4th edition, 1788.

——   *The Critical Review, or, Annals of Literature*, vol. 37, January-June 1774; vol. 41, January-June 1776

GM   *The Gentleman's Magazine, and Historical Chronicle*, vol. xlvi [46], for the year MDCCLXXVI [1776]

LM   *The London Magazine or Gentleman's Monthly Intelligencer*, vol. xlv [45], for the year 1776

OM   *The Oxford Magazine, or Universal Museum*, vol. x [10], January-June 1773

——   *The Political Register and Impartial Review of New Books*, vol. 1, 1767

TCM   *The Town and Country Magazine, or Universal Repository of Knowledge, Instruction, and Entertainment*, vol. v [5] for the year 1773 (anonymous 'Account of England' published in the February to November issues); vol. viii [8] for the year 1776

WM   *The Westminster Magazine, or, The Pantheon of Taste*, vol. v [5], 1777

iv. Printed books &c.

This list includes all other works cited in the source notes, additional books from which illustrations have been drawn, and a few of the other works consulted.

Place of publication is London unless indicated.

[n.d.] indicates no publication date given. Dates and author names in square brackets indicate information lacking from original editions.

AA — *American Archives ... A Documentary History of the English Colonies in North America* ed. Peter Force. 4th series, vols 1-6, Washington DC, 1837-1846; 5th series, vols 1-3, Washington DC, 1848-1853

The A to Z of Georgian London, introduction by Ralph Hyde, London Topographical Society, 1982. Reprints John Rocque's 1747 plan.

The A to Z of Regency London, introduction by Paul Laxton, London Topographical Society, 1985. Reprints William Faden's 1813 revision of Richard Horwood's 1790s plan.

Abington Life — *The Life of Mrs Abington* by the editor of the 'Life of Quin', 1888

Abler, Thomas S., et al., 'Guy Johnson, Benjamin West, and Cohoes Falls: Issues of (Mis)Identification', *New York History*, vol. 89, no. 2, Spring 2008, pp190-203

An Account of the Rise, Progress, and Present State of the Magdalen Hospital ... together with Dr Dodd's Sermons, 5th edition, 1776

Adam Works — *The Works in Architecture of Robert and James Adam, Esquires*, vols 1 and 2, 1778, 1779

Adams, John: *Familiar Letters of John Adams to his wife Abigail Adams, during the Revolution* ed. Charles Francis Adams, Boston, Massachusetts, 1875

Aitken Life — *The Life of James Aitken, commonly called John the Painter, an Incendiary ...*, 2nd edition, Winchester [1777]

Alden, John R., *Stephen Sayre: American Revolutionary Adventurer*, Baton Rouge, Louisiana, 1983

Allen, Ethan: *A Narrative of Col. Ethan Allen's Captivity* , written by himself, Walpole, New Hampshire, 1807

Altick, Richard D., *The Shows of London*, Cambridge, Massachusetts, 1978

The Ambulator, or, The Stranger's Companion in a Tour round London, 1774

American Archives ed. Peter Force — see AA

ANB — American National Biography Online

Andrew, Donna T., and McGowen, Randall, *The Perreaus and Mrs Rudd: Forgery and Betrayal in Eighteenth-Century London*, Berkeley, Los Angeles, 2001

Angelo, Henry: *Reminiscences of Henry Angelo*, 2 vols, 1828, 1830

[Anstey, Christopher] *An Election Ball, in Poetical Letters, from Mr Inkle, at Bath, to his wife at Glocester*, 3rd edition, Bath, 1776

The Antiquary, vol. 4, July to December 1873, 1873. Contributions relating to location of Tyburn gallows, including pp205-206, 239.

Archenholz, M. d' [Johann Wilhelm von Archenholz], *A Picture of England*, Dublin, 1790. Archenholz does not state directly when he was in England but refers (pp99, 135, 137, 145, 251) to witnessing events in 1770, 1775, 1776, 1777 and 1778.

Armstrong, Walter, *Gainsborough and his Place in English Art*, 1898

Asmodeus [n.d.]. Anonymous poem attributed to William Jackson. Usually dated to 1776 but there seems to have been an earlier edition: PA 13 Dec 1775 1d has advertisement saying 'This day is published ...'

Australian Dictionary of Biography ed. Douglas Pike, vol. 1, Carlton, Victoria, 1966. 'Bligh, William', by Alexander Huey, p118 et seq.

Bailyn, Bernard, '1776: A Year of Challenge — A World Transformed', *Journal of Law and Economics*, vol. 19, no. 3, October 1976, pp437-466

Bakewell, Sarah, *The Smart: The Story of Margaret Caroline Rudd and the Unfortunate Perreau Brothers*, 2001

Bangs, Isaac, 'Extract from the Journal of ...', in *Proceedings of the New Jersey Historical Society*, vol. viii [8], 1856-1859, Newark, New Jersey, 1859, pp120-125

Baretti European Mag. — Baretti, Joseph [Giuseppe], 'On Signora Pozzi's Publication of Dr Johnson's Letters'. 'Stricture the First', in *The European Magazine*, vol. 13, May 1788, pp313-317; 'Stricture the Second', in vol. 13, June 1788, pp393-399; 'Stricture the Third', in vol. 14, August 1788, pp89-99.

Baretti, Joseph [Giuseppe], *A Guide through the Royal Academy* [1781]

Barnard, Edward, *The New, Comprehensive and Complete History of England* [1783]

Barrington, Shute (ed.), *The Political Life of William Wildman, Viscount Barrington*, 1815

Baxter, James Phinney, *The British Invasion from the North: The Campaigns of Generals Carleton and Burgoyne from Canada, 1776-1777, with the Journal of Lieut. William Digby*, Albany, New York, 1887

BBT — Bell's British Theatre, consisting of the most esteemed English Plays, 21 vols, 1776-1781

BCE — *Beaumarchais et le Courier de l'Europe* ed. Gunnar and Mavis von Proschwitz, 2 vols, Oxford, 1990

BD — *A Brief Description of the Cities of London and Westminster ... To which are added, Some proper Cautions ...* by Sir John Fielding, 1776. Straight reprint of LWG (see below) with Fielding's Cautions tacked on at the end. Presence of Fielding's name on title page has sometimes led to the whole work being attributed to him in error.

BDA — *A Biographical Dictionary of Actors, Actresses, Musicians, Dancers, Managers and other Stage Personnel in London, 1660-1800* by Philip H. Highfill, Jr., Kalman A. Burnim, and Edward A. Langhans, 16 vols, Carbondale, Illinois, 1973-1993

Beaglehole, J. C., *The Life of Captain James Cook*, Stanford, California, 1974

Beauchamp, William M., *Metallic Ornaments of the New York Indians*, New York State Museum, Bulletin 73, Albany, New York, 1903

Beaumarchais Correspondance ed. Brian N. Morton, vol. 2, Paris, 1969

Beaumarchais et le Courier de l'Europe — see BCE

Bell, Walter George, *Fleet Street in Seven Centuries*, 1912

Bell's British Theatre — see BBT

Bemis, Samuel Flagg, 'British Secret Service and the French-American Alliance', *American Historical Review*, vol. 29, no. 3, April 1924, pp474-495

Bentham, Jeremy: *The Correspondence of Jeremy Bentham*, vol. 1, 1752–1776, ed. Timothy L. S. Sprigge, 1968

[Bentham, Jeremy] *A Fragment on Government, being an examination of what is delivered on the subject of Government in general, in the Introduction to Sir William Blackstone's Commentaries*, 1776

Bentley, William: *The Diary of William Bentley, D.D.*, Pastor of the East Church, Salem, vol. 2, Salem, Massachusetts, 1907

Berry, Helen, *The Castrato and his Wife*, Oxford, 2011

Besant, Walter, *Captain Cook*, 1890

Biographia Dramatica, or, A Companion to the Playhouse, originally compiled by David Erskine Baker, continued by Isaac Reed and Stephen Jones, 3 vols, 1812-1813

A Biographical Dictionary of Actors — see BDA

Black, Clementina, *The Linleys of Bath*, 1911

Bleackley, Horace, *Casanova in England*, 1923

Bleackley, Horace, *Life of John Wilkes*, 1917

Bleackley, Horace, *Some Distinguished Victims of the Scaffold*, 1905

BM Satires — Frederic George Stephens, *Catalogue of Prints and Drawings in the British Museum ... Political and Personal Satires*, vol. 3 pt. 1 (1734-*c*.1750, nos. 2016 to 3116), 1877, vol. 3 pt. 2 (1751-1760, nos. 3117 to 3804), 1877, and vol. 4 (1761-1770, nos. 3805 to 4838), 1883; Mary Dorothy George, *Catalogue of Political and Personal Satires preserved in ... the British Museum*, vol. 5 (1771-1783, nos. 4839 to 6360), 1935, and vol. 6 (1784-1792, nos. 6361 to 8263), 1938

Boaden, James, *Memoirs of Mrs Siddons*, 2 vols, 1827

Bolton, Arthur T., *The Architecture of Robert and James Adam*, 2 vols, London, 1922

Boswell 1931 — Private Papers of James Boswell from Malahide Castle, ed. Geoffrey Scott and Frederick A. Pottle, vol. 11: *The Journal of James Boswell, 1775-1776*, privately printed ... in the United States of America, 1931

Boswell Club — *The Correspondence of James Boswell with Certain Members of The Club* ed. Charles N. Fifer, 1976

Boswell LJ — *Boswell's Life of Johnson* ed. George Birkbeck Hill, 6 vols, Oxford, 1887

Boswell OY — *Boswell: The Ominous Years, 1774-1776* ed. Charles Ryskamp and Frederick A. Pottle, New York [1963]

Boswell in Extremes, 1776-1778 ed. Charles McC. Weis and Frederick A. Pottle, 1971

Boswell: The Applause of the Jury, 1782-1785 ed. Irma S. Lustig and Frederick A. Pottle, 1981

Boswell: The English Experiment, 1785-1789 ed. Irma S. Lustig and Frederick A. Pottle, 1986

Boucher, Jonathan: *Reminiscences of an American Loyalist, 1738-1789, being the Autobiography of the Revd. Jonathan Boucher*, edited by his grandson, Jonathan Bouchier, Boston, Massachusetts, 1925

Boucher Letters — 'Letters of Rev. Jonathan Boucher', in *Maryland Historical Magazine*, vols 7 to 10 , Baltimore, Maryland, 1912-1915

Boutaric, M. E. (ed.), *Correspondance secrète inédite de Louis XV*, 2 vols, Paris, 1866

Brenellerie, Gudin de, *Histoire de Beaumarchais* ed. Maurice Tourneux, Paris, 1888

Brewer, John, *Sentimental Murder: Love and Madness in the Eighteenth Century*, 2004

A Brief Description of the Cities of London and Westminster, 1776 — see BD

Briggs, Richard, *The English Art of Cookery, according to the Present Practice*, 1788

Britain and the American Revolution ed. H. T. Dickinson, 2016. First published 1998.

British Diplomatic Instructions 1689-1789, vol. 7: France, pt. 4, 1745-1789, ed. L G. Wickham Legg, Camden Society, 3rd series, vol. xlix [49], 1934

British Museum satires, catalogues of — see BM Satires

British Portrait Painters and Engravers of the Eighteenth Century ed. Edmund Gosse, 1906

Broadley, A. M., *Doctor Johnson and Mrs Thrale*, 1910

Brougham, Henry, Lord, *Historical Sketches of Statesmen who Flourished in the Time of George III*, 1st series, vol. 1, 1839. Appendix III, Letter from Lady Charlotte Lindsay on Lord North.

Bryant, William Clement, *Captain Brant and the Old King*, a paper read before the Buffalo Historical Society, 1 April 1889, Buffalo, New York, 1889

Brydone, P[atrick], *A Tour through Sicily and Malta ...*, a new edition, vol. 2, 1775

Buckland, Francis T., *Curiosities of Natural History*, 4th series, 1875

Buckle, Henry Thomas, *History of Civilization in England*, vol. 1, 1857

Burgoyne, John, *A State of the Expedition from Canada*, 1780

Burke, Bernard, *A Genealogical and Heraldic Dictionary of the Peerage and Baronetage of the British Empire*, 31st edition, 1869

Burke, Edmund: *The Correspondence of Edmund Burke*, vol. 3, ed. George H. Guttridge, Cambridge, 1961

Burke, Edmund: *Correspondence of the Right Honourable Edmund Burke* ed. Charles William, Earl Fitzwilliam, and Sir Richard Bourke, vol. 2, 1844

Burke, Edmund: *Speech of Edmund Burke, Esq., on moving his resolutions for Conciliation with the Colonies, March 22 1775*, 2nd edition, 1775

Burke, John, *A General and Heraldic Dictionary of the Peerage and Baronetage of the British Empire*, 3rd edition, 1830

Burney, Charles, *A General History of Music, from the Earliest Ages to the Present Period*, vol. 1, 1776; 2nd edition, 1789

Burney, Frances: *Diary and Letters of Madame d'Arblay edited by her niece* [Charlotte Barrett], vol. 4, 1842

Burney, Frances: *The Early Diary of Frances Burney, 1768-1778* ed. Annie Raine Ellis, 2 vols, 1889

Burney, Frances: *The Early Journals and Letters of Fanny Burney* ed. Lars E. Troide, vol. 2, Oxford, 1990

Burney, Frances — see also *Memoirs of Dr Burney*

Burrows, Simon, *Blackmail, Scandal, and Revolution: London's French libellistes, 1758-1792*, Manchester, 2006

Burrows, Simon, *The Life of Charles Théveneau de Morande, Blackmailer, Scandalmonger and Master-Spy*, 2010

Burton, John Hill, *Life and Correspondence of David Hume*, vol. 2, Edinburgh, 1846
Butler, John, *A Sermon preached before the House of Commons ... on Friday, December 13, 1776*, 1777
Calendar of Home Office Papers of the Reign of George III — see CHOP
Campbell, Thomas, *Life of Mrs Siddons*, vol. 1, 1834
Carlyle, Alexander: *Autobiography of the Rev. Dr Alexander Carlyle*, Edinburgh, 1860
Carter, Harold B., *Sir Joseph Banks, 1743-1820*, 1988
A Catalogue of the Rarities to be seen at Don Saltero's Coffee House in Chelsea, 23rd edition [n.d.]
Cavendish Debates — *Sir Henry Cavendish's Debates of the House of Commons during the thirteenth parliament of Great Britain* ed. J. Wright, vol. 2, 1841
CCR — *Court and City Register, or, Gentleman's Complete Annual Calendar, for the year 1776*, a new edition (corrected to the 1st of March 1776) [1776]
Chaloner Smith, John, *British Mezzotinto Portraits*, 4 vols, 1884
Chancellor, E. Beresford, *The Annals of Fleet Street: Its Traditions and Associations*, 1912
Chancellor, E. Beresford, *The Annals of the Strand*, 1912
Chancellor, E. Beresford, *The XIIIth Century in London* [*c.* 1920]
Chitty, Joseph, *A Treatise on the Game Laws, and on Fisheries*, 2nd edition, 1826
CHOP — *Calendar of Home Office Papers of the Reign of George III, 1773-1775*, vol. 1, ed. Joseph Redington, 1878; vol. 4, ed. Richard Arthur Roberts, 1899
Coke, David, and Borg, Alan, *Vauxhall Gardens: A History*, 2011
Collections of the Massachusetts Historical Society, 4th series, vol. 10, Boston, 1871. Includes some American reactions to the Stamp Act.
Collins's Peerage of England ed. Sir Egerton Brydges, vol. 5, 1812
Collison-Morley, Lacy, *Giuseppe Baretti*, 1909
Colombo, Claire Miller, '"This Pen of Mine Will Say Too Much": Public Performance in the Journals of Anna Larpent', *Texas Studies in Literature and Language*, vol. 38, no. 3/4, Fall/Winter 1996, pp285-301
A Companion to every Place of Curiosity and Entertainment in and about Westminster, 1767
The Complete Dictionary of Arts and Sciences with parts by Temple Henry Croker, Thomas Williams, Samuel Clark, et al., 1766
The Complete Peerage by G. E. C[okayne], rev. Vicary Gibbs, vol. 4, 1916
Compston, H. F. B., *The Magdalen Hospital: The Story of a Great Charity*, 1917
Cone, Carl B., *Torchbearer of Freedom: The Influence of Richard Price on Eighteenth Century Thought*, Lexington, Kentucky, 1952
Congreve, William, *The Old Batchelour*, 6th edition, corrected, 1697
Connoisseur, The, vol. v [5], January-April 1903; vol. vii [7], September-December 1903; vol. cxxvi [126], July-December 1950 (A. V. Sutherland-Graeme, '"Hashley's" (Astley's) Amphitheatre')
Cook, James: The Journals of Captain James Cook on his Voyages of Discovery. Vol. 3 pts. 1 and 2: *The Voyage of the* Resolution *and* Discovery, *1776-1780* ed. J. C. Beaglehole, Hakluyt Society Extra Series 36a and 36b, Cambridge, 1967
Cook, James, *A Voyage towards the South Pole and Round the World ... in the years 1772, 1773, 1774, and 1775*, vol. 1, 2nd edition, 1777
Cook, James, and King, James, *A Voyage to the Pacific Ocean ... in the years 1776, 1777, 1778, 1779, and 1780*, 4 vols (1 and 2 by Cook; 3 and 4 by Cook and King), 1784
Cooke, William, *Memoirs of Samuel Foote, Esq.*, 3 vols, 1805

Country Life, 1932 (issue dated 24th December); 1937 (issue dated 20th March)

Court and City Register — see CCR

Craddock, Patricia B., *Edward Gibbon: Luminous Historian, 1772-1794*, Baltimore, Maryland, 1989

Cradock, Joseph, *Literary and Miscellaneous Memoirs*, vol. 1, 2nd edition, 1826; vol. 4, 1828

A Critical Review of the Public Buildings, Statues, and Ornaments in and about London and Westminster, originally written by — Ralph, architect, and now reprinted with very large additions, 1783. Ralph's *Critical Review* was first published in 1734. Material quoted is from the anonymous 1783 additions.

Cross, David A., *A Striking Likeness: The Life of George Romney*, Aldershot, 2000

The Cumberland Letters, being the Correspondence of Richard Dennison Cumberland and George Cumberland between the years 1771 and 1774 ed. Clementina Black, 1912

Cunningham, Allan, *The Lives of the Most Eminent British Painters, Sculptors, and Architects*, vol. 5, 1832

Curwen, Samuel: *Journal and Letters of the late Samuel Curwen ... An American Refugee in England, from 1775 to 1784* ed. George Atkinson Ward, New York, 1842

Curwen, Samuel: *The Journal and Letters of Samuel Curwen, An American in England, from 1775 to 1783* ed. George Atkinson Ward, 4th edition, Boston, Massachusetts, 1864

Curwen, Samuel: *The Journal of Samuel Curwen, Loyalist* ed. Andrew Oliver, 2 vols, Cambridge, Massachusetts, 1972

DAR — *Documents of the American Revolution 1770-1783*, vol. 10 (Calendar) and vol. 12 (Transcripts), ed. K. G. Davies, Dublin, 1976

Dasent, Arthur Irwin, *The History of St James's Square*, 1895

DCHNY — *Documents relative to the Colonial History of the State of New-York*, vol. 8, ed. E. B. O'Callaghan, Albany, New York, 1857

Deane, Silas: *The Deane Papers* ed. Charles Isham, forming *Collections of the New-York Historical Society* for the years 1886-1888, New York, 1887-1889

Debrett's Peerage of Great Britain and Ireland, revised, corrected, and continued by George William Collen, 1840

Delany, Mary: *The Autobiography and Correspondence of Mary Granville, Mrs Delany* ed. Lady Llanover, 2nd series, vol. 2, 1862

Desc. Mid. — *A Description of the County of Middlesex*, 1775

Dickens, Charles, *Sketches by Boz*, 2nd series, 2nd edition, 1837. 'Vauxhall Gardens by Day', pp211-224.

Dobson — *Diary and Letters of Madame D'Arblay* ed. Charlotte Barrett, with preface and notes by Austin Dobson, 6 vols, 1904-1905. Illustration source only.

Documents of the American Revolution — see DAR

Documents relative to the Colonial History of the State of New-York — see DCHNY

Dodd Life — *An Account of the Life and Writings of William Dodd, LL.D.*, 1777

Dodd Trial — *A Full and Circumstantial Account of the Trial of the Rev. Doctor Dodd* [1777]

Doniol, Henri (ed.), *Histoire de La Participation de la France à L'établissement des États-Unis D'Amérique: Correspondance Diplomatique et Documents*, 2 vols, Paris, 1886

Doran, John, rev. Robert W. Lowe, *Their Majesties Servants: Annals of the English Stage from Thomas Betterton to Edmund Kean*, vol. 2, 1888

Drinkwater, John, *A History of the late Siege of Gibraltar*, 3rd edition, 1786

Dunlap, William, *History of the Rise and Progress of the Arts of Design in the United States*, 2 vols, New York, 1834

Einstein, Lewis, *Divided Loyalties: Americans in England during the War of Independence*, 1933

Elmes, James, *A Topographical Dictionary of London and its Environs*, 1831

Erffa, Helmut von, and Staley, Allen, *The Paintings of Benjamin West*, New Haven, Connecticut, 1986

Ewen, C. L'Estrange, *Lotteries and Sweepstakes: An Historical, Legal, and Ethical Survey*, 1932

Field, Rev. J., *The Life of John Howard*, 1850

Fitzgerald, Percy, *A Famous Forgery, being the story of 'the unfortunate' Doctor Dodd*, 1865

Fitzgerald, Percy, *Samuel Foote: A Biography*, 1910

Fonblanque, Edward Barrington de, *Political and Military Episodes in the ... Life and Correspondence of ... John Burgoyne*, 1876

Foote Memoirs — *Memoirs of the Life and Writings of Samuel Foote, Esq.*, 1778

Foote, Samuel, *A Trip to Calais ... to which is annexed, The Capuchin*, 1778

Foreman, Amanda, *Georgiana, Duchess of Devonshire*, 1998

Fortescue, Sir John (ed.), *The Correspondence of King George the Third*, 6 vols, 1928

Foster, Joseph, *The Peerage, Baronetage, and Knightage of the British Empire for 1881* [1881]

Frame, Paul, *Liberty's Apostle: Richard Price, His Life and Times*, Cardiff, 2015

The Francis Letters by Sir Philip Francis and other members of the family, ed. Beata Francis and Eliza Keary, 2 vols, 1901

Franklin, Benjamin: *The Works of Benjamin Franklin* ed. Jared Sparks, vol. 8, Boston, Massachusetts, 1856

Frith, Walter, '*Autour D'Evelina*. Some Unpublished Letters of Fanny Burney', *Cornhill Magazine*, new series, vol. xviii [18], January to June 1905, pp454-465

Frothingham, Thomas G., *Washington: Commander in Chief*, Boston, Massachusetts, 1930

Gage, Thomas: *The Correspondence of General Thomas Gage* ed. Clarence Edwin Carter, 2 vols, New Haven, Connecticut, 1931, 1933

Gaillardet, Frédéric, *Mémoires du Chevalier D'Éon, publiés pour la première fois ...*, 2 vols, Paris, 1836

Gaillardet, Frédéric, *Mémoires sur la Chevalière D'Éon ... suivis de Douze Lettres Inédites de Beaumarchais*, Paris, 1866

Gainsborough, Thomas: *The Letters of Thomas Gainsborough* ed. John Hayes, 2001

Garrick, David: *The Letters of David Garrick* ed. David M. Little and George M. Kahrl, vol. 3, 1963

Garrick, David: *The Private Correspondence of David Garrick with the most Celebrated Persons of his Time*, vol. 2, 1832

Gerhold, Dorian, *Westminster Hall: Nine Hundred Years of History*, 1999

Gervat, Claire, *Elizabeth: The Scandalous Life of the Duchess of Kingston*, 2003

Gibbon, Edward: *The Autobiographies of Edward Gibbon* ed. John Murray, 1896

Gibbon, Edward, *The History of the Decline and Fall of the Roman Empire*, vol. 1, 1776; new edition, vol. 1, 1848 (for Gibbon portrait only)

Gibbon, Edward: *The Letters of Edward Gibbon* ed. J. E. Norton, vol. 2, 1956

Gibbon, Edward: *The Miscellaneous Works of Edward Gibbon, Esq. with Memoirs of his Life and Writings* ed. John, Lord Sheffield, vol. 2, 1814

Gibbon PL — *Private Letters of Edward Gibbon* ed. Rowland E. Prothero, vol. 1, 1896

Gibbs, George, 'Account of the Statue of George III, formerly standing in the Bowling Green, New York', *Proceedings of the New York Historical Society for the year 1844*, New York, 1845, pp168-175

Gilbert, Christopher, *The Life and Works of Thomas Chippendale*, 2 vols, 1978

Gilchrist, Alexander, *Life of William Blake*, vol. 1, 1880

Glenbervie, Lord: *The Diaries of Sylvester Douglas (Lord Glenbervie)* ed. Francis Bickley, vol. 1, 1928

Gordon, Charles, *The Old Bailey and Newgate*, 1902

Graves, Algernon, *The Royal Academy of Arts: A Complete Dictionary of Contributors and their work from its foundation in 1769 to 1904*, 8 vols, 1905-1906

Graves, Algernon, and Cronin, William Vine, *A History of the Works of Sir Joshua Reynolds, P.R.A.*, 4 vols, 1899-1901

The Grenville Papers, being the Correspondence of Richard Grenville, Earl Temple, K.G., and the Right Hon. George Grenville, their friends and contemporaries ed. William James Smith, 4 vols, 1852

Griffiths, Arthur, *The Chronicles of Newgate*, vol. 1, 1884

Griffiths, Arthur, *Mysteries of Police and Crime*, subscription edition, vol. 2 [*c.* 1898]

Grosley, M. [Pierre-Jean], *A Tour to London, or New Observations on England and its Inhabitants*, 2 vols, 1772

Hamilton, Milton W., 'Joseph Brant, "The Most Painted Indian"', *New York History*, vol. 39, no. 2, April 1958, pp119-132

Hampden, John (ed.), *An Eighteenth-Century Journal, Being a Record of the Years 1774-1776*, 1940

Harris's List of Covent-Garden Ladies: or Man of Pleasure's Kalendar, for the year 1773, 1773

Harrison, Walter, *New and Universal History, Description and Survey of the Cities of London and Westminster*, 1776. Described in advertisement (MC 17 May 4c) as 'an entire new work' to be published in seventy weekly parts from 18 May 1776 i.e. publication straddled 1776 and 1777. Despite adjustments and additions the text is evidently based on *A New and Compleat History and Survey of the Cities of London and Westminster ... to the beginning of the year 1770 ...* by a society of gentlemen, revised ... by Henry Chamberlain, published *c.* 1770 by the same printer, J. Cooke at Shakespeare's Head in Paternoster Row.

Hawkins, Sir John, *The Life of Samuel Johnson, LL.D.*, 1787

Hemlow, Joyce, *The History of Fanny Burney*, Oxford, 1958

Hervey, Augustus: *Augustus Hervey's Journal* ed. David Erskine, 1953

Hickey, William: *Memoirs of William Hickey* ed. Alfred Spencer, 4 vols, 1913-1925

Hill, Constance, *The House in St Martin's Street, being Chronicles of the Burney Family*, 1907

Histoire de la vie et des aventures de la Duchesse de Kingston, nouvelle edition, Londres, 1789

Historical Records of New South Wales, vol. 1 pt. 1 (Cook, 1762-1780), Sydney, 1893

The History of North America, containing an exact account of their first settlements, 1776

History of Parliament, The — see HPHC

HMC Abergavenny — *The Manuscripts of the Marquess of Abergavenny, Lord Braye, G. F. Luttrell, Esq., &c.*, Historical Manuscripts Commission, 1887

HMC American — *Report on American Manuscripts in the Royal Institution of Great Britain*, Historical Manuscripts Commission, 2 vols, 1904, 1906

HMC Carlisle — *The Manuscripts of the Earl of Carlisle, preserved at Castle Howard*, Historical Manuscripts Commission, 1897

HMC Dartmouth — *The Manuscripts of the Earl of Dartmouth*, Historical Manuscripts Commission, 3 vols, 1887-1896

HMC Rutland — *The Manuscripts of his Grace the Duke of Rutland*, Historical Manuscripts Commission, vol. 4, 1905

HMC Stopford-Sackville — *Report on the Manuscripts of Mrs Stopford-Sackville, of Drayton House, Northamptonshire*, Historical Manuscripts Commission, 2 vols, 1904, 1910

HMC Various — *Report on Manuscripts in Various Collections*, Historical Manuscripts Commission, vols 5 and 6, 1909

Hogarth's Drawings ed. Michael Ayrton, with notes by Bernard Denvir, 1948

Holliday, John, *The Life of William, late Earl of Mansfield*, 1797

Holt — James Stonehouse, 'Mr John Holt', *Historic Society of Lancashire and Cheshire, Proceedings and Papers*, vol. 6, 1854, pp57-63. Includes extracts from Holt's diary recording a visit to London in April 1777.

The Holyoke Diaries, 1709-1856 ed. George Francis Dow, Salem, Massachusetts, 1911

Horwood, Richard, *Plan of the Cities of London and Westminster, the Borough of Southwark, and Parts adjoining*, 1792-1799

Howard, John, *The State of the Prisons in England and Wales ...*, Warrington, 1777

Howson, Gerald, *The Macaroni Parson: A Life of the Unfortunate Dr Dodd*, 1973

HPHC — The History of Parliament. *The House of Commons 1754-1790* by Sir Lewis Namier and John Brooke, 3 vols, 1964

Hume, David: *The Letters of David Hume* ed. J. Y. T. Greig, vol. 2, Oxford, 1932

Hume, David: *Letters of David Hume to William Strahan* ed. George Birkbeck Hill, Oxford, 1888

Hutchinson, Thomas: *The Diary and Letters of ... Thomas Hutchinson, Esq.* ed. Peter Orlando Hutchinson, 2 vols, Boston, Massachusetts, 1884

Hutchinson, Thomas, *The History of the Province of Massachusetts Bay, from 1749 to 1774*, edited by his grandson, the Rev. John Hutchinson, 1828

Inglis, Lucy, *Georgian London: Into the Streets*, 2013

Jackson, William, *The New and Complete Newgate Calendar*, vol. 5 [*c.* 1793]

Jasanoff, Maya, *Liberty's Exiles: The Loss of America and the Remaking of the British Empire*, 2011

Jeffares, Neil, *Dictionary of Pastellists before 1800*, 2006. Online edition.

Jesse, John Heneage, *George Selwyn and his Contemporaries*, vol. 1, 1843

Johnson, Samuel: *Letters of Samuel Johnson* ed. George Birkbeck Hill, 2 vols, Oxford, 1892

Johnson, Samuel: *The Letters of Samuel Johnson* ed. R. W. Chapman, vol. 2, Oxford, 1952

[Johnson, Samuel] *Taxation no Tyranny: An Answer to the Resolutions and Address of the American Congress*, 1775

Johnson, Samuel: *The Works of Samuel Johnson, LL.D.*, vol. 9, 1823

Johnson, Samuel: The Yale Edition of the Works of Samuel Johnson, vol. 1: *Diaries, Prayers, and Annals* ed. E. L. McAdam, Jr., New Haven, Connecticut, 1958

Johnsonian Miscellanies ed. George Birkbeck Hill, 2 vols, Oxford, 1897

Johnson's England: An Account of the Life and Manners of his Age ed. A. S. Turberville, 2 vols, Oxford, 1933

Jones, E. Alfred, *The Loyalists of Massachusetts: Their Memorials, Petitions and Claims*, 1930

Journals of Congress, containing the Proceedings from January 1, 1776, to January 1, 1777, vol. 2, York-Town, Pennsylvania, 1778

Journals of the House of Commons, vol. 35 (29 November 1774 to 15 October 1776), 1803; vol. 36 (31 October 1776 to 1 October 1778), 1803

Journals of the House of Lords, vol. 34 (13 January 1774 to 15 October 1776) [n.d.]; vol. 35 (13 October 1776 to 7 October 1779) [n.d.]

Kates, Garry, *Monsieur d'Eon is a Woman*, New York, 1995

KD — *Kent's Directory for the year 1776*, 1776

Kelly, Ian, *Mr Foote's Other Leg*, 2012

Kelsay, Isabel Thompson, *Joseph Brant, 1743-1807, Man of Two Worlds*, Syracuse, New York, 1984

Kent's Directory — see KD

Kidson, Alex, *George Romney: A Complete Catalogue of his Paintings*, 3 vols, New Haven, Connecticut, 2015

Kielmansegge, Count Frederick, *Diary of a Journey to England in the years 1761-1762*, trans. Countess Kielmansegg, 1902

King, Richard, *The Frauds of London Detected* [c. 1780]

Kingsford, William, *The History of Canada*, vols 5 and 6, Toronto, 1892, 1893

Kingston Detail — *An Authentic Detail of Particulars relative to the late Duchess of Kingston*, a new edition, 1788

Kinservik, Matthew J., 'Satire, Censorship, and Sodomy in Samuel Foote's *The Capuchin* (1776)', *Review of English Studies*, new series, vol. 54, no. 217, November 2003, pp639-660

Kinservik, Matthew J., *Sex, Scandal, and Celebrity in Late Eighteenth-Century England*, Basingstoke, 2007

Kippis, Andrew, *The Life of Captain James Cook*, 1788

Kite, Elizabeth S., *Beaumarchais and the War of American Independence*, 2 vols, Boston, Massachusetts, 1918

Kitson, Arthur, *Captain James Cook, R.N, F.R.S., 'The Circumnavigator'*, 1907

Knight, Cornelia, *Autobiography of Miss Cornelia Knight*, vol. 1, 3rd edition, 1861

Langford, Paul, *A Polite and Commercial People: England 1727-1783*, Oxford, 1989

Larpent, Anna: *'The Production of a Female Pen': Anna Larpent's Account of the Duchess of Kingston's Bigamy Trial of 1776*, a facsimile edition, ed. Matthew J. Kinservik, New Haven, Connecticut, 2004

Lawson, Philip, and Phillips, Jim, '"Our Execrable Banditti": Perceptions of Nabobs in Mid-Eighteenth Century Britain', *Albion*, vol. 16, no. 3, Autumn 1984, pp225-241

LD — *The London Directory for the year 1776, containing an Alphabetical List of the Names and Places of Abode of the Merchants and Principal Traders ...*, 9th edition, 1776

Lee, Richard Henry, *Life of Arthur Lee, LL.D.*, 2 vols, Boston, Massachusetts, 1829

Lennox, Lady Sarah: *The Life and Letters of Lady Sarah Lennox, 1745-1826* ed. the Countess of Ilchester and Lord Stavordale, vol. 1, 1901

Leslie, Charles Robert, and Taylor, Tom, *Life and Times of Sir Joshua Reynolds*, 2 vols, 1865

Leslie-Melville, R., *The Life and Work of Sir John Fielding*, 1934

Letters of David Garrick and Georgiana Countess Spencer, 1759-1779 ed. Earl Spencer and Christopher Dobson, Cambridge, for the Roxburghe Club, 1960

The Letters of Junius ed. John Wade, 2 vols, 1894

Lever, Maurice, trans. Susan Emanuel, *Beaumarchais: A Biography*, New York, 2009

Lever, Maurice, *Pierre-Augustin Caron de Beaumarchais*, 3 vols, Paris, 1999, 2003, 2004

LG — *The London Guide, describing Public and Private Buildings* [n.d.]. Internal references (e.g. pp168, 176, 212) indicate publication in spring or summer 1782.

Lichtenberg trans. Noel — Tom Taylor, 'Actors in England in 1775', with translations from Lichtenberg by R. Noel, *Victoria Magazine*, vol. 1, May to October, 1863

Lichtenbergs Briefe ed. Albert Leitzmann and Carl Schüddekopf, vol. 1, 1901, Leipzig

Lichtenberg's Visits to England as described in his Letters and Diaries trans. Margaret L. Mare and W. H. Quarrell, Oxford, 1938

Lillywhite, Bryant, *London Coffee Houses: A Reference Book*, 1963

Loménie, Louis de, trans. Henry S. Edwards, *Beaumarchais and his Times*, New York, 1857

The London and Westminster Guide — see LWG

The London Directory for the Year 1776 — see LD

The London Encyclopaedia ed. Ben Weinreb et al., 3rd edition, 2008

The London Guide — see LG

LS — *The London Stage 1660-1800: A Calendar of Plays ...*, pt. 4 vol. 3, ed. George Winchester Stone, Jr.; pt. 5 vol. 1, ed. Charles Beecher Hogan; Carbondale, Illinois, 1962, 1968

Lucas, Reginald, *Lord North*, 2 vols, 1913

LWG — *The London and Westminster Guide, through the Cities and Suburbs*, 1768. Reprinted in 1776 as *A Brief Description*: see BD above.

Lysons, Daniel, *The Environs of London*, vol. 3, County of Middlesex, 1815

Mackenzie, Frederick: *Diary of Frederick Mackenzie, giving a daily narrative of his military service*, vol. 1, Cambridge, Massachusetts, 1930

Maitland, William, *The History and Survey of London from its Foundation to the Present Time*, 2 vols, 1756

The Malefactor's Register, or, the Newgate and Tyburn Calendar, vol. 3, 1779

Malmesbury Diaries — *Diaries and Correspondence of James Harris, First Earl of Malmesbury*, vol. 1, 1844

Malmesbury Letters — *A Series of Letters of the First Earl of Malmesbury* [James Harris], edited by his grandson, the Earl of Malmesbury, vol. 1, 1870

Mannings, David, *Sir Joshua Reynolds: A Complete Catalogue of his Paintings*, 2 vols, 2000

The Mansfield Manuscripts and the Growth of English Law in the Eighteenth Century ed. James Oldham, vol. 2, Chapel Hill, North Carolina, 1992

Mawhood, William: *The Mawhood Diary* ed. E. E. Reynolds, Catholic Record Society, 1956

McClure, Ruth K., *Coram's Children: The London Foundling Hospital in the Eighteenth Century*, New Haven, Connecticut, 1981

McCormick, E. H., *Omai, Pacific Envoy*, Auckland, 1977

McCullough, David, *1776: America and Britain at War*, 2005

McIntyre, Ian, *Garrick*, 1999

McIntyre, Ian, *Joshua Reynolds: The Life and Times of the First President of the Royal Academy*, 2003

Melville, Lewis, *The Trial of the Duchess of Kingston*, 1927

Memoirs of Doctor Burney, arranged ... by his daughter, Madame D'Arblay [Fanny Burney], 3 vols, 1832

Memorials and Correspondence of Charles James Fox ed. Lord John Russell, vol. 1, 1853

MGL — Phillips, Hugh, *Mid-Georgian London*, 1964

Miles, Ellen G., et al., *American Paintings of the Eighteenth Century*, National Gallery of Art, Washington DC, 1995

Montresor, John: 'Journals of Capt. John Montresor', ed. G. D. Scull, forming *Collections of the New-York Historical Society for the year 1881*, New York, 1882

Moore, Thomas, *Memoirs of the Life of ... Richard Brinsley Sheridan*, 1825

More ed. Roberts — Roberts, William, *Memoirs of the Life and Correspondence of Mrs Hannah More*, vol. 1, New York, 1835

Moritz — *Travels, chiefly on foot, through several parts of England in 1782*, described in Letters to a Friend by Charles P. Moritz, a literary gentleman of Berlin, translated from the German by a lady, 2nd edition, 1797

Morton, Brian N., and Spinelli, Donald C., *Beaumarchais and the American Revolution*, Lanham, Maryland, 2003

NDAR — *Naval Documents of the American Revolution*, vols 3 and 4 ed. William Bell Clark; vols 5, 6, 7, 8 ed. William James Morgan; Washington DC, 1968-1980

The New Present State of Great-Britain, 2nd edition, 1776

The Newcastle Magazine, vol. 1, January to December 1822, Newcastle, 1822. Contributions relating to Dr Dodd and his execution: pp18-19, 127-128, 138-139, 207-209.

Nigh, Douglas Julian, 'Lesser Luminaries: Samuel Foote and the Little Theatre in the Haymarket, from 1766 through 1777', Ph.D. thesis, University of California, 1971

Noorthouck, John, *A New History of London including Westminster and Southwark*, 1773

Northcote, James, *The Life of Sir Joshua Reynolds*, 2 vols, 2nd edition, 1818

Norton, Mary Beth, *The British-Americans: The Loyalist Exiles in England, 1774-1789*, 1974

OBP — *The Whole Proceedings ... held at Justice Hall in the Old Bailey ...*, 10 vols [1776, 1777]. Each sessions published separately, from 'Wednesday the 9th of January 1776, and the following days' to 'Wednesday the 19th of February 1777, and the following days'. During mayoralty of John Sawbridge each volume 'revised and published by John Glynn, Serjeant at Law, and Recorder of London'; during mayoralty of Sir Thomas Halifax each volume (December 1776 onwards) 'taken in short-hand by Joseph Gurney'. Also other years as indicated.

ODNB — *Oxford Dictionary of National Biography*, online edition

O'Donoghue, Edward Geoffrey, *The Story of Bethlehem Hospital from its foundation in 1247*, 1914

OED — *Oxford English Dictionary*, online edition

Old Bailey Proceedings — see OBP

O'Keeffe, John: *Recollections of the Life of John O'Keeffe, written by himself*, 2 vols, 1826

Omiah's Farewell, inscribed to the Ladies of London, 1776. Anonymous poem.

O'Shaughnessy, Andrew, *The Men Who Lost America: British Command during the Revolutionary War and the Preservation of the Empire*, 2013

Oxford Dictionary of National Biography — see ODNB

Oxford English Dictionary — see OED

The Oxford History of the British Empire, vol. 2, *The Eighteenth Century* ed. P. J. Marshall, Oxford, 1998

Oxnard 1872 — 'Edward Oxnard's Journal' ed. Edward S. Moseley, in *New-England Historical and Genealogical Register ... for the year 1872*, vol. xxvi [26], Boston, Massachusetts, 1872, pp3-10, 115-121, 254-259

[Paine, Thomas] *Common Sense*
   i. *Common Sense, addressed to the Inhabitants of America*, written by an Englishman, 2nd edition, Philadelphia, Pennsylvania, 1776
   ii. *Common Sense* ... A New Edition, with several Additions in the Body of the Work, and an introduction dated 14 February, Philadelphia, Pennsylvania, 1776
   iii. *Common Sense* [as ii. above] with *Plain Truth*, reprinted by J. Almon, London, 1776 ('The Fourth Edition, Corrected.')
[Paine, Thomas] *The Crisis*, in *The Writings of Thomas Paine* ed. Moncure Daniel Conway, vol. 1, New York, 1894, pp168-380. Generally known as *The American Crisis*. A series of thirteen papers published between December 1776 and April 1783, plus 'A Supernumerary Crisis' dated December 1783.
Parl. Hist. — *The Parliamentary History of England from the Earliest Period to the year 1803*, vol. 15 (1753-1765), vol. 18 (1774-1777), vol. 19 (1777-1778), vol. 24 (1783-1785), 1813-1815
Parliamentary Papers of John Robinson 1774-1784 ed. William Thomas Laprade, 1922
Parl. Reg. Commons — *The Parliamentary Register, or, History of the Proceedings and Debates of the House of Commons*, vol. 3 (26 October 1775 to 6 May 1776), 1776; vol. 4 (7 May to 23 May 1776), 1776; vol. 6 (31 October 1776 to 25 February 1777), 1777
Parl. Reg. Lords — *The Parliamentary Register, or, History of the Proceedings and Debates of the House of Lords*, vol. 2 (30 Nov 1774 to 26 May 1775), 1775; vol. 5 (26 October 1775 to 23 May 1776), 1776; vol. 7 (31 October 1776 to 6 June 1777), 1777
Parsons, Mrs Clement, *Garrick and his Circle*, 1906
Paston, George, *Social Caricature in the Eighteenth Century*, 1905
Peake, Richard Brinsley, *Memoirs of the Colman Family*, 2 vols, 1841
Pelleport, Anne-Gédéon la Fite de, *Le Diable dans un Bénitier*, Paris [1784]
Perreau Trials — *The Trials of Robert and Daniel Perreau's* [with trial of Mrs Rudd appended], printed for T. Bell, 1775
Philosophical Transactions, giving some Account of the Present Undertakings ... of the Ingenious, printed for the Royal Society. Vol. lxiii [63], for the year 1773, pt. 2, 1774; includes John Walsh, 'Of the electric Property of the Torpedo', pp461-480. Vol lxv [65], for the year 1775, pt. 2, 1775; includes John Hunter, 'An Account of the Gymnotus Electricus', pp395-407.
Philosophical Transactions of the Royal Society of London, vol. lxvi [66], for the year 1776, pt. 1, 1776, pt. 2, 1777; vol. lxvii [67], for the year 1777, pt. 1, 1777, pt. 2, 1778
Phillips, Hugh — see MGL
Phillips, Sir Richard, *A Morning's Walk from London to Kew*, 1817
Pieces Rélatives aux Démêlés entre Mademoiselle d'Eon de Beaumont ... et le Sieur Caron dit de Beaumarchais, [? Amsterdam], 1778
Plain Truth: Addressed to the Inhabitants of America, containing Remarks on a late Pamphlet, intitled Common Sense, written by Candidus, Philadelphia, 1776; reprinted London, 1776
Porter, Anna — see under Larpent
Posthumous Letters from various Celebrated Men, addressed to Francis Colman and George Colman the Elder ed. George Colman the younger, 1820
[Pottinger, Israel?] *The Duenna: A Comic Opera, in Three Acts, As it is performed by his Majesty's Servants*, a new edition [1776]. Political satire inspired by Sheridan's work of the same name.

Potts, Louis W., *Arthur Lee: A Virtuous Revolutionary*, Baton Rouge, Louisiana, 1981

Price, Munro, *Preserving the Monarchy: The Comte de Vergennes, 1774-1787*, Cambridge, 1995

Price, Richard: *The Correspondence of Richard Price* ed. D. O. Thomas and Bernard Peach, vol. 1, Durham, North Carolina, 1983

Price, Richard, *Observations on the Nature of Civil Liberty, the Principles of Government, and the Justice and Policy of the War with America*. To which is added an Appendix, containing a State of the National Debt. 4th edition, 1776

Priestley, Joseph, *The Theological and Miscellaneous Works* ed. John Towill Rutt, vol. 1 pt. 1, 1817

Prown, Jules David, *John Singleton Copley in England 1774-1815*, vol. 2, Cambridge, Massachusetts, 1966

Pynchon, William: *The Diary of William Pynchon of Salem* ed. Fitch Edward Oliver, Boston, Massachusetts, 1890

Quincy, Samuel: Diary of Samuel Quincy in *Proceedings of the Massachusetts Historical Society*, vol. 19, 1881-1882, Boston, Massachusetts, 1882, pp211-223

Rae, John, *Life of Adam Smith*, 1895

Registers of Marriages of St Mary le Bone, Middlesex, 1775-1783 ed. W. Bruce Bannerman and R. R. Bruce Bannerman, pt. 3, Harleian Society vol. 51, 1921

Registers of St Mary Le Bowe, Cheapside, All Hallows, Honey Lane, and of St Pancras, Soper Lane, London, pt. 1: Baptisms and Burials, ed. W. Bruce Bannerman, Harleian Society Registers vol. 44, 1914

Registers of St Paul's Church, Covent Garden, London, vol. 2: Christenings, 1752-1837, ed. Rev. William H. Hunt, Harleian Society Registers vol. 34, 1906

Registers, Westminster Abbey — *The Marriage, Baptismal, and Burial Registers of the ... Abbey of St Peter, Westminster* ed. Joseph Lemuel Chester, Harleian Society vol. 10, 1876

Reinhardt, Leslie, 'British and Indian Identities in a Picture by Benjamin West', *Eighteenth-Century Studies*, vol. 31, no. 3, Spring 1998, pp283-305

Reynolds, Frederick: *The Life and Times of Frederick Reynolds, written by himself*, vol. 1, 1826

Reynolds, Sir Joshua: *The Works of Sir Joshua Reynolds, Knight*, with a Life by Edmond Malone, 3 vols, 3rd edition, 1801

Reynolds ed. Nicholas Penny, Royal Academy of Arts catalogue, 1986

Riedesel, Frederika: *Letters and Memoirs relating to the War of American Independence ... by Madame de Riedesel*, translated from the original German, New York, 1827

Riggs, A. R., 'Arthur Lee, a Radical Virginian in London, 1768-1776', *Virginia Magazine of History and Biography*, vol. 78, no. 3, July 1970, pp268-280

Roberts, S. C., *The Story of Doctor Johnson*, Cambridge, 1919

Robinson, Mary, *Memoirs of the late Mrs Robinson, written by herself*, 2 vols, 1803

Robiquet, Paul, *Theveneau de Morande*, Paris, 1882

Rocque, John, *A Plan of the Cities of London and Westminster and Borough of Southwark*, 1746 [1747]

Ross, Ian Simpson, *The Life of Adam Smith*, Oxford, 1995

[Rudd, Margaret Caroline] *Facts, or, A Plain and Explicit Narrative of the Case of Mrs Rudd, published from her own Manuscript* [1775]

Rudd, Margaret Caroline, *Mrs M. C. Rudd's Genuine Letter to Lord Weymouth, with several Authentic Anecdotes of the late Messrs. Perreaus*, 1776

[Rudd, Margaret Caroline] *Mrs Stewart's Case, written by herself*, 1788
Russell, Charles E., *English Mezzotint Portraits and their States*, vol. 1, 1926
Rutter, Owen, *Turbulent Journey: A Life of William Bligh, Vice-Admiral of the Blue*, 1936
Sackville Trial — *The Trial of the Right Honourable Lord George Sackville, at a Court-Martial held at the Horse-Guards, February 29, 1760 ... being charged with Disobedience of Orders, while he commanded the British Horse in Germany* [1760]
Sampson, William, *The Trial of the Rev. William Jackson ... on Thursday the 23d of April, 1795*, Dublin, 1795
Samwell, David, *A Narrative of the Death of Captain James Cook*, 1786
Sandby, William, *The History of the Royal Academy of Arts, from its foundation to the present time*, vol. 1, 1862
Sands, Mollie, *The Eighteenth-Century Pleasure Gardens of Marylebone, 1737-1777*, 1987
Sandwich Papers — *The Private Papers of John, Earl of Sandwich, First Lord of the Admiralty*, vol. 1: August 1770 – March 1778, ed. G. R. Barnes and J. H. Owen, Navy Records Society vol. 69, 1932
Schaeper, Thomas J., *Edward Bancroft: Scientist, Author, Spy*, New Haven, Connecticut, 2011
Schama, Simon, *Citizens: A Chronicle of the French Revolution*, 1989
Schofield, Robert E., *The Enlightened Joseph Priestley: A Study of his Life and Work from 1773 to 1804*, University Park, Pennsylvania, 2004
Scholes, Percy A., *The Great Dr Burney*, vol. 1, Oxford, 1948
The Secret History of the Green-Room, anonymous, a new edition, 2 vols, 1795
Sellers, Charles Coleman, *Patience Wright: American Artist and Spy in George III's London*, Middletown, Connecticut, 1976
Sewall, Jonathan: 'Letters of Jonathan Sewall', in *Proceedings of the Massachusetts Historical Society*, 2nd series, vol. x [10], 1895-1896, Boston, 1896, pp407-427
SF — B. F. Stevens's *Facsimiles of Manuscripts in European Archives relating to America, 1773-1783*, 25 vols, 1889-1898
Sharp, Granville: *Memoirs of Granville Sharp, Esq., composed from his own Manuscripts* ed. Prince Hoare, 1820
Sheridan, Richard Brinsley: *The Letters of Richard Brinsley Sheridan* ed. Cecil Price, vol. 1, Oxford, 1966
Shewmake, Antoinette (ed.), *For the Good of Mankind: Pierre-Augustin Caron de Beaumarchais: Political Correspondence relative to the American Revolution*, Lanham, Maryland, 1987
Sichel, Walter, *Sheridan, from new and original material*, vol. 1, 1909
Smith, Adam: *The Correspondence of Adam Smith* ed. Ernest Campbell Mossner and Ian Simpson Ross, Oxford, 1977
Smith, Adam, *Wealth of Nations* — see WN
Smith, Charles John, *Historical and Literary Curiosities*, 1840
Smith, H. Clifford, *Buckingham Palace: Its Furniture, Decoration and History*, 1931
Smith, John Thomas, *Antiquities of Westminster*, 1807
Smith, John Thomas, *Nollekens and his Times*, 2 vols, 1828
Smith, Thomas, *A Topographical and Historical Account of the Parish of St Mary-le-Bone*, 1833
Smith, William, *State of the Gaols in London, Westminster, and Borough of Southwark*, 1776. Advertised 5 November 1776 (MC 5 Nov 4c) as published 'this day'.
Sodom and Onan: A Satire [1776]. Anonymous poem, attributed to William Jackson.

SOL — Survey of London

    vol. iii [3] The Parish of St Giles-in-the-Fields, pt. 1: Lincoln's Inn Fields, 1912

    vol. x [10] The Parish of St Margaret, Westminster, pt. 1, 1926

    vol. xiii [13] The Parish of St Margaret, Westminster, pt. 2: Neighbourhood of Whitehall, vol. 1, 1930

    vol. xiv [14] The Parish of St Margaret, Westminster, pt. 3: Neighbourhood of Whitehall, vol. 2, 1931

    vol. xvi [16] Charing Cross: The Parish of St Martin-in-the-Fields, pt. 1, 1935

    vol. xviii [18] The Strand: The Parish of St Martin-in-the-Fields, pt. 2, 1937

    vol. xx [20] Trafalgar Square and Neighbourhood: The Parish of St Martin-in-the-Fields, pt. 3, 1940

    vol. xxi [21] Tottenham Court Road and Neighbourhood: The Parish of St Pancras, pt. 3, 1949

    vol. xxii [22] Bankside, 1950

    vol. xxiii [23] South Bank and Vauxhall: The Parish of St Mary Lambeth, pt. 1, 1951

    vol. xxiv [24] King's Cross Neighbourhood: The Parish of St Pancras, pt. 4, 1952

    vol. xxix [29] The Parish of St James, Westminster, pt. 1: South of Piccadilly, 1960

    vol. xxx [30] The Parish of St James, Westminster, pt. 1: South of Piccadilly, 1960 (continuation)

    vol. xxxi [31] The Parish of St James, Westminster: pt. 2: North of Piccadilly, 1963

    vol. xxxiii [33] The Parish of St Anne Soho, 1966

    vol. xxxv [35] The Theatre Royal, Drury Lane, and the Royal Opera House, Covent Garden, 1970

    vol. xxxvi [36] The Parish of St Paul, Covent Garden, 1970

    vol. xl [40] The Grosvenor Estate in Mayfair, pt. 2: The Buildings, 1980

    vol. xlvii [47] Northern Clerkenwell and Pentonville, 2008

Spielmann, M. H., *British Portrait Painting to the opening of the Nineteenth Century*, 2 vols, 1910

Spinelli, Donald C., 'Beaumarchais and d'Eon: What an Affair', in *The Chevalier d'Eon and his Worlds* ed. Simon Burrows et al., 2010, pp57-72

'Squire Randal's Excursion round London, or, A Week's Frolic in the year 1776, with the Remarks of John Trusty, in a series of Letters to their Friends and Bottle Companions in the Country, 1777

ST — *A Complete Collection of State Trials ...* compiled by T. B. Howell, vol. 20, 1816. Includes: pp355-652, 'The Trial of Elizabeth, calling herself Duchess Dowager of Kingston, for Bigamy', printed under an order of the House of Lords; pp1285-1316, 'The Trial of an Action brought by Stephen Sayre ... for False Imprisonment', published from Mr Gurney's short-hand notes; pp1317-1368, 'The Trial of James Hill ... known also by the name of John the Painter', taken in short-hand by Joseph Gurney.

The Statutes at Large, vol. 8 ('From the seventh year ... to the eighteenth year of King George the Third'), 1786

Stevens's Facsimiles — see SF

Stevens, Todd, and Cumming, Edward, *Ghosts of Rosevear and the Wreck of the* Nancy Packet, [? England], 2008

Stone, William L., *Life of Joseph Brant (Thayendanegea)*, 2 vols, New York, 1838

Street, G. S., 'The Betting Book at Brooks's', *North American Review*, vol. 173, no. 536, July 1901, pp44-55

[Stuart, James] *Critical Observations on the Buildings and Improvements of London*, 1771

Sumbel, Mary: *Memoirs of the Life of Mrs Sumbel, late Wells ... by herself*, vol. 3, 1811

Survey of London — see SOL

Sutherland, Lucy S., *The East India Company in Eighteenth-Century Politics*, Oxford, 1952

Swinburne, Henry, *The Courts of Europe at the Close of the Last Century*, vol. 1, 1841

Tayler, Alistair, and Tayler, Henrietta, *Lord Fife and his Factor, being the Correspondence of James, second Lord Fife, 1729-1809*, 1925

Taylor, John, *Records of My Life*, 2 vols, 1832

Telfer, J. Buchan, *The Strange Career of the Chevalier d'Eon de Beaumont*, 1885

Thicknesse, Philip: *Memoirs and Anecdotes of Philip Thicknesse*, Dublin, 1790

Thompson, Henry, *The Life of Hannah More*, 1838

Timbs, John [writing as 'Horace Foote'], *A Companion to the Theatres*, 2nd edition, 1829

The Torpedo, A Poem to the Electrical Eel, addressed to Mr John Hunter, Surgeon, 1777

Treloar, William Purdie, *Wilkes and the City*, 1917

The Trial of James Hill, commonly called John the Painter ..., printed by J. Wilkes, Winchester [1777]

Trials for Adultery, or, The History of Divorces, being Select Trials at Doctors Commons, taken in short-hand by a civilian, vol. 1, 1779; vol. 2, 1780; vol. 7, 1780

Trusler, Rev. Dr [John], *The London Adviser and Guide*, 1786

Turgot, Anne Robert Jacques, *Oeuvres de Turgot, nouvelle édition*, vol. 2, Paris, 1844

Tyne, C. H. van, 'French Aid before the Alliance of 1778', *American Historical Review*, vol. 31, no. 1, October 1925, pp20-40

Tyne, C. H. van, 'Influences which Determined the French Government to make the Treaty with America, 1778', *American Historical Review*, vol. 21, no. 3, April 1916, pp528-541

Valentine, Alan, *Lord George Germain*, Oxford, 1962

Valentine, Alan, *Lord North*, 2 vols, Norman, Oklahoma, 1967

Vardy, John, *Some Designs of Mr Inigo Jones and Mr Wm. Kent*, 1744

The Vauxhall Affray, or, The Macaronies Defeated, 1773

Vauxhall sale catalogues — *A Catalogue of the valuable Fixtures, Fittings, and Building Materials, of the Royal Gardens, Vauxhall* ...which will be sold by auction, by Messrs. Driver, on the premises, on Monday, August 22nd ..., 1859 [first portion]. Catalogue for second portion bears same title except for date: 'on Monday, the 29th of August'.

Villette, John, *A Genuine Account of the Behaviour and Dying-Words of Daniel Perreau and Robert Perreau* [1776]

Vincent, William, *A Plain and Succinct narrative of the late Riots and Disturbances*, 3rd edition, 1780

Walcott, Mackenzie E. C., *The Memorials of Westminster*, a new edition, 1851

Walford, Edward, *Old and New London*, vol. 6, a new edition [*c.* 1885]

Walker, Ralph S., and Oates, J. C. T., 'Charles Burney's Theft of Books at Cambridge', *Transactions of the Cambridge Bibliographical Society*, vol. 3, no. 4, 1962, pp313-326

Wall, A. J., 'The Statues of King George III and the Honorable William Pitt erected in New York City 1770', *New-York Historical Society Quarterly Bulletin*, vol. 4, July 1920, pp37-57

Walpole, Horace, *Memoirs of the Reign of King George the Third* ed. G. F. Russell Barker, vol. 3, 1894

Walpole, Horace: The Yale edition of Horace Walpole's correspondence ed. W. S. Lewis, 48 vols, New Haven, Connecticut, 1937-1983

Walpole Letters — *The Letters of Horace Walpole ... Chronologically arranged* ed. Mrs Paget Toynbee, 16 vols, Oxford, 1903-1905

Walpole LJ — *The Last Journals of Horace Walpole during the reign of George III from 1771 to 1783* ed. A. Francis Steuart, 2 vols, 1910

Walpole to Mann — *Letters of Horace Walpole, Earl of Orford, to Sir Horace Mann*, vol. 3, 1844. Illustration source only.

Ward, Humphry, and Roberts, W., *Romney: A Biographical and Critical Essay, with a Catalogue Raisonné of his Works*, 2 vols, 1904

Warner, Jessica, *John the Painter: Terrorist of the American Revolution*, 2005

Waterhouse, Ellis K., *Reynolds*, 1941

Webb, Samuel Blachley: *Correspondence and Journals of Samuel Blachley Webb* ed. Worthington Chauncey Ford, vol. 1, New York, 1893

Weber, Kaylin Haverstock, 'The Studio and Collection of the "American Raphael": Benjamin West, P.R.A. (1738-1820)', Ph.D thesis, University of Glasgow, 2013

Webster, Mary, *Johann Zoffany, 1733-1810*, New Haven, Connecticut, 2011

Weitzman, Sophia, *Warren Hastings and Philip Francis*, Manchester, 1929

Wendel, Jacques M., 'Turgot and the American Revolution', *Modern Age*, vol. 23, no. 3, Summer 1979, pp282-289

Werkmeister, Lucyle, *The London Daily Press 1772-1792*, Lincoln, Nebraska, 1963

Werkmeister, Lucyle, 'Notes for a Revised Life of William Jackson' and 'A Postscript', *Notes and Queries*, ccvi [206], February 1961, pp43-47, and July 1961, pp266-267

Wesley, John: *The Journal of the Rev. John Wesley*, vol. 4, 1827

Wharton, Francis (ed.), *The Revolutionary Diplomatic Correspondence of the United States*, vols 1-3, Washington DC, 1889

Wheatley, Henry B., *London Past and Present*, 3 vols, 1891. Based upon *The Handbook of London* by Peter Cunningham, first published 1849.

White, Jerry, *London in the Eighteenth Century: A Great and Monstrous Thing*, 2012

Whitehead, Thomas, *Original Anecdotes of the late Duke of Kingston and Miss Chudleigh, alias Mrs Harvey, alias Countess of Bristol, alias Duchess of Kingston*, 1792

Whitley, William T., *Artists and their Friends in England, 1700-1799*, 2 vols, 1928

Whitley, William T., *Thomas Gainsborough*, 1915

Wilkes, John: *The Correspondence of John Wilkes, with his Friends* ed. John Almon, 5 vols, 1805

Wilkes, John: *The Diaries of John Wilkes 1770-1797* ed. Robin Eagles, London Record Society vol. 49, 2014

Wilkes, John: *Letters ... of John Wilkes, Esq. addressed to his Daughter, the late Miss Wilkes*, 4 vols, 1804

Wilkinson, James, *Memoirs of My Own Times*, vol. 1, Philadelphia, Pennsylvania, 1816

Williamson, George C., *Richard Cosway, R.A., and his Wife and Pupils*, 1897

Winslow Papers, A.D. 1776-1826 ed. W. O. Raymond, St John, New Brunswick, 1901

WN — Smith, Adam, *An Inquiry into the Nature and Causes of the Wealth of Nations*, 2 vols, 1776

Wraxall, Sir Nathaniel: *The Historical and the Posthumous Memoirs of Sir Nathaniel William Wraxall, 1772-1784* ed. Henry B. Wheatley, 5 vols, 1884

Wraxall, Nathaniel, *A Tour through some of the Northern Parts of Europe*, 3rd edition, 1776

Wroth, Warwick, *The London Pleasure Gardens of the Eighteenth Century*, 1896

Zimmer, Anne Y., *Jonathan Boucher, Loyalist in Exile*, Detroit, Michigan, 1978

Index

Symbols and abbreviations used:

>   'see under' or 'see also under'

~   references occur often within the page range listed but not on every page

fn.   footnote

P   plate (*P1* etc)

Italic indicates pages or page ranges including one or more related illustrations. References to married couples are usually listed once, under the first name to appear. In most cases ranks and titles are given as at the start of 1776.

Entries for individual **clubs**, **coffee-houses**, **inns and taverns** and **newspapers and periodicals** are gathered under those headings.

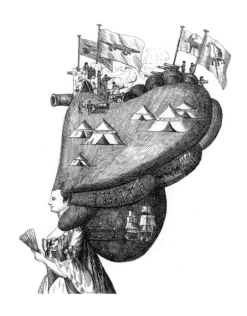